AF...

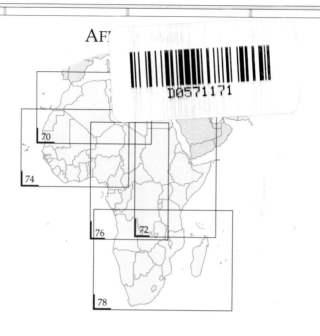

D0571171

70

74

76

72

78

EUROPE 80-81

84

82

94

98

108

106

88

86

90

100

110

92

96

104

102

A DORLING KINDERSLEY BOOK
www.dk.com

FOR THE SECOND EDITION

EDITOR-IN-CHIEF Andrew Heritage
SENIOR MANAGING ART EDITOR Philip Lord
SENIOR CARTOGRAPHIC MANAGER David Roberts
MANAGING EDITOR Punita Singh
SENIOR CARTOGRAPHIC EDITOR Simon Mumford
PROJECT CARTOGRAPHERS James Anderson, Alok Pathak
SYSTEMS COORDINATOR Philip Rowles
PRODUCTION Joanna Bull

DORLING KINDERSLEY CARTOGRAPHY

PROJECT CARTOGRAPHY AND DESIGN
Julia Lunn, Julie Turner

CARTOGRAPHERS
James Anderson, Roger Bullen, Martin Darlison,
Simon Mumford, John Plumer, Peter Winfield

DESIGN
Katy Wall

INDEX-GAZETTEER
Natalie Clarkson, Ruth Duxbury, Margaret Hynes, Margaret Stevenson

PRODUCTION
Hilary Stephens, David Proffit

EDITORIAL DIRECTION
Andrew Heritage

ART DIRECTION
Chez Picthall

First published in Great Britain in 1997 by Dorling Kindersley Limited
80 Strand, London WC2R 0RL
Reprinted with revisions 1998. Second Edition 2001. Reprinted with revisions 2003

Previously published as the Concise World Atlas
Copyright © 1997, 1998, 2001, 2003 Dorling Kindersley Limited, London

A Penguin Company

A CIP catalogue record for this book is available from the British Library

ISBN 0 7513 4884 8

Reproduced by GRB, Italy
Printed and bound in Slovakia by TBB s.r.o.

For the very latest information, visit:
www.dk.com and click on the Maps & Atlases icon

KEY TO MAP SYMBOLS

PHYSICAL FEATURES

Elevation

4,000m/13,124ft
2,000m/6,562ft
1,000m/3,281ft
500m/1,640ft
250m/820ft
100m/328ft
0
Below sea level

△   Mountain

▽   Depression

◬   Volcano

)(Pass/tunnel

     Sandy desert

DRAINAGE FEATURES

Major perennial river

Minor perennial river

Seasonal river

Canal

Waterfall

Perennial lake

Seasonal lake

Wetland

ICE FEATURES

Permanent ice cap/ice shelf

Winter limit of pack ice

Summer limit of pack ice

BORDERS

Full international border

Disputed *de facto* border

Territorial claim border

Cease-fire line

Undefined boundary

Internal administrative boundary

COMMUNICATIONS

Major road

Minor road

Rail

✈   International airport

SETTLEMENTS

◉   Over 500,000

◉   100,000 - 500,000

○   50,000 - 100,000

○   Less than 50,000

●   National capital

◉   Internal administrative capital

MISCELLANEOUS FEATURES

+   Site of interest

ᴠᴠᴠᴠᴠᴠ   Ancient wall

GRATICULE FEATURES

Line of latitude/longitude/ Equator

Tropic/Polar circle

25°   Degrees of latitude/ longitude

NAMES

Physical features

Andes

Sahara   Landscape features

Ardennes

Land's End   Headland

Mont Blanc 4,807m   Elevation/volcano/pass

Blue Nile   River/canal/waterfall

Ross Ice Shelf   Ice feature

PACIFIC OCEAN

Sulu Sea   Sea features

Palk Strait

Chile Rise   Undersea feature

Regions

FRANCE   Country

JERSEY
(to UK)   Dependent territory

KANSAS   Administrative region

Dordogne   Cultural region

Settlements

PARIS   Capital city

SAN JUAN   Dependent territory capital city

Chicago

Kettering   Other settlements

Burke

INSET MAP SYMBOLS

Urban area

City

Park

▪   Place of interest

▫   Suburb/district

CONTENTS

THE WORLD TODAY

Flags of the World 6-7
The Political World 8-9
The Physical World 10-11
Time Zones 12-13
Geology & Structure 14-15
World Climate 16-17
Ocean Currents 18-19
Life Zones 20-21
Population 22-23
Languages 24-25
Religion 26-27
The Global Economy 28-29
Global Conflict 30-31

THE WORLD'S REGIONS

NORTH & CENTRAL AMERICA

North & Central America 34-35
Western Canada & Alaska 36-37
Eastern Canada 38-39
USA: The Northeast 40-41
USA: The Southeast 42-43
  Bermuda
USA: Central States 44-45
USA: The West 46-47
  Los Angeles & Hawaii

USA: The Southwest 48-49
Mexico 50-51
Central America 52-53
The Caribbean 54-55
  Jamaica, St. Lucia, & Barbados

SOUTH AMERICA

South America 56-57
Northern South America 58-59
Western South America 60-61
  Galapagos Islands
Brazil 62-63
Southern South America 64-65
The Atlantic Ocean 66-67

AFRICA

Africa 68-69
Northwest Africa 70-71
Northeast Africa 72-73
West Africa 74-75
Central Africa 76-77
  Sao Tome & Principe
Southern Africa 78-79

EUROPE

Europe .80-81
The North Atlantic 82-83
Scandinavia & Finland 84-85
The Low Countries 86-87
The British Isles 88-89
  London

continued....

EUROPE *continued*

France, Andorra, & Monaco 90-91
  Paris, Andorra, & Monaco
Spain & Portugal 92-93
  Azores & Gibraltar
Germany & the Alpine States . . .94-95
  Liechtenstein
Italy 96-97
  San Marino & Vatican City
Central Europe 98-99
Southeast Europe 100-101
  Bosnia & Herzegovina
The Mediterranean 102-103
  Malta & Cyprus
Bulgaria & Greece 104-105
The Baltic States & Belarus 106-107
Ukraine, Moldova,
  & Romania 108-109
European Russia 110-111

NORTH & WEST ASIA

North & West Asia 112-113
Russia & Kazakhstan 114-115
Turkey & the Caucasus 116-117
The Near East 118-119
  West Bank
The Middle East 120-121
Central Asia 122-123

SOUTH & EAST ASIA

South & East Asia 124-125
Western China & Mongolia . . .126-127

Eastern China & Korea 128-129
  Hong Kong (Xianggang)
Japan .130-131
  Tōkyō & Nansei-Shotō
South India & Sri Lanka 132-133
North India, Pakistan,
  & Bangladesh 134-135
Mainland Southeast Asia 136-137
Maritime Southeast Asia 138-139
  Singapore
The Indian Ocean 140-141

AUSTRALASIA & OCEANIA

Australasia & Oceania 142-143
The Southwest Pacific 144-145
Western Australia 146-147
Eastern Australia 148-149
  Sydney
New Zealand 150-151
The Pacific Ocean 152-153
Antarctica 154
The Arctic Ocean 155

INDEX – GAZETTEER

Overseas Territories
  & Dependencies 156-159
Glossary of Geographical
  Terms 160-161
Continental Factfiles 162-163
Geographical Comparisons . . .164-166
Index-Gazetteer of Places
  & Countries 167-256

FLAGS OF THE WORLD

NORTH & CENTRAL AMERICA

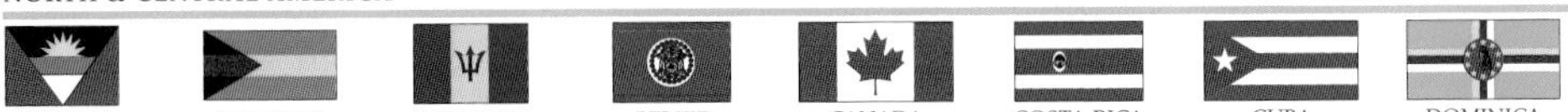

ANTIGUA & BARBUDA PAGES 54-55
BAHAMAS PAGES 54-55
BARBADOS PAGES 54-55
BELIZE PAGES 52-53
CANADA PAGES 36-39
COSTA RICA PAGES 52-53
CUBA PAGES 54-55
DOMINICA PAGES 54-55

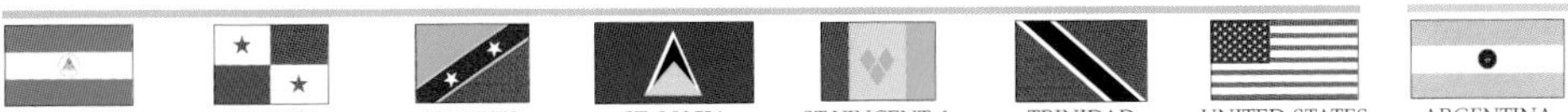

NICARAGUA PAGES 52-53
PANAMA PAGES 52-53
ST. KITTS & NEVIS PAGES 54-55
ST. LUCIA PAGES 54-55
ST.VINCENT & THE GRENADINES PAGES 54-55
TRINIDAD & TOBAGO PAGES 54-55
UNITED STATES OF AMERICA PAGES 40-49

SOUTH AMERICA

ARGENTINA PAGES 64-65

SURINAME PAGES 58-59
URUGUAY PAGES 64-65
VENEZUELA PAGES 58-59

AFRICA

ALGERIA PAGES 70-71
ANGOLA PAGES 78-79
BENIN PAGES 74-75
BOTSWANA PAGES 78-79
BURKINA FASO PAGES 74-75

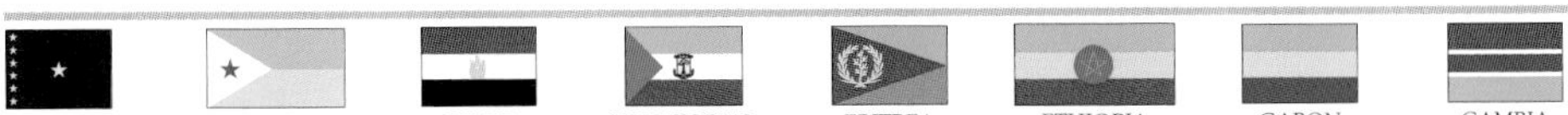

DEM. REP. CONGO PAGES 76-77
DJIBOUTI PAGES 72-73
EGYPT PAGES 72-73
EQUATORIAL GUINEA PAGES 76-77
ERITREA PAGES 72-73
ETHIOPIA PAGES 72-73
GABON PAGES 76-77
GAMBIA PAGES 74-75

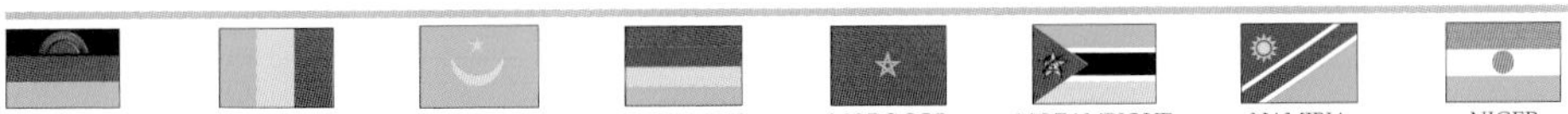

MALAWI PAGES 78-79
MALI PAGES 74-75
MAURITANIA PAGES 74-75
MAURITIUS PAGES 78-79
MOROCCO PAGES 70-71
MOZAMBIQUE PAGES 78-79
NAMIBIA PAGES 78-79
NIGER PAGES 74-75

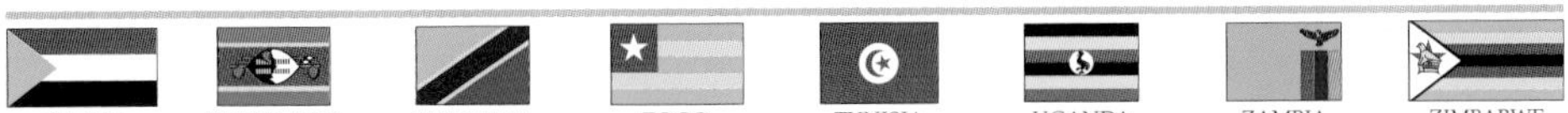

SUDAN PAGES 72-73
SWAZILAND PAGES 78-79
TANZANIA PAGES 72-73
TOGO PAGES 74-75
TUNISIA PAGES 70-71
UGANDA PAGES 72-73
ZAMBIA PAGES 78-79
ZIMBABWE PAGES 78-79

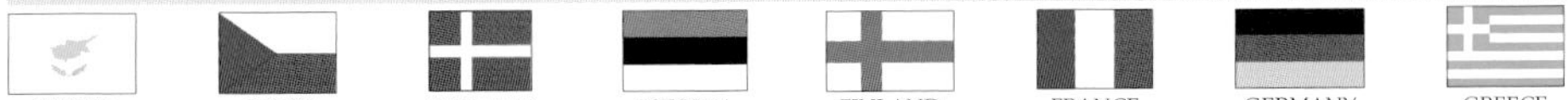

CYPRUS PAGES 102-103
CZECH REPUBLIC PAGES 98-99
DENMARK PAGES 84-85
ESTONIA PAGES 106-107
FINLAND PAGES 84-85
FRANCE PAGES 90-91
GERMANY PAGES 94-95
GREECE PAGES 104-105

MALTA PAGES 96-97
MOLDOVA PAGES 108-109
MONACO PAGES 90-91
NETHERLANDS PAGES 86-87
NORWAY PAGES 84-85
POLAND PAGES 98-99
PORTUGAL PAGES 92-93
REPUBLIC OF IRELAND PAGES 88-89

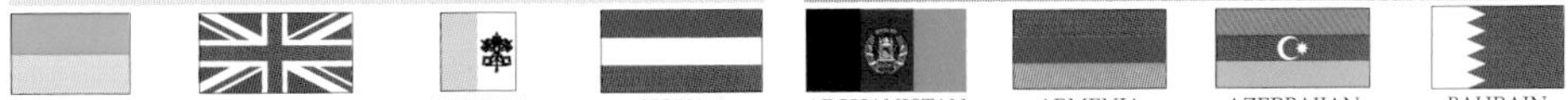

UKRAINE PAGES 108-109
UNITED KINGDOM PAGES 88-89
VATICAN CITY PAGES 96-97
SERBIA & MONTENEGRO (YUGOSLAVIA) PAGES 100-101

ASIA

AFGHANISTAN PAGES 122-123
ARMENIA PAGES 116-117
AZERBAIJAN PAGES 116-117
BAHRAIN PAGES 120-121

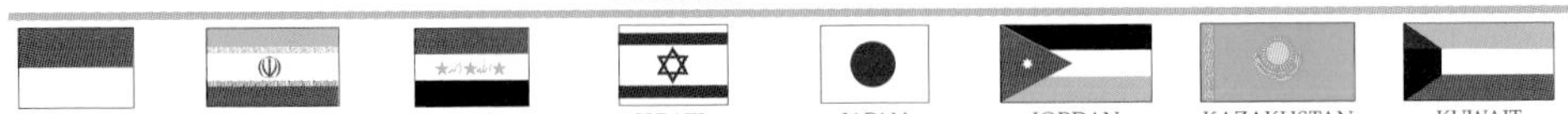

INDONESIA PAGES 138-139
IRAN PAGES 120-121
IRAQ PAGES 120-121
ISRAEL PAGES 118-119
JAPAN PAGES 130-131
JORDAN PAGES 118-119
KAZAKHSTAN PAGES 114-115
KUWAIT PAGES 120-121

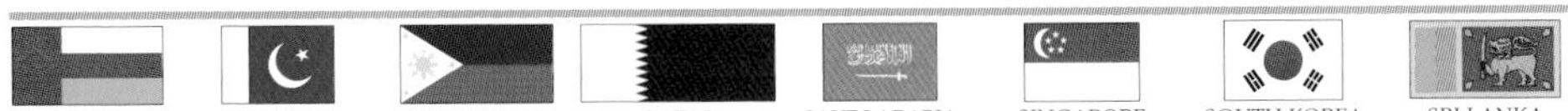

OMAN PAGES 120-121
PAKISTAN PAGES 134-135
PHILIPPINES PAGES 138-139
QATAR PAGES 120-121
SAUDI ARABIA PAGES 120-121
SINGAPORE PAGES 138-139
SOUTH KOREA PAGES 128-129
SRI LANKA PAGES 132-133

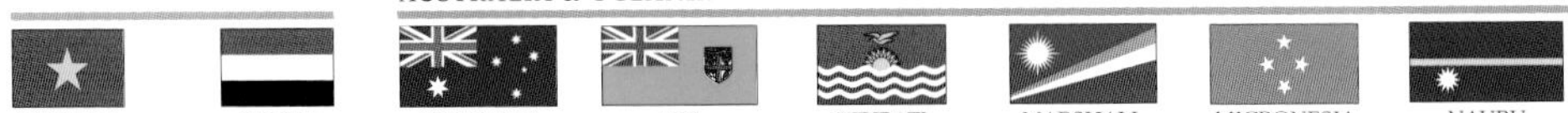

VIETNAM PAGES 136-137
YEMEN PAGES 120-121

AUSTRALIA & OCEANIA

AUSTRALIA PAGES 146-149
FIJI PAGES 144-145
KIRIBATI PAGES 144-145
MARSHALL ISLANDS PAGES 144-145
MICRONESIA PAGES 144-145
NAURU PAGES 144-145

DOMINICAN REPUBLIC PAGES 54-55
EL SALVADOR PAGES 52-53
GRENADA PAGES 54-55
GUATEMALA PAGES 52-53
HAITI PAGES 54-55
HONDURAS PAGES 52-53
JAMAICA PAGES 54-55
MEXICO PAGES 50-51

BOLIVIA PAGES 60-61
BRAZIL PAGES 62-63
CHILE PAGES 64-65
COLOMBIA PAGES 58-59
ECUADOR PAGES 60-61
GUYANA PAGES 58-59
PARAGUAY PAGES 64-65
PERU PAGES 60-61

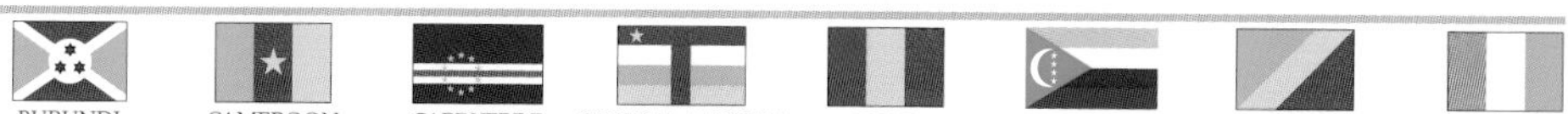

BURUNDI PAGES 72-73
CAMEROON PAGES 76-77
CAPE VERDE PAGES 74-75
CENTRAL AFRICAN REPUBLIC PAGES 76-77
CHAD PAGES 76-77
COMOROS PAGES 78-79
CONGO PAGES 76-77
CÔTE D'IVOIRE PAGES 74-75

GHANA PAGES 74-75
GUINEA PAGES 74-75
GUINEA-BISSAU PAGES 74-75
KENYA PAGES 72-73
LESOTHO PAGES 78-79
LIBERIA PAGES 74-75
LIBYA PAGES 70-71
MADAGASCAR PAGES 78-79

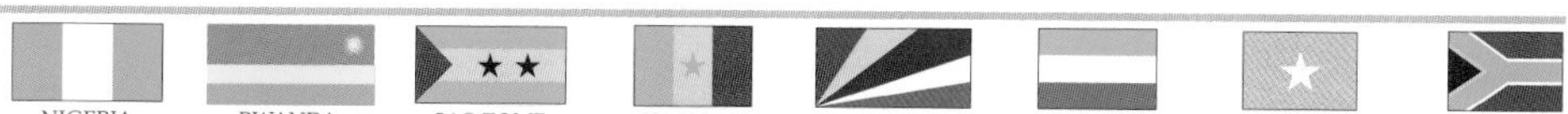

NIGERIA PAGES 74-75
RWANDA PAGES 72-73
SAO TOME & PRINCIPE PAGES 76-77
SENEGAL PAGES 74-75
SEYCHELLES PAGES 78-79
SIERRA LEONE PAGES 74-75
SOMALIA PAGES 72-73
SOUTH AFRICA PAGES 78-79

EUROPE

ALBANIA PAGES 100-101
ANDORRA PAGES 90-91
AUSTRIA PAGES 94-95
BELARUS PAGES 106-107
BELGIUM PAGES 86-87
BOSNIA & HERZEGOVINA PAGES 100-101
BULGARIA PAGES 104-105
CROATIA PAGES 100-101

HUNGARY PAGES 98-99
ICELAND PAGES 82-83
ITALY PAGES 96-97
LATVIA PAGES 106-107
LIECHTENSTEIN PAGES 94-95
LITHUANIA PAGES 106-107
LUXEMBOURG PAGES 86-87
MACEDONIA PAGES 100-101

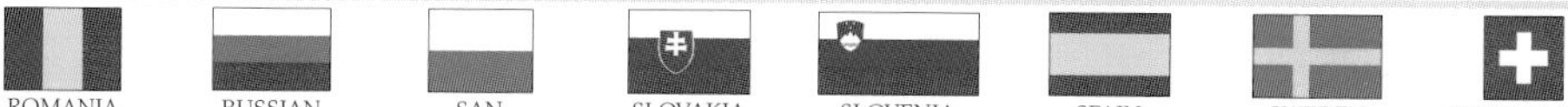

ROMANIA PAGES 108-109
RUSSIAN FEDERATION PAGES 110-111
SAN MARINO PAGES 96-97
SLOVAKIA PAGES 94-95
SLOVENIA PAGES 94-95
SPAIN PAGES 92-93
SWEDEN PAGES 84-85
SWITZERLAND PAGES 94-95

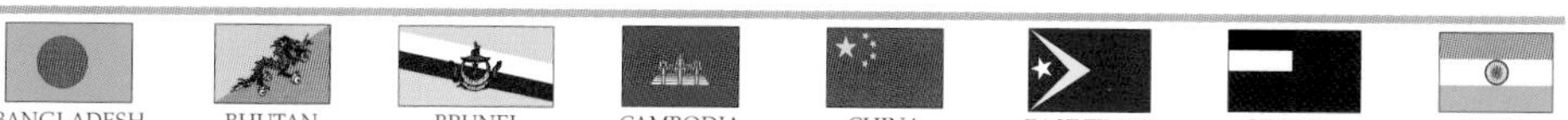

BANGLADESH PAGES 134-135
BHUTAN PAGES 134-135
BRUNEI PAGES 138-139
CAMBODIA PAGES 136-137
CHINA PAGES 126-129
EAST TIMOR PAGES 138-139
GEORGIA PAGES 116-117
INDIA PAGES 132-135

KYRGYZSTAN PAGES 122-123
LAOS PAGES 136-137
LEBANON PAGES 118-119
MALAYSIA PAGES 138-139
MALDIVES PAGES 132-133
MONGOLIA PAGES 126-127
MYANMAR (BURMA) PAGES 136-137
NEPAL PAGES 134-135
NORTH KOREA PAGES 128-129

SYRIA PAGES 118-119
TAIWAN PAGES 128-129
TAJIKISTAN PAGES 122-123
THAILAND PAGES 136-137
TURKEY PAGES 116-117
TURKMENISTAN PAGES 122-123
UNITED ARAB EMIRATES PAGES 120-121
UZBEKISTAN PAGES 122-123

NEW ZEALAND PAGES 150-151
PALAU PAGES 144-145
PAPUA NEW GUINEA PAGES 144-145
SAMOA PAGES 144-145
SOLOMON ISLANDS PAGES 144-145
TONGA PAGES 144-145
TUVALU PAGES 144-145
VANUATU PAGES 144-145

THE POLITICAL WORLD

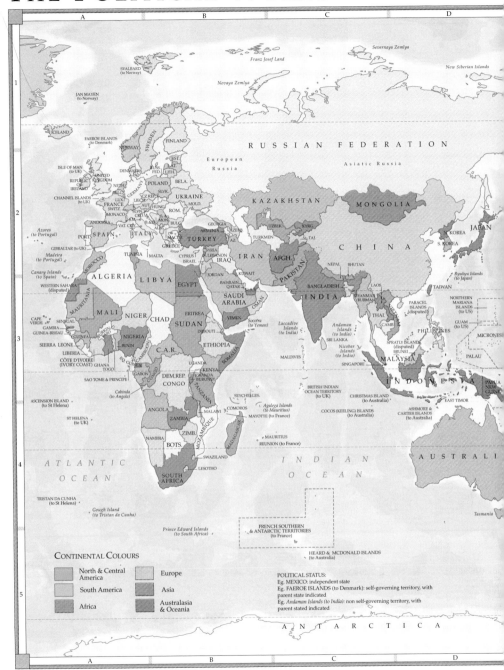

CONTINENTAL COLOURS

- North & Central America
- South America
- Africa
- Europe
- Asia
- Australasia & Oceania

POLITICAL STATUS:
Eg. MEXICO: independent state
Eg. FAEROE ISLANDS (to Denmark): self-governing territory, with parent state indicated
Eg. *Andaman Islands (to India)*: non self-governing territory, with parent stated indicated

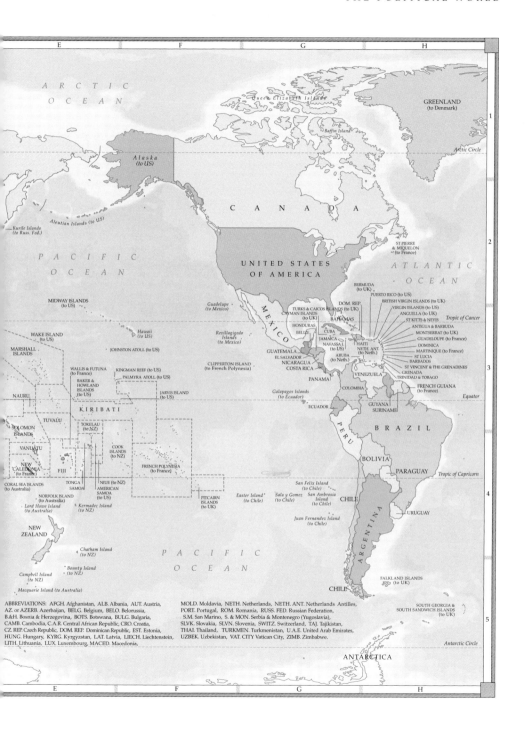

THE PHYSICAL WORLD

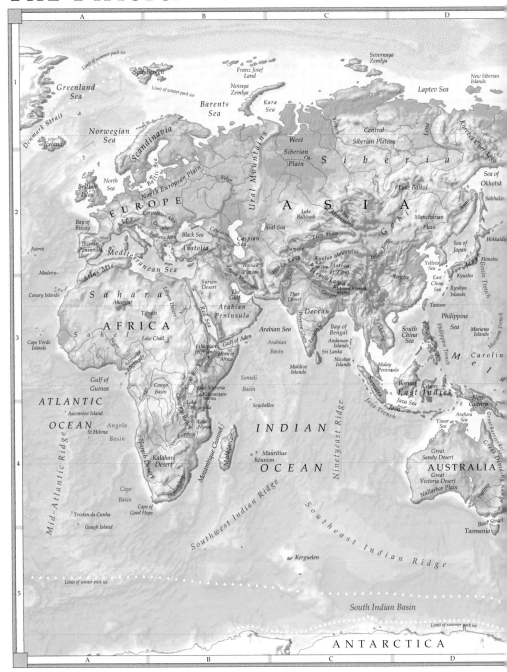

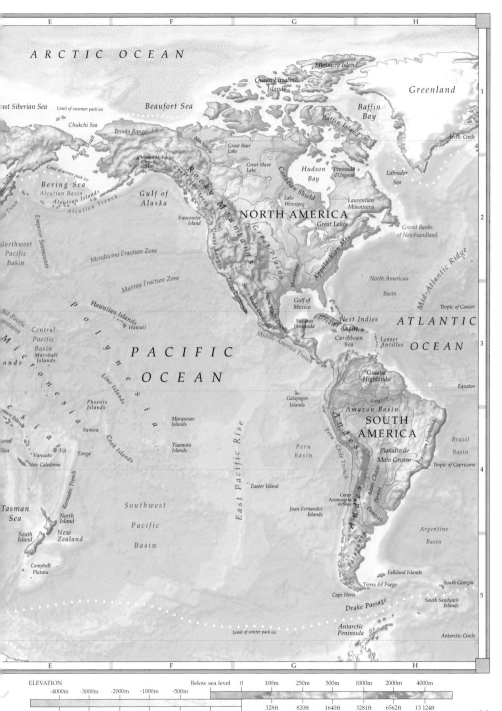

E F G H

ARCTIC OCEAN

East Siberian Sea Limit of summer pack ice

Chukchi Sea

Beaufort Sea

Queen Elizabeth
Islands

Ellesmere Island

Greenland

1

Brooks Range

Baffin Island

*Baffin
Bay*

Bering Strait

Mackenzie

Great Bear
Lake

Arctic Circle

Limit of winter pack ice

Mount McKinley
(Denali)
6194m

Great Slave
Lake

*Hudson
Bay*

Péninsula
d'Ungava

*Labrador
Sea*

Bering Sea

Aleutian Basin

Aleutian Islands

*Gulf of
Alaska*

Canadian Shield

Laurentian
Mountains

Aleutian Trench

Vancouver
Island

Lake
Winnipeg

NORTH AMERICA

Grand Banks
of Newfoundland

2

Emperor Seamounts

Coast Ranges

Rocky Mountains

Great Plains

Great Lakes

*Northwest
Pacific
Basin*

Mendocino Fracture Zone

Appalachian Mts.

North American

Mid-Atlantic Ridge

Murray Fracture Zone

Mississippi

Sierra Madre Occidental

Basin

Tropic of Cancer

Hawaiian Islands

Sierra Madre Oriental

Gulf of
Mexico

Hawaii

Yucatan
Peninsula

Greater Antilles

West Indies

ATLANTIC

3

*Mid-Pacific
Mountains*

*Central
Pacific
Basin*

Micronesia

Marshall
Islands

Middle America Trench

Caribbean
Sea

Lesser
Antilles

OCEAN

*P
o
l
y
n
e
s
i
a*

Line Islands

PACIFIC

OCEAN

Guiana
Highlands

Equator

Phoenix
Islands

Galapagos
Islands

Amazon

Marquesas
Islands

SOUTH
AMERICA

Samoa

Cook Islands

Tuamotu
Islands

Peru
Basin

Andes

Amazon Basin

Brazilian Highlands

*Brazil
Basin*

Vanuatu Fiji

Tonga

Planalto de
Mato Grosso

New Caledonia

Peru-Chile Trench

Gran Chaco

Pantanal

Tropic of Capricorn

4

East Pacific Rise

Easter Island

Cerro
Aconcagua
6959m

*Tasman
Sea*

North
Island

*Southwest

Pacific

Basin*

Juan Fernandez
Islands

Pampas

Patagonia

*Argentine
Basin*

South
Island

New
Zealand

Andes

Campbell
Plateau

Falkland Islands

South Georgia

Tierra del Fuego

Cape Horn

South Sandwich
Islands

5

Limit of winter pack ice

Drake Passage

Antarctic
Peninsula

Antarctic Circle

E F G H

ELEVATION					Below sea level	0	100m	250m	500m	1000m	2000m	4000m
-4000m	-3000m	-2000m	-1000m	-500m								
-13 124ft	-9843ft	-6562ft	-3281ft	-1640ft	-820ft/-250m	0	328ft	820ft	1640ft	3281ft	6562ft	13 124ft

11

TIME ZONES

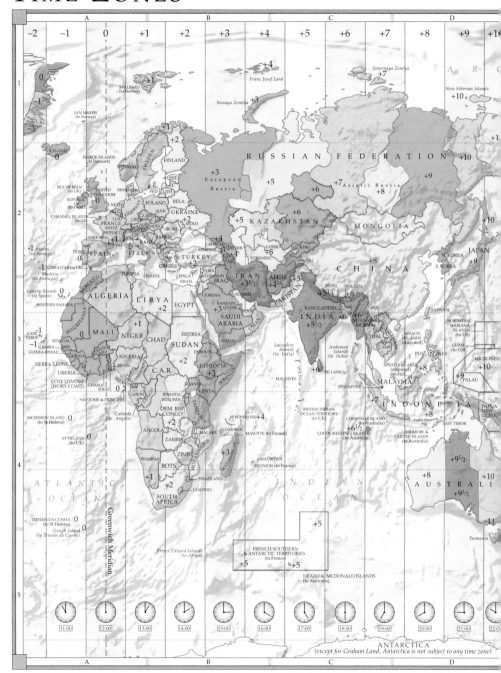

The numbers represented thus: +2/-2, indicate the number of hours each time zone is ahead or behind GMT (Greenwich Mean Time)

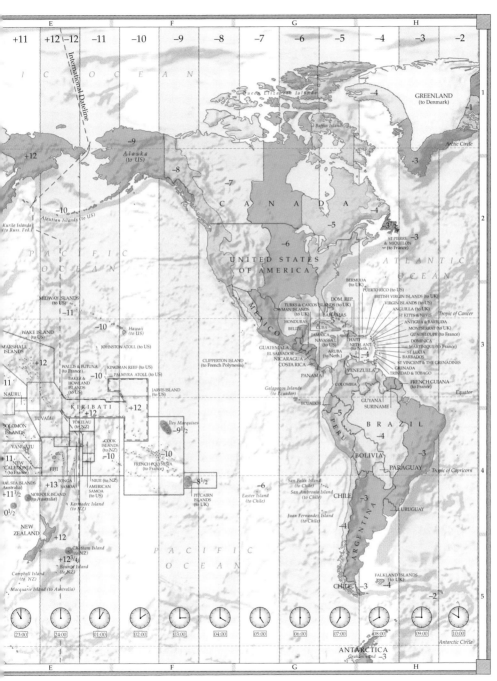

The clocks and 24-hour times given at the bottom of the map show the time in each time zone when it is 12.00 hours noon GMT

GEOLOGY & STRUCTURE

GEOLOGICAL REGIONS — Continental shield — Igneous rock types — **MOUNTAIN RANGES** — Hercynian (290 to 362 Ma) — Ma= millions of years ago

Sedimentary rocks — Coral formation — Alpine (5 to 23 Ma) — Caledonian (386 to 439 Ma)

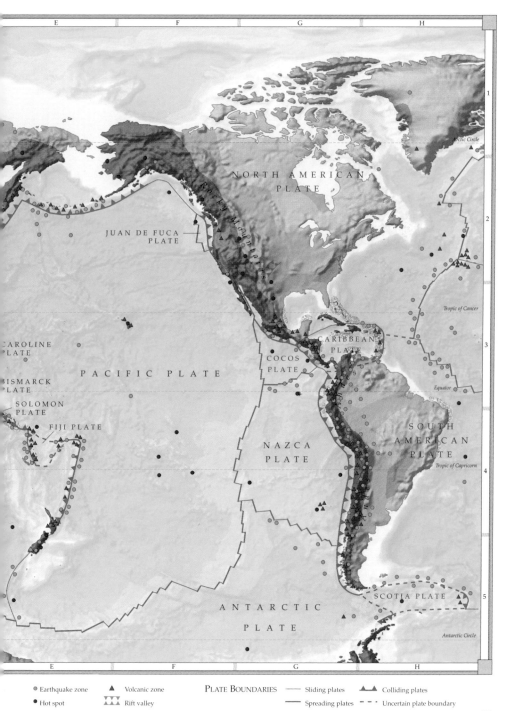

E   F   G   H

Arctic Circle

NORTH AMERICAN
PLATE

JUAN DE FUCA
PLATE

Rocky Mountains

Tropic of Cancer

CAROLINE
PLATE

CARIBBEAN
PLATE

COCOS
PLATE

PACIFIC PLATE

BISMARCK
PLATE

SOLOMON
PLATE

FIJI PLATE

Equator

SOUTH
AMERICAN
PLATE

NAZCA
PLATE

Tropic of Capricorn

SCOTIA PLATE

ANTARCTIC

PLATE

Antarctic Circle

E   F   G   H

● Earthquake zone   ▲ Volcanic zone   PLATE BOUNDARIES   — Sliding plates   ▲▲ Colliding plates

● Hot spot   ▲▲▲ Rift valley   — Spreading plates   - - - Uncertain plate boundary

15

WORLD CLIMATE

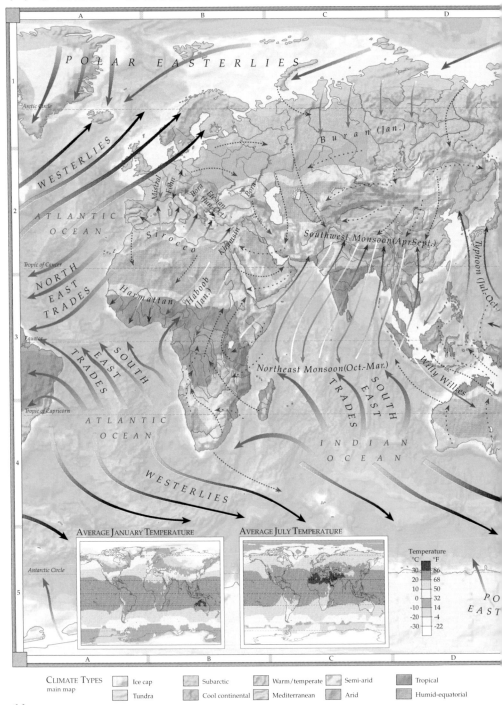

POLAR EASTERLIES

Arctic Circle

WESTERLIES

Buran (Jan.)

ATLANTIC
OCEAN

Mistral
Föhn
Bora
Etesian
Han (Oct.)
Bora

Tropic of Cancer

Sirocco

Khamsin

Southwest Monsoon (Apr.-Sept.)

Typhoon (Jul.-Oct.)

NORTH
EAST
TRADES

Harmattan

Haboob
(Jan.)

Equator

SOUTH
EAST
TRADES

Northeast Monsoon (Oct.-Mar.)

SOUTH
EAST
TRADES

Willy Willies

Tropic of Capricorn

ATLANTIC
OCEAN

INDIAN
OCEAN

WESTERLIES

AVERAGE JANUARY TEMPERATURE

AVERAGE JULY TEMPERATURE

Temperature
°C	°F
30	86
20	68
10	50
0	32
-10	14
-20	-4
-30	-22

Antarctic Circle

PO
EAST

CLIMATE TYPES
main map

Ice cap	Subarctic	Warm/temperate	Semi-arid	Tropical
Tundra	Cool continental	Mediterranean	Arid	Humid-equatorial

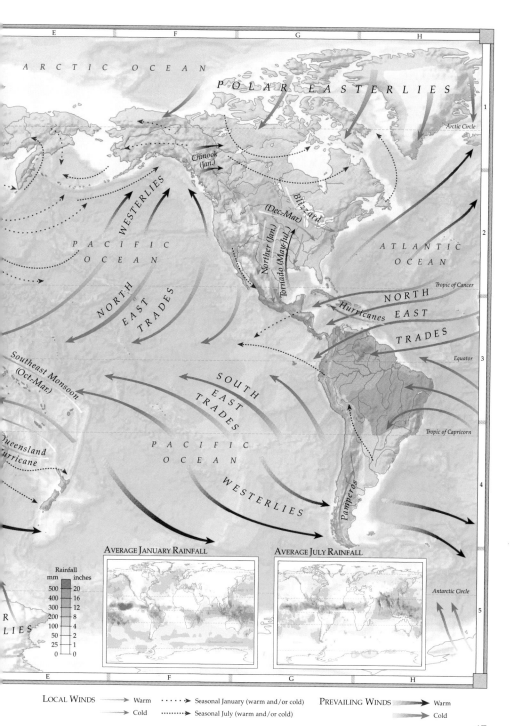

OCEAN CURRENTS

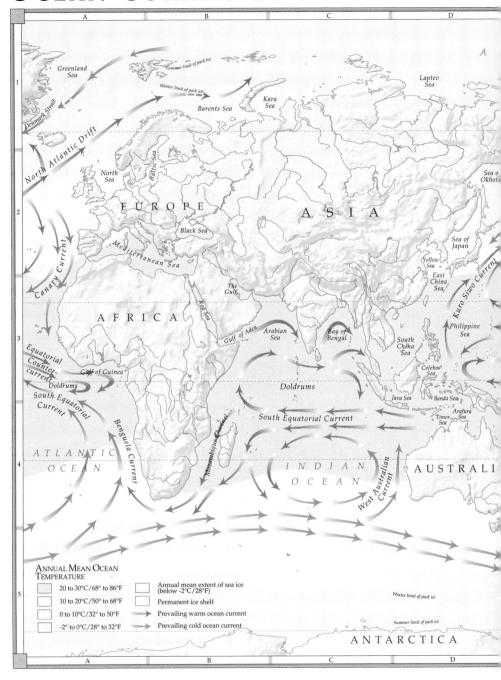

ANNUAL MEAN OCEAN TEMPERATURE

- 20 to 30°C/68° to 86°F
- 10 to 20°C/50° to 68°F
- 0 to 10°C/32° to 50°F
- -2° to 0°C/28° to 32°F
- Annual mean extent of sea ice (below -2°C/28°F)
- Permanent ice shelf
- Prevailing warm ocean current
- Prevailing cold ocean current

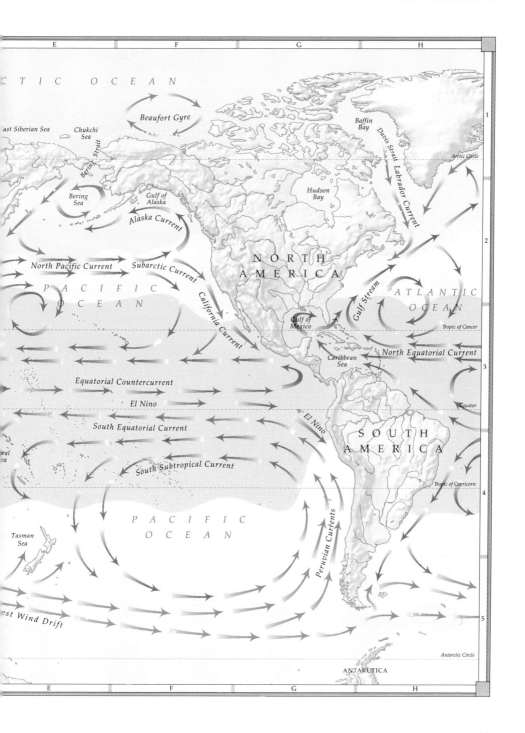

LIFE ZONES

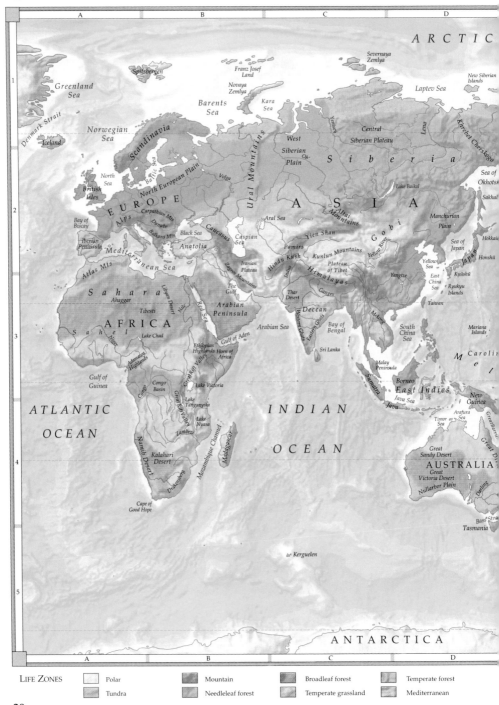

LIFE ZONES
| | Polar | | Mountain | | Broadleaf forest | | Temperate forest |
| | Tundra | | Needleleaf forest | | Temperate grassland | | Mediterranean |

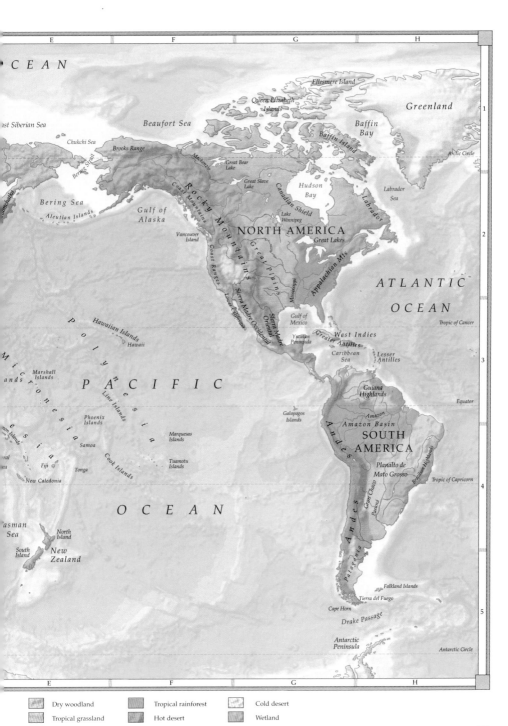

E   F   G   H

OCEAN

Ellesmere Island

Queen Elizabeth
Islands

Greenland

1

East Siberian Sea

Beaufort Sea

Baffin
Bay

Chukchi Sea

Baffin Island

Brooks Range

Arctic Circle

Mackenzie

Bering Strait

Great Bear
Lake

Great Slave
Lake

Hudson
Bay

Labrador
Sea

Bering Sea

Rocky Mountains

Canadian Shield

Labrador

Aleutian Islands

Gulf of
Alaska

Coast Mountains

Lake
Winnipeg

2

Vancouver
Island

NORTH AMERICA

Great Lakes

ATLANTIC

Coast Ranges

Great Plains

Appalachian Mts

OCEAN

Hawaiian Islands

Sierra Nevada

Sierra Madre
Occidental

Mississippi

Gulf of
Mexico

Tropic of Cancer

Hawaii

Yucatan
Peninsula

Sierra Madre
Oriental

West Indies
Greater Antilles

3

PACIFIC

Marshall
Islands

Line Islands

Caribbean
Sea

Lesser
Antilles

Micronesia

Polynesia

Galapagos
Islands

Guiana
Highlands

Equator

Phoenix
Islands

Amazon

Amazon Basin

SOUTH
AMERICA

Samoa

Marquesas
Islands

Andes

Fiji

Cook Islands

Tuamotu
Islands

Planalto de
Mato Grosso

New Caledonia

Tonga

Brazilian Highlands

Gran Chaco

Paraná

Tropic of Capricorn

4

OCEAN

Tasman
Sea

North
Island

South
Island

New
Zealand

Patagonia

Falkland Islands

Tierra del Fuego

Cape Horn

5

Drake Passage

Antarctic
Peninsula

Antarctic Circle

E   F   G   H

Dry woodland   Tropical rainforest   Cold desert

Tropical grassland   Hot desert   Wetland

POPULATION

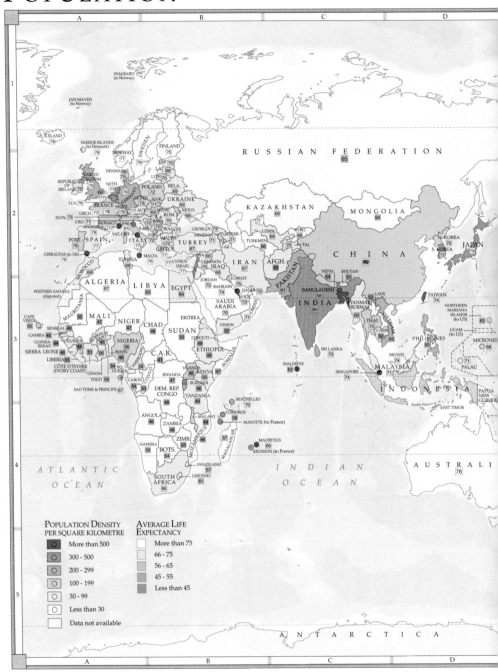

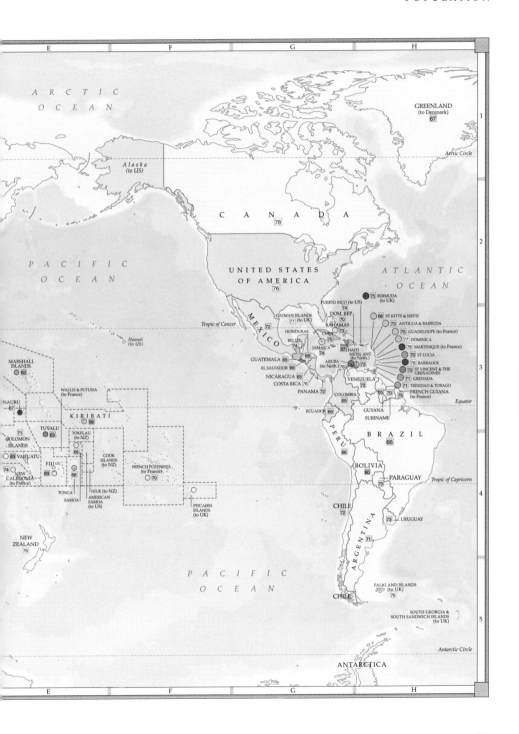

ARCTIC
OCEAN

GREENLAND
(to Denmark)
67

Arctic Circle

Alaska
(to US)

PACIFIC
OCEAN

C A N A D A
78

UNITED STATES
OF AMERICA
76

ATLANTIC
OCEAN

BERMUDA
(to UK)
75

PUERTO RICO (to US)
74

CAYMAN ISLANDS
(to UK) 77

Tropic of Cancer

DOM. REP.
70

ST KITTS & NEVIS 66
ANTIGUA & BARBUDA 73
GUADELOUPE (to France) 75
DOMINICA 77
MARTINIQUE (to France) 76
ST LUCIA 70
BARBADOS 76
ST VINCENT & THE GRENADINES 72
GRENADA 71
TRINIDAD & TOBAGO 71
FRENCH GUIANA (to France) 75

M E X I C O
72

HONDURAS
74

BELIZE
74

CUBA
75

JAMAICA
74

BAHAMAS
73

HAITI
57

NETH. ANT.
(to Neth.)

GUATEMALA 65
EL SALVADOR 68
NICARAGUA 65
COSTA RICA 76

68

ARUBA
(to Neth.) 76

73

Hawaii
(to US)

MARSHALL
ISLANDS
63

PANAMA 72

COLOMBIA
69

VENEZUELA
72

65 70
75

Equator

NAURU
67

WALLIS & FUTUNA
(to France)

KIRIBATI

ECUADOR 69

GUYANA
SURINAME

SOLOMON
ISLANDS
71

TUVALU
63

TOKELAU
(to NZ)
68

P E R U
66

B R A Z I L
66

VANUATU
63

74
NEW
CALEDONIA
(to France)

FIJI
63

COOK
ISLANDS
(to NZ)

68

FRENCH POLYNESIA
(to France)
70

BOLIVIA
60

PARAGUAY
70

Tropic of Capricorn

TONGA

SAMOA

NIUE (to NZ)

AMERICAN
SAMOA
(to US)

PITCAIRN
ISLANDS
(to UK)

CHILE
72

URUGUAY
73

NEW
ZEALAND
76

ARGENTINA
71

PACIFIC

OCEAN

CHILE

FALKLAND ISLANDS
(to UK)
76

SOUTH GEORGIA &
SOUTH SANDWICH ISLANDS
(to UK)

Antarctic Circle

ANTARCTICA

23

LANGUAGES

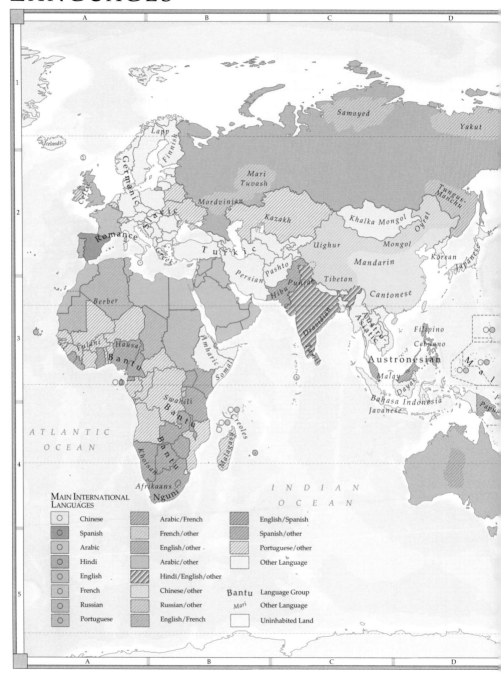

MAIN INTERNATIONAL LANGUAGES

○	Chinese		Arabic/French		English/Spanish
○	Spanish		French/other		Spanish/other
○	Arabic		English/other		Portuguese/other
○	Hindi		Arabic/other		Other Language
○	English		Hindi/English/other		
○	French		Chinese/other	**Bantu**	Language Group
○	Russian		Russian/other	*Mari*	Other Language
○	Portuguese		English/French		Uninhabited Land

Map labels: Icelandic, Lapp, Finnish, Germanic, Celtic, Slavic, Romance, Greek, Turkic, Berber, Mordvinian, Mari, Tuvash, Kazakh, Samoyed, Yakut, Khalka Mongol, Oyrat, Tungus-Manchu, Uighur, Mongol, Mandarin, Korean, Japanese, Persian, Pashto, Tibetan, Cantonese, Punjabi, Hibu, Dravidian, Tamil, Austro-Asiatic, Amharic, Somali, Fulani, Hausa, Bantu, Swahili, Khoisan, Afrikaans, Nguni, Filipino, Cebuano, Austronesian, Malay, Dayak, Bahasa Indonesia, Javanese, Papua, Malagasy, Creoles

ATLANTIC OCEAN

INDIAN OCEAN

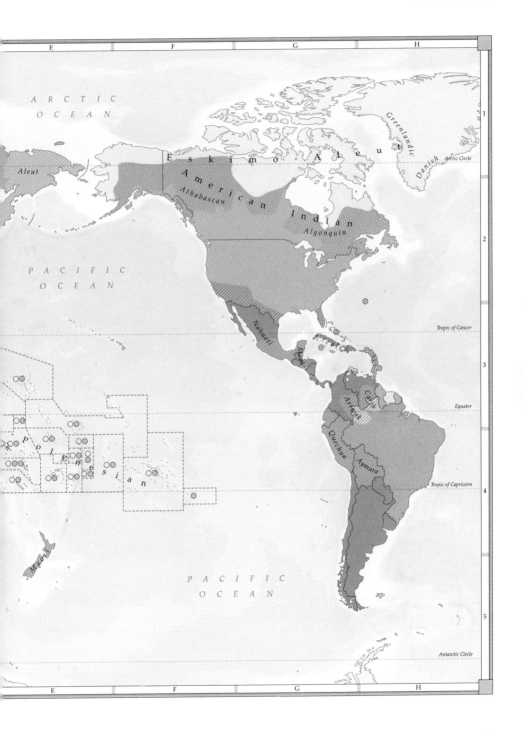

ARCTIC
OCEAN

Greenlandic

Aleut

Danish Arctic Circle

E s k i m o - A l e u t

A m e r i c a n

Athabascan

I n d i a n

Algonquin

PACIFIC
OCEAN

Tropic of Cancer

Nahuatl

Creole

Maya

Carib

Arawak

Equator

Quechua

Aymara

Tropic of Capricorn

P o l y n e s i a n

Maori

PACIFIC
OCEAN

Antarctic Circle

25

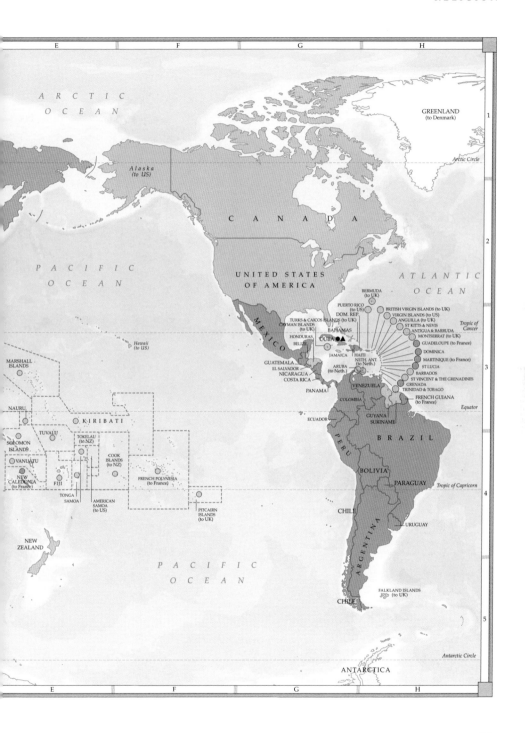

THE GLOBAL ECONOMY

ECONOMIC PERFORMANCE

GNP per capita, 1995 ($US)

- more than 20 000
- 10 000 to 20 000
- 5000 to 10 000
- 1000 to 5000
- 500 to 1000
- 250 to 500
- less than 250
- data not available

Human Development Index (HDI)

- high human development
- poor human development

HDI is one of the best indicators of economic development. The single index is reached by measuring life expectancy at birth, per capita purchasing power, literacy rates and years of schooling

FRENCH SOUTHERN & ANTARCTIC TERRITORIES (to France)

GLOBAL CONFLICT

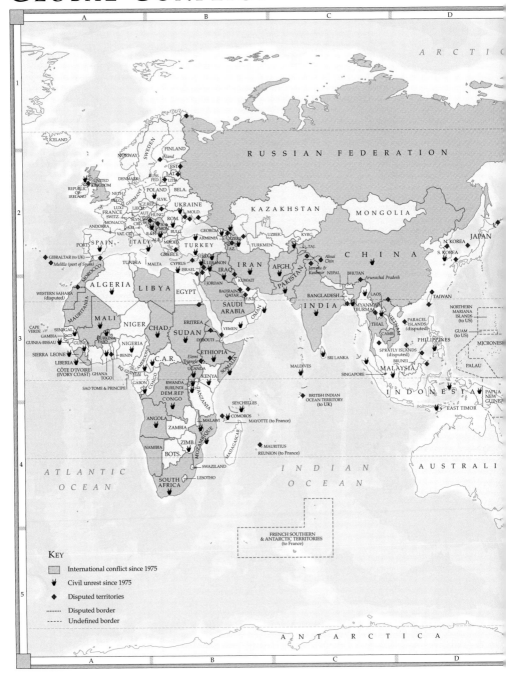

KEY

International conflict since 1975

Civil unrest since 1975

Disputed territories

Disputed border

Undefined border

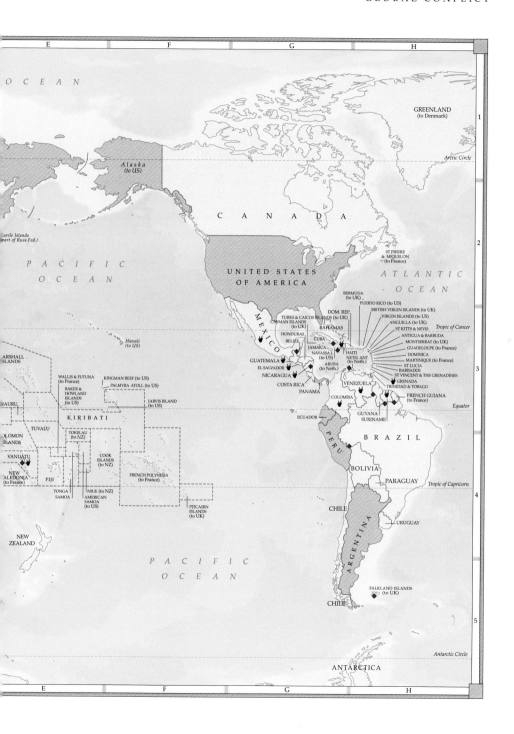

THE
WORLD'S
REGIONS

NORTH & CENTRAL AMERICA

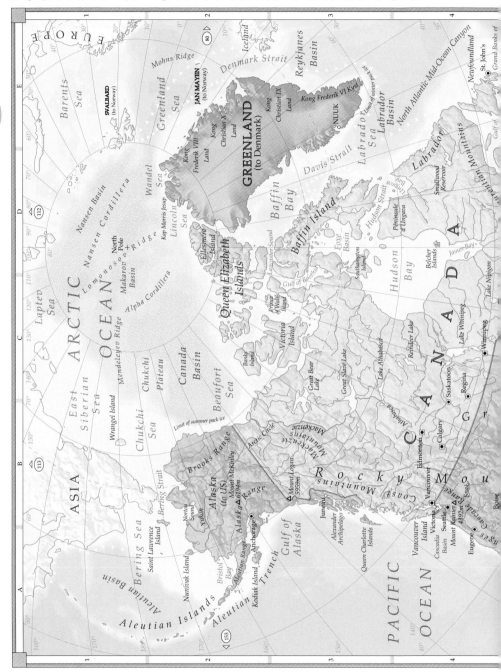

0 km 1000
0 miles 1000

POPULATION   ● National capital

○ Less than 50,000   ○ 50,000 -100,000   ◉ 100,000 - 500,000   ◼ Over 500,000

34

WESTERN CANADA & ALASKA

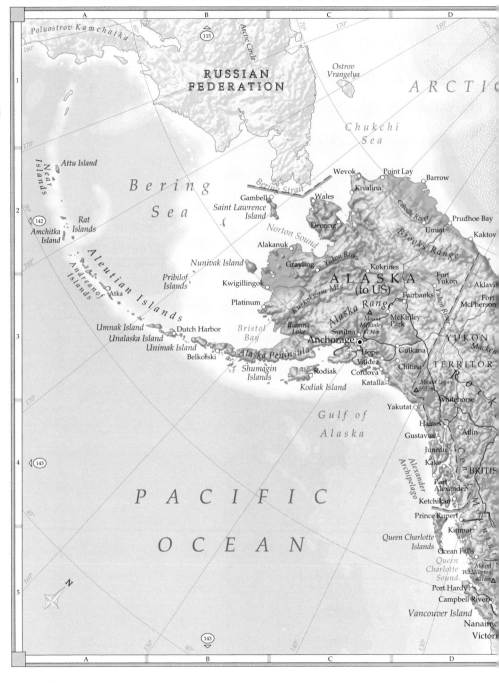

POPULATION

○ Less than 50,000   ○ 50,000 -100,000   ◉ 100,000 - 500,000   ◼ Over 500,000

⦿ Internal administrative capital

0 km   400

0 miles   400

GREENLAND
(to Denmark)

Knud Rasmussen Land

Alert

Ellesmere Island

Axel Heiberg
Island

OCEAN

Baffin
Bay

Prince Patrick
Island

Ellef Ringnes
Island
Isachsen

Amund
Ringnes
Island

Mould Bay

Queen Elizabeth Islands

Devon Island

Davis Strait

Arctic Circle

eaufort

Bathurst
Island Cornwallis
Island

Melville
Island

Lancaster Sound

Resolute

Sea

Banks
Island

Viscount Melville
Sound

Somerset
Island

Brodeur
Peninsula

Baffin Island

Sachs Harbour

McClintock Channel

Prince of
Wales Island

Gulf of Boothia

Cumberland Sound

uktoyaktuk

Amundsen
Gulf

Holman

Boothia
Peninsula

Igloolik

Nettilling
Lake

vik
Paulatuk

Victoria
Island

King William
Island

Pelly Bay

Melville
Peninsula

Amadjuak
Lake

Iqaluit

Fort
Good Hope

Kugluktuk

Cambridge Bay

Gjoa Haven

Foxe
Basin

Repulse Bay

Southampton
Island

Hudson Strait

Great
Bear
Lake

Echo Bay

Burnside

NUNAVUT

Coral
Harbour

Péninsule
d'Ungava

Back

Garry Lake

NORTHWEST

Baker Lake

Coats
Island

Mansel
Island

TERRITORIES

ngsten

Edzo

Yellowknife

Reliance

Rankin Inlet

QUEBEC

Fort Simpson

Great Slave
Lake

Lutselk'e

Whale Cove

Fort Providence

Hudson

Fort Liard

Hay River

Arviat

Fort Nelson

Fort Smith

Bay

OLUMBIA

Lake Athabasca

Churchill

are

Fort Vermilion

Wollaston Lake

Belcher
Islands

CAN

Fort St. John

Fort
McMurray

Fox Mine

Reindeer Lake

Southern
Indian Lake

Nelson

A D A

James
Bay

ALBERTA

Grande Prairie

Buffalo
Narrows

Thompson

Prince George

SASKATCHEWAN

Athabasca

Flin Flon

ONTARIO

Edmonton

Mount Robson
3954m

Leduc

North Saskatchewan

The Pas

Lake
Winnipeg

Red Deer

Kamloops

Calgary

Kindersley

Prince Albert
Saskatoon

Yorkton

MANITOBA

Kelowna

Medicine Hat

Regina

Lake
Manitoba

Brandon

Winnipeg

Cranbrook

Lethbridge

Weyburn

Melita

Lake
of the Woods

Lake Superior

Lake
Huron

ncouver

Milk River

Estevan

Lake
Michigan

UNITED   STATES   OF   AMERICA

ELEVATION

| -4000m | -3000m | -2000m | -1000m | -500m | Below sea level | 0 | 100m | 250m | 500m | 1000m | 2000m | 4000m |

| -13 124ft | -9843ft | -6562ft | -3281ft | -1640ft | -820ft/-250m | 0 | 328ft | 820ft | 1640ft | 3281ft | 6562ft | 13 124ft |

37

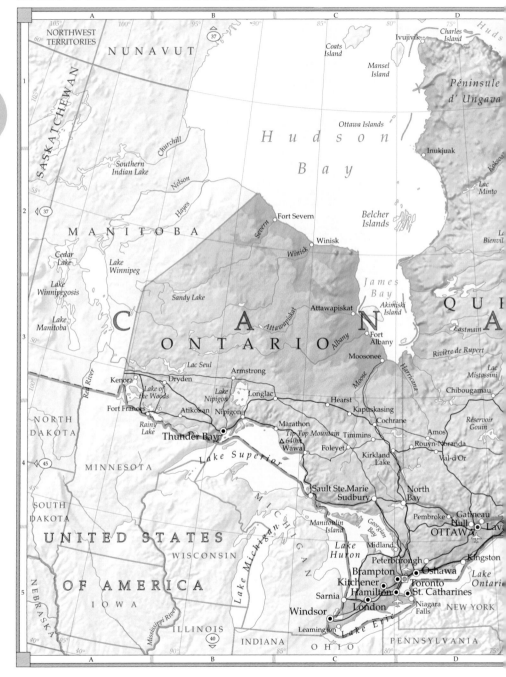

NORTHWEST TERRITORIES

NUNAVUT

SASKATCHEWAN

Huds

Charles Island

Ivujivik

Coats Island

Mansel Island

Péninsule d' Ungava

Ottawa Islands

H u d s o n

B a y

Inukjuak

Lac Minto

Kokso

Churchill

Southern Indian Lake

Nelson

Hayes

Severn

Fort Severn

Winisk

Winisk

Belcher Islands

L Bienvil

MANITOBA

Cedar Lake

Lake Winnipeg

Sandy Lake

J a m e s B a y

Akimiski Island

QU

Lake Winnipegosis

Attawapiskat

Attawapiskat

Eastmain

Lake Manitoba

C

A

ONTARIO

N

A

Albany

Fort Albany

Moosonee

Rivière de Rupert

Lac Mistassini

Red River

Lac Seul

Armstrong

Moose

Harricana

Chibougamau

Kenora

Dryden

Lake of the Woods

Lake Nipigon

Longlac

Hearst

Kapuskasing

Cochrane

Réservoir Gouin

NORTH DAKOTA

Fort Frances

Rainy Lake

Atikokan

Nipigon

Marathon

Tip Top Mountain
△ 640m

Timmins

Amos

Rouyn-Noranda

Val-d'Or

Thunder Bay

Wawal

Foleyet

Kirkland Lake

MINNESOTA

Lake Superior

MICHIGAN

Sault Ste.Marie

Sudbury

North Bay

Pembroke

Gatineau

Null

Lava

OTTAWA

SOUTH DAKOTA

NEBRASKA

UNITED STATES

WISCONSIN

Manitoulin Island

Georgian Bay

Lake Huron

Midland

Peterborough

Kingston

OF AMERICA

IOWA

Lake Michigan

Brampton

Kitchener

Sarnia

Hamilton

London

Oshawa

Toronto

St. Catharines

Lake Ontari

NEW YORK

Windsor

Leamington

Lake Erie

Niagara Falls

ILLINOIS

INDIANA

OHIO

PENNSYLVANIA

0 km   400

0 miles   400

POPULATION   ● National capital   ○ Internal administrative capital

○ Less than 50,000   ○ 50,000 -100,000   ◉ 100,000 - 500,000   ◼ Over 500,000

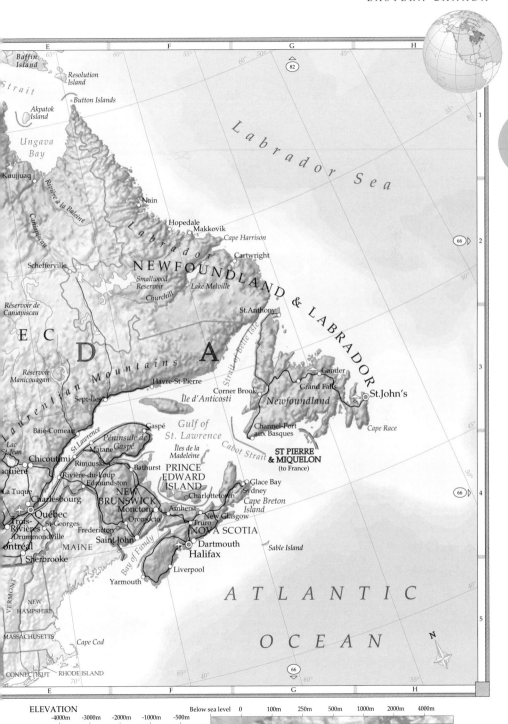

Baffin
Island
Resolution
Island
Button Islands
Akpatok
Island
Ungava
Bay
Strait

Labrador Sea

Kuujjuaq
Rivière à la Baleine
Caniapiscau
Nain
Hopedale
Makkovik
Cape Harrison
Scheffferville
Cartwright
NEWFOUNDLAND & LABRADOR
Smallwood
Reservoir
Lake Melville
Churchill
Réservoir de
Caniapiscau
St.Anthony
E C D A
Laurentian Mountains
Réservoir
Manicouagan
Havre-St-Pierre
Strait of Belle Isle
Sept-Îles
Gander
Île d'Anticosti
Corner Brook
Grand Falls
Newfoundland
St.John's
Baie-Comeau
St.Lawrence
Gaspé
Gulf of
St. Lawrence
Channel-Port
aux Basques
Cape Race
Lac
St-Jean
Matane
Péninsule de
Gaspé
Îles de la
Madeleine
Cabot Strait
ST PIERRE
& MIQUELON
(to France)
Chicoutimi
Rimouski
aquière
Rivière-du-Loup
Bathurst
PRINCE
EDWARD
ISLAND
Glace Bay
Sydney
La Tuque
Edmundston
NEW
BRUNSWICK
Charlottetown
Cape Breton
Island
Charlesbourg
Moncton
Amherst
Québec
St-Georges
Oromocto
New Glasgow
Trois-
Rivières
Fredericton
Truro
NOVA SCOTIA
Drummondville
Saint John
Sable Island
ontréal
MAINE
Dartmouth
Halifax
Sherbrooke
Bay of Fundy
Liverpool
VERMONT
Yarmouth
NEW
HAMPSHIRE
ATLANTIC
MASSACHUSETTS
Cape Cod
OCEAN
N
CONNECTICUT
RHODE ISLAND

ELEVATION
Below sea level   0   100m   250m   500m   1000m   2000m   4000m
-4000m   -3000m   -2000m   -1000m   -500m
328ft   820ft   1640ft   3281ft   6562ft   13 124ft
-13 124ft   -9843ft   -6562ft   -3281ft   -1640ft   -820ft/-250m   0

USA: THE NORTHEAST

Upper Red Lake
Lower Red Lake
Namakan Lake
Isle Royale
Lake Superior
Keweenaw Peninsula
Apostle Islands
Houghton
MINNESOTA
ONTARIO
CANADA
Superior
Ashland
Ironwood
Marquette
Gogebic Range
MICHIGAN
Sault Sainte Marie
North Channel
Georgian Bay
Mille Lacs Lake
Woodruff
Rhinelander
Iron Mountain
Escanaba
Saint Ignace
Cheboygan
Rice Lake
Ladysmith
Beaver Island
Petoskey
Alpena
Lake Huron
WISCONSIN
River Falls
Eau Claire
Wausau
Door Peninsula
Traverse City
Roscommon
Saginaw Bay
Bay City
Mississippi River
Wisconsin Rapids
Stevens Point
Green Bay
Beulah
Cadillac
Midland
Saginaw
Port Huron
IOWA
Tomah
La Crosse
Oshkosh
Fond du Lac
Lake Winnebago
Appleton
West Bend
Sheboygan
Ludington
Muskegon
Mount Pleasant
Grand Rapids
Flint
Lake Saint Clair
Wisconsin River
Madison
Milwaukee
Waukesha
Racine
Wyoming
Lansing
Pontiac
Livonia
Warren
Detroit
Lake Erie
Janesville
Rockford
Kenosha
Waukegan
Evanston
Kalamazoo
Ann Arbor
Adrian
Toledo
Cleveland
Euclid
Warren
Sterling
Elgin
Chicago
South Bend
Elkhart
Sandusky
Akron
Youngstown
Aliquippa
Rock Island
Galesburg
Aurora
Joliet
Gary
Valparaiso
Bowling Green
Findlay
Mansfield
Canton
Ottawa
Kankakee
Fort Wayne
Wabash
Van Wert
Marion
Wheeling
Macomb
Peoria
Bloomington
INDIANA
Kokomo
Sidney
Delaware
Cambridge
OHIO
Quincy
Pekin
Lafayette
Anderson
Muncie
Springfield
Columbus
Zanesville
WEST VIRGINIA
Champaign
Carmel
Delaware
Springfield
Jacksonville
Decatur
ILLINOIS
Indianapolis
Dayton
Kettering
Columbus
Athens
Clarksburg
Alton
Effingham
Terre Haute
Cincinnati
Wilmington
Chillicothe
Parkersburg
Ohio River
East Saint Louis
Bloomington
Columbus
Vincennes
Newport
Portsmouth
Charleston
Lake of the Ozarks
Belleville
Mount Vernon
Wabash River
New Albany
Ohio River
Huntington
Saint Albans
MISSOURI
Missouri River
Carbondale
Evansville
Owensboro
Louisville
Frankfort
Lexington
Richmond
Beckley
Mississippi River
Alton
Paducah
Henderson
Elizabethtown
KENTUCKY
Pikeville
Bluefield
Pulaski
Ozark Plateau
Hopkinsville
Kentucky Lake
Green River
Somerset
London
Bristol
Appalachia
ARKANSAS
Bowling Green
Middlesboro
TENNESSEE

0 km   200
0 miles   200

40

POPULATION
● National capital   ◎ Internal administrative capital
○ Less than 50,000   ◉ 50,000 -100,000   ● 100,000 - 500,000   ■ Over 500,000

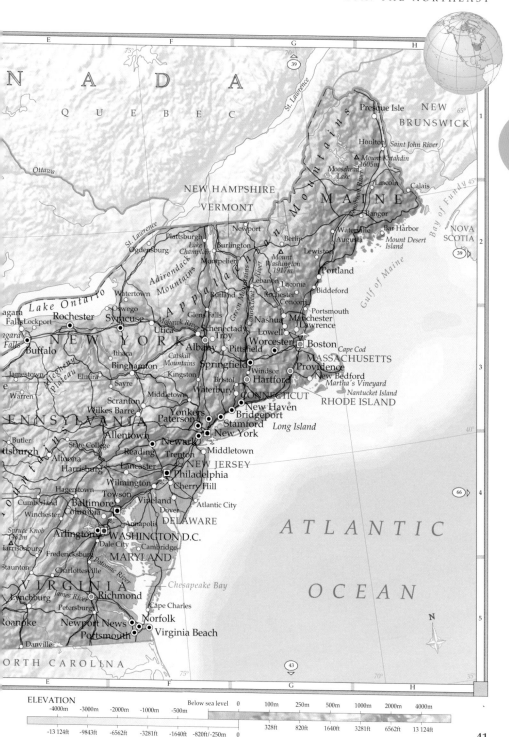

ELEVATION

-4000m	-3000m	-2000m	-1000m	-500m	Below sea level 0	100m	250m	500m	1000m	2000m	4000m
-13 124ft	-9843ft	-6562ft	-3281ft	-1640ft	-820ft/-250m 0	328ft	820ft	1640ft	3281ft	6562ft	13 124ft

USA: THE SOUTHEAST

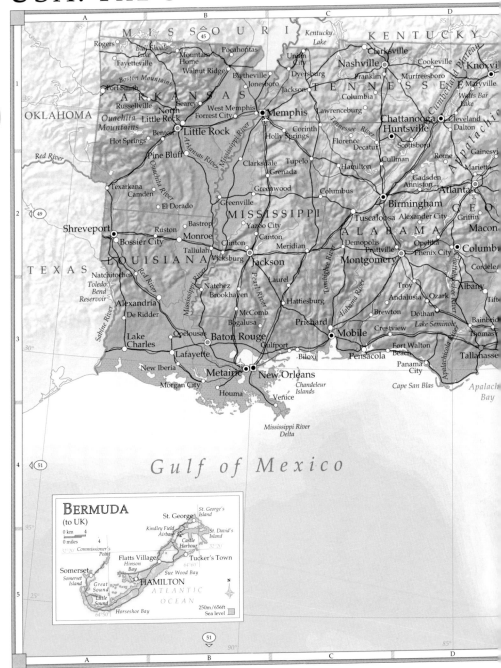

POPULATION

○ Less than 50,000   ○ 50,000 -100,000   ◉ 100,000 - 500,000   ◼ Over 500,000

⦿ Internal administrative capital

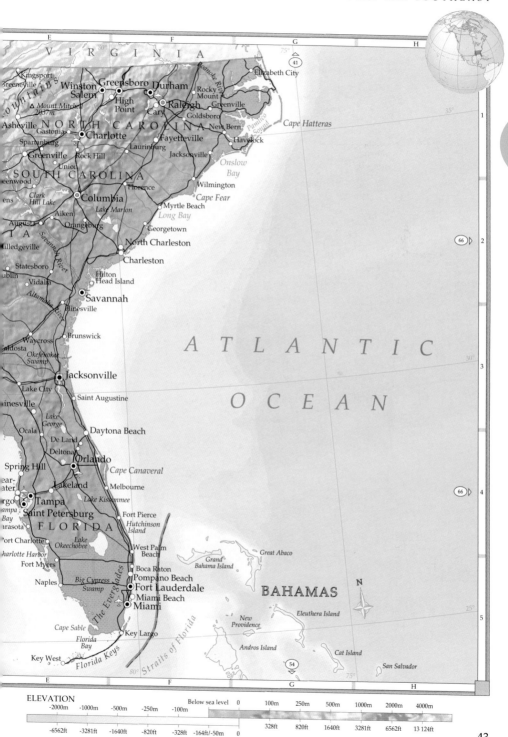

VIRGINIA

41

Kingsport
Greenville
Winston Salem
Greensboro
Durham
High Point
Raleigh
Cary
Rocky Mount
Elizabeth City
△ Mount Mitchell 2037m
NORTH CAROLINA
Asheville
Gastonia
Charlotte
Fayetteville
Goldsboro
Greenville
New Bern
Cape Hatteras
Havelock
Spartanburg
Laurinburg
Jacksonville
Greenville
Rock Hill
Onslow Bay
Union
SOUTH CAROLINA
eenwood
ens
Clark Hill Lake
Columbia
Lake Marion
Florence
Wilmington
Cape Fear
Aiken
Orangeburg
Myrtle Beach
Long Bay
A
Augusta
Georgetown
illedgeville
North Charleston
Charleston
Statesboro
Hilton Head Island
ublin
Vidalia
Savannah
Hinesville
Brunswick
Waycross
aldosta
Okefenokee Swamp
Jacksonville
Lake City
inesville
Saint Augustine
Lake George
Ocala
Daytona Beach
De Land
Deltona
Orlando
Spring Hill
Cape Canaveral
ear-
ater
Lakeland
Melbourne
rgo
Tampa
Lake Kissimmee
ampa Bay
Saint Petersburg
Fort Pierce
arasota
FLORIDA
Hutchinson Island
ort Charlotte
Lake Okeechobee
West Palm Beach
harlotte Harbor
Fort Myers
Big Cypress Swamp
Boca Raton
Pompano Beach
Naples
Fort Lauderdale
Miami Beach
The Everglades
Miami
Cape Sable
Key Largo
Florida Bay
Florida Keys
Key West
Straits of Florida

Roanoke River

Pamlico Sound

Savannah River

Altamaha River

ATLANTIC

OCEAN

BAHAMAS

Grand Bahama Island
Great Abaco
New Providence
Eleuthera Island
Andros Island
Cat Island
San Salvador

N

54

ELEVATION

-2000m	-1000m	-500m	-250m	-100m	Below sea level 0	100m	250m	500m	1000m	2000m	4000m
-6562ft	-3281ft	-1640ft	-820ft	-328ft	-164ft/-50m 0	328ft	820ft	1640ft	3281ft	6562ft	13 124ft

USA: CENTRAL STATES

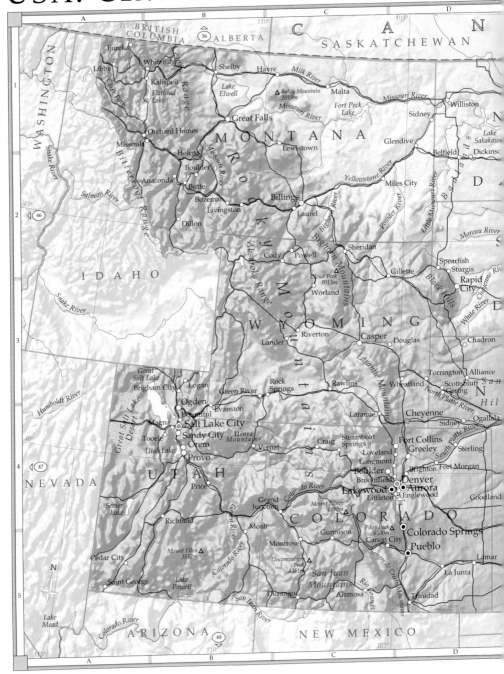

BRITISH COLUMBIA
ALBERTA
36
CANADA
SASKATCHEWAN

WASHINGTON

Eureka
Libby
Whitefish
Kalispell
Flathead Lake
Shelby
Havre
Milk River
Malta
Missouri River
Fort Peck Lake
Sidney
Williston
Lake Sakakawe

Missoula
Orchard Homes
Great Falls
Buffalo Mountain 2019m
Missouri River
MONTANA
Lewistown
Glendive
Belfield
Dickinso

Helena
Boulder
Anaconda
Butte
Bozeman
Livingston
Billings
Laurel
Yellowstone River
Miles City
Powder River
Little Missouri River

Dillon
Absaroka Range
Cody
Powell
Sheridan
Spearfish
Sturgis
Moreau River

IDAHO
Snake River
Cloud Peak 4013m
Worland
Bighorn Mountains
Gillette
Black Hills
Rapid City

Salmon River
ROCKY
WYOMING
Riverton
Casper
Douglas
Chadron

Lander
Laramie Mountains
Torrington
Alliance
San

Great Salt Lake
Brigham City
Logan
Green River
Rock Springs
Rawlins
Wheatland
Scottsbluff
Gering
North Platte River
Hil

Ogden
Evanston
Laramie
Cheyenne
Sidney
Ogalla

Magna
Bountiful
Salt Lake City
Sandy City
Orem
Uinta Mountains
Vernal
Craig
Steamboat Springs
Loveland
Longmont
Fort Collins
Greeley
South Platte River
Sterling

Tooele
Utah Lake
Provo
Mountains
Boulder
Broomfield
Brighton
Fort Morgan

NEVADA
Price
Grand Junction
Colorado River
Mount Elbert 4399m
Lakewood
Littleton
Denver
Aurora
Englewood
Goodland

Sevier Lake
Richfield
Moab
Gunnison
Pikes Peak 4300m
Canon City
COLORADO
Colorado Springs
Lamar

Cedar City
Mount Ellen 3512m
Montrose
Uncompahgre Peak 4361m
San Juan Mountains
Pueblo
La Junta

Saint George
Lake Powell
Durango
Alamosa
Rio Grande
Trinidad

Lake Mead
Colorado River
ARIZONA
48
San Juan River
NEW MEXICO

0 km   200
0 miles   200

POPULATION

○ Less than 50,000   ○ 50,000 -100,000   ◉ 100,000 - 500,000   ■ Over 500,000

◉ Internal administrative capital

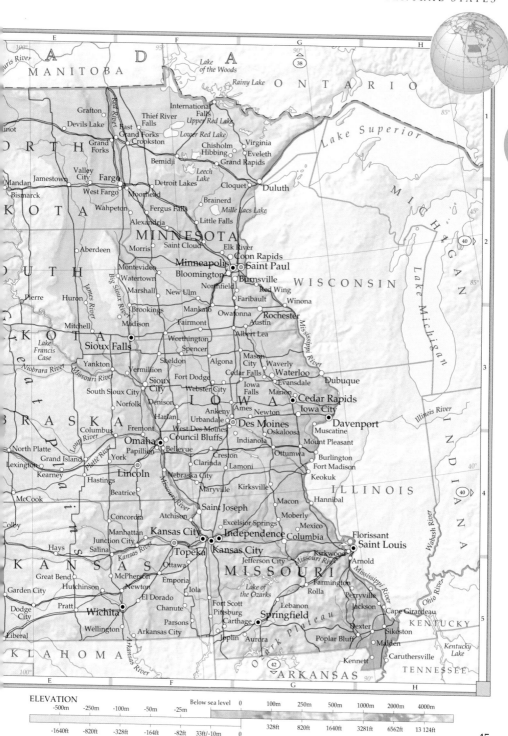

ELEVATION

				Below sea level	0	100m	250m	500m	1000m	2000m	4000m
-500m	-250m	-100m	-50m	-25m							
-1640ft	-820ft	-328ft	-164ft	-82ft	33ft/-10m	0	328ft	820ft	1640ft	3281ft	6562ft	13 124ft

USA: THE WEST

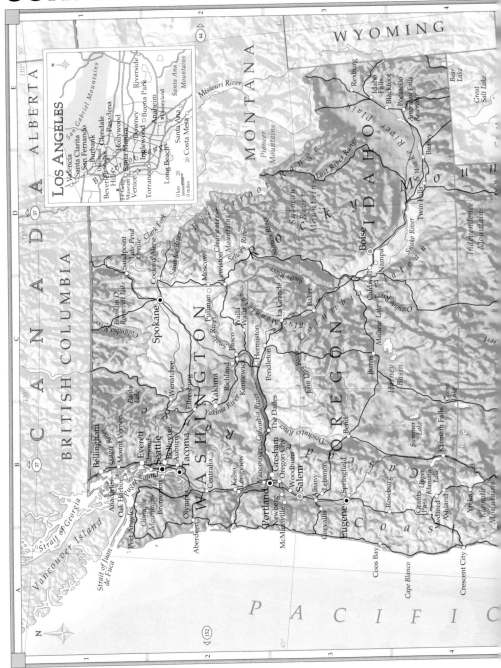

POPULATION

○ Less than 50,000 ○ 50,000 -100,000 ◉ 100,000 - 500,000 ■ Over 500,000

◉ Internal administrative capital

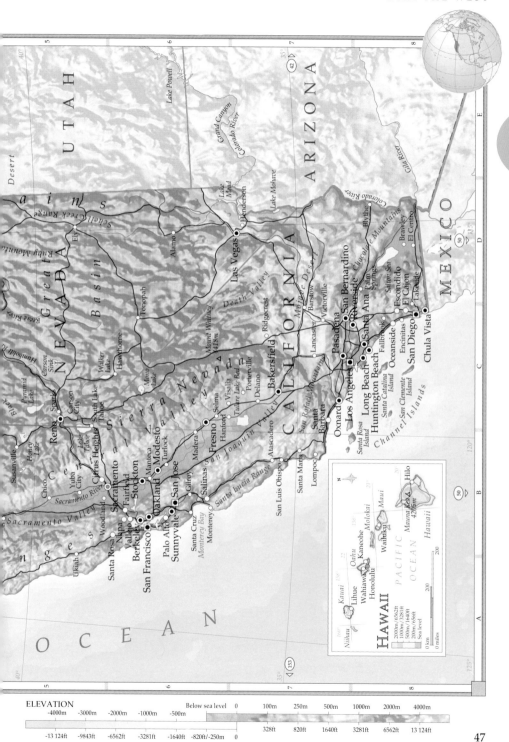

UTAH

ARIZONA

NEVADA

CALIFORNIA

MEXICO

Great Basin

Sierra Nevada

San Joaquin Valley

Central Valley

Sacramento Valley

Mojave Desert

Death Valley

Desert

Ruby Mountains

Schell Creek Range

Grand Canyon

Colorado River

Lake Powell

Lake Mead

Lake Mohave

Gila River

Colorado River

Chocolate Mountains

San Rafael Mountains

Santa Lucia Range

Monterey Bay

Reese River

Humboldt River

Carson River

Walker Lake

Mono Lake

South Lake Tahoe

Lake Tahoe

Tulare Lake Bed

Mount Whitney 4418m

Ely
Alamo
Las Vegas
Henderson
Blythe
San Bernardino
Riverside
Palm Springs
Escondido
El Chon
Brawley
El Centro
La Quinta
San Diego
Chula Vista
Santa Ana
Long Beach
Huntington Beach
Oceanside
Encinitas
Fallbrook
Los Angeles
Pasadena
Victorville
Barstow
Lancaster
Bakersfield
Ridgecrest
Delano
Porterville
Visalia
Selma
Hanford
Madera
Fresno
Atascadero
San Luis Obispo
Santa Maria
Lompoc
Santa Barbara
Oxnard
Tonopah
Hawthorne
Carson City
Sparks
Reno
Susanville
Chico
Ukiah
Santa Rosa
Napa
Vallejo
Fairfield
Woodland
Citrus Heights
Sacramento
Stockton
Manteca
Modesto
Turlock
Gilroy
Salinas
Santa Cruz
Monterey
San Jose
Sunnyvale
Palo Alto
Berkeley
Oakland
San Francisco
Honey Lake
Pyramid Lake
Black Rock
Yuba City
Sacramento River

Channel Islands
Santa Rosa Island
Santa Catalina Island
San Clemente Island

PACIFIC

OCEAN

HAWAII

Niihau
Kauai
Lihue
Oahu
Wahiawa
Honolulu
Kaneohe
Molokai
Wailuku
Maui
Hawaii
Hilo
Mauna Kea 4205m

PACIFIC OCEAN

N

2000m / 6562ft
1000m / 3281ft
500m / 1640ft
200m / 656ft
Sea level

0 km   200
0 miles   200

ELEVATION

-4000m	-3000m	-2000m	-1000m	-500m	Below sea level 0	100m	250m	500m	1000m	2000m	4000m
-13 124ft	-9843ft	-6562ft	-3281ft	-1640ft	-820ft/-250m 0	328ft	820ft	1640ft	3281ft	6562ft	13 124ft

USA: THE SOUTHWEST

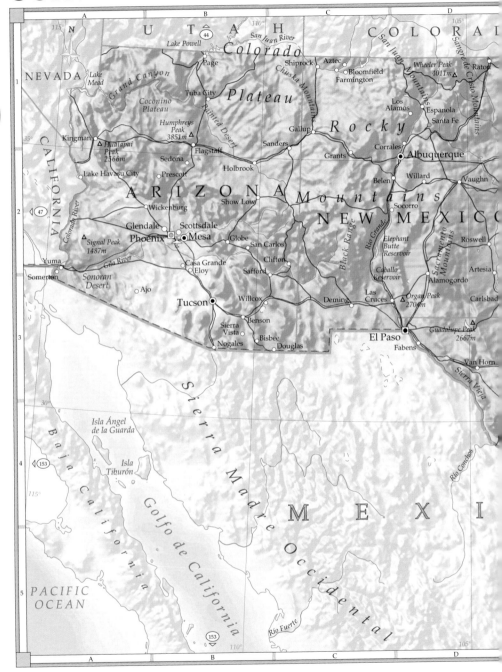

NEVADA

UTAH

COLORADO

CALIFORNIA

ARIZONA

NEW MEXICO

MEXICO

Colorado Plateau

Rocky Mountains

Lake Powell
San Juan River
Page
Shiprock
Aztec
Bloomfield
Farmington
Wheeler Peak
4011m
Raton
Sangre de Cristo Mountains

Lake Mead
Grand Canyon
Tuba City
Chuska Mountains
Los Alamos
Espanola
Santa Fe

Coconino Plateau
Painted Desert
Gallup
Corrales
Albuquerque

Kingman
Humphreys Peak
3851m
Sanders
Grants
Belen
Willard
Vaughn

Hualapai Peak
2566m
Flagstaff
Sedona
Holbrook
Socorro
Roswell

Lake Havasu City
Prescott
Show Low
Elephant Butte Reservoir
Black Range
Rio Grande

Wickenburg
Glendale
Scottsdale
Globe
San Carlos
Clifton
Caballo Reservoir
Sacramento Mountains
Artesia

Colorado River
Signal Peak
1487m
Phoenix
Mesa
Safford
Alamogordo

Yuma
Gila River
Casa Grande
Eloy
Deming
Las Cruces
Organ Peak
2704m
Carlsbad

Somerton
Sonoran Desert
Ajo
Willcox
El Paso
Guadalupe Peak
2667m

Tucson
Sierra Vista
Benson
Bisbee
Fabens
Van Horn

Nogales
Douglas
Sierra Vieja

Isla Ángel de la Guarda

Isla Tiburón

Sierra Madre Occidental

Baja California

Golfo de California

Río Conchos

Río Fuerte

PACIFIC OCEAN

0 km   200
0 miles   200

POPULATION

○ Less than 50,000

○ 50,000 -100,000

◉ Internal administrative capital

◉ 100,000 - 500,000

■ Over 500,000

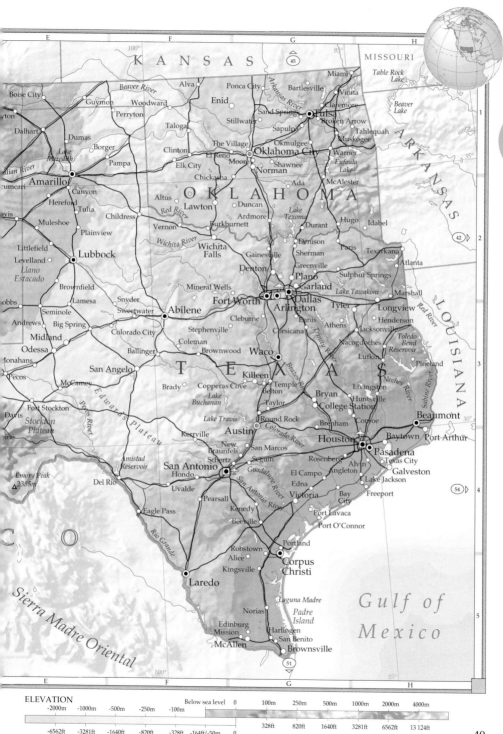

ELEVATION

-2000m	-1000m	-500m	-250m	-100m	Below sea level 0	100m	250m	500m	1000m	2000m	4000m
-6562ft	-3281ft	-1640ft	-820ft	-328ft	-164ft/-50m 0	328ft	820ft	1640ft	3281ft	6562ft	13 124ft

MEXICO

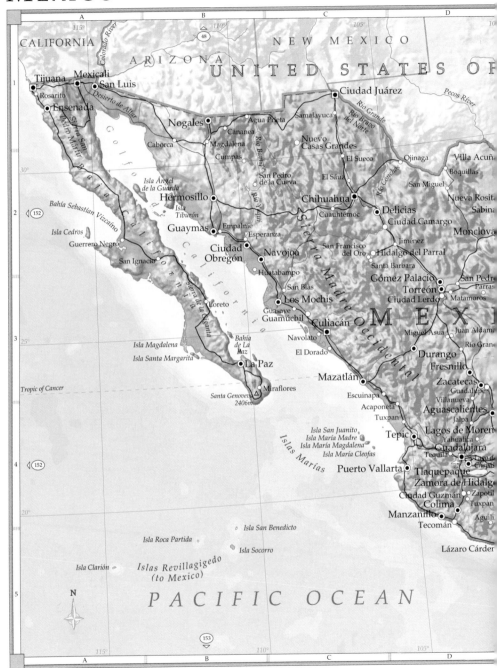

POPULATION ● National capital
○ Less than 50,000 ◐ 50,000 -100,000 ◉ 100,000 - 500,000 ◼ Over 500,000

AMERICA

T E X A S

Brazos River

Colorado River

Red River

Sabine River

Mississippi River

LOUISIANA

MISSISSIPPI

ALABAMA

FLORIDA

Mississippi River Delta

Piedras Negras

Río Grande

Nuevo Laredo

Padre Island

Gulf of

Mexico

Sabinas Hidalgo

Ciudad Miguel Alemán

Reynosa

Río Bravo

Matamoros

Monterrey

Montemorelos

Laguna Madre

Saltillo

Linares

Sierra Madre Oriental

Ciudad Victoria

Tropic of Cancer

85°

Ciudad Mante

Ciudad Madero

Yucatan Channel

Cancún

San Luis Potosí

Pánuco

Tampico

Río Lagartos

Tizimín

Isla Cozumel

Ciudad Valles

Progreso

Motul

Río Verde

Laguna de Tamiahua

Mérida

Dolores Hidalgo

Tamazunchale

Umán

Ticul

Valladolid

Tuxpán

Peto

Guanajuato

Poza Rica

Bahía de Campeche

Oxkutzcab

Teka

Campeche

Felipe Carrillo Puerto

Irapuato

Querétaro

Pachuca

Papantla

Champotón

Yucatan Peninsula

Morelia

Tulancingo

Teziutlán

Laguna de Términos

Chetumal

MEXICO

(MEXICO CITY)

Perote

Xalapa

Toluca

Tlaxcala

Veracruz

Frontera

Fransisco Escárcega

Cuernavaca

Popocatépetl 5452m

Puebla

Alvarado

Comalcalco

Carmen

BELIZE

Zacatepec

Córdoba

San Andrés Tuxtla

Coatzacoalcos

Villahermosa

Uruapan

Taxco

Tehuacán

Macuspana

Río Usumacinta

Gulf of Honduras

Presa del Infiernillo

Iguala

Cuautla

Tuxtepec

Minatitlán

Teapa

Río Balsas

Chilpancingo

Huajuapan

Istmo de Tehuantepec

San Cristóbal de Las Casas

Ixtapa

Sierra Madre del Sur

Oaxaca

Tuxtla

Chiapa de Corzo

Comitán

Tecpan

Ixtepec

Matías Romero

Acapulco

Pinotepa Nacional

Tehuantepec

Juchitán

Arriaga

Presa de la Angostura

Miahuatlán

Salina Cruz

Pijijiapán

GUATEMALA

HONDURAS

Puerto Escondido

Puerto Ángel

Golfo de Tehuantepec

Escuintla

Huixtla

Tapachula

Ciudad Hidalgo

EL SALVADOR

42

66

52

153

ELEVATION

					Below sea level	0	100m	250m	500m	1000m	2000m	4000m
-4000m	-3000m	-2000m	-1000m	-500m								
-13 124ft	-9843ft	-6562ft	-3281ft	-1640ft	-820ft/-250m	0	328ft	820ft	1640ft	3281ft	6562ft	13 124ft

51

CENTRAL AMERICA

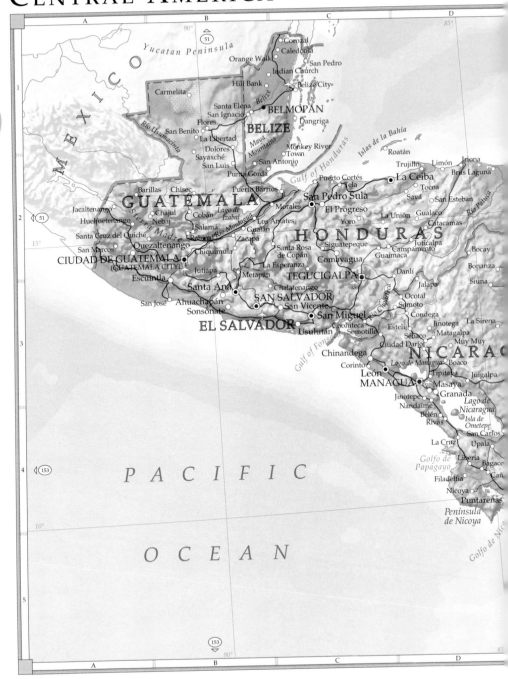

MEXICO

Yucatan Peninsula

Corozal
Caledonia
Orange Walk
San Pedro
Indian Church
Hill Bank
Belize City
Carmelita
Santa Elena
San Ignacio
BELMOPAN
Flores
Dangriga
La Libertad
BELIZE
Dolores
Monkey River Town
Sayaxché
San Antonio
San Luis
Roatán
Punta Gorda
Islas de la Bahía
Barillas
Chisec
Puerto Barrios
Trujillo
Limón
Iriona
Jacaltenango
Chajul
Cobán
Morales
Puerto Cortés
Tela
La Ceiba
Brus Laguna
Huehuetenango
Nebaj
Lago de Izabal
San Pedro Sula
Tocoa
GUATEMALA
Salamá
Los Amates
El Progreso
Savá
San Esteban
Santa Cruz del Quiché
Rabinal
Gualán
Yoro
La Unión
Gualaco
San Marcos
Zacapa
Catacamas
Quezaltenango
Chiquimula
Santa Rosa de Copán
Siguatepeque
Campamento
Juticalpa
Bocay
CIUDAD DE GUATEMALA
(GUATEMALA CITY)
HONDURAS
Comayagua
Guaimaca
Bonanza
Escuintla
Jutiapa
La Esperanza
Danlí
Siuna
Metapán
TEGUCIGALPA
Jalapa
Santa Ana
Chalatenango
Ocotal
San José
Ahuachapán
SAN SALVADOR
Somoto
Condega
Sonsonate
San Vicente
Choluteca
Esteli
Jinotega
La Sirena
EL SALVADOR
San Miguel
Somotillo
Sebaco
Matagalpa
Muy Muy
Usulután
Chinandega
Ciudad Darío
NICARAG
Corinto
Lago de Managua
Boaco
León
Tipitapa
Juigalpa
MANAGUA
Masaya
Jinotepe
Granada
Nandaime
Lago de Nicaragua
Belén
Rivas
Isla de Ometepe
La Cruz
San Carlos
Upala
Liberia
Bagace
Golfo de Papágayo
Filadelfia
Cañ
Nicoya
Puntarenas
Península de Nicoya
Golfo de Nic

Gulf of Honduras

Gulf of Fonseca

PACIFIC

OCEAN

90°
85°
15°
10°

51
153

0 km 200
0 miles 200

POPULATION

○ Less than 50,000 ○ 50,000 -100,000 ◉ 100,000 - 500,000 ■ Over 500,000

● National capital

Islas Santanilla
(to Honduras)

Bajo Nuevo
(to Colombia)

Cayo de Serranilla
(to Colombia)

15°

una de Caratasca

Puerto Lempira

Cayo de Serrana
(to Colombia)

ío Coco

Vaspam

Cayos Miskitos

75°

Yablis
Tuapi
Puerto Cabezas

C   a   r   i   b   b   e   a   n

Prinzapolka

Isla de Providencia
(to Colombia)

Barra de Río Grande

S   e   a

Mosquito Coast

Isla de San Andrés
(to Colombia)

JA

Laguna de Perlas

Rama

Islas del Maíz

Bluefields

Punta Gorda

San Juan del Norte

10°

San Juan
rto
iejo

COSTA RICA
Siquirres
Istmo de Panamá

El Porvenir

uesada
Heredia

ela
SAN JOSÉ   Limón

Portobelo
Colón
Cristóbal

Gulf of
Darien

Cartago
Guabito

Ailigandí

Cordillera de San Blas

Cerro Chirripó
Grande
3819m

Almirante

Golfo de los
Mosquitos

Panama Canal
Lago Gatún

Lago Bayano

Puerto Obaldía

pos
Buenos Aires
Cortés

Laguna
de Chiriquí

Balboa
San Miguelito

Chimán

Serranía del Darién

Cordillera de
Talamanca

Palmar Sur
Bahía
Coronado

Boquete

Volcán Barú 3475m

Capira
PANAMÁ
(PANAMA CITY)

La Palma

Yaviza

Cordillera Central

Penonomé

Archipiélago
de las Perlas

Isla
del Rey

El Real

COLOMBIA

La Concepción
David   P   A   N   A   M   A

Garachiné

nínsula de Osa

Aguadulce
Santiago

Golfo Dulce

Golfo
de Chiriquí

Guarumal

Ocú
Chitré

Golfo
de Panamá

Las Tablas

Jaqué

Isla de Coiba

Península de
Azuero

Isla
Cébaco

80°

ELEVATION

-4000m	-3000m	-2000m	-1000m	-500m	Below sea level	0	100m	250m	500m	1000m	2000m	4000m
-13 124ft	-9843ft	-6562ft	-3281ft	-1640ft	-820ft/-250m	0	328ft	820ft	1640ft	3281ft	6562ft	13 124ft

THE CARIBBEAN

N

UNITED STATES OF AMERICA

Gulf of Mexico

Tropic of Cancer

The Everglades

Grand Bahama Island
Freeport
Marsh Harbour
Great Abaco

Bimini Islands
Berry Islands
Nicholls Town
NASSAU
New Providence
Eleuthera Island

Florida Keys

Straits of Florida

Andros Town
Rock Sound
Cat Island

Cay Sal
Andros Island

Anguilla Cays

Exuma Cays
Exuma Sound

San Salvador

BAHAMAS

George Town
Rum Cay

LA HABANA (HAVANA)
Guanabacoa
Cárdenas
Matanzas
Sagua la Grande
Santa Clara

Great Exuma Island
Long Island
Clarence Town
Crooked Island

Artemisa
Pinar del Río
Consolación del Sur
La Fé
Cienfuegos
Placetas
Archipiélago de Camagüey

Ragged Island Range
Acklins Island

Mayaguan
Caicos Passage

Nueva Gerona
Isla de la Juventud
Archipiélago de los Canarreos
Cayo Largo
Sancti Spíritus
Ciego de Ávila
Morón

Bahía de Cochinos
Cayo Largo

CUBA
Camagüey
Nuevitas

Las Tunas
Holguín
Little Inagua
Lake Rosa

Archipiélago de los Jardines de la Reina
Manzanillo
Bayamo
Matthew Town
Great Inagua

Palma Soriano
Santiago de Cuba
Guantánamo
Cap-Haïtien
Gonaïves

Little Cayman
Cayman Brac
Guantánamo Bay (to US)

GEORGE TOWN
Grand Cayman

CAYMAN ISLANDS (to UK)

NAVASSA ISLAND (to US)
Île de la Gonâve
Jérémie
PORT-AU-PRINCE
HAITÍ

Montego Bay
Cayes
Jacm

Spanish Town
Portmore
KINGSTON

JAMAICA
Pedro Cays

Caribbean Sea

HONDURAS

NICARAGUA

COSTA RICA

COLOMBIA

JAMAICA inset

JAMAICA

Montego Bay
Lucea
Falmouth
Runaway Bay
St Ann's Bay
Caribbean Sea

Cambridge
The Cockpit Country
Ocho Rios
Annotto Bay
Buff Bay
Port Antonio

Savanna-La-Mar
Christiana
Ewarton
Blue Mountain Peak △ 2256m

Black River
Mandeville
May Pen
Spanish Town
KINGSTON
Old Harbour
Portmore
Morant Bay

Portland Bight

Caribbean Sea

0 km   20
0 miles   20

2000m/6562ft
1000m/3281ft
500m/1640ft
200m/656ft
Sea level

POPULATION
● National capital
○ Less than 50,000
○ 50,000 -100,000
◉ 100,000 - 500,000
■ Over 500,000

0 km   200
0 miles   200

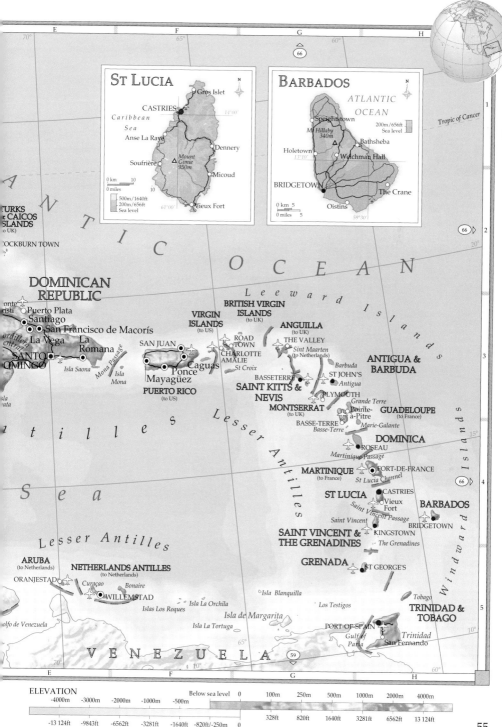

ST LUCIA

- Gros Islet
- CASTRIES
- *Caribbean Sea*
- Anse La Raye
- Dennery
- Soufrière
- △ Mount Gimie 950m
- Micoud
- Vieux Fort

0 km 10
0 miles 10

500m/1640ft
200m/656ft
Sea level

BARBADOS

ATLANTIC OCEAN

- Speightstown
- Mt Hillaby 340m △
- Bathsheba
- Holetown
- Watchman Hall
- BRIDGETOWN
- The Crane
- Oistins

200m/656ft
Sea level

0 km 5
0 miles 5

13°10'
59°30'

ATLANTIC OCEAN

Leeward Islands

DOMINICAN REPUBLIC

- Puerto Plata
- Santiago
- San Francisco de Macorís
- La Vega
- La Romana
- SANTO DOMINGO
- Isla Saona

Cordillera Central

Mona Passage
Isla Mona

SAN JUAN
Caguas
Ponce
Mayagüez
PUERTO RICO
(to US)

VIRGIN ISLANDS
(to US)

BRITISH VIRGIN ISLANDS
(to UK)

ROAD TOWN
CHARLOTTE AMALIE
St Croix

ANGUILLA
(to UK)
THE VALLEY
Sint Maarten
(to Netherlands)

Barbuda
ANTIGUA & BARBUDA
ST JOHN'S
Antigua

BASSETERRE
SAINT KITTS & NEVIS
MONTSERRAT
(to UK)
PLYMOUTH

Grande Terre
GUADELOUPE
(to France)
Pointe-à-Pitre
BASSE-TERRE
Basse-Terre
Marie-Galante

DOMINICA
ROSEAU

Martinique Passage

MARTINIQUE
(to France)
FORT-DE-FRANCE
St Lucia Channel

ST LUCIA
CASTRIES
Vieux Fort

BARBADOS
BRIDGETOWN

Saint Vincent
Saint Vincent Passage

SAINT VINCENT & THE GRENADINES
KINGSTOWN
The Grenadines

GRENADA
ST GEORGE'S

Lesser Antilles
Windward Islands

ARUBA
(to Netherlands)
ORANJESTAD

NETHERLANDS ANTILLES
(to Netherlands)
Curaçao
Bonaire
WILLEMSTAD

Isla La Orchila
Isla Blanquilla
Los Testigos
Isla de Margarita
Isla La Tortuga

Tobago

TRINIDAD & TOBAGO

PORT-OF-SPAIN
Gulf of Paria
Trinidad
San Fernando

Golfo de Venezuela
VENEZUELA

TURKS & CAICOS ISLANDS
(to UK)
COCKBURN TOWN

Lesser Antilles

Caribbean Sea

ELEVATION

-4000m	-3000m	-2000m	-1000m	-500m	Below sea level 0	100m	250m	500m	1000m	2000m	4000m
-13 124ft	-9843ft	-6562ft	-3281ft	-1640ft	-820ft/-250m 0	328ft	820ft	1640ft	3281ft	6562ft	13 124ft

SOUTH AMERICA

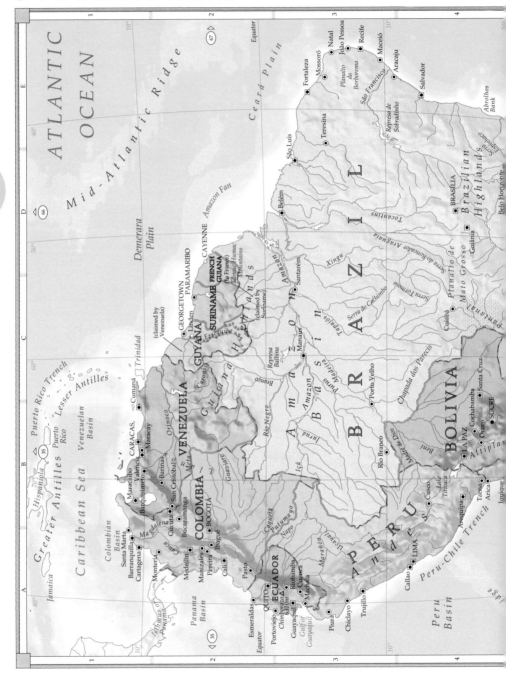

ATLANTIC OCEAN

Mid-Atlantic Ridge

Demerara Plain

Ceará Plain

Amazon Fan

BRAZIL

Brazilian Highlands

Equator

Mossoró
Fortaleza
Natal
João Pessoa
Recife
Maceió
Aracaju
Salvador

Teresina
São Luís
Belém

Planalto da Borborema
São Francisco
Represa de Sobradinho

Abrolhos Bank

BRASÍLIA
Goiânia
Belo Horizonte

Tocantins

Santarém
Xingu
Serra do Roncador
Araguaia
Planalto de Mato Grosso
Serra Tormosa

Serra do Cachimbo

Tapajós

A m a z o n

Manaus
Amazon Basin

Represa Balbina

Porto Velho
Chapada dos Parecis
Chapada dos Pareis

Pantanal
Cuiabá

Madeira
Rio Branco

BOLIVIA
Santa Cruz
Cochabamba
SUCRE
LA PAZ
Oruro
Altipla

Beni
Mamoré

Purus
Juruá
Içá
Amazon
Rio Negro
Branco

Guiana Highlands

Atlantic–Tumac Humac Mountains

CAYENNE
FRENCH GUIANA (to France)
PARAMARIBO
SURINAME
GEORGETOWN
Linden
Essequibo
GUYANA
(claimed by Venezuela)
(claimed by Suriname)

Trinidad
Cumaná
Caroni
Orinoco
VENEZUELA
CARACAS
Maracay
Valencia
Barinas
San Cristóbal
Maracaibo
Barquisimeto

Puerto Rico Trench
Puerto Rico
Venezuelan Basin
Lesser Antilles
Greater Antilles
Caribbean Sea
Jamaica
Hispaniola

Colombian Basin
Santa Marta
Barranquilla
Cartagena
Montería
Magdalena
Cauca
Medellín
Manizales
Pereira
Ibagué
Cali
Pasto

COLOMBIA
BOGOTÁ
Bucaramanga
Cúcuta
Meta
Guaviare
Caquetá
Putumayo
Napo
Marañón
Ucayali

ECUADOR
QUITO
Chimborazo
Cuenca
Machala
Guayaquil
Portoviejo
Esmeraldas
Gulf of Guayaquil
Riobamba
Babahoyo

PERU
LIMA
Callao
Cusco
Lake Titicaca
Arequipa
Tacna
Arica
Trujillo
Chiclayo
Chimbote
Piura

A n d e s

Peru–Chile Trench

Peru Basin

Panama Basin
Isthmus of Panama

Equator

POPULATION

● National capital

○ Less than 50,000   ◎ 50,000 -100,000   ◉ 100,000 - 500,000   ◼ Over 500,000

0 km   500
0 miles   500

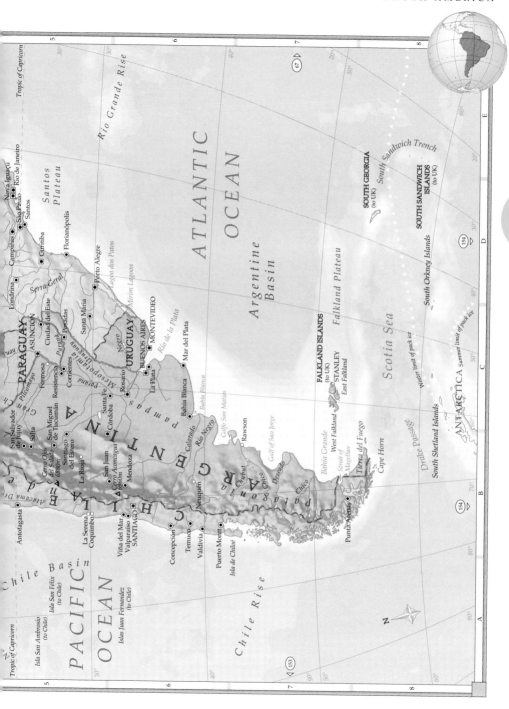

SOUTH AMERICA

Tropic of Capricorn

Rio Grande Rise

ATLANTIC

OCEAN

Nova Iguaçu
Rio de Janeiro
São Paulo
Santos
Santos
Plateau
Campinas
Curitiba
Florianópolis

Londrina
Serra Geral
Porto Alegre

Laguna dos Patos

PARAGUAY
ASUNCIÓN
Ciudad del Este
Posadas
Santa Maria
Paraná
Mirim Lagoon

Formosa
Corrientes
Resistencia
Mesopotamia
URUGUAY
MONTEVIDEO
BUENOS AIRES
Río de la Plata
Mar del Plata

San Salvador
de Jujuy
Salta
Cerro Ojos
del Salado
6880m
San Miguel
de Tucumán
Santiago
del Estero
Santa Fe
Río Negro
Córdoba
Rosario
La Plata

Pampas

Argentine
Basin

Atacama Des.
La Rioja
San Juan
Cerro Aconcagua
6960m
Mendoza
Bahía Blanca
Bahía Blanca

A R G E N T I N A

Antofagasta

Chile Basin
Isla San Félix
(to Chile)

La Serena
Coquimbo

Colorado
Río Negro

Gulf of San Jorge

Rawson

Falkland
Plateau

FALKLAND ISLANDS
(to UK)
STANLEY
East Falkland
West Falkland

Bahía Grande

South Shetland Islands

Viña del Mar
Valparaíso
SANTIAGO

Neuquén
Chico

Desado
Chico

Patagonia

Concepción
Temuco
Valdivia
Puerto Montt

Isla de Chiloé

Punta Arenas
Strait of Magellan
Tierra del Fuego
Cape Horn

Drake Passage

Scotia Sea

Winter limit of pack ice

SOUTH GEORGIA
(to UK)

South Sandwich Trench

SOUTH SANDWICH
ISLANDS
(to UK)

South Orkney Islands

Summer limit of pack ice

ANTARCTICA

PACIFIC

OCEAN

Chile Rise

Islas Juan Fernández
(to Chile)

Isla San Ambrosio
(to Chile)

Tropic of Capricorn

Golfo San Matías

N

NORTHERN SOUTH AMERICA

Caribbean Sea

Lesser Ant

ARUBA
(to Netherlands)

NETHERLANDS ANTILLES
(to Netherlands)

Curaçao · Bonaire

Islas Los Roques

Isla La Orch

Península de la Guajira

Golfo de Venezuela

Puerto López

Punto Fijo

Puerto

Cimarebo

Maicao

Coro

Ríohacha

Santa Marta

Barranquilla

Ciénaga

Pico Cristóbal Colón
5775m △

Sabanalarga

La Concepción

Dabajuro

Sabaneta

San Felipe

Puerto Cabello

CARACA

Cartagena

Soledad

Valledupar

Maracaibo

Cabimas

Maracay

Maracay

El Carmen de Bolívar

Machiques

Ciudad Ojeda

Carora

Barquisimeto

Valencia

San Juan de los Morr

Gulf of Darién

Sincelejo

Magangué

San Carlos del Zulia

Lago de Maracaibo

Barinas

Valera

Acarigua

Valle de la Pascua

Cereté

Montería

Planeta Rica

El Vigía

Mérida

Guanare

Calabozo

San Fernan

Aguachica

Ocaña

△ Pico Bolívar
5007m

Río Guanare

Panama Canal

PANAMA

Caucasia

Cúcuta

Pamplona

San Cristóbal

Río Apure

Dabeiba

Yarumal

Bucaramanga

Arauca

Río Arauca

VENI

Golfo de Panamá

Bello

Barrancabermeja

Río Meta

Puerto Carreño

Nuquí

Medellín

Itagüí

Puerto Berrío

Río Magdalena

PACIFIC OCEAN

Quibdó

Manizales

Sogamoso

Tunja

Yopal

Puerto Ayacuch

Pereira

Zipaquirá

Río Meta

Armenia

Tuluá

Ibagué

Girardot

BOGOTÁ

Villavicencio

Río Guaviare

Puerto Inírida

Buenaventura

Buga

Palmira

Espinal

COLOMBIA

Cali

Neiva

Popayán

Garzón

San José del Guaviare

Tumaco

Pitalito

Nevada de Cumbal
4764m △

Pasto

Mocoa

Florencia

Río Vaupés

Mitú

Ipiales

Orito

Río Apaporis

Equator

Río Putumayo

Río Caquetá

Río Japurá

ECUADOR

Río Napo

Río Içá

Río Iça

Andes

PERU

Amazon

Río Iu

0 km   200

0 miles   200

POPULATION   ● National capital

○ Less than 50,000   ○ 50,000 -100,000   ◉ 100,000 - 500,000   ◼ Over 500,000

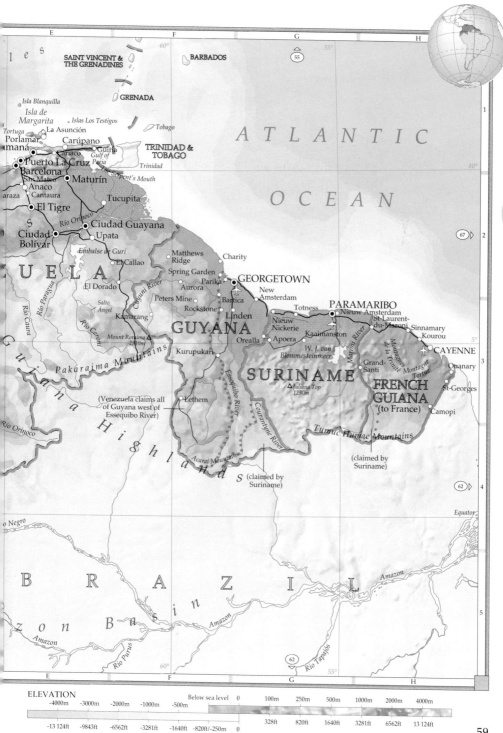

ATLANTIC

OCEAN

SAINT VINCENT &
THE GRENADINES

BARBADOS

GRENADA

Isla Blanquilla

Isla de
Margarita

Islas Los Testigos

Tobago

Tortuga

La Asunción

Porlamar

Carúpano

TRINIDAD &
TOBAGO

imaná

Cumaná

Gulf of
Paria

Cariaco

Güiria

Trinidad

Puerto La Cruz

Barcelona

San Mateo

Serpent's Mouth

Maturín

Anaco

Cantaura

araza

Tucupita

El Tigre

Río Orinoco

Ciudad Guayana

Upata

Ciudad
Bolívar

Embalse de Guri

El Callao

Matthews
Ridge

Charity

UELA

Spring Garden

Parika

GEORGETOWN

El Dorado

Cuyuni River

Aurora

New
Amsterdam

Río Paragua

Salto
Angel

Peters Mine

Bartica

Rockstone

PARAMARIBO

Totness

Nieuw Amsterdam

Kamarang

Río Caroní

Linden

St-Laurent-
du-Maroni

Sinnamary

Río Caura

GUYANA

Nieuw
Nickerie

Kourou

Mount Roraima
2810m

Orealla

Apoera

Kaaimanston

CAYENNE

Pakaraima Mountains

Kurupukari

W. J. van
Blommesteinmeer

Grand-
Santi

Oñanary

Guiana

St-Georges

Río Orinoco

SURINAME

Montagnes de la Trinité

Montagne Tortue

**FRENCH
GUIANA**
(to France)

Camopi

(Venezuela claims all
of Guyana west of
Essequibo River)

Lethem

Juliana Top
1230m

Essequibo River

Courantyne River

Tumuc-Humac Mountains

(claimed by
Suriname)

Highlands

Acarai Mountains

Maroni River

(claimed by
Suriname)

Equator

o Negro

B   R   A   Z   I   L

Amazon

z o n   B a s i n

Amazon

Amazon

Río Purús

Río Tapajós

60°

55°

10°

5°

1

2

3

4

5

E   F   G   H

60°   55°

ELEVATION

-4000m -3000m -2000m -1000m -500m   Below sea level   0   100m 250m 500m 1000m 2000m 4000m

-13 124ft -9843ft -6562ft -3281ft -1640ft -820ft/-250m 0   328ft 820ft 1640ft 3281ft 6562ft 13 124ft

WESTERN SOUTH AMERICA

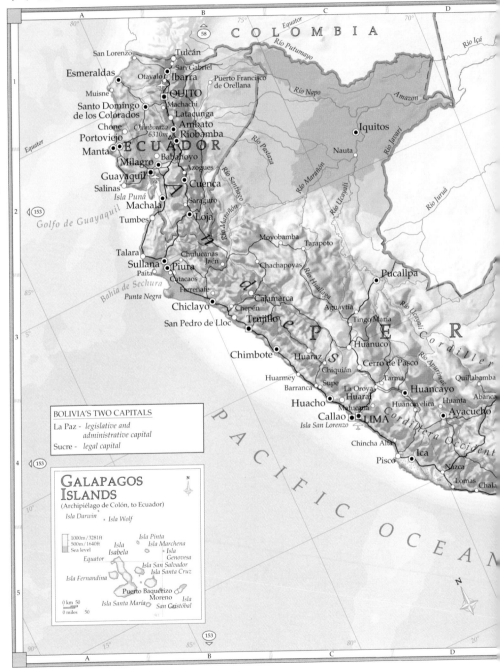

COLOMBIA

San Lorenzo
Tulcán
58
Esmeraldas
San Gabriel
Muisne
Otavalo Ibarra
Puerto Francisco
de Orellana
QUITO
Santo Domingo
de los Colorados
Machachi
Latacunga
Chone
Chimborazo
Ambato
Riobamba
Portoviejo
6310m
ECUADOR
Manta
Bahahoyo
Milagro
Guayaquil
Azogues
Salinas
Isla Puná
Cuenca
153
Machala
Saraguro
Golfo de Guayaquil
Tumbes
Loja

Río Putumayo
Río Napo
Amazon
Iquitos
Nauta
Río Pastaza
Río Marañón
Río Santiago
Río Ucayali
Río Juruá
Río Içá

Equator

Moyobamba
Tarapoto
Talara
Chulucanas
Jaén
Chachapoyas
Pucallpa
Sullana
Piura
Paita
Cataccos
Cajamarca
Aguaytía
Río Huallaga
Río Ucayali
Ferreñafe
Chiclayo
Chepén
Tingo María
San Pedro de Lloc
Trujillo
PERU
Huánuco
Cerro de Pasco
Río Apurímac
Chimbote
Huaraz
Huarmey
Chiquián
Tarma
Huancayo
Quillabamba
Barranca
Supe
La Oroya
Huanta
Abanca
Huacho
Huaral
Huancavelica
Ayacucho
Callao
LIMA
Matucana
Isla San Lorenzo
Cordillera Occidental
Chincha Alta
Pisco
Ica
Nazca
Lomas
Chala

PACIFIC OCEAN

Bahía de Sechura
Punta Negra

153

BOLIVIA'S TWO CAPITALS

La Paz - *legislative and administrative capital*

Sucre - *legal capital*

GALAPAGOS ISLANDS
(Archipiélago de Colón, to Ecuador)

Isla Darwin
Isla Wolf

1000m/3281ft	
500m/1640ft	
Sea level	

Isla Pinta
Isla Marchena
Isla Isabela
Isla Genovesa
Equator
Isla San Salvador
Isla Santa Cruz
Isla Fernandina
Puerto Baquerizo
Moreno
Isla Santa María
Isla San Cristóbal

0 km 50
0 miles 50

0 km 400
0 miles 400

POPULATION ● National capital

○ Less than 50,000   ○ 50,000 -100,000   ◉ 100,000 - 500,000   ■ Over 500,000

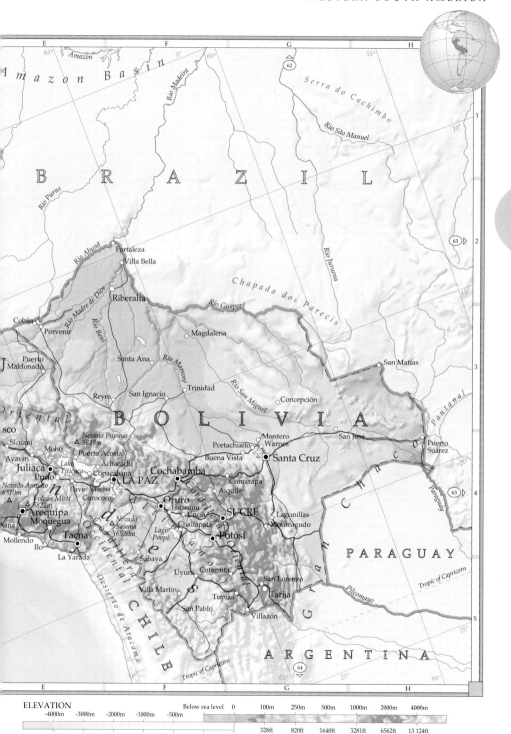

E   F   G   H
65°   5°   60°   55°

Amazon   *Rio Madeira*   △ 62

A m a z o n   B a s i n

Serra do Cachimbo

Rio São Manuel   10°   1

B   R   A   Z   I   L   63 ▷   2

Rio Purus

Rio Juruena   15°

△ 63

Rio Abunā   Fortaleza   *C h a p a d a   d o s   p a r e c i s*   55°
Villa Bella

Rio Madre de Dios   Riberalta   *Rio Guaporé*

Cobija   Magdalena
Porvenir   *Rio Beni*

Puerto   Santa Ana   *Rio Mamoré*   San Matías   3
Maldonado

Orien tal   Reyes   San Ignacio   Trinidad   *Rio San Miguel*   Concepción   *Pantanal*

sco   Nevado Pupuya   Montero   San José   Puerto
△ 5818m   Portachuelo   Warnes   Suárez   20°
Sicuani   Puerto Acosta   Buena Vista   Santa Cruz   63 ▷   4
Ayaviri   Achacachi   *Lago*   Comarapa
Juliaca   Moho   Copacabana   Cochabamba   Aiquile   *Chaco*
Pulo   *Lake*   Vlacha   Oruro   Lagunillas   *Paraguay*
Titicaca   LA PAZ   Huanuni   Corocoro   SUCRE   Monteagudo
Nevado Ampato   Ilave   Vlacha   Uncia   Challapata   Potosí
6310m   △ Volcán Misti   Nevado   *Lago*   *Gran*
5822m   Sajama   *Poopó*   San Lorenzo   PARAGUAY
Arequipa   6520m   Uyuni   Cotagaita   Tarija
Moquegua   Sabaya   Villa Martín   Tupiza
Mollendo   La Yarada   San Pablo   Villazón   25°   5
Ilo   *Desierto de Atacama*   *Pilcomayo*   Tropic of Capricorn

Occidental   CHILE   *Gran*   A R G E N T I N A

Tropic of Capricorn   65°   60°

E   F   G   H

ELEVATION
-4000m   -3000m   -2000m   -1000m   -500m   Below sea level   0   100m   250m   500m   1000m   2000m   4000m

-13 124ft   -9843ft   -6562ft   -3281ft   -1640ft   -820ft/-250m   0   328ft   820ft   1640ft   3281ft   6562ft   13 124ft

BRAZIL

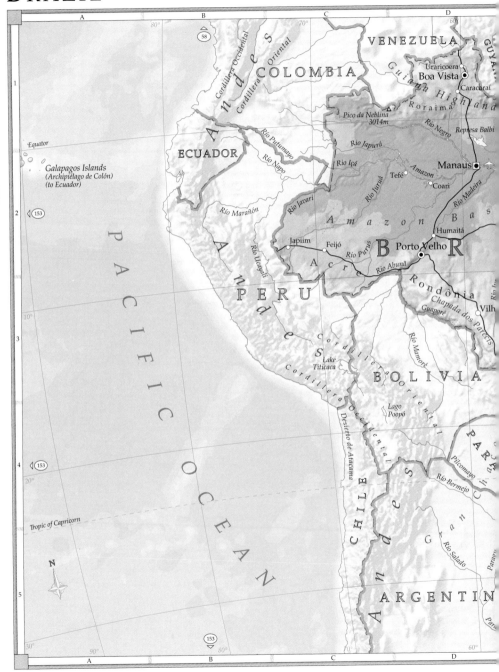

A B C D

58

VENEZUELA

COLOMBIA

Uraricoera

Boa Vista

Caracaraí

Guiana Highlands

1

Equator

Galapagos Islands
(Archipiélago de Colón)
(to Ecuador)

ECUADOR

Rio Putumayo

Rio Napo

Rio Japurá

Rio Içá

Pico da Neblina
3014m

Roraima

Rio Negro

Represa Balbi

Tefé

Coari

Manaus

Amazon

Rio Madeira

153

2

Rio Marañón

Rio Javari

Rio Juruá

A m a z o n

B a s

Humaitá

Japiim

Feijó

Rio Purus

B Porto Velho R

Rio Abunã

A c r e

Rio

Rondônia

Chapada dos Parecis

Vilh

Guaporé

P E R U

A n d e s

Rio Ucayali

3

Cordillera Occidental

Cordillera Oriental

Lake
Titicaca

B O L I V I A

Rio Mamoré

Lago
Poopó

P A R

153

4

P A C I F I C   O C E A N

Desierto de Atacama

Pilcomayo

Río Bermejo

C H I L E

Río Salado

Paran

N

5

A R G E N T I N

A B C D

0 km   600

0 miles   600

POPULATION   ● National capital

○ Less than 50,000   ○ 50,000 -100,000   ◉ 100,000 - 500,000   ■ Over 500,000

ATLANTIC OCEAN

Equator

ATLANTIC OCEAN

Tropic of Capricorn

FRENCH GUIANA (to France)

SURINAME

Tumuc Humac Mountains

A m a p á
Macapá
Ilha de Marajó
Belém
Baía de Marajó
Baía de São Marco
Mouths of the Amazon
Ilha Caviana de Fora

Obidos
Santarém
Itaituba
Amazon

Altamira

P a r á

B R A Z I L

Serra do Cachimbo

Marabá
Represa de Tucuruí

Imperatriz
M a r a n h ã o

São Luís
Parnaíba
Camocim
Fortaleza
Atol das Rocas
San Fernando de Noronha (to Brazil)

Bacabal
Piripiri
Teresina
Mossoró
Cabo de São Roque

C e a r á
Açu
Rio Grande do Norte
Natal

Floriano
Juazeiro do Norte
João Pessoa
Campina Grande

Carolina
Picos
P i a u í
Pernambuco
Alagoas
Recife

Balsas
Represa de Sobradinho
Juazeiro
Maceió

Rio São Francisco
Chapada Diamantina

Taguatinga

T o c a n t i n s
B a h i a
Aracaju
Estância

Feira de Santana
Salvador
Baía de Todos os Santos

Cuiabá
Planalto
Central
BRASÍLIA
Anápolis
Jananba
Itabuna
Canavieiras
Vitória da Conquista

Rondonópolis
Jataí
Goiânia
Montes Claros
Araçuaí
G o i á s

M a t o   G r o s s o
do Sul
Araguari
M i n a s   G e r a i s
Governador Valadares
Espírito Santo

Campo Grande
Uberlândia
Uberaba
Belo Horizonte

Aquidauana
Presidente Epitácio
Ribeirão Preto
Divinópolis
Juiz de Fora
Vitória

Marília
Campinas
Campos

Londrina
São Paulo
Nova Iguaçu
Rio de Janeiro

Maringá
P a r a n á
Santos

PARAGUAY
Represa de Itaipu
Ponta Grossa
Curitiba

Salto do Iguaçu
Rio Iguaçu
Joinville

Paraná
S a n t a   C a t a r i n a
Blumenau
Florianópolis

Rio Negro
URUGUAY
Passo Fundo

Santa Maria
Canoas
Rio Grande do Sul
Porto Alegre

Bagé
Lagoa dos Patos

Rio Grande
Mirim Lagoon

ELEVATION

								Below sea level	0	100m	250m	500m	1000m	2000m	4000m
-4000m	-3000m	-2000m	-1000m	-500m						328ft	820ft	1640ft	3281ft	6562ft	13 124ft
-13 124ft	-9843ft	-6562ft	-3281ft	-1640ft	-820ft/-250m	0									

SOUTHERN SOUTH AMERICA

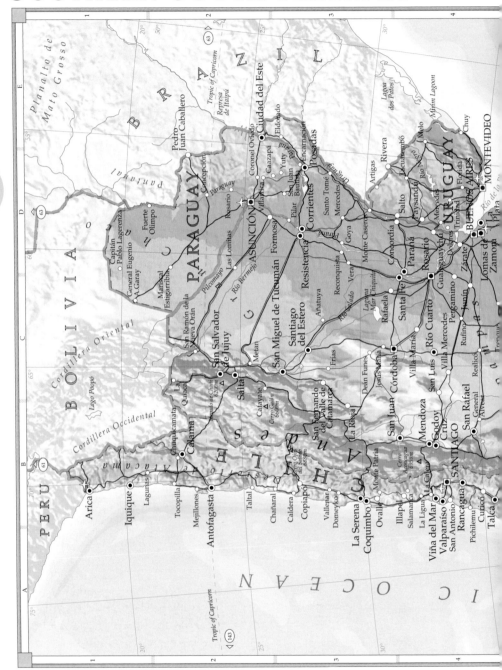

0 km   200
0 miles   200

POPULATION   ● National capital

○ Less than 50,000   ○ 50,000 -100,000   ◉ 100,000 - 500,000   ▣ Over 500,000

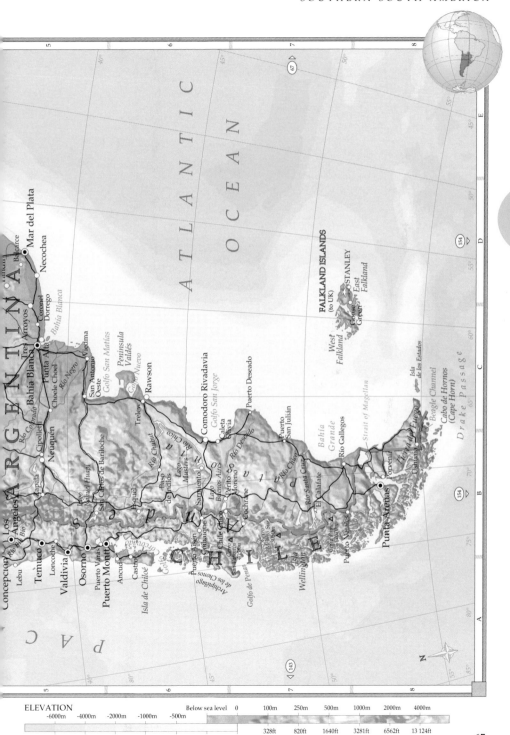

ATLANTIC OCEAN

ARGENTINA

REPUBLIC

CHILE

PACIFIC

FALKLAND ISLANDS
(to UK)

West
Falkland

East
Falkland

Grass
Green

STANLEY

Mar del Plata
Balcarce
Necochea
Coronel
Dorrego
Tres Arroyos
Bahía Blanca
Punta Alta
Bahía Blanca
Choele Choel
Cipolletti
Río Colorado
Viedma
San Antonio
Oeste
Golfo San Matías
Península
Valdés
Golfo Nuevo
Rawson
Río Negro
Neuquén
Zapala
Trelew
Nahuel Huapí
San Carlos de Bariloche
Paso
de Indios
Río Chubut
Esquel
Lago
Musters
Sarmiento
Comodoro Rivadavia
Golfo San Jorge
Caleta
Olivia
Río Chico
Río Deseado
Puerto Deseado
Puerto
San Julián
Bahía
Grande
Río Gallegos
Lago
Buenos Aires
Perito
Moreno
Cochrane
Chile Chico
El Calafate
Río Santa Cruz
El Chaltén
Puerto Natales
Cerro
San Valentín
3910m
Cerro
Mercedario
Punta Arenas
Porvenir
Tierra del Fuego
Ushuaia
Beagle Channel
Cabo de Hornos
(Cape Horn)
Isla
de los Estados
Strait of Magellan
Drake Passage

Concepción
Los
Ángeles
Río Bío Bío
Lebu
Temuco
Loncoche
Valdivia
Osorno
Puerto Varas
Puerto Montt
Ancud
Castro
Isla de Chiloé
Golfo
Corcovado
Puerto Aysén
Coyhaique
Archipiélago
de los Chonos
Golfo de Penas
Isla
Wellington

40°

45°

50°

55°

ELEVATION

-6000m	-4000m	-2000m	-1000m	-500m	Below sea level	0	100m	250m	500m	1000m	2000m	4000m

| -19 686ft | -13 124ft | -6562ft | -3281ft | -1640ft | -820ft/-250m | 0 | 328ft | 820ft | 1640ft | 3281ft | 6562ft | 13 124ft |

THE ATLANTIC OCEAN

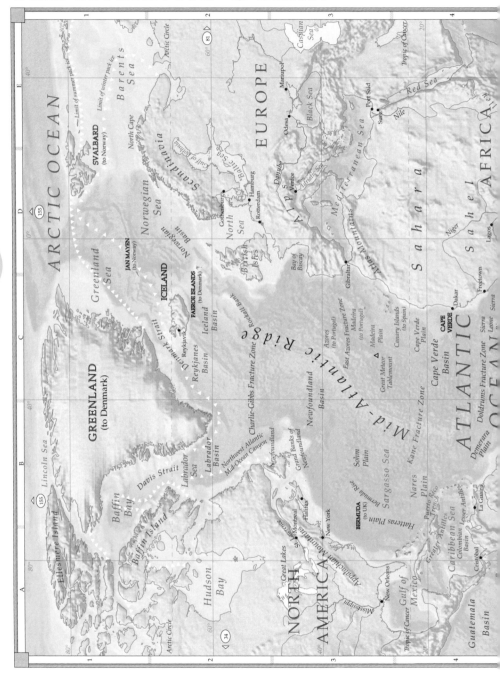

0 km   1000

0 miles   1000

• Major port

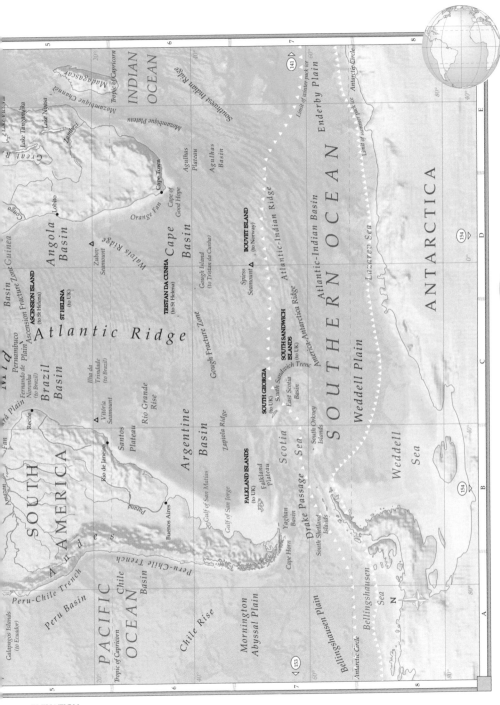

SOUTHERN OCEAN

ANTARCTICA

INDIAN OCEAN

PACIFIC OCEAN

SOUTH AMERICA

Mid Atlantic Ridge

Angola Basin

Brazil Basin

Argentine Basin

Cape Basin

Scotia Sea

Weddell Sea

Weddell Plain

Enderby Plain

Lazarev Sea

Bellingshausen Sea

Drake Passage

Madagascar

Mozambique Channel

Mozambique Plateau

Southwest Indian Ridge

Atlantic-Indian Ridge

Atlantic-Indian Basin

America-Antarctica Ridge

Agulhas Plateau

Agulhas Basin

Cape Town

Cape of Good Hope

Orange Fan

Zaïre Seamount

Walvis Ridge

Guinea Basin

Ascension Fracture Zone

ASCENSION ISLAND (to St Helena)

ST HELENA (to UK)

TRISTAN DA CUNHA (to St Helena)

Gough Island (to Tristan da Cunha)

Spiess Seamount

BOUVET ISLAND (to Norway)

SOUTH SANDWICH ISLANDS (to UK)

South Sandwich Trench

East Scotia Basin

SOUTH GEORGIA (to UK)

South Orkney Islands

Falkland Plateau

FALKLAND ISLANDS (to UK)

Gulf of San Matías

Gulf of San Jorge

Zapiola Ridge

Yaghan Basin

Cape Horn

South Shetland Islands

Bellingshausen Plain

Mornington Abyssal Plain

Chile Rise

Chile Basin

Peru-Chile Trench

Peru-Chile Trench

Peru Basin

Galápagos Islands (to Ecuador)

Amazon

Recife

Fernando de Noronha (to Brazil)

Ilha da Trindade (to Brazil)

Vitória Seamount

Santos Plateau

Rio Grande Rise

Rio de Janeiro

Paraná

Buenos Aires

Andes

Pernambuco Plain

Gough Fracture Zone

Congo

Lubito

Lake Victoria

Lake Tanganyika

Lake Nyasa

Zambezi

Great R.

Tropic of Capricorn

Tropic of Capricorn

Antarctic Circle

Antarctic Circle

Limit of winter pack-ice

Limit of summer pack-ice

N

ELEVATION

-6000m	-4000m	-2000m	-1000m	-500m	-250m	0
-19 686ft	-13 124ft	-6562ft	-3281ft	-1640ft	-820ft	0

AFRICA

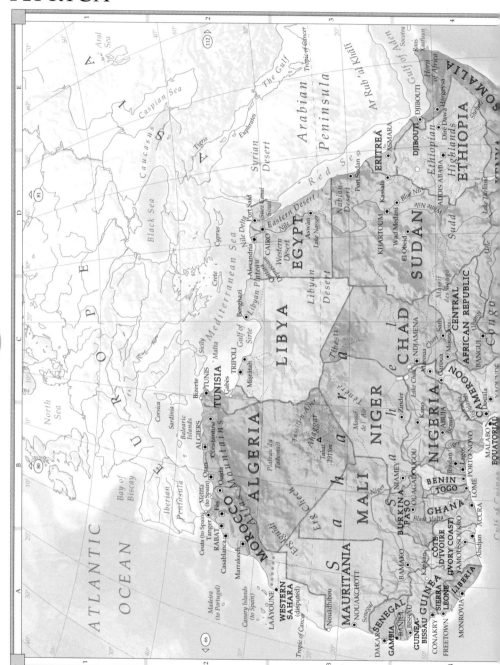

POPULATION ● National capital

○ Less than 50,000   ○ 50,000 -100,000   ◉ 100,000 - 500,000   ◼ Over 500,000

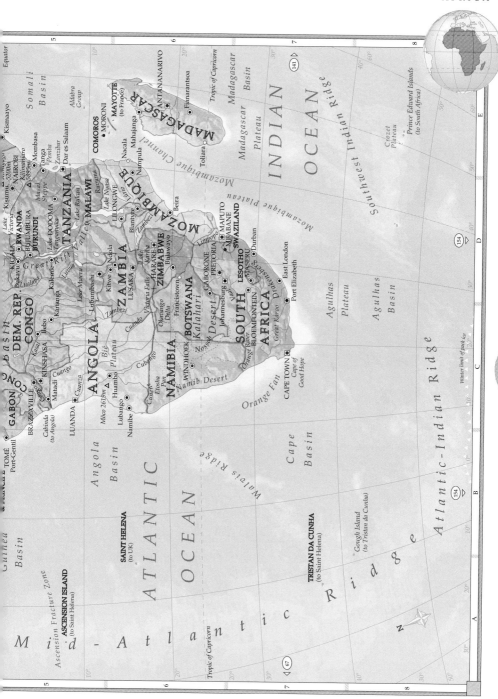

Equator

Somali Basin

Kismaayo

Mombasa
Tanga
Zanzibar
Dar es Salaam

NAIROBI

Kilimanjaro
5895m

Kisumu

KIGALI
RWANDA
BUJUMBURA
BURUNDI

Bukavu

DODOMA
TANZANIA

Masai Steppe

Lake Victoria

Lake Rukwa

Lake Nyasa

MALAWI
LILONGWE

Blantyre

Pemba

COMOROS
● **MORONI**

Aldabra Group

Aldabra

MAYOTTE
(to France)

ANTANANARIVO

Fianarantsoa

Tropic of Capricorn

MADAGASCAR

Madagascar Basin

Mahajanga

Nacala
Nampula

Toliara

Madagascar Plateau

Mozambique Channel

Beira

MAPUTO

MBABANE
SWAZILAND

Durban

INDIAN

OCEAN

Southwest Indian Ridge

Crozet Plateau

Prince Edward Islands
(to South Africa)

Kananga

Kalemie

Lubumbashi

Kitwe ● Ndola

LUSAKA

ZAMBIA

Victoria Falls

Lake Kariba

HARARE

Bulawayo

ZIMBABWE

Zambezi

Limpopo

PRETORIA

Johannesburg

GABORONE

BOTSWANA

Kalahari Desert

SOUTH

BLOEMFONTEIN

LESOTHO
MASERU

Drakensberg

East London

Port Elizabeth

Agulhas Plateau

Agulhas Basin

Atlantic-Indian Ridge

Winter limit of pack ice

GABON

BRAZZAVILLE

Cabinda
(to Angola)

Matadi

KINSHASA

DEM. REP.

CONGO

Kasai

Luanda

Kwango

Cuango

ANGOLA

Bié Plateau

Môco 2619m

Huambo

Lubango

Namibe

Cuanza

Cubango

Cunene

Etosha Pan

WINDHOEK

NAMIBIA

Nossob

Namib Desert

Okavango Delta

Cuando

Zambezi

CAPE TOWN
Cape of Good Hope

Great Karoo

Orange River

AFRICA

Cape Basin

Orange Fan

Walvis Ridge

ATLANTIC

OCEAN

SAINT HELENA
(to UK)

ASCENSION ISLAND
(to Saint Helena)

Ascension Fracture Zone

Guinea Basin

Angola Basin

SÃO TOMÉ
Port-Gentil

Gough Island
(to Tristan da Cunha)

TRISTAN DA CUNHA
(to Saint Helena)

Tropic of Capricorn

Mid-Atlantic Ridge

NORTHWEST AFRICA

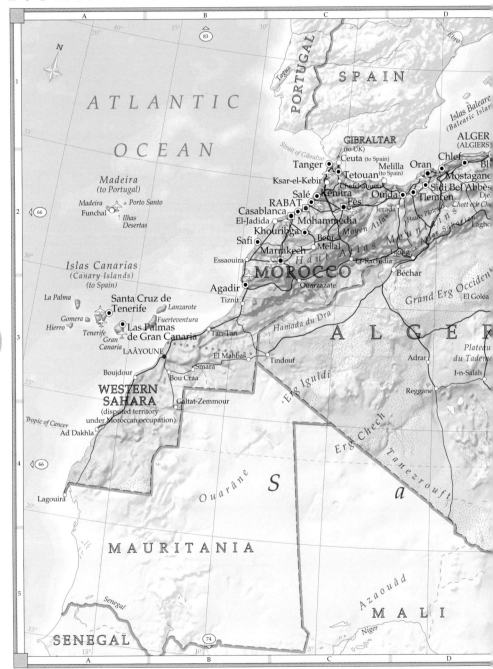

ATLANTIC

OCEAN

SPAIN

PORTUGAL

GIBRALTAR
(to UK)

Strait of Gibraltar

Tanger
Ceuta (to Spain)
Ksar-el-Kebir
Chefchaouen
Melilla
Tetouan (to Spain)

ALGER
(ALGIERS)

Oran
Chlef
Bli
Mostagane
Sidi Bel Abbès
Tlemcen
Dje

Islas Baleare
(Balearic Islar

Madeira
(to Portugal)

Madeira
Porto Santo
Funchal
Ilhas
Desertas

Salé
Kenitra
RABAT
Casablanca
El-Jadida
Mohammedia
Khouribga
Safi
Essaouira
Fès
Beni
Mellal

MOROCCO

Oujda
Jerada

Marrakech
Agadir
Tiznit

Haut
Ouarzazate
Er-Rachidia

Béchar

Figuig
Laghe

Chott ech Che

Haut Plateau

Moyen Atla
Atlas Saharien

Grand Erg Occiden
El Goléa

Islas Canarias
(Canary Islands)
(to Spain)

La Palma
Gomera
Hierro
Tenerife
Gran
Canaria

Santa Cruz de
Tenerife

Lanzarote
Fuerteventura

Las Palmas
de Gran Canaria

LAÂYOUNE

Boujdour

Bou Craa

WESTERN
SAHARA
(disputed territory
under Moroccan occupation)

Tropic of Cancer

Ad Dakhla

Galtat-Zemmour

Tan-Tan

Hamada du Dra

El Mahbas
Smara

Tindouf

'Erg Iguîdi

ALGER

Adrar

I-n-Salah

Reggane

Plateau
du Tadem

Erg Chech

Tanezrouft

Lagouira

Ouarâne

S

a

MAURITANIA

Senegal

SENEGAL

MALI

Niger

Azaouâd

0 km   400
0 miles   400

POPULATION   ● National capital
○ Less than 50,000   ○ 50,000 -100,000   ◉ 100,000 - 500,000   ■ Over 500,000

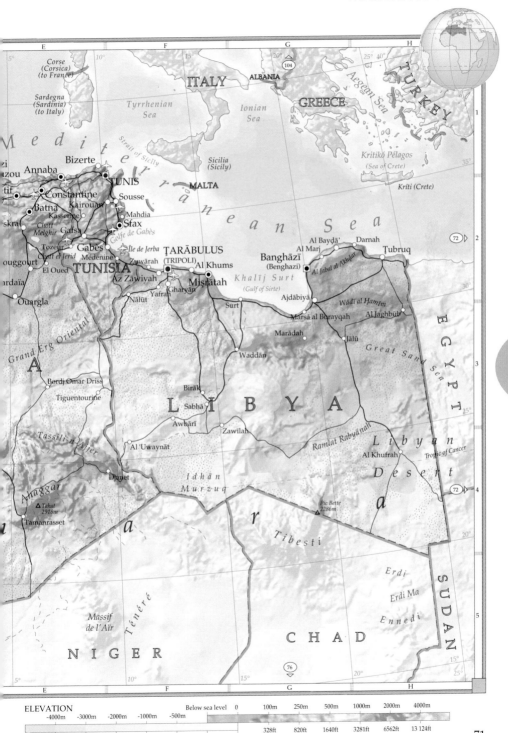

ELEVATION

| Below sea level | 0 | 100m | 250m | 500m | 1000m | 2000m | 4000m |

-4000m -3000m -2000m -1000m -500m

-13 124ft -9843ft -6562ft -3281ft -1640ft -820ft/-250m 0   328ft 820ft 1640ft 3281ft 6562ft 13 124ft

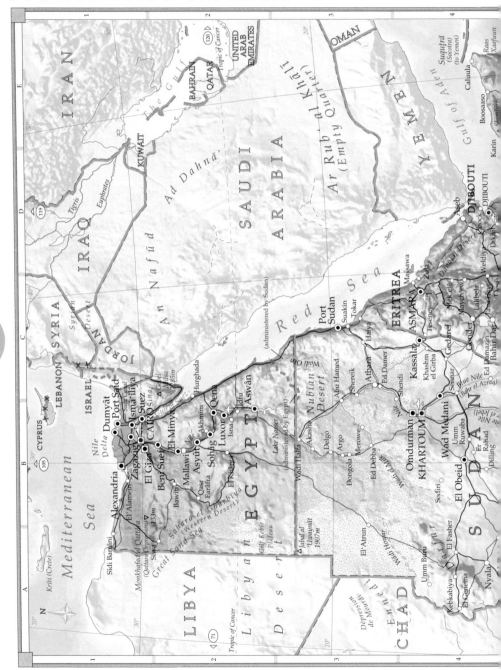

0 km   400
0 miles   400

POPULATION   ● National capital

○ Less than 50,000   ◉ 50,000 -100,000   ◉ 100,000 - 500,000   ■ Over 500,000

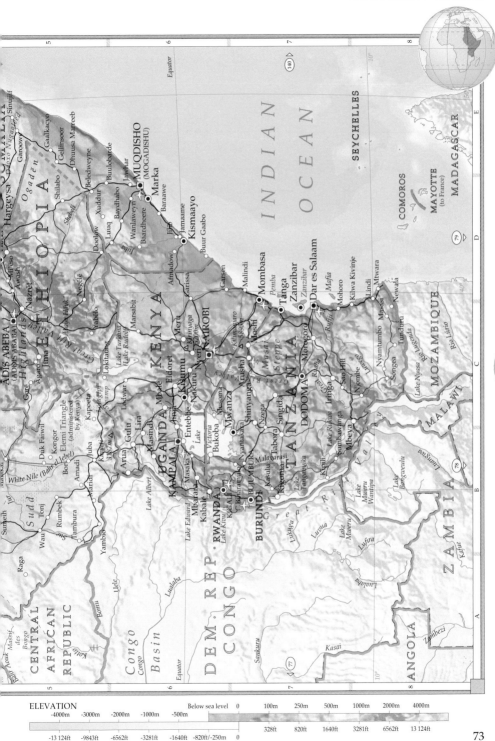

ELEVATION

Below sea level	0	100m	250m	500m	1000m	2000m	4000m
-4000m	-3000m	-2000m	-1000m	-500m			

			328ft	820ft	1640ft	3281ft	6562ft	13 124ft
-13 124ft	-9843ft	-6562ft	-3281ft	-1640ft	-820ft/-250m	0		

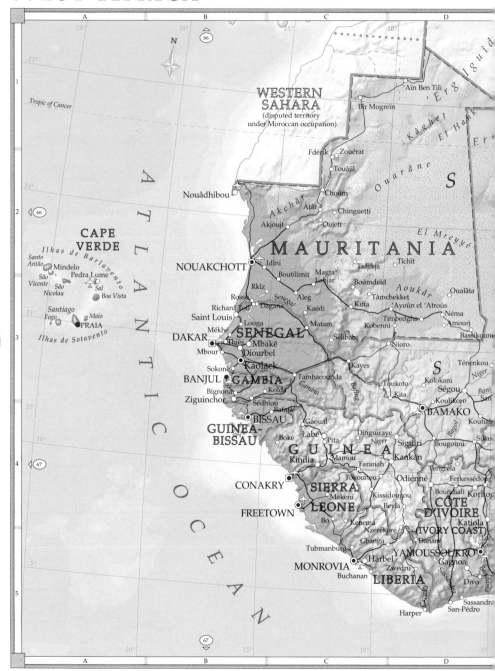

A   B   C   D

25°

20°

N

Tropic of Cancer

WESTERN SAHARA
(disputed territory
under Moroccan occupation)

Aïn Ben Tili

Bir Mogrein

Erg Iguid

Kâġhet El Ḥank

Er

Fdérik   Zouérat

Touâjil

Nouâdhibou

Choûm

Akchâr

Atâr

Chinguetti

Akjoujt

Oujeft

MAURITANIA

S

Ouarâne

El Mreyyé

CAPE VERDE

Ilhas de Barlavento

Santo Antão

Mindelo

Pedra Lume

São Vicente

São Nicolau

Sal

Boa Vista

Santiago

Fogo

Maio

PRAIA

Ilhas de Sotavento

A T L A N T I C

Idini

Boutilimit

NOUAKCHOTT

Rkíz

Magta Lahjar

Boúmdeïd

Tidjikja

Tîchît

Aoukâr

Tâmchekket

'Ayoûn el 'Atroûs

Oualâta

Rosso

Senegal

Aleg

Kaédi

Kiffa

Timbedgha

Kôbenni

Néma

Amourj

Richard Toll

Dagana

Saint Louis

Louga

Matam

Sélibabi

Nioro

Bassikoun

Mékhé

DAKAR

Thiès

Mbaké

SENEGAL

Diourbel

Mbour

Kaolack

Sokone

BANJUL

GAMBIA

Bignona

Ziguinchor

Sédhiou

Kolda

Tambacounda

Kayes

Toukoto

Kita

Koulikoro

Koutiala

S

Ténenkou

Niger

Kolokani

Ségou

Bani

San

BAMAKO

BISSAU

GUINEA-BISSAU

Gaoual

Boké

Labé

Pita

Dinguiraye

Niger

Siguiri

Bougouni

Sikasso

Kindia

Mamou

G U I N E A

Faranah

Kankan

Odienné

Tengréla

Ferkessédougou

CONAKRY

Tokounou

Makeni

Kissidougou

Beyla

Boundiali

Korhogo

CÔTE D'IVOIRE

FREETOWN

SIERRA LEONE

Bo

Kenema

Nzérékoré

Gbanga

Danané

Katiola

(IVORY COAST)

Tubmanburg

Harbel

MONROVIA

Buchanan

Zwedru

YAMOUSSOUKRO

Gagnoal

LIBERIA

Divo

Sassandra

Harper

San-Pédro

0 km   400

0 miles   400

POPULATION   ● National capital

○ Less than 50,000   ○ 50,000 -100,000   ◉ 100,000 - 500,000   ◼ Over 500,000

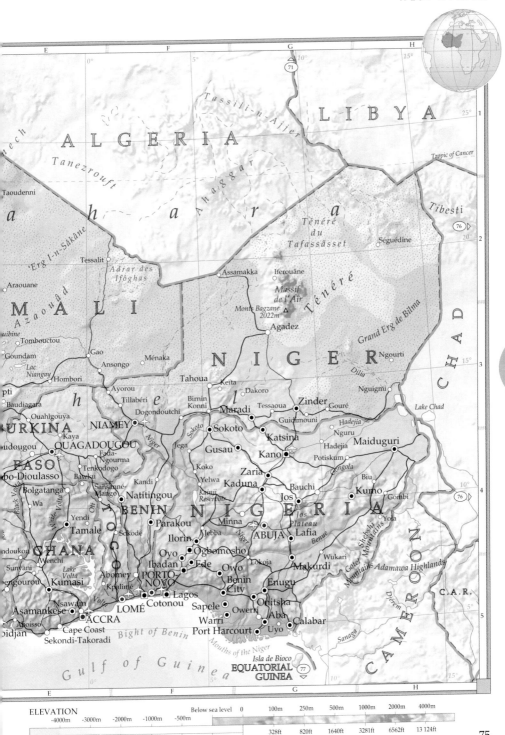

ELEVATION

					Below sea level	0	100m	250m	500m	1000m	2000m	4000m
-4000m	-3000m	-2000m	-1000m	-500m								
							328ft	820ft	1640ft	3281ft	6562ft	13 124ft
-13 124ft	-9843ft	-6562ft	-3281ft	-1640ft	-820ft/-250m	0						

75

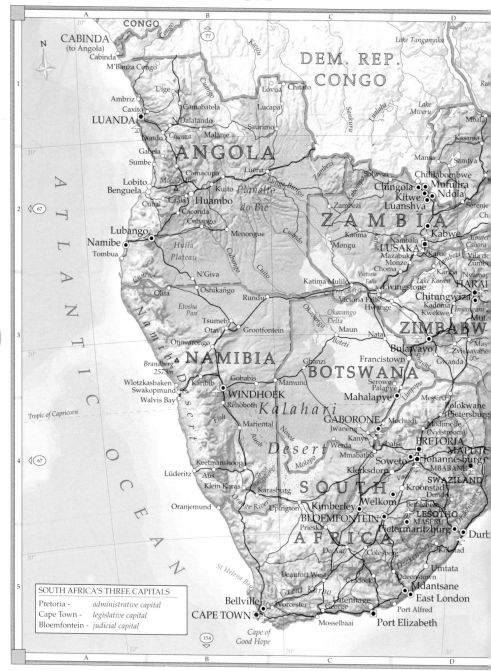

SOUTH AFRICA'S THREE CAPITALS

Pretoria -   *administrative capital*
Cape Town -   *legislative capital*
Bloemfontein - *judicial capital*

POPULATION   ● National capital

○ Less than 50,000   ○ 50,000 -100,000   ◉ 100,000 - 500,000   ■ Over 500,000

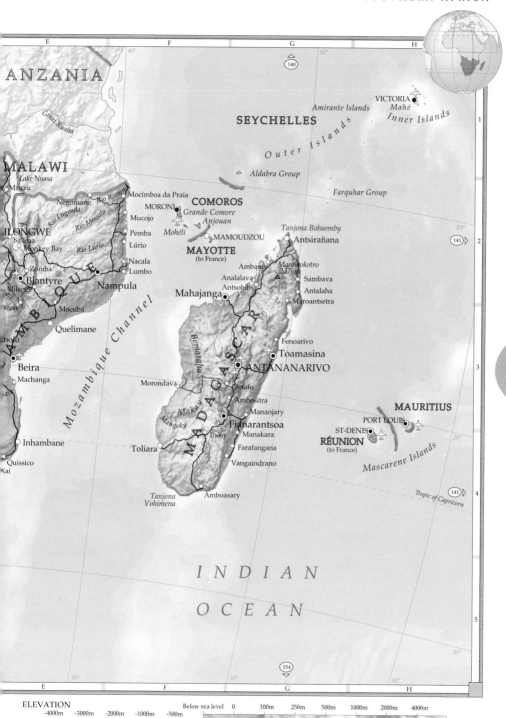

TANZANIA

Great Ruaha

MALAWI

Lake Nyasa
Mzuzu

ILONGWE
Salima
Monkey Bay
Zomba
Milange
Blantyre
Mocuba
Nampula

Quelimane

Beira

Machanga

Inhambane

Quissico
Xai

MOZAMBIQUE

Mozambique Channel

Negomane *Rio Rovuma*
Rio Lugenda
Rio Messalo
Mocímboa da Praia
Mucojo
Pemba
Rio Lúrio
Lúrio
Nacala
Lumbo

MORONI
Mucojo

COMOROS
Grande Comore
Anjouan
Mohéli
MAMOUDZOU
MAYOTTE
(to France)

SEYCHELLES

Amirante Islands
VICTORIA
Mahé
Inner Islands

Outer Islands

Aldabra Group

Farquhar Group

Tanjona Bobaomby
Antsirañana

Ambanja
Analalava
Antsohihy
Mahajanga

Maromokotro
2876ft
Sambava
Antalaha
Maroantsetra

MADAGASCAR

Bemaraha

Morondava

Betafo

Fenoarivo
Toamasina

ANTANANARIVO

Ambositra

Makay
Mangoky

Mananjary
Fianarantsoa
Ihosy
Manakara
Farafangana

Vangaindrano

Toliara

Tanjona
Vohimena

Amboasary

MAURITIUS
PORT LOUIS
ST-DENIS
RÉUNION
(to France)

Mascarene Islands

Tropic of Capricorn

INDIAN

OCEAN

ELEVATION

-4000m	-3000m	-2000m	-1000m	-500m	Below sea level	0	100m	250m	500m	1000m	2000m	4000m
-13 124ft	-9843ft	-6562ft	-3281ft	-1640ft	-820ft/-250m	0	328ft	820ft	1640ft	3281ft	6562ft	13 124ft

EUROPE

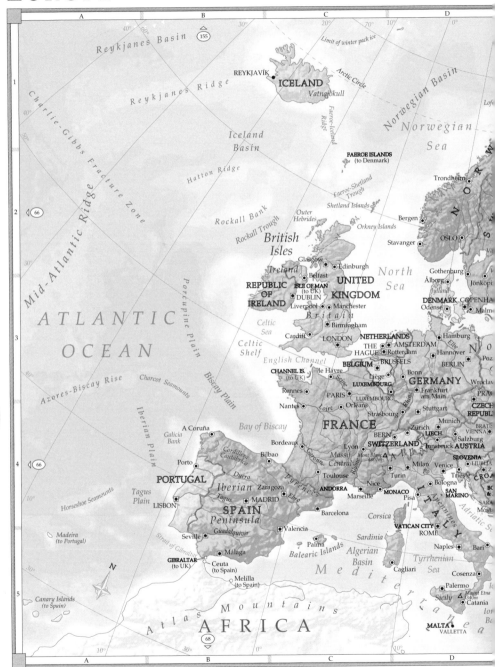

Reykjanes Basin

155

Limit of winter pack ice

Charlie-Gibbs Fracture Zone

Reykjanes Ridge

REYKJAVÍK

ICELAND
Vatnajökull

Arctic Circle

Norwegian Basin

Norwegian Sea

Iceland Basin

Faeroe-Iceland Ridge

FAEROE ISLANDS
(to Denmark)

Hatton Ridge

Trondheim

NORWAY

Mid-Atlantic Ridge

Rockall Bank

Rockall Trough

Faeroe-Shetland Trough

Shetland Islands

Outer Hebrides

Orkney Islands

Bergen

Stavanger

OSLO

Lofo

British Isles

North Sea

Gothenburg

Älborg

Jönkö

ATLANTIC OCEAN

Porcupine Plain

Glasgow

Edinburgh

Ireland

Belfast

Jylland

DENMARK COPENHA

Odense

Malmö

Celtic Sea

REPUBLIC OF IRELAND

ISLE OF MAN
(to UK)
DUBLIN

UNITED KINGDOM

Liverpool

Manchester

Britain

Cardiff

Birmingham

LONDON

NETHERLANDS

Hamburg

Elbe

N

Celtic Shelf

English Channel

THE HAGUE

AMSTERDAM

Rotterdam

Hannover

Poz

Azores-Biscay Rise

Charcot Seamounts

Biscay Plain

CHANNEL IS.
(to UK)

le Havre

BELGIUM

BRUSSELS

Liège

BERLIN

Bonn

Seine

LUXEMBOURG

LUXEMBOURG

GERMANY

Wrocła

PRA

Iberian Plain

Rennes

PARIS

Frankfurt
am Main

CZECH
REPUBLI

Nantes

Loire

Orléans

Strasbourg

Stuttgart

A Coruña

Bay of Biscay

FRANCE

Zürich

Munich

BRATIS
VIENNA

Galicia Bank

Bordeaux

Massif Central

Mont Blanc
4807m

BERN

SWITZERLAND

LIECH.

Salzburg

AUSTRIA

Tagus Plain

Cordillera Cantábrica

Bilbao

Lyon

SLOVENIA

Horseshoe Seamounts

PORTUGAL

Iberian

Duero

Zaragoza

Toulouse

ANDORRA

Nice

Milan

Turin

Po

Venice

Innsbruck

LJUBLIA

CRO

Porto

Douro

Pyrenees

Garonne

Rhône

Bologna

SAN MARINO

Madeira
(to Portugal)

LISBON

Tagus

MADRID

Ebro

Marseille

MONACO

Pisa

ITALY

SARA

Most

SPAIN

Peninsula

Barcelona

Corsica

VATICAN CITY

ROME

Adriatic Sea

Madeira
(to Portugal)

Guadalquivir

Valencia

Sardinia

Naples

Bari

Canary Islands
(to Spain)

Seville

Palma

Balearic Islands

Algerian Basin

Cagliari

Tyrrhenian Sea

Cosenza

Málaga

GIBRALTAR
(to UK)

Ceuta
(to Spain)

Strait of Gibraltar

Mediterra

Palermo

Sicily

Mount Etna
3340m

Catania

Melilla
(to Spain)

Atlas Mountains

AFRICA

68

MALTA
VALLETTA

0 km   500

0 miles   500

POPULATION   • National capital

○ Less than 50,000   ○ 50,000 -100,000   ◉ 100,000 - 500,000   ◼ Over 500,000

81

THE NORTH ATLANTIC

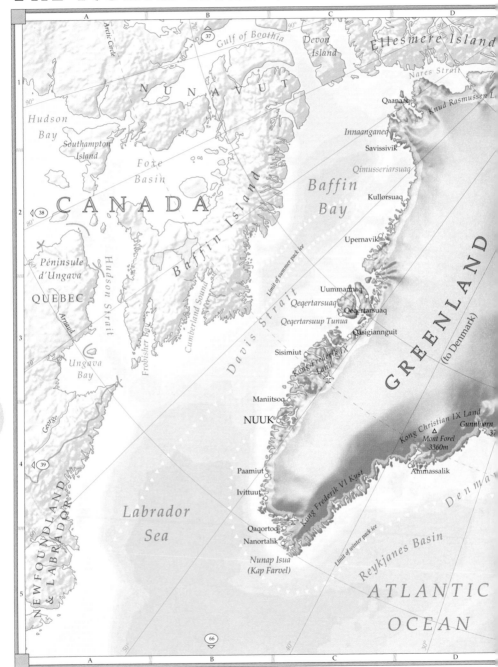

Arctic Circle

Gulf of Boothia

Devon Island

Ellesmere Island

Nares Strait

N U N A V U T

Qaanaaq

Knud Rasmussen L.

Hudson Bay

Innaanganeq

Southampton Island

Savissivik

Foxe Basin

Qimusseriarsuaq

Baffin Bay

Kullorsuaq

C A N A D A

Upernavik

Péninsule d'Ungava

QUEBEC

Baffin Island

Hudson Strait

Limit of summer pack ice

Uummannaq

Qeqertarsuaq

Qeqertarsuaq

Cumberland Sound

Qeqertarsuup Tunua

Qasigiannguit

G R E E N L A N D

(to Denmark)

Arnaud

Ungava Bay

Frobisher Bay

Davis Strait

Sisimiut

Kong Frederik IX Land

George

Maniitsoq

Kong Christian IX Land

Gunnbjørn

NUUK

Mont Forel 3360m

Paamiut

Kong Frederik VI Kyst

Ammassalik

N E W F O U N D L A N D & L A B R A D O R

Ivittuut

Denma

Labrador Sea

Qaqortoq

Nanortalik

Nunap Isua (Kap Farvel)

Limit of winter pack ice

Reykjanes Basin

ATLANTIC

OCEAN

0 km 400

0 miles 400

POPULATION ● National capital

○ Less than 50,000   ○ 50,000 -100,000   ◉ 100,000 - 500,000   ◼ Over 500,000

ARCTIC OCEAN

Lincoln Sea

Kap Morris Jesup

Wandel Sea

Independence Fjord

Nord

SVALBARD
(to Norway)

Kong Frederik VIII Land

Spitsbergen

LONGYEARBYEN
Barentsberg

Kvitøya

Nordaustlandet

Kong Karls Land

Barentsøya

Edgeøya

Storfjorden

Limit of winter pack ice

Zemlya Frantsa-Iosifa

Novaya Zemlya

Barents Sea

Greenland Sea

Kong Christian X Land

△ *Petermann Bjerg*
   2940m

Daneborg

Limit of summer pack ice

Kong Oscar Fjord

Bjørnøya
(to Norway)

Nordkapp
(North Cape)

Mohns Ridge

FINLAND

Ittoqqortoormiit

Kangikajik

Kangertittivaq

JAN MAYEN
(to Norway)

Norwegian Basin

Norwegian Sea

Vestfjorden

Arctic Circle

trait

ICELAND

Bolungarvík
Siglufjördhur Raufarhöfn
fjördhur
         Húsavík
      Akureyri
Stykkishólmur Seydhisfjördhur
         Neskaupstadhur
flói
REYKJAVÍK
  Selfoss Vatnajökull
orlákshöfn   Djúpivogur
      △ *Hvannadalshnúkur*
         2119m
Surtsey Vestmannaeyjar

N

SWEDEN

Gulf of Bothnia

FAEROE ISLANDS
(to Denmark)

○ TÓRSHAVN

NORWAY

Shetland Islands

ELEVATION

-4000m	-3000m	-2000m	-1000m	-500m	Below sea level 0	100m	250m	500m	1000m	2000m	4000m

-13 124ft	-9843ft	-6562ft	-3281ft	-1640ft	-820ft/-250m 0	328ft	820ft	1640ft	3281ft	6562ft	13 124ft

SCANDINAVIA & FINLAND

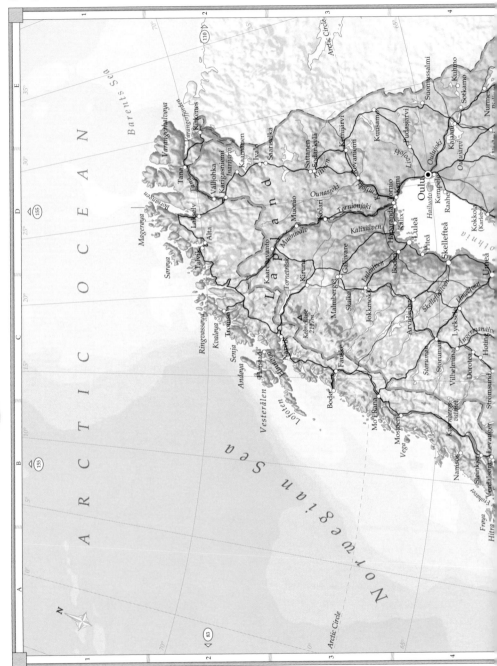

POPULATION   ● National capital

○ Less than 50,000   ○ 50,000 -100,000   ◉ 100,000 - 500,000   ◼ Over 500,000

ELEVATION

-2000m	-1000m	-500m	-250m	-100m	Below sea level	0	100m	250m	500m	1000m	2000m	4000m
-6562ft	-3281ft	-1640ft	-820ft	-328ft	-164ft/-50m	0	328ft	820ft	1640ft	3281ft	6562ft	13 124ft

THE LOW COUNTRIES

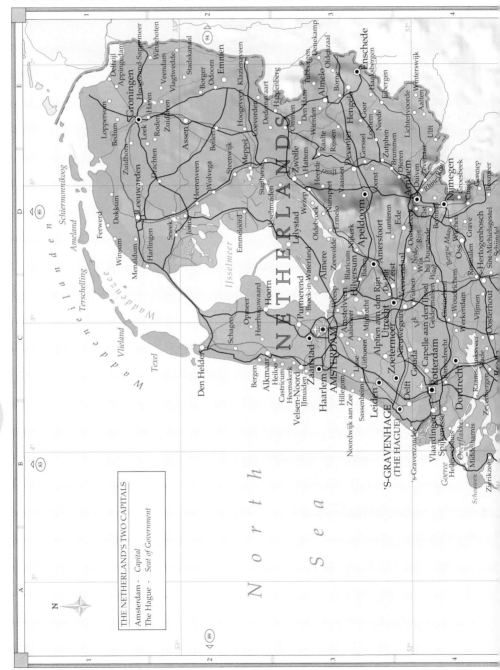

THE NETHERLAND'S TWO CAPITALS

Amsterdam - *Capital*
The Hague - *Seat of Government*

N

North Sea

Waddenzee

Wadden Eilanden

Schiermonnikoog
Ameland
Terschelling
Vlieland
Texel

IJsselmeer

NETHERLANDS

Den Helder
Groningen
Leeuwarden
Assen
Emmen
Zwolle
Apeldoorn
Enschede
Amersfoort
Nijmegen
Utrecht
AMSTERDAM
Haarlem
Leiden
'S-GRAVENHAGE (THE HAGUE)
Rotterdam
Dordrecht

0 km   50
0 miles   50

POPULATION   ● National capital

○ Less than 50,000   ○ 50,000 -100,000   ◉ 100,000 - 500,000   ◼ Over 500,000

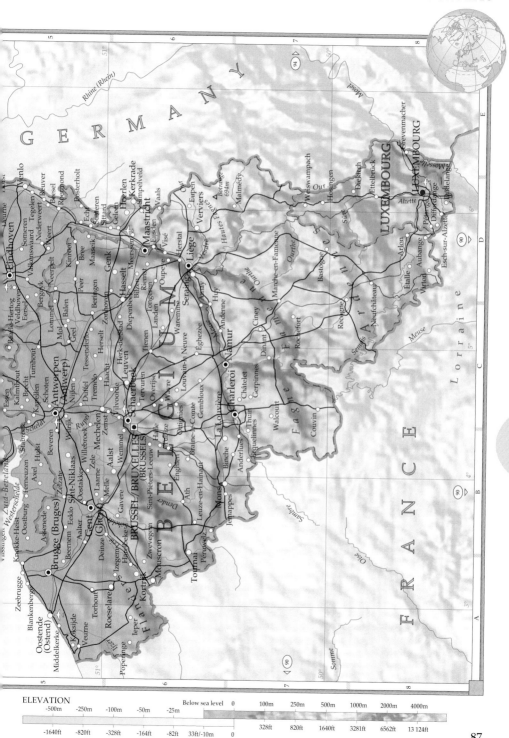

ELEVATION

-500m	-250m	-100m	-50m	-25m	Below sea level	0	100m	250m	500m	1000m	2000m	4000m
-1640ft	-820ft	-328ft	-164ft	-82ft	33ft/-10m	0	328ft	820ft	1640ft	3281ft	6562ft	13 124ft

THE BRITISH ISLES

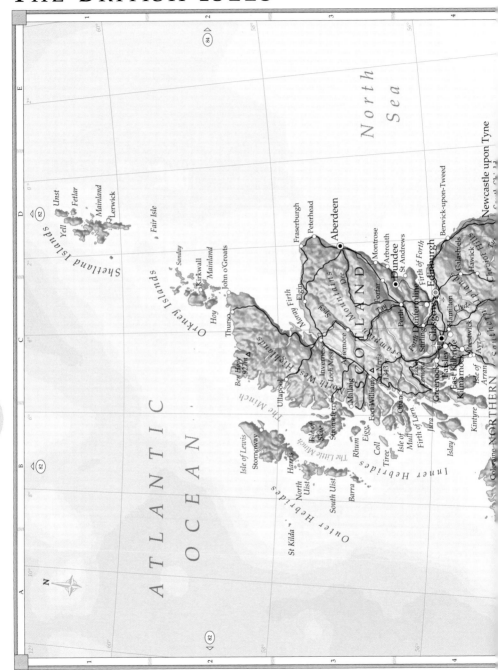

North Sea

Newcastle upon Tyne

Berwick-upon-Tweed

Fraserburgh
Peterhead
Aberdeen
Montrose
Arbroath
Dundee
St Andrews
Forfar
Firth of Forth
Edinburgh
Galashiels
Hawick
Dunfermline
Perth
Stirling
Glasgow
Hamilton
Paisley
Greenock
East Kilbride
Kilmarnock
Coatbridge
Ayr

Elgin
Dee
Grampian Mountains
Spey
Tay
Forth
Loch Lomond
Clyde

Moray Firth
Inverness
Aviemore
Loch Ness
North West Highlands
Fort William
1343
Oban
Mallaig
Firth of Lorn

SCOTLAND

Thurso
John o'Groats
Mainland
Kirkwall
Hoy
Sanday
Orkney Islands

Ben Hope
927m
Ullapool
Stornoway
Isle of Lewis
Harris
North Uist
South Uist
Barra
Outer Hebrides
St Kilda

Isle of Skye
Stromeferry
Rhum
Eigg
Coll
Tiree
Isle of Mull
Jura
Islay
Kintyre
Isle of Arran
Inner Hebrides
The Little Minch
The Minch

Fair Isle
Lerwick
Mainland
Fetlar
Unst
Yell
Shetland Islands

ATLANTIC

OCEAN

NORTHERN
Coleraine

Cheviot Hills
Southern Uplands

N

0 km   100

0 miles   100

POPULATION   ● National capital   ◎ Internal administrative capital

○ Less than 50,000   ○ 50,000 -100,000   ◉ 100,000 - 500,000   ◼ Over 500,000

ELEVATION

-2000m	-1000m	-500m	-250m	-100m	Below sea level	0	100m	250m	500m	1000m	2000m	4000m
-6562ft	-3281ft	-1640ft	-820ft	-328ft	-164ft/-50m	0	328ft	820ft	1640ft	3281ft	6562ft	13 124ft

89

FRANCE, ANDORRA & MONACO

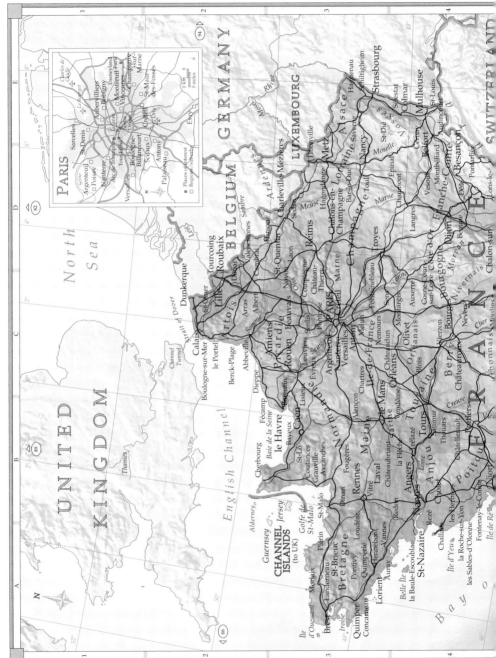

PARIS

POPULATION   ● National capital

○ Less than 50,000   ○ 50,000 -100,000   ◉ 100,000 - 500,000   ◼ Over 500,000

0 km   100

0 miles   100

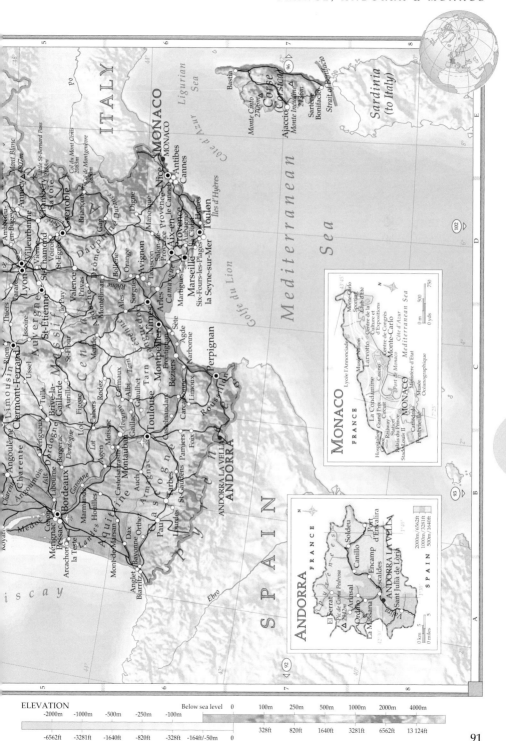

ITALY

MONACO

Ligurian Sea

Côte d'Azur

Bastia
Monte Cinto
2710m △
Corse
(Corsica)
Monte Incudine
2136m △
Sartène
Ajaccio
Bonifacio
Strait of Bonifacio

Sardinia
(to Italy)

Mont Blanc
4807m
Little St-Bernard Pass
Col du Mont Cenis
Col de Montgenèvre

Mediterranean Sea

Annecy
Chambéry
Grenoble
Briançon
Gap
Digne
Nice
Antibes
Cannes
Aix-en-Provence
Toulon
la Seyne-sur-Mer
Six-Fours-les-Plages
Hyères
Îles d'Hyères

Lyon
Villeurbanne
Vienne
St-Étienne
Valence
Privas
Montélimar
Orange
Avignon
Salon-de-Provence
Martigues
Marseille
Arles
Nîmes
Tarascon
Sète
Agde
Béziers
Narbonne
Perpignan
Montpellier

MONACO

Lycée l'Annonciade
Musée National
Larvotto
Centre de Culture et d'Expositions
Monte-Carlo
Sporting Club d'Été
Monte-Carlo
Casino
Centre de Congrès
La Condamine
Grand Prix Circuit
Palais du Prince
Railway
MONACO
Ministère d'État
Port de Monaco
Côte d'Azur
Musée Océanographique
Stade Louis II
Cathédrale
Fontvieille

Mediterranean Sea

FRANCE

0 m   500
0 yds 750

Clermont-Ferrand
Angoulême
Limousin
Brive-la-Gaillarde
Tulle
Aurillac
St-Flour
Rodez
Cahors
Figeac
Albi
Castres
Carcassonne
Limoux
Foix
Pamiers
Castelnaudary
Toulouse
Montauban
Moissac
Agen
Auch
Tarbes
St-Gaudens
Lourdes

Bordeaux
Libourne
Bergerac
Périgueux
Angoulême
Charente

Arcachon
la Teste
Pessac
Mérignac
Marmande
Mont-de-Marsan
Dax
Anglet
Bayonne
Biarritz

ANDORRA LA VELLA
ANDORRA

SPAIN

ANDORRA
FRANCE

El Serrat
Pic de Coma Pedrosa
2942m △
Arinsal
Ordino
La Massana
Canillo
Soldeu
Encamp
Escaldes
Port d'Envalira
ANDORRA LA VELLA
Sant Julià de Lòria

SPAIN

2000m /6562ft
1000m /3281ft
500m /1640ft

0 km   5
0 miles 5

Ebro

Biscay

ELEVATION

				Below sea level	0	100m	250m	500m	1000m	2000m	4000m
-2000m	-1000m	-500m	-250m	-100m							
-6562ft	-3281ft	-1640ft	-820ft	-328ft	-164ft/-50m	0	328ft	820ft	1640ft	3281ft	6562ft	13 124ft

SPAIN & PORTUGAL

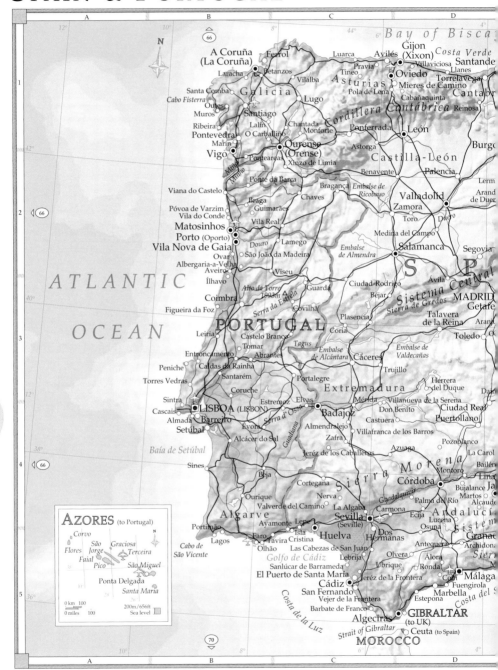

Bay of Biscay

Gijón (Xixon) · *Costa Verde*
Luarca · Avilés · Villaviciosa · Santander
Pravia · Tineo · Oviedo · Llanes · Torrelavega
A Coruña (La Coruña) · Ferrol · Pola de Lena · Mieres de Camino
Laracha · Betanzos · Cabañaquinta · Reinosa
Vilalba · **Asturias** · Cordillera Cantábrica · Cantabria
Santa Comba · *Galicia* · Lugo
Cabo Fisterra · Ounes · Ponferrada · León · Burgos
Muros · Santiago · Chantada · Monforte
Ribeira · Lalín · O Carballino · Astorga · **Castilla-León**
Pontevedra · Ourense (Orense) · Benavente · Palencia
Marín · Ponteareas · Xinzo de Limia · Lermo
Vigo · Miño · Braganca · *Embalse de Ricobayo* · Valladolid · Aranda de Duero
Viana do Castelo · Chaves · Zamora
Póvoa de Varzim · Braga · Guimarães · Toro · Duero
Vila do Conde · Vila Real · Medina del Campo
Matosinhos · Lamego · Salamanca · Segovia
Porto (Oporto) · Douro · São João da Madeira · *Embalse de Almendra* · Ávila · **SP**
Vila Nova de Gaia · Ovar · Viseu · Guarda · Ciudad-Rodrigo · Béjar · MADRID · Getafe
Albergaria-a-Velha · Ílhavo · Alto da Torre · *Sistema Central* · Sierra de Gredos
Aveiro · 1993m · *Serra da Estrela* · Covilhã · Plasencia · Talavera de la Reina · Aranjuez
Coimbra · Guarda
Figueira da Foz · Coria · Toledo

ATLANTIC

OCEAN

Leiria · **PORTUGAL** · Castelo Branco · *Tagus* · *Embalse de Valdecañas*
Entroncamento · Tomar · Abrantes · *Embalse de Alcántara* · Cáceres
Peniche · Caldas da Rainha · Trujillo · Herrera del Duque
Torres Vedras · Santarém · Portalegre · **Extremadura**
Coruche · Mérida · Villanueva de la Serena · Ciudad Real
Sintra · Estremoz · Elvas · Badajoz · Don Benito · Puertollano
Cascais · LISBOA (LISBON) · Évora · Castuera
Almada · Barreiro · Alcácer do Sal · Almendralejo · Villafranca de los Barros · Pozoblanco
Setúbal · Zafra · La Carolina
Baía de Setúbal · Jeréz de los Caballeros · Azuaga · Bailén
Sines · Beja · Cortegana · *Sierra Morena* · Córdoba · Montoro · Linares
Ourique · Nerva · Bujalance · Jaén
Valverde del Camino · Guadalquivir · Palma del Río · Martos · Alcaudete
Algarve · La Algaba · Carmona · Ecija · **Andalucía**
Portimão · Ayamonte · Lepe · Sevilla (Seville) · Osuna · Lucena · Sistema
Lagos · Faro · Tavira · Isla Cristina · Huelva · Dos Hermanas · Antequera · Archidona
Cabo de São Vicente · Olhão · Las Cabezas de San Juan · Olvera · Álora · Sierra
Golfo de Cádiz · Lebrija · Ubrique · Ronda · Coín · Málaga
Sanlúcar de Barrameda · Fuengirola · *Costa del Sol*
El Puerto de Santa María · Jeréz de la Frontera · Marbella
Cádiz · Vejer de la Frontera · Estepona
San Fernando
Costa de la Luz · Barbate de Franco · GIBRALTAR (to UK)
Algeciras · *Strait of Gibraltar* · Ceuta (to Spain)
MOROCCO

AZORES (to Portugal)

Corvo
Flores · São Jorge · Graciosa
Faial · Terceira
Pico · São Miguel
Ponta Delgada
Santa Maria

0 km 100
0 miles 100

200m/656ft
Sea level

0 km 100
0 miles 100

POPULATION
● National capital
○ Less than 50,000
○ 50,000 -100,000
◉ 100,000 - 500,000
■ Over 500,000

FRANCE

Bermeo
Zarautz
Donostia-San Sebastián
Eibar
Irún
Bergara
Tolosa
País Vasco
Pamplona
(Iruña)
itoria-Gasteiz
Miranda
de Ebro
Estella-Lizarra
Jaca
ogroño
Navarra
Monte Perdido
3348m
La Seu d'Urgel
ANDORRA
Golfe du Lion
Arnedo
Calahorra
Huesca
Berga
Ripoll
Figueres
Girona
(Gerona)
La Rioja
Tudela
Ejea de
los Caballeros
Barbastro
Monzón
Cataluña
Vic
Banyoles
Palafrugell
Tarazona
Soria
Cervera
Balaguer
Lleida
(Lérida)
Sabadell
Blanes
Arenys de Mar
Burgo
Osma
Zaragoza
Fraga
Tàrrega
Terrassa
Mataró
Costa Brava
Calatayud
Vilafranca del Penedès
Barcelona
Aragón
Daroca
Valls
Sitges
L'Hospitalet de Llobregat
Medinaceli
Alcañiz
Reus
El Vendrell
Guadalajara
Teruel
Tortosa
Tarragona
calá de Henares
ejón de Ardoz
Amposta
Sant Carles de la Ràpita
Cuenca
Javalambre
2020m
Vinaròs
Ciutadella de Menorca
Menorca
(Minorca)
Tarancón
Onda
Castelló de la Plana
Pollença
Sa Pola
Mahón
astilla-La Mancha
Burriana
Vall d' Uxó
Golfo de
Valencia
Palma
Manacor
Mota del Cuervo
Campo de Criptana
Burjassot
Sagunto
Valencia
Llucmajor
Felanitx
Socuéllamos
Torrente
Catarroja
Mallorca
(Majorca)
La Roda
Sueca
Cullera
Cabrera
Tomelloso
Algemesí
Xàtiva
Gandía
Islas Baleares
(Balearic Islands)
anzanares
Albacete
Almansa
Oliva
Denia
Eivissa
(Ibiza)
a Solana
peñas
Villanueva de los Infantes
Ontinyent
Alcoy
Villena
Benidorm
Eivissa
Hellín
Jumilla
Elda
Villajoyosa
Formentera
Beas de Segura
Monóvar
San Juan de Alicante
Moratalla
Cieza
Elche
Alicante
Villacarrillo
Mula
Callosa de Segura
Cazorla
Orihuela
Murcia
Huéscar
Totana
La Unión
Baza
Lorca
Guadix
Aguilas
Cartagena
Mojácar
Mediterranean Sea
Berja
Almería
Adra

ALGERIA

ELEVATION

					Below sea level	0	100m	250m	500m	1000m	2000m	4000m
-4000m	-3000m	-2000m	-1000m	-500m								
-13 124ft	-9843ft	-6562ft	-3281ft	-1640ft	-820ft/-250m	0	328ft	820ft	1640ft	3281ft	6562ft	13 124ft

93

GERMANY & THE ALPINE STATES

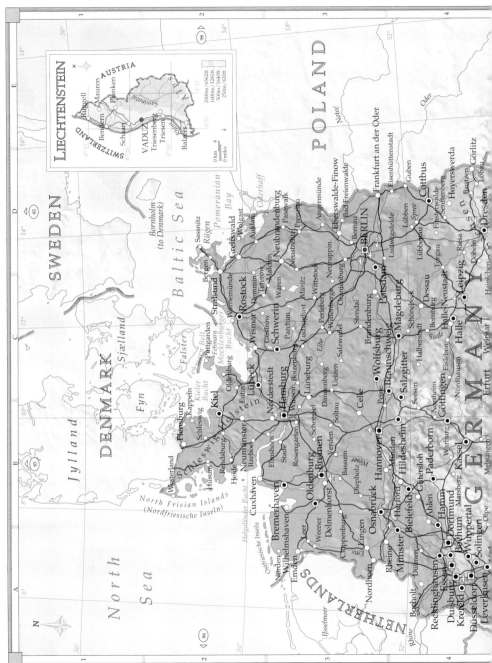

POPULATION   ● National capital

○ Less than 50,000   ○ 50,000 -100,000   ◉ 100,000 - 500,000   ◼ Over 500,000

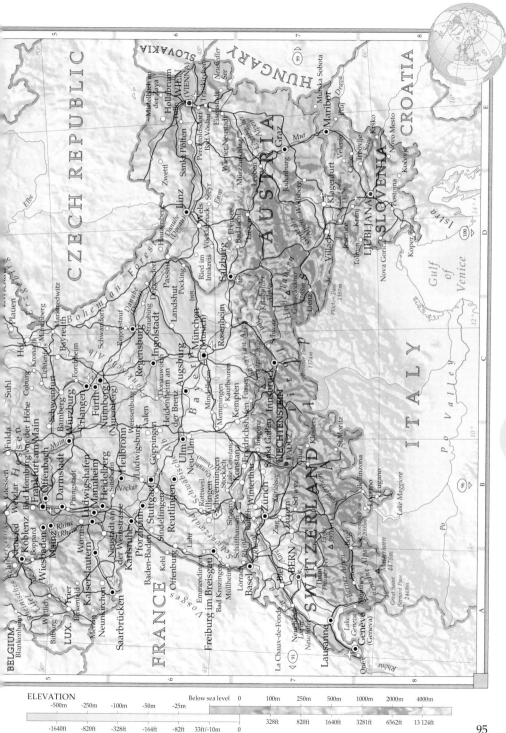

ELEVATION

-500m	-250m	-100m	-50m	-25m	Below sea level	0	100m	250m	500m	1000m	2000m	4000m

| -1640ft | -820ft | -328ft | -164ft | -82ft | 33ft/-10m | 0 | 328ft | 820ft | 1640ft | 3281ft | 6562ft | 13 124ft |

ITALY

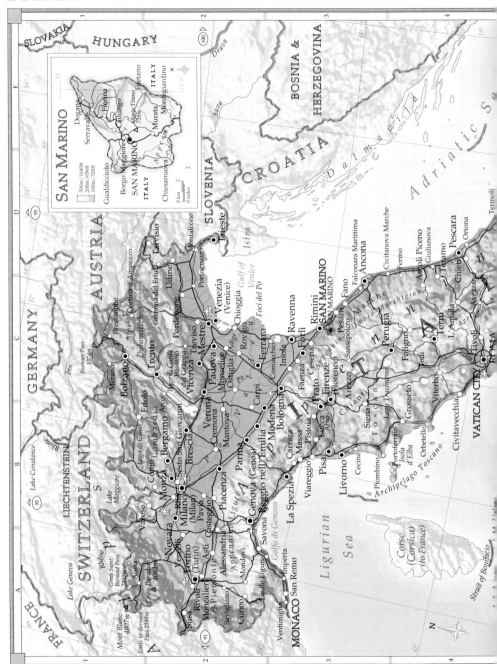

SAN MARINO

Dogana
Serravalle
Fiorina
Cailungo
ITALY
Gualdicciolo
Borgo Maggiore
SAN MARINO
ITALY
Chiesanuova
Acqua Viva
Monte Titano
739m
Murata
Montegiardino
Faetano

500m/1641ft
200m/656ft
100m/328ft

0 km   2
0 miles   2

SLOVAKIA
HUNGARY
Drava
AUSTRIA
GERMANY
LIECHTENSTEIN
SWITZERLAND
FRANCE
MONACO

BOSNIA &
HERZEGOVINA
CROATIA
Dalma_tia
SLOVENIA
Adriatic Sea

Brenner Pass
1374m
Merano
Bressanone
Bolzano
Alpi
Dolomitiche
Edolo
Trento
Arco
Lago di Garda
Bérgamo
Brescia
Sesto San Giovanni
Monza
Milano
(Milan)
Pavia
Como
Lombardia
Lago di Como
Lago
Maggiore
Varese
Novara
Vercelli
Torino
(Turin)
Asti
Alessandria
Mondovì
Cuneo
Savigliano
Moncalieri
Susa
Rivoli
Gran Paradiso
4061m
Aosta
Great Saint
Bernard Pass
Little St-Bernard
Pass 2188m
Mont Blanc
4807m
Rhône
Lake Geneva
Rhine
Lake Constance
Inn
Piemonte
Appennino Ligure
Finale Ligure
Imperia
San Remo
Ventimiglia
Savona
Golfo di Genoza
La Spezia
Genova (Genoa)
Castello
Piacenza
Cremona
Mántova
Verona
Parma
Reggio nell'Emilia
Módena
Carpi
Bologna
Emilia
Romagna
Ferrara
Comacchio
Imola
Faenza
Forlì
Cesena
Ravenna
Rimini
SAN MARINO
SAN MARINO
Pesaro
Fano
Senigallia
Ancona
Falconara Marittima
Civitanova Marche
Fermo
Áscoli Piceno
Giulianova
Téramo
Chieti
Pescara
Ortona
Téramo
Marche
Umbro-Marchigiana
Perugia
Fóligno
Todi
Spoleto
Terni
L'Aquila
Rivoli
Arezzo
Sansepolcro
Lago Trasimeno
Viterbo
Orbetello
Grosseto
Civitavecchia
VATICAN CITY
Appennino
Umbria
Lazio
Tevere
Arno
Chianti
Toscana
Siena
Firenze
(Florence)
Prato
Pistoia
Lucca
Pisa
Viareggio
Livorno
Cecina
Piombino
Portoferraio
Isola
d'Elba
Grosseto
Massa
Carrara
Massa
Arno
Archipelago Toscano
Corse
(Corsica)
(to France)
Ligurian
Sea
Strait of Bonifacio
Trieste
Istra
Montfalcone
Gorizia del Friuli
Gemona del Friuli
Tarvisio
Udine
Pordenone
Portogruaro
Treviso
Conegliano
Vittorio Veneto
Bassano
del Grappa
Vicenza
Padova
Mestre
Venezia
(Venice)
Chioggia
Gulf of
Venice
Foci del Po
Rovigo
Ostiglia
Po
Adige
Piave

0 km   100
0 miles   100

POPULATION ● National capital

○ Less than 50,000   ○ 50,000 -100,000   ◉ 100,000 - 500,000   ◼ Over 500,000

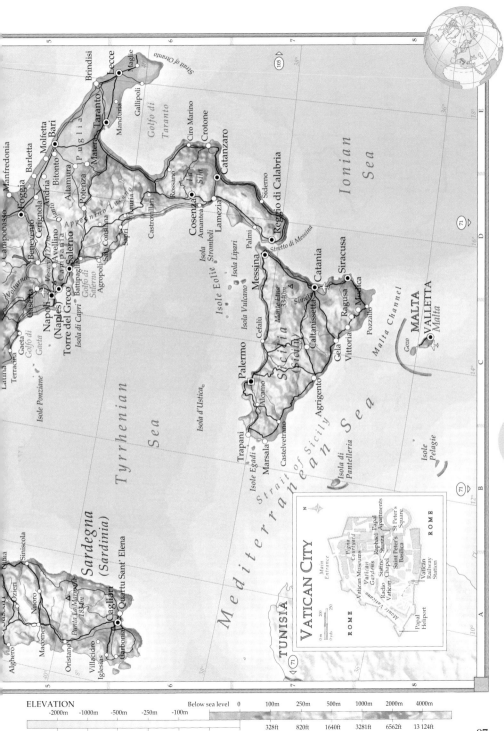

SOUTHEAST EUROPE

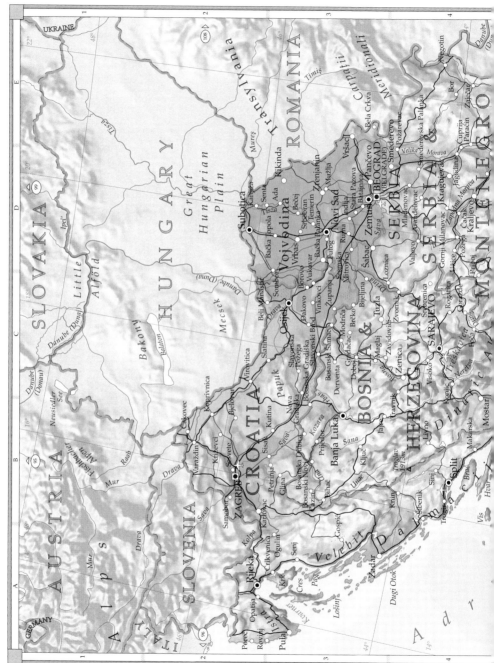

0 km   100

0 miles   100

POPULATION   ● National capital

○ Less than 50,000   ○ 50,000 -100,000   ◉ 100,000 - 500,000   ◼ Over 500,000

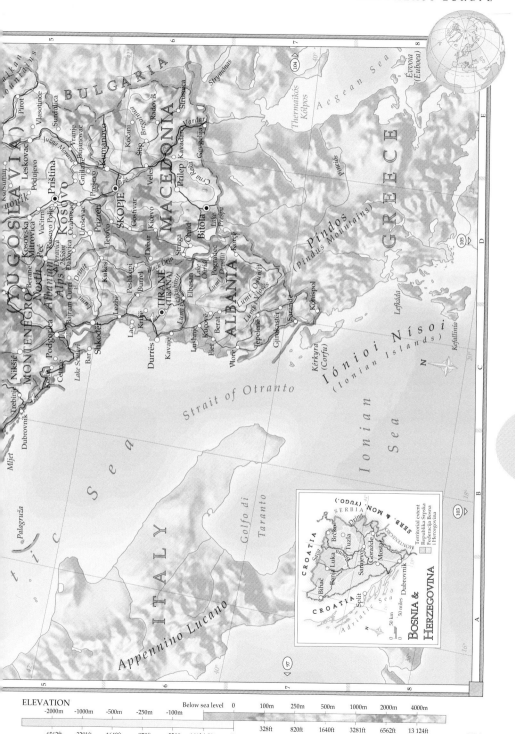

Balkan Mountains
BULGARIA
Pirot
Vlasotince
Surdulica
Kuršumlij
Leskovac
Podujevo
Vranje
Pčinja
Kumanovo
Kriva Reka
PRIŠTINA
KOSOVO
Gnjilane-Bujanovac
Preševo
Kočani
Štip
Bregalnica
Radoviš
Strumica
Kosovska Mitrovica
Vučitrn
Kosovo Polje
Obiliq
Uroševac
SKOPJE
Veles
Crna Reka
Prilep
Kavadarci
Gevgelija
Vardar
Strymónas
Strymónas
Thermaïkós Kólpos
Aegean Sea
Evvoia (Euboea)
YUGOSLAVIA
MONTENEGRO
Peć
Drenica
Prizren
Drim
Gostivar
Kičevo
Debar
Lake Ohrid
BITOLA
Crna Reka
MACEDONIA
Pindós
Pindós Mountains (Pindus Mountains)
Penéios
GREECE
North Albanian Alps
Berane
Balkan Cami
Drni
Peshkopi
Burrel
Black Drim
Struga
Ohrid
Pogradec
Lumi i Drinit
Korçë
Andrijevica
Đakovica
Kukës
Lezhë
TIRANË
(TIRANA)
Elbasan
Lumi i Shkumbinit
Lumi i Osumit
ALBANIA
Lumi i Devollit
Nikšić
Trebinje
Dubrovnik
Podgorica
Cetinje
Bar
Lake Scutari
Lake Skadar
Shkodër
Lac
Krujë
Durrës
Kavajë
Lushnjë
Fier
Berat
Vlorë
Tepelenë
Gjirokastër
Sarandë
Këlcyrë
Konispol
Kérkyra (Corfu)
Iónioi Nísoi (Ionian Islands)
Lefkáda
Kefallinía
Palagruža
Mljet
Adriatic Sea
Strait of Otranto
Golfo di Taranto
Ionian Sea
ITALY
Appennino Lucano
N

ELEVATION

					Below sea level	0	100m	250m	500m	1000m	2000m	4000m
-2000m	-1000m	-500m	-250m	-100m								
-6562ft	-3281ft	-1640ft	-820ft	-328ft	-164ft/-50m	0	328ft	820ft	1640ft	3281ft	6562ft	13 124ft

BOSNIA & HERZEGOVINA

Territorial extent
Republika Srpska
Federacija Bosna i Hercegovina

CROATIA
SERBIA
SERB. & MON. (YUGO.)
MONTENEGRO
Bihać
Banja Luka
Brčko
Bijeljina
Tuzla
Goražde
Sarajevo
Mostar
Split
Dubrovnik
Adriatic Sea
Drina
50 km
50 miles
0
0

101

THE MEDITERRANEAN

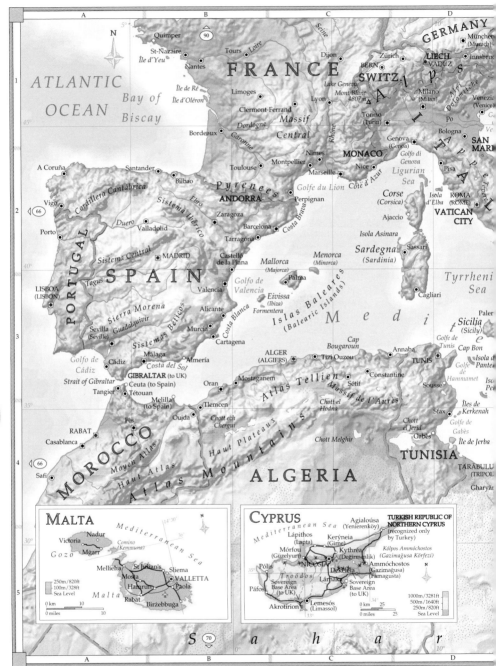

ATLANTIC OCEAN

Bay of Biscay

FRANCE

GERMANY

Quimper
St-Nazaire
Île d'Yeu
Nantes
Tours
Dijon
Zürich
BERN
München (Munich)
LIECH. VADUZ
Innsbruck
SWITZ.
Limoges
Lake Geneva
Mont Blanc 4807m
Milano (Milan)
Venezia (Venice)
A L P S
Clermont-Ferrand
Lyon
Torino (Turin)
Po
Dolomitiche
Bordeaux
Massif Central
Rhône
Genova (Genoa)
Bologna
SAN MARI
A Coruña
Santander
Bilbao
Nîmes
MONACO
Nice
Golfo di Genova
Pisa
ROMA (ROME)
Appennino
Vigo
Cordillera Cantábrica
Pyrenees
ANDORRA
Perpignan
Montpellier
Marseille
Côte d'Azur
Ligurian Sea
Corse (Corsica)
Isola d'Elba
VATICAN CITY
Porto
Duero
Valladolid
Sistema Ibérico
Ebro
Zaragoza
Barcelona
Costa Brava
Ajaccio
Isola Asinara
Sardegna (Sardinia)
Sassari
Tyrrheni Sea
PORTUGAL
Sistema Central
MADRID
Tagus
Castelló de la Plana
Mallorca (Majorca)
Menorca (Minorca)
Palma
Cagliari
SPAIN
LISBOA (LISBON)
Valencia
Golfo de Valencia
Sierra Morena
Guadalquivir
Alicante
Eivissa (Ibiza)
Formentera
Islas Baleares (Balearic Islands)
M e d i t e
Sicilia (Sicily)
Paler
Sistemas Béticos
Murcia
Costa Blanca
Cartagena
Cap Bougaroun
ALGER (ALGIERS)
Tizi Ouzou
Annaba
Golfe de Tunis
Cap Bon
Isola di Pante
Málaga
Almería
Golfo de Cádiz
Cádiz
Costa del Sol
GIBRALTAR (to UK)
Ceuta (to Spain)
Tangier
Tétouan
Melilla (to Spain)
Oran
Mostaganem
Constantine
Sétif
TUNIS
Sousse
Golfe de Hammamet
Iso Pen
Strait of Gibraltar
RABAT
Casablanca
Fès
Oujda
Tlemcen
Chott ech Chergui
Atlas Tellien
Massif de l'Aurès
Chott el Hodna
Sfax
Îles de Kerkenah
Safi
MOROCCO
Moyen Atlas
Haut Atlas
Haut Plateaux
Chott Melghir
Chott el Jerid
Golfe de Gabès
Gabès
Île de Jerba
Atlas Mountains
ALGERIA
TUNISIA
TARĀBULU (TRIPOL
Gharyān

90
66
66
70

MALTA

Mediterranean Sea
Nadur
Victoria
Gozo
Comino (Kemmuna)
Mgarr
Mellieha
St Julian's
Mosta
Sliema
VALLETTA
Hamrun
Paola
Malta
Rabat
Birżebbuġa

250m/820ft
100m/328ft
Sea Level
0 km   10
0 miles   10

CYPRUS

Mediterranean Sea
Agialoúsa (Yenierenköy)
TURKISH REPUBLIC OF NORTHERN CYPRUS
(recognized only by Turkey)
Lápithos (Lapta)
Kerýneia (Girne)
Mórfou (Güzelyurt)
Kythréa (Degirmenlik)
Kólpos Ammóchostos (Gazimağusa Körfezi)
Pólis
NICOSIA
Ammóchostos (Gazimağusa/Famagusta)
Troódos
Dekélia
Sovereign Base Area (to UK)
Páfos
Lárnaka
Sovereign Base Area (to UK)
Akrotírion
Lemesós (Limassol)

1000m/3281ft
500m/1640ft
250m/820ft
Sea Level
0 km   25
0 miles   25

S a h a r

0 km   400
0 miles   400

POPULATION   ● National capital

○ Less than 50,000   ○ 50,000 -100,000   ◉ 100,000 - 500,000   ◼ Over 500,000

SLOVAKIA
WIEN
(VIENNA)
USTRIA
BUDAPEST
Satu Mare
HUNGARY
Great
Hungarian
Plain
Danube
LJUBLJANA
LVN.
ZAGREB
CROATIA
Novi Sad
Rijeka
Sava
BOSNIA
& HERZ.
BEOGRAD
(BELGRADE)
SARAJEVO
SERBIA &
MONTENEGRO
(YUGOSLAVIA)
Prishtina
TIRANË
(TIRANA)
Bari
Napoli (Naples)
Vesuvio 1277m
Lecce
*Golfo di
Taranto*
Cosenza
ALBANIA
Catanzaro
*Monte Etna
3340m*
Catania
Siracusa
VALLETTA
ALTA

Târgu Mures
ROMANIA
Carpatii Meridonali
Danube
BUCUREȘTI
(BUCHAREST)
BULGARIA
Balkan Mountains
SOFIYA
(SOFIA)
SKOPJE
MACED.
*Rhodope
Mountains*
Thessaloníki
(Salónica)
Lárisa
GREECE
ATHÍNA
(ATHENS)
*Pindos
Oros Mts*
*Strait of
Otranto*
Kérkyra
(Corfu)
*Ionian
Sea*
Kefallinía
Zákynthos
Kýthira

Bălti
108
UKRAINE
*Kakhos'ka
Vodoskhovyshche*
MOLD.
CHIŞINĂU
Dniester
Galaţi
Varna
Burgas
Edirne
İstanbul
Boğazı
(Bosporus)
İstanbul
*Marmara
Denizi*
Bursa
Balıkesir
İzmir
*Aegean
Sea*
Chíos
Sámos
*Dodekánisos
(Dodecanese)*
*Kykládes
(Cyclades)*
Mirtóo
Pélagos
*Kritikó Pélagos
(Sea of Crete)*
Irákleio
*Kríti
(Crete)*
Límnos

Odesa
Dnieper
Berdyans'k
Sea of Azov
*Kryms'kyy
Pivostrov*
Kerch
Sevastopol'
Constanţa
Black Sea
Zonguldak
Küre Dağları
Samsun
ANKARA
Kızıl Irmak
Ordu
TURKEY
*Tuz
Gölü*
Kayseri
Antalya
Toros Dağları
*Antalya
Körfezi*
Gaziantep
Adana
İskenderun Körfezi
NICOSIA
CYPRUS
Lárnaka
Lemesós
(Limassol)
Halab
(Aleppo)
SYRIA
LEBANON
BEYROUTH
(BEIRUT)
DIMASHQ
(DAMASCUS)
Hefa
Tel Aviv-Yafo
ISRAEL
AMMAN
JERUSALEM
Gaza
Dead Sea
JORDAN

RUSS.
FED.
Novorossiysk
117
Euphrates
119

Mişrātah
*Khalīj Surt
(Gulf of Sirte)*
Surt
Ajdābiyā
Waddān
LIBYA
*Libyan
Desert*
Banghāzī
(Benghazi)
Darnah
Ţubruq
*Libyan
Plateau*
Great Sand Sea
*Munkhafad al Qattâra
(Qattâra Depression)*
Alexandria
*Nile
Delta*
El Giza
CAIRO
Suez
El Alamein
Port Said
*Suez
Canal*
EGYPT
Nile
*Sahara el Sharqiya
(Eastern Desert)*
Sinai
Suez
Elat
Al 'Aqabah
SAUDI
ARABIA
*Red
Sea*
72

Adriatic Sea
Dalmacija
scara

E   F   G   H
1
2
3
4
5

ELEVATION

-4000m	-3000m	-2000m	-1000m	-500m	Below sea level	0	100m	250m	500m	1000m	2000m	4000m
-13 124ft	-9843ft	-6562ft	-3281ft	-1640ft	-820ft/-250m	0	328ft	820ft	1640ft	3281ft	6562ft	13 124ft

BULGARIA & GREECE

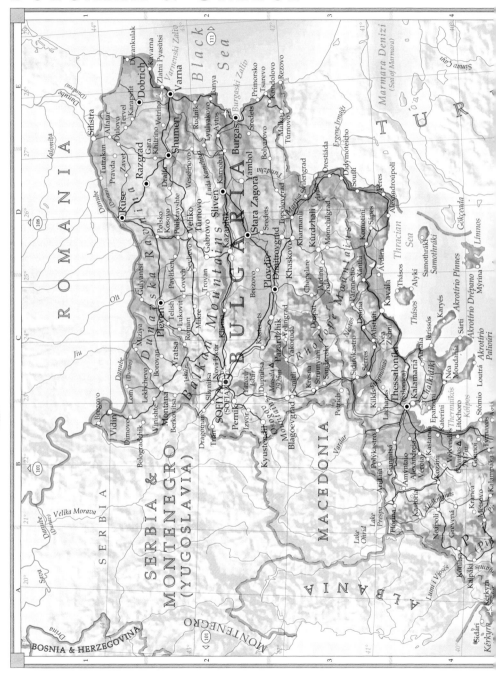

POPULATION   ● National capital

○ Less than 50,000   ◌ 50,000 –100,000   ◉ 100,000 - 500,000   ◼ Over 500,000

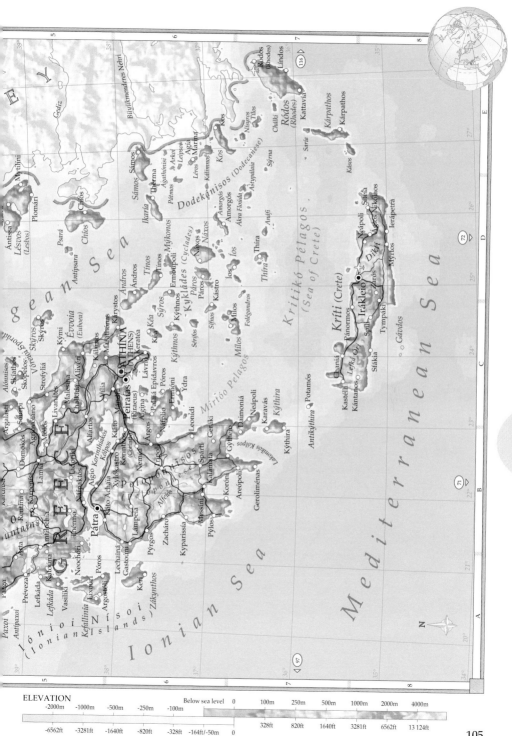

ELEVATION

-2000m	-1000m	-500m	-250m	-100m	Below sea level 0	100m	250m	500m	1000m	2000m	4000m
-6562ft	-3281ft	-1640ft	-820ft	-328ft	-164ft/-50m	0	328ft	820ft	1640ft	3281ft	6562ft	13 124ft

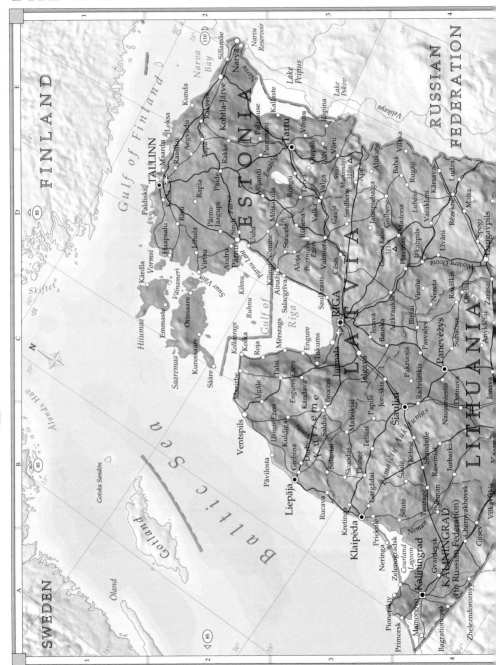

POPULATION • National capital

○ Less than 50,000 ○ 50,000 -100,000 ◉ 100,000 - 500,000 ▣ Over 500,000

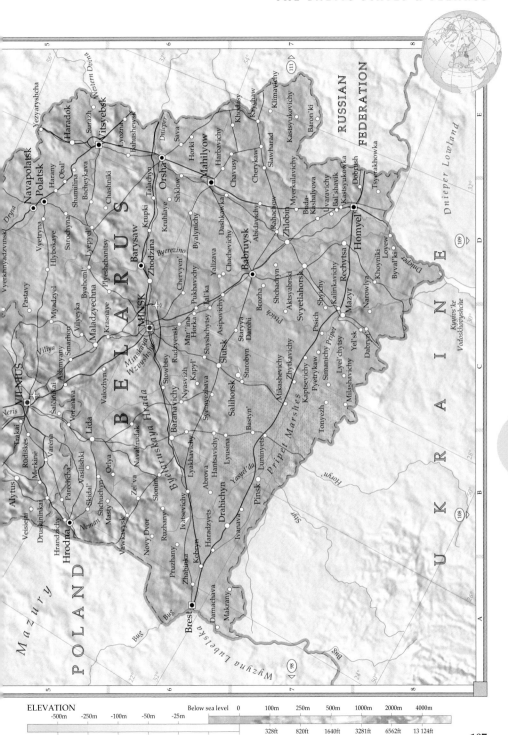

RUSSIAN
FEDERATION

UKRAINE

POLAND

Mazury

Wyżyna Lubelska

Dnieper Lowland

BELARUS

Byelaruskaya Hrada

Minskaya Wzvyshsha

Pripet Marshes

Vilnius

Navapolatsk
Polatsk
Harodok
Vitsyebsk
Surazh
Lyozna
Jahushewski
Yezyvryshcha

Harany
Obal'
Bacheykava
Shumilina
Sarochyna

Mahilyow
Orsha
Shklow
Horki
Harbavichy
Chavusy
Cherykaw

Homyel
Zhlobin
Babruysk
Mazyr

Pinsk
Brest

Mahilyow

ELEVATION

				Below sea level	0	100m	250m	500m	1000m	2000m	4000m
-500m	-250m	-100m	-50m	-25m							
-1640ft	-820ft	-328ft	-164ft	-82ft	33ft/-10m	0	328ft	820ft	1640ft	3281ft	6562ft	13 124ft

UKRAINE, MOLDOVA & ROMANIA

POPULATION   ● National capital

○ Less than 50,000   ○ 50,000 -100,000   ◉ 100,000 - 500,000   ◼ Over 500,000

Black Sea

ELEVATION

				Below sea level	0	100m	250m	500m	1000m	2000m	4000m
-2000m	-1000m	-500m	-250m	-100m							
-6562ft	-3281ft	-1640ft	-820ft	-328ft/-50m	0	328ft	820ft	1640ft	3281ft	6562ft	13 124ft

EUROPEAN RUSSIA

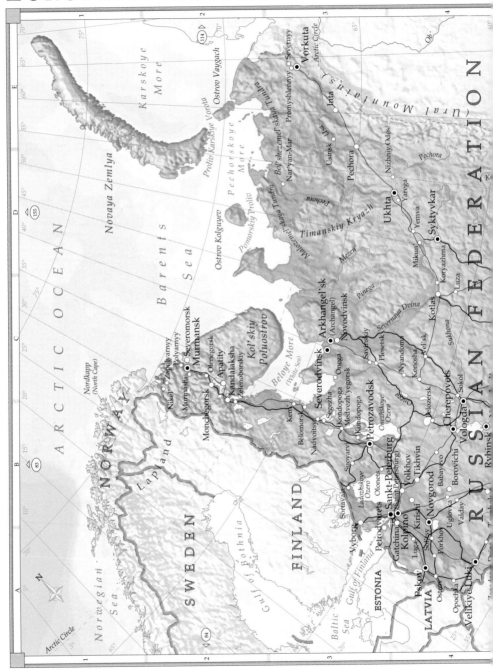

Karskoye More

Novaya Zemlya

Ostrov Vaygach

Proliv Karskiye Vorota

Pechorskoye More

Ostrov Kolguyev

Pomorskiy Proliv

Barents Sea

ARCTIC OCEAN

Nordkapp (North Cape)

NORWAY

Lapland

SWEDEN

Norwegian Sea

Arctic Circle

Gulf of Bothnia

FINLAND

Baltic Sea

ESTONIA

LATVIA

Severnyy
Vorkuta
Arctic Circle
Promyshlennyy
Inta
Usa'
Usinsk
Nar'yan-Mar
Bol'shezemel'skaya Tundra
Pechora
Nizhniy Odes
Pechora
Yarega
Ukhta
Syktyvkar
Mikun'
Yemva
Koryazhma
Luza
Timanskiy Kryazh
Mezen'
Pinega
Kotlas
Sukhona
Severnaya Dvina
Arkhangel'sk
(Archangel)
Novodvinsk
Onega
Savinskiy
Yel'sk
Plesetsk
Nyandoma
Konosha
Malozemel'skaya Tundra

Ural Mountains

RUSSIAN FEDERATION

Kol'skiy Poluostrov
Murmansk
Severomorsk
Polyarnyy
Zapolyarnyy
Nikel'
Murmashi
Olenegorsk
Apatity
Kandalaksha
Zelenoborskiy
Monchegorsk
Kem'
Belomorsk
Nadvoitsy
Segezha
Kondopoga
Medvezh'yegorsk
Beloye More
(White Sea)
Severodvinsk
Onega
Kondopoga
Belozersk
Vologda
Cherepovets
Sokol
Petrozavodsk
Onezhskoye Ozero
Sheksna
Rybinsk
Ladozhskoye Ozero
Olonets
Svatavla
Sortavala
Priozersk
Vyborg
Sankt-Peterburg
(St Petersburg)
Kolpino
Gatchina
Volkhov
Tikhvin
Kirishi
Babayevo
Borovichi
Ugolvka
Valday
Velikiye Luki
Pskov
Opochka
Ostrov
Soltsy
Luga
Novgorod
Porkhov
Petrodvorets

POPULATION

● National capital

○ Less than 50,000 ○ 50,000 – 100,000 ◉ 100,000 – 500,000 ◼ Over 500,000

0 km   400
0 miles   400

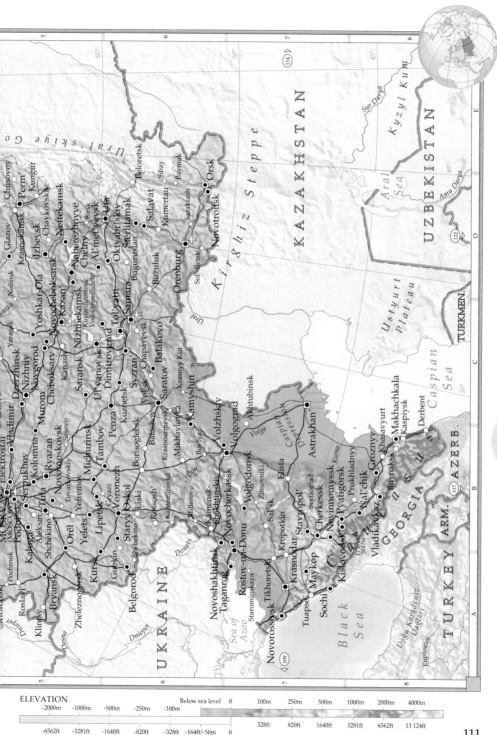

ELEVATION

					Below sea level	0	100m	250m	500m	1000m	2000m	4000m
-2000m	-1000m	-500m	-250m	-100m								
-6562ft	-3281ft	-1640ft	-820ft	-328ft	-164ft/-50m	0	328ft	820ft	1640ft	3281ft	6562ft	13 124ft

NORTH & WEST ASIA

A · R · C · T · I
Franz Josef Land
Severnaya Zem
Ostrov Komsomolets
Ostrov Oktyabr'skoy Revolyutsii
Ostrov Bol'shevik
Summer limit of pack ice
Poluostrov Taymyr
Winter limit of pack ice
North Siberi
Norwegian Sea
North Cape
Barents Sea
Novaya Zemlya
East Novaya Zemlya Trench
Kara Sea
Poluostrov Yamal
Ostrov Kolguyev
Noril'sk
Central Siberian Plateau
Murmansk
Kola Peninsula
White Sea
Kureyka
Lower Tunguska
Arctic Circle
Archangel
R · U · S · S · I · A · N · F
West Siberian Plain
Stony Tunguska
Lake Onega
Northern Dvina
Ob'
Irtysh
Ob'
Angara
S·i
Saint Petersburg
Vologda
Perm'
Yekaterinburg
Chulym
Tomsk
Krasnoyarsk
Gulf of Bothnia
Yaroslavl
Nizhniy Novgorod
Volga
Chelyabinsk
Novosibirsk
Baltic Sea
Kazan'
Ufa
Omsk
Novokuznetsk
Kaliningrad
MOSCOW
Central Russian Upland
Ul'yanovsk
Samara
Ishim
KALININGRAD (to Russ. Fed.)
Voronezh
Saratov
Orenburg
ASTANA
Sayanskiy Khrebet
EUROPE
Volgograd
Ural'sk
Kirghiz Steppe
Karaganda
Semipalatinsk
A
Rostov-na-Donu
Don
Astrakhan'
Ural
KAZAKHSTAN
Kazakh Uplands
Ozero Zaysan
Altai Mountains
Danube
Stavropol'
Aral'sk
Sur Darya
Lake Balkhash
El'brus 5642m
Caucasus
Aktau
Ustyurt Plateau
Aral Sea
Kyzyl Kum
Kyzylorda
Taraz
Almaty
Ili
Black Sea
Istanbul
Sûre Daglari
GEORGIA
BILISI
Dashkhovuz
UZBEKISTAN
Tien Shan
Anatolia
ANKARA
ARMENIA
YEREVAN
AZERB.
BAKU
TURKMENISTAN
Amu Darya
TASHKENT
KYRGYZSTAN
BISHKEK
TURKEY
Lake Van
Kara Kum
DUSHANBE
Adana
Gaziantep
Tabriz
ASHGABAT
TAJIKISTAN
CYPRUS
Aleppo
Mosul
TEHRAN
KABUL
Hindu Kush
Jalalabad
Kunlun Mountains
BEIRUT
SYRIA
IRAQ
Qom
IRAN
Herat
AFGHANISTAN
Khyber Pass
LEBANON
DAMASCUS
BAGHDAD
Isfahan
Iranian Plateau
ISRAEL
AMMAN
Syrian Desert
Euphrates
Tigris
Zagros Mountains
Himalayas
JERUSALEM
JORDAN
Basra
Thar Desert
KUWAIT
KUWAIT
Shiraz
Zahedan
Ganges
An Nafud
Bandar-e 'Abbas
MANAMA
Gulf
Dubai
Ganges Fan
Tropic of Cancer
BAHRAIN
RIYADH
DOHA
U.A.E.
Gulf of Oman
MUSCAT
Indus Fan
QATAR
ABU DHABI
Sur
SAUDI ARABIA
Arabian Peninsula
Murray Ridge
At Ta'if
Red Sea
Nile
Ar Rub' al Khali
OMAN
Ganges
AFRICA
Arabian Sea
Bay of Bengal
SANA
YEMEN
Socotra (to Yemen)
Ta'izz
Aden
Gulf of Aden

0 km   800
0 miles   800

POPULATION   ● National capital

○ Less than 50,000   ○ 50,000 -100,000   ◉ 100,000 - 500,000   ◙ Over 500,000

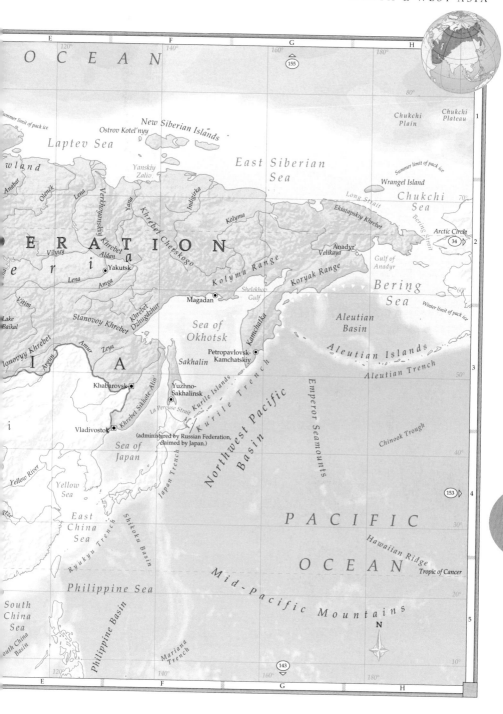

O C E A N

120°

140°

160°

180°

155

80°

Summer limit of pack ice

New Siberian Islands

Ostrov Kotel'nyy

Laptev Sea

wland

Anabar

Olenek

Lena

Yanskiy
Zaliv

Yana

Indigirka

Khrebet Cherskogo

Verkhoyanskiy Khrebet

East Siberian
Sea

Kolyma

Chukchi
Plain

Chukchi
Plateau

1

Summer limit of pack ice

Wrangel Island

Long Strait

Chukchi
Sea

Ekiatapskiy Khrebet

Bering Strait

70°

Arctic Circle

34

2

E R A T I O N

e r i a

Vilyuy

Aldan

Yakutsk

Lena

Amga

Kolyma Range

Anadyr
Velikaya

Koryak Range

Gulf of
Anadyr

Bering
Sea

60°

Winter limit of pack ice

Vitim

Lake
Baikal

Stanovoy Khrebet

Khrebet
Dzhugdzhur

Shelekhov
Gulf

Magadan

Sea of
Okhotsk

Kamchatka

Aleutian
Basin

Aleutian Islands

Aleutian Trench

50°

lonovyy Khrebet

Amur

Zeya

Argun

Khabarovsk

Khrebet Sikhote-Alin'

Yuzhno-
Sakhalinsk

Kurile Islands

La Perouse Strait

Kurile Trench

Northwest Pacific
Basin

Emperor Seamounts

Chinook Trough

40°

153

4

i

Vladivostok

Petropavlovsk-
Kamchatskiy

Sakhalin

(administered by Russian Federation,
claimed by Japan.)

Japan Trench

Sea of
Japan

Yellow River

Yellow
Sea

East
China
Sea

Shikoku Basin

Ryukyu Trench

Shikoku Basin

P A C I F I C

30°

O C E A N

Hawaiian Ridge

Tropic of Cancer

South
China
Sea

outh China
Basin

Philippine Sea

Philippine Basin

Mid-Pacific Mountains

20°

N

Mariana
Trench

143

10°

120°

140°

160°

180°

E

F

G

H

RUSSIA & KAZAKHSTAN

POPULATION

● National capital

0 km   800
0 miles   800

○ Less than 50,000   ○ 50,000 -100,000   ◉ 100,000 - 500,000   ■ Over 500,000

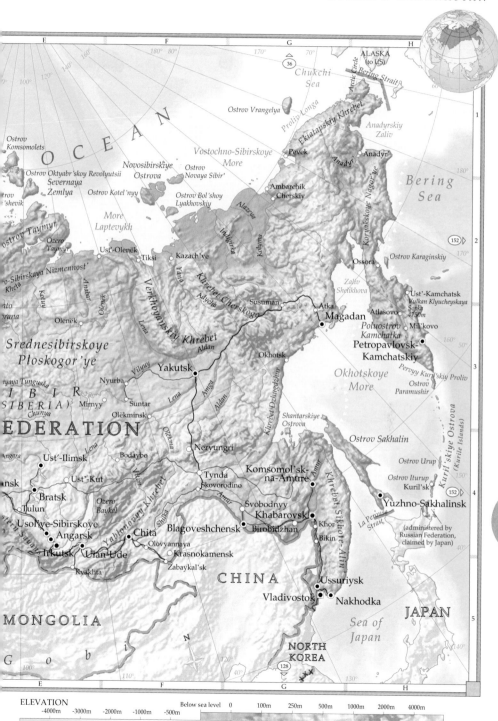

ELEVATION

-4000m	-3000m	-2000m	-1000m	-500m	Below sea level 0	100m	250m	500m	1000m	2000m	4000m

| -13 124ft | -9843ft | -6562ft | -3281ft | -1640ft | -820ft/-250m | 0 | 328ft | 820ft | 1640ft | 3281ft | 6562ft | 13 124ft |

TURKEY & THE CAUCASUS

ROMANIA

Iacul Razim
Iacul Sinoie

N
108

UKRAINE
Kryms'kyy
Pivostriv

Danube

BULGARIA

Varnenski
Zaliv

Black Sea

Burgaski
Zaliv

Maritsa

104 Edirne
Kırklareli

Cide Inebolu Sinop
Gerze

Çorlu
Ergene Nehri

Zonguldak Bartın Küre Dağları Bafra

Karabük Kastamonu Samsun

Tekirdağ İstanbul Devrek Kargı Ünye

Marmara Denizi İzmit Adapazarı Çerkeş Merzifon Ord

Bandırma Yalova Bolu Gerede Çankırı Kızıl Irmak Corum

Çanakkale İznik Gölü Bursa Tokat

Çanakkale Boğazı Bilecik Alaca Yıldızeli

Balıkesir Bozüyük Eskişehir ANKARA Kalecik Sorgun Siva

Edremit Kütahya Polatlı Kırıkkale Şarkışla

Simav Hirfanlı Barajı Boğazlıyan

Akhisar Gediz Kulu Tuz Gölü Bünyan Hek

Manisa Uşak Afyon Cihanbeyli İncesu Gürün

İzmir Aksaray Nevşehir Kayseri

Menemen Alaşehir Akşehir Gü

Ödemiş Nazilli Konya Niğde Göksun

Aydın Dinar Beyşehir Kahramanma

Söke Denizli Isparta Ereğli

Milas Burdur Karaman Gazi

Bodrum Tavas Burdur Gölü Süğla Gölü Toros Dağları Ceyhan

Marmaris Muğla Antalya Tarsus Osmaniye

Dalaman Manavgat Mersin Adana

Fethiye Alanya Mut İskenderun Kilis

Kaş Silifke Antakya Kırıkhan

Finike Anamur

Ródos Antalya Körfezi

Kárpathos

GREECE

Lésvos
Chíos
Sámos

Dodekánisos
(Dodecánese)

Mediterranean
Sea

CYPRUS

TURKISH REPUBLIC OF
NORTHERN CYPRUS
(recognised only by Turkey)

Orontes

LEBANON

72

0 km 200
0 miles 200

POPULATION • National capital
○ Less than 50,000 ○ 50,000 -100,000 ◉ 100,000 - 500,000 ◼ Over 500,000

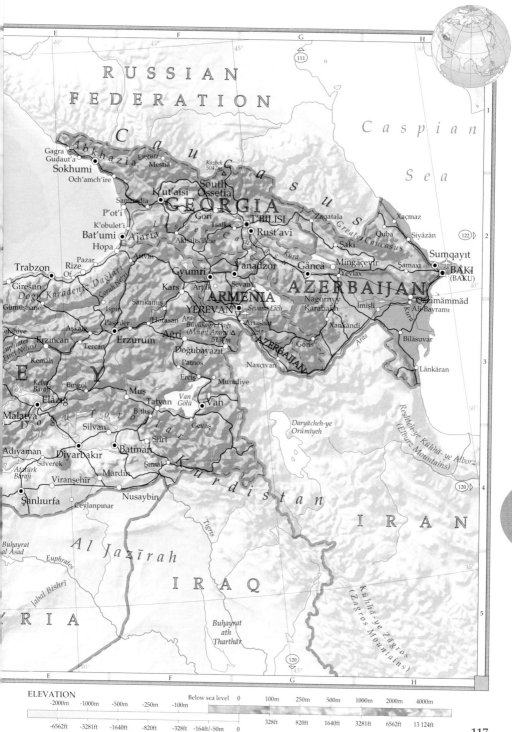

THE MIDDLE EAST

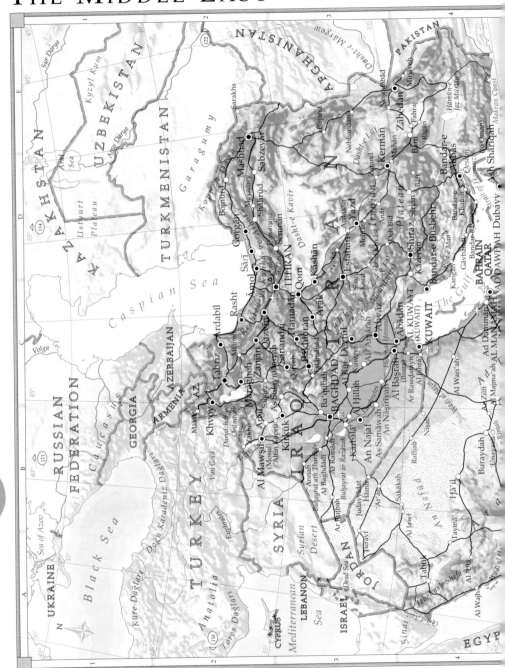

POPULATION
- ● National capital
- ○ Less than 50,000
- ◎ 50,000 -100,000
- ◉ 100,000 - 500,000
- ◼ Over 500,000

0 km   400

0 miles   400

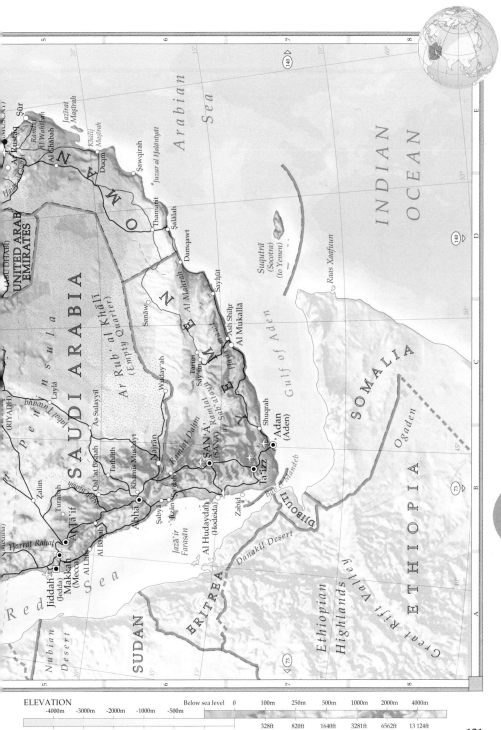

ELEVATION

-4000m	-3000m	-2000m	-1000m	-500m	Below sea level	0	100m	250m	500m	1000m	2000m	4000m

				328ft	820ft	1640ft	3281ft	6562ft	13 124ft
-13 124ft	-9843ft	-6562ft	-3281ft	-1640ft	-820ft/-250m	0			

CENTRAL ASIA

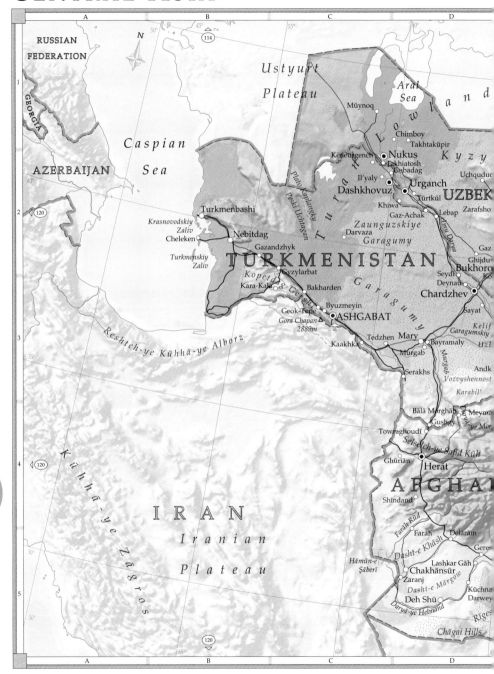

RUSSIAN
FEDERATION

GEORGIA

Caspian

Sea

AZERBAIJAN

Ustyurt

Plateau

Aral
Sea

Müynoq

Chimboy

Takhtaküpir

Keneurgench

Lakhiatosh

Gubadag

Nukus

Il'yaly

Urganch

Dashkhovuz

UZBEK

Khiwa

Türtkül

Uchquduc

Gaz-Achak

Zarafsho

Lebap

Turkmenbashi

Krasnovodskiy
Zaliv

Cheleken

Nebitdag

Darvaza

Zaunguzskiye

Garagumy

Gazandzhyk

Gaz

Turkmenskiy
Zaliv

Kyzylarbat

Seydi

Ghjdu

Bukhoro

Kara-Kala

Bakharden

Garagumy

Deynau

Chardzhev

Sayat

Geok-Tepe

Byuzmeyin

Gora Chapan
2889m

ASHGABAT

Tedzhen

Mary

Bayramaly

Kelif

Garagumskiy

Kaakhka

Mürgab

Serakhs

Andk
Vozvyshennost

Karabil'

Bālā Morghāb

Meyma

Gushgy

Towraghoudī

Ghūriān

Herāt

AFGHA

Shīndand

I R A N

Iranian

Plateau

Farāh Rūd

Farah

Delaram

Geres

Dasht-e Khāsh

Hāmūn-e
Şāberī

Lashkar Gāh

Chakhānsūr

Zaranj

Deh Shū

Kūchna
Darwey

Darya-ye Helmand

Rīge

Chāgai Hills

| 0 km | | 200 |
| 0 miles | | 200 |

POPULATION   ● National capital

○ Less than 50,000   ○ 50,000 -100,000   ◉ 100,000 - 500,000   ◼ Over 500,000

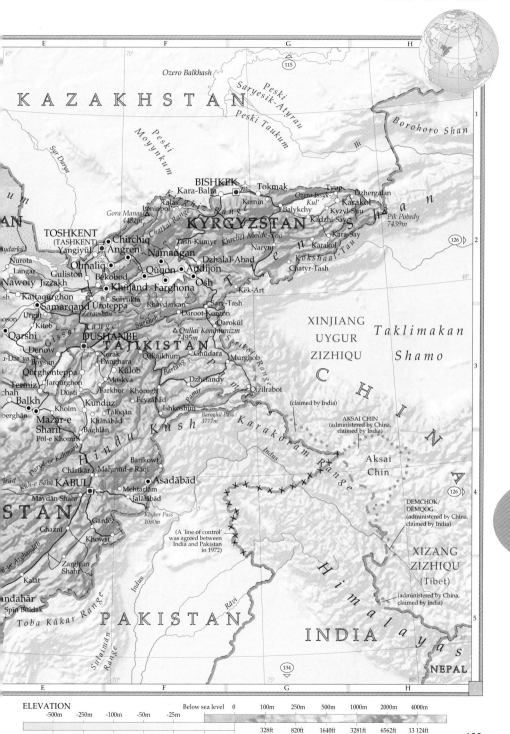

KAZAKHSTAN

Ozero Balkhash

Peski Saryesik-Atyrau

Peski Moyynkum

Peski Taukum

Borohoro Shan

Ili

Syr Darya

BISHKEK
Kara-Balta · Tokmak · Tyup · Dzhergalan
Talas · Kemin · *Ozero Issyk-Kul'* · Karakol
Jeninpol · Balykchy · Kyzyl-Suu
Gora Manas · *Kyrgyz Range* · Kadzhi-Sayg · *Pik Pobedy*
4482m · KYRGYZSTAN · Kara-Say · 7439m

TOSHKENT
(TASHKENT) · Chirchiq · Tash-Kumyr · *Khrebet Molde-Too* · Karakol
Yangiyŭl · Angren · Namangan · Naryn · Karakol-Tau
Aydarkŭl · Olmaliq · Dzhalal-Abad · *Kokshaal-Tau*
Nurota · Guliston · Bekobod · Qŭqon · Andijon · Chatyr-Tash
Langar · Jizzakh · Khŭjand · Farghona · Osh
Nawoiy · Kattaqŭrghon · Ŭroteppa · Kŭk-Art · XINJIANG
Qarshi · Samarqand · *Zeravshan* · Sŭlyukta · UYGUR · *Taklimakan*
Urgut · Kitob · Khavdarkan · Sary-Tash · ZIZHIQU · *Shamo*
oson · *Gissar Range* · DUSHANBE · Daroot-Korgon · Qarokŭl
Denow · TAJIKISTAN · △ *Qullai Kommunizm* · C
ı-Dar'ya · Boysun · Norak · Qal'aikhum · Ghŭdara · 7495m · H
ı · Qŭrghonteppa · Danghara · Murghob · I
Termiz · Jarqŭrghon · Kŭlob · Moskva · Dzhelandy · N
chah · Dŭsti · Farkhor · Khorugh · Qizilrabot · A
Balkh · Kunduz · Feyzabad · Ishkoshim · *Baroghil Pass*
berghān · Kholm · Tāloqān · 3777m · (claimed by India)
Mazār-e · Khānabād · *Karakoram Range* · AKSAI CHIN
Sharif · Baghlān · (administered by China,
Pol-e Khomrī · claimed by India)
Darya-ye Kunduz · *Indus* · Aksai
Kūh-e Bābā · Barīkowt · Chin
Charīkar · Mahmūd-e Rāqī · 126
KABUL · Asadābād · DEMCHOK/
Maydān Shahr · Mehtarlām · DÊMQOG
Jalālābād · (administered by China,
Khyber Pass · claimed by India)
Ghaznī · Gardēz · 1080m
Khowst · XIZANG
(A 'line of control' · ZIZHIQU
Zarghūn · was agreed between · (Tibet)
Shahr · India and Pakistan
in 1972) · (administered by China,
Kalāt · claimed by India)
ndahār
Spin Būldak · *Indus* · *Rāvi* · H
Toba Kākar Range · *i m a l a y a s*
Sulaimān Range · PAKISTAN · INDIA · NEPAL

134

ELEVATION

				Below sea level	0	100m	250m	500m	1000m	2000m	4000m
-500m	-250m	-100m	-50m	-25m							

| -1640ft | -820ft | -328ft | -164ft | -82ft | 33ft/-10m | 0 | 328ft | 820ft | 1640ft | 3281ft | 6562ft | 13 124ft |

SOUTH & EAST ASIA

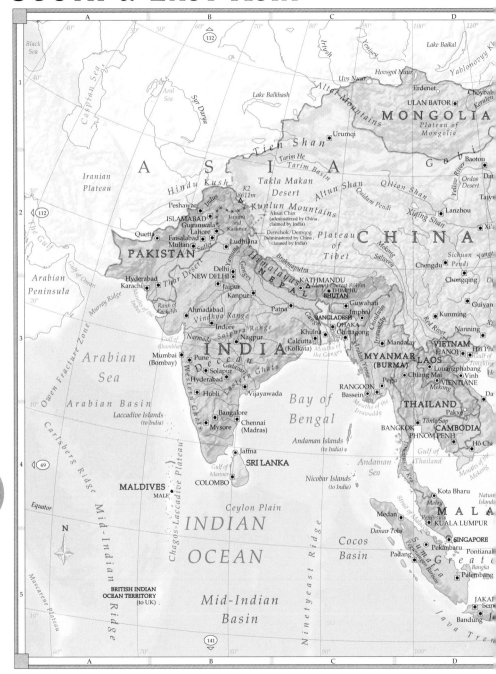

Black
Sea

40°

50°

60°

70°

80°

90°

100°

110°

112

40°

Aral
Sea

Lake Balkhash

Lake Baikal

Hovsgol Nuur

Uvs Nuur

Erdenet

Choybalsan

1

Caspian Sea

Syr Darya

Altai Mountains

ULAN BATOR

MONGOLIA

Kerulen

Yablonovyy Kh

Irtysh

Yenisey

Plateau of
Mongolia

Urumqi

Gobi

Baotou

Da

Iranian
Plateau

Tien Shan

Tarim He

Tarim Basin

Takla Makan
Desert

Altun Shan

Qilian Shan

Ordos
Desert

Xiying Shan

Yellow River

Lanzhou

Taiy

30°

112

Hindu Kush

Peshawar

Indus

K2
8611m

Kunlun Mountains

Aksai Chin
(administered by China,
claimed by India)

Plateau
of
Tibet

Mekong

Salween

Chengdu

Sichuan
Pendi

Yangt

C H I N A

Xi

2

The Gulf

ISLAMABAD

Gujranwala

Lahore

Jammu
and
Kashmir

Demchok/Demqog
(administered by China,
claimed by India)

Chongqing

Guiyan

Quetta

Faisalabad

Multan

Sutlej

Ludhiana

Brahmaputra

Kunming

Nanning

Xi

PAKISTAN

Delhi

Yamuna

Ganges

Himalayas

NEPAL

Mount Everest 8848m

KATHMANDU

THIMPHU

BHUTAN

Guwahati

Imphal

Mandalay

VIETNAM

HANOI

Hai Ph

20°

Arabian
Peninsula

Hyderabad

Karachi

Thar Desert

NEW DELHI

Jaipur

Kanpur

Patna

Ganges

BANGLADESH

DHAKA

Chittagong

Chindwin

Irrawaddy

Red River

Gulf of
Tongking

Gulf of Oman

Murray Ridge

Rann of
Kachchh

Ahmadabad

Vindhya Range

Indore

Satpura Range

Khulna

Calcutta
(Kolkata)

Mouths of
the Ganges

LAOS

Louangphabang

Vinh

Da

Mouths of the

Narmada

Arabian
Sea

Gulf of
Khambhat

Mumbai
(Bombay)

Pune

Deccan

Godavari

I N D I A

Solapur

Arakan Yoma

MYANMAR
(BURMA)

Chiang Mai

VIENTIANE

Mekong

RANGOON

Pegu

Indus

Owen Fracture Zone

Hyderabad

Eastern Ghats

Bassein

THAILAND

10°

Arabian Basin

Hubli

Vijayawada

Bay of

Pakxe

Laccadive Islands
(to India)

Western Ghats

Bangalore

Chennai
(Madras)

Bengal

Andaman Islands
(to India)

BANGKOK

CAMBODIA

Carlsberg Ridge

Mysore

Hô Chi

PHNOM PENH

Gulf of

69

Jaffna

Andaman
Sea

Equator

MALDIVES

MALE

Gulf of
Mannar

SRI LANKA

COLOMBO

Nicobar Islands
(to India)

Mouths of the
Mekong

Kota Bharu

Natun
Islands

Malay
Peninsula

M A L A

Mid-Indian Ridge

Chagos-Laccadive Plateau

Ceylon Plain

INDIAN

Medan

Danau Toba

Strait of Malacca

KUALA LUMPUR

Cocos
Basin

SINGAPORE

Pekanbaru

Pontiana

N

OCEAN

Ninetyeast Ridge

Padang

Sumatra

Greate

Bangka

5

10°

BRITISH INDIAN
OCEAN TERRITORY
(to UK)

Mid-Indian

Basin

Palembang

JAKA

Sem

Java Tren

Mascarene Plateau

Bandung

141

60°

70°

80°

90°

100°

0 km   1000

0 miles   1000

POPULATION   ● National capital

○ Less than 50,000   ○ 50,000 -100,000   ◉ 100,000 - 500,000   ◻ Over 500,000

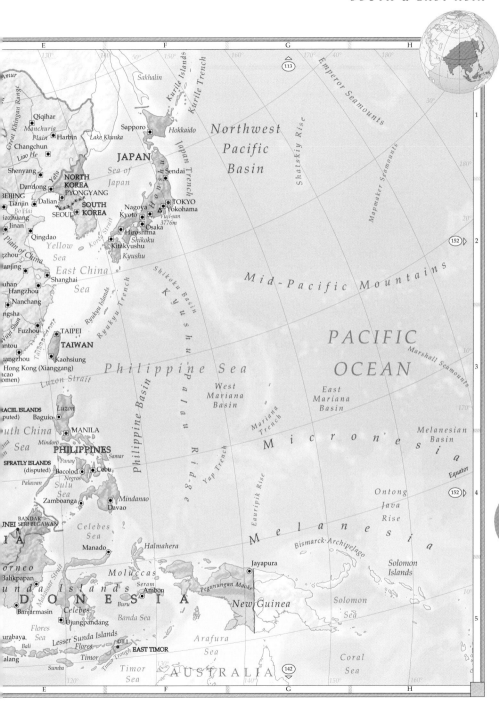

E | F | G | H

130° | 140° | 150° | 160° | 170° | 40° | 180°

113

Amur

Qiqihar

Great Khingan Range

Manchuria
Plain — Harbin | *Lake Khanka*

Sakhalin

Kurile Islands

Kurile Trench

Sapporo

Hokkaido

Northwest
Pacific
Basin

Shatskiy Rise

Emperor Seamounts

Changchun

Liao He

Shenyang

Yalu

BEIJING
Tianjin — Dandong — Dalian

NORTH
KOREA
PYONGYANG

SOUTH
KOREA

SEOUL

JAPAN

Sendai

Honshu

Japan Trench

Sea of
Japan

Mapmaker Seamounts

180°

30°

20°

iazhuang

Jinan

Qingdao

Nagoya **TOKYO**
Kyoto Yokohama
Osaka *Fuji-san*
3776m

TAIPEI

Korea Strait

Hiroshima
Kitakyushu
Shikoku
Kyushu

Bo Hai

Plain of
China

zhou | *Yellow*
Sea

anjing

Shanghai

East China
Sea

Shikoku Basin

Mid-Pacific Mountains

152

2

uhan
Hangzhou

Nanchang

ngsha

Fuzhou

Wuyi Shan

ntou

iangzhou

TAIPEI

TAIWAN

Kaohsiung

Hong Kong (Xianggang)

omen)

Ryukyu Islands

Ryukyu Trench

Taiwan Strait

Luzon Strait

Philippine Sea

Philippine Basin

Kyushu-Palau Ridge

PACIFIC

OCEAN

Marshall Seamounts

10°

3

170°

RACEL ISLANDS
puted)

Baguio

Luzon

uth China
Sea

MANILA

Mindoro

PHILIPPINES

West
Mariana
Basin

East
Mariana
Basin

M i c r o n e s
i
a

Melanesian
Basin

SPRATLY ISLANDS
(disputed)

Palawan

Bacolod *Panay* Cebu
Negros Samar

Mariana
Trench

Yap Trench

Equator

152

4

170°

Zamboanga

Mindanao
Davao

Sulu
Sea

Eauripik Rise

Ontong
Java
Rise

Melanesia

JNEI
BANDAR
SERI BEGAWAN

IA

orneo

Balikpapan

Celebes
Sea

Manado

Moluccas

Halmahera

Seram
Ambon

Buru

Jayapura

Pegunungan Maoke

Bismarck Archipelago

Solomon
Islands

Solomon
Sea

10°

5

Banjarmasin

Makassar Strait

I N D O N E S I A

Celebes

Ujungpandang

Banda Sea

New Guinea

Flores
urabaya Sea
Bali

alang

Lesser Sunda Islands
Flores

Sumba

Timor

DILI

EAST TIMOR

Timor
Sea

Timor Trough

Arafura
Sea

Coral
Sea

AUSTRALIA

142

120° | 130° | 140° | 150° | 160°

E | F | G | H

WESTERN CHINA & MONGOLIA

RUSSIAN FEI

KAZAKHSTAN

Kulunda Steppe

Kazakhskiy Melkosopochnik

Ozero Balkhash

Ozero Zaysan

Altay

Uvs Nuur

Ulaangom

Ölgiy

Chars Nuur

Hyargas Nuur

Har Nuur

Hovd

Hövsgöl Nuur

More

Tsetserleg

M O N

Altay

Bayanhongor

G

Aj Bogd Uul 3802m

Alag Bogd 2702m

Haygayn Nuruu

Karamay

Gurbantünggüt Shamo

Kuytun

Shihezi

Fukang

Jimsar

Qitai

Ürümqi

Bogro Shan

Yining

Tien Shan

Ozero Issyk-Kul'

KYRGYZSTAN

Pik Pobedy 7439m

Tarim He

Korla

Turpan

Turpan Pendi

Hami

Xingxingxia

Ejin Q

Bosten Hu

Kuruktag

Kashi

Yengisar

Shache

Tarim Basin

XINJIANG UYGUR

ZIZHIQU

Ruoqiang

Lop Nur

GANSU

Qilian Shan

Danghe Nanshan

Qinghai Hi

TAJIKISTAN

AFGH.

Yecheng
(claimed
by India)

Pishan

Moyu

Hotan

Qira

Taklimakan

Shamo

Altun Shan

Qaidam Pendi

Golmud

Burhan Budai Shan

Dulan

A...magens S

C

H

QINGHAI

Karakoram Range

**K2
8611m**

**AKSAI
CHIN**

AKSAI CHIN
(administered by
China, claimed
by India)

Kunlun Shan

Rutog

Qingzang Gaoyuan

(Plateau of Tibet)

Tongtian He

Bayan Har Sha

Yushu

PAKISTAN

K a s h m i r

**JAMMU
AND
KASHMIR**

DEMCHOK/DÊMQOG
(administered by China,
claimed by India)

Gar

Zanda

XIZANG

ZIZHIQU

(Tibet)

Nyima

Tangra Yumco

Ngangzê Co

Siling Co

Tanggula Shan

Amdo

Gyaring Co

Nam Co

Nagqu

Damxung

Nyainqêntanglha Shan

Qamdo

Saluem

Jinsha Jiang

Bishunai Shan

Indus

Rutog

Yamuna

Ganges

Brahmaputra

NEPAL

Lhazê

Xigazê

Maizhokunggar

Lhasa

Gonggar

Gyangzê

Mount Everest 8848m

H   i   m   a   l   a   y   a   s

BHUTAN

INDIA

**MYANMAR
(BURMA)**

INDIA

0 km   400

0 miles   400

POPULATION   ● National capital   ◉ Internal administrative capital

○ Less than 50,000   ○ 50,000 -100,000   ◉ 100,000 - 500,000   ■ Over 500,000

RUSS. FED.

Ozero Baykal

RATION

Shilka

Amur (Heilong Jiang)

Ergun
Zuoqi

Jagdaqi

Argun (Ergun He)

Onon

Hailar

Manzhouli

HEILONGJIANG

Selenga

Sühbaatar

Darhan

Onon Gol

Choybalsan

Hulun
Nur

Lake
Khanka

Erdenet

gan

ULAANBAATAR
(ULAN BATOR)

Dzuunmod

Öndörhaan

Menengiyn
Tal

Hulingol

JILIN

OLIA

Kerulen

Baruun-Urt

128

Tongliao

Saynshand

Xilinhot

Liao He

Sea of
Japan

Dalandzadgad

Erenhot

Chifeng

LIAONING

NORTH
KOREA

yn Nuruu

Nei

Jining

BEIJING

Korea
Bay

SOUTH
KOREA

Lang Shan

Huang He

Hohhot

Baotou

TIANJIN

Bo Hai

0130

JAPAN

Wuhai

Mu Us
Shamo

HEBEI

Great Wall of China

Yellow
Sea

Tengger
Shamo

NINGXIA
HUIZU
ZIZHIQU

ning

SHANXI

SHANDONG

N

A

Huang He (Yellow River)

JIANGSU

GANSU

SHAANXI

HENAN

Han Shui

East
China
Sea

ANHUI

SHANGHAI

HUBEI

Chang Jiang (Yangtze)

ZHEJIANG

SICHUAN

CHONGQING

JIANGXI

HUNAN

FUJIAN

129

YUNNAN

GUIZHOU

Tropic of Cancer

TAIWAN

ELEVATION

| -2000m | -1000m | -500m | -250m | -100m | Below sea level | 0 | 100m | 250m | 500m | 1000m | 2000m | 4000m |

| -6562ft | -3281ft | -1640ft | -820ft | -328ft | -164ft/-50m | 0 | 328ft | 820ft | 1640ft | 3281ft | 6562ft | 13 124ft |

127

EASTERN CHINA & KOREA

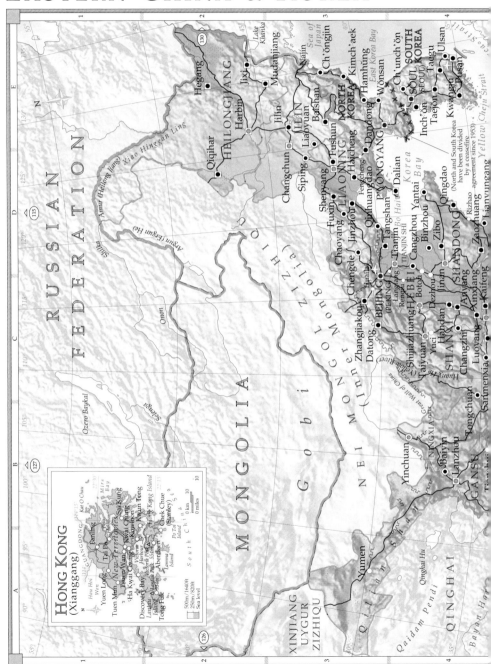

POPULATION ● National capital ◉ Internal administrative capital

○ Less than 50,000 ○ 50,000 -100,000 ◉ 100,000 - 500,000 ■ Over 500,000

0 km 400

0 miles 400

ELEVATION

| -2000m | -1000m | -500m | -250m | -100m | Below sea level 0 | 100m | 250m | 500m | 1000m | 2000m | 4000m |

| -6562ft | -3281ft | -1640ft | -820ft | -328ft | -164ft/-50m | 0 | 328ft | 820ft | 1640ft | 3281ft | 6562ft | 13 124ft |

JAPAN

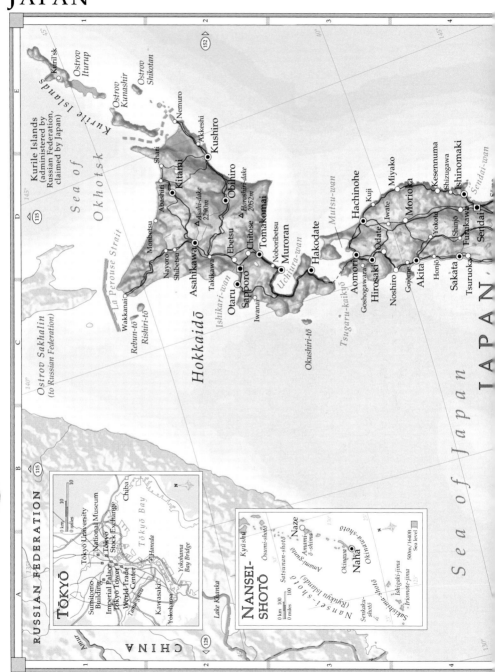

RUSSIAN FEDERATION

Kurile Islands
(administered by
Russian Federation,
claimed by Japan)

Kurile Islands

Kurilsk

Ostrov
Iturup

Ostrov
Kunashir

Ostrov
Shikotan

Nemuro

*Sea
of
Okhotsk*

Akkeshi

Kushiro

Shari

Abashiri

Kitami

Monbetsu

Asahi-dake
2290m

Obihiro

Eniwa-dake
2052m

La Perouse Strait

Nayoro

Shibetsu

Ebetsu

Chitose

Tomakomai

Noboribetsu

Muroran

Wakkanai

Asahikawa

Takikawa

Otaru

Sapporo

Iwanai

Ishikari-wan

Uchiura-wan

Hakodate

Rebun-tō

Rishiri-tō

Ostrov Sakhalin
(to Russian Federation)

Hokkaidō

Okushiri-tō

Tsugaru-kaikyō

Mutsu-wan

Hachinohe

Kuji

Miyako

Morioka

Kesennuma

Ishinomaki

Sendai-wan

Shizugawa

Goshogawara

Aomori

Odate

Hirosaki

Iwate

Yokote

Shinjō

Funakawa

Sendai

Noshiro

Gojōme

Akita

Honjō

Sakata

Tsuruoka

JAPAN

Sea of Japan

Amur

Lake Khanka

CHINA

TŌKYŌ

Chiba

Tōkyō Bay

Tōkyō University

National Museum

Tōkyō
Stock Exchange

Sumitomo
Building

Imperial Palace

Tōkyō Tower

World Trade
Center

Haneda

Yokohama
Bay Bridge

Kawasaki

Yokohama

NANSEI-
SHOTŌ

Kyūshū

Ōsumi-shotō

Naze

Amami-
ō-shima

Amami-guntō

Satsunan-shotō

Nansei-shotō
(Ryūkyū Islands)

Okinawa

Naha

Okinawa

Sakishima-shotō

Ishigaki-jima

Iriomote-jima

*Senkaku-
shotō*

500m/1640ft
Sea level

0 km   200

0 miles   200

POPULATION   ● National capital

○ Less than 50,000   ◎ 50,000 –100,000   ◉ 100,000 – 500,000   ◼ Over 500,000

Honshū

Iwaki
Hitachi
Utsunomiya
Mito
Chōshi
Ōyama
Chiba
TOKYO
Yokohama
Kawasaki
Sukagawa
Maebashi
Kōfu
Kawasaki
Nagaoka
Jōetsu
Nagano
Toyama
Matsumoto
Shizuoka
Hamamatsu
Takaoka
Kanazawa
Gifu
Toyota
Okazaki
Ise
Komatsu
Nagoya
Tsu
Fukui
Tsuruga
Kyōto
Ōtsu
Wakayama
Owase
Shingū
Ōsaka
Kōbe
Kobe
Tottori
Himeji
Tanabe
Gobō
Yonago
Okayama
Tokushima
Matsue
Kurashiki
Kōchi
Nakamura
Kure
Minami
Matsuyama
Sukumo
Fukuyama
Hiroshima
Iwakuni
Nobeoka
Miyakonojō
Gotsu
Hōfu
Ōita
Shikoku
Kyūshū
Miyazaki
Hamada
Nagato
Ube
Bungo-suidō
Masuda
Yamaguchi
Usuki
Nichinan
Shimonoseki
Kurume
Ōmuta
Kitakyūshū
Kumamoto
Sendai
Kagoshima
Fukuoka
Kumamoto
Yatsushiro
Saga
Sasebo
Nagasaki

Izu-shotō
Hachijō-jima
Miyake-jima
Mikura-jima
Nii-jima
Ō-shima
Kōzu-shima

P A C I F I C

O C E A N

Oki-shotō
Dōgo
Dōzen

Liancourt Rocks
(claimed by Japan
& South Korea)

SOUTH
KOREA

Korea Strait

East China Sea

Kagoshima-wan
Ōsumi-shotō
Tanega-shima
Yaku-shima
Shibushi-wan

Amakusa-nada
Koshikijima-rettō
Gotō-rettō
Iki
Tsushima
Kō-saki

ELEVATION

						Below sea level	0	100m	250m	500m	1000m	2000m	4000m
-4000m	-3000m	-2000m	-1000m	-500m									
-13 124ft	-9843ft	-6562ft	-3281ft	-1640ft	-820ft/-250m	0		328ft	820ft	1640ft	3281ft	6562ft	13 124ft

SOUTHERN INDIA & SRI LANKA

N

Arabian

Sea

Amīndīvi Islands

*Lakshadweep
(Laccadive Islands)
(to India)*

Kavaratti Island

Kalpeni Island

Nine Degree Channel

Minicoy Island

Eight Degree Channel

Ihavandippolhu Atoll

MALDIVES

Faadhippolhu Atoll

Horsburgh Atoll

Ari Atoll

Male' Atoll
MALE'

Felidhu Atoll

Mulaku Atoll

Kolhumadulu Atoll

Hadhdhunmathi Atoll

North Huvadhu Atoll

South Huvadhu Atoll

Equator

Addu Atoll

Gan

Kalyān
Mumbai
(Bombay)
Pune Ahmadnagar Nānded
Bārāmati Nizāmābād
Solāpur
Sāngli
Kolhāpur
Gulbarga Hyderābād
Belgaum Rāichūr
Pānji Gadag Kurnool
Hubli Nandyāl
Tungabhadra Reservoir Tādpatri
Dāvangere Anantapur Cuddapah
Shimoga
Bhadrāvati
Udupi Tumkūr
Mangalore Bangalore Vellore
Kāsargod Mandya
Cannanore Krishnagiri Tiruppatūr
Mysore
Calicut Erode Salem
Coimbatore Neyveli
Trichūr Tiruchchirāppalli
Ernākulam Dindigul
Cochin Madurai
Alleppey
Quilon Rājapālaiyam Mannar
Trivandrum Tuticorin
Nāgercoil

Nandyāl
Godāvari
Secunderābād
Karimnagar
Vizianagaram
Visākhapatn
Rājahmund
Kākināc
Vijayawāda
Machilīpatnam
Chīrāla
Ongole
Kāvali
Nellore

Chennai
(Madras)
Kānchīpuram
Pondicherry

SRI LANK
Jaffna
Vavuniya
Trincomalee
Anurādhapura
Batticaloa
Puttalam
Matale
Negombo
Kandy
COLOMBO Sri Jayawardanapura
Kalutara Ratnapura
Galle
Matara

Gulf of Mannar

Coromandel Coast

Malabār Coast

Pak Strait

INDIA
Deccan
Karnātaka
Western Ghats
Tamil Nādu
Andhra Pradesh
Krishna

INDIAN

0 km   300
0 miles   300

POPULATION   ● National capital

○ Less than 50,000   ○ 50,000 -100,000   ◉ 100,000 - 500,000   ■ Over 500,000

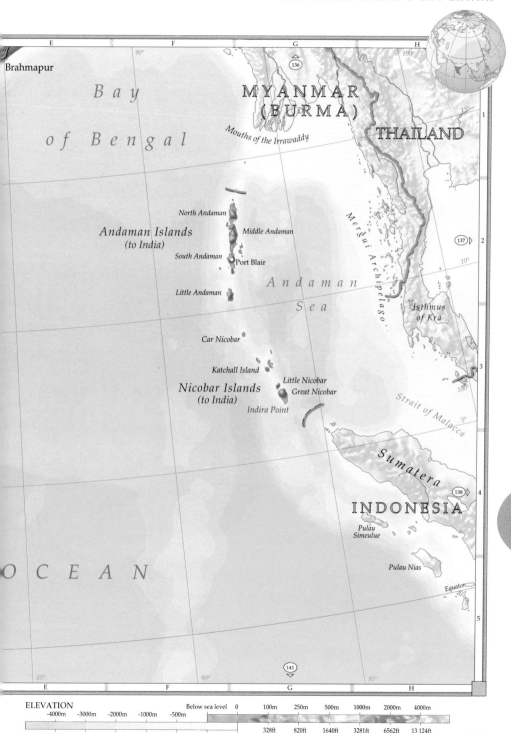

Brahmapur

B a y

o f   B e n g a l

MYANMAR
(BURMA)

THAILAND

Mouths of the Irrawaddy

North Andaman

Andaman Islands
(to India)

Middle Andaman

South Andaman

Port Blair

Little Andaman

A n d a m a n

S e a

Mergui Archipelago

Isthmus
of Kra

Car Nicobar

Katchall Island

Nicobar Islands
(to India)

Little Nicobar
Great Nicobar

Indira Point

Strait of Malacca

S u m a t e r a

INDONESIA

O C E A N

Pulau
Simeulue

Pulau Nias

Equator

ELEVATION

-4000m	-3000m	-2000m	-1000m	-500m	Below sea level 0	100m	250m	500m	1000m	2000m	4000m

-13 124ft	-9843ft	-6562ft	-3281ft	-1640ft	-820ft/-250m 0	328ft	820ft	1640ft	3281ft	6562ft	13 124ft

133

NORTHERN INDIA, PAKISTAN & BANGLADESH

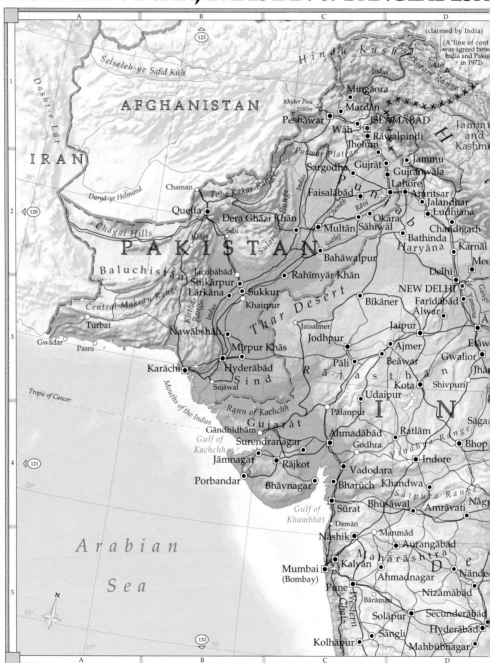

AFGHANISTAN

IRAN

Dasht-e Lūt

Selseleh-ye Safīd Kūh

Hindu Kush

Karakoram Range

(claimed by India)

(A "line of cont
was agreed betw
India and Pakis
in 1972)

K2
8611m

Indus

Mingāora

Khyber Pass
1080m

Peshāwar

Mardān

ISLĀMĀBĀD

Wāh

Rāwalpindi

Jhelum

Jammu
and
Kashmir

Daryā-ye Helmand

Chaman

Toba Kākar Range

Potwar Plateau

Sargodha

Gujrāt

Jammu

Gujrānwāla

Chāgai Hills

Quetta

Dera Ghāzi Khān

Sibi

Multān

Sāhīwāl

Okāra

Lahore

Amritsar

Jalandhar

Ludhiāna

Chandīgarh

Kālat

Sulaimān Range

Sutlej

Chenāb

Rāvi

Faisalābād

Bahāwalpur

Bathinda

Haryāna

Karnāl

Mee

Delhi

PAKISTAN

Baluchistan

Jacobābād

Shikārpur

Lārkāna

Sukkur

Khairpur

Rahīmyār Khān

NEW DELHI

Farīdābād

Alwar

Bīkāner

Central Makrān Range

Kirthar Range

Indus

Turbat

Nawābshāh

Thar Desert

Jaisalmer

Jodhpur

Jaipur

Ajmer

Beāwar

Gwalior

Etaw

Jha

Gwādar

Pasni

Mīrpur Khās

Pāli

Mouths of the Indus

Karāchi

Hyderābād

Sujāwal

Sind

Rāja sthān

Kota

Shivpuri

Tropic of Cancer

Rann of Kachchh

Udaipur

I

N

Pālanpur

Gandhīdhām

Gujarāt

Ahmadābād

Ratlām

Sāga

Gulf of
Kachchh

Surendranagar

Godhra

Bhop

Jāmnagar

Rājkot

Vadodara

Indore

Vindhya Range

Porbandar

Bhāvnagar

Bharūch

Khandwa

Sātpura Range

Nag

Sūrat

Bhusāwal

Amrāvati

Gulf of
Khambhāt

Dāman

Surat

Manmād

Aurangābād

Nāshik

Mahārāshtra

D

e

Arabian

Mumbai
(Bombay)

Kalyān

Ahmadnagar

Nānde

Sea

Pune

Nizāmābād

Bārāmati

N

Secunderābād

Solāpur

Hyderābād

Kolhāpur

Sāngli

Mahbūbnagar

Western Ghats

0 km   300

0 miles   300

POPULATION   ● National capital

○ Less than 50,000   ○ 50,000 -100,000   ◉ 100,000 - 500,000   ◼ Over 500,000

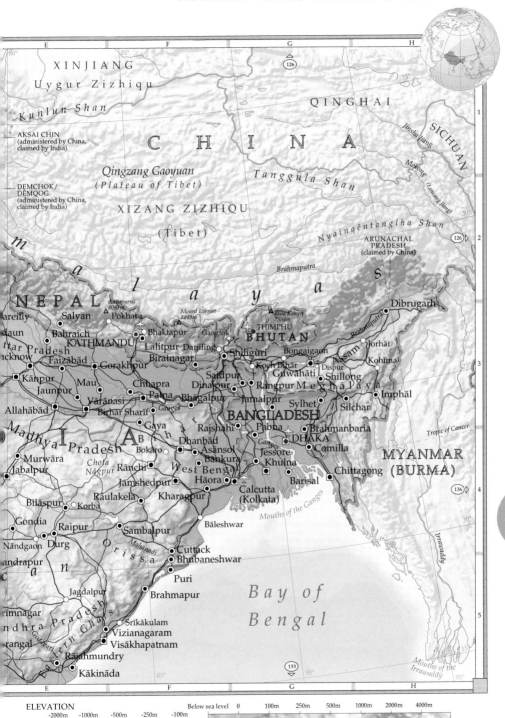

XINJIANG
Uygur Zizhiqu

Kunlun Shan

QINGHAI

AKSAI CHIN
(administered by China,
claimed by India)

C H I N A

Qingzang Gaoyuan
(Plateau of Tibet)

Tanggula Shan

Jinsha Jiang

SICHUAN

Mekong (Lancang Jiang)

DEMCHOK/
DÊMQOG
(administered by China,
claimed by India)

XIZANG ZIZHIQU

(Tibet)

Nyainqêntanglha Shan

ARUNACHAL
PRADESH
(claimed by China)

m
a
l
a
y
a
s

Brahmaputra

NEPAL

Annapurna
8091m

areilly
Salyan
Pokhara

Mount Everest
8848m

Kula Kangri
7554m

Dibrugarh

Brahmaputra

daun
Bahraich

ttar Pradesh
icknow
Faizabad
Kanpur
Jaunpur
Mau

Bhaktapur
KATHMANDU
Lalitpur
Biratnagar
Gorakhpur
Chhapra

Gangtok

Darjiling
Siliguri

THIMPHU

BHUTAN

Koch Bihar

Jorhat

Assam

Bongaigaon

Kohima

Guwahati

Dispur

Shillong
Meghalaya
Sylhet
Silchar

Imphal

Dinajpur
Rangpur
Saidpur
Jamalpur

Allahabad
Birhar Sharif

Patna
Bhagalpur
Varanasi
Gaya
Ganges

BANGLADESH

Rajshahi
Pabna
Brahmanbaria

Madhya I Pradesh
Murwara
Jabalpur
Bilaspur
Korba

Chota
Nagpur
Bokaro
Ranchi
Jamshedpur
Raulakela

Dhanbad
Asansol
Bankura
West Bengal
Haora

DHAKA
Comilla
Ganges
Jessore
Khulna

MYANMAR
(BURMA)

Tropic of Cancer

Kharagpur
Calcutta
(Kolkata)
Barisal

Chittagong

Gondia
Raipur

Nandgaon
Durg
Orissa

Sambalpur
Baleshwar

Mouths of the Ganges

Mahanadi

Irrawaddy

andrapur
a
n

Jagdalpur

Cuttack
Bhubaneshwar

Puri

Bay of
Bengal

rimnagar
ndhra Pradesh
rangal

Godavari

Srikakulam
Vizianagaram
Visakhapatnam
Rajahmundry
Kakinada

Mouths of the
Irrawaddy

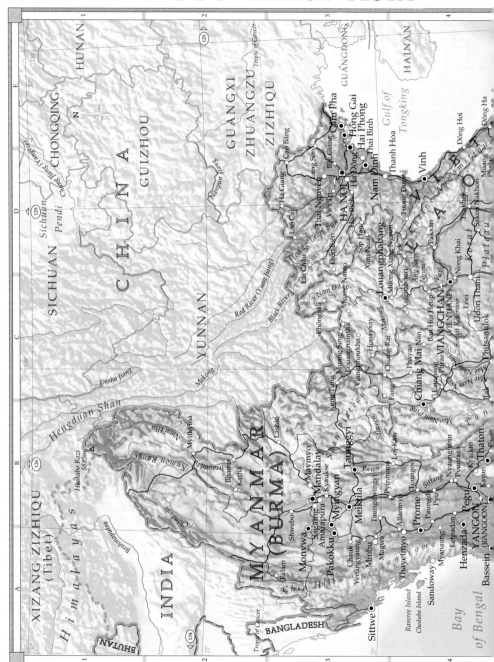

POPULATION   ● National capital

○ Less than 50,000   ○ 50,000 -100,000   ◉ 100,000 - 500,000   ■ Over 500,000

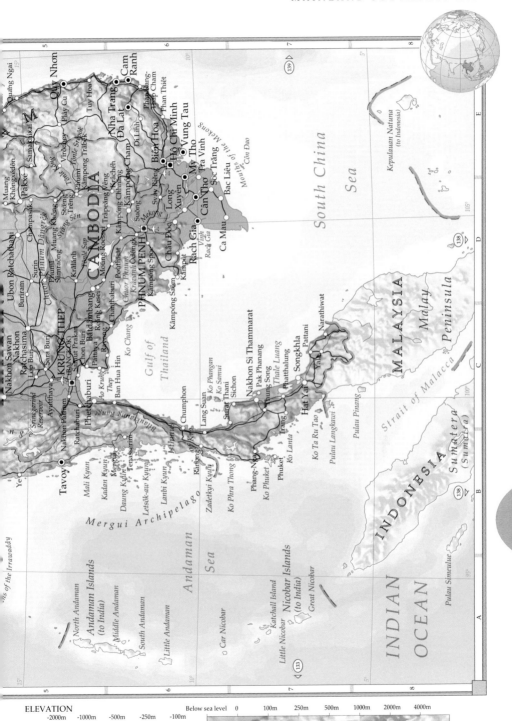

ELEVATION

					Below sea level	0	100m	250m	500m	1000m	2000m	4000m
-2000m	-1000m	-500m	-250m	-100m								

-6562ft	-3281ft	-1640ft	-820ft	-328ft	-164ft/-50m	0	
					328ft	820ft	1640ft	3281ft	6562ft	13 124ft

137

MARITIME SOUTHEAST ASIA

SINGAPORE

MALAYSIA

Johore Strait

Causeway

Lim Chu
Kang

Pulau
Tekong

Pulau
Ubin

Bukit Panjang

Hougang

New Town

Choa Chu
Kang

Changi

Bukit Timah 176m

Queenstown

Bedok
New Town

City

Jurong
Industrial
Estate

Telok Blangah

Selat Pandan

Sentosa

Pulau Sudong

Pulau Pandan

Strait of Singapore

Pulau Pawai

Urban areas
Open areas
Nature reserves

MYANMAR
(BURMA)

Gulf of
Tongking

Hainan Dao
(to China)

THAILAND

LAOS

VIETNAM

CAMBODIA

Mekong

PARACEL ISLANDS
(disputed by China, Taiwan and Vietnam)

South Chin

Sea

*Andaman
Sea*

Gulf of
Thailand

*Mouths of
the Mekong*

SPRATLY ISLANDS
(disputed by China, Malaysia,
Philippines, Taiwan and Vietnam)

Isthmus of Kra

*Nicobar Islands
(to India)*

Bandaaceh

Sigli

George
Town

Kota Bharu

Balaba

Gunung Kinaba

Kota Kinabalu

410

Sab

Langsa

Meulaboh

Butterworth

*Pulau
Pinang*

Taiping

Ipoh

Kuala Terengganu

Dungun

Cukai

BANDAR SERI
BEGAWAN

BRUNEI

Miri

Strait of Malacca

Kuantan

Medan

Tebingtinggi

Klang

*Kepulauan
Natuna*

Bintulu

Ta

Pematangsiantar

KUALA LUMPUR

MALAYSIA

Pulau Simeulue

*Danau
Toba*

Seremban

Melaka

Sibolga

*Kepulauan
Banyak*

Muar

Keluang

Batu Pahat

Johor Bahru

Selat Serasan

Sibu

Batang Raja

Kuching

Sarawak

Sungai Kayan

Equator

Pulau Nias

SINGAPORE

Sri Aman

Pekanbaru

Singkawang

Solok

Rengat

Padang

Pulau Siberut

*Kepulauan
Lingga*

Singkawang

Sidas

Pontianak

Sungai Kapuas

Batang Hari

Kualatungkal

Jambi

Bangka

Selat Karimata

Kuching

*Pegunungan
Muller*

Borneo

Samarinda

Balikpapan

*Kepulauan
Mentawai*

Sungaipenuh

Pangkalpinang

Kalimantan

Sungai Barito

Sungai Mahaka

Palembang

Lahat

I

N

D

Sampit

Amuntai

Kandang

Bengkulu

Kotabumi

*Pulau
Belitung*

Banjarmasin

*Pulau
Laut*

Sumatera
(Sumatra)

Bandarlampung

Cirebon

Tegal

Java Sea

Mak

Serang

JAKARTA

Pekalongan

Selat Sunda

Bogor

Sukabumi

Semarang

Kudus

*Pulau
Madura*

Surabaya

Probolinggo

N

Bandung

Tasikmalaya

Jumber Matar

Jawa
(Java)

Cilacap

Magelang

Yogyakarta

Surakarta

Kediri

Madiun

Malang

Denpas

Bali

*Pulau
Lombok*

INDIAN

OCEAN

0 km   400
0 miles   400

POPULATION   ● National capital

○ Less than 50,000   ○ 50,000 -100,000   ◉ 100,000 - 500,000   ■ Over 500,000

ELEVATION

				Below sea level	0	100m	250m	500m	1000m	2000m	4000m
-4000m	-3000m	-2000m	-1000m	-500m							
-13 124ft	-9843ft	-6562ft	-3281ft	-1640ft	-820ft/-250m	0	328ft	820ft	1640ft	3281ft	6562ft	13 124ft

THE INDIAN OCEAN

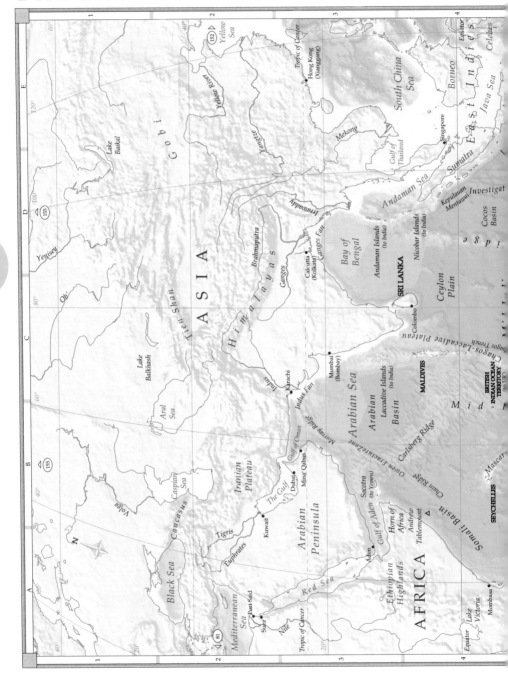

60°

20°

E

40°

1

2

Yellow
Sea

152

Yellow River

Tropic of Cancer

Hong Kong
(Xiangang)

3

South China
Sea

Equator

Celebes

Borneo

Java Sea

East Indies

Sumatra

Singapore

Gulf of
Thailand

Mekong

Andaman Sea

Kepulauan
Mentawai

Investigat

Cocos
Basin

100

155

D

Gobi

Yangtze

Irrawaddy

Andaman Islands
(to India)

Nicobar Islands
(to India)

idg e

Yenisey

Brahmaputra

Ganges Fan

Bay of
Bengal

Calcutta
(Kolkata)

Ganges

SRI LANKA

Ceylon
Plain

Ob

80°

A S I A

H i m a l a y a s

Colombo

C

Tien Shan

Chagos-Laccadive Plateau

Sunda Trench

Lake
Balkhash

Mumbai
(Bombay)

Arabian Sea

Laccadive Islands
(to India)

MALDIVES

Mid

Karachi

Indus Fan

Arabian
Basin

60°

Aral
Sea

Indus

Murray Ridg e

Carlsberg Ridge

Mascar

155

B

Iranian
Plateau

Gulf of Oman

Owen Fracture Zone

Chain Ridge

SEYCHELLES

Caspian
Sea

The Gulf

Dubai

Mina' Qabus

Socotra
(to Yemen)

Somali Basin

40°

Volga

Arabian
Peninsula

Gulf of Aden

Horn of
Africa

Andrew
Tablemount

Tigris

Kuwait

Aden

Caucasus

Euphrates

Ethiopian
Highlands

A

Black Sea

Red Sea

A F R I C A

Mombasa

Mediterranean
Sea

Port Said

Nile

Equator

Lake
Victoria

81

Suez

Tropic of Cancer

20°

1

2

3

4

60°

20°

40°

0 km   1500

● Major port

0 miles   1500

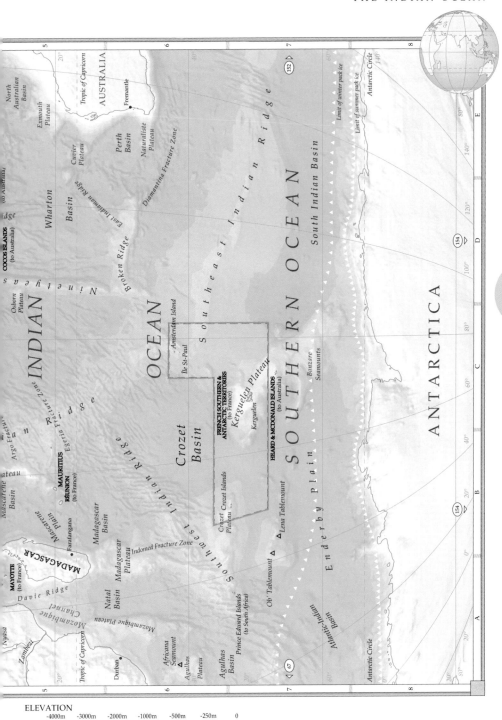

ELEVATION

| -4000m | -3000m | -2000m | -1000m | -500m | -250m | 0 |

| -13 124ft | -9843ft | -6562ft | -3281ft | -1640ft | -820ft | 0 |

AUSTRALASIA & OCEANIA

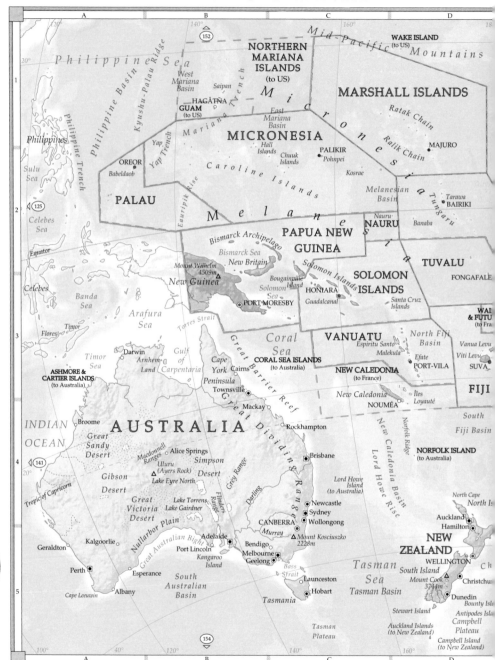

Philippine Sea
Philippine Basin Ridge
West Mariana Basin
Saipan
NORTHERN MARIANA ISLANDS (to US)
HAGÅTÑA
GUAM (to US)
East Mariana Basin
Mid-Pacific Mountains
WAKE ISLAND (to US)
MARSHALL ISLANDS
Ratak Chain
Ralik Chain
MAJURO
Philippines
Kyushu-Palau Ridge
Mariana Trench
Yap
Yap Trench
MICRONESIA
Hall Islands
Chuuk Islands
PALIKIR
Pohnpei
Philippine Trench
OREOR
Babeldaob
Caroline Islands
Kosrae
Melanesian Basin
Tarawa
BAIRIKI
Sulu Sea
Eauripik Rise
PALAU
Celebes Sea
Melanesia
Nauru
NAURU
Banaba
Tungaru
Equator
Bismarck Archipelago
PAPUA NEW GUINEA
TUVALU
FONGAFALE
Celebes
Bismarck Sea
New Britain
Mount Wilhelm 4509m
New Guinea
Bougainville Island
Solomon Islands
SOLOMON ISLANDS
WAI & FUTU (to Fra)
Flores
Banda Sea
Arafura Sea
Solomon Sea
HONIARA
Guadalcanal
Santa Cruz Islands
North Fiji Basin
Vanua Levu
Timor
Timor Sea
Torres Strait
PORT MORESBY
VANUATU
Espiritu Santo
Malakula
Efate
PORT-VILA
Viti Levu
SUVA
FIJI
Darwin
Arnhem Land
Gulf of Carpentaria
Cape York Peninsula
Cairns
CORAL SEA ISLANDS (to Australia)
Coral Sea
NEW CALEDONIA (to France)
New Caledonia
NOUMÉA
Îles Loyauté
ASHMORE & CARTIER ISLANDS (to Australia)
Townsville
Great Barrier Reef
South Fiji Basin
INDIAN OCEAN
Broome
Great Sandy Desert
AUSTRALIA
Macdonnell Ranges
Alice Springs
Uluru (Ayers Rock)
Lake Eyre North
Simpson Desert
Grey Range
Mackay
Rockhampton
Great Dividing Range
Brisbane
New Caledonia Basin
Norfolk Ridge
NORFOLK ISLAND (to Australia)
South Fiji Basin
Tropic of Capricorn
Gibson Desert
Great Victoria Desert
Lake Torrens
Lake Gairdner
Flinders Range
Darling
Lord Howe Island (to Australia)
Lord Howe Rise
North Cape
North Island
Auckland
Hamilton
Geraldton
Kalgoorlie
Nullarbor Plain
Great Australian Bight
Adelaide
Port Lincoln
Kangaroo Island
Bendigo
Melbourne
Geelong
Murray
Newcastle
Sydney
Wollongong
CANBERRA
Mount Kosciuszko 2228m
NEW ZEALAND
WELLINGTON
Perth
Esperance
Albany
Cape Leeuwin
South Australian Basin
Launceston
Hobart
Bass Strait
Tasman Sea
South Island
Mount Cook 3744m
Christchurch
Dunedin
Bounty Isla
Tasmania
Tasman Basin
Stewart Island
Antipodes Islands
Campbell Plateau
Tasman Plateau
Auckland Islands (to New Zealand)
Campbell Island (to New Zealand)

0 km 1000
0 miles 1000

POPULATION   ● National capital

○ Less than 50,000   ○ 50,000 -100,000   ◉ 100,000 - 500,000   ◼ Over 500,000

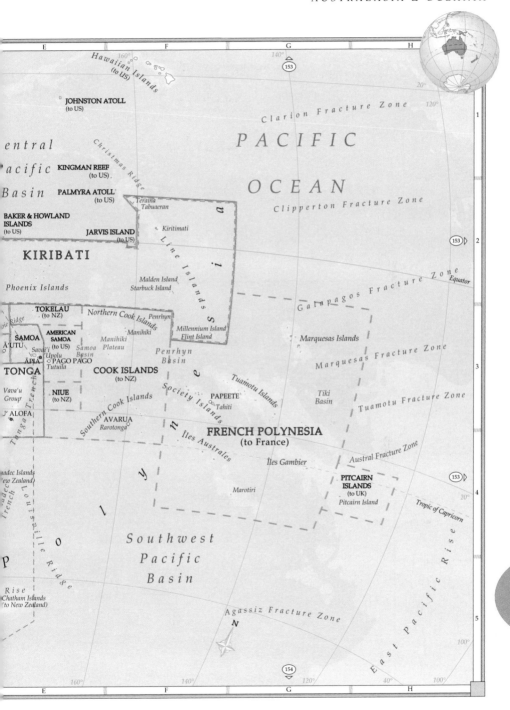

E   F   G   H

Hawaiian Islands
(to US)

153

JOHNSTON ATOLL
(to US)

Clarion Fracture Zone

PACIFIC

entral

Pacific

Basin

Christmas Ridge

KINGMAN REEF
(to US)

PALMYRA ATOLL
(to US)

OCEAN

Clipperton Fracture Zone

Teraina
Tabuaeran

BAKER & HOWLAND
ISLANDS
(to US)

JARVIS ISLAND
(to US)

Kiritimati

Line Islands

KIRIBATI

153

Phoenix Islands

Malden Island
Starbuck Island

Galapagos Fracture Zone

Equator

Shoe Ridge

TOKELAU
(to NZ)

Northern Cook Islands

Penrhyn

Manihiki

Marquesas Islands

Ā'UTU

SAMOA

AMERICAN
SAMOA
(to US)

Manihiki
Plateau

Samoa
Basin

Penrhyn
Basin

Marquesas Fracture Zone

Savai'i

Upolu

ĀPIA

PAGO PAGO

Tutuila

TONGA

COOK ISLANDS
(to NZ)

Tuamotu Islands

Tiki
Basin

Tuamotu Fracture Zone

Vava'u
Group

NIUE
(to NZ)

Society Islands

PAPEETE
Tahiti

J' ALOFA

Southern Cook Islands

AVARUA
Rarotonga

Îles Australes

FRENCH POLYNESIA
(to France)

Austral Fracture Zone

Tanga Trench

Îles Gambier

PITCAIRN
ISLANDS
(to UK)
Pitcairn Island

153

Tropic of Capricorn

adec Islands
ew Zealand)

Marotiri

Louisville Ridge

Southwest
Pacific
Basin

Trench

Rise

Chatham Islands
(to New Zealand)

Agassiz Fracture Zone

N

East Pacific Rise

154

THE SOUTHWEST PACIFIC

NORTHERN MARIANA ISLANDS (to US)

Tinian • Saipan
Rota

GUAM (to US)
HAGÁTÑA

MARSHALL ISLANDS

Enewetak Atoll
Bikini Atoll
Rongelap Atoll
Ailuk Atoll
Ujelang Atoll
Wotje Atoll
Kwajalein Atoll
Maloelap
Namu Atoll
Majuro Atoll
Ailinglaplap Atoll
Jaluit Atoll
Mili Atoll

MICRONESIA

Yap

Babeldaob
OREOR

PALAU

Chuuk Islands

PALIKIR
Pohnpei

Caroline Islands

Kosrae

Ebon Atoll

Makin

Taraw
BAIRIKI

Abemar
Nonou

NAURU
Banaba

Equator

Admiralty Islands
St.Matthias Group

Bismarck Archipelago

New Guinea
Bismarck Sea
New Ireland

INDONESIA

Madang
Central Range
Mount Wilhelm 4509m
Lae
New Britain

Bougainville Island

Choiseul
Santa Isabel

SOLOMON

New Georgia Islands
Malaita
HONIARA

ISLANDS

Arafura Sea

Owen Stanley Range
Gulf of Papua

PORT MORESBY

Solomon Sea

Guadalcanal

San Cristobal
Rennell

Santa Cruz Islands

Torres Strait

D'Entrecasteaux Islands

Louisiade Archipelago

Arnhem Land
Groote Eylandt

Gulf of Carpentaria

Coral Sea

Banks Islands

VANUATU

Espíritu Santo
Maéwo
Pentecost
Malekula
Ambrym
Epi
Efate
PORT-VILA

Cape York Peninsula

CORAL SEA ISLANDS (to Australia)

NEW CALEDONIA (to France)

Erromango
Tanna
Aneityum

Barkly Tableland

Tropic of Capricorn

NORTHERN

TERRITORY

Macdonnell Ranges

QUEENSLAND

Ouvéa
New Caledonia
Lifou
Maré
Îles Loyauté

NOUMÉA

A U S T R A L I A

New Guinea

Bismarck Sea

PAPUA NEW GUINEA

Melanesia

0 km   750
0 miles   750

POPULATION   ● National capital
○ Less than 50,000   ○ 50,000 -100,000   ◉ 100,000 - 500,000   ◼ Over 500,000

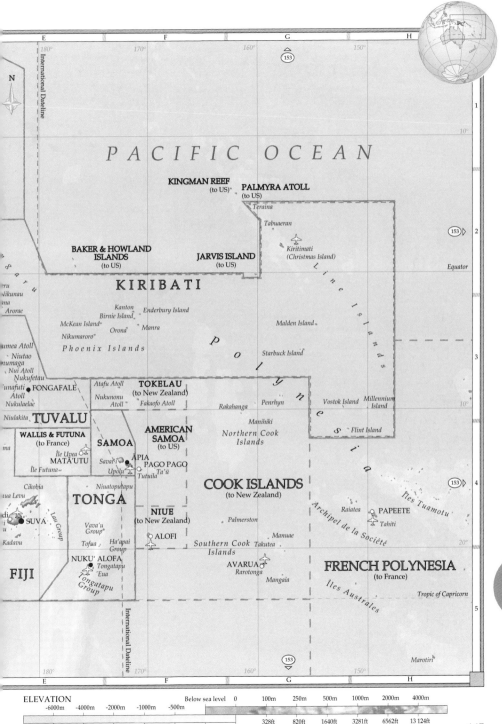

PACIFIC OCEAN

KINGMAN REEF
(to US)
PALMYRA ATOLL
(to US)

Teraina

Tabuaeran

BAKER & HOWLAND
ISLANDS
(to US)

JARVIS ISLAND
(to US)

Kiritimati
(Christmas Island)

Equator

KIRIBATI

eru
Nikunau
ana
Arorae

Kanton
Birnie Island
McKean Island
Nikumaroro
Orona
Enderbury Island
Manra

Malden Island

Line Islands

mea Atoll
Niutao
umaga
Nui Atoll
Nukufetau

P h o e n i x   I s l a n d s

Starbuck Island

P o l y n e s i a

unafuti
Atoll
Nukulaelae
FONGAFALE

Atafu Atoll
Nukunonu
Atoll
Fakaofo Atoll

TOKELAU
(to New Zealand)

Rakahanga
Penrhyn

Vostok Island
Millennium
Island

Niulakita
TUVALU

WALLIS & FUTUNA
(to France)
Île Uvea
MATA'UTU
Île Futuna

AMERICAN
SAMOA
(to US)

SAMOA
Savai'i
ĀPIA
Upolu
PAGO PAGO
Ta'ū
Tutuila

Manihiki

Northern Cook
Islands

Flint Island

ma

Cikobia
ua Levu

Niuatoputapu

TONGA

COOK ISLANDS
(to New Zealand)

Raiatea
PAPEETE
Tahiti

Archipel de la Société

Îles Tuamotu

di
SUVA

Lau Group

Vava'u
Group
Tofua
Ha'apai
Group

NIUE
(to New Zealand)
ALOFI

Palmerston

Manuae
Takutea

FRENCH POLYNESIA
(to France)

FIJI

Kadavu

NUKU'ALOFA
Tongatapu
'Eua
Tongatapu
Group

Southern Cook
Islands

AVARUA
Rarotonga
Mangaia

Îles Australes

Tropic of Capricorn

Marotiri

ELEVATION

| -6000m | -4000m | -2000m | -1000m | -500m | Below sea level | 0 | 100m | 250m | 500m | 1000m | 2000m | 4000m |

| -19 686ft | -13 124ft | -6562ft | -3281ft | -1640ft | -820ft/-250m | 0 | | 328ft | 820ft | 1640ft | 3281ft | 6562ft | 13 124ft |

145

WESTERN AUSTRALIA

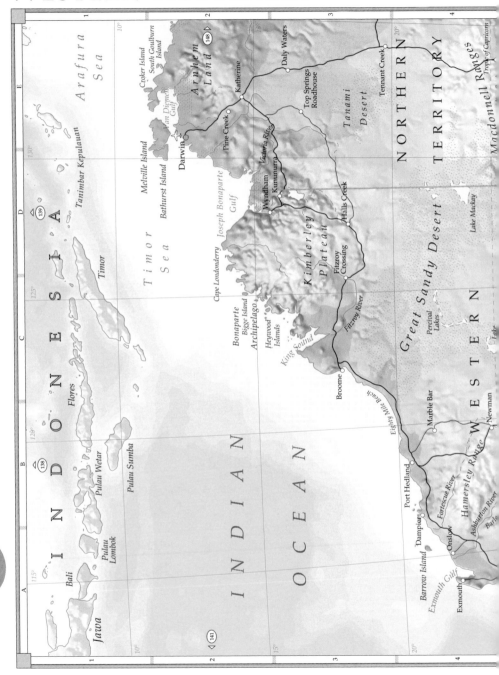

Arafura Sea

INDONESIA

Timor Sea

INDIAN

OCEAN

Java
Bali
Pulau Lombok
Pulau Sumba
Pulau Wetar
Flores
Timor
Tanimbar Kepulauan

Croker Island
South Goulburn Island
Melville Island
Bathurst Island
Van Diemen Gulf
Arnhem Land
Darwin
Pine Creek
Katherine
Daly Waters
Top Springs Roadhouse
Tennant Creek

NORTHERN TERRITORY

Macdonnell Ranges
Tropic of Capricorn

Tanami Desert

Joseph Bonaparte Gulf
Cape Londonderry
Wyndham
Kununurra
Victoria River
Halls Creek

Bonaparte Archipelago
Bigge Island
Heywood Islands
King Sound
Kimberley Plateau
Fitzroy Crossing
Fitzroy River

Great Sandy Desert
Percival Lakes
Lake Mackay

Broome
Eighty Mile Beach
Marble Bar
Newman

WESTERN

Port Hedland
Dampier
Onslow
Barrow Island
Exmouth Gulf
Exmouth
Fortescue River
Ashburton River
Hamersley Range

0 km 400
0 miles 400

POPULATION ● National capital ◉ Internal administrative capital
○ Less than 50,000 ○ 50,000 -100,000 ◉ 100,000 - 500,000 ▣ Over 500,000

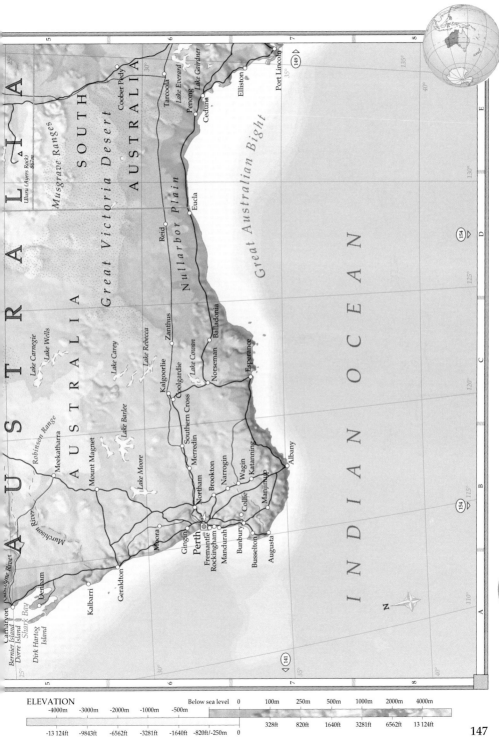

AUSTRALIA

SOUTH

AUSTRALIA

Musgrave Ranges

△ Uluru (Ayers Rock) 867m

Great Victoria Desert

Coober Pedy

Tarcoola

Penong

Lake Everard

Lake Gairdner

Ceduna

Elliston

Port Lincoln

Great Australian Bight

Nullarbor Plain

Eucla

Reid

Zanthus

INDIAN OCEAN

Lake Wells

Lake Carnegie

Lake Carey

Lake Rebecca

Kalgoorlie

Coolgardie

Lake Cowan

Balladonia

Norseman

Esperance

Robinson Range

Meekatharra

Lake Barlee

Southern Cross

Merredin

Mount Magnet

Lake Moore

Albany

Northam

Brookton

Narrogin

Wagin

Katanning

Manjimup

Murchison River

Moora

Gingin

Perth

Fremantle

Rockingham

Mandurah

Bunbury

Collie

Busselton

Augusta

Gascoyne River

Carnarvon

Bernier Island

Dorre Island

Shark Bay

Dirk Hartog Island

Denham

Kalbarri

Geraldton

N

ELEVATION

					Below sea level	0	100m	250m	500m	1000m	2000m	4000m
-4000m	-3000m	-2000m	-1000m	-500m								
-13 124ft	-9843ft	-6562ft	-3281ft	-1640ft	-820ft/-250m	0	328ft	820ft	1640ft	3281ft	6562ft	13 124ft

EASTERN AUSTRALIA

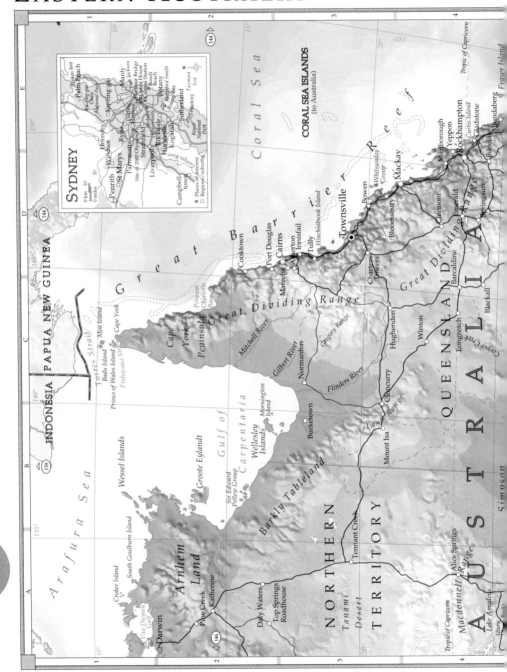

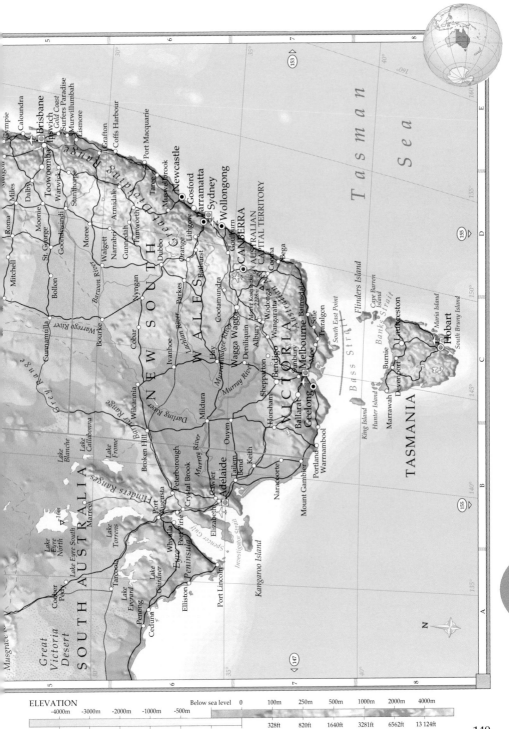

Tasman Sea

Bass Strait

TASMANIA

NEW SOUTH WALES

VICTORIA

SOUTH AUSTRALIA

AUSTRALIAN CAPITAL TERRITORY

Great Victoria Desert

Flinders Island

King Island

Kangaroo Island

Brisbane
Ipswich
Toowoomba
Warwick
Stanthorpe
Gympie
Caloundra
Gold Coast
Surfers Paradise
Murwillumbah
Lismore
Grafton
Coffs Harbour
Port Macquarie
Taree
Newcastle
Gosford
Parramatta
Sydney
Wollongong
Lithgow
Orange
Bathurst
Goulburn
CANBERRA
Cooma
Bega

Roma
Miles
Dalby
Moonie
Goondiwindi
Mitchell
St. George
Bollon
Cunnamulla
Bourke
Walgett
Narrabri
Gunnedah
Moree
Armidale
Tamworth
Muswellbrook
Dubbo
Nyngan
Cobar
Ivanhoe
Parkes
Cootamundra
Wagga Wagga
Deniliquin
Albury
Wangaratta
Wodonga
Shepparton
Bendigo
Ballarat
Geelong
MELBOURNE
Sale
Bairnsdale
Traralgon
Moe
Horsham
Ouyen
Mildura
Balranald
Hay
Corowa

Great Dividing Range
Flinders Ranges
Barrier Range
Grey Range

Murray River
Darling River
Lachlan River
Murrumbidgee River
Warrego River
Barwon River

Mount Kosciuszko
2228m

South East Point

Cape Barren Island
Hunter Island
Burnie
Marrawah
Devonport
Launceston
Maria Island
Hobart
South Bruny Island

Lake Eyre North
Lake Eyre South
Lake Torrens
Lake Gairdner
Lake Everard
Lake Frome
Lake Blanche
Lake Callabonna

Adelaide
Elizabeth
Gawler
Murray Bridge
Tailem Bend
Keith
Naracoorte
Mount Gambier
Portland
Warrnambool
Peterborough
Crystal Brook
Port Pirie
Port Augusta
Whyalla
Cowell
Elliston
Port Lincoln
Ceduna
Penong
Tarcoola
Coober Pedy
Marree

Spencer Gulf
Investigator Strait
Eyre Peninsula

N

ELEVATION

Below sea level	0	100m	250m	500m	1000m	2000m	4000m
-4000m	-3000m	-2000m	-1000m	-500m			

		328ft	820ft	1640ft	3281ft	6562ft	13 124ft
-13 124ft	-9843ft	-6562ft	-3281ft	-1640ft	-820ft/-250m	0	

149

NEW ZEALAND

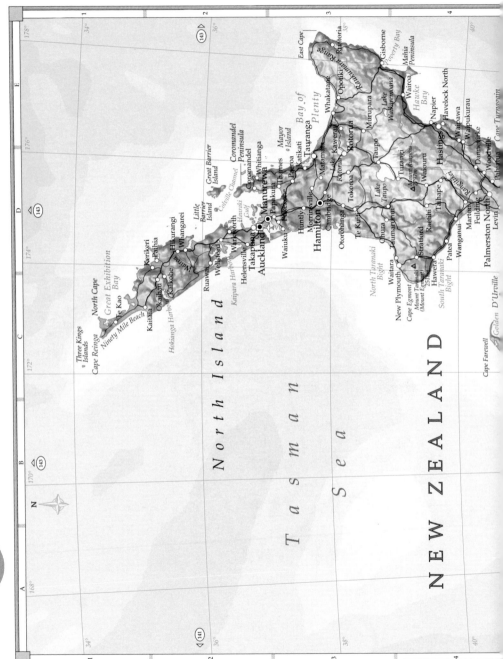

Three Kings Islands

Cape Reinga
Te Kao
North Cape
Great Exhibition Bay

Ninety Mile Beach
Kaitaia
Hokianga Harbour
Okaihau
Kaikohe
Kerikeri
Paihia
Hikurangi
Whangarei
Waitematā
Ruawai
Wellsford
Warkworth
Helensville
Takapuna
Auckland
Papakura
Manurewa
Waiuku
Morrinsville
Huntly
Hamilton
Cambridge
Te Kuiti
Otorohanga
Tokoroa
Te Awamutu

Little Barrier Island
Great Barrier Island
Colville Channel
Coromandel
Coromandel Peninsula
Hauraki Gulf
Whitianga
Thames
Mayor Island
Katikati
Tauranga
Matamata
Rotorua
Lake Rotorua
Kawerau
Bay of Plenty
Whakatane
Opotiki
East Cape
Ruatoria
Raukumara Range
Gisborne
Poverty Bay
Mahia Peninsula
Wairoa
Hawke Bay
Napier
Havelock North
Hastings
Waipawa
Waipukurau
Dannevirke
Woodville
Cape Turnagain

Turangi
Lake Taupo
Taupo
Mount Ruapehu 2797m
Waiouru
Taihape
Raetihi
Ohakune
Taumarunui
Wanganui
Marton
Feilding
Martinborough
Palmerston North
Levin

North Taranaki Bight
New Plymouth
Cape Egmont
Mount Taranaki (Mount Egmont) 2517m
Stratford
Hawera
Patea
Waitara
Waverley
South Taranaki Bight

North Island

T a s m a n   S e a

Cape Farewell
Golden Bay
Cape D'Urville

NEW ZEALAND

N

0 km — 100
0 miles — 100

POPULATION ● National capital
○ Less than 50,000   ○ 50,000 -100,000   ◉ 100,000 - 500,000   ■ Over 500,000

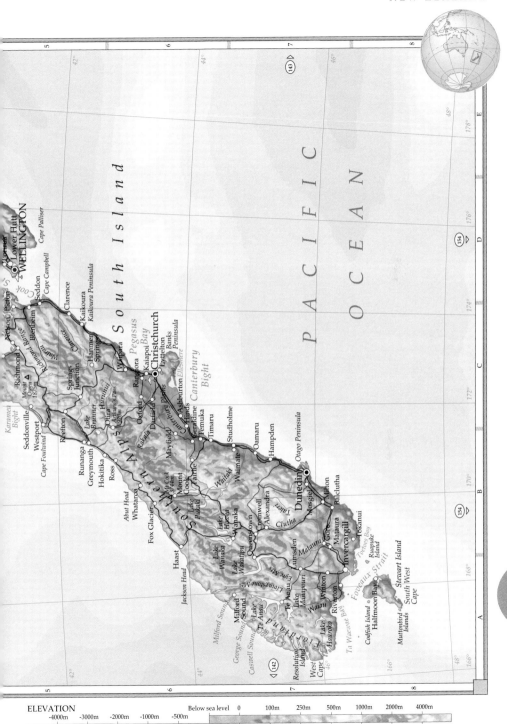

South Island

PACIFIC OCEAN

WELLINGTON
Lower Hutt
Cape Palliser
Cape Campbell
Seddon
Blenheim
Picton
Richmond
Mount Owen 1875m
Clarence
Kaikoura
Kaikoura Peninsula
Springs Junction
Hanmer Springs
Waipara
Pegasus
Kaiapoi Bay
Christchurch
Lyttelton
Banks Peninsula
Rangiora
Reefton
Lake Brunner
Otira
Arthur's Pass 920m
Oxford
Darfield
Ashburton
Methven
Canterbury Bight
Greymouth
Hokitika
Ross
Geraldine
Temuka
Timaru
Waimate
Studholme
Oamaru
Hampden
Otago Peninsula
Mount Cook 3754m
Lake Pukaki
Fairlie
Fox Glacier
Lake Tekapo
Dunedin
Milton
Mosgiel
Balclutha
Haast
Lake Hawea
Lake Wanaka
Cromwell
Alexandra
Lumsden
Mataura
Gore
Clinton
Tokanui
Jackson Head
Lake Wakatipu
Queenstown
Eyre Mts
Mataura
Invercargill
Toetoes Bay
Ruapuke Island
Stewart Island
South West Cape
Milford Sound
Te Anau
Lake Te Anau
Lake Manapouri
Winton
Riverton
Foveaux Strait
Codfish Island
Halfmoon Bay
Mutton bird Islands
Resolution Island
West Cape
Lake Hauroko
Te Waewae Bay

Karamea Bight
Seddonville
Westport
Cape Foulwind
Runanga
Abut Head
Whataroa

ELEVATION

				Below sea level	0	100m	250m	500m	1000m	2000m	4000m
-4000m	-3000m	-2000m	-1000m	-500m							
-13 124ft	-9843ft	-6562ft	-3281ft	-1640ft	-820ft/-250m	0	328ft	820ft	1640ft	3281ft	6562ft	13 124ft

THE PACIFIC OCEAN

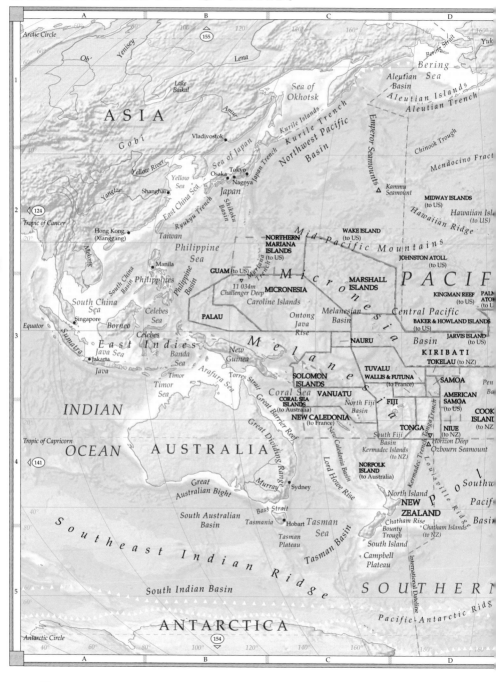

0 km   2000

0 miles   2000

● Major port

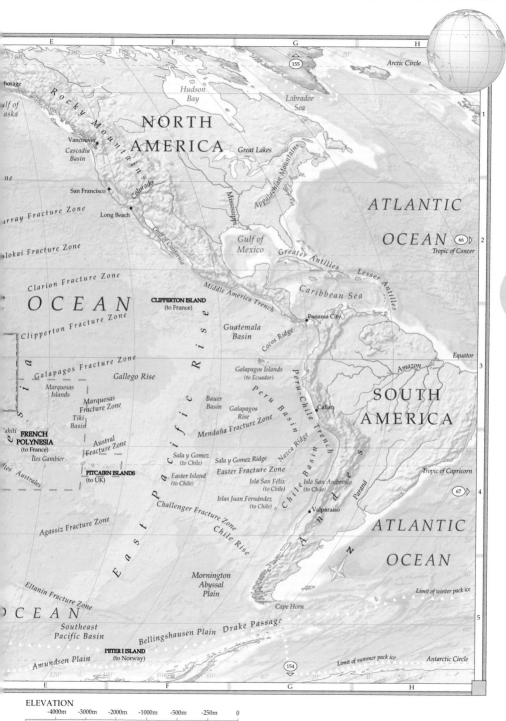

E F G H

Arctic Circle

horage

Gulf of aska

Rocky Mountains

Hudson Bay

Labrador Sea

155

1

Vancouver
Cascadia Basin

NORTH AMERICA

Great Lakes

ne

San Francisco

Colorado

Appalachian Mountains

ATLANTIC

Long Beach

rray Fracture Zone

Gulf of California

Mississippi

OCEAN 66

2

Tropic of Cancer

okai Fracture Zone

Gulf of Mexico

Greater Antilles

Lesser Antilles

Clarion Fracture Zone

O C E A N

CLIPPERTON ISLAND
(to France)

Middle America Trench

Caribbean Sea

Clipperton Fracture Zone

Guatemala Basin

Cocos Ridge

Panama City

Galapagos Fracture Zone

Gallego Rise

*Galapagos Islands
(to Ecuador)*

East Pacific Rise

Equator

Amazon

3

ia

Marquesas Islands

Marquesas Fracture Zone

Bauer Basin

Galapagos Rise

Peru Basin

SOUTH

Callao

AMERICA

Tiki Basin

Mendaña Fracture Zone

Peru–Chile Trench

Tahiti FRENCH POLYNESIA
(to France)

Austral Fracture Zone

Íles Gambier

*Sala y Gomez
(to Chile)*

Sala y Gomez Ridge

Nazca Ridge

es Australes

PITCAIRN ISLANDS
(to UK)

*Easter Island
(to Chile)*

Easter Fracture Zone

Tropic of Capricorn

*Isla San Félix
(to Chile)*

Chile Basin

*Isla San Ambrosio
(to Chile)*

Paraná

67

4

*Islas Juan Fernández
(to Chile)*

Challenger Fracture Zone

Valparaíso

Andes

Agassiz Fracture Zone

Chile Rise

ATLANTIC

Eltanin Fracture Zone

Mornington Abyssal Plain

OCEAN

OCEAN

Southeast Pacific Basin

Bellingshausen Plain *Drake Passage*

Cape Horn

Limit of winter pack ice

5

PETER I ISLAND
(to Norway)

154

Limit of summer pack ice

Antarctic Circle

Amundsen Plain

E F G H

ELEVATION

| -4000m | -3000m | -2000m | -1000m | -500m | -250m | 0 |

| -13 124ft | -9843ft | -6562ft | -3281ft | -1640ft | -820ft | 0 |

153

ANTARCTICA

A   B   C   D

30°   20°   10°   55°   0°   10°   20°

67

Limit of winter pack ice

ATLANTIC

OCEAN

South Sandwich Trench

America-Antarctica Ridge

60°

SOUTHERN

SOUTH GEORGIA
(to UK)

SOUTH SANDWICH
ISLANDS
(to UK)

OCEAN

Atlantic-Indian Basin

*Scotia
Sea*

Lazarev Sea

Antarctic Circle

65

40°

Enderby Plain

1

Orcadas
(Argentina)

Weddell Plain

Sanae
(South Africa)

Novolazarevskaya
(Russian Federation)

South Orkney
Islands

Signy
(UK)

Georg von Neumayer
(Germany)

*Lützow
Holmbukta*

Molodezhnaya
(Russian Federation)

South Shetland
Islands

Limit of summer pack ice

70°

*Dronning Maud
Land*

Syowa
(Japan)

*Enderby
Land*

Esperanza
(Argentina)

Halley
(UK)

75°

80°

Mawson
(Australia)

Capitán Arturo Prat
(Chile)

*Weddell
Sea*

Belgrano II
(Argentina)

Coats
Land

Cape Darnley

Palmer
(US)

Antarctic Peninsula

Berkner
Island

*Mackenzie
Bay*

Prydz Bay

2

Rothera
(UK)

San Martin
(Argentina)

Palmer Land

Ronne
Ice Shelf

85°

Princess
Elizabeth
Land

Davis
(Australia)

Alexander
Island

ANTARCTICA

*Davis
Sea*

80°

Bellingshausen

Vinson Massif
4897m △

Sea

Amundsen-Scott
(US)

Greater

Mirny
(Russian Federation)

PETER I ISLAND
(to Norway)

*Ellsworth
Land*

South
Pole

*Shackleton
Ice Shelf*

90°

Lesser

South
Geomagnetic
Pole

Vostok
(Russian Federation)

Antarctica

3

Antarctica

Marie Byrd Land

Mount Kirkpatrick
4528m △

*Wilkes
Land*

Casey
(Australia)

*Amundsen
Sea*

Mount Sidley
4181m △

Mount Markham
4351m △

*Ross Ice
Shelf*

Cape
Poinsett

100°

Mount Siple
3100m △

*Roosevelt
Island*

Scott Base
(N.Z.)

McMurdo Base
(US)

Mount Erebus
3794m △

Victoria Land

*Terre
Adélie*

153

110°

*Amundsen
Plain*

*Ross
Sea*

George V
Land

*South
Indian*

4

SOUTHERN

Cape Adare

Dumont d'Urville
(France)

120°

Leningradskaya
(Russian Federation)

Basin

OCEAN

Scott Island

Balleny Islands

*Macquarie
Ridge*

Pacific-Antarctic Ridge

Limit of winter pack ice

Udintsev Fracture Zone

152

Eltanin Fracture Zone

5

○ Antarctic research station

150°   160°   170°   180°   170°   160°   150°

A   B   C   D

0 km   500

0 miles   500

ELEVATION

Below sea level   0   100m   250m   500m   1000m 2000m 4000m

-4000m -3000m -2000m -1000m   -500m

328ft   820ft   1640ft 3281ft 6562ft 13 124ft

-13 124ft -9843ft -6562ft -3281ft -1640ft -820ft/-250m

ARCTIC OCEAN

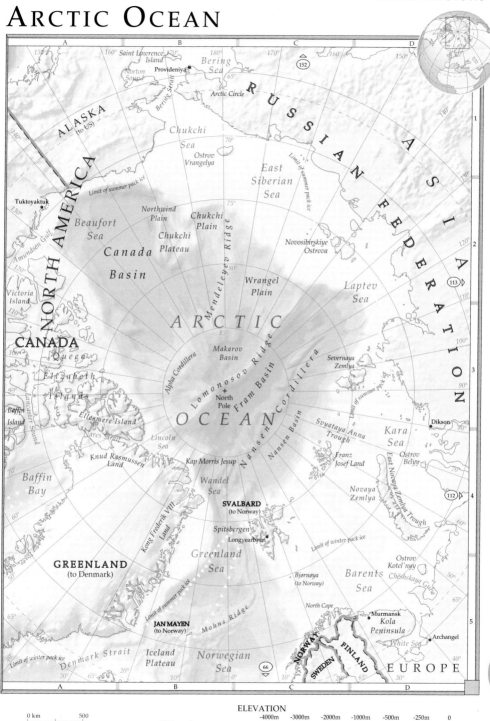

A · B · C · D

Saint Lawrence Island
Norton Sound
Provideniya
Bering Strait
Bering Sea
152
Arctic Circle

ALASKA (to US)

R U S S I A N   F E D E R A T I O N

Chukchi Sea
Ostrov Vrangelya
East Siberian Sea
Limit of summer pack ice

Tuktoyaktuk

Limit of summer pack ice

Northwind Plain
Chukchi Plain
Chukchi Plateau

Beaufort Sea

Novosibirskiye Ostrova

NORTH AMERICA

Amundsen Gulf

Canada Basin

Wrangel Plain

Laptev Sea

113

Victoria Island

A R C T I C

CANADA

Alpha Cordillera
Makarov Basin

Severnaya Zemlya

Queen

Mendeleyev Ridge

Lomonosov Ridge
North Pole
Fram Basin

Dikson

Elizabeth Islands

O C E A N

Nansen Cordillera

Nansen Basin

Kara Sea

Baffin Island

Ellesmere Island
Nares Strait
Lincoln Sea

Svyataya Anna Trough

Ostrov Belyy

Lancaster Sound

Knud Rasmussen Land

Kap Morris Jesup

Franz Josef Land

East Novaya Zemlya Trough

Baffin Bay

Wandel Sea

SVALBARD (to Norway)

Novaya Zemlya

112

Kong Frederik VIII Land

Spitsbergen
Longyearbyen

Limit of winter pack ice

Ostrov Kotel'nyy
Chëshskaya Guba

GREENLAND (to Denmark)

Greenland Sea

Bjørnøya (to Norway)

Barents Sea

White Sea

Limit of summer pack ice

North Cape

Murmansk
Kola Peninsula

Archangel

JAN MAYEN (to Norway)

Mohns Ridge

NORWAY
FINLAND

Limit of winter pack ice

Denmark Strait

Iceland Plateau

Norwegian Sea

66

SWEDEN

E U R O P E

0 km   500
0 miles   500

• Major port

ELEVATION
-4000m -3000m -2000m -1000m -500m -250m 0
-13 124ft -9843ft -6562ft -3281ft -1640ft -820ft 0

155

OVERSEAS TERRITORIES & DEPENDENCIES

DESPITE THE RAPID process of global decolonization since the Second World War, around 10 million people in more than 50 territories around the world continue to live under the protection of France, Australia, the Netherlands, Denmark, Norway, New Zealand, the UK, or the USA. These remnants of former colonial empires may have persisted for economic, strategic or political reasons and are administered in a variety of ways.

AUSTRALIA

AUSTRALIA'S OVERSEAS TERRITORIES have not been an issue since Papua New Guinea became independent in 1975. Consequently there is no overriding policy toward them. Norfolk Island is inhabited by descendants of the H.M.S Bounty mutineers and more recent Australian migrants.

ASHMORE & CARTIER ISLANDS
Indian Ocean
STATUS: External territory
CLAIMED: 1978
CAPITAL: Not applicable
POPULATION: None
AREA: 5.2 sq km
(2 sq miles)

CHRISTMAS ISLAND
Indian Ocean
STATUS: External territory
CLAIMED: 1958
CAPITAL: Flying Fish Cove
POPULATION: 1,275
AREA: 134.6 sq km
(52 sq miles)

COCOS ISLANDS
Indian Ocean
STATUS: External territory
CLAIMED: 1955
CAPITAL: No official capital
POPULATION: 670
AREA: 14.24 sq km
(5.5 sq miles)

CORAL SEA ISLANDS
South Pacific
STATUS: External territory
CLAIMED: 1969
CAPITAL: None
POPULATION: 8 (meteorologists)
AREA: Less than 3 sq km
(1.16 sq miles)

HEARD & McDONALD IS.
Indian Ocean
STATUS: External territory
CLAIMED: 1947
CAPITAL: Not applicable
POPULATION: None
AREA: 417 sq km
(161 sq miles)

NORFOLK ISLAND
South Pacific
STATUS: External territory
CLAIMED: 1774
CAPITAL: Kingston
POPULATION: 2,181
AREA: 34.4 sq km
(13.3 sq miles)

DENMARK

THE FAEROE ISLANDS have been under Danish administration since Queen Margreth I of Denmark inherited Norway in 1380. The Home Rule Act of 1948 gave the Faeroese control over all their internal affairs. Greenland first came under Danish rule in 1380. Today, Denmark is responsible for the island's foreign affairs and defense.

FAEROE ISLANDS
North Atlantic
STATUS: External territory
CLAIMED: 1380
CAPITAL: Tórshavn
POPULATION: 43,382
AREA: 1,399 sq km
(540 sq miles)

GREENLAND
North Atlantic
STATUS: External territory
CLAIMED: 1380
CAPITAL: Nuuk
POPULATION: 56,076
AREA: 2,175,516 sq km
(840,000 sq miles)

FRANCE

FRANCE HAS DEVELOPED economic ties with its overseas territories, thereby stressing interdependence over independence. Overseas *départements*, officially part of France, have their own governments. Territorial *collectivités* and overseas *territoires* have varying degrees of autonomy.

CLIPPERTON ISLAND
East Pacific
STATUS: Dependency of French Polynesia
CLAIMED: 1930
CAPITAL: Not applicable
POPULATION: None
AREA: 7 sq km
(2.7 sq miles)

FRENCH GUIANA
South America
STATUS: Overseas department
CLAIMED: 1817
CAPITAL: Cayenne
POPULATION: 152,300
AREA: 90,996 sq km
(35,135 sq miles)

FRENCH POLYNESIA
South Pacific
STATUS: Overseas territory
CLAIMED: 1843
CAPITAL: Papeete
POPULATION: 219,521
AREA: 4,165 sq km
(1,608 sq miles)

GUADELOUPE
West Indies
STATUS: Overseas department
CLAIMED: 1635
CAPITAL: Basse-Terre
POPULATION: 419,500
AREA: 1,780 sq km
(687 sq miles)

MARTINIQUE
West Indies
STATUS: Overseas department
CLAIMED: 1635
CAPITAL: Fort-de-France
POPULATION: 381,200
AREA: 1,100 sq km
(425 sq miles)

MAYOTTE
Indian Ocean
STATUS: Territorial collectivity
CLAIMED: 1843
CAPITAL: Mamoudzou
POPULATION: 131,320
AREA: 374 sq km
(144 sq miles)

NEW CALEDONIA
South Pacific
STATUS: Overseas territory
CLAIMED: 1853
CAPITAL: Nouméa
POPULATION: 196,836
AREA: 19,103 sq km
(7,374 sq miles)

RÉUNION
Indian Ocean
STATUS: Overseas department
CLAIMED: 1638
CAPITAL: Saint-Denis
POPULATION: 632,000
AREA: 2,512 sq km
(970 sq miles)

ST. PIERRE & MIQUELON
North America
STATUS: Territorial collectivity
CLAIMED: 1604
CAPITAL: Saint-Pierre
POPULATION: 6,600
AREA: 242 sq km
(93.4 sq miles)

WALLIS & FUTUNA
South Pacific
STATUS: Overseas territory
CLAIMED: 1842
CAPITAL: Matā'Utu
POPULATION: 15,000
AREA: 274 sq km
(106 sq miles)

NETHERLANDS

THE COUNTRY'S TWO REMAINING overseas territories were formerly part of the Dutch West Indies. Both are now self-governing, but the Netherlands remains responsible for their defense.

ARUBA
West Indies
STATUS: Autonomous part of the Netherlands
CLAIMED: 1643
CAPITAL: Oranjestad
POPULATION: 88,000
AREA: 194 sq km (75 sq miles)

NETHERLANDS ANTILLES
West Indies
STATUS: Autonomous part of the Netherlands
CLAIMED: 1816
CAPITAL: Willemstad
POPULATION: 207,175
AREA: 800 sq km (308 sq miles)

NEW ZEALAND

NEW ZEALAND'S GOVERNMENT has no desire to retain any overseas territories. However, the economic weakness of its dependent territory Tokelau and its freely associated states, Niue and the Cook Islands, has forced New Zealand to remain responsible for their foreign policy and defense.

COOK ISLANDS
South Pacific
STATUS: Associated territory
CLAIMED: 1901
CAPITAL: Avarua
POPULATION: 20,200
AREA: 293 sq km
(113 sq miles)

NIUE
South Pacific
STATUS: Associated territory
CLAIMED: 1901
CAPITAL: Alofi
POPULATION: 2,080
AREA: 264 sq km
(102 sq miles)

TOKELAU
South Pacific
STATUS: Dependent territory
CLAIMED: 1926
CAPITAL: Not applicable
POPULATION: 1,577
AREA: 10.4 sq km (4 sq miles)

NORWAY

IN 1920, 41 nations signed the Spitsbergen Treaty recognizing Norwegian sovereignty over Svalbard. There is a NATO base on Jan Mayen. Bouvet Island is a nature reserve.

BOUVET ISLAND
South Atlantic
STATUS: Dependency
CLAIMED: 1928
CAPITAL: Not applicable
POPULATION: None
AREA: 58 sq km (22 sq miles)

JAN MAYEN
North Atlantic
STATUS: Dependency
CLAIMED: 1929
CAPITAL: Not applicable
POPULATION: None
AREA: 381 sq km (147 sq miles)

PETER I. ISLAND
Southern Ocean
STATUS: Dependency
CLAIMED: 1931
CAPITAL: Not applicable
POPULATION: None
AREA: 180 sq km (69 sq miles)

SVALBARD
Arctic Ocean
STATUS: Dependency
CLAIMED: 1920
CAPITAL: Longyearbyen
POPULATION: 3,231
AREA: 62,906 sq km
(24,289 sq miles)

Continued on p.158

UNITED KINGDOM

THE UK STILL has the largest number of overseas territories. These are locally-governed by a mixture of elected representatives and appointed officials, and they all enjoy a large measure of internal self-government, but certain powers, such as foreign affairs and defense, are reserved for Governors of the British Crown.

ANGUILLA
West Indies
STATUS: Dependent territory
CLAIMED: 1650
CAPITAL: The Valley
POPULATION: 10,300
AREA: 96 sq km
(37 sq miles)

ASCENSION ISLAND
South Atlantic
STATUS: Dependency of St. Helena
CLAIMED: 1673
CAPITAL: Georgetown
POPULATION: 1,099
AREA: 88 sq km
(34 sq miles)

BERMUDA
North Atlantic
STATUS: Crown colony
CLAIMED: 1612
CAPITAL: Hamilton
POPULATION: 60,144
AREA: 53 sq km
(20.5 sq miles)

BRITISH INDIAN OCEAN TERRITORY
STATUS: Dependent territory
CLAIMED: 1814
CAPITAL: Diego Garcia
POPULATION: 930
AREA: 60 sq km
(23 sq miles)

BRITISH VIRGIN ISLANDS
West Indies
STATUS: Dependent territory
CLAIMED: 1672
CAPITAL: Road Town
POPULATION: 17,896
AREA: 153 sq km
(59 sq miles)

CAYMAN ISLANDS
West Indies
STATUS: Dependent territory
CLAIMED: 1670
CAPITAL: George Town
POPULATION: 35,000
AREA: 259 sq km (100 sq miles)

FALKLAND ISLANDS
South Atlantic
STATUS: Dependent territory
CLAIMED: 1832
CAPITAL: Stanley
POPULATION: 2,564
AREA: 12,173 sq km
(4,699 sq miles)

GIBRALTAR
Southwest Europe
STATUS: Crown colony
CLAIMED: 1713
CAPITAL: Gibraltar
POPULATION: 27,086
AREA: 6.5 sq km (2.5 sq miles)

GUERNSEY
Channel Islands
STATUS: Crown dependency
CLAIMED: 1066
CAPITAL: St. Peter Port
POPULATION: 56,681
AREA: 65 sq km (25 sq miles)

ISLE OF MAN
British Isles
STATUS: Crown dependency
CLAIMED: 1765
CAPITAL: Douglas
POPULATION: 71,714
AREA: 572 sq km (221 sq miles)

JERSEY
Channel Islands
STATUS: Crown dependency
CLAIMED: 1066
CAPITAL: St. Helier
POPULATION: 85,150
AREA: 116 sq km (45 sq miles)

MONTSERRAT
West Indies
STATUS: Dependent territory
CLAIMED: 1632
CAPITAL: Plymouth
(currently uninhabitable)
POPULATION: 2,850
AREA: 102 sq km (40 sq miles)

PITCAIRN ISLANDS
South Pacific
STATUS: Dependent territory
CLAIMED: 1887
CAPITAL: Adamstown
POPULATION: 55
AREA: 3.5 sq km (1.35 sq miles)

ST. HELENA
South Atlantic
STATUS: Dependent territory
CLAIMED: 1673
CAPITAL: Jamestown
POPULATION: 6,472
AREA: 122 sq km (47 sq miles)

SOUTH GEORGIA & THE SOUTH SANDWICH ISLANDS
South Atlantic
STATUS: Dependent territory
CLAIMED: 1775
CAPITAL: Not applicable
POPULATION: No permanent residents
AREA: 3,592 sq km (1,387 sq miles)

TRISTAN DA CUNHA
South Atlantic
STATUS: Dependency of St. Helena
CLAIMED: 1612
CAPITAL: Edinburgh
POPULATION: 297
AREA: 98 sq km (38 sq miles)

TURKS & CAICOS ISLANDS
West Indies
STATUS: Dependent territory
CLAIMED: 1766
CAPITAL: Cockburn Town
POPULATION: 13,800
AREA: 430 sq km (166 sq miles)

UNITED STATES OF AMERICA

AMERICA'S OVERSEAS TERRITORIES
have been seen as strategically
useful, if expensive, links with its
"backyards." The US has, in most
cases, given the local population
a say in deciding their own status.
A US Commonwealth territory, such
as Puerto Rico, has a greater level
of independence than that of a US
unincorporated or external territory.

AMERICAN SAMOA
South Pacific
STATUS: Unincorporated
territory
CLAIMED: 1900
CAPITAL: Pago Pago
POPULATION: 60,000
AREA: 195 sq km (75 sq miles)

BAKER & HOWLAND ISLANDS
South Pacific
STATUS: Unincorporated
territory
CLAIMED: 1856
CAPITAL: Not applicable
POPULATION: None
AREA: 1.4 sq km (0.54 sq miles)

GUAM
West Pacific
STATUS: Unincorporated
territory
CLAIMED: 1898
CAPITAL: Hagåtña
POPULATION: 149,249
AREA: 549 sq km (212 sq miles)

JARVIS ISLAND
South Pacific
STATUS: Unincorporated
territory
CLAIMED: 1856
CAPITAL: Not applicable
POPULATION: None
AREA: 4.5 sq km (1.7 sq miles)

JOHNSTON ATOLL
Central Pacific
STATUS: Unincorporated
territory
CLAIMED: 1858
CAPITAL: Not applicable
POPULATION: 327
AREA: 2.8 sq km (1 sq mile)

KINGMAN REEF
Central Pacific
STATUS: Administered territory
CLAIMED: 1856
CAPITAL: Not applicable
POPULATION: None
AREA: 1 sq km
(0.4 sq miles)

MIDWAY ISLANDS
Central Pacific
STATUS: Administered
territory
CLAIMED: 1867
CAPITAL: Not applicable
POPULATION: 453
AREA: 5.2 sq km
(2 sq miles)

NAVASSA ISLAND
West Indies
STATUS: Unincorporated
territory
CLAIMED: 1856
CAPITAL: Not applicable
POPULATION: None
AREA: 5.2 sq km (2 sq miles)

NORTHERN MARIANA ISLANDS
West Pacific
STATUS: Commonwealth
territory
CLAIMED: 1947
CAPITAL: Saipan
POPULATION: 58,846
AREA: 457 sq km (177 sq miles)

PALMYRA ATOLL
Central Pacific
STATUS: Unincorporated
territory
CLAIMED: 1898
CAPITAL: Not applicable
POPULATION: None
AREA: 12 sq km (5 sq miles)

PUERTO RICO
West Indies
STATUS: Commonwealth
territory
CLAIMED: 1898
CAPITAL: San Juan
POPULATION: 3.8 million
AREA: 8,959 sq km
(3,458 sq miles)

VIRGIN ISLANDS
West Indies
STATUS: Unincorporated
territory
CLAIMED: 1917
CAPITAL: Charlotte Amalie
POPULATION: 101,809
AREA: 355 sq km
(137 sq miles)

WAKE ISLAND
Central Pacific
STATUS: Unincorporated
territory
CLAIMED: 1898
CAPITAL: Not applicable
POPULATION: 302
AREA: 6.5 sq km
(2.5 sq miles)

GLOSSARY OF GEOGRAPHICAL TERMS

THE FOLLOWING GLOSSARY lists all geographical terms occuring on the maps and in the main-entry names in the Index–Gazetteer. These terms may precede, follow or be run together with the proper elements of the name; where they precede it the term is reversed for indexing purposes – thus Poluostov Yamal is indexed as Yamal, Poluostrov.

A

Å *Danish, Norwegian*, River
Alpen *German*, Alps
Altiplanicie *Spanish*, Plateau
Älv(en) *Swedish*, River
Anse *French*, Bay
Archipiélago *Spanish*, Archipelago
Arcipelago *Italian*, Archipelago
Arquipélago *Portuguese*, Archipelago
Aukštuma *Lithuanian*, Upland

B

Bahía *Spanish*, Bay
Baía *Portuguese*, Bay
Baḥr *Arabic*, River
Baie *French*, Bay
Bandao *Chinese*, Peninsula
Banjaran *Malay*, Mountain range
Batang *Malay*, Stream
-berg *Afrikaans, Norwegian*, Mountain
Birket *Arabic* , Lake
Boğazı *Turkish*, Strait
Bucht *German*, Bay
Bugten *Danish*, Bay
Buḥayrat *Arabic*, Lake, reservoir
Buḥeiret *Arabic*, Lake
Bukit *Malay*, Mountain
-bukta *Norwegian*, Bay
bukten *Swedish*, Bay
Burnu *Turkish*, Cape, point
Buuraha *Somali*, Mountains

C

Cabo *Portuguese*, Cape
Cap *French*, Cape
Cascada *Portuguese*, Waterfall
Cerro *Spanish*, Mountain
Chaîne *French*, Mountain range
Chau *Cantonese*, Island
Chāy *Turkish*, Stream
Chhâk *Cambodian*, Bay
Chhu *Tibetan*, River
-chôsuji *Korean*, Reservoir

Chott *Arabic*, Salt lake, depression
Ch'ün-tao *Chinese*, Island group
Cambodian, Mountains
Cordillera *Spanish*, Mountain range
Costa *Spanish*, Coast
Côte *French*, Coast
Cuchilla *Spanish*, Mountains

D

Dağı *Azerbaijani, Turkish*, Mountain
Dağları *Azerbaijani, Turkish*, Mountains
-dake *Japanese*, Peak
Danau *Indonesian*, Lake
Đao *Vietnamese*, Island
Daryā *Persian*, River
Daryācheh *Persian*, Lake
Dasht *Persian*, Plain, desert
Dawḥat *Arabic*, Bay
Dere *Turkish*, Stream
Dili *Azerbaijani*, Spit
-do *Korean*, Island
Dooxo *Somali*, Valley
Düzü *Azerbaijani*, Steppe
-dwīp *Bengali*, Island

E

Embalse *Spanish*, Reservoir
Erg *Arabic*, Dunes
Estany *Catalan*, Lake
Estrecho *Spanish*, Strait
-ey *Icelandic*, Island
Ezero *Bulgarian, Macedonian*, Lake

F

Fjord *Danish*, Fjord
-fjorden *Norwegian*, Fjord
-fjordhur *Faeroese*, Fjord
Fleuve *French*, River
Fliegu *Maltese*, Channel
-fljór *Icelandic*, River

G

-gang *Korean*, River
Ganga *Nepali, Sinhala*, River
Gaoyuan *Chinese*, Plateau
-gawa *Japanese*, River
Gebel *Arabic*, Mountain

-gebirge *German*, Mountains
Ghubbat *Arabic*, Bay
Gjiri *Albanian*, Bay
Gol *Mongolian*, River
Golfe *French*, Gulf
Golfo *Italian, Spanish*, Gulf
Gora *Russian, Serbian*, Mountain
Gory *Russian*, Mountains
Guba *Russian*, Bay
Gunung *Malay*, Mountain

H

Ḥadd *Arabic*, Spit
-haehyŏp *Korean*, Strait
Haff *German*, Lagoon
Hai *Chinese*, Sea, bay
Ḥammādat *Arabic*, Plateau
Hāmūn *Persian*, Lake
Hawr *Arabic*, Lake
Hāyk' *Amharic*, Lake
He *Chinese*, River
Helodrano *Malagasy*, Bay
-hegység *Hungarian*, Mountain range
Hka *Burmese*, River
-ho *Korean*, Lake
Hô *Korean*, Reservoir
Holot *Hebrew*, Dunes
Hora *Belorussian*, Mountain
Hrada *Belorussian*, Mountains, ridge
Hsi *Chinese*, River
Hu *Chinese*, Lake

I

Île(s) *French*, Island(s)
Ilha(s) *Portuguese*, Island(s)
Ilhéu(s) *Portuguese*, Islet(s)
Irmak *Turkish*, River
Isla(s) *Spanish*, Island(s)
Isola (Isole) *Italian*, Island(s)

J

Jabal *Arabic*, Mountain
Jāl *Arabic*, Ridge
-järvi *Finnish*, Lake
Jazīrat *Arabic*, Island
Jazīreh *Persian*, Island
Jebel *Arabic*, Mountain

Jezero *Serbian/Croatian*, Lake
Jiang *Chinese*, River
-joki *Finnish*, River
-jökull *Icelandic*, Glacier
Juzur *Arabic*, Islands

K

Kaikyō *Japanese*, Strait
-kaise *Lappish*, Mountain
Kali *Nepali*, River
Kalnas *Lithuanian*, Mountain
Kalns *Latvian*, Mountain
Kang *Chinese*, Harbor
Kangri *Tibetan*, Mountain(s)
Kaôh *Cambodian*, Island
Kapp *Norwegian*, Cape
Kavīr *Persian*, Desert
K'edi *Georgian*, Mountain range
Kediet *Arabic*, Mountain
Kepulauan *Indonesian, Malay*, Island group
Khalîg, Khalīj *Arabic*, Gulf
Khawr *Arabic*, Inlet
Khola *Nepali*, River
Khrebet *Russian*, Mountain range
Ko *Thai*, Island
Kolpos *Greek*, Bay
-kopf *German*, Peak
Körfäzi *Azerbaijani*, Bay
Körfezi *Turkish*, Bay
Kõrgustik *Estonian*, Upland
Koshi *Nepali*, River
Kowtal *Persian*, Pass
Kūh(hā) *Persian*, Mountain(s)
-kundo *Korean*, Island group
-kysten *Norwegian*, Coast
Kyun *Burmese*, Island

L

Laaq *Somali*, Watercourse
Lac *French*, Lake
Lacul *Romanian*, Lake
Lago *Italian, Portuguese, Spanish*, Lake
Laguna *Spanish*, Lagoon, Lake

160

Laht *Estonian*, Bay
Laut *Indonesian*, Sea
Lembalemba *Malagasy*, Plateau
Lerr *Armenian*, Mountain
Lerrnashght'a *Armenian*, Mountain range
Les *Czech*, Forest
Lich *Armenian*, Lake
Liqeni *Albanian*, Lake
Lumi *Albanian*, River
Lyman *Ukrainian*, Estuary

M

Mae Nam *Thai*, River
-mägi *Estonian*, Hill
Maja *Albanian*, Mountain
-man *Korean*, Bay
Marios *Lithuanian*, Lake
-meer *Dutch*, Lake
Melkosopochnik *Russian*, Plain
-meri *Estonian*, Sea
Mifraz *Hebrew*, Bay
Monkhafad *Arabic*, Depression
Mont(s) *French*, Mountain(s)
Monte *Italian*, *Portuguese*, Mountain
More *Russian*, Sea
Mörön *Mongolian*, River

N

Nagor'ye *Russian*, Upland
Nahal *Hebrew*, River
Nahr *Arabic*, River
Nam *Laotian*, River
Nehri *Turkish*, River
Nevado *Spanish*, Mountain (snow-capped)
Nisoi *Greek*, Islands
Nizmennost' *Russian*, Lowland, plain
Nosy *Malagasy*, Island
Nur *Mongolian*, Lake
Nuruu *Mongolian*, Mountains
Nuur *Mongolian*, Lake
Nyzovyna *Ukrainian*, Lowland, plain

O

Ostrov(a) *Russian*, Island(s)
Oued *Arabic*, Watercourse
-oy *Faeroese*, Island
-oy(a) *Norwegian*, Island
Oya *Sinhala*, River
Ozero *Russian*, *Ukrainian*, Lake

P

Passo *Italian*, Pass
Pegunungan *Indonesian*, *Malay*, Mountain range
Pelagos *Greek*, Sea
Penisola *Italian*, Peninsula
Peski *Russian*, Sands
Phanom *Thai*, Mountain
Phou *Laotian*, Mountain
Pic *Catalan*, Peak
Pico *Portuguese*, *Spanish*, Peak
Pik *Russian*, Peak
Planalto *Portuguese*, Plateau
Planina, Planini *Bulgarian*, *Macedonian*, *Serbian, Croatian*, Mountain range
Ploskogor'ye *Russian*, Upland
Poluostrov *Russian*, Peninsula
Potamos *Greek*, River
Proliv *Russian*, Strait
Pulau *Indonesian*, *Malay*, Island
Pulu *Malay*, Island
Punta *Portuguese*, *Spanish*, Point

Q

Qā' *Arabic*, Depression
Qolleh *Persian*, Mountain

R

Raas *Somali*, Cape
-rags *Latvian*, Cape
Ramlat *Arabic*, Sands
Ra's *Arabic*, Cape, point, headland
Ravnina *Bulgarian*, *Russian*, Plain
Récif *French*, Reef
Represa (Rep.) *Spanish*, *Portuguese*, Reservoir
-rettō *Japanese*, Island chain
Riacho *Spanish*, Stream
Riban' *Malagasy*, Mountains
Rio *Portuguese*, River
Río *Spanish*, River
Riu *Catalan*, River
Rivier *Dutch*, River
Rivière *French*, River
Rowd *Pashtu*, River
Rūd *Persian*, River
Rudohorie *Slovak*, Mountains
Ruisseau *French*, Stream

S

Sabkhat *Arabic*, Salt marsh
Şaḥrā' *Arabic*, Desert
Samudra *Sinhala*, Reservoir
-san *Japanese, Korean*, Mountain
-sanchi *Japanese*, Mountains
-sanmaek *Korean*, Mountains
Sarīr *Arabic*, Desert
Sebkha, Sebkhet *Arabic*, Salt marsh, depression
See *German*, Lake
Selat *Indonesian*, Strait
-selkä *Finnish*, Ridge
Selseleh *Persian*, Mountain range
Serra *Portuguese*, Mountain
Serranía *Spanish*, Mountain
Sha'īb *Arabic*, Watercourse
Shamo *Chinese*, Desert
Shan *Chinese*, Mountain(s)
Shan-mo *Chinese*, Mountain range
Shaṭṭ *Arabic*, Distributary
-shima *Japanese*, Island
Shui-tao *Chinese*, Channel
Sierra *Spanish*, Mountains
Sôn *Vietnamese*, Mountain
Sông *Vietnamese*, River
-spitze *German*, Peak
Štít *Slovak*, Peak
Stoeng *Cambodian*, River
Stretto *Italian*, Strait
Su Anbarı *Azerbaijani*, Reservoir
Sungai *Indonesian*, *Malay*, River
Suu *Turkish*, River

T

Tal *Mongolian*, Plain
Tandavan' *Malagasy*, Mountain range
Tangorombohitr' *Malagasy*, Mountain massif
Tao *Chinese*, Island
Tassili *Berber*, Plateau, mountain
Tau *Russian*, Mountain(s)
Taungdan *Burmese*, Mountain range
Teluk *Indonesian*, *Malay*, Bay

Terara *Amharic*, Mountain
Tog *Somali*, Valley
Tônlé *Cambodian*, Lake
Top *Dutch*, Peak
-tunturi *Finnish*, Mountain
Tur'at *Arabic*, Channel

V

Väin *Estonian*, Strait
-vatn *Icelandic*, Lake
-vesi *Finnish*, Lake
Vinh *Vietnamese*, Bay
Vodokhranilishche (Vdkhr.) *Russian*, Reservoir
Vodoskhovyshche (Vdskh.) *Ukrainian*, Reservoir
Volcán *Spanish*, Volcano
Vozvyshennost' *Russian*, Upland, plateau
Vrh *Macedonian*, Peak
Vysochyna *Ukrainian*, Upland
Vysočina *Czech*, Upland

W

Waadi *Somali*, Watercourse
Wādī *Arabic*, Watercourse
Wâḥat, Wâhat *Arabic*, Oasis
Wald *German*, Forest
Wan *Chinese*, Bay
Wyżyna *Polish*, Upland

X

Xé *Laotian*, River

Y

Yarımadası *Azerbaijani*, Peninsula
Yazovir *Bulgarian*, Reservoir
Yoma *Burmese*, Mountains
Yü *Chinese*, Island

Z

Zaliv *Bulgarian*, *Russian*, Bay
Zatoka *Ukrainian*, Bay
Zemlya *Russian*, Land

CONTINENTAL FACTFILES

NORTH & CENTRAL AMERICA

POLITICAL FEATURES

■ TOTAL AREA:
9,400,000 sq miles
(24,346,000 sq km)

TOTAL NUMBER
OF COUNTRIES: 23

TOTAL POPULATION:
466.2 million

LARGEST CITY WITH
POPULATION: Mexico
City, Mexico 18 million

COUNTRY WITH HIGHEST
POPULATION DENSITY: Barbados
1,614 people per sq mile
(623 people per sq km)

LARGEST COUNTRY:
Canada 3,851,788 sq miles
(9,976,140 sq km)

SMALLEST COUNTRY:
Grenada 131 sq miles
(340 sq km)

PHYSICAL FEATURES

LARGEST LAKE: Lake Superior,
Canada/ USA 32,150 sq miles
(83,270 sq km)

LONGEST RIVER: Mississippi-
Missouri, USA 3,740 miles
(6,019 km)

HIGHEST POINT: Mt. McKinley
(Denali), Alaska, USA 20,322 ft
(6,194 m)

LOWEST POINT: Death Valley,
California, USA
282 ft (86 m) below sea level

SOUTH AMERICA

POLITICAL FEATURES

■ TOTAL AREA:
6,880,000 sq miles
(17,819,000 sq km)

TOTAL NUMBER
OF COUNTRIES: 12

TOTAL POPULATION:
332.3 million

LARGEST CITY WITH
POPULATION: São Paulo,
Brazil 10.1 million

COUNTRY WITH HIGHEST
POPULATION DENSITY:
Ecuador 118 people per sq mile
(45 people per sq km)

LARGEST COUNTRY:
Brazil 3,286,469 sq miles
(8,511,965 sq km)

SMALLEST COUNTRY:
Suriname 63,039 sq miles
(163,270 sq km)

PHYSICAL FEATURES

LARGEST LAKE: Lake Titicaca,
Bolivia/Peru 3,220 sq miles
(8,340 sq km)

LONGEST RIVER: Amazon,
Brazil 4,050 miles
(6,516 km)

HIGHEST POINT: Cerro
Aconcagua, Argentina
22,833 ft (6,959 m)

LOWEST POINT: Peninsula
Valdés, Argentina
131 ft (40 m) below sea level

AFRICA

POLITICAL FEATURES

■ TOTAL AREA:
11,677,250 sq miles
(30,244,050 sq km)

TOTAL NUMBER
OF COUNTRIES: 53

TOTAL POPULATION:
776.5 million

LARGEST CITY WITH
POPULATION: Cairo,
Egypt 6.4 million

COUNTRY WITH HIGHEST
POPULATION DENSITY: Mauritius
1,671 people per sq mile
(645 people per sq km)

LARGEST COUNTRY:
Sudan 967,493 sq miles
(2,505,810 sq km)

SMALLEST COUNTRY:
Seychelles 176 sq miles
(455 sq km)

PHYSICAL FEATURES

LARGEST LAKE: Lake Victoria,
Uganda, Kenya, Tanzania,
26,828 sq miles (69,484 sq km)

LONGEST RIVER: Nile,
Uganda/Sudan/Egypt
4,160 miles (6,695 km)

HIGHEST POINT: Kilimanjaro,
Tanzania 19,341 ft
(5,895 m)

LOWEST POINT: Lac',
Assal, Djibouti 512 ft
(156 m) below sea level

EUROPE

POLITICAL FEATURES

■ TOTAL AREA:
4,809,200 sq miles
(12,456,000 sq km)

TOTAL NUMBER
OF COUNTRIES: 43

TOTAL POPULATION:
582.5 million

LARGEST CITY WITH
POPULATION: Moscow,
European Russia 9 million

COUNTRY WITH HIGHEST
POPULATION DENSITY: Monaco
42,104 people per sq mile
(16,256 people per sq km)

LARGEST COUNTRY: European
Russia 1,527,341 sq miles
(3,955,818 sq km)

SMALLEST COUNTRY:
Vatican City, Italy 0.17 sq miles
(0.44 sq km)

PHYSICAL FEATURES

LARGEST LAKE: Ladoga,
European Russia
7,100 sq miles (18,390 sq km)

LONGEST RIVER: Volga,
European Russia
2,290 miles (3,688 km)

HIGHEST POINT: El' brus,
Caucasus Mts, European
Russia 18,510 ft (5,642 m)

LOWEST POINT: Volga Delta,
Caspian Sea, European Russia
92 ft (28 m) below sea level

162

NORTH & WEST ASIA

POLITICAL FEATURES

 TOTAL AREA: 9,585,550 sq miles (24,826,600 sq km)

TOTAL NUMBER OF COUNTRIES: 24

TOTAL POPULATION: 478.6 million

LARGEST CITY WITH POPULATION: Istanbul, Turkey 6.5 million

 **COUNTRY WITH HIGHEST POPULATION DENSITY:** Bahrain 2,724 people per sq mile (1,052 people per sq km)

LARGEST COUNTRY: Asiatic Russia 5,065,471 square miles (13,119,582 sq km)

SMALLEST COUNTRY: Bahrain 239 sq miles (620 sq km)

PHYSICAL FEATURES

 LARGEST LAKE: Caspian Sea 142,243 sq miles (371,000 sq km)

 LONGEST RIVER: Ob'-Irtysh, Asiatic Russia 3,461 miles (5,570 km)

 HIGHEST POINT: Pik Pobedy, Kyrgyzstan/China 24,408 ft (7,439 m)

LOWEST POINT: Dead Sea, Israel/Jordan 1,286 ft (392 m) below sea level

SOUTH & EAST ASIA

POLITICAL FEATURES

TOTAL AREA: 7,936,200 sq miles (20,554,700 sq km)

TOTAL NUMBER OF COUNTRIES: 24

 TOTAL POPULATION: 3,300 million

LARGEST CITY WITH POPULATION: Tokyo, Japan 18.1 million

COUNTRY WITH HIGHEST POPULATION DENSITY: Singapore 16,400 people per sq mile (6,332 people per sq km)

LARGEST COUNTRY: China 3,705,386 sq miles (9,596,960 sq km)

SMALLEST COUNTRY: Maldives 116 sq miles (300 sq km)

PHYSICAL FEATURES

 LARGEST LAKE: Tônlé Sap, Cambodia 100 sq miles (2,850 sq km)

 LONGEST RIVER: Chang Jiang (Yangtze), China 3,965 miles (6,380 km)

 HIGHEST POINT: Mount Everest, Nepal 29,030 ft (8,848 m)

 LOWEST POINT: Turpan Hami (Turfan Basin), China 505 ft (154 m) below sea level

AUSTRALASIA & OCEANIA

POLITICAL FEATURES

TOTAL AREA: 3,376,700 sq miles (8,745,750 sq km)

 TOTAL NUMBER OF COUNTRIES: 14

TOTAL POPULATION: 28.6 million

LARGEST CITY WITH POPULATION: Sydney, Australia 3.7 million

 COUNTRY WITH HIGHEST POPULATION DENSITY: Nauru 1,455 people per sq mile (562 people per sq km)

LARGEST COUNTRY: Australia 2,967,892 sq miles (7,686,850 sq km)

SMALLEST COUNTRY: Nauru 8 sq miles (21 sq km)

PHYSICAL FEATURES

 LARGEST LAKE: Lake Eyre, Australia 3,430 sq miles (8,884 sq km)

 LONGEST RIVER: Murray-Darling, Australia 2,330 miles (3,750 km)

HIGHEST POINT: Mt. Wilhelm Papua New Guinea 14,794 ft (4,509 m)

LOWEST POINT: Lake Eyre, Australia 52 ft (16 m) below sea level

ANTARCTICA

POLITICAL FEATURES

 TOTAL AREA: 5,405,500 sq miles (14,000,000 sq km) of which approx. 324,300 sq miles (840,000 sq km) is ice-free

 TOTAL NUMBER OF COUNTRIES: The Antarctic Treaty has 30 participating nations and 14 with observer status. Claims by Australia, France, New Zealand, Norway, Argentina, Chile and the UK are not recognized by other member states.

TOTAL POPULATION: No indigenous population. 74 research stations, (42 are staffed all year-round). Population varies between about 1,000 (winter) and 4,000 (summer).

PHYSICAL FEATURES

 TOTAL VOLUME OF ICE: 7,200,000 cu miles (30,000,000 cu km): contains 90% of the Earth's fresh water

SEA ICE: 1,158,300 sq miles (3,000,000 sq km) in February. 7,722,000 sq miles (20,000,000 sq km) in October

LOWEST TEMPERATURE: Vostok Station -89.5°C (-129°F)

HIGHEST POINT: Vinson Massif 16,072 ft (4,897 m)

LOWEST POINT: Coastline 0ft/m

GEOGRAPHICAL COMPARISONS

LARGEST COUNTRIES

Russ. Fed. . . . . .6,592,735 sq miles . .(17,075,200 sq km)
Canada . . . . . . .3,851,788 sq miles . . .(9,976,140 sq km)
USA . . . . .3,717,792 sq miles . . .(9,629,091 sq km)
China . . . . .3,705,386 sq miles . . .(9,596,960 sq km)
Brazil . . . . .3,286,470 sq miles . . .(8,511,965 sq km)
Australia . . . . . .2,967,893 sq miles . . .(7,686,893 sq km)
India . . . . .1,269,339 sq miles . . .(3,287,590 sq km)
Argentina . . . . .1,068,296 sq miles . . .(2,766,890 sq km)
Kazakhstan . . . .1,049,150 sq miles . . .(2,717,300 sq km)
Sudan . . . . .967,493 sq miles . . .(2,505,810 sq km)

SMALLEST COUNTRIES

Vatican City . . . . .0.17 sq miles . . . .(0.44 sq km)
Monaco . . . . .0.75 sq miles . . . .(1.95 sq km)
Nauru . . . . .8 sq miles . . . .(21 sq km)
Tuvalu . . . . .10 sq miles . . . .(26 sq km)
San Marino . . . . .24 sq miles . . . .(61 sq km)
Liechtenstein . . . . .62 sq miles . . . .(160 sq km)
Marshall Islands . . . . .70 sq miles . . . .(181 sq km)
St. Kitts & Nevis . . . . .101 sq miles . . . .(261 sq km)
Maldives . . . . .116 sq miles . . . .(300 sq km)
Malta . . . . .122 sq miles . . . .(316 sq km)

LARGEST ISLANDS

(TO THE NEAREST 1,000 - OR 100,000 FOR THE LARGEST)

Greenland . . . . . .849,400 sq miles . . .(2,200,000 sq km)
New Guinea . . . . .312,000 sq miles . . . .(808,000 sq km)
Borneo . . . . .292,222 sq miles . . . .(757,050 sq km)
Madagascar . . . . .229,300 sq miles . . . .(594,000 sq km)
Sumatra . . . . .202,300 sq miles . . . .(524,000 sq km)
Baffin Island . . . .183,800 sq miles . . . .(476,000 sq km)
Honshu . . . . .88,800 sq miles . . . .(230,000 sq km)
Britain . . . . .88,700 sq miles . . . .(229,800 sq km)
Victoria Island . . . .81,900 sq miles . . . .(212,000 sq km)
Ellesmere Island . .75,700 sq miles . . . .(196,000 sq km)

RICHEST COUNTRIES

(GNP PER CAPITA, IN US$)

Luxembourg 42.930
Liechtenstein 40,000
Switzerland 38,380
Norway 33,470
Denamrk 32,050
Japan 32,030
USA 31,910
Germany 25,620
Austria 25,430
Singapore 24,150

POOREST COUNTRIES

(GNP PER CAPITA, IN US$)

Somalia 100
Ethiopia 100
Congo, Dem. Rep. 110
Sierra Leone 130
Malawi 180
Niger 190
Mozambique 220
Burundi 240
Rwanda 250
Tanzania 260

MOST POPULOUS COUNTRIES

China 1,290,000,000
India 1,030,000,000
USA 281,400,000
Indonesia 214,000,000
Brazil 172,600,000
Pakistan 145,000,000
Russian Federation 144,700,000
Bangladesh 140,400,000
Japan 127,300,000
Nigeria 116,900,000

LEAST POPULOUS COUNTRIES

Vatican City 524
Tuvalu 10,800
Nauru 11,800
Palau 19,100
San Marino 26,900
Liechtenstein 32,200
Monaco 31,700
St. Kitts & Nevis 41,000
Antigua & Barbuda .66,400
Andorra 66,800

MOST DENSELY POPULATED COUNTRIES

Monaco . . . .42,104 people per sq mile . .(16,256 per sq km)
Singapore . .16,400 people per sq mile . .(6,332 per sq km)
Malta . . . . . .3,213 people per sq mile . .(2,241 per sq km)
Vatican City 3,084 people per sq mile . .(1,191 per sq km)
Bahrain . . . .2,724 people per sq mile . .(1,052 per sq km)
Maldives . .2,590 people per sq mile . .(1,000 per sq km)
Bangladesh 2,525 people per sq mile . . .(975 per sq km)
Mauritius . .1,671 people per sq mile . . . .(645 per sq km)
Barbados . .1,614 people per sq mile . . . .(623 per sq km)
Taiwan . . . .1,598 people per sq mile . . . .(617 per sq km)

MOST SPARSELY POPULATED COUNTRIES

Mongolia . . . . .4 people per sq mile . . . . . .(2 per sq km)
Namibia . . . . . .6 people per sq mile . . . . . .(2 per sq km)
Australia . . . . .7 people per sq mile . . . . . .(3 per sq km)
Mauritania . . . .7 people per sq mile . . . . . .(3 per sq km)
Suriname . . . . .7 people per sq mile . . . . . .(3 per sq km)
Botswana . . . . .7 people per sq mile . . . . . .(3 per sq km)
Iceland . . . . . . .7 people per sq mile . . . . . .(3 per sq km)
Libya . . . . .8 people per sq mile . . . . . .(3 per sq km)
Canada . . . . . . .8 people per sq mile . . . . . .(3 per sq km)
Guyana . . . . . . .9 people per sq mile . . . . . .(4 per sq km)

MOST WIDELY SPOKEN LANGUAGES

1. Chinese (Mandarin) 6. Arabic
2. English 7. Bengali
3. Hindi 8. Portuguese
4. Spanish 9. Malay-Indonesian
5. Russian 10. French

COUNTRIES WITH THE MOST LAND BORDERS

14: China *(Afghanistan, Bhutan, Myanmar, India,*
Kazakhstan, Kyrgyzstan, Laos, Mongolia,
Nepal, North Korea, Pakistan, Russian
Federation, Tajikistan, Vietnam)

14: Russian Federation *(Azerbaijan, Belarus,*
China, Estonia, Finland, Georgia, Kazakhstan,
Latvia, Lithuania, Mongolia, North Korea,
Norway, Poland, Ukraine)

10: Brazil *(Argentina, Bolivia, Colombia, French*
Guiana, Guyana, Paraguay, Peru, Suriname,
Uruguay, Venezuela)

9: Congo, Dem. Rep. *(Angola, Burundi,*
Central African Republic, Congo, Rwanda,
Sudan, Tanzania, Uganda, Zambia)

9: Germany *(Austria, Belgium, Czech Republic,*
Denmark, France, Luxembourg,
Netherlands, Poland, Switzerland)

9: Sudan *(Central African Republic, Chad,*
Congo, Dem. Rep., Egypt, Eritrea, Ethiopia,
Kenya, Libya, Uganda)

8: Austria *(Czech Republic, Germany, Hungary, Italy,*
Liechtenstein, Slovakia, Slovenia, Switzerland)

8: France *(Andorra, Belgium, Germany, Italy,*
Luxembourg, Monaco, Spain, Switzerland)

8: Tanzania *(Burundi, Congo, Dem. Rep.,*
Kenya, Malawi, Mozambique, Rwanda,
Uganda, Zambia)

8: Turkey *(Armenia, Azerbaijan, Bulgaria, Georgia,*
Greece, Iran, Iraq, Syria)

8: Zambia *(Angola, Botswana, Congo, Dem. Rep.,*
Malawi, Mozambique, Namibia,
Tanzania, Zimbabwe)

LONGEST RIVERS

Nile (NE Africa) . . . . .4,160 miles . . . .(6,695 km)
Amazon (South America) . .4,049 miles . . . .(6,516 km)
Yangtze (China) . . . . .3,915 miles . . . .(6,299 km)
Mississippi/Missouri (US) .3,710 miles . . . .(5,969 km)
Ob'-Irtysh (Russ. Fed.) . . .3,461 miles . . . .(5,570 km)
Yellow River (China) . . . . .3,395 miles . . . .(5,464 km)
Congo (Central Africa) . . .2,900 miles . . . .(4,667 km)
Mekong (Southeast Asia) . .2,749 miles . . . .(4,425 km)
Lena (Russian Federation) . .2,734 miles . . . .(4,400 km)
Mackenzie (Canada) . . . . .2,640 miles . . . .(4,250 km)
Yenisey (Russ. Federation) .2,541 miles . . . .(4,090 km)

HIGHEST MOUNTAINS

(HEIGHT ABOVE SEA LEVEL)

Everest . . . . .29,030 ft . . . .(8,848 m)
K2 . . . . .28,253 ft . . . .(8,611 m)
Kanchenjunga I . . . . .28,210 ft . . . .(8,598 m)
Makalu I . . . . .27,767 ft . . . .(8,463 m)
Cho Oyu . . . . .26,907 ft . . . .(8,201 m)
Dhaulagiri I . . . . .26,796 ft . . . .(8,167 m)
Manaslu I . . . . .26,783 ft . . . .(8,163 m)
Nanga Parbat I . . . . .26,661 ft . . . .(8,126 m)
Annapurna I . . . . .26,547 ft . . . .(8,091 m)
Gasherbrum I . . . . .26,471 ft . . . .(8,068 m)

LARGEST BODIES OF INLAND WATER

(WITH AREA AND DEPTH)

Caspian Sea
143,243 sq miles (371,000 sq km) . . .3,215 ft (980 m)
Lake Superior
32,150 sq miles (83,270 sq km) . . . . .1,289 ft (393 m)
Lake Victoria
26,828 sq miles (69,484 sq km) . . . . . .328 ft (100 m)
Lake Huron
23,436 sq miles (60,700 sq km) . . . . . .751 ft (229 m)
Lake Michigan
22,402 sq miles (58,020 sq km) . . . . . .922 ft (281 m)
Lake Tanganyika
12,703 sq miles (32,900 sq km) . . . .4,700 ft (1,435 m)
Great Bear Lake
12,274 sq miles (31,790 sq km) . . . . .1,047 ft (319 m)
Lake Baikal
11,776 sq miles (30,500 sq km) . . . .5,712 ft (1,741 m)
Great Slave Lake
10,981 sq miles (28,440 sq km) . . . . . .459 ft (140 m)
Lake Erie
9,915 sq miles (25,680 sq km) . . . . .197 ft (60 m)

. . . . . .*continued on p.166*

DEEPEST OCEAN FEATURES

Challenger Deep, Marianas Trench (Pacific)
36,201 ft . . . .(11,034 m)
Vityaz III Depth, Tonga Trench (Pacific)
35,704 ft . . . .(10,882 m)
Vityaz Depth, Kurile-Kamchatka Trench (Pacific)
34,588 ft . . . .(10,542 m)
Cape Johnson Deep, Philippine Trench (Pacific)
34,441 ft . . . .(10,497 m)
Kermadec Trench (Pacific)
32,964 ft . . . .(10,047 m)
Ramapo Deep, Japan Trench (Pacific)
32,758 ft . . . .(9,984 m)
Milwaukee Deep, Puerto Rico Trench (Atlantic)
30,185 ft . . . .(9,200 m)
Argo Deep, Torres Trench (Pacific)
30,070 ft . . . .(9,165 m)
Meteor Depth, South Sandwich Trench (Atlantic)
30,000 ft . . . .(9,144 m)
Planet Deep, New Britain Trench (Pacific)
29,988 ft . . . .(9,140 m)

GREATEST WATERFALLS

(MEAN FLOW OF WATER)

Boyoma (Congo) . . . . . 600,400 cu. ft/sec (17,000 cu.m/sec)
Khône (Laos/Cambodia) 410,000 cu. ft/sec (11,600 cu.m/sec)
Niagara (USA/Canada) 195,000 cu. ft/sec (5,500 cu.m/sec)
Grande (Uruguay) . . . .160,000 cu. ft/sec (4,500 cu.m/sec)
Paulo Afonso (Brazil) 100,000 cu. ft/sec (2,800 cu.m/sec)
Urubupunga (Brazil) . .97,000 cu. ft/sec (2,750 cu.m/sec)
Iguaçu (Argentina/Brazil) 62,000 cu. ft/sec (1,700 cu.m/sec)
Maribondo (Brazil) . . . .53,000 cu. ft/sec (1,500 cu.m/sec)
Victoria (Zimbabwe) . . .39,000 cu. ft/sec (1,100 cu.m/sec)
Kabalega (Uganda) . . . .42,000 cu. ft/sec (1,200 cu.m/sec)
Churchill (Canada) . . . .35,000 cu. ft/sec (1,000 cu.m/sec)
Cauvery (India) . . . . . .33,000 cu. ft/sec (900 cu.m/sec)

HIGHEST WATERFALLS

Angel (Venezuela) . . . . .3,212 ft . . . .(979 m)
Tugela (South Africa) . . . . . .3,110 ft . . . .(948 m)
Utigard (Norway) . . . . .2,625 ft . . . .(800 m)
Mongefossen (Norway) . . . .2,539 ft . . . .(774 m)
Mtarazi (Zimbabwe) . . . . . .2,500 ft . . . .(762 m)
Yosemite (USA) . . . . .2,425 ft . . . .(739 m)
Ostre Mardola Foss (Norway) 2,156 ft . . . .(657 m)
Tyssestrengane (Norway) . .2,119 ft . . . .(646 m)
*Cuquenan (Venezuela) . . .2,001 ft . . . .(610 m)
Sutherland (New Zealand) . .1,903 ft . . . .(580 m)
*Kjellfossen (Norway) . . . . .1,841 ft . . . .(561 m)

* indicates that the total height is a single leap

LARGEST DESERTS

Sahara . . . . .3,450,000 sq miles . .(9,065,000 sq km)
Gobi . . . . .500,000 sq miles . .(1,295,000 sq km)
Ar Rub al Khali . .289,600 sq miles . . . .(750,000 sq km)
Great Victorian . .249,800 sq miles . . . .(647,000 sq km)
Sonoran . . . . . . .120,000 sq miles . . . .(311,000 sq km)
Kalahari . . . . . . .120,000 sq miles . . . .(310,800 sq km)
Kara Kum . . . . . .115,800 sq miles . . . .(300,000 sq km)
Takla Makan . . . . .100,400 sq miles . . . .(260,000 sq km)
Namib . . . . .52,100 sq miles . . . .(135,000 sq km)
Thar . . . . .33,670 sq miles . . . .(130,000 sq km)
NB – Most of Antarctica is a polar desert, with only
50 mm of precipitation annually

HOTTEST INHABITED PLACES

Djibouti (Djibouti) . . . . .86° F . . . .(30 °C)
Timbouctou (Mali) . . . . . .84.7° F . . . .(29.3 °C)
Tirunelveli (India)
Tuticorin (India)
Nellore (India) . . . . .84.5° F . . . .(29.2 °C)
Santa Marta (Colombia)
Aden (Yemen) . . . . .84° F . . . .(28.9 °C)
Madurai (India)
Niamey (Niger)
Hodeida (Yemen) . . . . .83.8° F . . . .(28.8 °C)
Ouagadougou (Burkina Faso)
Thanjavur (India)
Tiruchchirappalli (India)

DRIEST INHABITED PLACES

Aswân (Egypt) . . . . .0.02 in . . . .(0.5 mm)
Luxor (Egypt) . . . . .0.03 in . . . .(0.7 mm)
Arica (Chile) . . . . .0.04 in . . . .(1.1 mm)
Ica (Peru) . . . . .0.1 in . . . .(2.3 mm)
Antofagasta (Chile) . . . . .0.2 in . . . .(4.9 mm)
El Minya (Egypt) . . . . .0.2 in . . . .(5.1 mm)
Asyût (Egypt) . . . . .0.2 in . . . .(5.2 mm)
Callao (Peru) . . . . .0.5 in . . . . . .(12.0 mm)
Trujillo (Peru) . . . . .0.55 in . . . . . .(14.0 mm)
El Faiyûm (Egypt) . . . . .0.8 in . . . . . .(19.0 mm)

WETTEST INHABITED PLACES

Buenaventura (Colombia) . . . .265 in . . . . . .(6,743 mm)
Monrovia (Liberia) . . . . .202 in . . . . . .(5,131 mm)
Pago Pago (American Samoa) . . .196 in . . .(4,990 mm)
Moulmein (Myanmar) . . . . . . .191 in . . . . .(4,852 mm)
Lae (Papua New Guinea) . . . . . .183 in . . . . .(4,645 mm)
Baguio (Luzon Island, Philippines)180 in . . .(4,573 mm)
Sylhet (Bangladesh) . . . . .176 in . . . . .(4,457 mm)
Padang (Sumatra, Indonesia) . . . .166 in . . . . .(4,225 mm)
Bogor (Java, Indonesia) . . . . . . .166 in . . . . .(4,225 mm)
Conakry (Guinea) . . . . .171 in . . . . .(4,341 mm)

GLOSSARY OF ABBREVIATIONS

This Glossary provides a comprehensive guide to the abbreviations used in this Atlas, and in the Index.

A
abbrev. abbreviated
Afr. Afrikaans
Alb. Albanian
Amh. Amharic
anc. ancient
Ar. Arabic
Arm. Armenian
Az. Azerbaijani

B
Basq. Basque
Bel. Belorussian
Ben. Bengali
Bibl. Biblical
Bret. Breton
Bul. Bulgarian
Bur. Burmese

C
Cam. Cambodian
Cant. Cantonese
Cast. Castilian
Cat. Catalan
Chin. Chinese
Cro. Croat
Cz. Czech

D
Dan. Danish
Dut. Dutch

E
Eng. English
Est. Estonian
est. estimated

F
Faer. Faeroese
Fij. Fijian
Fin. Finnish
Flem. Flemish
Fr. French
Fris. Frisian

G
Geor. Georgian
Ger. German
Gk. Greek
Guj. Gujarati

H
Haw. Hawaiian
Heb. Hebrew
Hind. Hindi
hist. historical
Hung. Hungarian

I
Icel. Icelandic
Ind. Indonesian
In. Inuit
Ir. Irish
It. Italian

J
Jap. Japanese

K
Kaz. Kazakh
Kir. Kirghiz
Kor. Korean
Kurd. Kurdish

L
Lao. Laotian
Lapp. Lappish
Lat. Latin
Latv. Latvian
Lith. Lithanian
Lus. Lusatian

M
Mac. Macedonian
Mal. Malay
Malg. Malagasy
Malt. Maltese
Mong. Mongolian

N
Nepali. Nepali
Nor. Norwegian

O
off. officially

P
Pash. Pashtu
Per. Persian
Pol. Polish
Port. Portuguese
prev. previously

R
Rmsch. Romansch
Roman. Romanian
Rus. Russian

S
SCr. Serbo - Croatian
Serb. Serbian
Slvk. Slovak
Slvn. Slovene
Som. Somali
Sp. Spanish
Swa. Swahili
Swe. Swedish

T
Taj. Tajik
Th. Thai
Tib. Tibetan
Turk. Turkish
Turkm. Turkmenistan

U
Uigh. Uighur
Ukr. Ukrainian
Uzb. Uzbek

V
var. variant
Vtn. Vietnamese

W
Wel. Welsh

X
Xh. Xhosa

Y
Yugo. Yugoslavia

Key to country factboxes within the Index:

Formation
Date of independence

Population
Total population / population density - based on total land area .

Calorie consumption
Average number of calories consumed daily per person.

A

Aachen *94 A4 Dut.* Aken, *Fr.* Aix-la-Chapelle; *anc.* Aquae Grani, Aquisgranum. Nordrhein-Westfalen, W Germany
Aaiún *see* Laâyoune
Aalborg *see* Ålborg
Aalen *95 B6* Baden-Württemberg, S Germany
Aalsmeer *86 C3* Noord-Holland, C Netherlands
Aalst *87 B6 Fr.* Alost. Oost-Vlaanderen, C Belgium
Aalten *86 E4* Gelderland, E Netherlands
Aalter *87 B5* Oost-Vlaanderen, NW Belgium
Äänekoski *85 D5* Länsi-Suomi, W Finland
Aar *see* Aare
Aare *95 A7 var.* Aar. *River* W Switzerland
Aarhus *see* Århus
Aat *see* Ath
Aba *75 G5* Abia, S Nigeria
Aba *77 E5* Orientale, NE Dem. Rep. Congo
Abā as Su'ūd *see* Najrān
Abaco Island *see* Great Abaco
Ābādān *120 C4* Khūzestān, SW Iran
Abai *see* Blue Nile
Abakan *114 D4* Respublika Khakasiya, S Russian Federation
Abancay *60 D4* Apurímac, SE Peru
Abariringa *see* Kanton
Abashiri *130 D2 var.* Abasiri. Hokkaidō, NE Japan
Abasiri *see* Abashiri
Ābaya Hāyk' *73 C5 Eng.* Lake Margherita, *It.* Abbaia. *Lake* SW Ethiopia
Ābay Wenz *see* Blue Nile
Abbeville *90 C2 anc.* Abbatis Villa. Somme, N France
'Abd al 'Azīz, Jabal *118 D2 mountain range* NE Syria
Abéché *76 C3 var.* Abécher, Abeshr. Ouaddaï, SE Chad
Abécher *see* Abéché
Abela *see* Ávila
Abemama *144 D2 var.* Apamama; *prev.* Roger Simpson Island. *Atoll* Tungaru, W Kiribati
Abengourou *75 E5* E Côte d'Ivoire
Aberdeen *88 D3 anc.* Devana. NE Scotland, UK
Aberdeen *45 E2* South Dakota, N USA
Aberdeen *46 B2* Washington, NW USA
Abergwaun *see* Fishguard
Abertawe *see* Swansea
Aberystwyth *89 C6* W Wales, UK
Abeshr *see* Abéché
Abhā *121 B6* 'Asīr, SW Saudi Arabia
Abidavichy *107 D7 Rus.* Obidovichi. Mahilyowskaya Voblasts', E Belarus
Abidjan *75 E5* S Côte d'Ivoire
Abilene *49 F3* Texas, SW USA
Abingdon *see* Pinta, Isla
Abkhazia *117 E1 autonomous republic* NW Georgia
Åbo *85 D6* Länsi-Suomi, W Finland
Aboisso *75 E5* SE Côte d'Ivoire
Abo, Massif d' *76 B1 mountain range* NW Chad
Abomey *75 F5* S Benin
Abou-Déïa *76 C3* Salamat, SE Chad
Abrantes *92 B3 var.* Abrántes. Santarém, C Portugal
Abrolhos Bank *56 E4 undersea feature* W Atlantic Ocean
Abrova *107 B6 Rus.* Obrovo. Brestskaya Voblasts', SW Belarus
Abrud *108 B4 Ger.* Gross-Schlatten, *Hung.* Abrudbánya. Alba, SW Romania

Abruzzese, Appennino *96 C4 mountain range* C Italy
Absaroka Range *44 B2 mountain range* Montana/Wyoming, NW USA
Abū aḍ Ḍuhūr *118 B3 Fr.* Aboudouhour. Idlib, NW Syria
Abu Dhabi *see* Abū Ẓaby
Abu Hamed *72 C3* River Nile, N Sudan
Abuja *75 G4 country capital* (Nigeria) Federal Capital District, C Nigeria
Abū Kamāl *118 E3 Fr.* Abou Kémal. Dayr az Zawr, E Syria
Abula *see* Ávila
Abunã, Rio *62 C2 var.* Río Abuná. *River* Bolivia/Brazil
Abut Head *151 B6 headland* South Island, NZ
Ābuyē Mēda *72 D4 mountain* C Ethiopia
Abū Ẓabī *see* Abū Ẓaby
Abū Ẓaby *121 C5 var.* Abū Ẓabī, *Eng.* Abu Dhabi. *Country capital* (UAE) Abū Ẓaby, C UAE
Abyla *see* Ávila
Acalayong *77 A5* SW Equatorial Guinea
Acaponeta *50 D4* Nayarit, C Mexico
Acapulco *51 E5 var.* Acapulco de Juárez. Guerrero, S Mexico
Acapulco de Juárez *see* Acapulco
Acarai Mountains *59 F4 Sp.* Serra Acaraí. *Mountain range* Brazil/Guyana
Acarigua *58 D2* Portuguesa, N Venezuela
Accra *75 E5 country capital* (Ghana) SE Ghana
Achacachi *61 E4* La Paz, W Bolivia
Acklins Island *54 C2 island* SE Bahamas
Aconcagua, Cerro *64 B4 mountain* W Argentina
Açores *see* Azores
A Coruña *92 B1 Cast.* La Coruña, *Eng.* Corunna; *anc.* Caronium. Galicia, NW Spain
Acre *62 C2 off.* Estado do Acre. *State* W Brazil
Açu *63 G2 var.* Assu. Rio Grande do Norte, E Brazil
Ada *49 G2* Oklahoma, C USA
Ada *100 D3* Serbia, N Serbia and Montenegro (Yugo.)
Adalia, Gulf of *see* Antalya Körfezi
Adama *see* Nazrēt
Adamawa Highlands *76 B4 plateau* NW Cameroon
'Adan *121 B7 Eng.* Aden. SW Yemen
Adana *116 D4 var.* Seyhan. Adana, S Turkey
Adapazarı *116 B2 prev.* Ada Bazar. Sakarya, NW Turkey
Adare, Cape *154 B4 headland* Antarctica
Ad Dahnā' *120 C4 desert* E Saudi Arabia
Ad Dakhla *70 A4 var.* Dakhla. SW Western Sahara
Ad Dalanj *see* Dilling
Ad Damar *see* Ed Damer
Ad Damazin *see* Ed Damazin
Ad Dāmir *see* Ed Damer
Ad Dammām *120 C4 var.* Dammām. Ash Sharqīyah, NE Saudi Arabia
Ad Dawādimī *see* Damoûr
Ad Dawhah *120 C4 Eng.* Doha. *Country capital* (Qatar) C Qatar
Aḍ Ḍiffah *see* Libyan Plateau
Addis Ababa *see* Ādīs Ābeba
Addu Atoll *132 A5 atoll* S Maldives
Adelaide *149 B6 state capital* South Australia
Aden *see* 'Adan
Aden, Gulf of *121 C7 gulf* SW Arabian Sea

Amami-ō-shima *130 A3 island*
S Japan
Amantea *97 D6* Calabria, SW Italy
Amapá *63 E1* Amapá, NE Brazil
Amara *see* Al 'Amārah
Amarapura *136 B3* Mandalay,
C Myanmar
Amarillo *49 E2* Texas, SW USA
Amay *87 C6* Liège, E Belgium
Amazon *63 E1 Sp.* Amazonas. *River*
Brazil/Peru
Amazon Basin *62 D2 basin* N South
America
Amazon, Mouths of the *63 F1 delta*
NE Brazil
Ambam *77 B5* Sud, S Cameroon
Ambanja *79 G2* Antsiranana,
N Madagascar
Ambarchik *115 G2* Respublika
Sakha (Yakutiya), NE Russian
Federation
Ambato *60 B1* Tungurahua,
C Ecuador
Ambérieu-en-Bugey *91 D5* Ain,
E France
Amboasary *79 F4* Toliara,
S Madagascar
Ambon *139 F4 prev.* Amboina,
Amboyna. Pulau Ambon,
E Indonesia
Ambositra *79 G3* Fianarantsoa,
SE Madagascar
Ambrim *see* Ambrym
Ambriz *78 A1* Bengo, NW Angola
Ambrym *144 D4 var.* Ambrim.
Island C Vanuatu
Amchitka Island *36 A2 island*
Aleutian Islands, Alaska, USA
Amdo *126 C5* Xizang Zizhiqu,
W China
Ameland *86 D1 Fris.* It Amelân.
Island Waddeneilanden,
N Netherlands
America-Antarctica Ridge *67 C7*
undersea feature S Atlantic Ocean
American Falls Reservoir *46 E4*
reservoir Idaho, NW USA
American Samoa *145 E4 US*
unincorporated territory
W Polynesia
Amersfoort *86 D3* Utrecht,
C Netherlands
Ames *45 F3* Iowa, C USA
Amfilochía *105 A5 var.* Amfilokhía.
Dytiki Ellás, C Greece
Amfilokhía *see* Amfilochía
Amga *115 F3 river* NE Russian
Federation
Amherst *39 F4* Nova Scotia,
SE Canada
Amida *see* Diyarbakır
Amiens *90 C3 anc.* Ambianum,
Samarobriva. Somme, N France
Amíndaion *see* Amýntaio
Amindeo *see* Amýntaio
Amīndīvi Islands *132 A2 island*
group Lakshadweep, India,
N Indian Ocean
Amirante Islands *79 G1 var.*
Amirantes Group. *Island group*
C Seychelles
Amirantes Group *see* Amirante
Islands
Amistad Reservoir *49 F4 var.* Presa
de la Amistad. *Reservoir*
Mexico/USA
'Ammān *119 B6 var.* Amman; *anc.*
Philadelphia, *Bibl.* Rabbah
Ammon, Rabbath Ammon.
Country capital (Jordan) 'Ammān,
NW Jordan
Amman *see* 'Ammān
Ammassalik *82 D4 var.*
Angmagssalik. S Greenland
Ammóchostos *102 D5 var.*
Famagusta, Gazimağusa.
E Cyprus
Āmol *120 D2 var.* Amul.
Māzandarān, N Iran
Amorgós *105 D6 island* Kykládes,
Greece, Aegean Sea
Amorgós *105 D6* Amorgós,
Kykládes, Greece, Aegean Sea
Amos *38 D4* Quebec, SE Canada
Amourj *74 D3* Hodh ech Chargui,
SE Mauritania
Amoy *see* Xiamen

Ampato, Nevado *61 E4 mountain*
S Peru
Amposta *93 F2* Cataluña,
NE Spain
Amrāvati *134 D4 prev.* Amraoti.
Mahārāshtra, C India
Amritsar *134 D2* Punjab, N India
Amstelveen *86 C3* Noord-Holland,
C Netherlands
Amsterdam *86 C3 country capital*
(Netherlands) Noord-Holland,
C Netherlands
Amsterdam Island *141 C6 island*
NE French Southern and
Antarctic Territories
Am Timan *76 C3* Salamat,
SE Chad
Amu Darya *122 D2 Rus.*
Amudar'ya, *Taj.* Dar''yoi Amu,
Turkm. Amyderya, *Uzb.*
Amudaryo; *anc.* Oxus. *River*
C Asia
Amu-Dar'ya *123 E3* Lebapskiy
Velayat, NE Turkmenistan
Amul *see* Āmol
Amund Ringnes Island *37 F2 island*
Nunavut, N Canada
Amundsen Basin *see* Fram Basin
Amundsen Gulf *37 E2 gulf*
Northwest Territories, N Canada
Amundsen Plain *154 A4 undersea*
feature S Pacific Ocean
Amundsen-Scott *154 B3 US research*
station Antarctica
Amundsen Sea *154 A4 sea* S Pacific
Ocean
Amuntai *138 D4 prev.* Amoentai.
Borneo, C Indonesia
Amur *115 G4 Chin.* Heilong Jiang.
River China/Russian Federation
Amvrosiyivka *109 H3 Rus.*
Amvrosiyevka. Donets'ka Oblast',
SE Ukraine
Amýntaio *104 B4 var.* Amindeo;
prev. Amíndaion. Dytikí
Makedonía, N Greece
Anabar *115 E2 river* NE Russian
Federation
An Abhainn Mhór *see* Blackwater
Anaco *59 E2* Anzoátegui,
NE Venezuela
Anaconda *44 B2* Montana, NW USA
Anacortes *46 B1* Washington,
NW USA
Anadolu Dağları *see* Doğu
Karadeniz Dağları
Anadyr' *115 G1 river* NE Russian
Federation
Anadyr' *115 H1* Chukotskiy
Avtonomnyy Okrug, NE Russian
Federation
Anadyr, Gulf of *see* Anadyrskiy
Zaliv
Anadyrskiy Zaliv *115 H1 Eng.* Gulf
of Anadyr. *Gulf* NE Russian
Federation
Anáfi *105 D7 anc.* Anaphe. *Island*
Kykládes, Greece, Aegean Sea
'Ānah *see* 'Annah
Anaheim *46 E2* California, W USA
Anaiza *see* 'Unayzah
Analalava *79 G2* Mahajanga,
NW Madagascar
Anamur *116 C5* İçel, S Turkey
Anantapur *132 C2* Andhra Pradesh,
S India
Anápolis *63 F3* Goiás, C Brazil
Anār *120 D3* Kermān, C Iran
Anatolia *116 C4 plateau* C Turkey
Anatom *see* Aneityum
Añatuya *64 C3* Santiago del Estero,
N Argentina
An Bhearú *see* Barrow
Anchorage *36 C3* Alaska, USA
Ancona *96 C3* Marche, C Italy
Ancud *65 B6 prev.* San Carlos de
Ancud. Los Lagos, S Chile
Åndalsnes *85 A5* Møre og Romsdal,
S Norway
Andalucía *92 D4 cultural region*
S Spain
Andalusia *42 C3* Alabama, S USA
Andaman Islands *124 B4 island*
group India, NE Indian Ocean
Andaman Sea *124 C4 sea* NE Indian
Ocean
Andenne *87 C6* Namur, SE Belgium

Anderlues *87 B7* Hainaut,
S Belgium
Anderson *40 C4* Indiana, N USA
Andes *64 B3 mountain range*
W South America
Andhra Pradesh *135 E5 state*
E India
Andijon *123 F2 Rus.* Andizhan.
Andijon Wiloyati, E Uzbekistan
Andikíthira *see* Antikýthira
Andipaxi *see* Antípaxoi
Andípsara *see* Antípsara
Ándissa *see* Ántissa
Andkhvoy *122 D3* Fāryāb,
N Afghanistan
Andorra *91 A7 Cat.* Valls
d'Andorra, *Fr.* Vallée d'Andorre.
Country SW Europe

Andorra 91

Official name Principality of
Andorra
Formation 1278
Capital Andorra la Vella
Population 66,800 / 370 people
per sq mile (143 people per sq km)
Total area 181 sq miles (468 sq km)
Languages Catalan, Spanish,
French, Portuguese
Religions Roman Catholic 94%,
other 6%
Ethnic mix Spanish 46%, Andorrian
28%, other 18%, French 8%
Government Parliamentary
democracy
Currency Euro (French franc and
Spanish peseta until 2002)
Literacy rate 99%
Calorie consumption not available

Andorra *see* Andorra la Vella
Andorra la Vella *91 A8 var.*
Andorra, *Fr.* Andorre la Vielle, *Sp.*
Andorra la Vieja. *Country capital*
(Andorra) C Andorra
Andorra la Vieja *see* Andorra la
Vella
Andorre la Vielle *see* Andorra la
Vella
Andover *89 D7* S England, UK
Andøya *84 C2 island* C Norway
Andreanof Islands *36 A3 island*
group Aleutian Islands, Alaska,
USA
Andrews *49 E3* Texas, SW USA
Andrew Tablemount *140 A4 var.*
Gora Andrew. *Undersea feature*
W Indian Ocean
Andria *97 D5* Puglia, SE Italy
Ándros *105 C6 island* Kykládes,
Greece, Aegean Sea
Ándros *105 D6* Ándros, Kykládes,
Greece, Aegean Sea
Andros Island *54 B2 island*
NW Bahamas
Andros Town *54 C1* Andros Island,
NW Bahamas
Aneityum *144 D5 var.* Anatom; *prev.*
Kéamu. *Island* S Vanuatu
Ānewetak *see* Enewetak Atoll
Angara *115 E4 river* C Russian
Federation
Angarsk *115 E4* Irkutskaya Oblast',
S Russian Federation
Ånge *85 C5* Västernorrland,
C Sweden
Ángel de la Guarda, Isla *50 B2*
island NW Mexico
Angeles *139 E1 off.* Angeles City.
Luzon, N Philippines
Angel Falls *see* Ángel, Salto
Ángel, Salto *59 E3 Eng.* Angel Falls.
Waterfall E Venezuela
Ångermanälven *84 C4 river*
N Sweden
Angermünde *94 D3* Brandenburg,
NE Germany
Angers *90 B4 anc.* Juliomagus.
Maine-et-Loire, NW France
Anglesey *89 C5 island*
NW Wales, UK
Anglet *91 A6* Pyrénées-Atlantiques,
SW France
Angleton *49 H4* Texas, SW USA

Angmagssalik *see* Ammassalik
Ang Nam Ngum *136 C4 lake* C Laos
Angola *78 B2 prev.* People's
Republic of Angola, Portuguese
West Africa. *Country* SW Africa

Angola 78

Official name Republic of Angola
Formation 1975
Capital Luanda
Population 13.5 million /28 people
per sq mile (11 people per sq km)
Total area 481,351 sq miles
(1,246,700 sq km)
Languages Portuguese, Umbundu,
Kimbundu, Kikongo
Religions Roman Catholic 50%,
other 30%, Protestant 20%
Ethnic mix Ovimbundu 37%, other
25%, Kimbundu 25%, Bakongo 13%
Government Presidential regime
Currency Readjusted kwanza =
100 lwei
Literacy rate 40%
Calorie consumption 1,903
kilocalories

Angola Basin *69 B5 undersea feature*
E Atlantic Ocean
Angostura, Presa de la *51 G5*
reservoir SE Mexico
Angoulême *91 B5 anc.* Iculisma.
Charente, W France
Angoumois *91 B5 cultural region*
W France
Angren *123 F2* Toshkent Wiloyati,
E Uzbekistan
Anguilla *55 G3 UK dependent*
territory E West Indies
Anguilla Cays *54 B2 islets*
SW Bahamas
Anhui *128 C5 var.* Anhui Sheng,
Anhwei, Wan. Admin. region
province E China
Anhui Sheng *see* Anhui
Anhwei *see* Anhui
Anina *108 A4 Ger.* Steierdorf, *Hung.*
Stájerlakanina; *prev.* Staierdorf-
Anina, Steierdorf-Anina,
Steyerlak-Anina. Caraş-Severin,
SW Romania
Anjou *90 B4 cultural region*
NW France
Anjouan *79 F2 var.* Nzwani,
Johanna Island. *Island*
SE Comoros
Ankara *116 C3 prev.* Angora, *anc.*
Ancyra. *Country capital* (Turkey)
Ankara, C Turkey
Ankeny *45 F3* Iowa, C USA
Anklam *94 D2* Mecklenburg-
Vorpommern, NE Germany
Anykščiai *106 C4* Anykščiai,
E Lithuania
An Longfort *see* Longford
An Mhuir Cheilteach *see* Celtic Sea
An Nafūd *120 B4 desert* NW Saudi
Arabia
'Annah *120 B3 var.* 'Ānah. NW Iraq
An Najaf *120 B3 var.* Najaf. S Iraq
Annamitique, Chaîne *136 D4*
mountain range C Laos
Annapolis *41 F4 state capital*
Maryland, NE USA
Annapurna *135 E3 mountain*
C Nepal
An Nāqūrah *see* En Nâqoûra
Ann Arbor *40 C3* Michigan, N USA
An Nāşiriyah *120 C3 var.* Nasiriya.
SE Iraq
Annecy *91 D5 anc.* Anneciacum.
Haute-Savoie, E France
An Nîl al Azraq *see* Blue Nile
Anniston *42 D2* Alabama, S USA
Annotto Bay *54 B4* C Jamaica
An Ómaigh *see* Omagh
Anqing *128 D5* Anhui, E China
Anse La Raye *55 F1* NW Saint
Lucia
Anshun *128 B6* Guizhou, S China
Ansongo *75 E3* Gao, E Mali
An Srath Bán *see* Strabane
Antakya *116 D4 anc.* Antioch,
Antiochia. Hatay, S Turkey

Australia (continued)

Ethnic mix European 95%, Asian 4%, Aboriginal and other 1%
Government Parliamentary democracy
Currency Australian dollar = 100 cents
Literacy rate 99%
Calorie consumption 3,176 kilocalories

Australian Alps 149 C7 *mountain range* SE Australia
Australian Capital Territory 149 D7 *prev.* Federal Capital Territory. *Territory* SE Australia
Austral Islands *see* Australes, Îles
Austria 95 D7 *Ger.* Österreich. *Country* C Europe

Austria 95

Official name Republic of Austria
Formation 1918
Capital Vienna
Population 8.1 million / 250 people per sq mile (97 people per sq km)
Total area 32,378 sq miles (83,858 sq km)
Languages German, Croatian, Slovenian
Religions Roman Catholic 78%, non-religious 9%, Protestant 5%, other (including Muslim and Jewish) 8%
Ethnic mix German 93%, Croat, Slovene, Hungarian 6%, other 1%
Government Parliamentary democracy
Currency Euro (Austrian schilling until 2002)
Literacy rate 99%
Calorie consumption 3,757 kilocalories

Auvergne 91 C5 *cultural region* C France
Auxerre 90 C4 *anc.* Autesiodorum, Autissiodorum. Yonne, C France
Avarua 145 G5 *dependent territory capital* (Cook Islands) Rarotonga, S Cook Islands
Ávdira 104 C3 Anatolikí Makedonía kai Thráki, NE Greece
Aveiro 92 B2 *anc.* Talabriga. Aveiro, W Portugal
Avela *see* Ávila
Avellino 97 D5 *anc.* Abellinum. Campania, S Italy
Avesta 85 C6 Kopparberg, C Sweden
Aveyron 91 C6 *river* S France
Avezzano 96 C4 Abruzzo, C Italy
Aviemore 88 C3 N Scotland, UK
Avignon 91 D6 *anc.* Avenio. Vaucluse, SE France
Avila *see* Ávila
Ávila 92 D3 *var.* Avila; *anc.* Abela, Abula, Abyla, Avela. Castilla-León, C Spain
Avilés 92 C1 Asturias, NW Spain
Avranches 90 B3 Manche, N France
Awaji-shima 131 C6 *island* , SW Japan
Āwash 73 D5 *var.* Hawash. *River* C Ethiopia
Awbārī 71 F3 SW Libya
Ax *see* Dax
Axel 87 B5 Zeeland, SW Netherlands
Axel Heiberg Island 37 E1 *var.* Axel Heiburg. *Island* Nunavut, N Canada
Axel Heiburg *see* Axel Heiberg Island
Ayacucho 60 D4 Ayacucho, S Peru
Ayagoz 130 D4 *var.* Ayaguz, *Kaz.* Ayaköz; *prev.* Sergiopol. Vostochnyy Kazakhstan, E Kazakhstan
Ayaguz *see* Ayagoz
Ayaköz *see* Ayagoz
Ayamonte 92 C4 Andalucía, S Spain

Ayaviri 61 E4 Puno, S Peru
Aydarkül 123 E2 *Rus.* Ozero Aydarkul'. *Lake* C Uzbekistan
Aydın 116 A4 *var.* Aidin; *anc.* Tralles. Aydın, SW Turkey
Ayers Rock *see* Uluru
Ayeyarwady *see* Irrawaddy
Ayiá *see* Agiá
Áyios Evstrátios *see* Efstrátios, Ágios
Áyios Nikólaos *see* Ágios Nikólaos
Ayorou 75 E3 Tillabéri, W Niger
'Ayoûn el 'Atroûs 74 D3 *var.* Aïoun el Atrous, Aïoun el Atroûss. Hodh el Gharbi, SE Mauritania
Ayr 88 C4 W Scotland, UK
Ayteke Bi 130 B4 . *Kaz.* Zhangaqazaly, *prev.* Novokazalinsk Kyzylorda, SW Kazakhstan
Aytos 104 E2 Burgas, E Bulgaria
Ayutthaya 137 C5 *var.* Phra Nakhon Si Ayutthaya. Phra Nakhon Si Ayutthaya, C Thailand
Ayvalık 116 A3 Balıkesir, W Turkey
Azahar, Costa del 93 F3 *coastal region* E Spain
Azaouâd 75 E3 *desert* C Mali
A'zāz 118 B2 Ḥalab, NW Syria
Azerbaijan 117 G2 *Az.* Azärbaycan, Azärbaycan Respublikasi; *prev.* Azerbaijan SSR. *Country* SE Asia

Azerbaijan 117

Official name Republic of Azerbaijan
Formation 1991
Capital Baku
Population 8.1 million / 242 people per sq mile (94 people per sq km)
Total area 33,436 sq miles (86,600 sq km)
Languages Azeri, Russian
Religions Shi'a ithna Muslims 61%, Sunni Muslims 26%, Armenian and Russian Orthodox 11%, other 2%
Ethnic mix Azeri 90%, Russian 3%, Daghestani 3%, Armenian 2%, other 2%
Government Multiparty republic
Currency Manat = 100 gopik
Literacy rate 96%
Calorie consumption 2,468 kilocalories

Azimabad *see* Patna
Azogues 60 B2 Cañar, S Ecuador
Azores 92 A4 *var.* Açores, Ilhas dos Açores, *Port.* Arquipélago dos Açores. *Island group* Portugal, NE Atlantic Ocean
Azores-Biscay Rise 80 A3 *undersea feature* E Atlantic Ocean
Azoum, Bahr 76 C3 *seasonal river* SE Chad
Azov, Sea of 103 H1 *Rus.* Azovskoye More, *Ukr.* Azovs'ke More. *Sea* NE Black Sea
Azraq, Wāḩat al 135 C6 *oasis* N Jordan
Aztec 48 C1 New Mexico, SW USA
Azuaga 92 C4 Extremadura, W Spain
Azuero, Península de 53 F5 *peninsula* S Panama
Azul 65 D5 Buenos Aires, E Argentina
Azur, Côte d' 107 E6 *Coastal region* SE France
Az Zaqāzīq *see* Zagazig
Az Zarqā' 119 B6 *var.* Zarqa. Az Zarqā', NW Jordan
Az Zāwiyah 71 F2 *var.* Zawia. NW Libya
Az Zilfī 120 B4 Ar Riyāḍ, N Saudi Arabia
Æsernia *see* Isernia

B

Ba 100 D3 *prev.* Mba. Viti Levu, W Fiji
Baalbek 118 B4 *var.* Ba'labakk; *anc.* Heliopolis. E Lebanon
Bá an Daingin *see* Dingle Bay

Baardheere 73 D6 *var.* Bardere, *It.* Bardera. Gedo, SW Somalia
Baarle-Hertog 87 C5 Antwerpen, N Belgium
Baarn 86 C3 Utrecht, C Netherlands
Babadag 108 D5 Tulcea, SE Romania
Babahoyo 60 B2 *prev.* Bodegas. Los Ríos, C Ecuador
Bābā, Kūh-e 123 E4 *mountain range* C Afghanistan
Babayevo 110 B4 Vologodskaya Oblast', NW Russian Federation
Babeldaob 144 A1 *var.* Babeldaop, Babelthuap. *Island* N Palau
Babeldaop *see* Babeldaob
Bab el Mandeb 121 B7 *strait* Gulf of Aden/Red Sea
Babelthuap *see* Babeldaob
Bá Bheanntraí *see* Bantry Bay
Babruysk 107 D7 *Rus.* Bobruysk. Mahilyowskaya Voblasts', E Belarus
Babuyan Channel 139 E1 *channel* N Philippines
Babuyan Island 139 E1 *island* N Philippines
Bacabal 63 F2 Maranhão, E Brazil
Bacău 108 C4 *Hung.* Bákó. Bacău, NE Romania
Bắc Giang 136 D3 Ha Bắc, N Vietnam
Bacheykava 107 D5 *Rus.* Bocheykovo. Vitsyebskaya Voblasts', N Belarus
Back 37 F3 *river* Nunavut, N Canada
Bačka Palanka 100 D3 *prev.* Palanka. Serbia, NW Serbia and Montenegro (Yugo.)
Bačka Topola 100 D3 *Hung.* Topolya; *prev. Hung.* Bácstopolya. Serbia, N Serbia and Montenegro (Yugo.)
Bạc Liêu 137 D6 *var.* Vinh Loi. Minh Hai, S Vietnam
Bacolod 125 E4 *off.* Bacolod City. Negros, C Philippines
Bacolod City *see* Bacolod
Bácsszenttamás *see* Srbobran
Badajoz 92 C4 *anc.* Pax Augusta. Extremadura, W Spain
Baden-Baden 95 B6 *anc.* Aurelia Aquensis. Baden-Württemberg, SW Germany
Bad Freienwalde 94 D3 Brandenburg, E Germany
Bad Hersfeld 94 B4 Hessen, C Germany
Bad Homburg *see* Bad Homburg vor der Höhe
Bad Homburg vor der Höhe 95 B5 *var.* Bad Homburg. Hessen, W Germany
Bá Dhún na nGall *see* Donegal Bay
Bad Ischl 95 D7 Oberösterreich, N Austria
Bad Krozingen 95 A6 Baden-Württemberg, SW Germany
Badlands 44 D2 *physical region* North Dakota, N USA
Badu Island 148 C1 *island* Queensland, NE Australia
Bad Vöslau 95 E6 Niederösterreich, NE Austria
Baetic Cordillera *see* Béticos, Sistemas
Baetic Mountains *see* Béticos, Sistemas
Bafatá 74 C4 C Guinea-Bissau
Baffin Bay 37 G2 *bay* Canada/Greenland
Baffin Island 37 G2 *island* Nunavut, NE Canada
Bafing 74 C3 *river* W Africa
Bafoussam 76 A4 Ouest, W Cameroon
Bafra 116 D2 Samsun, N Turkey
Bāft 120 D4 Kermān, S Iran
Bagaces 52 D4 Guanacaste, NW Costa Rica
Bagdad *see* Baghdād
Bagé 63 E5 Rio Grande do Sul, S Brazil
Baghdād 120 B3 *var.* Bagdad, *Eng.* Baghdad. *Country capital* (Iraq) C Iraq

Baghlān 123 E3 Baghlān, NE Afghanistan
Bago *see* Pegu
Bagoé 74 D4 *river* Côte d'Ivoire/Mali
Bagrationovsk 106 A4 *Ger.* Preussisch Eylau. Kaliningradskaya Oblast', W Russian Federation
Bagrax Hu *see* Bosten Hu
Baguio 139 E1 *off.* Baguio City. Luzon, N Philippines
Bagzane, Monts 75 F3 *mountain* N Niger
Bahama Islands *see* Bahamas

Bahamas 54

Official name Commonwealth of the Bahamas
Formation 1973
Capital Nassau
Population 308,000 / 57 people per sq mile (22 people per sq km)
Total area 5,382 sq miles (13,940 sq km)
Languages English, English Creole, French Creole
Religions Baptist 32%, Anglican 20%, Roman Catholic 19%, Church of God 6%, Methodist 6%, other 17%
Ethnic mix Black African 85%, Other 15%
Government Parliamentary democracy
Currency Bahamian dollar = 100 cents
Literacy rate 95.7%
Calorie consumption 2,443 kilocalories

Bahamas 54 C2 *Country* N West Indies
Bahamas 35 D6 *var.* Bahama Islands. *Island group* N West Indies
Bahāwalpur 134 C2 Punjab, E Pakistan
Bahía 63 F3 *off.* Estado da Bahia. *State* E Brazil
Bahía Blanca 65 C5 Buenos Aires, E Argentina
Bahía, Islas de la 52 C1 *Eng.* Bay Islands. *Island group* N Honduras
Bahir Dar 72 C4 *var.* Bahr Dar, Bahrdar Giyorgis. NW Ethiopia
Bahraich 135 E3 Uttar Pradesh, N India

Bahrain 120

Official name State of Bahrain
Formation 1971
Capital Manama
Population 652,000 / 2,724 people per sq mile (1,052 people per sq km)
Total area 239 sq miles (620 sq km)
Languages Arabic
Religions Muslim (mainly Shi'a) 99%, other 1%
Ethnic mix Bahraini 70%, Iranian, Indian, Pakistani 24%, other Arab 4%, European 2%
Government Constitutional monarchy
Currency Bahraini dinar = 1,000 fils
Literacy rate 87.6%
Calorie consumption not available

Bahrain 120 C4 *Ar.* Al Baḩrayn; *prev.* Bahrein, *anc.* Tylos or Tyros. *Country* SW Asia
Baḩr al Milḩ *see* Razāzah, Buḩayrat ar
Baḩrat Lūt *see* Dead Sea
Bahrat Tabariya *see* Tiberias, Lake
Bahr Dar *see* Bahir Dar
Bahrdar Giyorgis *see* Bahir Dar
Bahr el Azraq *see* Blue Nile
Bahr el Jebel *see* White Nile
Bahret Lut *see* Dead Sea
Bahr Tabariya, Sea of *see* Tiberias, Lake

Bahushewsk 107 E6 *Rus.*
Bogushévsk. Vitsyebskaya
Voblasts', NE Belarus
Baia Mare 108 B3 *Ger.* Frauenbach,
Hung. Nagybánya; *prev.* Neustadt.
Maramureş, NW Romania
Baia Sprie 108 B3 *Ger.* Mittelstadt,
Hung. Felsőbánya. Maramureş,
NW Romania
Baïbokoum 76 B4 Logone-Oriental,
SW Chad
Baidoa *see* Baydhabo
Baie-Comeau 39 E3 Quebec,
SE Canada
Baikal, Lake *see* Baykal, Ozero
Baile Átha Luain *see* Athlone
Bailén 92 D4 Andalucía, S Spain
Baile na Mainistreach *see*
Newtownabbey
Băileşti 108 B5 Dolj, SW Romania
Ba Illi 76 B3 Chari-Baguirmi,
SW Chad
Bainbridge 42 D3 Georgia, SE USA
Bă'ir *see* Bāyir
Baireuth *see* Bayreuth
Bairiki 144 D2 *country capital*
(Kiribati) Tarawa, NW Kiribati
Bairnsdale 149 C7 Victoria,
SE Australia
Baishan 129 E3 *prev.* Hunjiang. Jilin,
NE China
Baiyin 128 B4 Gansu, C China
Baja 99 C7 Bács-Kiskun, S Hungary
Baja California 48 A4 *Eng.* Lower
California. *Peninsula* NW Mexico
Baja California 50 B2 *state*
NW Mexico
Bajo Boquete *see* Boquete
Bajram Curri 101 D5 Kukës,
N Albania
Bakala 76 C4 Ouaka, C Central
African Republic
Bakan *see* Shimonoseki
Baker 46 C3 Oregon, NW USA
Baker and Howland Islands 145 E2
US unincorporated territory
W Polynesia
Baker Lake 37 F3 Nunavut,
N Canada
Bakersfield 47 C7 California, W USA
Bakharden 122 C3 *Turkm.* Bäherden;
prev. Bakherden. Akhalskiy
Velayat, C Turkmenistan
Bakhchysaray 109 F5 *Rus.*
Bakhchisaray. Respublika Krym,
S Ukraine
Bakhmach 109 F1 Chernihivs'ka
Oblast', N Ukraine
Bäkhtarän 120 C3 *prev.*
Kermānshāh, Qahremānshahr.
Kermānshāh. W Iran
Bakı 117 H2 *Eng.* Baku. *Country
capital* (Azerbaijan) E Azerbaijan
Bakony 99 C7 *Eng.* Bakony
Mountains, *Ger.* Bakonywald.
Mountain range W Hungary
Baku *see* Bakı
Balabac Island 129 C8 *island*
W Philippines
Balabac Strait 138 D2 *var.* Selat
Balabac. *Strait*
Malaysia/Philippines
Ba'labakk *see* Baalbek
Balaguer 93 F2 Cataluña,
NE Spain
Balakovo 111 C6 Saratovskaya
Oblast', W Russian Federation
Bālā Morghāb 122 D4 Laghmān,
NW Afghanistan
Balashov 111 B6 Saratovskaya
Oblast', W Russian Federation
Balaton C7 *var.* Lake Balaton, *Ger.*
Plattensee. *Lake* W Hungary
Balaton, Lake *see* Balaton
Balbina, Represa 62 D1 *reservoir*
NW Brazil
Balboa 53 G4 Panamá, C Panama
Balcarce 65 D5 Buenos Aires,
E Argentina
Balclutha 151 B7 Otago, South
Island, NZ
Baldy Mountain 44 C1 *mountain*
Montana, NW USA
Bâle *see* Basel
Baleares, Islas 93 G3 *Eng.* Balearic
Islands. *Island group* Spain,
W Mediterranean Sea

Balearic Islands *see* Baleares, Islas
Balearic Plain *see* Algerian Basin
Baleine, Rivière à la 39 E2 *river*
Quebec, E Canada
Balen 87 C5 Antwerpen, N Belgium
Bāleshwar 135 F4 *prev.* Balasore.
Orissa, E India
Bali 138 D5 *island* C Indonesia
Balıkesir 116 A3 Balıkesir,
W Turkey
Balīkh, Nahr 118 C2 *river* N Syria
Balikpapan 138 D4 Borneo,
C Indonesia
Balkan Mountains 104 C2
Bul./Scr. Stara Planina. *Mountain
range* Bulgaria/Serbia and
Montenegro (Yugo.)
Balkh 123 E3 *anc.* Bactra. Balkh,
N Afghanistan
Balkhash 114 C5 *Kaz.* Balqash.
Karaganda, SE Kazakhstan
Balkhash, Lake *see* Balkhash,
Ozero
Balkhash, Ozero 114 C5 *Eng.* Lake
Balkhash, *Kaz.* Balqash. *Lake*
SE Kazakhstan
Balladonia 147 C6 Western
Australia
Ballarat 149 C7 Victoria,
SE Australia
Balleny Islands 154 B5 *island group*
Antarctica
Ballinger 49 F3 Texas, SW USA
Balochistān *see* Baluchistān
Balş 108 B5 Olt, S Romania
Balsas 63 F2 Maranhão, E Brazil
Balsas, Río 51 E5 *var.* Río Mexcala.
River S Mexico
Bal'shavik 107 D7 *Rus.* Bol'shevik.
Homyel'skaya Voblasts',
SE Belarus
Balta 108 D3 Odes'ka Oblast',
SW Ukraine
Bălţi 108 D3 *Rus.* Bel'tsy.
N Moldova
Baltic Sea 85 C7 *Ger.* Ostee, *Rus.*
Baltiskoye More. *Sea* N Europe
Baltimore 41 F4 Maryland, NE USA
Baltkrievija *see* Belarus
Baluchistān 134 B3 *var.* Balochistān,
Beluchistan. Admin. region
province SW Pakistan
Balvi 106 D4 Balvi, NE Latvia
Balykchy 123 G2 *Kir.* Ysyk-Köl;
prev. Issyk-Kul', Rybach'ye. Issyk-
Kul'skaya Oblast', NE Kyrgyzstan
Balzers 94 E2 S Liechtenstein
Bam 120 E4 Kermān, SE Iran
Bamako 74 D4 *country capital* (Mali)
Capital District, SW Mali
Bambari 76 C4 Ouaka, C Central
African Republic
Bamberg 95 C5 Bayern, SE Germany
Bamenda 76 A4 Nord-Ouest,
W Cameroon
Banaba 144 D2 *var.* Ocean Island.
Island Tungaru, W Kiribati
Bandaaceh 138 A3 *var.* Banda
Atjeh; *prev.* Koetaradja,
Kutaradja, Kutaraja. Sumatera,
W Indonesia
Banda Atjeh *see* Bandaaceh
Bandama 74 D5 *var.* Bandama
Fleuve. *River* S Côte d'Ivoire
Bandama Fleuve *see* Bandama
Bandar 'Abbās *see* Bandar-e 'Abbās
Bandarbeyla 73 E5 *var.* Bender
Beila, Bender Beyla. Bari,
NE Somalia
Bandar-e 'Abbās 120 D4 *var.*
Bandar 'Abbās; *prev.* Gombroon.
Hormozgān, S Iran
Bandar-e Büshehr 120 C4 *var.*
Büshehr, *Eng.* Bushire. Büshehr,
S Iran
Bandar-e Khamīr 120 D4
Hormozgān, S Iran
Bandar-e Langeh 120 D4 *var.*
Bandar-e Lengeh, Lingeh.
Hormozgān, S Iran
Bandar-e Lengeh *see* Bandar-e
Langeh
Bandar Kassim *see* Boosaaso
Bandarlampung 138 C4 *prev.*
Tanjungkarang, Teloekbetoeng,
Telukbetung. Sumatera,
W Indonesia

Bandar Maharani *see* Muar
Bandar Masulipatnam *see*
Machilipatnam
Bandar Seri Begawan 138 D3 *prev.*
Brunei Town. *Country capital*
(Brunei) N Brunei
Bandar Sri Aman *see* Sri Aman
Banda Sea 139 F5 *var.* Laut Banda.
Sea E Indonesia
Bandiagara 75 E3 Mopti, C Mali
Bandırma 116 A3 *var.* Penderma.
Balıkesir, NW Turkey
Bandundu 77 C6 *prev.* Banningville.
Bandundu, W Dem. Rep. Congo
Bandung 138 C5 *prev.* Bandoeng.
Jawa, C Indonesia
Bangalore 132 C2 Karnātaka, S India
Bangassou 76 D4 Mbomou,
SE Central African Republic
Banggai, Kepulauan 139 E4 *island
group* C Indonesia
Banghāzī 71 G2 *Eng.* Bengazi,
Benghazi, *It.* Bengasi. NE Libya
Bangka, Pulau 138 C4 *island*
W Indonesia
Bangkok *see* Krung Thep
Bangkok, Bight of *see* Krung Thep,
Ao
Bangladesh 135 G3 *prev.* East
Pakistan. *Country* S Asia

Bangladesh 135

Official name People's Republic of
Bangladesh
Formation 1971
Capital Dhaka
Population 140.4 million /2,525
people per sq mile (975 people per
sq km)
Total area 55,598 sq miles
(144,000 sq km)
Languages Bengali, Urdu, Chakma,
Marma (Magh), Garo, Khasi,
Santhali, Tripuri, Mro
Religions Muslim (mainly Sunni)
87%, Hindu 12%, other 1%
Ethnic mix Bengali 98%, other 2%
Government Parliamentary
democracy
Currency Taka = 100 paisa
Literacy rate 41.4%
Calorie consumption 2,103
kilocalories

Bangor 89 B5 *Ir.* Beannchar.
E Northern Ireland, UK
Bangor 41 G2 Maine, NE USA
Bangor 89 C6 NW Wales, UK
Bangui 77 B5 *country capital*
(Central African Republic)
Ombella-Mpoko, SW Central
African Republic
Bangweulu, Lake 78 D1 *var.* Lake
Bengweulu. *Lake* N Zambia
Ban Hat Yai *see* Hat Yai
Ban Hin Heup 136 C4 Viangchan,
C Laos
Ban Houaxay *see* Houayxay
Ban Houei Sai *see* Houayxay
Ban Hua Hin 137 C6 *var.* Hua Hin.
Prachuap Khiri Khan,
SW Thailand
Bani 74 D3 *river* S Mali
Bāniyās *see* Bāniyās
Banī Suwayf *see* Beni Suef
Bāniyās 118 B3 *var.* Banias, Baniyas,
Paneas. Ṭarṭūs, W Syria
Baniyas *see* Bāniyās
Banja Luka 100 B3 Republika
Srpska, NW Bosnia and
Herzegovina
Banjarmasin 138 D4 *prev.*
Bandjarmasin. Borneo,
C Indonesia
Banjul 74 B3 *prev.* Bathurst. *Country
capital* (Gambia) W Gambia
Banks Island 37 E2 *island* Banks
Island, Northwest Territories,
NW Canada
Banks Islands 144 D4 *Fr.* Îles
Banks. *Island group* N Vanuatu
Banks Lake 46 B1 *reservoir*
Washington, NW USA
Banks Peninsula 151 C6 *peninsula*
South Island, NZ

Banks Strait 149 C8 *strait*
SW Tasman Sea
Bänkura 135 F4 West Bengal,
NE India
Ban Mak Khaeng *see* Udon Thani
Banmo *see* Bhamo
Bañolas *see* Banyoles
Ban Pak Phanang *see* Pak Phanang
Ban Sichon *see* Sichon
Banská Bystrica 99 C6 *Ger.*
Neusohl, *Hung.* Besztercebánya.
Banskobystrický Kraj, C Slovakia
Bantry Bay 89 A7 *Ir.* Bá Bheanntraí.
Bay SW Ireland
Banya 104 E2 Burgas, E Bulgaria
Banyak, Kepulauan 138 A3 *prev.*
Kepulauan Banjak. *Island group*
NW Indonesia
Banyo 76 B4 Adamaoua,
NW Cameroon
Banyoles 93 G2 *var.* Bañolas.
Cataluña, NE Spain
Banzare Seamounts 141 C7 *undersea
feature* S Indian Ocean
Baoji 128 B4 *var.* Pao-chi, Paoki.
Shaanxi, C China
Baoro 76 B4 Nana-Mambéré,
W Central African Republic
Baoshan 128 A6 *var.* Pao-shan.
Yunnan, SW China
Baotou 127 F3 *var.* Pao-t'ou,
Paotow. Nei Mongol Zizhiqu,
N China
Ba'qūbah 120 B3 *var.* Qubba. C Iraq
Baquerizo Moreno *see* Puerto
Baquerizo Moreno
Bar 101 C5 *It.* Antivari.
Montenegro, SW Serbia and
Montenegro (Yugo.)
Baraawe 73 D6 *It.* Brava.
Shabeellaha Hoose, S Somalia
Baraji, Hirfanli 116 C3 *lake*
C Turkey
Bārāmati 134 C5 Mahārāshtra, W India
Baranavichy 107 B6 *Pol.*
Baranowicze, *Rus.* Baranovichi.
Brestskaya Voblasts', SW Belarus
Barbados 55 G1 *country*
SE West Indies

Barbados 55

Official name Barbados
Formation 1966
Capital Bridgetown
Population 268,000 /1,614 people
per sq mile (623 people per sq km)
Total area 166 sq miles (430 sq km)
Languages English, Bajan
(Barbadian English)
Religions Anglican 40%, other 24%,
non-religious 17%, Pentecostal 8%,
Methodist 7%, Roman Catholic 4%
Ethnic mix Black African 90%,
other 10%
Government Parliamentary
democracy
Currency Barbados dollar = 100
cents
Literacy rate 98%
Calorie consumption 3,022
kilocalories

Barbastro 93 F2 Aragón, NE Spain
Barbate de Franco 92 C5 Andalucía,
S Spain
Barbuda 55 G3 *island* N Antigua
and Barbuda
Barcaldine 148 C4 Queensland,
E Australia
Barce *see* Al Marj
Barcelona 93 G2 *anc.* Barcino,
Barcinona. Cataluña, E Spain
Barcelona 59 E2 Anzoátegui,
NE Venezuela
Barcoo *see* Cooper Creek
Barcs 99 C7 Somogy, SW Hungary
Bardaï 76 C1 Borkou-Ennedi-
Tibesti, N Chad
Bardejov 99 D5 *Ger.* Bartfeld,
Hung. Bártfa. Prešovský Kraj,
E Slovakia
Bardera *see* Baardheere
Bardere *see* Baardheere
Bareilly 135 E3 *var.* Bareli. Uttar
Pradesh, N India

Bareli *see* Bareilly
Barendrecht 86 *C4* Zuid-Holland, SW Netherlands
Barentin 90 *C3* Seine-Maritime, N France
Barentsberg 83 *G2* Spitsbergen, W Svalbard
Barentsøya 83 *G2 island* E Svalbard
Barents Sea 110 *C2 Nor.* Barents Havet, *Rus.* Barentsevo More. *Sea* Arctic Ocean
Barents Trough 81 *E1 undersea feature* SW Barents Sea
Bar Harbor 41 *H2* Mount Desert Island, Maine, NE USA
Bari 97 *E5 var.* Bari delle Puglie; *anc.* Barium. Puglia, SE Italy
Bāridah *see* Al Bāridah
Bari delle Puglie *see* Bari
Barikot *see* Barīkowṭ
Barīkowṭ 123 *F4 var.* Barikot. Kunar, NE Afghanistan
Barillas 52 *A2 var.* Santa Cruz Barillas. Huehuetenango, NW Guatemala
Barinas 58 *C2* Barinas, W Venezuela
Barisal 135 *G4* Khulna, S Bangladesh
Barisan, Pegunungan 138 *B4 mountain range* Sumatera, W Indonesia
Barito, Sungai 138 *D4 river* Borneo, C Indonesia
Barium *see* Bari
Barka *see* Al Marj
Barkly Tableland 148 *B3 plateau* Northern Territory/Queensland, N Australia
Bârlad 108 *D4 prev.* Bîrlad. Vaslui, E Romania
Barlavento, Ilhas de 74 *A2 var.* Windward Islands. *Island group* N Cape Verde
Bar-le-Duc 90 *D3 var.* Bar-sur-Ornain. Meuse, NE France
Barlee, Lake 147 *B6 lake* Western Australia
Barlee Range 146 *A4 mountain range* Western Australia
Barletta 97 *D5 anc.* Barduli. Puglia, SE Italy
Barlinek 98 *B3 Ger.* Berlinchen. Zachodniopomorskie, NW Poland
Barmouth 89 *C6* NW Wales, UK
Barnaul 114 *D4* Altayskiy Kray, C Russian Federation
Barnet 89 *F7* SE England, UK
Barnstaple 89 *C7* SW England, UK
Baroghil Pass 123 *F1 var.* Kowtal-e Barowghīl. *Pass* Afghanistan/Pakistan
Baron'ki 107 *E7 Rus.* Boron'ki. Mahilyowskaya Voblasts', E Belarus
Barquisimeto 58 *C2* Lara, NW Venezuela
Barra 88 *B3 island* NW Scotland, UK
Barra de Río Grande 53 *E3* Región Autónoma Atlántico Sur, E Nicaragua
Barragem de Sobradinho *see* Sobradinho, Represa de
Barranca 60 *C3* Lima, W Peru
Barrancabermeja 58 *B2* Santander, N Colombia
Barranquilla 58 *B1* Atlántico, N Colombia
Barreiro 92 *B4* Setúbal, W Portugal
Barrier Range 149 *C6 hill range* New South Wales, SE Australia
Barrow 89 *B6 Ir.* An Bhearú. *River* SE Ireland
Barrow 36 *D2* Alaska, USA
Barrow-in-Furness 89 *C5* NW England, UK
Barrow Island 146 *A4 island* Western Australia
Barstow 47 *C7* California, W USA
Bar-sur-Ornain *see* Bar-le-Duc
Bartang 123 *F3 river* SE Tajikistan
Bartica 59 *F3* N Guyana
Bartın 116 *C2* Bartın NW Turkey
Bartlesville 49 *G1* Oklahoma, C USA
Bartoszyce 98 *D2 Ger.* Bartenstein. Warmińsko-Mazurskie, NE Poland

Baruun-Urt 127 *F2* Sühbaatar, E Mongolia
Barú, Volcán 53 *E5 var.* Volcán de Chiriquí. *Volcano* W Panama
Barwon River 149 *D5 river* New South Wales, SE Australia
Barysaw 107 *D6 Rus.* Borisov. Minskaya Voblasts', NE Belarus
Basarabeasca 108 *D4 Rus.* Bessarabka. SE Moldova
Basel 95 *A7 Eng.* Basle, *Fr.* Bâle. Basel-Stadt, NW Switzerland
Basilan 139 *E3 island* SW Philippines
Basle *see* Basel
Basra *see* Al Baṣrah
Bassano del Grappa 96 *C2* Veneto, NE Italy
Bassein 136 *A4 var.* Pathein. Irrawaddy, SW Myanmar
Basse-Terre 55 *G4 dependent territory capital* (Guadeloupe) Basse Terre, SW Guadeloupe
Basse Terre 55 *G4 island* W Guadeloupe
Basseterre 55 *G3 country capital* (Saint Kitts and Nevis) Saint Kitts, Saint Kitts and Nevis
Bassikounou 74 *D3* Hodh ech Chargui, SE Mauritania
Bass Strait 149 *C7 strait* SE Australia
Bassum 94 *B3* Niedersachsen, NW Germany
Bastia 91 *E7* Corse, France, C Mediterranean Sea
Bastogne 87 *D7* Luxembourg, SE Belgium
Bastrop 42 *B2* Louisiana, S USA
Bastyn' 107 *B7 Rus.* Bostyn'. Brestskaya Voblasts', SW Belarus
Basuo *see* Dongfang
Bata 77 *A5* NW Equatorial Guinea
Batabanó, Golfo de 54 *A2 gulf* W Cuba
Batajnica 100 *D3* Serbia, N Serbia and Montenegro (Yugo.)
Batangas 139 *E2 off.* Batangas City. Luzon, N Philippines
Bătdâmbâng 137 *C5 prev.* Battambang. Bătdâmbâng, NW Cambodia
Batéké, Plateaux 77 *B6 plateau* S Congo
Bath 89 *D7 hist.* Akermanceaster, *anc.* Aquae Calidae, Aquae Solis. SW England, UK
Bathinda 134 *D2* Punjab, NW India
Bathsheba 55 *G1* E Barbados
Bathurst 39 *F4* New Brunswick, SE Canada
Bathurst 149 *D6* New South Wales, SE Australia
Bathurst Island 146 *D2 island* Northern Territory, N Australia
Bathurst Island 37 *F2 island* Parry Islands, Nunavut, N Canada
Bāṭin, Wādī al 124 *C4 dry watercourse* SW Asia
Batman 117 *E4 var.* Iluh. Batman, SE Turkey
Batna 71 *E2* NE Algeria
Baton Rouge 42 *B3 state capital* Louisiana, S USA
Batroûn 118 *A4 var.* Al Batrūn. N Lebanon
Batticaloa 132 *D3* Eastern Province, E Sri Lanka
Battipaglia 97 *D5* Campania, S Italy
Bat'umi 117 *F2* W Georgia
Batu Pahat 138 *B3 prev.* Bandar Penggaram. Johor, Peninsular Malaysia
Bauchi 75 *G4* Bauchi, NE Nigeria
Bauer Basin 153 *F3 undersea feature* E Pacific Ocean
Bauska 106 *C3 Ger.* Bauske. Bauska, S Latvia
Bautzen 94 *D4 Lus.* Budyšin. Sachsen, E Germany
Bavarian Alps 95 *C7 Ger.* Bayrische Alpen. *Mountain range* Austria/Germany
Bavispe, Río 50 *C2 river* NW Mexico
Bawîtî 72 *B2* N Egypt
Bawku 75 *E4* N Ghana

Bayamo 54 *C3* Granma, E Cuba
Bayan Har Shan 126 *D4 var.* Bayan Khar. *Mountain range* C China
Bayanhongor 126 *D2* Bayanhongor, C Mongolia
Bayan Khar *see* Bayan Har Shan
Bayano, Lago 53 *G4 lake* E Panama
Bay City 40 *C3* Michigan, N USA
Bay City 49 *G4* Texas, SW USA
Baydhabo 73 *D6 var.* Baydhowa, Isha Baydhabo, *It.* Baidoa. Bay, SW Somalia
Baydhowa *see* Baydhabo
Bayern 95 *C6 cultural region* SE Germany
Bayeux 90 *B3 anc.* Augustodurum. Calvados, N France
Bāyir 119 *C7 var.* Bā'ir. Ma'ān, S Jordan
Baykal, Ozero 115 *E4 Eng.* Lake Baikal. *Lake* S Russian Federation
Baymak 111 *D6* Respublika Bashkortostan, W Russian Federation
Bayonne 91 *A6 anc.* Lapurdum. Pyrénées-Atlantiques, SW France
Bayramaly 122 *D3 prev.* Bayram-Ali. Maryyskiy Velayat, S Turkmenistan
Bayreuth 95 *C5 var.* Baireuth. Bayern, SE Germany
Bayrūt *see* Beyrouth
Baytown 49 *H4* Texas, SW USA
Baza 93 *E4* Andalucía, S Spain
Beagle Channel 65 *C8 channel* Argentina/Chile
Béal Feirste *see* Belfast
Beannchar *see* Bangor
Bear Lake 46 *E4 lake* Idaho/Utah, NW USA
Beas de Segura 93 *E4* Andalucía, S Spain
Beata, Isla 55 *E3 island* SW Dominican Republic
Beatrice 45 *F4* Nebraska, C USA
Beaufort Sea 36 *D2 sea* Arctic Ocean
Beaufort West 78 *C5 Afr.* Beaufort-Wes. Western Cape, SW South Africa
Beaumont 49 *H3* Texas, SW USA
Beaune 90 *D4* Côte d'Or, C France
Beauvais 90 *C3 anc.* Bellovacum, Caesaromagus. Oise, N France
Beaver Island 40 *C2 island* Michigan, N USA
Beaver Lake 49 *H1 reservoir* Arkansas, C USA
Beaver River 49 *F1 river* Oklahoma, C USA
Beāwar 134 *C3* Rājasthān, N India
Bečej 100 *D3 Ger.* Altbetsche, *Hung.* Óbecse, Rácz-Becse; *prev.* Magyar-Becse, Stari Bečej. Serbia, N Serbia and Montenegro (Yugo.)
Béchar 70 *D2 prev.* Colomb-Béchar. W Algeria
Beckley 40 *D5* West Virginia, NE USA
Bedford 89 *D6* E England, UK
Bedum 86 *E1* Groningen, NE Netherlands
Be'ér Menuḥa 119 *B7 var.* Be'er Menukha. Southern, S Israel
Be'er Menukha *see* Be'ér Menuḥa
Beernem 87 *A5* West-Vlaanderen, NW Belgium
Beersheba *see* Be'ér Sheva'
Be'ér Sheva' 119 *A7 var.* Beersheba, *Ar.* Bir es Saba. Southern, S Israel
Beesel 87 *D5* Limburg, SE Netherlands
Beeville 49 *G4* Texas, SW USA
Bega 149 *D7* New South Wales, SE Australia
Beida *see* Al Bayḍā'
Beihai 128 *B6* Guangxi Zhuangzu Zizhiqu, S China
Beijing 128 *C3 var.* Pei-ching, *Eng.* Peking; *prev.* Pei-p'ing. *Country/municipality capital* (China) Beijing Shi, E China
Beilen 86 *E2* Drenthe, NE Netherlands
Beira 79 *E3* Sofala, C Mozambique
Beirut *see* Beyrouth
Beit Leḥm *see* Bethlehem

Beiuş 108 *B3 Hung.* Belényes. Bihor, NW Romania
Beja 92 *B4 anc.* Pax Julia. Beja, SE Portugal
Béjar 92 *C3* Castilla-León, N Spain
Bejraburi *see* Phetchaburi
Békéscsaba 99 *D7 Rom.* Bichiş-Ciaba. Békés, SE Hungary
Bekobod 123 *E2 Rus.* Bekabad; *prev.* Begovat. Toshkent Wiloyati, E Uzbekistan
Bela Crkva 100 *E3 Ger.* Weisskirchen, *Hung.* Fehértemplom. Serbia, W Serbia and Montenegro (Yugo.)
Belarus 107 *B6 var.* Belorussia, *Latv.* Baltkrievija; *prev.* Belorussian SSR, *Rus.* Belorusskaya SSR. *Country* E Europe

---

Belarus 107

Official name	Republic of Belarus
Formation	1991
Capital	Minsk
Population	10.1 million / 126 people per sq mile (49 people per sq km)
Total area	80,154 sq miles (207,600 sq km)
Languages	Belorussian, Russian
Religions	Russian Orthodox 60%, other (including Muslim, Jews and Protestant) 32% Roman Catholic 8%
Ethnic mix	Belorussian 78%, Russian 13%, Polish 4%, Ukrainian 3%, other 2%
Government	Presidential regime
Currency	Belorussian rouble = 100 kopeks
Literacy rate	99%
Calorie consumption	2,902 kilocalories

Belau *see* Palau
Belchatow *see* Bełchatów
Bełchatów 98 *C4 var.* Belchatow. Łódzkie, C Poland
Belcher Islands 38 *C2 Fr.* Îles Belcher. *Island group* Northwest Territories, SE Canada
Beledweyne 73 *D5 var.* Belet Huen, *It.* Belet Uen. Hiiraan, C Somalia
Belém 63 *F1 var.* Pará. *State capital* Pará, N Brazil
Belen 48 *D2* New Mexico, SW USA
Belén 52 *D4* Rivas, SW Nicaragua
Belet Huen *see* Beledweyne
Belet Uen *see* Beledweyne
Belfast 89 *B5 Ir.* Béal Feirste. *Admin capital* E Northern Ireland, UK
Belfield 44 *D2* North Dakota, N USA
Belfort 90 *E4* Territoire-de-Belfort, E France
Belgaum 132 *B1* Karnātaka, W India
Belgium 87 *B6 Dut.* België, *Fr.* Belgique. *Country* NW Europe

---

Belgium 87

Official name	Kingdom of Belgium
Formation	1830
Capital	Brussels
Population	10.1 million / 874 people per sq mile (338 people per sq km)
Total area	11,780 sq miles 30,510 sq km)
Languages	Dutch, French, German
Religions	Roman Catholic 88%, Muslim 2%, other 10%
Ethnic mix	Fleming 58%, Walloon 33%, Italian 2%, Moroccan 1%, other 6%
Government	Parliamentary democracy
Currency	Euro (Belgian franc until 2002)
Literacy rate	99%
Calorie consumption	3,701 kilocalories

Belgorod 111 *A6* Belgorodskaya Oblast', W Russian Federation

Belgrade *see* Beograd
Belgrano II 154 A2 *Argentinian research station* Antarctica
Belice *see* Belize City
Beligrad *see* Berat
Beli Manastir 100 C3 *Hung.* Pélmonostor; *prev.* Monostor. Osijek-Baranja, NE Croatia
Bélinga 77 B5 Ogooué-Ivindo, NE Gabon
Belitung, Pulau 138 C4 *island* W Indonesia
Belize 52 B1 *Sp.* Belice; *prev.* British Honduras, Colony of Belize. *Country* Central America

Belize 52

Official name Belize
Formation 1981
Capital Belmopan
Population 200,000 /23 people per sq mile (9 people per sq km)
Total area 8,867 sq miles (22,966 sq km)
Languages English, English Creole, Spanish, Mayan, Garifuna (Carib)
Religions Roman Catholic 62%, Anglican 12%, Mennonite 4%, Methodist 6%, other 16%
Ethnic mix Mestizo 44%, Creole 30%, Maya 11%, Garifuna 7%, Asian Indian 4%, other 4%
Government Parliamentary democracy
Currency Belizean dollar = 100 cents
Literacy rate 93.2%
Calorie consumption 2,888 kilocalories

Belize 52 B1 *river* Belize/Guatemala
Belize *see* Belize City
Belize City 52 C1 *var.* Belize, *Sp.* Belice. Belize, NE Belize
Belkofski 36 B3 Alaska, USA
Belle Île 90 A4 *island* NW France
Belle Isle, Strait of 39 G3 *strait* Newfoundland and Labrador, E Canada
Belleville 40 B4 Illinois, N USA
Bellevue 45 F4 Iowa, C USA
Bellevue 46 B2 Washington, NW USA
Bellingham 46 B1 Washington, NW USA
Belling Hausen Mulde *see* Southeast Pacific Basin
Bellingshausen Abyssal Plain *see* Bellingshausen Plain
Bellingshausen Plain 153 F5 *var.* Bellingshausen Abyssal Plain. *Undersea feature* SE Pacific Ocean
Bellingshausen Sea 154 A3 *sea* Antarctica
Bellinzona 95 B8 *Ger.* Bellenz. Ticino, S Switzerland
Bello 58 B2 Antioquia, W Colombia
Bellville 78 B5 Western Cape, SW South Africa
Belmopan 52 C1 *country capital* (Belize) Cayo, C Belize
Belogradchik 104 B1 Vidin, NW Bulgaria
Belo Horizonte 63 F4 *prev.* Bello Horizonte. *State capital* Minas Gerais, SE Brazil
Belomorsk 110 B3 Respublika Kareliya, NW Russian Federation
Beloretsk 111 D6 Respublika Bashkortostan, W Russian Federation
Belorussia/Belorussian SSR *see* Belarus
Belorusskaya SSR *see* Belarus
Beloye More 110 C3 *Eng.* White Sea. *Sea* NW Russian Federation
Belozersk 110 B4 Vologodskaya Oblast', NW Russian Federation
Belton 49 G3 Texas, SW USA
Beluchistan *see* Baluchistān
Belukha, Gora 114 D5 *mountain* Kazakhstan/Russian Federation
Belyy, Ostrov 114 D2 *island* N Russian Federation

Bemaraha 79 F3 *var.* Plateau du Bemaraha. *Mountain range* W Madagascar
Bemidji 45 F1 Minnesota, N USA
Bemmel 86 D4 Gelderland, SE Netherlands
Benaco *see* Garda, Lago di
Benavente 92 D2 Castilla-León, N Spain
Bend 46 B3 Oregon, NW USA
Bender Beila *see* Bandarbeyla
Bender Beyla *see* Bandarbeyla
Bender Cassim *see* Boosaaso
Bendern 94 E1 NW Liechtenstein
Bender Qaasim *see* Boosaaso
Bendigo 149 C7 Victoria, SE Australia
Benešov 99 B5 *Ger.* Beneschau. Středočeský Kraj, W Czech Republic
Benevento 97 D5 *anc.* Beneventum, Malventum. Campania, S Italy
Bengal, Bay of 124 C4 *bay* N Indian Ocean
Bengbu 128 D5 *var.* Peng-pu. Anhui, E China
Benghazi *see* Banghāzī
Bengkulu 138 B4 *prev.* Bengkoeloe, Benkoelen, Benkulen. Sumatera, W Indonesia
Benguela 78 A2 *var.* Benguella. W Angola
Benguella *see* Benguela
Bengweulu, Lake *see* Bangweulu, Lake
Ben Hope 88 B2 *mountain* N Scotland, UK
Beni 56 B4 *var.* El Beni. Admin. region *department* N Bolivia
Beni 77 E5 Nord Kivu, NE Dem. Rep. Congo
Benidorm 93 F4 País Valenciano, SE Spain
Beni-Mellal 70 C2 C Morocco
Benin 75 F4 *prev.* Dahomey. *Country* W Africa

Benin 75

Official name Republic of Benin
Formation 1960
Capital Porto-Novo
Population 6.4 million / 147 people per sq mile (57 people per sq km)
Total area 43,483 sq miles (112,620 sq km)
Languages French, Fon, Bariba, Yoruba, Adja, Houeda, Somba
Religions Indigenous beliefs 70%, Muslim 15%, Christian 15%
Ethnic mix Fon 47%, Baraba 10%, Adja 12%, other 31%
Government Presidential democracy
Currency CFA franc = 100 centimes
Literacy rate 40.3%
Calorie consumption 2,558 kilocalories

Benin, Bight of 75 F5 *gulf* W Africa
Benin City 75 F5 Edo, SW Nigeria
Beni, Río 61 F3 *river* N Bolivia
Beni Suef 72 B2 *var.* Banī Suwayf. N Egypt
Ben Nevis 88 C3 *mountain* N Scotland, UK
Benson 48 B3 Arizona, SW USA
Bent Jbaïl 119 A5 *var.* Bint Jubayl. S Lebanon
Benton 42 B1 Arkansas, C USA
Benue 76 B4 *Fr.* Bénoué. *River* Cameroon/Nigeria
Benue 75 G4 *state* SE Nigeria
Beograd 100 D3 *Eng.* Belgrade, *Ger.* Belgrad; *anc.* Singidunum. *Country capital* Serbia, N Serbia and Montenegro (Yugo.)
Berane 101 D5 *prev.* Ivangrad. Montenegro, SW Serbia and Montenegro (Yugo.)
Berat 101 C6 *var.* Berati, *SCr.* Beligrad. Berat, C Albania
Berati *see* Berat
Berau, Teluk 139 G4 *var.* MacCluer Gulf. *Bay* Papua, E Indonesia
Berbera 72 C4 Woqooyi Galbeed, NW Somalia

Berbérati 77 B5 Mambéré-Kadéï, SW Central African Republic
Berck-Plage 90 C2 Pas-de-Calais, N France
Berdyans'k 109 G4 *Rus.* Berdyansk; *prev.* Osipenko. Zaporiz'ka Oblast', SE Ukraine
Berdychiv 108 D2 *Rus.* Berdichev. Zhytomyrs'ka Oblast', N Ukraine
Berehove 108 B3 Cz. Berehovo, *Hung.* Beregszász, *Rus.* Beregovo. Zakarpats'ka Oblast', W Ukraine
Berettyó 99 D7 *Rom.* Barcău; *prev.* Berătău, Beretău. *River* Hungary/Romania
Berettyóújfalu 99 D6 Hajdú-Bihar, E Hungary
Berezhany 108 C2 *Pol.* Brzeżany. Ternopil's'ka Oblast', W Ukraine
Berezniki 111 D5 Permskaya Oblast', NW Russian Federation
Berga 93 G2 Cataluña, NE Spain
Bergamo 96 B2 *anc.* Bergomum. Lombardia, N Italy
Bergara 93 E1 País Vasco, N Spain
Bergen 85 A5 Hordaland, S Norway
Bergen 94 D2 Mecklenburg-Vorpommern, NE Germany
Bergen 86 C2 Noord-Holland, NW Netherlands
Bergerac 91 B5 Dordogne, SW France
Bergeyk 87 C5 Noord-Brabant, S Netherlands
Bergse Maas 86 D4 *river* S Netherlands
Beringen 87 C5 Limburg, NE Belgium
Bering Sea 36 A2 *sea* N Pacific Ocean
Bering Strait 36 C2 *Rus.* Beringov Proliv. *Strait* Bering Sea/Chukchi Sea
Berja 93 E5 Andalucía, S Spain
Berkeley 47 B6 California, W USA
Berkner Island 154 A2 *island* Antarctica
Berkovitsa 104 C2 Montana, NW Bulgaria
Berlin 94 D3 *country capital* (Germany) Berlin, NE Germany
Berlin 41 G2 New Hampshire, NE USA
Bermejo, Río 64 D2 *river* N Argentina
Bermeo 93 E1 País Vasco, N Spain
Bermuda 35 D6 *var.* Bermuda Islands, Bermudas; *prev.* Somers Islands. *UK crown colony* NW Atlantic Ocean
Bermuda Islands *see* Bermuda
Bermuda Rise 35 E6 *undersea feature* C Sargasso Sea
Bermudas *see* Bermuda
Bern 95 A7 *Fr.* Berne. *Country capital* (Switzerland) Bern, W Switzerland
Bernau 94 D3 Brandenburg, NE Germany
Bernburg 94 C4 Sachsen-Anhalt, C Germany
Berne *see* Bern
Berner Alpen 95 A7 *var.* Berner Oberland, *Eng.* Bernese Oberland. *Mountain range* SW Switzerland
Berner Oberland *see* Berner Alpen
Bernese Oberland *see* Berner Alpen
Bernier Island 147 A5 *island* Western Australia
Berry 90 C4 *cultural region* C France
Berry Islands 54 C1 *island group* N Bahamas
Bertoua 77 B5 Est, E Cameroon
Beru 145 E2 *var.* Peru. Atoll Tungaru, W Kiribati
Berwick-upon-Tweed 88 D4 N England, UK
Berytus *see* Beyrouth
Besançon 90 D4 *anc.* Besontium, Vesontio. Doubs, E France
Beskra *see* Biskra
Betafo 79 G3 Antananarivo, C Madagascar
Betanzos 92 B1 Galicia, NW Spain

Bethlehem 119 B6 *Ar.* Beit Laḥm, *Heb.* Bet Lehem. C West Bank
Bethlehem 78 D4 Free State, C South Africa
Béticos, Sistemas 92 D4 *var.* Sistema Penibético, *Eng.* Baetic Cordillera, Baetic Mountains. *Mountain range* S Spain
Bet Lehem *see* Bethlehem
Bétou 77 C5 La Likouala, N Congo
Bette, Pic 71 C4 Bīkkū Bīttī, *It.* Picco Bette. *Mountain* S Libya
Bette, Picco *see* Bette, Pic
Beulah 40 C2 Michigan, N USA
Beuthen *see* Bytom
Beveren 87 B5 Oost-Vlaanderen, N Belgium
Beverley 89 D5 E England, UK
Bexley 89 B8 SE England, UK
Beyla 74 D4 Guinée-Forestière, SE Guinea
Beyrouth 118 A4 *var.* Bayrūt, *Eng.* Beirut; *anc.* Berytus. *Country capital* (Lebanon) W Lebanon
Beyşehir 116 B4 Konya, SW Turkey
Beyşehir Gölü 116 B4 *lake* C Turkey
Béziers 91 C6 *anc.* Baeterrae, Baeterrae Septimanorum, Julia Beterrae. Hérault, S France
Bhadrāvati 132 C2 Karnātaka, SW India
Bhāgalpur 135 F3 Bihār, NE India
Bhaktapur 135 F3 Central, C Nepal
Bhamo 136 B2 *var.* Banmo. Kachin State, N Myanmar
Bharūch 134 C4 Gujarāt, W India
Bhāvnagar 134 C4 *prev.* Bhaunagar. Gujarāt, W India
Bhopāl 134 D4 Madhya Pradesh, C India
Bhubaneshwar 135 F5 *prev.* Bhubaneswar, Bhuvaneshwar. Orissa, E India
Bhuket *see* Phuket
Bhusāwal 134 D4 *prev.* Bhusaval. Mahārāshtra, C India
Bhutan 135 G3 *var.* Druk-yul. *Country* S Asia

Bhutan 135

Official name Kingdom of Bhutan
Formation 1656
Capital Thimpu
Population 2.1 million / 116 people per sq mile (45 people per sq km)
Total area 18,147 sq miles (47,000 sq km)
Languages Dzongkha, Nepali, Assamese
Religions Mahayana Buddhist 70%, Hindu 24%, other 6%
Ethnic mix Bhote 50%, Nepalese 25%, other 25%
Government Monarchy
Currency Ngultrum = 100 chetrum
Literacy rate 47.3%
Calorie consumption not available

Biak, Pulau 139 G4 *island* E Indonesia
Biała Podlaska 98 E3 Lubelskie, E Poland
Białogard 98 B2 Ger. Belgard. Zachodniopomorskie, NW Poland
Białystok 98 E3 *Rus.* Belostok, Bielostok. Podlaskie, NE Poland
Biarritz 91 A6 Pyrénées-Atlantiques, SW France
Bicaz 108 C3 *Hung.* Békás. Neamţ, NE Romania
Biddeford 41 G2 Maine, NE USA
Bideford 89 C7 SW England, UK
Biel 95 A7 *Fr.* Bienne. Bern, W Switzerland
Bielefeld 94 B4 Nordrhein-Westfalen, NW Germany
Bielsko-Biała 99 C5 *Ger.* Bielitz, Bielitz-Biala. Śląskie, S Poland
Bielsk Podlaski 98 E3 Podlaskie, NE Poland
Bien Bien *see* Điên Biên
Biên Hoa 137 E6 Đông Nai, S Vietnam

Bienville, Lac 38 D2 lake Quebec, C Canada
Bié, Planalto do 78 B2 var. Bié Plateau. Plateau C Angola
Bié Plateau see Bié, Planalto do
Big Cypress Swamp 43 E5 wetland Florida, SE USA
Bigge Island 146 C2 island Western Australia
Bighorn Mountains 44 C2 mountain range Wyoming, C USA
Bighorn River 44 C2 river Montana/Wyoming, NW USA
Bignona 74 B3 SW Senegal
Big Sioux River 45 E2 river Iowa/South Dakota, N USA
Big Spring 49 E3 Texas, SW USA
Bihać 100 B3 Federacija Bosna I Hercegovina, NW Bosnia and Herzegovina
Bihār 135 F4 prev. Behar. Admin. region state N India
Biharamulo 73 B7 Kagera, NW Tanzania
Bihosava 107 D5 Rus. Bigosovo. Vitsyebskaya Voblasts', NW Belarus
Bijeljina 100 C3 Republika Srpska, NE Bosnia and Herzegovina
Bijelo Polje 101 D5 Montenegro, SW Serbia and Montenegro (Yugo.)
Bikāner 134 C3 Rājasthān, NW India
Bikin 115 G4 Khabarovskiy Kray, SE Russian Federation
Bikini Atoll 144 C1 var. Pikinni. Atoll Ralik Chain, NW Marshall Islands
Bikku Bïttï see Bette, Pic
Bilāspur 135 E4 Madhya Pradesh, C India
Bilāsuvar 117 H3 Rus. Bilyasuvar; prev. Pushkino. SE Azerbaijan
Bila Tserkva 109 E2 Rus. Belaya Tserkov'. Kyyivs'ka Oblast', N Ukraine
Bilauktaung Range 137 C6 var. Thanintari Taungdan. Mountain range Myanmar/Thailand
Bilbao 93 E1 Basq. Bilbo. País Vasco, N Spain
Bilecik 116 B3 Bilecik, NW Turkey
Billings 44 C2 Montana, NW USA
Bilma, Grand Erg de 75 H3 desert NE Niger
Biloela 148 D4 Queensland, E Australia
Biloxi 42 C3 Mississippi, S USA
Biltine 76 C3 Biltine, E Chad
Bilwi see Puerto Cabezas
Bilzen 87 D6 Limburg, NE Belgium
Bimini Islands 54 C1 island group W Bahamas
Binche 87 B7 Hainaut, S Belgium
Bindloe Island see Marchena, Isla
Binghamton 41 F3 New York, NE USA
Bingöl 117 E3 Bingöl, E Turkey
Bint Jubayl see Bent Jbaïl
Bintulu 138 D3 Sarawak, East Malaysia
Binzhou 128 D4 Shandong, E China
Bío Bío, Río 65 B5 river C Chile
Bioco, Isla de 77 A5 var. Bioko, Eng. Fernando Po, Sp. Fernando Póo; prev. Macías Nguema Biyogo. Island NW Equatorial Guinea
Bioko see Bioco, Isla de
Birāk 71 F3 var. Brak. C Libya
Birao 76 D3 Vakaga, NE Central African Republic
Biratnagar 135 F3 Eastern, SE Nepal
Birhār Sharīf 135 F3 Bihar, N India
Birjand 120 E3 Khorāsān, E Iran
Birkenfeld 95 A5 Rheinland-Pfalz, SW Germany
Birkenhead 89 C5 NW England, UK
Birmingham 42 C2 Alabama, S USA
Birmingham 89 C6 C England, UK
Bir Moghreïn see Bîr Mogreïn
Bîr Mogreïn 74 C1 var. Bir Moghrein; prev. Fort-Trinquet. Tiris Zemmour, N Mauritania

Birnie Island 145 E3 atoll Phoenix Islands, C Kiribati
Birni-Nkonni see Birnin Konni
Birnin Konni 75 F3 var. Birni-Nkonni. Tahoua, SW Niger
Birobidzhan 115 G4 Yevreyskaya Avtonomnaya Oblast', SE Russian Federation
Birsk 111 D5 Respublika Bashkortostan, W Russian Federation
Biržai 106 C4 Ger. Birsen. Biržai, NE Lithuania
Birżebbuġa 102 B5 SE Malta
Bisbee 48 B3 Arizona, SW USA
Biscay, Bay of 80 B4 Sp. Golfo de Vizcaya, Port. Baía de Biscaia. Bay France/Spain
Biscay Plain 80 B3 undersea feature SE Bay of Biscay
Bishah, Wādī 121 B5 dry watercourse C Saudi Arabia
Bishkek 123 G2 var. Pishpek; prev. Frunze. Country capital (Kyrgyzstan) Chuyskaya Oblast', N Kyrgyzstan
Bishop's Lynn see King's Lynn
Bishrī, Jabal 118 D3 mountain range E Syria
Biskara see Biskra
Biskra 71 E2 var. Beskra, Biskara. NE Algeria
Biskupiec 98 D2 Ger. Bischofsburg. Warmińsko-Mazurskie, NE Poland
Bislig 139 F2 Mindanao, S Philippines
Bismarck 45 E2 state capital North Dakota, N USA
Bismarck Archipelago 144 B3 island group NE PNG
Bismarck Sea 144 B3 sea W Pacific Ocean
Bisnulok see Phitsanulok
Bissau 74 B4 country capital (Guinea-Bissau) W Guinea-Bissau
Bistrița 108 B3 Ger. Bistritz, Hung. Beszterce; prev. Nösen. Bistrița-Năsăud, N Romania
Bitam 77 B5 Woleu-Ntem, N Gabon
Bitburg 95 A5 Rheinland-Pfalz, SW Germany
Bitlis 117 F3 Bitlis, SE Turkey
Bitola 101 D6 Turk. Monastir; prev. Bitolj. S FYR Macedonia
Bitonto 97 D5 anc. Butuntum. Puglia, SE Italy
Bitterroot Range 46 D2 mountain range Idaho/Montana, NW USA
Bitung 139 F3 prev. Bitoeng. Sulawesi, C Indonesia
Biu 75 H4 Borno, E Nigeria
Biwa-ko 131 C6 lake Honshū, SW Japan
Bizerte 71 E1 Ar. Banzart, Eng. Bizerta. N Tunisia
Bjelovar 100 B2 Hung. Belovár. Bjelovar-Bilogora, N Croatia
Bjørnøya 83 F3 Eng. Bear Island. Island N Norway
Blackall 148 C4 Queensland, E Australia
Black Drin 101 D6 Alb. Lumi i Drinit të Zi, SCr. Crni Drim. River Albania/FYR Macedonia
Blackfoot 46 E4 Idaho, NW USA
Black Forest see Schwarzwald
Black Hills 44 D3 mountain range South Dakota/Wyoming, N USA
Blackpool 89 C5 NW England, UK
Black Range 48 C2 mountain range New Mexico, SW USA
Black River 135 C3 Chin. Babian Jiang, Lixian Jiang, Fr. Rivière Noire, Vtn. Sông Đa. River China/Vietnam
Black River 54 A5 W Jamaica
Black Rock Desert 47 C5 desert Nevada, W USA
Black Sand Desert see Garagumy
Black Sea 116 B1 var. Euxine Sea, Bul. Cherno More, Rom. Marea Neagrā, Rus. Chernoye More, Turk. Karadeniz, Ukr. Chorne More. Sea Asia/Europe
Black Sea Lowland 109 E4 Ukr. Prychornomors'ka Nyzovyna. Depression SE Europe

Black Volta 75 E4 var. Borongo, Mouhoun, Moun Hou, Fr. Volta Noire. River W Africa
Blackwater 89 A6 Ir. An Abhainn Mhór. River S Ireland
Blagoevgrad 104 C3 prev. Gorna Dzhumaya. Blagoevgrad, SW Bulgaria
Blagoveshchensk 115 G4 Amurskaya Oblast', SE Russian Federation
Blake Plateau 35 D6 var. Blake Terrace. Undersea feature W Atlantic Ocean
Blake Terrace see Blake Plateau
Blanca, Bahía 65 C5 bay E Argentina
Blanca, Costa 93 F4 physical region SE Spain
Blanche, Lake 149 B5 lake South Australia
Blanc, Mont 91 D5 It. Monte Bianco. Mountain France/Italy
Blanco, Cape 46 A4 headland Oregon, NW USA
Blanes 93 G2 Cataluña, NE Spain
Blankenberge 87 A5 West-Vlaanderen, NW Belgium
Blankenheim 95 A5 Nordrhein-Westfalen, W Germany
Blanquilla, Isla 59 E1 var. La Blanquilla. Island N Venezuela
Blantyre 79 E2 var. Blantyre-Limbe. Southern, S Malawi
Blantyre-Limbe see Blantyre
Blaricum 86 C3 Noord-Holland, C Netherlands
Blenheim 151 C5 Marlborough, South Island, NZ
Blida 70 D2 var. El Boulaida, El Boulaïda. N Algeria
Bloemfontein 78 C4 var. Mangaung. Country capital (South Africa-judicial capital) Free State, C South Africa
Blois 90 C4 anc. Blesae. Loir-et-Cher, C France
Bloomfield 48 C1 New Mexico, SW USA
Bloomington 40 B4 Illinois, N USA
Bloomington 40 C4 Indiana, N USA
Bloomington 45 F2 Minnesota, N USA
Bloomsbury 148 D3 Queensland, NE Australia
Bluefield 40 D5 West Virginia, NE USA
Bluefields 53 E3 Región Autónoma Atlántico Sur, SE Nicaragua
Blue Mountain Peak 54 B5 mountain E Jamaica
Blue Mountains 46 C3 mountain range Oregon/Washington, NW USA
Blue Nile 68 D4 var. Abai, Bahr el Azraq, Amh. Ābay Wenz, Ar. An Nīl al Azraq. River Ethiopia/Sudan
Blue Nile 72 C4 state E Sudan
Blumenau 63 E5 Santa Catarina, S Brazil
Blythe 47 D8 California, W USA
Blytheville 42 C1 Arkansas, C USA
Bo 74 C4 S Sierra Leone
Boaco 52 D3 Boaco, S Nicaragua
Boa Vista 74 A3 island Ilhas de Barlavento, E Cape Verde
Boa Vista 62 D1 state capital Roraima, NW Brazil
Bobaomby, Tanjona 79 G2 Fr. Cap d'Ambre. Headland N Madagascar
Bobigny 90 E1 Seine-St-Denis, N France
Bobo-Dioulasso 74 D4 SW Burkina faso
Bobrynets' 109 E3 Rus. Bobrinets. Kirovohrads'ka Oblast', C Ukraine
Boca Raton 43 F5 Florida, SE USA
Bocay 52 D2 Jinotega, N Nicaragua
Bocche del Po see Po, Foci del
Bocholt 94 A4 Nordrhein-Westfalen, W Germany
Bochum 94 A4 Nordrhein-Westfalen, W Germany
Bocşa 108 A4 Ger. Bokschen, Hung. Boksánbánya. Caraş-Severin, SW Romania

Bodaybo 115 F4 Irkutskaya Oblast', E Russian Federation
Boden 84 D4 Norrbotten, N Sweden
Bodmin 89 C7 SW England, UK
Bodø 84 C3 Nordland, C Norway
Bodrum 116 A4 Muğla, SW Turkey
Boende 77 C5 Equateur, C Dem. Rep. Congo
Boetoeng see Buton, Pulau
Bogale 136 B4 Irrawaddy, SW Myanmar
Bogalusa 42 B3 Louisiana, S USA
Bogatynia 98 B4 Ger. Reichenau. Dolnośląskie, SW Poland
Boğazlıyan 116 D3 Yozgat, C Turkey
Bogor 138 C5 Dut. Buitenzorg. Jawa, C Indonesia
Bogotá 58 B3 prev. Santa Fe, Santa Fe de Bogotá. Country capital (Colombia) Cundinamarca, C Colombia
Bo Hai 128 D4 var. Gulf of Chihli. Gulf NE China
Bohemia 99 A5 Cz. Čechy, Ger. Böhmen. Cultural and historical region W Czech Republic
Bohemian Forest 95 C5 Cz. Český Les, Šumava, Ger. Böhmerwald. Mountain range C Europe
Böhmisch-Krumau see Český Krumlov
Bohol Sea 139 E2 var. Mindanao Sea. Sea S Philippines
Bohoro Shan 126 B2 mountain range NW China
Bohuslav 109 E2 Rus. Boguslav. Kyyivs'ka Oblast', N Ukraine
Boise 46 D3 var. Boise City. State capital Idaho, NW USA
Boise City see Boise
Boise City 49 E1 Oklahoma, C USA
Boizenburg 94 C3 Mecklenburg-Vorpommern, N Germany
Bojador see Boujdour
Bojnūrd 120 D2 var. Bujnurd. Khorāsān, N Iran
Bokāro 135 F4 Bihār, N India
Boké 74 C4 Guinée-Maritime, W Guinea
Bokhara see Bukhoro
Boknafjorden 85 A6 fjord S Norway
Bol 76 B3 Lac, W Chad
Bolgatanga 75 E4 N Ghana
Bolhrad 108 D4 Rus. Bolgrad. Odes'ka Oblast', SW Ukraine
Bolívar, Pico 58 C2 mountain W Venezuela
Bolivia 61 F3 Country W South America
Bollène 91 D6 Vaucluse, SE France

Bolivia 61

Official name Republic of Bolivia
Formation 1825
Capital Sucre (judicial)/La Paz (administrative)
Population 8.5 million / 20 people per sq mile (8 people per sq km)
Total area 424,162 sq miles (1,098,580 sq km)
Languages Spanish, Aymara, Quechua
Religions Roman Catholic 93%, other 7%
Ethnic mix Quechua 37%, Aymara 32%, mixed 13%, European 10%, other 8%
Government Presidential democracy
Currency Boliviano = 100 centavos
Literacy rate 85.6%
Calorie consumption 2,218 kilocalories

Bollnäs 85 C5 Gävleborg, C Sweden
Bollon 149 D5 Queensland, C Australia
Bologna 96 C3 Emilia-Romagna, N Italy
Bol'shevik, Ostrov 115 E2 island Severnaya Zemlya, N Russian Federation

Bol'shezemel'skaya Tundra *110 E3 physical region* NW Russian Federation
Bol'shoy Lyakhovskiy, Ostrov *115 F2 island* NE Russian Federation
Bolton *89 D5 prev.* Bolton-le-Moors. NW England, UK
Bolu *116 B3* Bolu, NW Turkey
Bolungarvík *83 E4* Vestfirdhir, NW Iceland
Bolyarovo *104 D3 prev.* Pashkeni. Yámbol, E Bulgaria
Bolzano *96 C1 Ger.* Bozen; *anc.* Bauzanum. Trentino-Alto Adige, N Italy
Boma *77 B6* Bas-Zaïre, W Dem. Rep. Dem. Rep. Congo
Bombay *see* Mumbai
Bomu *76 D4 var.* Mbomou, Mbomu, M'Bomu. *River* Central African Republic/Dem. Rep. Congo
Bonaire *55 F5 island* E Netherlands Antilles
Bonanza *52 D2* Región Autónoma Atlántico Norte, NE Nicaragua
Bonaparte Archipelago *146 C2 island group* Western Australia
Bon, Cap *102 D3 headland* N Tunisia
Bonda *77 B6* Ogooué-Lolo, C Gabon
Bondoukou *75 E4* E Côte d'Ivoire
Bone *see* Watampone
Bone, Teluk *139 E4 bay* Sulawesi, C Indonesia
Bongaigaon *135 G3* Assam, NE India
Bongo, Massif des *76 D4 var.* Chaîne des Mongos. *Mountain range* NE Central African Republic
Bongor *76 B3* Mayo-Kébbi, SW Chad
Bonifacio *91 E7* Corse, France, C Mediterranean Sea
Bonifacio, Strait of *96 A4 Fr.* Bouches de Bonifacio, *It.* Bocche de Bonifacio. *Strait* C Mediterranean Sea
Bonn *95 A5* Nordrhein-Westfalen, W Germany
Bononia *see* Boulogne-sur-Mer
Boosaaso *72 F4 var.* Bandar Kassim, Bender Qaasim, Bosaso, *It.* Bender Cassim. Bari, N Somalia
Boothia, Gulf of *37 F2 gulf* Nunavut, NE Canada
Boothia Peninsula *37 F2 prev.* Boothia Felix. *Peninsula* Nunavut, NE Canada
Boppard *95 A5* Rheinland-Pfalz, W Germany
Boquete *53 E5 var.* Bajo Boquete. Chiriquí, W Panama
Boquillas *50 D2 var.* Boquillas del Carmen. Coahuila de Zaragoza, NE Mexico
Boquillas del Carmen *see* Boquillas
Bor *73 B5* Jonglei, S Sudan
Bor *100 E4* Serbia, E Serbia and Montenegro (Yugo.)
Borås *85 B7* Västra Götaland, S Sweden
Borborema, Planalto da *56 E3 plateau* NE Brazil
Bordeaux *91 B5 anc.* Burdigala. Gironde, SW France
Bordj Omar Driss *71 E3* E Algeria
Børgefjellet *84 C4 mountain range* C Norway
Borger *86 E2* Drenthe, NE Netherlands
Borger *49 E1* Texas, SW USA
Borgholm *85 C7* Kalmar, S Sweden
Borgo Maggiore *96 E1* NW San Marino
Borisoglebsk *111 B6* Voronezhskaya Oblast', W Russian Federation
Borlänge *85 C6* Kopparberg, C Sweden
Borne *86 E3* Overijssel, E Netherlands
Borneo *138 C4 island* Brunei/Indonesia/Malaysia
Bornholm *85 B8 island* E Denmark
Borohoro Shan *123 H1 mountain range* NW China

Borongo *see* Black Volta
Borovan *104 C2* Vratsa, NW Bulgaria
Borovichi *110 B4* Novgorodskaya Oblast', W Russian Federation
Borovo *100 C3* Vukovar-Srijem, NE Croatia
Borşa *108 C3 Hung.* Borsa. Maramureş, N Romania
Boryslav *108 B2 Pol.* Borysław, *Rus.* Borislav. L'vivs'ka Oblast', NW Ukraine
Bosanska Dubica *100 B3 var.* Kozarska Dubica. Republika Srpska, NW Bosnia and Herzegovina
Bosanska Gradiška *100 B3 var.* Gradiška. Republika Srpska, N Bosnia and Herzegovina
Bosanski Novi *100 B3 var.* Novi Grad. Republika Srpska, NW Bosnia and Herzegovina
Bosanski Šamac *100 C3 var.* Šamac. Republika Srpska, N Bosnia and Herzegovina
Bosaso *see* Boosaaso
Boskovice *99 B5 Ger.* Boskowitz. Brněnský Kraj, SE Czech Republic
Bosna *100 C4 river* N Bosnia and Herzegovina
Bosna I Hercegovina, Federacija Admin. region *republic* Bosnia and Herzegovina
Bosnia and Herzegovina *100 B3 Country* SE Europe

Bosnia and Herzegovina 100

Official name Bosnia and Herzegovina
Formation 1992
Capital Sarajevo
Population 4.1 million /208 people per sq mile (80 people per sq km)
Total area 19,741 sq miles (51,129 sq km)
Languages Serbo-Croat
Religions Muslim (mainly Sunni) 40%, Serbian Orthodox 31%, Roman Catholic 15%, Protestant 4%, other 10%
Ethnic mix Bosniak 44%, Serb 31%, Croat 17%, other 8%
Government Multiparty republic
Currency Marka = 100 pfenniga
Literacy rate 93%
Calorie consumption 2,661 kilocalories

Bōsō-hantō *131 D6 peninsula* Honshū, S Japan
Bosphorus *see* İstanbul Boğazı
Bosporus *see* İstanbul Boğazı
Bosporus Cimmerius *see* Kerch Strait
Bosporus Thracius *see* İstanbul Boğazı
Bossangoa *76 C4* Ouham, C Central African Republic
Bossembélé *76 C4* Ombella-Mpoko, C Central African Republic
Bossier City *42 A2* Louisiana, S USA
Bosten Hu *126 C3 var.* Bagrax Hu. *Lake* NW China
Boston *89 E6 prev.* St.Botolph's Town. E England, UK
Boston *41 G3 state capital* Massachusetts, NE USA
Boston Mountains *42 B1 mountain range* Arkansas, C USA
Botany *148 E2* New South Wales, SE Australia
Botany Bay *148 E2 inlet* New South Wales, SE Australia
Boteti *78 C3 var.* Botletle. *River* N Botswana
Bothnia, Gulf of *85 D5 Fin.* Pohjanlahti, *Swe.* Bottniska Viken. *Gulf* N Baltic Sea
Botletle *see* Boteti

Botoşani *108 C3 Hung.* Botosány. Botoşani, NE Romania
Botou *128 C4 prev.* Bozhen. Hebei, E China
Botrange *87 D6 mountain* E Belgium
Botswana *78 C3 Country* S Africa

Botswana 78

Official name Republic of Botswana
Formation 1966
Capital Gaborone
Population 1.6 million /7 people per sq mile (3 people per sq km)
Total area 231,803 sq miles (600,370 sq km)
Languages English, Tswana, Shona, San, Khoikhoi, Ndebele
Religions Traditional beliefs 50%, Christian (mainly Protestant) 30%, other (including Muslim) 20%
Ethnic mix Tswana 98% other 2%
Government Presidential democracy
Currency Pula = 100 thebe
Literacy rate 77.2%
Calorie consumption 2,255 kilocalories

Bouar *76 B4* Nana-Mambéré, W Central African Republic
Bou Craa *70 B3 var.* Bu Craa. NW Western Sahara
Bougainville Island *142 B3 island* NE PNG
Bougaroun, Cap *102 C3 headland* NE Algeria
Bougouni *74 D4* Sikasso, SW Mali
Boujdour *70 A3 var.* Bojador. W Western Sahara
Boulder *44 C4* Colorado, C USA
Boulder *44 B2* Montana, NW USA
Boulogne *see* Boulogne-sur-Mer
Boulogne-Billancourt *90 D1 prev.* Boulogne-sur-Seine. Hauts-de-Seine, N France
Boulogne-sur-Mer *90 C2 var.* Boulogne; *anc.* Bononia, Gesoriacum, Gessoriacum. Pas-de-Calais, N France
Boûmdeïd *74 C3 var.* Boumdeït. Assaba, S Mauritania
Boumdeït *see* Boûmdeïd
Boundiali *74 D4* N Côte d'Ivoire
Bountiful *44 B4* Utah, W USA
Bounty Basin *see* Bounty Trough
Bounty Islands *142 D5 island group* S NZ
Bounty Trough *152 C5 var.* Bounty Basin. *Undersea feature* S Pacific Ocean
Bourbonnais *90 C4* Illinois, N USA
Bourg *see* Bourg-en-Bresse
Bourgas *see* Burgas
Bourge-en-Bresse *see* Bourg-en-Bresse
Bourges *90 C4 anc.* Avaricum. Cher, C France
Bourgogne *90 C4 Eng.* Burgundy. *Cultural region* E France
Bourke *149 C5* New South Wales, SE Australia
Bournemouth *89 D7* S England, UK
Boutilimit *74 C3* Trarza, SW Mauritania
Bouvet Island *67 D7 Norwegian dependency* S Atlantic Ocean
Bowen *148 D3* Queensland, NE Australia
Bowling Green *40 B5* Kentucky, S USA
Bowling Green *40 C3* Ohio, N USA
Boxmeer *86 D4* Noord-Brabant, SE Netherlands
Boyarka *109 E2* Kyyivs'ka Oblast', N Ukraine
Boysun *123 E3 Rus.* Baysun. Surkhondaryo Wiloyati, S Uzbekistan

Bozeman *44 B2* Montana, NW USA
Bozüyük *116 B3* Bilecik, NW Turkey
Brač *100 B4 var.* Brach, *It.* Brazza; *anc.* Brattia. *Island* S Croatia
Brach *see* Brač
Bradford *89 D5* N England, UK
Brady *49 F3* Texas, SW USA
Braga *92 B2 anc.* Bracara Augusta. Braga, NW Portugal
Bragança *92 C2 Eng.* Braganza; *anc.* Julio Briga. Bragança, NE Portugal
Brahmanbaria *135 G4* Chittagong, E Bangladesh
Brahmapur *135 F5* Orissa, E India
Brahmaputra *135 H3 var.* Padma, Tsangpo, *Ben.* Jamuna, *Chin.* Yarlung Zangbo Jiang, *Ind.* Bramaputra, Dihang, Siang. *River* S Asia
Brăila *108 D4* Brăila, E Romania
Braine-le-Comte *87 B6* Hainaut, SW Belgium
Brainerd *45 F2* Minnesota, N USA
Brak *see* Brač
Bramaputra *see* Brahmaputra
Brampton *38 D5* Ontario, S Canada
Branco, Rio *56 C3 river* N Brazil
Brandberg *78 A3 mountain* NW Namibia
Brandenburg *94 C3 var.* Brandenburg an der Havel. Brandenburg, NE Germany
Brandenburg an der Havel *see* Brandenburg
Brandon *37 F5* Manitoba, S Canada
Braniewo *98 D2 Ger.* Braunsberg. Warmińsko-Mazurskie, NE Poland
Brasília *63 F3 country capital* (Brazil) Distrito Federal, C Brazil
Braşov *108 C4 Ger.* Kronstadt, *Hung.* Brassó; *prev.* Oraşul Stalin. Braşov, C Romania
Bratislava *99 C6 Ger.* Pressburg, *Hung.* Pozsony. *Country capital* (Slovakia) Bratislavský Kraj, SW Slovakia
Bratsk *115 E4* Irkutskaya Oblast', C Russian Federation
Brattia *see* Brač
Braunschweig *94 C4 Eng./Fr.* Brunswick. Niedersachsen, N Germany
Brava, Costa *93 H2 coastal region* NE Spain
Bravo del Norte *see* Grande, Rio
Bravo del Norte, Rio *see* Bravo, Rio
Bravo del Norte, Río *see* Grande, Rio
Bravo, Río *50 C1 var.* Rio Bravo del Norte, Rio Grande. *River* Mexico/USA
Bravo, Río *see* Grande, Rio
Brawley *47 D8* California, W USA
Brazil *62 C2 Port.* República Federativa do Brasil, *Sp.* Brasil; *prev.* United States of Brazil. *Country* South America

Brazil 62

Official name Federative Republic of Brazil
Formation 1822
Capital Brasília
Population 172.6 million / 53 people per sq mile (20 people per sq km)
Total area 3,286,470 sq miles (8,511,965 sq km)
Languages Portuguese, German, Italian, Spanish, Polish, Japanese
Religions Roman Catholic 74%, Protestant 15%, Atheist 7%, other 4%
Ethnic mix Black 53%, Mixed 40%, White 6%, other 1%
Government Presidential democracy
Currency Real = 100 centavos
Literacy rate 85.2%
Calorie consumption 2,985 kilocalories

Brazil Basin *67 C5 var.* Brazilian Basin, Brazil'skaya Kotlovina. *Undersea feature* W Atlantic Ocean

Brazilian Basin *see* Brazil Basin
Brazilian Highlands *see* Central,
Planalto
Brazil'skaya Kotlovina *see* Brazil
Basin
Brazos River *49 G3 river* Texas,
SW USA
Brazza *see* Brač
Brazzaville *77 B6 country capital*
(Congo) Capital District, S Congo
Brecht *87 C5* Antwerpen, N Belgium
Brecon Beacons *89 C6 mountain
range* S Wales, UK
Breda *86 C4* Noord-Brabant,
S Netherlands
Bree *87 D5* Limburg, NE Belgium
Bregalnica *101 E6 river* E FYR
Macedonia
Bregenz *57 B7 anc.* Brigantium.
Vorarlberg, W Austria
Bregovo *104 B1* Vidin, NW Bulgaria
Brčko *100 C3* Republika Srpska,
NE Bosnia and Herzegovina
Bremen *94 B3 Fr.* Brême. Bremen,
NW Germany
Bremerhaven *94 B3* Bremen,
NW Germany
Bremerton *46 B2* Washington,
NW USA
Brenham *49 G3* Texas, SW USA
Brenner Pass *96 C1 var.*
BrennerSattel, *Fr.* Col du Brenner,
Ger. Brennerpass, *It.* Passo del
Brennero. *Pass* Austria/Italy
Brennerpass *see* Brenner Pass
Brenner Sattel *see* Brenner Pass
Brescia *96 B2 anc.* Brixia.
Lombardia, N Italy
Bressanone *96 C1 Ger.* Brixen.
Trentino-Alto Adige, N Italy
Brest *107 A6 Pol.* Brześć nad
Bugiem, *Rus.* Brest-Litovsk; *prev.*
Brześć Litewski. Brestskaya
Voblasts', SW Belarus
Brest *90 A3* Finistère, NW France
Bretagne *90 A3 Eng.* Brittany; *Lat.*
Britannia Minor. *Cultural region*
NW France
Brewton *42 C3* Alabama, S USA
Brezovo *104 D2 prev.* Abrashlare.
Plovdiv, C Bulgaria
Bria *76 D4* Haute-Kotto, C Central
African Republic
Briançon *91 D5 anc.* Brigantio.
Hautes-Alpes, SE France
Bridgeport *41 F3* Connecticut,
NE USA
Bridgetown *55 G2 country capital*
(Barbados) SW Barbados
Bridlington *89 D5* E England, UK
Bridport *89 D7* S England, UK
Brig *95 A7 Fr.* Brigue, *It.* Briga.
Valais, SW Switzerland
Brigham City *44 B3* Utah,
W USA
Brighton *44 D4* Colorado, C USA
Brighton *89 E7* SE England, UK
Brindisi *97 E5 anc.* Brundisium,
Brundusium. Puglia, SE Italy
Brisbane *149 E5 state capital*
Queensland, E Australia
Bristol *89 D7 anc.* Bricgstow.
SW England, UK
Bristol *41 F3* Connecticut,
NE USA
Bristol *40 D5* Virginia, NE USA
Bristol Bay *36 B3 bay* Alaska, USA
Bristol Channel *89 C7 inlet*
England/Wales, UK
Britain *80 C3 var.* Great Britain.
Island
British Columbia *36 D4 Fr.*
Colombie-Britannique. *Province*
SW Canada
British Indian Ocean Territory *141
B5 UK dependent territory*
C Indian Ocean
British Isles *89 island group*
NW Europe
British Virgin Islands *55 F3 var.*
Virgin Islands. *UK dependent
territory* E West Indies
Brive-la-Gaillarde *91 C5 prev.* Brive,
anc. Briva Curretia. Corrèze,
C France
Brno *99 B5 Ger.* Brünn. Brněnský
Kraj, SE Czech Republic
Bročeni *106 B3* Saldus, SW Latvia

Brodeur Peninsula *37 F2 peninsula*
Baffin Island, Nunavut,
NE Canada
Brodnica *98 C3 Ger.* Buddenbrock.
Kujawski-pomorskie, C Poland
Broek-in-Waterland *86 C3* Noord-
Holland, C Netherlands
Broken Arrow *49 G1* Oklahoma,
C USA
Broken Bay *148 E1 bay* New South
Wales, SE Australia
Broken Hill *149 B6* New South
Wales, SE Australia
Broken Ridge *141 D6 undersea
feature* S Indian Ocean
Bromley *89 B8* SE England, UK
Brookhaven *42 B3* Mississippi,
S USA
Brookings *45 F3* South Dakota,
N USA
Brooks Range *36 D2 mountain range*
Alaska, USA
Brookton *147 B6* Western Australia
Broome *146 B3* Western Australia
Broomfield *44 D4* Colorado, C USA
Broucsella *see* Brussel
Brovary *109 E2* Kyyivs'ka Oblast',
N Ukraine
Brownfield *49 E2* Texas, SW USA
Brownville *49 G5* Texas, SW USA
Brownwood *49 F3* Texas, SW USA
Brozha *107 D7* Mahilyowskaya
Voblasts', E Belarus
Brugge *87 A5 Fr.* Bruges. West-
Vlaanderen, NW Belgium
Brummen *86 D3* Gelderland,
E Netherlands
Brunei *138 D3Mal.* Negara Brunei
Darussalam. *Country* SE Asia

Brunei 138

Official name Sultanate of Brunei
Formation 1984
Capital Bandar Seri Begawan
Population 335,000 /
150 people per sq mile (58 people
per sq km)
Total area 2,228 sq miles
(5,770 sq km)
Languages Malay, English,
Chinese
Religions Muslim 66%, Buddhist
14%, Christian 10%, other 10%
Ethnic mix Malay 67%, Chinese
16%, Indigenous 6%, other 11%
Government Monarchy
Currency Brunei dollar = 100 cents
Literacy rate 91.5%
Calorie consumption 2,832
kilocalories

Brunner, Lake *151 C5 lake* South
Island, NZ
Brunswick *43 E3* Georgia,
SE USA
Brusa *see* Bursa
Brus Laguna *52 D2* Gracias a Dios,
E Honduras
Brussa *see* Bursa
Brussel *var.* Brussels, *Fr.* Bruxelles,
Ger. Brüssel; *anc.* Broucsella.
Country capital (Belgium)
Brussels, C Belgium *see also*
Bruxelles
Brüssel *see* Brussel
Brussels *see* Brussel
Bruxelles *see* Brussel
Bryan *49 G3* Texas, SW USA
Bryansk *111 A5* Bryanskaya Oblast',
W Russian Federation
Brzeg *98 C4 Ger.* Brieg; *anc.* Civitas
Altae Ripae. Opolskie, S Poland
Bucaramanga *58 B2* Santander,
N Colombia
Buchanan *74 C5 prev.* Grand Bassa.
SW Liberia
Buchanan, Lake *49 F3 reservoir*
Texas, SW USA
Bucharest *see* București
Bu Craa *see* Bou Craa
București *108 C5 Eng.* Bucharest,
Ger. Bukarest; *prev.* Altenburg, *anc.*
Cetatea Dâmboviței. *Country
capital* (Romania) București,
S Romania

Buda-Kashalyova *107 D7 Rus.*
Buda-Koshelëvo. Homyel'skaya
Voblasts', SE Belarus
Budapest *99 C6 off.* Budapest
Főváros, *SCr.* Budimpešta.
Country capital (Hungary) Pest,
N Hungary
Budaun *134 D3* Uttar Pradesh,
N India
Buena Park *46 E2* California, W USA
Buenaventura *58 A3* Valle del
Cauca, W Colombia
Buena Vista *93 H5* S Gibraltar
Buena Vista *61 G4* Santa Cruz,
C Bolivia
Buenos Aires *64 D4 hist.* Santa
Maria del Buen Aire. *Country
capital* (Argentina) Buenos Aires,
E Argentina
Buenos Aires *53 E5* Puntarenas,
SE Costa Rica
Buenos Aires, Lago *65 B6 var.* Lago
General Carrera. *Lake*
Argentina/Chile
Buffalo *41 E3* New York, NE USA
Buffalo Narrows *37 F4*
Saskatchewan, C Canada
Buff Bay *54 B5* E Jamaica
Buftea *108 C5* București, S Romania
Bug *81 E3 Bel.* Zakhodni Buh, *Eng.*
Western Bug, *Rus.* Zapadnyy Bug,
Ukr. Zakhidnyy Buh. *River*
E Europe
Buga *58 B3* Valle del Cauca,
W Colombia
Bughotu *see* Santa Isabel
Buguruslan *111 D6* Orenburgskaya
Oblast', W Russian Federation
Buhayrat Nāṣir *see* Nasser, Lake
Buheiret Nâṣir *see* Nasser, Lake
Bujalance *92 D4* Andalucía, S Spain
Bujanovac *101 E5* Serbia, SE Serbia
and Montenegro (Yugo.)
Bujnurd *see* Bojnūrd
Bujumbura *73 B7 prev.* Usumbura.
Country capital (Burundi)
W Burundi
Bukavu *77 E6 prev.* Costermansville.
Sud Kivu, E Dem. Rep. Congo
Bukhara *see* Bukhoro
Bukhoro *122 D2 var.* Bokhara, *Rus.*
Bukhara. Bukhoro Wiloyati,
C Uzbekistan
Bukoba *73 B6* Kagera,
NW Tanzania
Bülach *95 B7* Zürich,
NW Switzerland
Bulawayo *78 D3 var.* Buluwayo.
Matabeleland North,
SW Zimbabwe
Buldur *see* Burdur
Bulgan *127 E2* Bulgan, N Mongolia
Bulgaria *104 C2 Bul.* Bǔlgariya; *prev.*
People's Republic of Bulgaria.
Country SE Europe

Bulgaria 104

Official name Republic of Bulgaria
Formation 1908
Capital Sofia
Population 7.9 million / 184 people
per sq mile (71 people per sq km)
Total area 42,822 sq miles
(110,910 sq km)
Languages Bulgarian, Turkish,
Macedonian, Romany
Religions Bulgarian Orthodox 84%,
Muslim 13%, Jewish 1%, Roman
Catholic 1%, other 1%
Ethnic mix Bulgarian 85%, Turkish
9%, Macedonian 3%, Romany 3%
Government Multiparty republic
Currency Lev = 100 stotinki
Literacy rate 98.4%
Calorie consumption 2,467
kilocalories

Bull Shoals Lake *42 B1 reservoir*
Arkansas/Missouri, C USA
Bulukumba *139 E4 prev.*
Boeloekoemba. Sulawesi,
C Indonesia
Buluwayo *see* Bulawayo
Bumba *77 D5* Equateur, N Dem.
Rep. Congo

Bunbury *147 A7* Western
Australia
Bundaberg *148 E4* Queensland,
E Australia
Bungo-suidō *131 B7 strait* SW Japan
Bunia *77 E5* Orientale, NE Dem.
Rep. Congo
Bünyan *116 D3* Kayseri, C Turkey
Buraida *see* Buraydah
Buraydah *120 B4 var.* Buraida.
Al Qaşīm, N Saudi Arabia
Burdur *116 B4 var.* Buldur. Burdur,
SW Turkey
Burdur Gölü *116 B4 salt lake*
SW Turkey
Burē *72 C4* C Ethiopia
Burgas *104 E2 var.* Bourgas. Burgas,
E Bulgaria
Burgaski Zaliv *104 E2 gulf*
E Bulgaria
Burgos *92 D2* Castilla-León,
N Spain
Burhan Budai Shan *126 D4
mountain range* C China
Buri Ram *see* Buriram
Buriram *137 D5 var.* Buri Ram,
Puriramya. Buri Ram, E Thailand
Burjassot *93 F3* País Valenciano,
E Spain
Burkburnett *49 F2* Texas, SW USA
Burketown *148 B3* Queensland,
NE Australia
Burkina *see* Burkina Faso
Burkina Faso *75 E4 var.* Burkina;
prev. Upper Volta. *Country*
W Africa

Burkina Faso 75

Official name Burkina Faso
Formation 1960
Capital Ouagadougou
Population 11.9 million / 112
people per sq mile
(43 people per sq km)
Total area 105,869 sq miles
(274,200 sq km)
Languages French, Mossi,
Fulani, Tuareg, Dyula, Songhai
Religions Traditional beliefs 55%,
Muslim 35%, Roman Catholic 9%,
other Christian 1%
Ethnic mix Mossi 50%, other 50%
Government Multiparty republic
Currency CFA franc = 100 centimes
Literacy rate 23.9%
Calorie consumption 2,293
kilocalories

Burley *46 D4* Idaho, NW USA
Burlington *45 G4* Iowa, C USA
Burlington *41 F2* Vermont, NE USA
Burma *see* Myanmar
Burnie *149 C8* Tasmania,
SE Australia
Burns *46 C3* Oregon, NW USA
Burnside *37 F3 river* Nunavut,
NW Canada
Burnsville *45 F2* Minnesota,
N USA
Burrel *101 D6 var.* Burreli. Dibër,
C Albania
Burreli *see* Burrel
Burriana *93 F3* País Valenciano,
E Spain
Bursa *116 B3 var.* Brussa; *prev.*
Brusa, *anc.* Prusa. Bursa,
NW Turkey
Burtnieks *see* Burtnieku Ezers
Burtnieku Ezers *106 C3 var.*
Burtnieks. *Lake* N Latvia
Burundi *73 B7 prev.* Kingdom of
Burundi, Urundi. *Country*
C Africa

Burundi 73

Official name Republic of Burundi
Formation 1962
Capital Bujumbura
Population 6.5 million /605 people
per sq mile (234 people per sq km)
Total area 10,745 sq miles
(27,830 sq km)
Languages Kirundi, French,
Kiswahili

Burundi (continued)

religions Christian 60%, Traditional beliefs 39%, Muslim 1%
Ethnic mix Hutu 85%, Tutsi 14%, Twa 1%
Government Transitional regime
Currency Burundi franc = 100 centimes
Literacy rate 48.3%
Calorie consumption 1,605 kilocalories

Buru, Pulau 139 F4 prev. Boeroe. Island E Indonesia
Buşayrah 118 D3 Dayr az Zawr, E Syria
Būshehr see Bandar-e Būshehr
Bushire see Bandar-e Būshehr
Busselton 147 A7 Western Australia
Buta 77 D5 Orientale, N Dem. Rep. Congo
Butembo 77 E5 Nord Kivu, NE Dem. Rep. Congo
Butler 41 E4 Pennsylvania, NE USA
Buton, Pulau 139 E4 var. Pulau Butung; prev. Boetoeng. Island C Indonesia
Butte 44 B2 Montana, NW USA
Butterworth 138 B3 Pinang, Peninsular Malaysia
Button Islands 39 E1 island group Northwest Territories, NE Canada
Butuan 139 F2 off. Butuan City. Mindanao, S Philippines
Buulobarde 73 D5 var. Buulo Berde. Hiiraan, C Somalia Africa
Buulo Berde see Buulobarde
Buur Gaabo 73 D6 Jubbada Hoose, S Somalia
Buynaksk 111 B8 Respublika Dagestan, SW Russian Federation
Büyükağrı Dağı 117 F3 var. Aghri Dagh, Agri Dagi, Koh I Noh, Masis, Eng. Great Ararat, Mount Ararat. Mountain E Turkey
Büyükmenderes Nehri 116 A4 river SW Turkey
Buzău 108 C4 Buzău, SE Romania
Buzuluk 111 D6 Akmola, C Kazakhstan
Byahoml' 107 D5 Rus. Begoml'. Vitsyebskaya Voblasts', N Belarus
Byalynichy 107 D6 Rus. Belynichi. Mahilyowskaya Voblasts', E Belarus
Bydgoszcz 98 C3 Ger. Bromberg. Kujawskie-pomorskie, C Poland
Byelaruskaya Hrada 107 B6 Rus. Belorusskaya Gryada. Ridge N Belarus
Byerezino 107 D6 Rus. Berezina. River C Belarus
Byron Island see Nikunau
Bytom 99 C5 Ger. Beuthen. Śląskie, S Poland
Bytča 99 C5 Žilinský Kraj, N Slovakia
Bytów 98 C2 Ger. Bütow. Pomorskie, N Poland
Byuzmeyin 122 C3 Turkm. Büzmeyin; prev. Bezmein. Akhalskiy Velayat, C Turkmenistan
Byval'ki 107 D8 Homyel'skaya Voblasts', SE Belarus
Byzantium see Istanbul

C

Caála 78 B2 var. Kaala, Robert Williams, Port. Vila Robert Williams. Huambo, C Angola
Caazapá 64 D3 Caazapá, S Paraguay
Caballo Reservoir 48 C3 reservoir New Mexico, SW USA
Cabañaquinta 92 D1 Asturias, N Spain
Cabanatuan 139 E1 off. Cabanatuan City. Luzon, N Philippines
Cabimas 58 C1 Zulia, NW Venezuela
Cabinda 78 A1 var. Kabinda. Cabinda, NW Angola
Cabinda 78 A1 var. Kabinda. Admin. region province NW Angola

Cabora Bassa, Lake see Cahora Bassa, Albufeira de
Caborca 50 B1 Sonora, NW Mexico
Cabot Strait 39 G4 strait E Canada
Cabras, Ilha das 76 E2 island S Sao Tome and Principe
Cabrera 93 G3 anc. Capraria. Island Islas Baleares, Spain, W Mediterranean Sea
Cáceres 92 C3 Ar. Qazris. Extremadura, W Spain
Cachimbo, Serra do 63 E2 mountain range C Brazil
Caconda 78 B2 Huíla, C Angola
Čadca 99 C5 Hung. Csaca. Žilinský Kraj, N Slovakia
Cadillac 40 C2 Michigan, N USA
Cadiz 139 E2 off. Cadiz City. Negros, C Philippines
Cádiz 92 C5 anc. Gades, Gadier, Gadir, Gadire. Andalucía, SW Spain
Cádiz, Golfo de 92 B5 Eng. Gulf of Cadiz. Gulf Portugal/Spain
Cadiz, Gulf of see Cádiz, Golfo de
Caen 90 B3 Calvados, N France
Caene see Qena
Caenepolis see Qena
Caerdydd see Cardiff
Caer Gybi see Holyhead
Caesarea Mazaca see Kayseri
Cafayate 64 C2 Salta, N Argentina
Cagayan de Oro 139 E2 off. Cagayan de Oro City. Mindanao, S Philippines
Cagliari 97 A6 anc. Caralis. Sardegna, Italy, C Mediterranean Sea
Caguas 55 F3 E Puerto Rico
Cahora Bassa, Albufeira de 78 D2 var. Lake Cabora Bassa. Reservoir NW Mozambique
Cahors 91 C5 anc. Cadurcum. Lot, S France
Cahul 108 D4 Rus. Kagul. S Moldova
Caicos Passage 54 D2 strait Bahamas/Turks and Caicos Islands
Caiffa see Hefa
Cailungo 96 E1 N San Marino
Caiphas see Hefa
Cairns 148 D3 Queensland, NE Australia
Cairo 72 B2 Ar. Al Qāhirah, var. El Qâhira. Country capital (Egypt) N Egypt
Caisleán an Bharraigh see Castlebar
Cajamarca 60 B3 prev. Caxamarca. Cajamarca, NW Peru
Čakovec 100 B2 Ger. Csakathurn, Hung. Csáktornya; prev. Ger. Tschakathurn. Međimurje, N Croatia
Calabar 75 G5 Cross River, S Nigeria
Calabozo 58 D2 Guárico, C Venezuela
Calafat 108 B5 Dolj, SW Romania
Calafate see El Calafate
Calahorra 93 E2 La Rioja, N Spain
Calais 41 H2 Maine, NE USA
Calais 90 C1 Pas-de-Calais, N France
Calama 64 B2 Antofagasta, N Chile
Calamianes see Calamian Group
Calamian Group 129 C7 var. Calamianes. Island group W Philippines
Cālāraş see Călăraşi
Călăraşi 108 D3 var. Călăras, Rus. Kalarash. C Moldova
Călăraşi 108 C5 Călăraşi, SE Romania
Calatayud 93 E2 Aragón, NE Spain
Calbayog 139 E2 off. Calbayog City. Samar, C Philippines
Calcutta 135 G4 var. Kolkata. West Bengal, NE India
Caldas da Rainha 92 B3 Leiria, W Portugal
Caldera 64 B3 Atacama, N Chile
Caldwell 46 C3 Idaho, NW USA
Caledonia see Catalan Bay
Caleta see Catalan Bay
Caleta Olivia 65 B6 Santa Cruz, SE Argentina

Calgary 37 E5 Alberta, SW Canada
Cali 58 B3 Valle del Cauca, W Colombia
Calicut 132 C2 var. Kozhikode. Kerala, SW India
California 47 B7 off. State of California; also known as El Dorado, The Golden State. State W USA
California, Golfo de 50 B2 Eng. Gulf of California; prev. Sea of Cortez. Gulf W Mexico
California, Gulf of see California, Golfo de
Călimăneşti 108 B4 Vâlcea, SW Romania
Callabonna, Lake 149 B5 lake South Australia
Callao 60 C4 Callao, W Peru
Callosa de Segura 93 F4 País Valenciano, E Spain
Calmar see Kalmar
Caloundra 149 E5 Queensland, E Australia
Caltanissetta 97 C7 Sicilia, Italy, C Mediterranean Sea
Caluula 72 E4 Bari, NE Somalia
Camabatela 78 B1 Cuanza Norte, NW Angola
Camacupa 78 B2 var. General Machado, Port. Vila General Machado. Bié, C Angola
Camagüey 54 C2 prev. Puerto Príncipe. Camagüey, C Cuba
Camagüey, Archipiélago de 54 C2 island group C Cuba
Camaná 61 E4 Arequipa, SW Peru
Camargue 91 D6 physical region SE France
Ca Mau 137 D6 prev. Quan Long. Minh Hai, S Vietnam
Cambodia 137 D5 var. Democratic Kampuchea, Roat Kampuchea, Cam. Kampuchea; prev. People's Democratic Republic of Kampuchea. Country SE Asia

Cambodia 137

Official name Kingdom of Cambodia
Formation 1953
Capital Phnom Penh
Population 13.4 million / 192 people per sq mile (74 people per sq km)
Total area 69,900 sq miles (181,040 sq km)
Languages Khmer, French, Chinese, Vietnamese, Cham
Religions Buddhist 93%, Muslim 6%, Christian 1%
Ethnic mix Khmer 90%, other 5% Vietnamese 4%, Chinese 1%,
Government Constitutional monarchy
Currency Riel = 100 sen
Literacy rate 37.4%
Calorie consumption 2,070 kilocalories

Cambrai 90 C2 Flem. Kambryk; prev. Cambray, anc. Cameracum. Nord, N France
Cambrian Mountains 89 C6 mountain range C Wales, UK
Cambridge 89 E6 Lat. Cantabrigia. E England, UK
Cambridge 41 F4 Maryland, NE USA
Cambridge 40 D4 Ohio, NE USA
Cambridge 54 A4 W Jamaica
Cambridge 150 D3 Waikato, North Island, NZ
Cambridge Bay 37 F3 district capital Victoria Island, Nunavut, NW Canada
Camden 42 B2 Arkansas, C USA
Cameroon 76 A4 Fr. Cameroun. Country W Africa

Cameroon

Official name Kingdom of Cambodia
Formation 1953

Cameroon (continued)

Capital Phnom Penh
Population 13.4 million / 192 people per sq mile (74 people per sq km)
Total area 69,900 sq miles (181,040 sq km)
Languages Khmer, French, Chinese, Vietnamese, Cham
Religions Buddhist 93%, Muslim 6%, Christian 1%
Ethnic mix Khmer 90%, other 5% Vietnamese 4%, Chinese 1%,
Government Constitutional monarchy
Currency Riel = 100 sen
Literacy rate 37.4%
Calorie consumption 2,070 kilocalories

Camocim 63 F2 Ceará, E Brazil
Camopi 59 H3 E French Guiana
Campamento 52 C2 Olancho, C Honduras
Campania 97 D5 cultural region SE Italy
Campbell, Cape 151 D5 headland South Island, NZ
Campbell Island 142 D5 island S NZ
Campbell Plateau 142 D5 undersea feature SW Pacific Ocean
Campbell River 36 D5 Vancouver Island, British Columbia, SW Canada
Campeche 51 G4 Campeche, SE Mexico
Campeche, Bahía de 51 F4 Eng. Bay of Campeche. Bay E Mexico
Câm Pha 136 E3 Quang Ninh, N Vietnam
Câmpina 108 C4 prev. Cîmpina. Prahova, SE Romania
Campina Grande 63 G2 Paraíba, E Brazil
Campinas 63 F4 São Paulo, S Brazil
Campobasso 97 D5 Molise, C Italy
Campo Criptana see Campo de Criptana
Campo de Criptana 93 E3 var. Campo Criptana. Castilla-La Mancha, C Spain
Campo dos Goitacazes see Campos
Campo Grande 63 E4 state capital Mato Grosso do Sul, SW Brazil
Campos 63 F4 var. Campo dos Goitacazes. Rio de Janeiro, SE Brazil
Câmpulung 108 B4 prev. Câmpulung-Muşcel, Cîmpulung. Argeş, S Romania
Campus Stellae see Santiago
Cam Ranh 137 E6 Khanh Hoa, S Vietnam
Canada 34 B4 country N North America

Canada 34

Official name Canada
Formation 1867
Capital Ottawa
Population 3.1 million /8 people per sq mile (3 people per sq km)
Total area 3,851,788 sq miles (9,976,140 sq km)
Languages English, French, Chinese, Italian, German, Ukranian, Inuktitut
Religions Roman Catholic 47%, Protestant 41%, non-religious 12%
Ethnic mix British origin 44%, French origin 25%, Other European 20%, other 11%
Government Parliamentary democracy
Currency Canadian dollar = 100 cents
Literacy rate 99%
Calorie consumption 3,174 kilocalories

Canada Basin 34 C2 *undersea feature* Arctic Ocean
Canadian River 49 E2 *river* SW USA
Çanakkale 116 A3 *var.* Dardanelli; *prev.* Chanak, Kale Sultanie. Çanakkale, W Turkey
Çanakkale Boğazı 116 A2 *Eng.* Dardanelles. *Strait* NW Turkey
Cananea 50 B1 Sonora, NW Mexico
Canarias, Islas 70 A2 *Eng.* Canary Islands. *Island group* Spain, NE Atlantic Ocean
Canarreos, Archipiélago de los 54 B2 *island group* W Cuba
Canary Islands *see* Canarias, Islas
Cañas 52 D4 Guanacaste, NW Costa Rica
Canaveral, Cape 43 E4 *headland* Florida, SE USA
Canavieiras 63 G3 Bahia, E Brazil
Canberra 142 C4 *country capital* (Australia) Australian Capital Territory, SE Australia
Cancún 51 H3 Quintana Roo, SE Mexico
Candia *see* Irákleio
Canea *see* Chaniá
Cangzhou 128 D4 Hebei, E China
Caniapiscau 39 E2 *river* Quebec, E Canada
Caniapiscau, Réservoir de 38 D3 *reservoir* Quebec, C Canada
Canik Dağları 116 D2 *mountain range* N Turkey
Canillo 91 A7 C Andorra
Çankırı 116 C3 *var.* Chankiri; *anc.* Gangra, Germanicopolis. Çankın, N Turkey
Cannanore 132 B2 *var.* Kananur, Kannur. Kerala, SW India
Cannes 91 D6 Alpes-Maritimes, SE France
Canoas 63 E5 Rio Grande do Sul, S Brazil
Canon City 44 C5 Colorado, C USA
Cantabria 92 D1 *cultural region* N Spain
Cantábrica, Cordillera 92 C1 *mountain range* N Spain
Cantaura 59 E2 Anzoátegui, NE Venezuela
Canterbury 89 E7 *hist.* Cantwaraburh, *anc.* Durovernum, *Lat.* Cantuaria. SE England, UK
Canterbury Bight 151 C6 *bight* South Island, NZ
Canterbury Plains 151 C6 *plain* South Island, NZ
Cân Thơ 137 E6 Can Tho, S Vietnam
Canton *see* Guangzhou
Canton 42 B2 Mississippi, S USA
Canton 40 D4 Ohio, N USA
Canton Island *see* Kanton
Canyon 49 E2 Texas, SW USA
Cao Băng 136 D3 *var.* Caobang. Cao Băng, N Vietnam
Caobang *see* Cao Băng
Cape Barren Island 149 C8 *island* Furneaux Group, Tasmania, SE Australia
Cape Basin 69 B7 *undersea feature* S Atlantic Ocean
Cape Breton Island 39 G4 *Fr.* Île du Cap-Breton. *Island* Nova Scotia, SE Canada
Cape Charles 41 F5 Virginia, NE USA
Cape Coast 75 E5 *prev.* Cape Coast Castle. S Ghana
Cape Farewell *see* Uummannarsuaq
Cape Girardeau 45 H5 Missouri, C USA
Cape Horn *see* Hornos, Cabo de
Capelle aan den IJssel 86 C4 Zuid-Holland, SW Netherlands
Cape Palmas *see* Harper
Cape Town 78 B5 *var.* Ekapa, *Afr.* Kaapstad, Kapstad. *Country capital* (South Africa-legislative capital) Western Cape, SW South Africa

Cape Verde 74 A2 *Port.* Cabo Verde, Ilhas do Cabo Verde. *Country* E Atlantic Ocean

Cape Verde 74

Official name Republic of Cape Verde
Formation 1975
Capital Praia
Population 437,000 / 281 people per sq mile (108 people per sq km)
Total area 1,557 sq miles (4,033 sq km)
Languages Portuguese Creole, Portuguese
Religions Roman Catholic 97%, Protestant (Church of Nazarene) 1%, other 2%
Ethnic mix Mestico 60%, African 30%, other 10%
Government Multiparty republic
Currency Cape Verde escudo = 100 centavos
Literacy rate 74.2%
Calorie consumption 3,278 kilocalories

Cape Verde Basin 66 C4 *undersea feature* E Atlantic Ocean
Cape Verde Plain 66 C4 *undersea feature* E Atlantic Ocean
Cape York Peninsula 148 C2 *peninsula* Queensland, N Australia
Cap-Haïtien 54 D3 *var.* Le Cap. N Haiti
Capira 53 G5 Panamá, C Panama
Capitán Arturo Prat 154 A2 *Chilean research station* South Shetland Islands, Antarctica
Capitán Pablo Lagerenza 64 D1 *var.* Mayor Pablo Lagerenza. Chaco, N Paraguay
Capri, Isola di 97 C5 *island* S Italy
Caprivi Strip 78 C3 *Ger.* Caprivizipfel; *prev.* Caprivi Concession. *Cultural region* NE Namibia
Caquetá 56 B3 *off.* Departamanto del Caquetá. *Province* S Colombia
Caquetá, Río 58 C5 *var.* Rio Japurá, Yapurá. *River* Brazil/Colombia *see also* Japurá, Rio
CAR *see* Central African Republic
Caracal 108 B5 Olt, S Romania
Caracaraí 62 D1 Rondônia, W Brazil
Caracas 58 D1 *country capital* (Venezuela) Distrito Federal, N Venezuela
Caratasca, Laguna de 53 E2 *lagoon* NE Honduras
Carballiño *see* O Carballiño
Carbondale 40 B5 Illinois, N USA
Carbonia 97 A6 *var.* Carbonia Centro. Sardegna, Italy, C Mediterranean Sea
Carbonia Centro *see* Carbonia
Carcassonne 91 C6 *anc.* Carcaso. Aude, S France
Cárdenas 54 B2 Matanzas, W Cuba
Cardiff 89 C7 *Wel.* Caerdydd. *Admin capital* S Wales, UK
Cardigan Bay 89 C6 *bay* W Wales, UK
Carei 108 B3 *Ger.* Gross-Karol, Karol, *Hung.* Nagykároly; *prev.* Careii-Mari. Satu Mare, NW Romania
Carey, Lake 147 B6 *lake* Western Australia
Cariaco 59 E1 Sucre, NE Venezuela
Caribbean Sea 54 C4 *sea* W Atlantic Ocean
Carlisle 88 C4 *anc.* Caer Luel, Luguvallium, Luguvallum. NW England, UK
Carlow 89 B6 *Ir.* Ceatharlach. SE Ireland
Carlsbad 48 D3 New Mexico, SW USA
Carlsberg Ridge 140 B4 *undersea feature* S Arabian Sea
Carlsruhe *see* Karlsruhe
Carmana *see* Kermān
Carmarthen 89 C6 SW Wales, UK
Carmaux 91 C6 Tarn, S France

Carmel 40 C4 Indiana, N USA
Carmelita 52 B1 Petén, N Guatemala
Carmen 51 G4 *var.* Ciudad del Carmen. Campeche, SE Mexico
Carmona 92 C4 Andalucía, S Spain
Carnaro *see* Kvarner
Carnarvon 147 A5 Western Australia
Carnegie, Lake 147 B5 *salt lake* Western Australia
Car Nicobar 133 F3 *island* Nicobar Islands, India, NE Indian Ocean
Caroço, Ilha 76 E1 *island* N Sao Tome and Principe
Carolina 63 F2 Maranhão, E Brazil
Caroline Island *see* Millennium Island
Caroline Islands 106 C2 *island group* C Micronesia
Caroní, Río 59 E3 *river* E Venezuela
Caronium *see* A Coruña
Carora 58 C1 Lara, N Venezuela
Carpathian Mountains 81 E4 *var.* Carpathians, *Cz./Pol.* Karpaty, *Ger.* Karpaten. *Mountain range* E Europe
Carpathians *see* Carpathian Mountains
Carpaţii Meridionali 108 B4 *var.* Alpi Transilvaniei, Carpaţii Sudici, *Eng.* South Carpathians, Transylvanian Alps, *Ger.* Südkarpaten, Transsylvanische Alpen, *Hung.* Déli-Kárpátok, Erdélyi-Havasok. *Mountain range* C Romania
Carpaţii Occidentali 99 E7 *Eng.* Western Carpathians. *Mountain range* W Romania
Carpaţii Sudici *see* Carpaţii Meridionali
Carpentaria, Gulf of 148 B2 *gulf* N Australia
Carpi 96 C2 Emilia-Romagna, N Italy
Carrara 96 B3 Toscana, C Italy
Carson City 47 C5 *state capital* Nevada, W USA
Carson Sink 47 C5 *salt flat* Nevada, W USA
Cartagena 93 F4 *anc.* Carthago Nova. Murcia, SE Spain
Cartagena 58 B1 *var.* Cartagena de los Indes. Bolívar, NW Colombia
Cartagena de los Indes *see* Cartagena
Cartago 53 E4 Cartago, C Costa Rica
Carthage 45 F5 Missouri, C USA
Cartwright 39 F2 Newfoundland and Labrador, E Canada
Carúpano 59 E1 Sucre, NE Venezuela
Caruthersville 45 H5 Missouri, C USA
Cary 43 F1 North Carolina, SE USA
Casablanca 70 C2 *Ar.* Dar-el-Beida. NW Morocco
Casa Grande 48 B2 Arizona, SW USA
Cascade Range 46 B3 *mountain range* Oregon/Washington, NW USA
Cascais 92 B4 Lisboa, C Portugal
Caserta 97 D5 Campania, S Italy
Casey 154 D4 *Australian research station* Antarctica
Casino 91 C8 New South Wales, SE Australia
Čáslav 99 B5 *Ger.* Tschaslau. Středočeský Kraj, C Czech Republic
Casper 44 C3 Wyoming, C USA
Caspian Depression 111 B7 *Kaz.* Kaspīy Mangy Oypaty, *Rus.* Prikaspiyskaya Nizmennost'. *Depression* Kazakhstan/Russian Federation
Caspian Sea 114 A4 *Az.* Xäzär Dänizi, *Kaz.* Kaspiy Tengizi, *Per.* Baḩr-e Khazar, Daryā-ye Khazar, *Rus.* Kaspiyskoye More. *Inland sea* Asia/Europe
Cassai *see* Kasai
Castamoni *see* Kastamonu

Casteggio 96 B2 Lombardia, N Italy
Castelló de la Plana 93 F3 *var.* Castellón. País Valenciano, E Spain
Castellón *see* Castelló de la Plana
Castelnaudary 91 C6 Aude, S France
Castelo Branco 92 C3 Castelo Branco, C Portugal
Castelsarrasin 91 B6 Tarn-et-Garonne, S France
Castelvetrano 97 C7 Sicilia, Italy, C Mediterranean Sea
Castilla-La Mancha 93 E3 *cultural region* NE Spain
Castilla-León 92 C2 *cultural region* NW Spain
Castlebar 89 A5 *Ir.* Caisleán an Bharraigh. W Ireland
Castleford 89 D5 N England, UK
Castle Harbour 42 B5 *inlet* Bermuda, NW Atlantic Ocean
Castricum 86 C3 Noord-Holland, W Netherlands
Castries 55 F1 *country capital* (Saint Lucia) N Saint Lucia
Castro 65 B6 Los Lagos, W Chile
Castrovillari 97 D6 Calabria, SW Italy
Castuera 92 D4 Extremadura, W Spain
Caswell Sound 151 A7 *sound* South Island, NZ
Catacamas 52 D2 Olancho, C Honduras
Catacaos 60 B3 Piura, NW Peru
Catalan Bay 93 H4 *var.* Caleta. *Bay* E Gibraltar
Cataluña 93 G2 *cultural region* N Spain
Catamarca *see* San Fernando del Valle de Catamarca
Catania 97 D7 Sicilia, Italy, C Mediterranean Sea
Catanzaro 97 D6 Calabria, SW Italy
Catarroja 93 F3 País Valenciano, E Spain
Cat Island 54 C1 *island* C Bahamas
Catskill Mountains 41 F3 *mountain range* New York, NE USA
Cauca, Río 58 B2 *river* N Colombia
Caucasia 58 B2 Antioquia, NW Colombia
Caucasus 81 G4 *Rus.* Kavkaz. *Mountain range* Georgia/Russian Federation
Caura, Río 59 E3 *river* C Venezuela
Cavalla 74 D5 *var.* Cavally, Cavally Fleuve. *River* Côte d'Ivoire/Liberia
Cavally *see* Cavalla
Cavally Fleuve *see* Cavalla
Caviana de Fora, Ilha 63 E1 *var.* Ilha Caviana. *Island* N Brazil
Caxito 78 B1 Bengo, NW Angola
Cayenne 59 H3 *dependent territory capital* (French Guiana) NE French Guiana
Cayes 54 D3 *var.* Les Cayes. SW Haiti
Cayman Brac 54 B3 *island* E Cayman Islands
Cayman Islands 54 B3 *UK dependent territory* W West Indies
Cay Sal 54 B2 *islet* SW Bahamas
Cazin 100 B3 Federacija Bosna I Hercegovina, NW Bosnia and Herzegovina
Cazorla 93 E4 Andalucía, S Spain
Ceadâr-Lunga *see* Ciadir-Lunga
Ceará 63 F2 *off.* Estado do Ceará. *State* E Brazil
Ceara Abyssal Plain *see* Ceará Plain
Ceará Plain 56 E3 *var.* Ceara Abyssal Plain. *Undersea feature* W Atlantic Ocean
Ceatharlach *see* Carlow
Cébaco, Isla 53 F5 *island* SW Panama
Cebu 139 E2 *off.* Cebu City. Cebu, C Philippines
Cecina 96 B3 Toscana, C Italy
Cedar City 44 A5 Utah, W USA
Cedar Falls 45 G3 Iowa, C USA
Cedar Lake 38 A2 *lake* Manitoba, C Canada

Cedar Rapids 45 G3 Iowa, C USA
Cedros, Isla 50 A2 *island* W Mexico
Ceduna 149 A6 South Australia
Cefalu 97 C7 *anc.* Cephaloedium. Sicilia, Italy, C Mediterranean Sea
Celebes *see* Sulawesi
Celebes Sea 139 E3 Ind. Laut Sulawesi. *Sea* Indonesia/Philippines
Celje 95 E7 Ger. Cilli. C Slovenia
Celldömölk 99 C6 Vas, W Hungary
Celle 94 B3 *var.* Zelle. Niedersachsen, N Germany
Celtic Sea 89 B7 Ir. An Mhuir Cheilteach. *Sea* W British Isles
Celtic Shelf 80 B3 *undersea feature* E Atlantic Ocean
Cenderawasih, Teluk 139 G4 *var.* Teluk Irian, Teluk Sarera. *Bay* W Pacific Ocean
Cenon 91 B5 Gironde, SW France
Central African Republic 76 C4 *var.* République Centrafricaine, *abbrev.* CAR; *prev.* Ubangi-Shari, Oub angui-Chari, Territoire de l'Oubangui-Chari. *Country* C Africa

---

Central African Republic 76

Official name Central African Republic
Formation 1960
Capital Bangui
Population 3.8 million / 16 people per sq mile (6 people per sq km)
Total area 240,534 sq miles (622,984 sq km)
Languages French, Sango, Banda, Gbaya
Religions Traditional beliefs 60%, Christian 35%, Muslim 5%
Ethnic mix Baya 34%, Banda 27%, Mandjia 21%, Sara 10%, other 8%
Government Multiparty republic
Currency CFA franc = 100 centimes
Literacy rate 46.7%
Calorie consumption 1,946 kilocalories

Central, Cordillera 55 E3 *mountain range* C Dominican Republic
Central, Cordillera 53 F5 *mountain range* C Panama
Central, Cordillera 139 E1 *mountain range* Luzon, N Philippines
Central, Cordillera 58 B3 *mountain range* W Colombia
Central Group *see* Inner Islands
Centralia 46 B2 Washington, NW USA
Central Indian Ridge *see* Mid-Indian Ridge
Central Makrán Range 134 A3 *mountain range* W Pakistan
Central Pacific Basin 142 D1 *undersea feature* C Pacific Ocean
Central, Planalto 63 F3 *var.* Brazilian Highlands. *Mountain range* E Brazil
Central Range 144 B3 *mountain range* NW PNG
Central Russian Upland *see* Srednerusskaya Vozvyshennost'
Central Siberian Plateau *see* Srednesibirskoye Ploskogor'ye
Central Siberian Uplands *see* Srednesibirskoye Ploskogor'ye
Central, Sistema 92 D3 *mountain range* C Spain
Central Valley 47 B6 *valley* California, W USA
Cephaloedium *see* Cefalu
Ceram *see* Seram, Pulau
Ceram Sea 139 F4 Ind. Laut Seram. *Sea* E Indonesia
Cerasus *see* Giresun
Cereté 58 B2 Córdoba, NW Colombia
Cerignola 97 D5 Puglia, SE Italy
Cerigo *see* Kýthira
Çerkeş 116 C2 Çankırı, N Turkey
Cernay 90 E4 Haut-Rhin, NE France

Cerro Chirripó *see* Chirripó Grande, Cerro
Cerro de Mulhacén *see* Mulhacén
Cerro de Pasco 60 C3 Pasco, C Peru
Cervera 93 F2 Cataluña, NE Spain
Cesena 96 C3 *anc.* Caesena. Emilia-Romagna, N Italy
Cēsis 106 D3 Ger. Wenden. Cēsis, C Latvia
České Budějovice 99 B5 Ger. Budweis. Budějovický Kraj, S Czech Republic
Český Krumlov 99 A5 *var.* Böhmisch-Krumau, Ger. Krummau. Budějovický Kraj, S Czech Republic
Cetinje 101 C5 It. Cettigne. Montenegro, SW Serbia and Montenegro (Yugo.)
Ceuta 70 C2 *enclave* Spain, N Africa
Cévennes 91 C6 *mountain range* S France
Ceyhan 116 D4 Adana, S Turkey
Ceylanpınar 117 E4 Şanlıurfa, SE Turkey
Ceylon Plain 124 B4 *undersea feature* N Indian Ocean
Ceyre to the Caribs *see* Marie-Galante
Chachapoyas 60 B2 Amazonas, NW Peru
Chachevichy 107 D6 Rus. Chechevichi. Mahilyowskaya Voblasts', E Belarus
Chaco *see* Gran Chaco
Chad 76 C3 Fr. Tchad. *Country* C Africa

Chad 76

Official name Republic of Chad
Formation 1960
Capital N'Djamena
Population 8.1 million / 16 people per sq mile (6 people per sq km)
Total area 495,752 sq miles (1,284,000 sq km)
Languages French, Arabic, Sara, Maba
Religions Muslim 50%, Traditional beliefs 43%, Christian 7%
Ethnic mix Nomads (Tuareg and Toubou) 38%, Sara 30, Arab 15%, Other 17%
Government Presidential democracy
Currency CFA franc = 100 centimes
Literacy rate 42.6%
Calorie consumption 2,046 kilocalories

Chad, Lake 76 B3 Fr. Lac Tchad. *Lake* C Africa
Chadron 44 D3 Nebraska, C USA
Chadyr-Lunga *see* Ciadir-Lunga
Chāgai Hills 134 A2 *var.* Chāh Gay. *Mountain range* Afghanistan/Pakistan
Chaghasarāy *see* Asadābād
Chagos-Laccadive Plateau 124 B4 *undersea feature* N Indian Ocean
Chagos Trench 141 C5 *undersea feature* N Indian Ocean
Chāh Gay *see* Chāgai Hills
Chaillu, Massif du 77 B6 *mountain range* C Gabon
Chaîne des Dangrek *see* Dângrêk, Chuŏr Phnum
Chaîne des Mitumba *see* Mitumba, Monts
Chaîne des Mongos *see* Bongo, Massif des
Chain Ridge 140 B4 *undersea feature* W Indian Ocean
Chajul 52 B2 Quiché, W Guatemala
Chakhānsūr 122 D5 Nīmrūz, SW Afghanistan
Chala 60 D4 Arequipa, SW Peru
Chalatenango 52 C3 Chalatenango, N El Salvador
Chalcidice *see* Chalkidikí
Chalcis *see* Chalkída
Chálki 105 E7 *island* Dodekánisos, Greece, Aegean Sea

Chalkída 105 C5 *var.* Halkida; *prev.* Khalkís, *anc.* Chalcis. Evvoia, E Greece
Chalkidikí 104 C4 *var.* Khalkidhikí; *anc.* Chalcidice. *Peninsula* NE Greece
Challans 90 B4 Vendée, NW France
Challapata 61 F4 Oruro, SW Bolivia
Challenger Deep 152 B3 *undersea feature* W Pacific Ocean
Challenger Fracture Zone 153 F4 *tectonic feature* SE Pacific Ocean
Châlons-en-Champagne 90 D3 *prev.* Châlons-sur-Marne, *hist.* Arcae Remorum, *anc.* Carolopois. Marne, NE France
Chalon-sur-Saône 90 D4 *anc.* Cabillonum. Saône-et-Loire, C France
Cha Mai *see* Thung Song
Chaman 134 B2 Baluchistān, SW Pakistan
Chambéry 91 D5 *anc.* Cambería. Savoie, E France
Champagne 90 D3 Yukon Territory, W Canada
Champaign 40 B4 Illinois, N USA
Champasak 137 D5 Champasak, S Laos
Champlain, Lake 41 F2 *lake* Canada/USA
Champotón 51 G4 Campeche, SE Mexico
Chanak *see* Çanakkale
Chañaral 64 B3 Atacama, N Chile
Chanchiang *see* Zhanjiang
Chandeleur Islands 42 C3 *island group* Louisiana, S USA
Chandīgarh 134 D2 Punjab, N India
Chandrapur 135 E5 Mahārāshtra, C India
Changan *see* Xi'an
Changane 79 E3 *river* S Mozambique
Changchun 128 D3 *var.* Ch'angch'un, Ch'ang-ch'un; *prev.* Hsinking. Jilin, NE China
Ch'angch'un *see* Changchun
Chang Jiang 128 B5 *var.* Yangtze Kiang, *Eng.* Yangtze. *River* C China
Changkiakow *see* Zhangjiakou
Chang, Ko 137 C6 *island* S Thailand
Changsha 128 C6 *var.* Ch'angsha, Ch'ang-sha. Hunan, S China
Ch'angsha *see* Changsha
Changzhi 128 C4 Shanxi, C China
Chaniá 105 C7 *var.* Hania, Khaniá, *Eng.* Canea; *anc.* Cydonia. Kríti, Greece, E Mediterranean Sea
Chañi, Nevado de 64 B2 *mountain* NW Argentina
Chankiri *see* Çankırı
Channel Islands 89 C8 Fr. Îles Normandes. *Island group* S English Channel
Channel Islands 47 B8 *island group* California, W USA
Channel-Port aux Basques 39 G4 Newfoundland, Newfoundland and Labrador, SE Canada
Channel, The *see* English Channel
Channel Tunnel 90 C2 *tunnel* France/UK
Chantabun *see* Chanthaburi
Chantaburi *see* Chanthaburi
Chantada 92 C1 Galicia, NW Spain
Chanthaburi 137 C6 *var.* Chantabun, Chantaburi. Chantaburi, S Thailand
Chanute 45 F5 Kansas, C USA
Chaouèn *see* Chefchaouen
Chaoyang 128 D3 Liaoning, NE China
Chapala, Lago de 50 D4 *lake* C Mexico
Chapan, Gora 122 B3 *mountain* C Turkmenistan
Chapayevsk 111 C6 Samarskaya Oblast', W Russian Federation
Chaplynka 109 F4 Khersons'ka Oblast', S Ukraine
Charcot Seamounts 80 B3 *undersea feature* E Atlantic Ocean

Chardzhev 122 D3 *prev.* Chardzhou, Chardzhui, Leninsk-Turkmenski, *Turkm.* Chärjew. Lebapskiy Velayat, E Turkmenistan
Charente 91 B5 *cultural region* W France
Charente 91 B5 *river* W France
Chari 76 B3 *var.* Shari. *River* Central African Republic/Chad
Chärīkār 123 E4 Parwān, NE Afghanistan
Charity 59 F2 NW Guyana
Charkhlik *see* Ruoqiang
Charkhliq *see* Ruoqiang
Charleroi 87 C7 Hainaut, S Belgium
Charlesbourg 39 E4 Quebec, SE Canada
Charles de Gaulle 90 E1 *international airport* (Paris) Seine-et-Marne, N France
Charles Island 38 D1 *island* Northwest Territories, NE Canada
Charles Island *see* Santa María, Isla
Charleston 40 D5 *state capital* West Virginia, NE USA
Charleston 43 F2 South Carolina, SE USA
Charleville 149 D5 Queensland, E Australia
Charleville-Mézières 90 D3 Ardennes, N France
Charlie-Gibbs Fracture Zone 66 B2 *tectonic feature* N Atlantic Ocean
Charlotte 43 E1 North Carolina, SE USA
Charlotte Amalie 55 F3 *prev.* Saint Thomas. *Dependent territory capital* (Virgin Islands (US)) Saint Thomas, N Virgin Islands (US)
Charlotte Harbor 43 E5 *inlet* Florida, SE USA
Charlottesville 41 E5 Virginia, NE USA
Charlottetown 39 F4 Prince Edward Island, Prince Edward Island, SE Canada
Charsk *see* Shar
Charters Towers 148 D3 Queensland, NE Australia
Chartres 90 C3 *anc.* Autricum, Civitas Carnutum. Eure-et-Loir, C France
Charus Nuur 126 C2 *lake* NW Mongolia
Chashniki 107 D5 Rus. Chashniki. Vitsyebskaya Voblasts', N Belarus
Châteaubriant 90 B4 Loire-Atlantique, NW France
Châteaudun 90 C3 Eure-et-Loir, C France
Châteauroux 90 C4 *prev.* Indreville. Indre, C France
Château-Thierry 90 C3 Aisne, N France
Châtelet 87 C7 Hainaut, S Belgium
Châtelherault *see* Châtellerault
Châtellerault 90 B4 *var.* Châtelherault. Vienne, W France
Chatham Island *see* San Cristóbal, Isla
Chatham Island Rise *see* Chatham Rise
Chatham Islands 143 E5 *island group* NZ, SW Pacific Ocean
Chatham Rise 142 D5 *var.* Chatham Island Rise. *Undersea feature* S Pacific Ocean
Chatkal Range 123 F2 Rus. Chatkal'skiy Khrebet. *Mountain range* Kyrgyzstan/Uzbekistan
Chattahoochee River 42 D3 *river* SE USA
Chattanooga 42 D1 Tennessee, S USA
Chatyr-Tash 123 G2 Narynskaya Oblast', C Kyrgyzstan
Châu Độc 137 D6 *var.* Chauphu, Chau Phu. An Giang, S Vietnam
Chauk 136 A3 Magwe, W Myanmar
Chaumont 90 D4 *prev.* Chaumont-en-Bassigny. Haute-Marne, N France
Chau Phu *see* Châu Độc
Chaves 92 C2 *anc.* Aquae Flaviae. Vila Real, N Portugal
Chávez, Isla *see* Santa Cruz, Isla

Chavusy *107 E6 Rus.* Chausy.
Mahilyowskaya Voblasts',
E Belarus
Chaykovskiy *111 D5* Permskaya
Oblast', NW Russian Federation
Cheb *99 A5 Ger.* Eger. Karlovarský
Kraj, W Czech Republic
Cheboksary *111 C5* Chuvashskaya
Respublika, W Russian Federation
Cheboygan *40 C2* Michigan, N USA
Chechaouèn *see* Chefchaouen
Chech, Erg *74 D1 desert*
Algeria/Mali
Che-chiang *see* Zhejiang
Cheduba Island *136 A4 island*
W Myanmar
Chefchaouen *70 C2 var.* Chaouèn,
Chechaouèn, *Sp.* Xauen.
N Morocco
Chefoo *see* Yantai
Cheju-do *129 E4 Jap.* Saishū;
prev. Quelpart. *Island* S South
Korea
Cheju Strait *129 E4 strait* S South
Korea
Chekiang *see* Zhejiang
Cheleken *122 B2* Balkanskiy
Velayat, W Turkmenistan
Chelkar *114 B4* Aktyubinsk,
W Kazakhstan
Chełm *98 E4 Rus.* Kholm.
Lubelskie, E Poland
Chełmno *98 C3 Ger.* Culm, Kulm.
Kujawski-pomorskie, C Poland
Chełmża *98 C3 Ger.* Culmsee,
Kulmsee. Kujawski-pomorskie, C
Poland
Cheltenham *89 D6* C England, UK
Chelyabinsk *114 C3*
Chelyabinskaya Oblast',
C Russian Federation
Chemnitz *94 D4 prev.* Karl-Marx-
Stadt. Sachsen, E Germany
Chenāb *134 C2 river* India/Pakistan
Chengchiatun *see* Liaoyuan
Ch'eng-chou *see* Zhengzhou
Chengchow *see* Zhengzhou
Chengde *128 D3 var.* Jehol. Hebei,
E China
Chengdu *128 B5 var.* Chengtu,
Ch'eng-tu. Sichuan, C China
Chenghsien *see* Zhengzhou
Ch'eng-tu *see* Chengdu
Chennai *132 D2 prev* Madras. Tamil
Nādu, S India
Chenxian *see* Chenzhou
Chen Xian *see* Chenzhou
Chen Xiang *see* Chenzhou
Chenzhou *128 C6 var.* Chenxian,
Chen Xian, Chen Xiang. Hunan,
S China
Chepelare *104 C3* Smolyan,
S Bulgaria
Chepén *60 B3* La Libertad, C Peru
Cher *90 C4 river* C France
Cherbourg *90 B3 anc.* Carusbur.
Manche, N France
Cherepovets *110 B4* Vologodskaya
Oblast', NW Russian Federation
Chergui, Chott ech *70 D2 salt lake*
NW Algeria
Cherkasy *109 E2 Rus.* Cherkassy.
Cherkas'ka Oblast', C Ukraine
Cherkessk *111 B7* Karachayevo-
Cherkesskaya Respublika,
SW Russian Federation
Chernihiv *109 E1 Rus.* Chernigov.
Chernihivs'ka Oblast',
NE Ukraine
Chernivtsi *108 C3 Ger.* Czernowitz,
Rom. Cernăuţi, *Rus.* Chernovtsy.
Chernivets'ka Oblast', W Ukraine
Cherno More *see* Black Sea
Chernoye More *see* Black Sea
Chernyakhovsk *106 A4 Ger.*
Insterburg. Kaliningradskaya
Oblast', W Russian Federation
Cherry Hill *41 F4* New Jersey,
NE USA
Cherski Range *see* Cherskogo,
Khrebet
Cherskiy *115 G2* Respublika Sakha
(Yakutiya), NE Russian
Federation
Cherskogo, Khrebet *115 F2 var.*
Cherski Range. *Mountain range*
NE Russian Federation

Chervonohrad *108 C2 Rus.*
Chervonograd. L'vivs'ka Oblast',
NW Ukraine
Chervyen' *107 D6 Rus.* Cherven'.
Minskaya Voblasts', C Belarus
Cherykaw *107 E7 Rus.* Cherikov.
Mahilyowskaya Voblasts',
E Belarus
Chesapeake Bay *41 F5 inlet*
NE USA
Chesha Bay *see* Chëshskaya Guba
Chëshskaya Guba *172 D5 var.*
Archangel Bay, Chesha Bay, Dvina
Bay. *Bay* NW Russian Federation
Chester *89 C6 Wel.* Caerleon; *hist.*
Legaceaster, *Lat.* Deva, Devana
Castra. C England, UK
Chetumal *51 H4 var.* Payo Obispo.
Quintana Roo, SE Mexico
Cheviot Hills *88 D4 hill range*
England/Scotland, UK
Cheyenne *44 D4 state capital*
Wyoming, C USA
Cheyenne River *44 D3 river* South
Dakota/Wyoming, N USA
Chhapra *135 F3 prev.* Chapra. Bihār,
N India
Chiai *128 D6 var.* Chia-i, Chiayi,
Kiayi, Jiayi, *Jap.* Kagi. C Taiwan
Chia-i *see* Chiai
Chiang-hsi *see* Jiangxi
Chiang Mai *136 B4 var.* Chiangmai,
Chiengmai, Kiangmai. Chiang
Mai, NW Thailand
Chiangmai *see* Chiang Mai
Chiang Rai *136 C3 var.* Chianpai,
Chienrai, Muang Chiang Rai.
Chiang Rai, NW Thailand
Chiang-su *see* Jiangsu
Chian-ning *see* Nanjing
Chianpai *see* Chiang Rai
Chianti *96 C3 cultural region*
C Italy
Chiapa *see* Chiapa de Corzo
Chiapa de Corzo *51 G5 var.* Chiapa.
Chiapas, SE Mexico
Chiayi *see* Chiai
Chiba *130 B1 var.* Tiba. Chiba,
Honshū, S Japan
Chibougamau *38 D3* Quebec,
SE Canada
Chicago *40 B3* Illinois, N USA
Ch'i-ch'i-ha-erh *see* Qiqihar
Chickasha *49 G2* Oklahoma, C USA
Chiclayo *60 B3* Lambayeque,
NW Peru
Chico *47 B5* California, W USA
Chico, Río *65 B6 river* S Argentina
Chico, Río *65 B7 river* SE Argentina
Chicoutimi *39 E4* Quebec,
SE Canada
Chiengmai *see* Chiang Mai
Chienrai *see* Chiang Rai
Chiesanuova *96 D2* SW San
Marino
Chieti *96 D4 var.* Teate. Abruzzo,
C Italy
Chifeng *127 G2 var.* Ulanhad. Nei
Mongol Zizhiqu, N China
Chih-fu *see* Yantai
Chihli *see* Hebei
Chihli, Gulf of *see* Bo Hai
Chihuahua *50 C2* Chihuahua,
NW Mexico
Childress *49 F2* Texas, SW USA
Chile *64 B3 Country* SW South
America

Chile 64

Official name Republic of Chile
Formation 1818
Capital Santiago
Population 15.4 million / 53 people
per sq mile (20 people per sq km)
Total area 292,258 sq miles
(756,950 sq km)
Languages Spanish, Amerindian
languages
Religions Roman Catholic 80%,
other and non-religious 20%
Ethnic mix Mixed and European
90%, Amerindian 10%
Government Multiparty republic
Currency Chilean peso = 100
centavos

Chile (continued)

Literacy rate 95.7%
Calorie consumption 2,882
kilocalories

Chile Basin *57 A5 undersea feature*
E Pacific Ocean
Chile Chico *65 B6* Aisén, W Chile
Chile Rise *57 A7 undersea feature*
SE Pacific Ocean
Chililabombwe *78 D2* Copperbelt,
C Zambia
Chi-lin *see* Jilin
Chillán *65 B5* Bío Bío, C Chile
Chillicothe *40 D4* Ohio, N USA
Chiloé, Isla de *65 A6 var.* Isla
Grande de Chiloé. *Island*
W Chile
Chilpancingo *51 E5 var.*
Chilpancingo de los Bravos.
Guerrero, S Mexico
Chilpancingo de los Bravos *see*
Chilpancingo
Chilung *128 D6 var.* Keelung, *Jap.*
Kirun, Kiirun; *prev. Sp. Santissima
Trinidad.* N Taiwan
Chimán *53 G5* Panamá, E Panama
Chimborazo *60 A1 volcano*
C Ecuador
Chimbote *60 C3* Ancash, W Peru
Chimboy *122 D1 Rus.* Chimbay.
Qoraqalpoghiston Respublikasi,
NW Uzbekistan
Chimoio *79 E3* Manica,
C Mozambique
China *124 C2 Chin.* Chung-hua Jen-
min Kung-ho-kuo, Zhonghua
Renmin Gongheguo; *prev.* Chinese
Empire. *Country* E Asia

China 124

Official name People's Republic
of China
Formation 960
Capital Beijing
Population 1.29 billion /
348 people per sq mile (134 people
per sq km)
Total area 3,705,386 sq miles
(9,596,960 sq km)
Languages Mandarin, Wu,
Cantonese, Hsiang, Min,
Hakka, Kan
Religions Non-religious 59%,
Traditional beliefs 20%, other 21%
Ethnic mix Han 93%, other 7%
Government One-party state
Currency Yuan (Renminbi) = 10 jiao
Literacy rate 84.2%
Calorie consumption 3,029
kilocalories

Chi-nan *see* Jinan
Chinandega *52 C3* Chinandega,
NW Nicaragua
Chincha Alta *60 D4* Ica, SW Peru
Chin-chiang *see* Quanzhou
Chin-chou *see* Jinzhou
Chinchow *see* Jinzhou
Chindwin *136 B2 river*
N Myanmar
Ch'ing Hai *see* Qinghai Hu
Chingola *78 D2* Copperbelt,
C Zambia
Ching-Tao *see* Qingdao
Chinguetti *74 C2 var.* Chinguetti.
Adrar, C Mauritania
Chin Hills *136 A3 mountain range*
W Myanmar
Chinhsien *see* Jinzhou
Chinnereth *see* Tiberias, Lake
Chinook Trough *113 H4 undersea
feature* N Pacific Ocean
Chioggia *96 C2 anc.* Fossa Claudia.
Veneto, NE Italy
Chíos *105 D5 var.* Hios, Khíos, *It.*
Scio, *Turk.* Sakiz-Adasi. Chíos,
E Greece
Chíos *105 D5 var.* Khíos. *Island*
E Greece
Chipata *78 D2 prev.* Fort Jameson.
Eastern, E Zambia

Chiquián *60 C3* Ancash, W Peru
Chiquimula *52 B2* Chiquimula,
SE Guatemala
Chīrāla *132 D1* Andhra Pradesh,
E India
Chirchiq *123 E2 Rus.* Chirchik.
Toshkent Wiloyati, E Uzbekistan
Chiriquí, Golfo de *53 E5 Eng.*
Chiriqui Gulf. *Gulf* SW Panama
Chiriquí, Laguna de *53 E5 lagoon*
NW Panama
Chirripó Grande, Cerro *52 D4 var.*
Cerro Chirripó. *Mountain*
SE Costa Rica
Chisec *52 B2* Alta Verapaz,
C Guatemala
Chisholm *45 F1* Minnesota, N USA
Chisimaio *see* Kismaayo
Chisimayu *see* Kismaayo
Chişinău *108 D4 Rus.* Kishinev.
Country capital (Moldova)
C Moldova
Chita *115 F4* Chitinskaya Oblast',
S Russian Federation
Chitato *78 C1* Lunda Norte,
NE Angola
Chitina *36 D3* Alaska, USA
Chitose *130 D2 var.* Titose.
Hokkaidō, NE Japan
Chitré *53 F5* Herrera, S Panama
Chittagong *135 G4 Ben.* Chāttagām.
Chittagong, SE Bangladesh
Chitungwiza *78 D3 prev.*
Chitangwiza. Mashonaland East,
NE Zimbabwe
Chlef *70 D2 var.* Ech Cheliff, Ech
Cleff; *prev.* Al-Asnam, El Asnam,
Orléansville. NW Algeria
Chocolate Mountains *47 D8
mountain range* California, W USA
Chodzież *98 C3* Wielkopolskie, C
Poland
Choele Choel *65 C5* Río Negro,
C Argentina
Choiseul *144 C3 var.* Lauru. *Island*
NW Solomon Islands
Chojnice *98 C2 Ger.* Knoitz.
Pomorskie, N Poland
Ch'ok'ē *72 C4 var.* Choke
Mountains. *Mountain range*
NW Ethiopia
Choke Mountains *see* Ch'ok'ē
Cholet *90 B4* Maine-et-Loire,
NW France
Choluteca *52 C3* Choluteca,
S Honduras
Choluteca, Río *52 C3 river*
SW Honduras
Choma *78 D2* Southern, S Zambia
Chomutov *98 A4 Ger.* Komotau.
Ústecký Kraj, NW Czech Republic
Chona *113 E2 river* C Russian
Federation
Chon Buri *137 C5 prev.* Bang Pla
Soi. Chon Buri, S Thailand
Chone *60 A1* Manabí, W Ecuador
Ch'ŏngjin *129 E3* NE North Korea
Chongqing *128 B5 var.* Ch'ung-
ching, Ch'ung-ch'ing, Chungking,
Pahsien, Tchongking, Yuzhou.
Chongqing, C China
Chongqing *128 B5 Admin. region
province* C China
Chonos, Archipiélago de los *65 A6
island group* S Chile
Chorne More *see* Black Sea
Chornomors'ke *109 E4 Rus.*
Chernomorskoye. Respublika
Krym, S Ukraine
Chortkiv *108 C2 Rus.* Chortkov.
Ternopil's'ka Oblast', W Ukraine
Chorum *see* Çorum
Chorzów *99 C5 Ger.* Königshütte;
prev. Królewska Huta. Śląskie,
S Poland
Chōshi *131 D5 var.* Tyōsi. Chiba,
Honshū, S Japan
Choszczno *98 B3 Ger.* Arnswalde.
Zachodniopomorskie, NW Poland
Chota Nāgpur *135 E4 plateau*
N India
Chott el-Hodna *see* Hodna, Chott El
Chott Melrhir *see* Melghir, Chott
Choûm *74 C2* Adrar, C Mauritania
Choybalsan *127 F2* Dornod,
E Mongolia
Christchurch *151 C6* Canterbury,
South Island, NZ

Christiana 54 B5 C Jamaica
Christiansand see Kristiansand
Christianshåb see Qasigianguit
Christiansund see Kristiansund
Christmas Island 141 D5 Australian external territory E Indian Ocean
Christmas Ridge 143 E1 undersea feature C Pacific Ocean
Chuan see Sichuan
Ch'u-chou see Quanzhou
Chubut 57 B7 off. Provincia de Chubut. Admin. region province S Argentina
Chubut, Río 65 B6 river SE Argentina
Ch'u-chiang see Shaoguan
Chūgoku-sanchi 131 B6 mountain range Honshū, SW Japan
Chuí see Chuy
Chukai see Cukai
Chukchi Plain 155 B2 undersea feature Arctic Ocean
Chukchi Plateau 34 C2 undersea feature Arctic Ocean
Chukchi Sea 34 B2 Rus. Chukotskoye More. Sea Arctic Ocean
Chula Vista 47 C8 California, W USA
Chulucanas 60 B2 Piura, NW Peru
Chulym 114 D4 river C Russian Federation
Chumphon 137 C6 var. Jumporn. Chumphon, SW Thailand
Ch'unch'ŏn 129 E4 Jap. Shunsen. N South Korea
Ch'ung-ching see Chongqing
Chungking see Chongqing
Chunya 115 E3 river C Russian Federation
Chuquicamata 64 B2 Antofagasta, N Chile
Chur 95 B7 Fr. Coire, It. Coira, Rmsch. Cuera, Quera; anc. Curia Rhaetorum. Graubünden, E Switzerland
Churchill 55 B3 river Manitoba/Saskatchewan, C Canada
Churchill 39 F2 river Newfoundland and Labrador, E Canada
Churchill 37 G4 Manitoba, C Canada
Chuska Mountains 48 C1 mountain range Arizona/New Mexico, SW USA
Chusovoy 111 D5 Permskaya Oblast', NW Russian Federation
Chuuk Islands 144 B2 var. Hogoley Islands; prev. Truk Islands. Island group Caroline Islands, C Micronesia
Chuy 64 E4 var. Chuí. Rocha, E Uruguay
Chyhyryn 109 E2 Rus. Chigirin. Cherkas'ka Oblast', N Ukraine
Ciadîr-Lunga 108 D4 var. Ceadâr-Lunga, Rus. Chadyr-Lunga. S Moldova
Cide 116 C2 Kastamonu, N Turkey
Ciechanów 98 D3 prev. Zichenau. Mazowieckie, C Poland
Ciego de Ávila 54 C2 Ciego de Ávila, C Cuba
Ciénaga 58 B1 Magdalena, N Colombia
Cienfuegos 54 B2 Cienfuegos, C Cuba
Cieza 93 E4 Murcia, SE Spain
Cihanbeyli 116 C3 Konya, C Turkey
Cikobia 145 E4 prev. Thikombia. Island N Fiji
Cilacap 138 C5 prev. Tjilatjap. Jawa, C Indonesia
Cill Airne see Killarney
Cill Chainnigh see Kilkenny
Cill Mhantáin see Wicklow
Cincinnati 40 C4 Ohio, N USA
Ciney 87 C7 Namur, SE Belgium
Cinto, Monte 91 E7 mountain Corse, France, C Mediterranean Sea
Cipolletti 65 B5 Río Negro, C Argentina
Cirebon 138 C4 prev. Tjirebon. Jawa, S Indonesia

Ciro Marino 97 E6 Calabria, S Italy
Cisnădie 108 B4 Ger. Heltau, Hung. Nagydisznód. Sibiu, SW Romania
Citlaltépetl see Orizaba, Volcán Pico de
Citrus Heights 47 B5 California, W USA
Ciudad Bolívar 59 E2 prev. Angostura. Bolívar, E Venezuela
Ciudad Acuña see Villa Acuña
Cuidad Camargo 50 D2 Chihuahua, N Mexico
Ciudad Cortés see Cortés
Ciudad Darío 52 D3 var. Dario. Matagalpa, W Nicaragua
Ciudad de Dolores Hidalgo see Dolores Hidalgo
Ciudad de Guatemala 52 B2 var. Gautemala City Eng. Guatemala City; prev. Santiago de los Caballeros. Country capital (Guatemala) Guatemala, C Guatemala
Ciudad del Carmen see Carmen
Ciudad del Este 64 E2 prev. Cuidad Presidente Stroessner, Presidente Stroessner, Puerto Presidente Stroessner. Alto Paraná, SE Paraguay
Ciudad Delicias see Delicias
Ciudad de México see México
Ciudad de Panamá see Panamá
Ciudad Guayana 59 E2 prev. San Tomé de Guayana, Santo Tomé de Guayana. Bolívar, NE Venezuela
Ciudad Guzmán 50 D4 Jalisco, SW Mexico
Ciudad Hidalgo 51 G5 Chiapas, SE Mexico
Ciudad Juárez 50 C1 Chihuahua, N Mexico
Ciudad Lerdo 50 D3 Durango, C Mexico
Ciudad Madero 51 E3 var. Villa Cecilia. Tamaulipas, C Mexico
Ciudad Mante 51 E3 Tamaulipas, C Mexico
Ciudad Miguel Alemán 51 E2 Tamaulipas, C Mexico
Ciudad Obregón 50 B2 Sonora, NW Mexico
Ciudad Ojeda 58 C1 Zulia, NW Venezuela
Ciudad Porfirio Díaz see Piedras Negras
Ciudad Quesada see Quesada
Ciudad Real 92 D3 Castilla-La Mancha, C Spain
Ciudad-Rodrigo 92 C3 Castilla-León, N Spain
Ciudad Valles 51 E3 San Luis Potosí, C Mexico
Ciudad Victoria 51 E3 Tamaulipas, C Mexico
Ciutadella see Ciutadella de Menorca
Ciutadella de Menorca 93 H3 var. Ciutadella. Menorca, Spain, W Mediterranean Sea
Civitanova Marche 96 D3 Marche, C Italy
Civitavecchia 96 C4 anc. Centum Cellae, Trajani Portus. Lazio, C Italy
Claremore 49 G1 Oklahoma, C USA
Clarence 151 C5 river South Island, NZ
Clarence 151 C5 Canterbury, South Island, NZ
Clarence Town 54 D2 Long Island, C Bahamas
Clarinda 45 F4 Iowa, C USA
Clarion Fracture Zone 153 E2 tectonic feature NE Pacific Ocean
Clarión, Isla 50 A5 island W Mexico
Clark Fork 44 A1 river Idaho/Montana, NW USA
Clark Hill Lake 43 E2 var. J.Storm Thurmond Reservoir. Reservoir Georgia/South Carolina, SE USA
Clarksburg 40 D4 West Virginia, NE USA
Clarksdale 42 B2 Mississippi, S USA

Clarksville 42 C1 Tennessee, S USA
Clayton 49 E1 New Mexico, SW USA
Clearwater 43 E4 Florida, SE USA
Clearwater Mountains 46 D2 mountain range Idaho, NW USA
Cleburne 49 G3 Texas, SW USA
Clermont 148 D4 Queensland, E Australia
Clermont-Ferrand 91 C5 Puy-de-Dôme, C France
Cleveland 40 D3 Ohio, N USA
Cleveland 42 D1 Tennessee, S USA
Clifton 48 C2 Arizona, SW USA
Clinton 42 B2 Mississippi, S USA
Clinton 49 F1 Oklahoma, C USA
Clipperton Fracture Zone 153 E3 tectonic feature E Pacific Ocean
Clipperton Island 35 A7 French dependency of French Polynesia E Pacific Ocean
Cloncurry 148 B3 Queensland, C Australia
Clonmel 89 B6 Ir. Cluain Meala. S Ireland
Cloppenburg 94 B3 Niedersachsen, NW Germany
Cloquet 45 G2 Minnesota, N USA
Cloud Peak 44 C3 mountain Wyoming, C USA
Clovis 49 E2 New Mexico, SW USA
Cluain Meala see Clonmel
Cluj-Napoca 108 B3 Ger. Klausenburg, Hung. Kolozsvár; prev. Cluj. Cluj, NW Romania
Clutha 151 B7 river South Island, NZ
Clyde 88 C4 river W Scotland, UK
Coari 62 D2 Amazonas, N Brazil
Coast Mountains 36 D4 Fr. Chaîne Côtière. Mountain range Canada/USA
Coast Ranges 46 A4 mountain range W USA
Coats Island 37 G3 island Nunavut, NE Canada
Coats Land 154 B2 physical region Antarctica
Coatzacoalcos 51 G4 var. Quetzalcoalco; prev. Puerto México. Veracruz-Llave, E Mexico
Cobán 52 B2 Alta Verapaz, C Guatemala
Cobar 149 C6 New South Wales, SE Australia
Cobija 61 E3 Pando, NW Bolivia
Coburg 95 C5 Bayern, SE Germany
Coca see Puerto Francisco de Orellana
Cochabamba 61 F4 hist. Oropeza. Cochabamba, C Bolivia
Cochin 132 C3 var. Kochi. Kerala, SW India
Cochinos, Bahía de 54 B2 Eng. Bay of Pigs. Bay SE Cuba
Cochrane 65 B7 Aisén, S Chile
Cochrane 38 C4 Ontario, S Canada
Cocibolca see Nicaragua, Lago de
Cockburn Town 55 E2 var. Grand Turk. dependent territory capital (Turks and Caicos Islands) Grand Turk Island, SE Turks and Caicos Islands
Cockpit Country, The 54 A4 physical region W Jamaica
Cocobeach 77 A5 Estuaire, NW Gabon
Coconino Plateau 48 B1 plain Arizona, SW USA
Coco, Río 53 E2 var. Río Wanki, Segoviao Wangkí. River Honduras/Nicaragua
Cocos Basin 124 C5 undersea feature E Indian Ocean
Cocos Island Ridge see Cocos Ridge
Cocos Islands 141 D5 island group E Indian Ocean
Cocos Ridge 35 C8 var. Cocos Island Ridge. Undersea feature E Pacific Ocean
Cod, Cape 41 G3 headland Massachusetts, NE USA
Codfish Island 151 A8 island SW NZ
Codlea 108 C4 Ger. Zeiden, Hung. Feketehalom. Braşov, C Romania

Cody 44 C2 Wyoming, C USA
Coeur d'Alene 46 C2 Idaho, NW USA
Coevorden 86 E2 Drenthe, NE Netherlands
Coffs Harbour 149 E6 New South Wales, SE Australia
Cognac 91 B5 anc. Compniacum. Charente, W France
Coiba, Isla de 53 E5 island SW Panama
Coihaique 65 B6 var. Coyhaique. Aisén, S Chile
Coimbatore 132 C3 Tamil Nādu, S India
Coimbra 92 B3 anc. Conimbria, Conimbriga. Coimbra, W Portugal
Coín 92 D5 Andalucía, S Spain
Coirib, Loch see Corrib, Lough
Colby 45 E4 Kansas, C USA
Colchester 89 E6 hist. Colneceaste, anc. Camulodunum. E England, UK
Col du Brenner see Brenner Pass
Coleman 49 F3 Texas, SW USA
Coleraine 88 B4 Ir. Cúil Raithin. N Northern Ireland, UK
Colesberg 78 C5 Northern Cape, C South Africa
Colima 50 D4 Colima, S Mexico
Coll 88 B3 island W Scotland, UK
College Station 49 G3 Texas, SW USA
Collie 147 A7 Western Australia
Colmar 90 E4 Ger. Kolmar. Haut-Rhin, NE France
Cöln see Köln
Cologne see Köln
Colombia 58 B3 Country N South America

Colombia 58

Official name Republic of Colombia
Formation 1819
Capital Bogotá
Population 42.8 million /97 people per sq mile (38 people per sq km)
Total area 439,733 sq miles (1,138,910 sq km)
Languages Spanish, Amerindian languages, English Creole
Religions Roman Catholic 95%, other 5%
Ethnic mix Mestizo 58%, White 20%, other 22%
Government Presidential democracy
Currency Colombian peso = 100 centavos
Literacy rate 91.8%
Calorie consumption 2,597 kilocalories

Colombian Basin 56 A1 undersea feature SW Caribbean Sea
Colombo 132 C3 country capital (Sri Lanka) Western Province, W Sri Lanka
Colón 53 G4 prev. Aspinwall. Colón, C Panama
Colonia Agrippina see Köln
Colón Ridge 35 B8 undersea feature E Pacific Ocean
Colorado 44 C4 off. State of Colorado; also known as Centennial State, Silver State. State C USA
Colorado City 49 F3 Texas, SW USA
Colorado Plateau 48 B1 plateau W USA
Colorado, Río 65 C5 river E Argentina
Colorado, Río see Colorado River
Colorado River 35 B5 var. Río Colorado. River Mexico/USA
Colorado River 49 G4 river Texas, SW USA
Colorado Springs 44 D5 Colorado, C USA
Columbia 46 B3 river Canada/USA

Columbia *43 E2 state capital* South
Carolina, SE USA
Columbia *41 E4* Maryland,
NE USA
Columbia *45 G4* Missouri, C USA
Columbia *42 C1* Tennessee, S USA
Columbia Plateau *46 C3 plateau*
Idaho/Oregon, NW USA
Columbus *40 D4 state capital* Ohio,
N USA
Columbus *42 D2* Georgia, SE USA
Columbus *40 C4* Indiana, N USA
Columbus *42 C4* Mississippi,
S USA
Columbus *45 F4* Nebraska, C USA
Colville Channel *150 D2 channel*
North Island, NZ
Colville River *36 D2 river* Alaska,
USA
Comacchio *96 C3 var.* Commachio;
anc. Comactium. Emilia-
Romagna, N Italy
Comactium *see* Comacchio
Comalcalco *51 G4* Tabasco,
SE Mexico
Coma Pedrosa, Pic de *91 A7*
mountain NW Andorra
Comarapa *61 F4* Santa Cruz,
C Bolivia
Comayagua *52 C2* Comayagua,
W Honduras
Comer See *see* Como, Lago di
Comilla *135 G4 Ben.* Kumillā.
Chittagong, E Bangladesh
Comino *102 A5 Malt.* Kemmuna.
Island C Malta
Comitán *51 G5 var.* Comitán de
Domínguez. Chiapas, SE Mexico
Comitán de Domínguez *see*
Comitán
Commachio *see* Comacchio
Commissioner's Point *42 A5*
headland W Bermuda
Communism Peak *see*
Kommunizm, Qullai
Como *96 B2 anc.* Comum.
Lombardia, N Italy
Comodoro Rivadavia *65 B6*
Chubut, SE Argentina
Como, Lago di *B2 var.* Lario, *Eng.*
Lake Como, *Ger.* Comer See. *Lake*
N Italy
Como, Lake *see* Como, Lago di
Comoros *79 F2 Fr.* République
Fédérale Islamique des Comores.
Country W Indian Ocean

Comoros 79

Official name Federal Islamic
Republic of the Comoros
Formation 1975
Capital Moroni
Population 727,000 / 868 people
per sq mile (335 people per sq km)
Total area 838 sq miles
(2,170 sq km)
Languages Arabic, French,
Comoran
Religions Muslim (mainly Sunni)
98%, Roman Catholic 1%, other 1%
Ethnic mix Comorian 97%,
other 3%
Government Presidential
democracy
Currency Comoros franc =
100 centimes
Literacy rate 59.6%
Calorie consumption 1,753
kilocalories

Compiègne *90 C3* Oise, N France
Compostella *see* Santiago
Comrat *108 D4 Rus.* Komrat.
S Moldova
Conakry *74 C4 country capital*
(Guinea) Conakry, SW Guinea
Concarneau *90 A3* Finistère,
NW France
Concepción *64 D2 var.* Villa
Concepción. Concepción,
C Paraguay
Concepción *see* La Concepción
Concepción *65 B5* Bío Bío, C Chile
Concepción *61 G3* Santa Cruz,
E Bolivia

Concepción de la Vega *see* La Vega
Conchos, Río *50 D2 river* C Mexico
Conchos, Río *48 D4 river*
NW Mexico
Concord *41 G3 state capital* New
Hampshire, NE USA
Concordia *64 D4* Entre Ríos,
E Argentina
Concordia *45 E4* Kansas, C USA
Côn Đao *137 E7 var.* Con Son. *Island*
S Vietnam
Condate *see* Cosne-Cours-sur-Loire
Condega *52 D3* Estelí,
NW Nicaragua

Congo 77

Official name Republic of the
Congo
Formation 1960
Capital Brazzaville
Population 3.1 million / 23 people
per sq mile (9 people per sq km)
Total area 132,046 sq miles
(342,000 sq km)
Languages French, Kongo, Teke,
Lingala
Religions Traditional beliefs 50%,
Christian 48%, Muslim 2%
Ethnic mix Bakongo 48%,
Sangha 20%, Teke 17%, Mbochi 12%,
other 3%
Government Presidential
democracy
Currency CFA franc = 100 centimes
Literacy rate 80.7%
Calorie consumption 2,223
kilocalories

Congo, Dem. Rep. *77 C6 prev.* Zaire,
Belgian Congo, Congo (Kinshasa).
Country C Africa

Congo, Dem. Rep. 77

Official name Democratic Republic
of the Congo
Formation 1960
Capital Kinshasa
Population 52.5 million / 58 people
per sq mile (22 people per sq km)
Total area 905,563 sq miles
(2,345,410 sq km)
Languages French, Kiswahili,
Tshiluba
Religions Traditional beliefs 50%,
Roman Catholic 37%, Protestant 13%
Ethnic mix Bantu and Hamitic 45%,
other 55%
Government Military-based regime
Currency franc = 100 centimes
Literacy rate 61.4%
Calorie consumption 1,514
kilocalories

Congo *77 C6 var.* Kongo, *Fr.* Zaire.
River C Africa
Congo Basin *77 C6 drainage basin*
W Dem. Rep. Congo
Connacht *see* Connaught
Connaught *89 A5 var.* Connacht, *Ir.*
Chonnacht, Cúige. *Cultural region*
W Ireland
Connecticut *41 F3 off.* State of
Connecticut; also known as Blue
Law State, Constitution State,
Land of Steady Habits, Nutmeg
State. *State* NE USA
Connecticut *41 G3 river*
Canada/USA
Conroe *49 G3* Texas, SW USA
Consolación del Sur *54 A2* Pinar
del Río, W Cuba
Con Son *see* Côn Đao
Constance *see* Konstanz
Constance, Lake *B7 Ger.* Bodensee.
Lake C Europe
Constanţa *108 D5 var.* Küstendje,
Eng. Constanza, *Ger.* Konstanza,
Turk. Küstence. Constanţa,
SE Romania
Constantia *see* Konstanz

Constantine *71 E2 var.* Qacentina,
Ar. Qoussantina. NE Algeria
Constantinople *see* İstanbul
Constanz *see* Konstanz
Constanza *see* Constanţa
Coober Pedy *149 A5* South
Australia
Cookeville *42 D1* Tennessee, S USA
Cook Islands *145 F4 territory in free*
association with NZ S Pacific Ocean
Cook, Mount *151 B6 prev.* Aoraki,
Aorangi. *Mountain* South Island,
NZ
Cook Strait *151 D5 var.* Raukawa.
Strait NZ
Cooktown *148 D2* Queensland,
NE Australia
Coolgardie *147 B6* Western
Australia
Cooma *149 D7* New South Wales,
SE Australia
Coon Rapids *45 F2* Minnesota,
N USA
Cooper Creek *148 C4 var.* Barcoo,
Cooper's Creek. *Seasonal river*
Queensland/South Australia
Cooper's Creek *see* Cooper Creek
Coos Bay *46 A3* Oregon, NW USA
Cootamundra *149 D6* New South
Wales, SE Australia
Copacabana *61 E4* La Paz,
W Bolivia
Copenhagen *see* København
Copiapó *64 B3* Atacama, N Chile
Copperas Cove *49 G3* Texas,
SW USA
Coppermine *see* Kugluktuk
Coquimbo *64 B3* Coquimbo,
N Chile
Corabia *108 B5* Olt, S Romania
Coral Harbour *37 G3* Southampton
Island, Nunavut, NE Canada
Coral Sea *142 B3 sea* SW Pacific
Ocean
Coral Sea Islands *144 B4 Australian*
external territory SW Pacific Ocean
Corantijn Rivier *see* Courantyne
River
Corcaigh *see* Cork
Corcovado, Golfo *65 B6 gulf* S Chile
Cordele *42 D3* Georgia, SE USA
Cordillera Ibérica *see* Ibérico,
Sistema
Córdoba *see* Córdoba
Córdoba *92 D4 var.* Cordoba, *Eng.*
Cordova; *anc.* Corduba.
Andalucía, SW Spain
Córdoba *64 C3* Córdoba,
C Argentina
Córdoba *51 F4* Veracruz-Llave,
E Mexico
Cordova *see* Córdoba
Cordova *36 C3* Alaska, USA
Corduba *see* Córdoba
Corentyne River *see* Courantyne
River
Corfu *see* Kérkyra
Coria *92 C3* Extremadura, W Spain
Corinth *42 C1* Mississippi, S USA
Corinth *see* Kórinthos
Corinth, Gulf of *see* Korinthiakós
Kólpos
Corinthiacus Sinus *see*
Korinthiakós Kólpos
Corinto *52 C3* Chinandega,
NW Nicaragua
Cork *89 A6 Ir.* Corcaigh. S Ireland
Çorlu *116 A2* Tekirdağ, NW Turkey
Corner Brook *39 G3*
Newfoundland, Newfoundland
and Labrador, E Canada
Corn Islands *see* Maíz, Islas del
Cornwallis Island *37 F2 island*
Nunavut, N Canada
Coro *58 C1 prev.* Santa Ana de Coro.
Falcón, NW Venezuela
Corocoro *61 F4* La Paz, W Bolivia
Coromandel *150 D2* Waikato, North
Island, NZ
Coromandel Coast *132 D2 coast*
E India
Coromandel Peninsula *150 D2*
peninsula North Island, NZ
Coronado, Bahía de *52 D5 bay*
S Costa Rica
Coronel Dorrego *65 C5* Buenos
Aires, E Argentina

Coronel Oviedo *64 D2* Caaguazú,
SE Paraguay
Corozal *52 C1* Corozal, N Belize
Corpus Christi *49 G4* Texas,
SW USA
Corrales *48 D2* New Mexico,
SW USA
Corrib, Lough *89 A5 Ir.* Loch
Coirib. *Lake* W Ireland
Corrientes *64 D3* Corrientes,
NE Argentina
Corriza *see* Korçë
Corse *91 E7 Eng.* Corsica. *Island*
France, C Mediterranean Sea
Corsica *see* Corse
Corsicana *49 G3* Texas, SW USA
Cortegana *92 C4* Andalucía,
S Spain
Cortés *53 E5 var.* Ciudad Cortés.
Puntarenas, SE Costa Rica
Cortina d'Ampezzo *96 C1* Veneto,
NE Italy
Coruche *92 B3* Santarém,
C Portugal
Çoruh Nehri *117 E3 Geor.* Chorokhi,
Rus. Chorokh. *River*
Georgia/Turkey
Çorum *116 D3 var.* Chorum. Çorum,
N Turkey
Corunna *see* A Coruña
Corvallis *46 B3* Oregon, NW USA
Corvo *92 A5 var.* Ilha do Corvo.
Island Azores, Portugal,
NE Atlantic Ocean
Cosenza *97 D6 anc.* Consentia.
Calabria, SW Italy
Cosne-Cours-sur-Loire *90 C4 var.*
Cosne-sur-Loire; *anc.* Condate.
Nièvre, C France
Cosne-sur-Loire *see* Cosne-Cours-
sur-Loire
Costa Mesa *46 D2* California,
W USA
Costa Rica *53 E4 Country* Central
America

Costa Rica 53

Official name Republic of Costa
Rica
Formation 1838
Capital San José
Population 4.1 million / 208 people
per sq mile (80 people per sq km)
Total area 19,730 sq miles
(51,100 sq km)
Languages Spanish, English Creole,
Bribri, Cabecar
Religions Roman Catholic 76%,
other (including Protestant) 24%
Ethnic mix Mesitzo and European
96%, Black 2%, Indian 1%,
Chinese 1%
Government Presidential
democracy
Currency Costa Rican colón =
100 centimos
Literacy rate 95.6%
Calorie consumption 2,783
kilocalories

Cotagaita *61 F5* Potosí, S Bolivia
Côte d'Ivoire *74 D4 Eng.* Ivory
Coast, Republic of the Ivory
Coast. *Country* W Africa

Côte d'Ivoire 74

Official name Republic of Côte
d'Ivoire
Formation 1960
Capital Yamoussoukro
Population 16.3 million / 131
people per sq mile (51 people
per sq km)
Total area 124,502 sq miles
(322,460 sq km)
Languages French, Akan, Kru,
Voltaic
Religions Traditional beliefs 23%,
Muslim 25%, Roman Catholic 18%,
Protestant 6%, other 23%
Ethnic mix Baoule 23%, Bete 18%,
Senufo 15% Agni-Ashanti 14%,
Mandinka 11%, other 19%

Côte d'Ivoire (continued)

Government Multiparty republic
Currency CFA franc = 100 centimes
Literacy rate 47.1%
Calorie consumption 2,590 kilocalories

Côte d'Or 90 D4 *cultural region* C France
Cotonou 75 F5 *var.* Kotonu. S Benin
Cotrone *see* Crotone
Cotswold Hills 89 D6 *var.* Cotswolds. *Hill range* S England, UK
Cotswolds *see* Cotswold Hills
Cottbus 94 D4 *prev.* Kottbus. Brandenburg, E Germany
Council Bluffs 45 F4 Iowa, C USA
Courantyne River 59 G4 *var.* Corantijn Rivier, Corentyne River. *River* Guyana/Suriname
Courland Lagoon 106 A4 Ger. Kurisches Haff, *Rus.* Kurskiy Zaliv. *Lagoon* Lithuania/Russian Federation
Coutances 90 B3 *anc.* Constantia. Manche, N France
Couvin 87 C7 Namur, S Belgium
Coventry 89 D6 *anc.* Couentrey. C England, UK
Covilhã 92 C3 Castelo Branco, E Portugal
Cowan, Lake 147 B6 *lake* Western Australia
Coxen Hole *see* Roatán
Coxin Hole *see* Roatán
Coyhaique *see* Coihaique
Cozumel, Isla 51 H3 *island* SE Mexico
Cradock 78 C5 Eastern Cape, S South Africa
Craig 44 C4 Colorado, C USA
Craiova 108 B5 Dolj, SW Romania
Cranbrook 37 E5 British Columbia, SW Canada
Crane *see* The Crane
Crawley 89 E7 SE England, UK
Cremona 96 B2 Lombardia, N Italy
Cres 100 A3 *It.* Cherso; *anc.* Crexa. *Island* W Croatia
Crescent City 46 A4 California, W USA
Crescent Group 128 C7 *island group* C Paracel Islands
Creston 45 F4 Iowa, C USA
Crestview 42 D3 Florida, SE USA
Crete *see* Kríti
Créteil 90 E2 Val-de-Marne, N France
Crete, Sea of *see* Kritikó Pélagos
Creuse 90 B4 *river* C France
Crewe 89 D6 C England, UK
Crikvenica 100 A3 *It.* Cirquenizza; *prev.* Cirkvenica, Crjkvenica. Primorje-Gorski Kotar, NW Croatia
Crimea 81 F4 *var.* Krym, *Eng.* Crimea, Crimean Oblast; *prev. Rus.* Krymskaya ASSR, Krymskaya Oblast'. Admin. region *province* SE Ukraine
Crimean Oblast *see* Crimea
Cristóbal 53 G4 Colón, C Panama
Cristóbal Colón, Pico 58 B1 *mountain* N Colombia
Cristuru Secuiesc 108 C4 *prev.* Cristur, Cristura Săcuiesc, Cristuru, *Ger.* Kreutz, *Hung.* Székelykeresztúr, Szitás-Keresztúr. Harghita, C Romania
Crna Reka 101 D6 *river* S FYR Macedonia
Croatia 100 B3 *Ger.* Kroatien, *SCr.* Hrvatska. *Country* SE Europe

Croatia 100

Official name Republic of Croatia
Formation 1991
Capital Zagreb
Population 4.7 million /215 people per sq mile (83 people per sq km)
Total area 21,831 sq miles (56,542 sq km)

Croatia 100

Languages Croatian
Religions Roman Catholic 76%, Orthodox 11%, Muslim 1%, other 12%
Ethnic mix Croat 78%, Serb 12%, Yugoslav 2%, other 8%
Government Parliamentary democracy
Currency Kuna = 100 lipa
Literacy rate 98.3%
Calorie consumption 2,843 kilocalories

Crocodile *see* Limpopo
Croia *see* Krujë
Croker Island 146 E2 *island* Northern Territory, N Australia
Cromwell 151 B7 Otago, South Island, NZ
Crooked Island 54 D2 *island* SE Bahamas
Crooked Island Passage 54 D2 *channel* SE Bahamas
Crookston 45 F1 Minnesota, N USA
Croton *see* Crotone
Crotona *see* Crotone
Crotone 97 E6 *var.* Cotrone; *anc.* Croton, Crotona. Calabria, SW Italy
Croydon 89 A8 SE England, UK
Crozet Basin 141 B6 *undersea feature* S Indian Ocean
Crozet Islands 141 B7 *island group* French Southern and Antarctic Territories
Crozet Plateau 141 B7 *var.* Crozet Plateaus. *Undersea feature* SW Indian Ocean
Crozet Plateaus *see* Crozet Plateau
Crystal Brook 149 B6 South Australia
Csorna 99 C6 Győr-Moson-Sopron, NW Hungary
Csurgó 99 C7 Somogy, SW Hungary
Cuando 78 C2 *var.* Kwando. *River* S Africa
Cuango 78 B1 *var.* Kwango. *River* Angola/Dem. Rep. Congo *see also* Kwango
Cuan na Gaillimhe *see* Galway Bay
Cuanza 78 B1 *var.* Kwanza. *River* C Angola
Cuauhtémoc 50 C2 Chihuahua, N Mexico
Cuautla 51 E4 Morelos, S Mexico
Cuba 54 B2 *Country* W West Indies

Cuba 54

Official name Republic of Cuba
Formation 1902
Capital Havana
Population 11.2 million /262 people per sq mile (101 people per sq km)
Total area 42,803 sq miles (110,860 sq km)
Languages Spanish
Religions Non-religious 49%, Roman Catholic 40%, Atheist 6%, Protestant 1%, other 4%
Ethnic mix White 66%, European-African 22%, Black 12%
Government One-party state
Currency Cuban peso = 100 centavos
Literacy rate 96.7%
Calorie consumption 2,564 kilocalories

Cubal 78 B2 Benguela, W Angola
Cubango 78 B2 *var.* Kavango, Kavengo, Kubango, Okavango, Okavanggo. *River* S Africa *see also* Okavango
Cubango 78 B2 *var.* Kavango, *Port.* Vila Artur de Paiva, Vila da Ponte. Huíla, SW Angola
Cúcuta 58 C2 *var.* San José de Cúcuta. Norte de Santander, N Colombia

Cuddapah 132 C2 Andhra Pradesh, S India
Cuenca 93 E3 *anc.* Conca. Castilla-La Mancha, C Spain
Cuenca 60 B2 Azuay, S Ecuador
Cuernavaca 51 E4 Morelos, S Mexico
Cuiabá 63 E3 *prev.* Cuyabá. *State capital* Mato Grosso, SW Brazil
Cúige *see* Connaught
Cúige Laighean *see* Leinster
Cúige Mumhan *see* Munster
Cuijck 86 D4 Noord-Brabant, SE Netherlands
Cúil Raithin *see* Coleraine
Cuito 78 B2 *var.* Kwito. *River* SE Angola
Cukai 138 B3 *var.* Chukai, Kemaman. Terengganu, Peninsular Malaysia
Culiacán 50 C3 *var.* Culiacán Rosales, Culiacán-Rosales. Sinaloa, C Mexico
Culiacán-Rosales *see* Culiacán
Cullera 93 F3 País Valenciano, E Spain
Cullman 42 C2 Alabama, S USA
Culmsee *see* Chełmża
Culpepper Island *see* Darwin, Isla
Cumaná 59 E1 Sucre, NE Venezuela
Cumbal, Nevada de 58 A4 *mountain* SW Colombia
Cumberland 41 F4 Maryland, NE USA
Cumberland Plateau 42 D1 *plateau* E USA
Cumberland Sound 37 H3 *inlet* Baffin Island, Nunavut, NE Canada
Cumpas 50 B2 Sonora, NW Mexico
Cunene 69 C6 *var.* Kunene. *River* Angola/Namibia *see also* Kunene
Cunene 78 A3 *province* S Angola
Cuneo 96 A2 Fr. Coni. Piemonte, NW Italy
Cunnamulla 149 C5 Queensland, E Australia
Ćuprija 100 E4 Serbia, E Serbia and Montenegro (Yugo.)
Curaçao 55 E5 *island* Netherlands Antilles
Curicó 64 B4 Maule, C Chile
Curitiba 63 E4 *prev.* Curytiba. *State capital* Paraná, S Brazil
Curtea de Argeș 108 C4 *var.* Curtea-de-Argeș, Argeș, S Romania
Curtea-de-Argeș *see* Curtea de Argeș
Curtici 108 A4 *Ger.* Kurtitsch, *Hung.* Kürtös. Arad, W Romania
Curtis Island 148 E4 *island* Queensland, SE Australia
Cusco 61 E4 *var.* Cuzco. Cuzco, C Peru
Cusset 91 C5 Allier, C France
Cutch, Gulf of *see* Kachchh, Gulf of
Cuttack 135 F4 Orissa, E India
Cuvier Plateau 141 E6 *undersea feature* E Indian Ocean
Cuxhaven 94 B3 Niedersachsen, NW Germany
Cuyuni, Río *see* Cuyuni River
Cuyuni River 59 F3 *var.* Río Cuyuni. *River* Guyana/Venezuela
Cuzco *see* Cusco
Cyclades *see* Kykládes
Cydonia *see* Chaniá
Cymru *see* Wales
Cyprus 102 C4 *Gk.* Kypros, *Turk.* Kıbrıs, Kıbrıs Cumhuriyeti. *Country* E Mediterranean Sea

Cyprus 102

Official name Republic of Cyprus
Formation 1960
Capital Nicosia
Population 790,000 / 221 people per sq mile (85 people per sq km)
Total area 3,571 sq miles (9,250 sq km)
Languages Greek, Turkish, English
Religions Greek Orthodox 73%, Muslim 23%, other 4%
Ethnic mix Greek 77%, Turkish 18%, other (mainly British) 5%

Cyprus (continued)

Government Presidential democracy
Currency Cyprus pound/Turkish lira
Literacy rate 97.1%
Calorie consumption 3,259 kilocalories

Cythera *see* Kýthira
Cythnos *see* Kýthnos
Czech Republic 99 A5 *Cz.* Česká Republika. *Country* C Europe

Czech Republic 99

Official name Czech Republic
Formation 1993
Capital Prague
Population 10.3 million / 338 people per sq mile (131 people per sq km)
Total area 30,450 sq miles (78,866 sq km)
Languages Czech, Slovak, Hungarian
Religions Atheist 38%, Roman Catholic 39%, Protestant 3%, Hussites 2%, other 18%
Ethnic mix Czech 81%, Moravian 13%, Slovak 6%
Government Parliamentary democracy
Currency Czech koruna = 100 halura
Literacy rate 99%
Calorie consumption 3,104 kilocalories

Częstochowa 98 C4 *Ger.* Czenstochau, Tschenstochau, *Rus.* Chenstokhov. Śląskie, S Poland
Człuchów 98 C3 *Ger.* Schlochau. Pomorskie, N Poland

D

Dabajuro 58 C1 Falcón, NW Venezuela
Dabeiba 58 B2 Antioquia, NW Colombia
Dąbrowa Tarnowska 99 D5 Małopolskie, S Poland
Dabryn' 107 C8 *Rus.* Dobryn'. Homyel'skaya Voblasts', SE Belarus
Dagana 74 B3 N Senegal
Dagda 106 D4 Krāslava, SE Latvia
Dagenham 89 88 SE England, UK
Dağlıq Qarabağ *see* Nagornyy Karabakh
Dagupan 139 E1 *off.* Dagupan City. Luzon, N Philippines
Da Hinggan Ling 127 G1 *Eng.* Great Khingan Range. *Mountain range* NE China
Dahm, Ramlat 121 B6 *desert* NW Yemen
Daimiel 92 D3 Castilla-La Mancha, C Spain
Daimoniá 105 B7 Pelopónnisos, S Greece
Dairen *see* Dalian
Dakar 74 B3 *country capital* (Senegal) W Senegal
Dakhla *see* Ad Dakhla
Dakoro 75 G3 Maradi, S Niger
Đakovica 101 D5 *var.* Djakovica, *Alb.* Gjakovë. Serbia, S Serbia and Montenegro (Yugo.)
Đakovo 100 C3 *var.* Djakovo, *Hung.* Diakovár. Osijek-Baranja, E Croatia
Dalai *see* Hulun Nur
Dalain Hob *see* Ejin Qi
Dalaman 116 A4 Muğla, SW Turkey
Dalandzadgad 127 E3 Ömnögovi, S Mongolia
Đa Lat 137 E6 Lâm Đồng, S Vietnam
Dalby 149 D5 Queensland, E Australia

Dale City 41 E4 Virginia, NE USA
Dalhart 49 E1 Texas, SW USA
Dali 128 A6 var. Xiaguan. Yunnan, SW China
Dalian 128 D4 var. Dairen, Dalien, Lüda, Ta-lien, Rus. Dalny. Liaoning, NE China
Dalien see Dalian
Dallas 49 G2 Texas, SW USA
Dalmacija 100 B4 Eng. Dalmatia, Ger. Dalmatien, It. Dalmazia. Cultural region S Croatia
Dalny see Dalian
Dalton 42 D1 Georgia, SE USA
Daly Waters 148 A2 Northern Territory, N Australia
Damachava 107 A6 var. Damachova, Pol. Domaczewo, Rus. Domachëvo. Brestskaya Voblasts', SW Belarus
Damachova see Damachava
Damān 134 C4 Damān and Diu, W India
Damara 76 C4 Ombella-Mpoko, S Central African Republic
Damas see Dimashq
Damasco see Dimashq
Damascus see Dimashq
Damāvand, Qolleh-ye 120 D3 mountain N Iran
Dammām see Ad Dammām
Damoûr 119 A5 var. Ad Dāmūr. W Lebanon
Dampier 146 A4 Western Australia
Dampier, Selat 139 F4 strait Papua, E Indonesia
Damqawt 121 D6 var. Damqut. E Yemen
Damqut see Damqawt
Damxung 126 C5 Xizang Zizhiqu, W China
Danakil Desert 72 D4 var. Afar Depression, Danakil Plain. Desert E Africa
Danakil Plain see Danakil Desert
Danané 74 D5 W Côte d'Ivoire
Đà Nẵng 137 E5 prev. Tourane. Quang Nam-Đa Nẵng, C Vietnam
Danborg see Daneborg
Dandong 128 D3 var. Tan-tung; prev. An-tung. Liaoning, NE China
Daneborg 83 E3 var. Danborg. N Greenland
Dänew see Deynau
Dangerous Archipelago see Tuamotu, Îles
Danghara 123 E3 Rus. Dangara. SW Tajikistan
Danghe Nanshan 126 D3 mountain range W China
Dangla see Tanggula Shan
Dângrêk, Chuōr Phnum 137 D5 var. Phanom Dang Raek, Phanom Dong Rak, Fr. Chaîne des Dangrek. Mountain range Cambodia/Thailand
Dangriga 52 C1 prev. Stann Creek. Stann Creek, E Belize
Danish West Indies see Virgin Islands (US)
Danlí 52 D2 El Paraíso, S Honduras
Danmarksstraedet see Denmark Strait
Dannenberg 94 C3 Niedersachsen, N Germany
Dannevirke 150 D4 Manawatu-Wanganui, North Island, NZ
Danube 81 E4 Bul. Dunav, Cz. Dunaj, Ger. Donau, Hung. Duna, Rom. Dunărea. River C Europe
Danville 41 E5 Virginia, NE USA
Dan Xian see Danzhou
Danxian/Dan Xian see Danzhou
Danzhou 128 C7 prev. Dan Xian, Danxian, Nada. Hainan, S China
Danziger Bucht see Danzig, Gulf of
Danzig, Gulf of 98 C2 var. Gulf of Pomerelia, Ger. Danziger Bucht, Pol. Zakota Pomorskiea, Rus. Gdan'skaya Bukhta. Gulf N Poland
Daqm see Duqm
Dar'a 119 B5 var. Der'a, Fr. Déraa. Dar'ā, SW Syria
Darabani 108 C3 Botoşani, NW Romania
Daraut-Kurgan see Daroot-Korgon

Dardanelli see Çanakkale
Dar es Salaam 73 C7 Dar es Salaam, E Tanzania
Darfield 151 C6 Canterbury, South Island, NZ
Darfur 72 A4 var. Darfur Massif. Cultural region W Sudan
Darfur Massif see Darfur
Darhan 127 E2 Selenge, N Mongolia
Darien, Gulf of 58 A2 Sp. Golfo del Darién. Gulf S Caribbean Sea
Darién, Serranía del 53 H5 mountain range Colombia/Panama
Dario see Ciudad Darío
Darjeeling see Darjiling
Darjiling 135 F3 prev. Darjeeling. West Bengal, NE India
Darling River 149 C6 river New South Wales, SE Australia
Darlington 89 D3 N England, UK
Darmstadt 95 B5 Hessen, SW Germany
Darnah 71 G2 var. Dérna. NE Libya
Darnley, Cape 154 D2 headland Antarctica
Daroca 93 E2 Aragón, NE Spain
Daroot-Korgon 123 F3 var. Daraut-Kurgan. Oshskaya Oblast', SW Kyrgyzstan
Dartford 89 B8 SE England, UK
Dartmoor 89 C7 moorland SW England, UK
Dartmouth 39 F4 Nova Scotia, SE Canada
Darvaza 122 C2 Turkm. Derweze. Akhalskiy Velayat, C Turkmenistan
Darwin 146 D2 prev. Palmerston, Port Darwin. Territory capital Northern Territory, N Australia
Darwin, Isla 60 A4 var. Culpepper Island. Island W Ecuador
Daryācheh-ye Hāmūn see Şāberī, Hāmūn-e
Daryācheh-ye Sīstān see Şāberī, Hāmūn-e
Daryā-ye Morghāb see Murgab
Daryā-ye Pāmīr see Pamir
Daryoi Pomir see Pamir
Dashkawka 107 D6 Rus. Dashkovka. Mahilyowskaya Voblasts', E Belarus
Dashkhovuz 122 C2 Turkm. Dashhowuz; prev. Tashauz. Dashkhovuzskiy Velayat, N Turkmenistan
Datong 128 C3 var. Tatung, Ta-t'ung. Shanxi, C China
Daugavpils 106 D4 Ger. Dünaburg; prev. Rus. Dvinsk. Municipality Daugvapils, SE Latvia
Daung Kyun 137 B6 island S Myanmar
Dauphiné 91 D5 cultural region E France
Davangere 132 C2 Karnātaka, W India
Davao 139 F3 off. Davao City. Mindanao, S Philippines
Davao Gulf 139 F3 gulf Mindanao, S Philippines
Davenport 45 G3 Iowa, C USA
David 53 E5 Chiriquí, W Panama
Davie Ridge 141 A5 undersea feature W Indian Ocean
Davis 154 D3 Australian research station Antarctica
Davis Sea 154 D3 sea Antarctica
Davis Strait 82 B3 strait Baffin Bay/Labrador Sea
Dawei see Tavoy
Dax 91 B6 var. Ax; anc. Aquae Augustae, Aquae Tarbelicae. Landes, SW France
Dayr az Zawr 118 D3 var. Deir ez Zor. Dayr az Zawr, E Syria
Dayton 40 C4 Ohio, N USA
Daytona Beach 43 E4 Florida, SE USA
De Aar 78 C5 Northern Cape, C South Africa
Dead Sea 119 B6 var. Bahret Lut, Lacus Asphaltites, Ar. Al Baḥr al Mayyit, Baḥrat Lūṭ, Heb. Yam HaMelaḥ. Salt lake Israel/Jordan
Dealnu see Tana
Deán Funes 64 C3 Córdoba, C Argentina

Death Valley 47 C7 valley California, W USA
Debar 101 D6 Ger. Dibra, Turk. Debre. W FYR Macedonia
Debica 99 D5 Podkarpackie, SE Poland
De Bildt see De Bilt
De Bilt 86 C3 var. De Bildt. Utrecht, C Netherlands
Dębno 98 B3 Zachodniopomorskie, NW Poland
Debrecen 99 D6 Ger. Debreczin, Rom. Debreţin; prev. Debreczen. Hajdú-Bihar, E Hungary
Decatur 42 C1 Alabama, S USA
Decatur 40 B4 Illinois, N USA
Deccan 134 D5 Hind. Dakshin. Plateau C India
Děčín 98 B4 Ger. Tetschen. Ústecký Kraj, NW Czech Republic
Dedeagaç see Alexandroúpoli
Dedeagach see Alexandroúpoli
Dedemsvaart 86 E3 Overijssel, E Netherlands
Dee 88 C3 river NE Scotland, UK
Deering 36 C2 Alaska, USA
Deggendorf 95 D6 Bayern, SE Germany
Değirmenlik 102 C5 N Cyprus
Deh Bīd 120 D3 Fārs, C Iran
Dehli see Delhi
Deh Shū 122 D5 var. Deshu. Helmand, S Afghanistan
Deinze 87 B5 Oost-Vlaanderen, NW Belgium
Deir ez Zor see Dayr az Zawr
Deirgeirt, Loch see Derg, Lough
Dej 108 B3 Hung. Dés; prev. Deés. Cluj, NW Romania
Dékoa 76 C4 Kémo, 188C Central African Republic
De Land 43 E4 Florida, SE USA
Delano 47 C7 California, W USA
Delārām 122 D5 Farāh, SW Afghanistan
Delaware 41 F4 off. State of Delaware; also known as Blue Hen State, Diamond State, First State. State NE USA
Delaware 40 D4 Ohio, N USA
Delft 86 B4 Zuid-Holland, W Netherlands
Delfzijl 86 E1 Groningen, NE Netherlands
Delgo 72 B3 Northern, N Sudan
Delhi 134 D3 var. Dehli, Hind. Dilli; hist. Shahjahanabad. Delhi, N India
Delicias 50 D2 var. Ciudad Delicias. Chihuahua, N Mexico
Déli-Kárpátok see Carpaţii Meridionali
Delmenhorst 94 B3 Niedersachsen, NW Germany
Del Rio 49 F4 Texas, SW USA
Deltona 43 E4 Florida, SE USA
Demba 77 C7 Kasai Occidental, C Dem. Rep. Congo
Dembia 76 D4 Mbomou, SE Central African Republic
Demchok see Dêmqog. Disputed region China/India see also Dêmqog
Demchok 126 A4 var. Dêmqog. China/India see also Dêmqog
Demerara Plain 56 C2 undersea feature W Atlantic Ocean
Deming 48 C3 New Mexico, SW USA
Demmin 94 C2 Mecklenburg-Vorpommern, NE Germany
Demopolis 42 C2 Alabama, S USA
Dêmqog var. Demchok. Disputed region China/India see also Demchok
Dender 87 B6 Fr. Dendre. River W Belgium
Denekamp 86 E3 Overijssel, E Netherlands
Den Haag see 's-Gravenhage
Den Ham 86 E3 Overijssel, E Netherlands
Den Helder 86 C2 Noord-Holland, NW Netherlands
Denham 147 A5 Western Australia
Den Helder see Den Helder
Denia 93 F4 País Valenciano, E Spain

Deniliquin 149 C7 New South Wales, SE Australia
Denison 45 F3 Iowa, C USA
Denison 49 G2 Texas, SW USA
Denizli 116 B4 Denizli, SW Turkey
Denmark 85 A7 Dan. Danmark; anc. Hafnia. Country N Europe

Denmark 85

Official name Kingdom of Denmark
Formation AD 950
Capital Copenhagen (København)
Population 5.3 million / 319 people per sq mile (123 people per sq km)
Total area 16,639 sq miles (43,094 sq km)
Languages Danish
Religions Evangelical Lutheran 89%, Roman Catholic 1%, other 10%
Ethnic mix Danish 96%, Faeroe and Inuit 1%, other (including Scandinavian) 3%
Government Parliamentary democracy
Currency Danish krone = 100 ore
Literacy rate 99%
Calorie consumption 3,396 kilocalories

Denmark Strait 82 D4 var. Danmarksstraedet. Strait Greenland/Iceland
Dennery 55 F1 E Saint Lucia
Denow 123 E3 Rus. Denau. Surkhondaryo Wiloyati, S Uzbekistan
Denpasar 138 D5 prev. Paloe. Bali, C Indonesia
Denton 49 G2 Texas, SW USA
D'Entrecasteaux Islands 144 B3 island group SE PNG
Denver 44 D4 state capital Colorado, C USA
Der'a see Dar'ā
Déraa see Dar'a
Dera Ghāzi Khān 134 C2 var. Dera Ghāzikhān. Punjab, C Pakistan
Dera Ghāzikhān see Dera Ghāzi Khān
Đeravica 101 D5 mountain S Serbia and Montenegro (Yugo.)
Derbent 111 B8 Respublika Dagestan, SW Russian Federation
Derby 89 D6 C England, UK
Dereli see Gónnoi
Derg, Lough 89 A6 Ir. Loch Deirgeirt. Lake W Ireland
Derhachi 109 G2 Rus. Dergachi. Kharkivs'ka Oblast', E Ukraine
De Ridder 42 A3 Louisiana, S USA
Dérna see Darnah
Derry see Londonderry
Derventa 100 B3 Republika Srpska, N Bosnia and Herzegovina
Deschutes River 46 B3 river Oregon, NW USA
Desē 72 C4 var. Desse, It. Dessie. N Ethiopia
Deseado, Río 65 B7 river S Argentina
Desertas, Ilhas 70 A2 island group Madeira, Portugal, NE Atlantic Ocean
Deshu see Deh Shū
Desierto de Altar see Sonoran Desert
Des Moines 45 F3 state capital Iowa, C USA
Desna 109 E2 river Russian Federation/Ukraine
Dessau 94 C4 Sachsen-Anhalt, E Germany
Desse see Desē
Dessie see Desē
Detroit 40 D3 Michigan, N USA
Detroit Lakes 45 F2 Minnesota, N USA
Deurne 87 D5 Noord-Brabant, SE Netherlands
Deva 108 B4 Ger. Diemrich, Hung. Déva. Hunedoara, W Romania
Đevđelija see Gevgelija

Deventer 86 D3 Overijssel,
E Netherlands
Devils Lake 45 E1 North Dakota,
N USA
Devoll see Devollit, Lumi i
Devollit, Lumi i 101 D6 var. Devoll.
River SE Albania
Devon Island 37 F2 prev. North
Devon Island. Island Parry
Islands, Nunavut, NE Canada
Devonport 149 C8 Tasmania,
SE Australia
Devrek 116 C2 Zonguldak,
N Turkey
Dexter 45 H5 Missouri, C USA
Deynau 122 D3 var. Dyanev, Turkm.
Dänew. Lebapskiy Velayat,
NE Turkmenistan
Dezfūl 120 C3 var. Dizful.
Khūzestān, SW Iran
Dezhou 128 D4 Shandong, E China
Dhaka 135 G4 prev. Dacca. Country
capital (Bangladesh) Dhaka,
C Bangladesh
Dhanbād 135 F4 Bihār, NE India
Dhekélia 102 C5 Eng. Dhekelia. Gk.
Dekéleia. UK air base SE Cyprus
Dhidhimótikhon see Didymóteicho
Dhíkti Ori see Díkti
Dhodhekánisos see Dodekánisos
Dhomokós see Domokós
Dhráma see Dráma
Dhrepanon, Akrotírio see Drépano
Akrotírio
Dhuusa Marreeb 73 E5 var. Dusa
Marreb, It. Dusa Mareb.
Galguduud, C Somalia
Diakovár see Đakovo
Diamantina, Chapada 63 F3
mountain range E Brazil
Diamantina Fracture Zone 141 E6
tectonic feature E Indian Ocean
Diarbekr see Diyarbakır
Dibrugarh 135 H3 Assam, NE India
Dickinson 44 D2 North Dakota,
N USA
Didimotiho see Didymóteicho
Didymóteicho 104 D3 var.
Dhidhimótikhon, Didimotiho.
Anatolikí Makedonía kai Thráki,
NE Greece
Diégo-Suarez see Antsirañana
Diekirch 87 D7 Diekirch,
C Luxembourg
Điên Biên 136 D3 var. Bien Bien,
Dien Bien Phu. Lai Châu,
N Vietnam
Dien Bien Phu see Điên Biên
Diepenbeek 87 D6 Limburg,
NE Belgium
Diepholz 94 B3 Niedersachsen,
NW Germany
Dieppe 90 C2 Seine-Maritime,
N France
Dieren 86 D4 Gelderland,
E Netherlands
Differdange 87 D8 Luxembourg,
SW Luxembourg
Digne 91 D6 var. Digne-les-Bains.
Alpes-de-Haute-Provence,
SE France
Digne-les-Bains see Digne
Digoin 90 C4 Saône-et-Loire,
C France
Digul, Sungai 139 H5 prev. Digoel.
River Papua, E Indonesia
Dihang see Brahmaputra
Dijon 90 D4 anc. Dibio. Côte d'Or,
C France
Dikhil 72 D4 SW Djibouti
Dikson 114 D2 Taymyrskiy
(Dolgano-Nenetskiy) Avtonomnyy
Okrug, N Russian Federation
Díkti 105 D8 var. Dhíkti Ori.
Mountain range Kríti, Greece,
E Mediterranean Sea
Dili 139 F5 var. Dilli, Dilly. Country
capital (East Timor), N East Timor
Dilia 75 G3 var. Dillia. River
SE Niger
Di Linh 137 E6 Lâm Đông,
S Vietnam
Dilli see Delhi
Dilli see Dili
Dillia see Dilia
Dilling 72 B4 var. Ad Dalanj.
Southern Kordofan, C Sudan

Dillon 44 B2 Montana, NW USA
Dilly see Dili
Dilolo 77 D7 Ngounié, S Gabon
Dimashq 119 B5 var. Ash Shām, Esh
Sham, Eng. Damascus, Fr. Damas,
It. Damasco. Country capital
(Syria) Dimashq, SW Syria
Dimitrovgrad 104 D3 Khaskovo,
S Bulgaria
Dimitrovgrad 111 C6
Ul'yanovskaya Oblast',
W Russian Federation
Dimovo 104 B1 Vidin, NW Bulgaria
Dinajpur 135 F3 Rajshahi,
NW Bangladesh
Dinan 90 B3 Côtes d'Armor,
NW France
Dinant 87 C7 Namur, S Belgium
Dinar 116 B4 Afyon, SW Turkey
Dinara see Dinaric Alps
Dinaric Alps 100 C4 var. Dinara.
Mountain range Bosnia and
Herzegovina/Croatia
Dindigul 132 C3 Tamil Nādu,
SE India
Dingle Bay 89 A6 Ir. Bá an Daingin.
Bay SW Ireland
Dinguiraye 74 C4 Haute-Guinée,
N Guinea
Diourbel 74 B3 W Senegal
Dirē Dawa 73 D5 E Ethiopia
Dirk Hartog Island 147 A5 island
Western Australia
Disappointment, Lake 146 C4 salt
lake Western Australia
Dispur 135 G3 Assam, NE India
Divinópolis 63 F4 Minas Gerais,
SE Brazil
Divo 74 D5 S Côte d'Ivoire
Diyarbakır 117 E4 var. Diarbekr;
anc. Amida. Diyarbakır, SE Turkey
Dizful see Dezfūl
Djajapura see Jayapura
Djakovica see Đakovica
Djakovo see Đakovo
Djambala 77 B6 Plateaux, C Congo
Djambi see Jambi
Djanet 71 E4 prev. Fort Charlet.
SE Algeria
Djéblé see Jablah
Djelfa 70 D2 var. El Djelfa. N Algeria
Djéma 76 D4 Haut-Mbomou,
E Central African Republic
Djérablous see Jarābulus
Djerba see Jerba, Île de
Djérem 76 B4 river C Cameroon
Djevdjelija see Gevgelija
Djibouti 72 D4 var. Jibuti; prev.
French Somaliland, French
Territory of the Afars and Issas,
Fr. Côte Française des Somalis,
Territoire Française des Afars et
des Issas. Country E Africa

Djibouti 72

Official name Republic of Djibouti
Formation 1977
Capital Djibouti
Population 644,000 / 76 people per
sq mile (29 people per sq km)
Total area 8,490 sq miles
(22,000 sq km)
Languages French, Arabic,
Somali, Afar
Religions Muslim 94%,
Christian 6%
Ethnic mix Issa 60%, Afar 35%,
other 5%
Government Presidential
democracy
Currency Djibouti franc =
100 centimes
Literacy rate 64.6%
Calorie consumption 2,050
kilocalories

Djibouti 72 D4 var. Jibuti. Country
capital (Djibouti) E Djibouti
Djourab, Erg du 76 C2 dunes
N Chad
Djúpivogur 83 E5 Austurland,
SE Iceland
Dnieper 81 F4 Bel. Dnyapro, Rus.
Dnepr, Ukr. Dnipro. River
E Europe

Dnieper Lowland 109 E2 Bel.
Prydnyaprowskaya Nizina, Ukr.
Prydniprovs'ka Nyzovyna.
Lowlands Belarus/Ukraine
Dniester 81 E4 Rom. Nistru, Rus.
Dnestr, Ukr. Dnister; anc. Tyras.
River Moldova/Ukraine
Dnipro see Dnieper
Dniprodzerzhyns'k 109 F3 Rus.
Dneprodzerzhinsk; prev.
Kamenskoye. Dnipropetrovs'ka
Oblast', E Ukraine
**Dniprodzerzhyns'ke
Vodoskhovyshche** 109 F3 Rus.
Dneprodzerzhinskoye
Vodokhranilishche. Reservoir
C Ukraine
Dnipropetrovs'k 109 F3 Rus.
Dnepropetrovsk; prev.
Yekaterinoslav. Dnipropetrovs'ka
Oblast', E Ukraine
Dniprorudne 109 F3 Rus.
Dneprorudnoye. Zaporiz'ka
Oblast', SE Ukraine
Doba 76 C4 Logone-Oriental,
S Chad
Döbeln 94 D4 Sachsen, E Germany
Doberai, Jazirah 139 G4 Dut.
Vogelkop. Peninsula Papua,
E Indonesia
Doboj 100 C3 Republika Srpska,
N Bosnia and Herzegovina
Dobre Miasto 98 D2 Ger. Guttstadt.
Warmińsko-Mazurskie, NE
Poland
Dobrich 104 E1 Rom. Bazargic; prev.
Tolbukhin. Dobrich, NE Bulgaria
Dobrush 107 D7 Homyel'skaya
Voblasts', SE Belarus
Dodécanèse see Dodekánisos
Dodekánisos 105 D6 var. Nóties
Sporádes, Eng. Dodecanese; prev.
Dhodhekánisos. Island group
SE Greece
Dodge City 45 E5 Kansas,
C USA
Dodoma 69 D5 country capital
(Tanzania) Dodoma, C Tanzania
Dodoma 73 C7 region C Tanzania
Dogana 96 E1 NE San Marino
Dōgo 131 B6 island Oki-shotō,
SW Japan
Dogondoutchi 75 F3 Dosso,
SW Niger
Doğubayazıt 117 F3 Ağrı,
E Turkey
Doğu Karadeniz Dağları 117 E3
var. Anadolu Dağları. Mountain
range NE Turkey
Doha see Ad Dawḥah
Doire see Londonderry
Dokkum 86 D1 Friesland,
N Netherlands
Dokuchayevs'k 109 G3 var.
Dokuchayevsk. Donets'ka Oblast',
SE Ukraine
Dokuchayevsk see Dokuchayevs'k
Doldrums Fracture Zone 66 C4
tectonic feature W Atlantic Ocean
Dôle 90 D4 Jura, E France
Dolisie 77 B6 prev. Loubomo. Le
Niari, S Congo
Dolomites see Dolomitiche, Alpi
Dolomiti see Dolomitiche, Alpi
Dolomitiche, Alpi 96 C1 var.
Dolomiti, Eng. Dolomites.
Mountain range NE Italy
Dolores 64 D4 Buenos Aires,
E Argentina
Dolores 52 B1 Petén, N Guatemala
Dolores 64 D4 Soriano,
SW Uruguay
Dolores Hidalgo 51 E4 var. Ciudad
de Dolores Hidalgo. Guanajuato,
C Mexico
Dolyna 108 B2 Rus. Dolina. Ivano-
Frankivs'ka Oblast', W Ukraine
Dolyns'ka 109 F3 Rus. Dolinskaya.
Kirovohrads'ka Oblast',
S Ukraine
Domachëvo see Damachava
Domaczewo see Damachava
Dombås 85 B5 Oppland,
S Norway
Domel Island see Letsôk-aw Kyun
Domeyko 64 B3 Atacama,
N Chile

Dominica 55 H4 Country
E West Indies

Dominica 55

Official name Commonwealth of
Dominica
Formation 1978
Capital Roseau
Population 73,000 / 251 people
per sq mile (97 people per sq km)
Total area 291 sq miles (754 sq km)
Languages English, French Creole
Religions Roman Catholic 77%,
Protestant 15%, other 8%
Ethnic mix Black 91%, Mixed 6%,
Indian 2%, other 1%
Government Parliamentary
democracy
Currency East Caribbean dollar =
100 cents
Literacy rate 94%
Calorie consumption 2,994
kilocalories

Dominica Channel see Martinique
Passage
Dominican Republic 55 E2 country
C West Indies

Dominican Republic 55

Official name Dominican Republic
Formation 1865
Capital Santo Domingo
Population 8.5 million / 452 people
per sq mile (174 people per sq km)
Total area 18,815 sq miles
(48,730 sq km)
Languages Spanish, French Creole
Religions Roman Catholic 92%,
other and non-religious 8%
Ethnic mix Mixed 75%, White 15%,
Black 10%
Government Presidential
democracy **Currency** Dominican
Republic peso = 100 centavos
Literacy rate 83.6%
Calorie consumption 2,325
kilocalories

Domokós 105 B5 var. Dhomokós.
Stereá Ellás, C Greece
Don 111 B6 var. Duna, Tanais. River
SW Russian Federation
Donau see Danube
Donauwörth 95 C6 Bayern,
S Germany
Don Benito 92 C3 Extremadura,
W Spain
Doncaster 89 D5 anc. Danum.
N England, UK
Dondo 78 B1 Cuanza Norte,
NW Angola
Donegal 89 B5 Ir. Dún na nGall.
NW Ireland
Donegal Bay 89 A5 Ir. Bá Dhún na
nGall. Bay NW Ireland
Donets 109 G2 var. Sivers'kyy
Donets', Rus. Severskiy Donets.
Serra Acaraí. river Russian
Federation/Ukraine
Donets'k 109 G3 Rus. Donetsk; prev.
Stalino. Donets'ka Oblast',
E Ukraine
Dongfang 128 B7 var. Basuo.
Hainan, S China
Dongguan 128 C6 Guangdong,
S China
Đông Ha 136 E4 Quang Tri,
C Vietnam
Đông Hơi 136 D4 Quang Binh,
C Vietnam
Dongliao see Liaoyuan
Dongola 72 B3 var. Donqola,
Dunqulah. Northern, N Sudan
Dongou 77 C5 La Likouala,
NE Congo
Dongting Hu 128 C5 var. Tung-t'ing
Hu. Lake S China
Donji Vakuf see Srbobran,
Federacija Bosna I Hercegovina,
N Serbia and Montenegro (Yugo.)
Donostia-San Sebastián 93 E1 País
Vasco, N Spain

188

Donqola *see* Dongola
Doolow 73 D5 E Ethiopia
Doornik *see* Tournai
Door Peninsula 40 C2 *peninsula* Wisconsin, N USA
Dooxo Nugaaleed 73 E5 *var.* Nogal Valley. *Valley* E Somalia
Dordogne 91 B5 *cultural region* SW France
Dordogne 91 B5 *river* W France
Dordrecht 86 C4 *var.* Dordt, Dort. Zuid-Holland, SW Netherlands
Dordt *see* Dordrecht
Dorohoi 108 C3 Botoşani, NE Romania
Dorotea 84 C4 Västerbotten, N Sweden
Dorre Island 147 A5 *island* Western Australia
Dort *see* Dordrecht
Dortmund 94 A4 Nordrhein-Westfalen, W Germany
Dos Hermanas 92 C4 Andalucía, S Spain
Dospad Dagh *see* Rhodope Mountains
Dospat 104 C3 Smolyan, S Bulgaria
Dothan 42 D3 Alabama, S USA
Dotnuva 106 B4 Kédainiai, C Lithuania
Douai 90 C2 *prev.* Douay, *anc.* Duacum. Nord, N France
Douala 77 A5 *var.* Duala. Littoral, W Cameroon
Douglas 89 C5 *dependent territory capital* (Isle of Man) E Isle of Man
Douglas 48 C3 Arizona, SW USA
Douglas 44 D3 Wyoming, C USA
Douro 92 B2 Sp. Duero. *River* Portugal/Spain *see also* Duero
Dover 89 E7 *Fr.* Douvres; *Lat.* Dubris Portus. SE England, UK
Dover 41 F4 *state capital* Delaware, NE USA
Dover, Strait of 90 C2 *var.* Straits of Dover, *Fr.* Pas de Calais. *Strait* England, UK/France
Dover, Straits of *see* Dover, Strait of
Dovrefjell 85 B5 *plateau* S Norway
Downpatrick 89 B5 *Ir.* Dún Pádraig. SE Northern Ireland, UK
Dōzen 131 B6 *island* Oki-shotō, SW Japan
Drač *see* Durrës
Drachten 86 D2 Friesland, N Netherlands
Drăgăşani 108 B5 Vâlcea, SW Romania
Dragoman 104 B2 Sofiya, W Bulgaria
Dra, Hamada du 70 C3 *var.* Hammada du Drâa, Haut Plateau du Dra. *Plateau* W Algeria
Drahichyn 107 B6 *Pol.* Drohiczyn Poleski, *Rus.* Drogichin. Brestskaya Voblasts', SW Belarus
Drakensberg 78 D5 *mountain range* Lesotho/South Africa
Drake Passage 57 B8 *passage* Atlantic Ocean/Pacific Ocean
Dralfa 104 D2 Tŭrgovishte, N Bulgaria
Dráma 104 C3 *var.* Dhráma. Anatolikí Makedonía kai Thráki, NE Greece
Drammen 85 B6 Buskerud, S Norway
Drau *see* Drava
Drava 100 C3 *var.* Drau, *Eng.* Drave, *Hung.* Dráva. *River* C Europe *see also* Drau
Dráva *see* Drava
Drave *see* Drava
Drawsko Pomorskie 98 B3 *Ger.* Dramburg. Zachodniopomorskie, NW Poland
Drépano, Akrotírio 104 C4 *var.* Akra Dhrepanon. *Headland* N Greece
Dresden 94 D4 Sachsen, E Germany
Drin *see* Drinit, Lumi i
Drina 100 C3 *river* Bosnia and Herzegovina/Serbia and Montenegro (Yugo.)

Drinit, Lumi i 101 D5 *var.* Drin. *River* NW Albania
Drobeta-Turnu Severin 108 B5 *prev.* Turnu Severin. Mehedinţi, SW Romania
Drogheda 89 B5 *Ir.* Droichead Átha. NE Ireland
Drohobych 108 B2 *Pol.* Drohobycz, *Rus.* Drogobych. L'vivs'ka Oblast', NW Ukraine
Droichead Átha *see* Drogheda
Drôme 91 D5 *cultural region* SE France
Dronning Maud Land 154 B2 *physical region* Antarctica
Drummondville 39 E4 Quebec, SE Canada
Druskininkai 107 B5 *Pol.* Druskienniki. Druskininkai, S Lithuania
Dryden 38 B3 Ontario, C Canada
Drysa 107 D5 *Rus.* Drissa. *River* N Belarus
Duala *see* Douala
Dubai *see* Dubayy
Dubăsari 108 D3 *Rus.* Dubossary. NE Moldova
Dubawnt 37 F4 *river* Northwest Territories/Nunavut, NW Canada
Dubayy 120 D4 *Eng.* Dubai. Dubayy, NE UAE
Dubbo 149 D6 New South Wales, SE Australia
Dublin 89 B5 *Ir.* Baile Átha Cliath; *anc.* Eblana. *Country capital* (Ireland), E Ireland
Dublin 43 E2 Georgia, SE USA
Dubno 108 C2 Rivnens'ka Oblast', NW Ukraine
Dubrovnik 101 B5 *It.* Ragusa. Dubrovnik-Neretva, SE Croatia
Dubuque 45 G3 Iowa, C USA
Dudelange 87 D8 *var.* Forge du Sud, *Ger.* Dudelingen. Luxembourg, S Luxembourg
Dudelingen *see* Dudelange
Duero 92 D2 *Port.* Douro. *River* Portugal/Spain *see also* Douro
Duesseldorf *see* Düsseldorf
Duffel 87 C5 Antwerpen, C Belgium
Dugi Otok 100 A4 *var.* Isola Grossa, *It.* Isola Lunga. *Island* W Croatia
Duisburg 94 A4 *prev.* Duisburg-Hamborn. Nordrhein-Westfalen, W Germany
Duiven 86 D4 Gelderland, E Netherlands
Duk Faiwil 73 B5 Jonglei, SE Sudan
Dulan 126 D4 *var.* Qagan Us. Qinghai, C China
Dulce, Golfo 53 E5 *gulf* S Costa Rica
Dülmen 94 A4 Nordrhein-Westfalen, W Germany
Dulovo 104 E1 Silistra, NE Bulgaria
Duluth 45 F2 Minnesota, N USA
Dūmā 119 B5 *Fr.* Douma. Dimashq, SW Syria
Dumas 49 E1 Texas, SW USA
Dumfries 88 C4 S Scotland, UK
Dumont d'Urville 154 C4 *French research station* Antarctica
Dumyât 72 B1 *Eng.* Damietta. N Egypt
Duna *see* Danube
Duna *see* Don
Dunaj *see* Danube
Dunaújváros 99 C7 *prev.* Dunapentele, Sztálinváros. Fejér, C Hungary
Dunav *see* Danube
Dunavska Ravnina 104 C2 *Eng.* Danubian Plain. *Plain* N Bulgaria
Duncan 49 G2 Oklahoma, C USA
Dundalk 89 B5 *Ir.* Dún Dealgan. NE Ireland
Dún Dealgan *see* Dundalk
Dundee 88 C4 E Scotland, UK
Dundee 78 D4 KwaZulu/Natal, E South Africa
Dunedin 151 B7 Otago, South Island, NZ
Dunfermline 88 C4 C Scotland, UK
Dungu 77 E5 Orientale, NE Dem. Rep. Congo

Dungun 138 B3 *var.* Kuala Dungun. Terengganu, Peninsular Malaysia
Dunkerque 90 C2 *Eng.* Dunkirk, *Flem.* Duinekerke; *prev.* Dunquerque. Nord, N France
Dún Laoghaire 89 B6 *Eng.* Dunleary; *prev.* Kingstown. E Ireland
Dún na nGall *see* Donegal
Dún Pádraig *see* Downpatrick
Dunqulah *see* Dongola
Dunărea *see* Danube
Dupnitsa 104 C2 *prev.* Marek, Stanke Dimitrov. Kyustendil, W Bulgaria
Duqm 121 E5 *var.* Daqm. E Oman
Durance 91 D6 *river* SE France
Durango 50 D3 *var.* Victoria de Durango. Durango, W Mexico
Durango 44 C5 Colorado, C USA
Durankulak 104 E1 *Rom.* Răcari; *prev.* Blatnitsa, Duranulac. Dobrich, NE Bulgaria
Durant 49 G2 Oklahoma, C USA
Durazzo *see* Durrës
Durban 78 D4 *var.* Port Natal. KwaZulu/Natal, E South Africa
Durbe 106 B3 *Ger.* Durben. Liepāja, W Latvia
Durg 135 E4 *prev.* Drug. Madhya Pradesh, C India
Durham 89 D5 *hist.* Dunholme. N England, UK
Durham 43 F1 North Carolina, SE USA
Durostorum *see* Silistra
Durrës 101 C6 *var.* Durrësi, Dursi, *It.* Durazzo, *SCr.* Drač, *Turk.* Draç. Durrës, W Albania
Durrësi *see* Durrës
Dursi *see* Durrës
Durūz, Jabal ad 119 C5 *mountain* SW Syria
D'Urville Island 150 C4 *island* C NZ
Dusa Mareb *see* Dhuusa Marreeb
Dusa Marreb *see* Dhuusa Marreeb
Dushanbe 123 E3 *var.* Dyushambe; *prev.* Stalinabad, *Taj.* Stalinobod. *Country capital* (Tajikistan) W Tajikistan
Düsseldorf 94 A4 *var.* Duesseldorf. Nordrhein-Westfalen, W Germany
Dústi 123 E3 *Rus.* Dusti. SW Tajikistan
Dutch Harbor 36 B3 Unalaska Island, Alaska, USA
Dutch New Guinea *see* Papua
Duzdab *see* Zāhedān
Dvina *see* Severnaya Dvina
Dvina Bay *see* Chëshskaya Guba
Dyanev *see* Deynau
Dyersburg 42 C1 Tennessee, S USA
Dyushambe *see* Dushanbe
Dza Chu *see* Mekong
Dzerzhinsk 111 C5 Nizhegorodskaya Oblast', W Russian Federation
Dzhalal-Abad 123 F2 *Kir.* Jalal-Abad. Dzhalal-Abadskaya Oblast', W Kyrgyzstan
Dzhambul *see* Taraz
Dzhankoy 109 F4 Respublika Krym, S Ukraine
Dzhelandy 123 F3 SE Tajikistan
Dzhergalan 123 G2 *Kir.* Jyrgalan. Issyk-Kul'skaya Oblast', NE Kyrgyzstan
Dzhugdzhur, Khrebet 115 G3 *mountain range* E Russian Federation
Dzhusaly 114 B4 *Kaz.* Zholsaly. Kyzylorda, SW Kazakhstan
Działdowo 98 D3 Warmińsko-Mazurskie, NE Poland
Dzuunmod 127 E2 Töv, C Mongolia

E

Eagle Pass 49 F4 Texas, SW USA
East Açores Fracture Zone *see* East Azores Fracture Zone
East Antarctica *see* Greater Antarctica
East Australian Basin *see* Tasman Basin

East Azores Fracture Zone 66 C3 *var.* East Açores Fracture Zone. *Tectonic feature* E Atlantic Ocean
Eastbourne 89 E7 SE England, UK
East Cape 150 E3 *headland* North Island, NZ
East China Sea 125 E2 *Chin.* Dong Hai. *Sea* W Pacific Ocean
Easter Fracture Zone 153 G4 *tectonic feature* E Pacific Ocean
Easter Island 153 F4 *var.* Rapa Nui, *island* E Pacific Ocean
Eastern Desert 68 D3 *var.* Aş Şaḥrā' ash Sharqīyah, *Eng.* Arabian Desert, Eastern Desert. *Desert* E Egypt
Eastern Ghats 124 B3 *mountain range* SE India
Eastern Sayans 115 E4 *Mong.* Dzüün Soyonī Nuruu, *Rus.* Vostochnyy Sayan. *Mountain range* Mongolia/Russian Federation
East Falkland 65 D8 *var.* Isla Soledad. *Island* E Falkland Islands
East Grand Forks 45 E1 Minnesota, N USA
East Indiaman Ridge 141 D6 *undersea feature* E Indian Ocean
East Indies 132 A3 *island group* SE Asia
East Kilbride 88 C4 S Scotland, UK
East Korea Bay 129 E3 *bay* E North Korea
Eastleigh 89 D7 S England, UK
East London 78 D5 *Afr.* Oos-Londen; *prev.* Emonti, Port Rex. Eastern Cape, S South Africa
Eastmain 38 D3 *river* Quebec, C Canada
East Mariana Basin 142 B1 *undersea feature* W Pacific Ocean
East Novaya Zemlya Trench 112 C1 *var.* Novaya Zemlya Trench. *Undersea feature* W Kara Sea
East Pacific Rise 153 F4 *undersea feature* E Pacific Ocean
East Saint Louis 40 B4 Illinois, N USA
East Scotia Basin 67 C7 *undersea feature* SE Scotia Sea
East Sea *see* Japan, Sea of
East Siberian Sea *see* Vostochno-Sibirskoye More
East Timor 139 F5 *var.* Loro Sae *prev.* Portuguese Timor, Timor Timur. *Country,* SE Asia

---

East Timor 139

Official name	East Timor
Formation	2002
Capital	Dili
Population	737,811 /196 people per sq mile (49 per sq km)
Total area	3,756 sq miles (14, 874 sq km)
Languages	Tetum (Portuguese/ Austronesian), Bahasa Indonesia, Portuguese
Religions	Roman Catholic 93%, other 7%
Ethnic mix	Various Papuan groups; 2% Chinese. In the 1990's Indonesian settlers became numerous, accounting for 20% of the population by 1999
Government	Multiparty republic
Currency	US dollar
Literacy rate	41 %
Calorie consumption	not available

Eau Claire 40 A2 Wisconsin, N USA
Eauripik Rise 142 B2 *undersea feature* W Pacific Ocean
Ebensee 95 D6 Oberösterreich, N Austria
Eberswalde-Finow 94 D3 Brandenburg, E Germany
Ebetsu 130 D2 *var.* Ebetu. Hokkaidō, NE Japan
Ebetu *see* Ebetsu
Ebolowa 77 A5 Sud, S Cameroon
Ebon Atoll 144 D2 *var.* Epoon. *Atoll* Ralik Chain, S Marshall Islands
Ebro 93 E2 *river* NE Spain
Ebusus *see* Eivissa

Ech Cheliff *see* Chlef
Ech Chleff *see* Chlef
Echo Bay 37 E3 Northwest Territories, NW Canada
Echt 87 D5 Limburg, SE Netherlands
Ecija 92 D4 *anc.* Astigi. Andalucía, SW Spain
Ecuador 60 B1 *Country* NW South America

Ecuador 60

Official name Republic of Ecuador
Formation 1830
Capital Quito
Population 12.9 million /118 people per sq mile (46 people per sq km)
Total area 109,483 sq miles (283,560 sq km)
Languages Spanish, Quechua, other Amerindian languages
Religions Roman Catholic 93%, Protestant, Jewish and other 7%
Ethnic mix Mestizo 55%, Indian 25%, Black 10%, White 10%
Government Presidential democracy
Currency US dollar
Literacy rate 91.3%
Calorie consumption 2,693 kilocalories

Ed Da'ein 72 A4 Southern Darfur, W Sudan
Ed Damazin 72 C4 *var.* Ad Damazīn. Blue Nile, E Sudan
Ed Damer 72 C3 *var.* Ad Damar, Ad Dāmir. River Nile, NE Sudan
Ed Debba 72 B3 Northern, N Sudan
Ede 86 D4 Gelderland, C Netherlands
Ede 75 F5 Osun, SW Nigeria
Edéa 77 A5 Littoral, SW Cameroon
Edeyin Murzuq *see* Murzuq, Idhān
Edfu *see* Idfu
Edgeoya 83 G2 *island* S Svalbard
Edgware 89 A7 SE England, UK
Edina 49 G5 Texas, SW USA
Edinburgh 88 C4 *admin capital* S Scotland, UK
Edirne 116 A2 Eng. Adrianople; *anc.* Adrianopolis, Hadrianopolis. Edirne, NW Turkey
Edmonds 46 B2 Washington, NW USA
Edmonton 37 E5 Alberta, SW Canada
Edmundston 39 E4 New Brunswick, SE Canada
Edna 49 G4 Texas, SW USA
Edolo 96 B1 Lombardia, N Italy
Edremit 116 A3 Balıkesir, NW Turkey
Edward, Lake 77 E5 *var.* Albert Edward Nyanza, Edward Nyanza, Lac Idi Amin, Lake Rutanzige. *Lake* Uganda / Zaire
Edward Nyanza *see* Edward, Lake
Edwards Plateau 49 F3 *plain* Texas, SW USA
Eeklo 87 B5 *var.* Eekloo. Oost-Vlaanderen, NW Belgium
Edzo 53 E4 *prev.* Rae-Edzo. Northwest Territories, NW Canada
Eekloo *see* Eeklo
Eersel 87 C5 Noord-Brabant, S Netherlands
Efate 144 D4 *var.* Éfaté Fr. Vaté; *prev.* Sandwich Island. *Island* C Vanuatu
Effingham 40 B4 Illinois, N USA
Eforie Sud 108 D5 Constanța, E Romania
Efstrátios, Ágios 104 D4 *var.* Ayios Evstratios. *Island* E Greece
Egadi, Isole 97 B7 *island group* S Italy
Eger 99 D6 Ger. Erlau. Heves, NE Hungary
Egeria Fracture Zone 141 C5 *tectonic feature* W Indian Ocean
Éghezèe 87 C6 Namur, C Belgium
Egina *see* Aígina
Egio *see* Aígio

Egmont, Mount *see* Taranaki, Mount
Egmont, Cape 150 C4 *headland* North Island, NZ
Egoli *see* Johannesburg
Egypt 72 B2 Ar. Jumhūrīyah Miṣr al 'Arabīyah; *prev.* United Arab Republic, *anc.* Aegyptus. *Country* NE Africa

Egypt 72

Official name Arab Republic of Egypt
Formation 1936
Capital Cairo
Population 69.1 million / 179 people per sq mile (69 people per sq km)
Total area 386,660 sq miles (1,001,450 sq km)
Languages Arabic, French, English, Berber
Religions Muslim (mainly Sunni) 94%, Coptic Christian and other 6%
Ethnic mix Eastern Hamitic 90%, other (Nubian, Armenian, Greek) 10%
Government Presidential democracy
Currency Egyptian pound = 100 piastres
Literacy rate 55.4%
Calorie consumption 3,346 kilocalories

Eibar 93 E1 País Vasco, N Spain
Eibergen 86 E3 Gelderland, E Netherlands
Eidfjord 85 A5 Hordaland, S Norway
Eier-Berg *see* Suur Munamägi
Eifel 95 A5 *plateau* W Germany
Eiger 95 B7 *mountain* C Switzerland
Eigg 88 B3 *island* W Scotland, UK
Eight Degree Channel 132 B3 *channel* India / Maldives
Eighty Mile Beach 146 B4 *beach* Western Australia
Eijsden 87 D6 Limburg, SE Netherlands
Eilat *see* Elat
Eindhoven 87 D5 Noord-Brabant, S Netherlands
Eipel *see* Ipel'
Eipel *see* Ipoly
Eisenhüttenstadt 94 D4 Brandenburg, E Germany
Eisenstadt 95 E6 Burgenland, E Austria
Eisleben 94 C4 Sachsen-Anhalt, C Germany
Eivissa 93 G3 *var.* Iviza, *Cast.* Ibiza; *anc.* Ebusus. *Island* Islas Baleares, Spain, W Mediterranean Sea
Eivissa 93 G3 *var.* Iviza, *Cast.* Ibiza; *anc.* Ebusus. Eivissa, Spain, W Mediterranean Sea
Ejea de los Caballeros 93 E2 Aragón, NE Spain
Ejin Qi 126 D3 *var.* Dalain Hob. Nei Mongol Zizhiqu, N China
Ekapa *see* Cape Town
Ekiatapskiy Khrebet 115 G1 *mountain range* NE Russian Federation
El 'Alamein 72 B1 *var.* Al 'Alamayn. N Egypt
El Asnam *see* Chlef
Elat 119 B8 *var.* Eilat, Elath. Southern, S Israel
Elat, Gulf of *see* Aqaba, Gulf of
Elath *see* Al 'Aqabah
Elath *see* Elat
El'Atrun 72 B3 Northern Darfur, NW Sudan
Elâzığ 117 E3 *var.* Elâziz. Elâzığ, E Turkey
Elâziz *see* Elâzığ
Elba, Isola d' 96 B4 *island* Archipelago Toscano, C Italy
Elbasan 101 D6 *var.* Elbasani. Elbasan, C Albania
Elbasani *see* Elbasan

Elbe 80 D3 Cz. Labe. *River* Czech Republic / Germany
El Beni *see* Beni
Elbert, Mount 44 C4 *mountain* Colorado, C USA
Elbing *see* Elblag
Elblag 98 C2 *var.* Elblag, Ger. Elbing. Warmińsko-Mazurskie, NE Poland
El Boulaida *see* Blida
El'brus 111 A8 *var.* Gora El'brus. *Mountain* SW Russian Federation
El Burgo de Osma 93 E2 Castilla-León, C Spain
El Cajon 47 C8 California, W USA
El Calafate 65 B7 *var.* Calafate. Santa Cruz, S Argentina
El Callao 59 E2 Bolívar, E Venezuela
El Campo 49 G4 Texas, SW USA
El Carmen de Bolívar 58 B2 Bolívar, NW Colombia
El Centro 47 D8 California, W USA
Elche 93 F4 *var.* Elx-Elche; *anc.* Ilici, *Lat.* Illicis. País Valenciano, E Spain
Elda 93 F4 País Valenciano, E Spain
El Djazaïr *see* Alger
El Djelfa *see* Djelfa
El Dorado 42 B2 Arkansas, C USA
El Dorado 59 F2 Bolívar, E Venezuela
El Dorado 45 F5 Kansas, C USA
El Dorado 50 C3 Sinaloa, C Mexico
Eldorado 64 E3 Misiones, NE Argentina
Eldoret 73 C6 Rift Valley, W Kenya
Elektrostal' 111 B5 Moskovskaya Oblast', W Russian Federation
Elemi Triangle 73 B5 *disputed region* Kenya / Sudan
Elephant Butte Reservoir 48 C2 *reservoir* New Mexico, SW USA
Eleuthera Island 54 C1 *island* N Bahamas
El Fasher 72 A4 *var.* Al Fāshir. Northern Darfur, W Sudan
El Ferrol *see* Ferrol
El Ferrol del Caudillo *see* Ferrol
El Gedaref *see* Gedaref
El Geneina 72 A4 *var.* Ajjinena, Al-Genain, Al Junaynah. Western Darfur, W Sudan
Elgin 40 B3 Illinois, N USA
Elgin 88 C3 NE Scotland, UK
El Gîza 72 B1 *var.* Al Jīzah, Gîza, Gizeh. N Egypt
El Goléa 70 D3 *var.* Al Golea. C Algeria
El Hank 74 D1 *cliff* N Mauritania
El Haseke *see* Al Ḥasakah
El-Jadida 70 C2 *prev.* Mazagan. W Morocco
Ełk 98 E2 Ger. Lyck. Warmińsko-Mazurskie, NE Poland
Elk City 49 F1 Oklahoma, C USA
El Kerak *see* Al Karak
El Khalîl *see* Hebron
El Khârga 72 B2 *var.* Al Khārijah. C Egypt
Elkhart 40 C3 Indiana, N USA
El Khartûm *see* Khartoum
Elk River 45 F2 Minnesota, N USA
El Kuneitra *see* Al Qunayṭirah
Ellef Ringnes Island 37 E1 *island* Nunavut, N Canada
Ellen, Mount 44 B5 *mountain* Utah, W USA
Ellensburg 46 B2 Washington, NW USA
Ellesmere Island 37 F1 *island* Queen Elizabeth Islands, Nunavut, N Canada
Ellesmere, Lake 151 C6 *lake* South Island, NZ
Elliston 149 A6 South Australia
Ellsworth Land 154 A3 *physical region* Antarctica

El Mahbas 70 B3 *var.* Mahbés. SW Western Sahara
El Mina 118 B4 *var.* Al Mīnā'. N Lebanon
El Minya 72 B2 *var.* Al Minyā, Minya. C Egypt
Elmira 41 E3 New York, NE USA
El Mreyyé 74 D2 *desert* E Mauritania
Elmshorn 94 B3 Schleswig-Holstein, N Germany
El Muglad 72 B4 Western Kordofan, C Sudan
El Obeid 72 B4 *var.* Al Obayyid, Al Ubayyiḍ. Northern Kordofan, C Sudan
El Ouâdi *see* El Oued
El Oued 71 E2 *var.* Al Oued, El Ouâdi, El Wad. NE Algeria
Eloy 48 B2 Arizona, SW USA
El Paso 48 D3 Texas, SW USA
El Porvenir 53 G4 San Blas, N Panama
El Progreso 52 C2 Yoro, NW Honduras
El Puerto de Santa María 92 C5 Andalucía, S Spain
El Quds *see* Jerusalem
El Quneitra *see* Al Qunayṭirah
El Queseir *see* Al Quṣayr
El Quweira *see* Al Quwayrah
El Rama 53 E3 Región Autónoma Atlántico Sur, SE Nicaragua
El Real 53 H5 *var.* El Real de Santa María. Darién, SE Panama
El Real de Santa María *see* El Real
El Reno 49 F1 Oklahoma, C USA
El Salvador 52 B3 *Country* Central America

El Salvador 52

Official name Republic of El Salvador
Formation 1841
Capital San Salvador
Population 6.4 million /788 people per sq mile (304 people per sq km)
Total area 8,124 sq miles (21,040 sq km)
Languages Spanish
Religions Roman Catholic 80%, Evangelical 18%, other 2%
Ethnic mix Mestizo 94%, Indian 5%, White 1%
Government Presidential democracy
Currency Salvadorean colón = 100 centavos
Literacy rate 78.8%
Calorie consumption 2,503 kilocalories

El Sáuz 50 C2 Chihuahua, N Mexico
El Serrat 91 A7 N Andorra
Elst 86 D4 Gelderland, E Netherlands
El Sueco 50 C2 Chihuahua, N Mexico
El Suweida *see* As Suwaydā'
Eltanin Fracture Zone 153 E5 *tectonic feature* SE Pacific Ocean
El Tigre 59 E2 Anzoátegui, NE Venezuela
Elvas 92 C4 Portalegre, C Portugal
El Vendrell 93 G2 Cataluña, NE Spain
El Vigía 58 C2 Mérida, NW Venezuela
El Wad *see* El Oued
Elwell, Lake 44 B1 *reservoir* Montana, NW USA
Elx-Elche *see* Elche
Ely 47 D5 Nevada, W USA
El Yopal *see* Yopal
Emajõgi 106 D3 Ger. Embach. *River* SE Estonia
Emba 114 B4 Kaz. Embi. Aktyubinsk, W Kazakhstan
Emba 114 B4 Kaz. Embi. *River* W Kazakhstan
Emden 94 A3 Niedersachsen, NW Germany
Emerald 148 D4 Queensland, E Australia
Emerald Isle *see* Montserrat

Emesa see Ḥimṣ
Emmaste 106 C2 Hiiumaa, W Estonia
Emmeloord 86 D2 Flevoland, N Netherlands
Emmen 86 E2 Drenthe, NE Netherlands
Emmendingen 95 A6 Baden-Württemberg, SW Germany
Emory Peak 49 E4 *mountain* Texas, SW USA
Empalme 50 B2 Sonora, NW Mexico
Emperor Seamounts 113 G3 *undersea feature* NW Pacific Ocean
Emporia 45 F5 Kansas, C USA
Empty Quarter see Ar Rub 'al Khālī
Ems 94 A3 *Dut.* Eems. *River* NW Germany
Encamp 91 A8 C Andorra
Encarnación 64 D3 Itapúa, S Paraguay
Encinitas 47 C8 California, W USA
Encs 99 D6 Borsod-Abaúj-Zemplén, NE Hungary
Endeavour Strait 148 C1 *strait* Queensland, NE Australia
Enderbury Island 145 F3 *atoll* Phoenix Islands, C Kiribati
Enderby Land 154 C2 *physical region* Antarctica
Enderby Plain 154 D2 *undersea feature* S Indian Ocean
Enewetak Atoll 144 C1 *var.* Änewetak, Eniwetok. *Atoll* Ralik Chain, W Marshall Islands
Enfield 89 A7 SE England, UK
Engannim see Jenin
Enghien 87 B6 *Dut.* Edingen. Hainaut, SW Belgium
England 89 D5 *Lat.* Anglia. *National region* UK
Englewood 44 D4 Colorado, C USA
English Channel 89 D8 *var.* The Channel, *Fr.* la Manche. *Channel* NW Europe
Engure 106 C3 Tukums, W Latvia
Engures Ezers 106 B3 *lake* NW Latvia
Enguri 117 F1 *Rus.* Inguri. *River* NW Georgia
Enid 49 F1 Oklahoma, C USA
Enikale Strait see Kerch Strait
Eniwetok see Enewetak Atoll
En Nâqoûra 119 A5 *var.* An Nâqūrah. SW Lebanon
Ennedi 76 D2 *plateau* E Chad
Ennis 89 A6 *Ir.* Inis. W Ireland
Ennis 49 G3 Texas, SW USA
Enniskillen 89 B5 *var.* Inniskilling, *Ir.* Inis Ceithleann. SW Northern Ireland, UK
Enns 95 D6 *river* C Austria
Enschede 86 E3 Overijssel, E Netherlands
Ensenada 50 A1 Baja California, NW Mexico
Entebbe 73 B6 S Uganda
Entroncamento 92 B3 Santarém, C Portugal
Enugu 75 G5 Enugu, S Nigeria
Eolie, Isole 97 C6 *var.* Isole Lipari, *Eng.* Aeolian Islands, Lipari Islands. *Island group* S Italy
Epanomí 104 B4 Kentrikí Makedonía, N Greece
Epéna 77 B5 La Likouala, NE Congo
Eperies see Prešov
Eperjes see Prešov
Epi 144 D4 *var.* Épi. *Island* C Vanuatu
Épi see Epi
Épinal 90 D4 Vosges, NE France
Epiphania see Ḥamāh
Epitoli see Pretoria
Epoon see Ebon Atoll
Epsom 89 A8 SE England, UK
Equatorial Guinea 77 A5 *Country* C Africa

Equatorial Guinea 77

Official name Republic of Equatorial Guinea
Formation 1968
Capital Malabo

Equatorial Guinea (continued)

Population 470,000 /43 people per sq mile (17 people per sq km)
Total area 10,830 sq miles (28,051 sq km)
Languages Spanish, Fang, Bubi
Religions Roman Catholic 90%, other 10%
Ethnic mix Fang 85%, Bubi 4%, other 11%
Government Presidential regime
Currency CFA franc = 100 centimes
Literacy rate 83.2%
Calorie consumption not available

Erautini see Johannesburg
Erbil see Arbīl
Erciş 117 F3 Van, E Turkey
Erdélyi-Havasok see Carpaţii Meridionali
Erdenet 127 E2 Bulgan, N Mongolia
Erdi 76 C2 *plateau* NE Chad
Erdi Ma 76 D2 *desert* NE Chad
Erebus, Mount 154 B4 *mountain* Ross Island, Antarctica
Ereğli 116 C4 Konya, S Turkey
Erenhot 127 F2 *var.* Erlian. Nei Mongol Zizhiqu, NE China
Erevan see Yerevan
Erfurt 94 C4 Thüringen, C Germany
Ergene Irmağı 116 A2 *var.* Ergene Irmağı. *River* NW Turkey
Erg Iguid see Iguidi, 'Erg
Ergun He see Argun
Ergun Zuoqi 127 F1 Nei Mongol Zizhiqu, N China
Erie 40 D3 Pennsylvania, NE USA
Erie, Lake 40 D3 *Fr.* Lac Érié. *Lake* Canada/USA
Eritrea 72 C4 *Tig.* Ērtra. *Country* E Africa

Eritrea 72

Official name State of Eritrea
Formation 1993
Capital Asmara
Population 3.8 million / 81 people per sq mile (31 people per sq km)
Total area 46,842 sq miles (121,320 sq km)
Languages Tigrinya, English, Tigre, Afar, Arabic, Bilen, Kunama, Nara, Saho, Hadareb
Religions Christian 45%, Muslim 45%, other 10%
Ethnic mix Tigray and Kunama 40%, Tigray 50%, Afar 4%, Saho 3%, other 4%
Government Transitional regime
Currency Nafka = 100 cents
Literacy rate 55.7%
Calorie consumption 1,665 kilocalories

Erivan see Yerevan
Erlangen 95 C5 Bayern, S Germany
Erlian see Erenhot
Ermelo 86 D3 Gelderland, C Netherlands
Ermióni 105 C6 Pelopónnisos, S Greece
Ermoúpoli 105 D6 *var.* Hermoupolis; *prev.* Ermoúpolis. Sýros, Kykládes, Greece, Aegean Sea
Ermoúpolis see Ermoúpoli
Ernákulam 132 C3 Kerala, SW India
Erode 132 C2 Tamil Nādu, SE India
Erquelinnes 87 B7 Hainaut, S Belgium
Er-Rachidia 70 C2 *var.* Ksar al Soule. E Morocco
Er Rahad 72 B4 *var.* Ar Rahad. Northern Kordofan, C Sudan
Erromango 144 D4 *island* S Vanuatu
Ertis see Irtysh
Erzgebirge 95 C5 *Cz.* Krušné Hory, *Eng.* Ore Mountains. *Mountain range* Czech Republic/Germany
see also Krušné Hory
Erzincan 117 E3 *var.* Erzinjan. Erzincan, E Turkey

Erzinjan see Erzincan
Erzurum 117 E3 *prev.* Erzerum. Erzurum, NE Turkey
Esbjerg 85 A7 Ribe, W Denmark
Escaldes 91 A8 C Andorra
Escanaba 40 C2 Michigan, N USA
Esch-sur-Alzette 87 D8 Luxembourg, S Luxembourg
Escondido 47 C8 California, W USA
Escuinapa 50 D3 *var.* Escuinapa de Hidalgo. Sinaloa, C Mexico
Escuinapa de Hidalgo see Escuinapa
Escuintla 51 G5 Chiapas, SE Mexico
Escuintla 52 B2 Escuintla, S Guatemala
Eşfahān 120 C3 *Eng.* Isfahan; *anc.* Aspadana. Eşfahān, C Iran
Esh Sham see Dimashq
Esh Sharā see Ash Sharāh
Eskişehir 116 B3 *var.* Eskishehr. Eskişehir, W Turkey
Eskishehr see Eskişehir
Eslāmābād 120 C3 *var.* Eslamābād-e Gharb; *prev.* Harunabad. Shāhābād. Kermānshāhān, W Iran
Eslāmābād-e Gharb see Eslāmābād
Esmeraldas 60 A1 Esmeraldas, N Ecuador
Esna see Isna
Espanola 48 D1 New Mexico, SW USA
Esperance 147 B7 Western Australia
Esperanza 154 A2 *Argentinian research station* Antarctica
Esperanza 50 B2 Sonora, NW Mexico
Espinal 58 B3 Tolima, C Colombia
Espinhaço, Serra do 56 D4 *mountain range* SE Brazil
Espírito Santo 63 F4 *off.* Estado do Espírito Santo. *State* E Brazil
Espiritu Santo 144 C4 *var.* Santo. *Island* W Vanuatu
Espoo 85 D6 *Swe.* Esbo. Etelä-Suomi, S Finland
Esquel 65 B6 Chubut, SW Argentina
Essaouira 70 B2 *prev.* Mogador. W Morocco
Es Semara see Smara
Essen 94 A4 *var.* Essen an der Ruhr. Nordrhein-Westfalen, W Germany
Essen 87 C5 Antwerpen, N Belgium
Essen an der Ruhr see Essen
Essequibo River 59 F3 *river* C Guyana
Es Suweida see As Suwaydā'
Estacado, Llano 49 E2 *plain* New Mexico/Texas, SW USA
Estados, Isla de los 65 C8 *prev. Eng.* Staten Island. *Island* S Argentina
Estância 63 G3 Sergipe, E Brazil
Estelí 52 D3 Estelí, NW Nicaragua
Estella see Estella-Lizarra
Estella-Lizarra 93 E1 *Bas.* Lizarra *var.* Estella. Navarra, N Spain
Estepona 92 D5 Andalucía, S Spain
Estevan 37 F5 Saskatchewan, S Canada
Estonia 106 D2 *Est.* Eesti Vabariik, *Ger.* Estland, *Latv.* Igaunija; *prev.* Estonian SSR, *Rus.* Éstonskaya SSR. *Country* NE Europe

Estonia 106

Official name Republic of Estonia
Formation 1991
Capital Tallinn
Population 1.4 million / 80 people per sq mile (31 people per sq km)
Total area 17,462 sq miles (45,226 sq km)
Languages Estonian, Russian
Religions Evangelical Lutheran 56%, Russian Orthodox 25%, Other 19%
Ethnic mix Estonian 62%, Russian 30%, other 8%
Government Parliamentary democracy
Currency Kroon = 100 cents
Literacy rate 99%
Calorie consumption 3 376 kilocalories

Estrela, Serra da 92 C3 *mountain range* C Portugal
Estremoz 92 C4 Évora, S Portugal
Esztergom 99 C6 *Ger.* Gran; *anc.* Strigonium. Komárom-Esztergom, N Hungary
Étalle 87 D8 Luxembourg, SE Belgium
Etāwah 134 D3 Uttar Pradesh, N India
Ethiopia 73 C5 *prev.* Abyssinia, People's Democratic Republic of Ethiopia. *Country* E Africa

Ethiopia 73

Official name Federal Democratic Republic of Ethiopia
Formation 1896
Capital Addis Ababa
Population 64.5 million / 148 people per sq mile (57 people per sq km)
Total area 435,184 sq miles (1,127,127 sq km)
Languages Amharic, Tigrinya, Galla
Religions Muslim 40%, Ethiopian Orthodox 40%, other 20%
Ethnic mix Oromo 40%, Amhara 25%, Sidamo 9%, Somali 6%, Berta 6%, other 14%
Government Multiparty republic
Currency Ethiopian birr = 100 cents
Literacy rate 38.4%
Calorie consumption 2,023 kilocalories

Ethiopian Highlands 73 C5 *var.* Ethiopian Plateau. *Plateau* N Ethiopia
Ethiopian Plateau see Ethiopian Highlands
Etna, Monte 97 C7 *Eng.* Mount Etna. *Volcano* Sicilia, Italy, C Mediterranean Sea
Etna, Mount see Etna, Monte
Etosha Pan 78 B3 *salt lake* N Namibia
Etoumbi 77 B5 Cuvette, NW Congo
Et Tafila 64 *see Aţ Ţafilah
Ettelbrück 87 D8 Diekirch, C Luxembourg
'Eua 145 E5 *prev.* Middleburg Island. *Island* Tongatapu Group, SE Tonga
Euboea see Évvoia
Eucla 147 D6 Western Australia
Euclid 40 D3 Ohio, N USA
Eufaula Lake 49 G1 *var.* Eufaula Reservoir. *Reservoir* Oklahoma, C USA
Eufaula Reservoir see Eufaula Lake
Eugene 46 B3 Oregon, NW USA
Eupen 87 D6 Liège, E Belgium
Euphrates 112 B4 *Ar.* Al Furāt, *Turk.* Firat Nehri. *River* SW Asia
Eureka 47 A5 California, W USA
Eureka 44 A1 Montana, NW USA
Europa Point 93 H5 *headland* S Gibraltar
Europe 34 E1 *continent*
Eutin 94 C2 Schleswig-Holstein, N Germany
Euxine Sea see Black Sea
Evansdale 45 G3 Iowa, C USA
Evanston 40 B4 Wyoming, C USA
Evanston 40 B3 Illinois, N USA
Evansville 40 B5 Indiana, N USA
Eveleth 45 G1 Minnesota, N USA
Everard, Lake 149 A6 *salt lake* South Australia
Everest, Mount 126 B5 *Chin.* Qomolangma Feng, *Nep.* Sagarmatha. *Mountain* China/Nepal
Everett 46 B2 Washington, NW USA
Everglades, The 43 F5 *wetland* Florida, SE USA
Evje 85 A6 Aust-Agder, S Norway
Évora 92 B4 *anc.* Ebora, *Lat.* Liberalitas Julia.Évora, C Portugal
Évreux 90 C3 *anc.* Civitas Eburovicum. Eure, N France
Évros see Maritsa
Évry 90 E2 Essonne, N France

Évvoia 101 E8 *Lat.* Euboea. *Island* C Greece
Ewarton 54 B5 C Jamaica
Excelsior Springs 45 F4 Missouri, C USA
Exe 89 C7 *river* SW England, UK
Exeter 89 C7 *anc.* Isca Damnoniorum. SW England, UK
Exmoor 89 C7 *moorland* SW England, UK
Exmouth 89 C7 SW England, UK
Exmouth 146 A4 Western Australia
Exmouth Gulf 146 A4 *gulf* Western Australia
Exmouth Plateau 141 E5 *undersea feature* E Indian Ocean
Extremadura 92 C3 *cultural region* W Spain
Exuma Cays 54 C1 *islets* C Bahamas
Exuma Sound 54 C1 *sound* C Bahamas
Eyre Mountains 151 A7 *mountain range* South Island, NZ
Eyre North, Lake 149 A5 *salt lake* South Australia
Eyre Peninsula 149 A6 *peninsula* South Australia
Eyre South, Lake 149 A5 *salt lake* South Australia

F

Faadhippolhu Atoll 132 B4 *var.* Fadiffolu, Lhaviyani Atoll. *Atoll* N Maldives
Fabens 48 D3 Texas, SW USA
Fada 76 C2 Borkou-Ennedi-Tibesti, E Chad
Fada-Ngourma 75 E4 E Burkina faso
Fadiffolu *see* Faadhippolhu Atoll
Faenza 96 C3 *anc.* Faventia. Emilia-Romagna, N Italy
Faeroe-Iceland Ridge 80 C1 *undersea feature* NW Norwegian Sea
Faeroe-Shetland Trough 80 C2 *undersea feature* NE Atlantic Ocean
Faeroes Islands 83 E5 *Dan.* Færøerne, *Faer.* Førøyar. *Danish external territory* N Atlantic Ocean
Faetano 96 E2 E San Marino
Făgăraş 108 C4 *Ger.* Fogarasch, *Hung.* Fogaras. Braşov, C Romania
Fagibina, Lake *see* Faguibine, Lac
Fagne 87 C7 *hill range* S Belgium
Faguibine, Lac 75 E3 *var.* Lake Fagibina. *Lake* NW Mali
Fahlun *see* Falun
Fahraj 120 E4 Kermān, SE Iran
Faial 92 A5 *var.* Ilha do Faial. *Island* Azores, Portugal, NE Atlantic Ocean
Fairbanks 36 D3 Alaska, USA
Fairfield 47 B6 California, W USA
Fair Isle 88 D2 *island* NE Scotland, UK
Fairlie 151 B6 Canterbury, South Island, NZ
Fairmont 45 F3 Minnesota, N USA
Faisalābād 134 C2 *prev.* Lyallpur. Punjab, NE Pakistan
Faizābād *see* Feyzābād
Faizābād 135 E3 Uttar Pradesh, N India
Fakaofo Atoll 145 F3 *island* SE Tokelau
Falam 136 A3 Chin State, W Myanmar
Falconara Marittima 96 C3 Marche, C Italy
Falkland Islands 65 D7 *var.* Falklands, Islas Malvinas. *UK dependent territory* SW Atlantic Ocean
Falkland Plateau 57 D7 *var.* Argentine Rise. *Undersea feature* SW Atlantic Ocean
Falklands *see* Falkland Islands
Fallbrook 47 C8 California, W USA
Falmouth 89 C7 SW England, UK
Falmouth 54 A4 W Jamaica
Falster 85 B8 *island* SE Denmark
Fălticeni 108 C3 *Hung.* Falticsén. Suceava, NE Romania

Falun 85 C6 *var.* Fahlun. Kopparberg, C Sweden
Famagusta *see* Ammóchostos
Famagusta Bay *see* Kólpos Ammóchostos
Famenne 87 C7 *physical region* SE Belgium
Fang 136 C3 Chiang Mai, NW Thailand
Fano 96 C3 *anc.* Colonia Julia Fanestris, Fanum Fortunae. Marche, C Italy
Farafangana 79 G4 Fianarantsoa, SE Madagascar
Farāh 122 D4 *var.* Farah, Fararud. Farāh, W Afghanistan
Farāh Rūd 122 D4 *river* W Afghanistan
Faranah 74 C4 Haute-Guinée, S Guinea
Fararud *see* Farāh
Farasān, Jazā'ir 121 A6 *island group* SW Saudi Arabia
Farewell, Cape 150 C4 *headland* South Island, NZ
Farewell, Cape *see* Nunap Isua
Farghona 123 F2 *Rus.* Fergana; *prev.* Novyy Margilan. Farghona Wiloyati, E Uzbekistan
Fargo 45 F2 North Dakota, N USA
Faribault 45 F2 Minnesota, N USA
Farīdābād 134 D3 Haryāna, N India
Farkhor 123 E3 *Rus.* Parkhar. SW Tajikistan
Farmington 45 G5 Missouri, C USA
Farmington 48 C1 New Mexico, SW USA
Faro 92 B5 Faro, S Portugal
Farquhar Group 79 G2 *island group* S Seychelles
Farvel, Kap *see* Nunap Isua
Fastiv 109 E2 *Rus.* Fastov. Kyyivs'ka Oblast', NW Ukraine
Fauske 84 C3 Nordland, C Norway
Faxaflói 82 D5 *Eng.* Faxa Bay. *Bay* W Iceland
Faya 76 C2 *prev.* Faya-Largeau, Largeau. Borkou-Ennedi-Tibesti, N Chad
Fayetteville 42 A1 Arkansas, C USA
Fayetteville 43 F1 North Carolina, SE USA
Fdérick *see* Fdérik
Fdérik 74 C2 *var.* Fdérick, *Fr.* Fort Gouraud. Tiris Zemmour, NW Mauritania
Fear, Cape 43 F2 *headland* Bald Head Island, North Carolina, SE USA
Fécamp 90 B3 Seine-Maritime, N France
Federation of the separate territories of *see* Malaysia
Fehérgyarmat 99 E6 Szabolcs-Szatmár-Bereg, E Hungary
Fehmarn 94 C2 *island* N Germany
Fehmarn Belt 94 C2 *Ger.* Fehmarnbelt. *Strait* Denmark/Germany
Feijó 62 C2 Acre, W Brazil
Feilding 150 D4 Manawatu-Wanganui, North Island, NZ
Feira *see* Feira de Santana
Feira de Santana 63 G3 *var.* Feira. Bahia, E Brazil
Felanitx 93 G3 *anc.* Canati, Felaniche. Mallorca, Spain, W Mediterranean Sea
Felidhu Atoll 132 B4 *atoll* C Maldives
Felipe Carrillo Puerto 51 H4 Quintana Roo, SE Mexico
Felixstowe 89 E6 E England, UK
Femunden 85 B5 *lake* S Norway
Fengcheng 128 D3 *var.* Feng-cheng, Fenghwangcheng. Liaoning, NE China
Feng-cheng *see* Fengcheng
Fenghwangcheng *see* Fengcheng
Fengtien *see* Liaoning
Fenoarivo 79 G3 Toamasina, E Madagascar
Fens, The 89 E6 *wetland* E England, UK

Feodosiya 109 F5 *var.* Kefe, *It.* Kaffa; *anc.* Theodosia. Respublika Krym, S Ukraine
Féres 104 D3 Anatolikí Makedonía kai Thráki, NE Greece
Fergus Falls 45 F2 Minnesota, N USA
Ferkessédougou 74 D4 N Côte d'Ivoire
Fermo 96 C4 *anc.* Firmum Picenum. Marche, C Italy
Fernandina, Isla 60 A5 *var.* Narborough Island. *Island* Galapagos Islands, Ecuador, E Pacific Ocean
Fernando de Noronha 63 H2 *island* E Brazil
Fernando Po *see* Bioco, Isla de
Fernando Póo *see* Bioco, Isla de
Ferrara 96 C2 *anc.* Forum Alieni. Emilia-Romagna, N Italy
Ferreñafe 60 B3 Lambayeque, W Peru
Ferro *see* Hierro
Ferrol 92 B1 *var.* El Ferrol; *prev.* El Ferrol del Caudillo. Galicia, NW Spain
Ferwerd 86 D1 *Fris.* Ferwert. Friesland, N Netherlands
Fès 70 C2 *Eng.* Fez. N Morocco
Feteşti 108 D5 Ialomiţa, SE Romania
Fethiye 116 B4 Muğla, SW Turkey
Fetlar 88 D1 *island* NE Scotland, UK
Feyzābād 123 F3 *var.* Faizabad, Faizābād, Feyzābād, Fyzabad. Badakhshān, NE Afghanistan
Fianarantsoa 79 F3 Fianarantsoa, C Madagascar
Fianga 76 B4 Mayo-Kébbi, SW Chad
Fier 101 C6 *var.* Fieri. Fier, SW Albania
Fieri *see* Fier
Figeac 91 C5 Lot, S France
Figig *see* Figuig
Figueira da Foz 92 B3 Coimbra, W Portugal
Figueres 93 G2 Cataluña, E Spain
Figuig 70 D2 *var.* Figig. E Morocco
Fiji 145 E5 *Fij.* Viti. *Country* SW Pacific Ocean

Fiji 145

Official name Republic of the Fiji Islands
Formation 1970
Capital Suva
Population 823,000 / 117 people per sq mile (45 people per sq km)
Total area 7,054 sq miles (18,270 sq km)
Languages Fijian, English, Hindi, Urdu, Tamil, Telegu
Religions Hindu 38%, Methodist 37%, Roman Catholic 9%, other 16%
Ethnic mix Melanesian 48%, Indian 46%, other 6%
Government Multiparty republic
Currency Fiji dollar = 100 cents
Literacy rate 92.9%
Calorie consumption 2,861 kilocalories

Filadelfia 52 D4 Guanacaste, W Costa Rica
Filiaşi 108 B5 Dolj, SW Romania
Filipstad 85 B6 Värmland, C Sweden
Finale Ligure 96 A3 Liguria, NW Italy
Finchley 89 A7 SE England, UK
Findlay 40 C4 Ohio, N USA
Finike 116 B4 Antalya, SW Turkey
Finland 84 D4 *Fin.* Suomen Tasavalta, Suomi. *Country* N Europe

Finland 84

Official name Republic of Finland
Formation 1917
Capital Helsinki

Finland (continued)

Population 5.2 million / 40 people per sq mile (15 people per sq km)
Total area 130,127 sq miles (337,030 sq km)
Languages Finnish, Swedish, Sami
Religions Evangelical Lutheran 89%, Finnish Orthodox 1%, Roman Catholic 1%, other 9%
Ethnic mix Finnish 93%, other (including Sami) 7%
Government Paliamentary democracy
Currency Euro (Markka until 2002)
Literacy rate 99%
Calorie consumption 3,227 kilocalories

Finland, Gulf of 85 D6 *Est.* Soome Laht, *Fin.* Suomenlahti, *Ger.* Finnischer Meerbusen, *Rus.* Finskiy Zaliv, *Swe.* Finska Viken. *Gulf* E Baltic Sea
Finnmarksvidda 84 D2 *physical region* N Norway
Finsterwalde 94 D4 Brandenburg, E Germany
Fiordland 151 A7 *physical region* South Island, NZ
Fiorina 96 E1 NE San Marino
Firenze 96 C3 *Eng.* Florence; *anc.* Florentia. Toscana, C Italy
Fischbacher Alpen 95 E7 *mountain range* E Austria
Fish 78 B4 *var.* Vis. *River* S Namibia
Fishguard 89 C6 *Wel.* Abergwaun. SW Wales, UK
Fisterra, Cabo 92 B1 *headland* NW Spain
Fitzroy Crossing 146 C3 Western Australia
Fitzroy River 146 C3 *river* Western Australia
Flagstaff 48 B2 Arizona, SW USA
Flanders 87 A6 *Dut.* Vlaanderen, *Fr.* Flandre. *Cultural region* Belgium/France
Flathead Lake 44 B1 *lake* Montana, NW USA
Flat Island 128 C8 *island* NE Spratly Islands
Flatts Village 42 B5 *var.* The Flatts Village. C Bermuda
Flensburg 94 B2 Schleswig-Holstein, N Germany
Flinders Island 149 C8 *island* Furneaux Group, Tasmania, SE Australia
Flinders Ranges 149 B6 *mountain range* South Australia
Flinders River 148 C3 *river* Queensland, NE Australia
Flin Flon 37 F5 Manitoba, C Canada
Flint 40 C3 Michigan, N USA
Flint Island 145 G4 *island* Line Islands, E Kiribati
Floreana, Isla *see* Santa María, Isla
Florence *see* Firenze
Florence 42 C1 Alabama, S USA
Florence 43 F2 South Carolina, SE USA
Florencia 58 B4 Caquetá, S Colombia
Florentia *see* Firenze
Flores 92 A5 *island* Azores, Portugal, NE Atlantic Ocean
Flores 139 E5 *island* Nusa Tenggara, C Indonesia
Flores 52 B1 Petén, N Guatemala
Flores Sea 138 D5 *Ind.* Laut Flores. *Sea* C Indonesia
Floriano 63 F2 Piauí, E Brazil
Florianópolis 63 F5 *prev.* Destêrro. *State capital* Santa Catarina, S Brazil
Florida 43 E4 *off.* State of Florida; also known as Peninsular State, Sunshine State. *State* SE USA
Florida 64 D4 Florida, S Uruguay
Florida Bay 43 E5 *bay* Florida, SE USA
Florida Keys 43 E5 *island group* Florida, SE USA
Florida, Straits of 54 B1 *strait* Atlantic Ocean/Gulf of Mexico

Flórina 104 B4 *var.* Phlórina. Dytikí Makedonía, N Greece
Florissant 45 G4 Missouri, C USA
Floúda, Akrotírio 105 D7 *headland* Astypálaia, Kykládes, Greece, Aegean Sea
Foča 100 C4 *var.* Srbinje, Republika Srpska, SE Bosnia and Herzegovina
Focşani 108 C4 Vrancea, E Romania
Foggia 97 D5 Puglia, SE Italy
Fogo 74 A3 *island* Ilhas de Sotavento, SW Cape Verde
Foix 91 B6 Ariège, S France
Folégandros 105 C7 *island* Kykládes, Greece, Aegean Sea
Foleyet 38 C4 Ontario, S Canada
Foligno 96 C4 Umbria, C Italy
Folkestone 89 E7 SE England, UK
Fond du Lac 40 B2 Wisconsin, N USA
Fongafale 145 E3 *var.* Funafuti. *Country capital* (Tuvalu) Funafuti Atoll, SE Tuvalu
Fonseca, Gulf of 52 C3 *Sp.* Golfo de Fonseca. *Gulf* Central America
Fontainebleau 90 C3 Seine-et-Marne, N France
Fontenay-le-Comte 90 B4 Vendée, NW France
Fontvieille 91 B8 SW Monaco
Fonyód 99 C7 Somogy, W Hungary
Foochow *see* Fuzhou
Forchheim 95 C5 Bayern, SE Germany
Forel, Mont 82 D4 *mountain* SE Greenland
Forfar 88 C3 E Scotland, UK
Forge du Sud *see* Dudelange
Forlì 96 C3 *anc.* Forum Livii. Emilia-Romagna, N Italy
Formentera 93 G4 *anc.* Ophiusa, *Lat.* Frumentum. *Island* Islas Baleares, Spain, W Mediterranean Sea
Formosa 64 D2 Formosa, NE Argentina
Formosa, Serra 63 E3 *mountain range* C Brazil
Formosa Strait *see* Taiwan Strait
Forrest City 42 B1 Arkansas, C USA
Fort Albany 38 C3 Ontario, C Canada
Fortaleza 63 G2 *prev.* Ceará. *State capital* Ceará, NE Brazil
Fortaleza 61 F2 Pando, N Bolivia
Fort-Bayard *see* Zhanjiang
Fort-Cappolani *see* Tidjikja
Fort Collins 44 D4 Colorado, C USA
Fort Davis 49 E3 Texas, SW USA
Fort-de-France 55 H4 *prev.* Fort-Royal. *Dependent territory capital* (Martinique) W Martinique
Fort Dodge 45 F3 Iowa, C USA
Fortescue River 146 A4 *river* Western Australia
Fort Frances 38 B4 Ontario, S Canada
Fort Good Hope 37 E3 *var.* Good Hope. Northwest Territories, NW Canada
Fort Gouraud *see* Fdérik
Forth 88 C4 *river* C Scotland, UK
Forth, Firth of 88 C4 *estuary* E Scotland, UK
Fort-Lamy *see* Ndjamena
Fort Lauderdale 43 F5 Florida, SE USA
Fort Liard 37 E4 *var.* Liard. Northwest Territories, W Canada
Fort Madison 45 G4 Iowa, C USA
Fort McMurray 37 E4 Alberta, C Canada
Fort McPherson 36 D3 *var.* McPherson. Northwest Territories, NW Canada
Fort Morgan 44 D4 Colorado, C USA
Fort Myers 43 E5 Florida, SE USA
Fort Nelson 37 E4 British Columbia, W Canada
Fort Peck Lake 44 C1 *reservoir* Montana, NW USA
Fort Pierce 43 F4 Florida, SE USA
Fort Providence 37 E4 *var.* Providence. Northwest Territories, W Canada

Fort St.John 37 E4 British Columbia, W Canada
Fort Scott 45 F5 Kansas, C USA
Fort Severn 38 C2 Ontario, C Canada
Fort-Shevchenko 114 A4 Mangistau, W Kazakhstan
Fort Simpson 37 E4 *var.* Simpson. Northwest Territories, W Canada
Fort Smith 37 E4 *district capital* Northwest Territories, W Canada
Fort Smith 42 B1 Arkansas, C USA
Fort Stockton 49 E3 Texas, SW USA
Fort-Trinquet *see* Bîr Mogreïn
Fort Vermilion 37 E4 Alberta, W Canada
Fort Walton Beach 42 C3 Florida, SE USA
Fort Wayne 40 C4 Indiana, N USA
Fort William 88 C3 N Scotland, UK
Fort Worth 49 G2 Texas, SW USA
Fort Yukon 36 D3 Alaska, USA
Fougamou 77 A6 Ngounié, C Gabon
Fougères 90 B3 Ille-et-Vilaine, NW France
Foulwind, Cape 151 B5 *headland* South Island, NZ
Foumban 76 A4 Ouest, NW Cameroon
Fou-shan *see* Fushun
Foveaux Strait 151 A8 *strait* S NZ
Foxe Basin 37 G3 *sea* Nunavut, N Canada
Fox Glacier 151 B6 West Coast, South Island, NZ
Fox Mine 37 F4 Manitoba, C Canada
Fraga 93 F2 Aragón, NE Spain
Fram Basin 155 C3 *var.* Amundsen Basin. *Undersea feature* Arctic Ocean
France 90 B4 *It./Sp.* Francia; *prev.* Gaul, Gaule, *Lat.* Gallia. *Country* W Europe

France 90

Official name French Republic
Formation 987
Capital Paris
Population 59.5 million /282 people per sq mile (109 people per sq km)
Total area 211,208 sq miles (547,030 sq km)
Languages French, Provenial, German, Breton, Catalan, Basque
Religions Roman Catholic 88%, Muslim 8%, Protestant 2%, other 2%
Ethnic mix French 90%, North African 6%, German 2%, other 2%
Government Multiparty republic
Currency Euro (French franc until 2002)
Literacy rate 99%
Calorie consumption 3,591 kilocalories

Franceville 77 B6 *var.* Massoukou, Masuku. Haut-Ogooué, E Gabon
Francfort *prev. see* Frankfurt am Main
Franche-Comté 90 D4 *cultural region* E France
Francis Case, Lake 45 E3 *reservoir* South Dakota, N USA
Francisco Escárcega 51 G4 Campeche, SE Mexico
Francistown 78 D3 North East, NE Botswana
Franconian Jura *see* Fränkische Alb
Frankenalb *see* Fränkische Alb
Frankenstein *see* Ząbkowice Śląskie
Frankenstein in Schlesien *see* Ząbkowice Śląskie
Frankfort 40 C5 *state capital* Kentucky, S USA
Frankfort on the Main *see* Frankfurt am Main
Frankfurt *see* Frankfurt am Main
Frankfurt am Main 95 B5 *var.* Frankfurt, *Fr.* Francfort; *prev. Eng.* Frankfort on the Main. Hessen, SW Germany

Frankfurt an der Oder 94 D3 Brandenburg, E Germany
Fränkische Alb 95 C6 *var.* Frankenalb, *Eng.* Franconian Jura. *Mountain range* S Germany
Franklin 42 C1 Tennessee, S USA
Franklin D.Roosevelt Lake 46 C1 *reservoir* Washington, NW USA
Frantsa-Iosifa, Zemlya 114 D1 *Eng.* Franz Josef Land. *Island group* N Russian Federation
Franz Josef Land *see* Frantsa-Iosifa, Zemlya
Fraserburgh 88 D3 NE Scotland, UK
Fraser Island 148 E4 *var.* Great Sandy Island. Island Queensland, E Australia
Fredericksburg 41 E5 Virginia, NE USA
Fredericton 39 F4 New Brunswick, SE Canada
Frederikshåb *see* Paamiut
Frederikstad 85 B6 Østfold, S Norway
Freeport 54 C1 Grand Bahama Island, N Bahamas
Freeport 49 H4 Texas, SW USA
Freetown 74 C4 *country capital* (Sierra Leone) W Sierra Leone
Freiburg *see* Freiburg im Breisgau
Freiburg im Breisgau 95 A6 *var.* Freiburg, *Fr.* Fribourg-en-Brisgau. Baden-Württemberg, SW Germany
Fremantle 147 A6 Western Australia
Fremont 45 F4 Nebraska, C USA
French Guiana 59 H3 *var.* Guyane. *French overseas department* N South America
French Polynesia 143 F4 *French overseas territory* C Polynesia
French Southern and Antarctic Territories 141 B7 *Fr.* Terres Australes et Antarctiques Françaises. *French overseas territory* S Indian Ocean
Fresnillo 50 D3 *var.* Fresnillo de González Echeverría. Zacatecas, C Mexico
Fresnillo de González Echeverría *see* Fresnillo
Fresno 47 C6 California, W USA
Frías 64 C3 Catamarca, N Argentina
Fribourg-en-Brisgau *see* Freiburg im Breisgau
Friedrichshafen 95 B7 Baden-Württemberg, S Germany
Frobisher Bay 82 B3 *inlet* Baffin Island, Northwest Territories, NE Canada
Frohavet 84 B4 *sound* C Norway
Frome, Lake 149 B6 *salt lake* South Australia
Frontera 51 G4 Tabasco, SE Mexico
Frontignan 91 C6 Hérault, S France
Frostviken *see* Kvarnbergsvattnet
Frøya 84 A4 *island* W Norway
Frunze *see* Bishkek
Frýdek-Místek 99 C5 *Ger.* Friedek-Mistek. Ostravský Kraj, E Czech Republic
Fu-chien *see* Fujian
Fu-chou *see* Fuzhou
Fuengirola 92 D5 Andalucía, S Spain
Fuerte Olimpo 64 D2 *var.* Olimpo. Alto Paraguay, NE Paraguay
Fuerte, Río 48 C5 *river* C Mexico
Fuerteventura 70 B3 *island* Islas Canarias, Spain, NE Atlantic Ocean
Fuhkien *see* Fujian
Fu-hsin *see* Fuxin
Fuji 131 D6 *var.* Huzi. Shizuoka, Honshū, S Japan
Fujian 128 D6 *var.* Fu-chien, Fuhkien, Fujian Sheng, Fukien, Min. Admin. region *province* SE China
Fujian Sheng *see* Fujian
Fuji-san 131 C6 *var.* Fujiyama, *Eng.* Mount Fuji. *Mountain* Honshū, SE Japan
Fujiyama *see* Fuji-san
Fukang 126 C2 Xinjiang Uygur Zizhiqu, W China

Fukien *see* Fujian
Fukui 131 C6 *var.* Hukui. Fukui, Honshū, SW Japan
Fukuoka 131 A7 *var.* Hukuoka; *hist.* Najima. Fukuoka, Kyūshū, SW Japan
Fukushima 130 D4 *var.* Hukusima. Fukushima, Honshū, C Japan
Fulda 95 B5 Hessen, C Germany
Funafuti *see* Fongafale
Funafuti Atoll 145 E3 *atoll* C Tuvalu
Funchal 70 A2 Madeira, Portugal, NE Atlantic Ocean
Fundy, Bay of 39 F5 *bay* Canada/USA
Furnes *see* Veurne
Fürth 95 C5 Bayern, S Germany
Furukawa 130 D4 *var.* Hurukawa. Miyagi, Honshū, C Japan
Fushun 128 D3 *var.* Fou-shan, Fu-shun. Liaoning, NE China
Fu-shun *see* Fushun
Fusin *see* Fuxin
Füssen 95 C7 Bayern, S Germany
Futog 100 D3 Serbia, NW Serbia and Montenegro (Yugo.)
Futuna, Île 145 E4 *island* S Wallis and Futuna
Fuxin 128 D3 *var.* Fou-hsin, Fu-hsin, Fusin. Liaoning, NE China
Fuzhou *see* Linchuan
Fuzhou 128 D6 *var.* Foochow, Fu-chou. Fujian, SE China
Fyn 85 B8 *Ger.* Fünen. *Island* C Denmark
Fyzabad *see* Feyzābād

G

Gaafu Alifu Atoll *see* North Huvadhu Atoll
Gaafu Dhaalu Atoll *see* South Huvadhu Atoll
Gaalkacyo 73 E5 *var.* Galka'yo, *It.* Galcaio. Mudug, C Somalia
Gabela 78 B2 Cuanza Sul, W Angola
Gabès 71 E2 *var.* Qābis. E Tunisia
Gabès, Golfe de 71 F2 *Ar.* Khalīj Qābis. *Gulf* E Tunisia
Gabon 77 B6 *Country* C Africa

Gabon 77

Official name Gabonese Republic
Formation 1960
Capital Libreville
Population 1.3 million / 13 people per sq mile (5 people per sq km)
Total area 103,346 sq miles (267,667 sq km)
Languages French, Fang, Punu, Sira, Nzebi, Mpongwe
Religions Christian 55%, Traditional beliefs 40%, Muslim 1%, other 4%
Ethnic mix Fang 35%, Eshira 25%, other Bantu 29%, other 11%
Government Multiparty republic
Currency CFA franc = 100 centimes
Literacy rate 70.8%
Calorie consumption 2,564 kilocalories

Gaborone 78 C4 *prev.* Gaberones. *Country capital* (Botswana) South East, SE Botswana
Gabrovo 104 D2 Gabrovo, N Bulgaria
Gadag 132 C1 Karnātaka, W India
Gadsden 42 D2 Alabama, S USA
Gaeta 97 C5 Lazio, C Italy
Gaeta, Golfo di 97 C5 *var.* Gulf of Gaeta. *Gulf* C Italy
Gaeta, Gulf of *see* Gaeta, Golfo di
Gäfle *see* Gävle
Gafsa 71 E2 *var.* Qafşah. W Tunisia
Gagnoa 74 D5 C Côte d'Ivoire
Gagra 117 F1 NW Georgia
Gaillac 91 C6 *var.* Gaillac-sur-Tarn. Tarn, S France
Gaillac-sur-Tarn *see* Gaillac
Gaillimh *see* Galway
Gainesville 43 E3 Florida, SE USA
Gainesville 42 D2 Georgia, SE USA
Gainesville 49 G2 Texas, SW USA

Gairdner, Lake 149 A6 *salt lake* South Australia
Gaiziņ *see* Gaizina Kalns
Gaizina Kalns 106 C3 *var.* Gaiziņ. *Mountain* E Latvia
Galán, Cerro 64 B3 *mountain* NW Argentina
Galanta 99 C6 *Hung.* Galánta. Trnavský Kraj, W Slovakia
Galapagos Fracture Zone 153 E3 *tectonic feature* E Pacific Ocean
Galapagos Islands 153 F3 *var.* Islas de los Galápagos,Tortoise Islands. *Island group* Ecuador, E Pacific Ocean
Galapagos Rise 153 F3 *undersea feature* E Pacific Ocean
Galashiels 88 C4 SE Scotland, UK
Galaţi 108 D4 *Ger.* Galatz. Galaţi, E Romania
Galcaio *see* Gaalkacyo
Galesburg 40 B3 Illinois, N USA
Galicia 92 B1 *cultural region* NW Spain
Galicia Bank 80 B4 *undersea feature* E Atlantic Ocean
Galilee, Sea of *see* Tiberias, Lake
Galka'yo *see* Gaalkacyo
Galle 132 D4 *prev.* Point de Galle. Southern Province, SW Sri Lanka
Gallego Rise 153 F3 *undersea feature* E Pacific Ocean
Gallegos *see* Río Gallegos
Gallipoli 97 E6 Puglia, SE Italy
Gällivare 84 C3 Norrbotten, N Sweden
Gallup 48 C1 New Mexico, SW USA
Galtat-Zemmour 70 B3 C Western Sahara
Galveston 49 H4 Texas, SW USA
Galway 89 A5 *Ir.* Gaillimh. W Ireland
Galway Bay 89 A6 *Ir.* Cuan na Gaillimhe. Bay W Ireland
Gambell 36 C2 Saint Lawrence Island, Alaska, USA
Gambia 74 C3 *Fr.* Gambie. *River* W Africa
Gambia 74 B3 *Country* W Africa

Gambia 74

Official name Republic of The Gambia
Formation 1965
Capital Banjul
Population 1.34 million / 307 people per sq mile (119 people per sq km)
Total area 4,363 sq miles (11,300 sq km)
Languages English, Mandinka, Fulani, Wolof, Jola, Soninke
Religions Sunni Muslim 90%, Christian 9%, Indigenous beliefs 1%
Ethnic mix Mandinka 42%, Fulani 18%, Wolof 16%, Jola 10%, Serahuli 9%, other 5%
Government Multiparty republic
Currency Dalasi = 100 butut
Literacy rate 36.6%
Calorie consumption 2,474 kilocalories

Gambier, Îles 143 G4 *island group* E French Polynesia
Gamboma 77 B6 Plateaux, E Congo
Gan *see* Gansu
Gan *see* Jiangxi
Gan 132 B5 Addu Atoll, C Maldives
Gäncä 117 G2 *Rus.* Gyandzha; *prev.* Kirovabad, Yelisavetpol. W Azerbaijan
Gandajika 77 D7 Kasai Oriental, S Dem. Rep. Congo
Gander 39 G3 Newfoundland, Newfoundland and Labrador, SE Canada
Gāndhīdhām 134 C4 Gujarāt, W India
Gandía 93 F3 País Valenciano, E Spain
Ganges 135 F3 *Ben.* Padma. *River* Bangladesh/India *see also* Padma
Ganges Cone *see* Ganges Fan

Ganges Fan 140 D3 *var.* Ganges Cone. *Undersea feature* N Bay of Bengal
Ganges, Mouths of the 135 G4 *delta* Bangladesh/India
Gangra *see* Çankırı
Gangtok 135 F3 Sikkim, N India
Gansu 128 B4 *var.* Gan, Gansu Sheng, Kansu. Admin. region *province* N China
Gansu Sheng *see* Gansu
Ganzhou 128 D6 Jiangxi, S China
Gao 75 E3 Gao, E Mali
Gaoual 74 C4 Moyenne-Guinée, N Guinea
Gaoxiong *see* Kaohsiung
Gap 91 D5 *anc.* Vapincum. Hautes-Alpes, SE France
Gar 126 A4 *var.* Gar Xincun. Xizang Zizhiqu, W China
Garachiné 53 G5 Darién, SE Panama
Garagum *see* Garagumy
Garagum Kanaly *see* Garagumskiy Kanal
Garagumskiy Kanal 122 D3 *var.* Kara Kum Canal, Karakumskiy Kanal, *Turkm.* Garagum Kanaly. *Canal* C Turkmenistan
Garagumy 122 C3 *var.* Qara Qum, *Eng.* Black Sand Desert, Kara Kum, *Turkm.* Garagum; *prev.* Peski Karakumy. *Desert* C Turkmenistan
Gara Khitrino 104 D2 Shumen, NE Bulgaria
Garda, Lago di C2 *var.* Benaco, *Eng.* Lake Garda, *Ger.* Gardasee. *Lake* NE Italy
Garda, Lake *see* Garda, Lago di
Gardasee *see* Garda, Lago di
Garden City 45 E5 Kansas, C USA
Gardeyz *see* Gardēz
Gardēz 123 E4 *var.* Gardeyz, Gordiaz. Paktīā, E Afghanistan
Gargždai 106 B3 Klaipėda, W Lithuania
Garissa 73 D6 Coast, E Kenya
Garland 49 G2 Texas, SW USA
Garman, Loch *see* Wexford
Garoe *see* Garoowe
Garonne 91 B5 *anc.* Garumna. *River* S France
Garoowe 73 E5 *var.* Garoe. Nugaal, N Somalia
Garoua 76 B4 *var.* Garua. Nord, N Cameroon
Garrygala *see* Kara-Kala
Garry Lake 37 F3 *lake* Nunavut, N Canada
Garsen 73 D6 Coast, S Kenya
Garua *see* Garoua
Garwolin 98 D4 Mazowieckie, C Poland
Gar Xincun *see* Gar
Gary 40 B3 Indiana, N USA
Garzón 64 B4 Huila, S Colombia
Gascogne 91 B6 *Eng.* Gascony. *Cultural region* S France
Gascoyne River 147 A5 *river* Western Australia
Gaspé 39 F3 Quebec, SE Canada
Gaspé, Péninsule de 39 E4 *var.* Péninsule de la Gaspésie. *Peninsula* Quebec, SE Canada
Gastonia 43 E1 North Carolina, SE USA
Gastoúni 105 B6 Dytikí Ellás, S Greece
Gatchina 110 B4 Leningradskaya Oblast', NW Russian Federation
Gatineau 38 D2 Quebec, SE Canada
Gatún, Lago 53 F4 *reservoir* C Panama
Gauja 106 D3 *Ger.* Aa. *River* Estonia/Latvia
Gauteng *see* Johannesburg
Gāvbandī 120 D4 Hormozgān, S Iran
Gávdos 105 C8 *island* SE Greece
Gavere 87 B6 Oost-Vlaanderen, NW Belgium
Gävle 85 C6 *var.* Gäfle; *prev.* Gefle. Gävleborg, C Sweden
Gawler 149 B6 South Australia
Gaya 135 F3 Bihār, N India
Gayndah 149 E5 Queensland, E Australia

Gaza 119 A6 *Ar.* Ghazzah, *Heb.* 'Azza. NE Gaza Strip
Gaz-Achak 122 D2 *Turkm.* Gazojak. Lebapskiy Velayat, NE Turkmenistan
Gazandzhyk 122 B2 *Turkm.* Gazanjyk; *prev.* Kazandzhik. Balkanskiy Velayat, W Turkmenistan
Gaza Strip 119 A7 *Ar.* Qiţā' Ghazzah. *Disputed region* SW Asia
Gazi Antep *see* Gaziantep
Gaziantep 116 D4 *var.* Gazi Antep; *prev.* Aintab, Antep. Gaziantep, S Turkey
Gazimağusa *see* Ammóchostos
Gazimağusa Körfezi *see* Kólpos Ammóchostos
Gazli 122 D2 Bukhoro Wiloyati, C Uzbekistan
Gbanga 74 D5 *var.* Gbarnga. N Liberia
Gbarnga *see* Gbanga
Gdansk 98 C2 *Fr.* Dantzig, *Ger.* Danzig. Pomorskie, N Poland
Gdan'skaya Bukhta *see* Danzig, Gulf of
Pomorskie, Gulf of *see* Danzig, Gulf of
Gdynia 98 C2 *Ger.* Gdingen. Pomorskie, N Poland
Gedaref 72 C4 *var.* Al Qaḑārif, El Gedaref. Gedaref, E Sudan
Gediz 116 B3 Kütahya, W Turkey
Gediz Nehri 116 A3 *river* W Turkey
Geel 87 C5 *var.* Gheel. Antwerpen, N Belgium
Geelong 149 C7 Victoria, SE Australia
Ge'e'mu *see* Golmud
Gefle *see* Gävle
Geilo 85 A5 Buskerud, S Norway
Gejiu 128 B6 *var.* Kochiu. Yunnan, S China
Gëkdepe *see* Geok-Tepe
Gela 97 C7 *prev.* Terranova di Sicilia. Sicilia, Italy, C Mediterranean Sea
Geldermalsen 86 C4 Gelderland, C Netherlands
Geleen 87 D6 Limburg, SE Netherlands
Gelinsoor *see* Gellinsoor
Gellinsoor 73 E5 *var.* Gelinsoor. Mudug, NE Somalia
Gembloux 87 C6 Namur, Belgium
Gemena 77 C5 Equateur, NW Dem. Rep. Congo
Gemona del Friuli 96 D2 Friuli-Venezia Giulia, NE Italy
Genck *see* Genk
General Alvear 64 B4 Mendoza, W Argentina
General Eugenio A.Garay 64 C1 Guairá, S Paraguay
General Machado *see* Camacupa
General Santos 139 F3 *off.* General Santos City. Mindanao, S Philippines
Geneva *see* Genève
Geneva, Lake 44 *Fr.* Lac de Genève, Lac Léman, le Léman, *Ger.* Genfer See. *Lake* France/Switzerland
Genève 91 D7 *Eng.* Geneva, *Ger.* Genf, *It.* Ginevra. Genève, SW Switzerland
Genf *see* Genève
Genk 87 D6 *var.* Genck. Limburg, NE Belgium
Gennep 86 D4 Limburg, SE Netherlands
Genoa *see* Genova
Genova 102 D1 *Eng.* Genoa, *Fr.* Gênes; *anc.* Genua. Liguria, NW Italy
Genova, Golfo di 96 A3 *Eng.* Gulf of Genoa. *Gulf* NW Italy
Genovesa, Isla 60 B5 *var.* Tower Island. *Island* Galapagos Islands, Ecuador, E Pacific Ocean
Gent 87 B5 *Eng.* Ghent, *Fr.* Gand. Oost-Vlaanderen, NW Belgium
Geok-Tepe 122 C3 *var.* Gëkdepe, *Turkm.* Gökdepe. Akhalskiy Velayat, C Turkmenistan

George 82 A4 *river* Newfoundland and Labrador/Quebec, E Canada
George 78 C5 Western Cape, S South Africa
George, Lake 43 E3 *lake* Florida, SE USA
Georges Bank 35 D5 *undersea feature* W Atlantic Ocean
George Sound 151 A7 *sound* South Island, NZ
Georges River 148 D2 *river* New South Wales, SE Australia
George Town 54 B3 *var.* Georgetown. *Dependent territory capital* (Cayman Islands) Grand Cayman, SW Cayman Islands
George Town 138 B3 *var.* Penang, Pinang. Pinang, Peninsular Malaysia
George Town 54 C2 Great Exuma Island, C Bahamas
Georgetown 59 F2 *country capital* (Guyana) N Guyana
Georgetown 43 F2 South Carolina, SE USA
George V Land 154 C4 *physical region* Antarctica
Georgia 117 F2 *Geor.* Sak'art'velo, *Rus.* Gruzinskaya SSR, Gruziya; *prev.* Georgian SSR. *Country* SW Asia

---

Georgia 117

Official name Georgia
Formation 1991
Capital Tbilisi
Population 5.2 million /193 people per sq mile (75 people per sq km)
Total area 26,911 sq miles (69,700 sq km)
Languages Georgian, Russian
Religions Georgian Orthodox 65%, Muslim 11%, Russian Orthodox 10%, Armenian Orthodox 8%, Unknown 6%
Ethnic mix Georgian 70%, Armenian 8%, Russian 6%, Azeri 6%, Ossetian 3%, other 7%
Government Presidential democracy
Currency Lari = 100 tetri
Literacy rate 99%
Calorie consumption 2,412 kilocalories

Georgia 42 D2 *off.* State of Georgia; also known as Empire State of the South, Peach State. *State* SE USA
Georgian Bay 40 D2 *lake bay* Ontario, S Canada
Georgia, Strait of 46 A1 *strait* British Columbia, W Canada
Georg von Neumayer 154 A2 *German research station* Antarctica
Gera 94 C4 Thüringen, E Germany
Geráki 105 B6 Pelopónnisos, S Greece
Geraldine 151 B6 Canterbury, South Island, NZ
Geraldton 147 A6 Western Australia
Geral, Serra 57 D5 *mountain range* S Brazil
Gerede 116 C2 Bolu, N Turkey
Gereshk 122 D5 Helmand, SW Afghanistan
Gering 44 D3 Nebraska, C USA
Germanicopolis *see* Çankırı
Germany 94 B4 *Ger.* Bundesrepublik Deutschland, Deutschland. *Country* N Europe

---

Germany 94

Official name Federal Republic of Germany
Formation 1871
Capital Berlin
Population 82 million / 595 people per sq mile (230 people per sq km)
Total area 137,846 sq miles (357,021 sq km)
Languages German, Turkish
Religions Protestant 34%, Roman Catholic 33%, Muslim 3%, other 30%

Germany (continued)

Ethnic mix German 92%, other 8%
Government Parliamentary democracy
Currency Euro (Deutsche Mark until 2002)
Literacy rate 99%
Calorie consumption 3,451 kilocalories

Geroliménas *105 B7* Pelopónnisos, S Greece
Gerona *see* Girona
Gerpinnes *87 C7* Hainaut, S Belgium
Gerunda *see* Girona
Gerze *116 D2* Sinop, N Turkey
Gesoriacum *see* Boulogne-sur-Mer
Gessoriacum *see* Boulogne-sur-Mer
Getafe *92 D3* Madrid, C Spain
Gevas *117 F3* Van, SE Turkey
Gevgeli *see* Gevgelija
Gevgelija *101 E6 var.* Devđelija, Djevdjelija, *Turk.* Gevgeli. SE FYR Macedonia
Ghaba *see* Al Ghābah
Ghana *75 E5 Country* W Africa

Ghana 75

Official name Republic of Ghana
Formation 1957
Capital Accra
Population 19.7 million / 214 people per sq mile (83 people per sq km)
Total area 92,100 sq miles (238,540 sq km)
Languages English, Twi, Fanti, Ewe, Ga, Adangbe, Gurma, Dagomba
Religions Christian 43%, Traditional beliefs 38%, Muslim 11%, other 8%
Ethnic mix Ashanti and Fanti 52%, Moshi-Dagomba 16%, Ewe 12%, Ga 8%, Yoruba 1%, other 11%
Government Presidential democracy
Currency Cedi = 100 pesewas
Literacy rate 71.5%
Calorie consumption 2,699 kilocalories

Ghanzi *78 C3 var.* Khanzi. Ghanzi, W Botswana
Gharandal *119 B7* Ma'ān, SW Jordan
Ghardaïa *70 D2* N Algeria
Gharvān *see* Gharyān
Gharyān *71 F2 var.* Gharvān. NW Libya
Ghaznī *123 E4 var.* Ghazni. Ghaznī, E Afghanistan
Ghazni *see* Ghaznī
Gheel *see* Geel
Gheorgheni *108 C4 prev.* Gheorghieni, Sînt-Miclăuș, *Ger.* Niklasmarkt, *Hung.* Gyergyószentmiklós. Harghita, C Romania
Ghijduwon *122 D2 Rus.* Gizhduvan. Bukhoro Wiloyati, C Uzbekistan
Ghūdara *123 F3 var.* Gudara, *Rus.* Kudara. SE Tajikistan
Ghurdaqah *see* Hurghada
Ghūrīān *122 D4* Herāt, W Afghanistan
Giannitsá *104 B4 var.* Yiannitsá. Kentrikí Makedonía, N Greece
Gibraltar *93 G4 UK dependent territory* SW Europe
Gibraltar, Bay of *93 G5 bay* Gibraltar/Spain
Gibraltar, Strait of *92 C5 Fr.* Détroit de Gibraltar, *Sp.* Estrecho de Gibraltar. *Strait* Atlantic Ocean / Mediterranean Sea
Gibson Desert *147 B5 desert* Western Australia
Giedraičiai *107 C5* Molėtai, E Lithuania

Giessen *95 B5* Hessen, W Germany
Gifu *131 C6 var.* Gihu. Gifu, Honshū, SW Japan
Giganta, Sierra de la *50 B3 mountain range* W Mexico
Gihu *see* Gifu
Gijón *92 D1 var.* Xixón. Asturias, NW Spain
Gilani *see* Gnjilane
Gila River *48 A2 river* Arizona, SW USA
Gilbert River *148 C3 river* Queensland, NE Australia
Gilf Kebir Plateau *72 A2 Ar.* Haḍabat al Jilf al Kabīr. *Plateau* SW Egypt
Gillette *44 D3* Wyoming, C USA
Gilroy *47 B6* California, W USA
Gimie, Mount *55 F1 mountain* C Saint Lucia
Gimma *see* Jīma
Ginevra *see* Genève
Gingin *147 A6* Western Australia
Giohar *see* Jawhar
Girardot *58 B3* Cundinamarca, C Colombia
Giresun *117 E2 var.* Kerasunt; *anc.* Cerasus, Pharnacia. Giresun, NE Turkey
Girin *see* Jilin
Girne *see* Kerýneia
Girona *93 G2 var.* Gerona; *anc.* Gerunda. Cataluña, NE Spain
Gisborne *150 E3* Gisborne, North Island, NZ
Gissar Range *123 E3 Rus.* Gissarskiy Khrebet. *Mountain range* Tajikistan/Uzbekistan
Githio *see* Gýtheio
Giulianova *96 D4* Abruzzo, C Italy
Giumri *see* Gyumri
Giurgiu *108 C5* Giurgiu, S Romania
Giza *see* El Gîza
Gizeh *see* El Gîza
Giżyeko *98 D2* Warmiúsko-Mazurskie, NE Poland
Gjakovë *see* Đakovica
Gjilan *see* Gnjilane
Gjinokastër *see* Gjirokastër
Gjirokastër *101 C7 var.* Gjirokastra; *prev.* Gjinokastër, *Gk.* Argyrokastron, *It.* Argirocastro. Gjirokastër, S Albania
Gjirokastra *see* Gjirokastër
Gjoa Haven *37 F3* King William Island, Nunavut, NW Canada
Gjøvik *85 B5* Oppland, S Norway
Glace Bay *39 G4* Cape Breton Island, Nova Scotia, SE Canada
Gladstone *148 E4* Queensland, E Australia
Glåma *85 B5 river* SE Norway
Glasgow *88 C4* S Scotland, UK
Glavn'a Morava *see* Velika Morava
Glazov *111 D5* Udmurtskaya Respublika, NW Russian Federation
Glendale *48 B2* Arizona, SW USA
Glendive *44 D2* Montana, NW USA
Glens Falls *41 F3* New York, NE USA
Glina *100 B3* Sisak-Moslavina, NE Croatia
Glittertind *85 A5 mountain* S Norway
Gliwice *99 C5 Ger.* Gleiwitz. Śląskie, S Poland
Globe *48 B2* Arizona, SW USA
Głogów *98 B4 Ger.* Glogau, Glogow. Dolnośląskie
Gloucester *89 D6 hist.* Caer Glou, *Lat.* Glevum. C England, UK
Głowno *98 D4* Łódź, C Poland
Gniezno *98 C3 Ger.* Gnesen. Wielkopolskie, C Poland
Gnjilane *101 D5 var.* Gilani, *Alb.* Gjilan. Serbia, S Serbia and Montenegro (Yugo.)
Goa *see* Panaji
Gobabis *78 B3* Omaheke, E Namibia
Gobi *126 D3 desert* China/Mongolia
Gobō *131 C6* Wakayama, Honshū, SW Japan
Godāvari *124 B3 var.* Godavari. *River* C India

Godhavn *see* Qeqertarsuaq
Godhra *134 C4* Gujarāt, W India
Godoy Cruz *64 B4* Mendoza, W Argentina
Godthaab *see* Nuuk
Godthåb *see* Nuuk
Goeree *86 B4 island* SW Netherlands
Goes *87 B5* Zeeland, SW Netherlands
Goettingen *see* Göttingen
Gogebic Range *40 B1 hill range* Michigan/Wisconsin, N USA
Goiânia *63 E3 prev.* Goyania. State capital Goiás, C Brazil
Goiás *63 E3* Goiás, C Brazil
Gojōme *130 D3* Akita, Honshū, NW Japan
Gökçeada *104 D4 var.* Imroz Adası, *Gk.* Imbros. *Island* NW Turkey
Gökdepe *see* Geok-Tepe
Göksun *116 D4* Kahramanmaraş, C Turkey
Gol *85 A5* Buskerud, S Norway
Golan Heights *119 B5 Ar.* Al Jawlān, *Heb.* HaGolan. *Mountain range* SW Syria
Gołdap *98 E2 Ger.* Goldap. Warmińsko-Mazurskie, NE Poland
Gold Coast *149 E5 cultural region* Queensland, E Australia
Golden Bay *150 C4 bay* South Island, NZ
Goldsboro *43 F1* North Carolina, SE USA
Goleniów *98 B3 Ger.* Gollnow. Zachodniopomorskie, NW Poland
Golmo *see* Golmud
Golub-Dobrzyń *98 C3* Kujawski-pomorskie, C Poland
Golmud *126 D4 var.* Ge'e'mu, Golmo, *Chin.* Ko-erh-mu. Qinghai, C China
Goma *77 E6* Nord Kivu, NE Dem. Rep. Congo
Gombi *75 H4* Adamawa, E Nigeria
Gombroon *see* Bandar-e 'Abbās
Gomera *70 A3 island* Islas Canarias, Spain, NE Atlantic Ocean
Gómez Palacio *50 D3* Durango, C Mexico
Gonaïves *54 D3 var.* Les Gonaïves. N Haiti
Gonâve, Île de la *54 D3 island* C Haiti
Gondar *see* Gonder
Gonder *72 C4 var.* Gondar. N Ethiopia
Gondia *135 E4* Mahārāshtra, C India
Gonggar *126 C5* Xizang Zizhiqu, W China
Gongola *75 G4 river* E Nigeria
Gonni *see* Gónnoi
Gónnoi *104 B4 var.* Gonni, Gónnos; *prev.* Dereli. Thessalía, C Greece
Gónnos *see* Gónnoi
Good Hope *see* Fort Good Hope
Good Hope, Cape of *78 B5 Afr.* Kaap de Goede Hoop, Kaap die Goeie Hoop. *Headland* SW South Africa
Goodland *44 D4* Kansas, C USA
Goondiwindi *149 D5* Queensland, E Australia
Goor *86 E3* Overijssel, E Netherlands
Goose Green *65 D7 var.* Prado del Ganso. East Falkland, Falkland Islands
Goose Lake *46 B4 var.* Lago dos Gansos. *Lake* California/Oregon, W USA
Göppingen *95 B6* Baden-Württemberg, SW Germany
Gora Andryu *see* Andrew Tablemount
Gora El'brus *see* El'brus
Góra Kalwaria *114 D4* Mazowieckie, C Poland
Gorakhpur *135 E3* Uttar Pradesh, N India
Goražde *100 C4* Federacija Bosna I Hercegovina, SE Bosnia and Herzegovina
Gordiaz *see* Gardēz

Gore *151 B7* Southland, South Island, NZ
Gorē *73 C5* C Ethiopia
Goré *76 C4* Logone-Oriental, S Chad
Gorgān *120 D2 var.* Astarabad, Astrabad, Gurgan; *prev.* Asterābād, *anc.* Hyrcania. Golestān, N Iran
Gori *117 F2* C Georgia
Gorinchem *86 C4 var.* Gorkum. Zuid-Holland, C Netherlands
Goris *117 G3* SE Armenia
Gorkum *see* Gorinchem
Görlitz *94 D4* Sachsen, E Germany
Gornji Milanovac *100 C4* Serbia, C Serbia and Montenegro (Yugo.)
Gorontalo *139 E4* Sulawesi, C Indonesia
Gorontalo, Teluk *see* Tomini, Gulf of
Gorssel *86 D3* Gelderland, E Netherlands
Gory Putorana *see* Putorana, Plato
Gorzów Wielkopolski *98 B3 Ger.* Landsberg, Landsberg an der Warthe. Lubuskie, W Poland
Gosford *149 D6* New South Wales, SE Australia
Goshogawara *130 D3 var.* Gosyogawara. Aomori, Honshū, C Japan
Gospić *100 A3* Lika-Senj, C Croatia
Gostivar *101 D6* W FYR Macedonia
Gosyogawara *see* Goshogawara
Göteborg *85 B7 Eng.* Gothenburg. Västra Götaland, S Sweden
Gotel Mountains *75 G5 mountain range* E Nigeria
Gotha *94 C4* Thüringen, C Germany
Gothenburg *see* Göteborg
Gothenburg *80 D3* Nebraska, C USA
Gotland *85 C7 island* SE Sweden
Gotō-rettō *131 A7 island group* SW Japan
Gotska Sandön *106 B1 island* SE Sweden
Gōtsu *131 B6 var.* Gōtu. Shimane, Honshū, SW Japan
Göttingen *94 B4 var.* Goettingen. Niedersachsen, C Germany
Gōtu *see* Gōtsu
Gouda *86 C4* Zuid-Holland, C Netherlands
Gough Fracture Zone *67 C6 tectonic feature* S Atlantic Ocean
Gough Island *69 B8 island* Tristan da Cunha, S Atlantic Ocean
Gouin, Réservoir *38 D4 reservoir* Quebec, SE Canada
Goulburn *149 D6* New South Wales, SE Australia
Goundam *75 E3* Tombouctou, NW Mali
Gouré *75 G3* Zinder, SE Niger
Governador Valadares *63 F4* Minas Gerais, SE Brazil
Govĭ Altayn Nuruu *127 E3 mountain range* S Mongolia
Goya *64 D3* Corrientes, NE Argentina
Goz Beïda *76 C3* Ouaddaï, SE Chad
Gozo *97 C8 Malt.* Ghawdex. *Island* N Malta
Graciosa *92 A5 var.* Ilha Graciosa. *Island* Azores, Portugal, NE Atlantic Ocean
Gradačac *100 C3* Federacija Bosna I Hercegovina, N Bosnia and Herzegovina
Gradaús, Serra dos *63 E3 mountain range* C Brazil
Gradiška *see* Bosanska Gradiška
Grafton *149 E5* New South Wales, SE Australia
Grafton *45 E1* North Dakota, N USA
Graham Land *154 A2 physical region* Antarctica
Grajewo *98 E3* Podlaskie, NE Poland
Grampian Mountains *88 C3 mountain range* C Scotland, UK
Granada *92 D5* Andalucía, S Spain
Granada *52 D3* Granada, SW Nicaragua

Gran Canaria 70 A3 var. Grand Canary. *Island* Islas Canarias, Spain, NE Atlantic Ocean
Gran Chaco 64 D2 var. Chaco. *Lowland plain* South America
Grand see Cockburn Town
Grand Bahama Island 54 B1 *island* N Bahamas
Grand Banks of Newfoundland 34 E4 *undersea feature* NW Atlantic Ocean
Grand Canary see Gran Canaria
Grand Canyon 48 A1 *canyon* Arizona, SW USA
Grand Cayman 54 B3 *island* SW Cayman Islands
Grande, Bahía 65 B7 *bay* S Argentina
Grande Comore 79 F2 var. Njazidja, Great Comoro. *Island* NW Comoros
Grande de Chiloé, Isla see Chiloé, Isla de
Grande Prairie 37 E4 Alberta, W Canada
Grand Erg Occidental 70 D3 *desert* W Algeria
Grand Erg Oriental 71 E3 *desert* Algeria/Tunisia
Grande, Rio 35 B6 var. Río Bravo, *Sp.* Río Bravo del Norte, Bravo del Norte. *River* Mexico/USA
Grande, Rio 49 F4 *river* Texas, SW USA
Grande, Rio see Bravo, Río
Grande, Río 51 E2 *river* S Mexico
Grande Terre 55 G3 *island* E West Indies
Grand Falls 39 G3 Newfoundland, Newfoundland and Labrador, SE Canada
Grand Forks 45 E1 North Dakota, N USA
Grand Island 45 E4 Nebraska, C USA
Grand Junction 44 C4 Colorado, C USA
Grand Rapids 40 C3 Michigan, N USA
Grand Rapids 45 F1 Minnesota, N USA
Grand-Santi 59 G3 W French Guiana
Gran Lago see Nicaragua, Lago de
Gran Malvina, Isla see West Falkland
Gran Paradiso 96 A2 Fr. Grand Paradis. *Mountain* NW Italy
Gran Santiago see Santiago
Grants 48 C2 New Mexico, SW USA
Grants Pass 46 B4 Oregon, NW USA
Granville 90 B3 Manche, N France
Graulhet 91 C6 Tarn, S France
Grave 86 D4 Noord-Brabant, SE Netherlands
Grayling 36 C2 Alaska, USA
Graz 95 E7 prev. Gratz. Steiermark, SE Austria
Great Abaco 54 C1 var. Abaco Island. *Island* N Bahamas
Great Alfold see Great Hungarian Plain
Great Ararat see Büyükağrı Dağı
Great Australian Bight 147 D7 *bight* S Australia
Great Barrier Island 150 D2 *island* N NZ
Great Barrier Reef 148 D2 *reef* Queensland, NE Australia
Great Basin 47 C5 *basin* W USA
Great Bear Lake 37 E3 Fr. Grand Lac de l'Ours. *Lake* Northwest Territories, NW Canada
Great Belt see Storebælt
Great Bend 45 E5 Kansas, C USA
Great Bermuda see Bermuda
Great Britain see Britain
Great Comoro see Grande Comore
Great Dividing Range 148 D4 *mountain range* NE Australia
Greater Antarctica 154 C3 var. East Antarctica. *Physical region* Antarctica
Greater Antilles 54 D3 *island group* West Indies

Greater Caucasus 117 G2 Az. Bas Qafqaz Silsiläsi, Geor. Kavkasioni, Rus. Bol'shoy Kavkaz. *Mountain range* Asia/Europe
Greater Sunda Islands 124 D5 var. Sunda Islands. *Island group* Indonesia
Great Exhibition Bay 150 C1 *inlet* North Island, NZ
Great Exuma Island 54 C2 *island* C Bahamas
Great Falls 44 B1 Montana, NW USA
Great Hungarian Plain 99 C7 var. Great Alfold, Plain of Hungary, Hung. Alföld. *Plain* SE Europe
Great Inagua 54 D2 var. Inagua Islands. *Island* S Bahamas
Great Indian Desert see Thar Desert
Great Karroo see Great Karoo
Great Lakes 35 C5 *lakes* Ontario, Canada/USA
Great Meteor Seamount see Great Meteor Tablemount
Great Meteor Tablemount 66 B3 var. Great Meteor Seamount. *Undersea feature* E Atlantic Ocean
Great Nicobar 133 G3 *island* Nicobar Islands, India, NE Indian Ocean
Great Plain of China 125 E2 *plain* E China
Great Plains 45 E3 var. High Plains. *Plains* Canada/USA
Great Rift Valley 73 C5 var. Rift Valley. *Depression* Asia/Africa
Great Ruaha 73 C7 *river* S Tanzania
Great Saint Bernard Pass 96 A1 Fr. Col du Grand-Saint-Bernard, It. Passo di Gran San Bernardo. *Pass* Italy/Switzerland
Great Salt Lake 44 B3 *salt lake* Utah, W USA
Great Salt Lake Desert 44 A4 *plain* Utah, W USA
Great Sand Sea 71 H3 *desert* Egypt/Libya
Great Sandy Desert 146 C4 *desert* Western Australia
Great Sandy Island see Fraser Island
Great Slave Lake 37 E4 Fr. Grand Lac des Esclaves. *Lake* Northwest Territories, NW Canada
Great Sound 42 A5 *bay* Bermuda, NW Atlantic Ocean
Great Victoria Desert 147 C5 *desert* South Australia/Western Australia
Great Wall of China 128 C4 *ancient monument* N China
Great Yarmouth 89 E6 var. Yarmouth. E England, UK
Gredos, Sierra de 92 D3 *mountain range* W Spain
Greece 105 A5 Gk. Ellás; anc. Hellas. *Country* SE Europe

Greece 105

Official name Hellenic Republic
Formation 1829
Capital Athens
Population 10.6 million / 208 people per sq mile (80 people per sq km)
Total area 50,942 sq miles (131,940 sq km)
Languages Greek, Turkish, Macedonian, Albanian
Religions Greek Orthodox 98%, Muslim 1%, other 1%
Ethnic mix Greek 98%, other 2%
Government Presidential democracy
Currency Euro (Drachma until 2002)
Literacy rate 97.3%
Calorie consumption 3,705 kilocalories

Greece 81 E5 New York, NE USA
Greeley 44 D4 Colorado, C USA

Green Bay 40 B2 *lake bay* Michigan/Wisconsin, N USA
Green Bay 40 B2 Wisconsin, N USA
Greeneville 43 E1 Tennessee, S USA
Greenland 82 D3 Dan. Grønland, Inuit Kalaallit Nunaat. *Danish external territory* NE North America
Greenland Sea 83 F2 *sea* Arctic Ocean
Green Mountains 41 G2 *mountain range* Vermont, NE USA
Greenock 88 C4 W Scotland, UK
Green River 40 C5 *river* Kentucky, C USA
Green River 44 B4 *river* Utah, W USA
Green River 44 B3 Wyoming, C USA
Greensboro 43 F1 North Carolina, SE USA
Greenville 42 B2 Mississippi, S USA
Greenville 43 F1 North Carolina, SE USA
Greenville 43 E1 South Carolina, SE USA
Greenville 49 G2 Texas, SW USA
Greenwich 89 B8 SE England, UK
Greenwood 42 B2 Mississippi, S USA
Greenwood 43 E2 South Carolina, SE USA
Gregory Range 148 C3 *mountain range* Queensland, E Australia
Greifswald 94 D2 Mecklenburg-Vorpommern, NE Germany
Grenada 55 G5 *country* SE West Indies

Grenada 55

Official name Grenada
Formation 1974
Capital St. George's
Population 98,000 /747 people per sq mile (288 people per sq km)
Total area 131 sq miles (340 sq km)
Languages English, English Creole
Religions Roman Catholic 68%, Anglican 17%, other 15%
Ethnic mix Black 82%, Mulatto 13%, Indian 3%, other 2%
Government Parliamentary democracy
Currency East Caribbean dollar = 100 cents
Literacy rate 96%
Calorie consumption 2,764 kilocalorie

Grenada 42 C2 Mississippi, S USA
Grenadines, The 55 H4 *island group* Grenada/St Vincent and the Grenadines
Grenoble 91 D5 anc. Cularo, Gratianopolis. Isère, E France
Gresham 46 B3 Oregon, NW USA
Grevená 104 B4 Dytikí Makedonía, N Greece
Grevenmacher 87 E8 Grevenmacher, E Luxembourg
Greymouth 151 B5 West Coast, South Island, NZ
Grey Range 149 C5 *mountain range* New South Wales/Queensland, E Australia
Greytown see San Juan del Norte
Griffin 42 D2 Georgia, SE USA
Grimari 76 C4 Ouaka, C Central African Republic
Grimsby 89 E5 prev. Great Grimsby. E England, UK
Grobiņa 106 B3 Ger. Grobin. Liepāja, W Latvia
Grodzisk Wielkopolski 98 B3 Wielkopolskie, C Poland
Groesbeek 86 D4 Gelderland, SE Netherlands
Grójec 98 D4 Mazowieckie, C Poland
Groningen 86 E1 Groningen, NE Netherlands
Groote Eylandt 148 B2 *island* Northern Territory, N Australia

Grootfontein 78 B3 Otjozondjupa, N Namibia
Groot Karasberge 78 B4 *mountain range* S Namibia
Groot Karoo see Great Karoo
Gros Islet 55 F1 N Saint Lucia
Grosse Morava see Velika Morava
Grosseto 96 B4 Toscana, C Italy
Grossglockner 95 C7 *mountain* W Austria
Groznyy 111 B8 Chechenskaya Respublika, SW Russian Federation
Grudziądz 98 C3 Ger. Graudenz. Kujawski-pomorskie, C Poland
Grums 85 B6 Värmland, C Sweden
Gryazi 111 B6 Lipetskaya Oblast', W Russian Federation
Gryfice 98 B2 Ger. Greifenberg, Greifenberg in Pommern. Zachodniopomorskie, NW Poland
Guabito 53 E4 Bocas del Toro, NW Panama
Guadalajara 93 E3 Ar. Wad Al-Hajarah; anc. Arriaca. Castilla-La Mancha, C Spain
Guadalajara 50 D4 Jalisco, C Mexico
Guadalcanal 144 C3 *island* C Solomon Islands
Guadalquivir 92 D4 *river* W Spain
Guadalupe 50 D3 Zacatecas, C Mexico
Guadalupe Peak 48 D3 *mountain* Texas, SW USA
Guadalupe River 49 G4 *river* SW USA
Guadarrama, Sierra de 93 E2 *mountain range* C Spain
Guadeloupe 55 H3 French overseas department E West Indies
Guadiana 92 C4 *river* Portugal/Spain
Guadix 93 E4 Andalucía, S Spain
Guaimaca 52 C2 Francisco Morazán, C Honduras
Guajira, Península de la 58 B1 *peninsula* N Colombia
Gualaco 52 D2 Olancho, C Honduras
Gualán 52 B2 Zacapa, C Guatemala
Gualdicciolo 96 D1 NW San Marino
Gualeguaychú 64 D4 Entre Ríos, E Argentina
Guam 144 B1 US unincorporated territory W Pacific Ocean
Guamúchil 50 C3 Sinaloa, C Mexico
Guanabacoa 54 B2 La Habana, W Cuba
Guanajuato 51 E4 Guanajuato, C Mexico
Guanare 58 C2 Portuguesa, N Venezuela
Guanare, Río 58 D2 *river* W Venezuela
Guangdong 128 C6 var. Guangdong Sheng, Kuang-tung, Kwangtung, Yue. Admin. region *province* S China
Guangdong Sheng see Guangdong
Guangxi see Guangxi Zhuangzu Zizhiqu
Guangxi Zhuangzu Zizhiqu 128 C6 var. Guangxi, Gui, Kuang-hsi, Kwangsi, Eng. Kwangsi Chuang Autonomous Region. Admin. region *autonomous region* S China
Guangyuan 128 B5 var. Kuang-yuan, Kwangyuan. Sichuan, C China
Guangzhou 128 C6 var. Kuang-chou, Kwangchow, Eng. Canton. Guangdong, S China
Guantánamo 54 D3 Guantánamo, SE Cuba
Guantánamo Bay 54 D3 US military installation, SE Cuba
Guaporé, Río 62 D3 var. Río Iténez. River Bolivia/Brazil see also Iténez, Río
Guarda 92 C3 Guarda, N Portugal
Guarumal 53 F5 Veraguas, S Panama
Guasave 50 C3 Sinaloa, C Mexico

Guatemala 52 A2 *Country* Central
America

Guatemala 52

Official name Republic of
Guatemala
Formation 1838
Capital Guatemala City
Population 11.7 million /
278 people per sq mile (107 people
per sq km)
Total area 42,042 sq miles
(108,890 sq km)
Languages Spanish, Quiché, Mam,
Cakchiquel, Kekchí
Religions Roman Catholic 65%,
Protestant 33%, other 2%
Ethnic mix Amerindian 60%,
Mestizo 30%, other 10%
Government Presidential
democracy
Currency Quetzal = 100 centavos
Literacy rate 68.8%
Calorie consumption 2,171
kilocalories

Guatemala Basin 35 B7 *undersea
feature* E Pacific Ocean
Guatemala City *see* Ciudad de
Guatemala
Guaviare 56 B2 *off.* Comisaría
Guaviare. *Province* S Colombia
Guaviare, Río 58 D3 *river* E Colombia
Guayaquil 60 A2 *var.* Santiago de
Guayaquil. Guayas, SW Ecuador
Guayaquil, Golfo de 60 A2 *var.* Gulf
of Guayaquil. *Gulf* SW Ecuador
Guayaquil, Gulf of *see* Guayaquil,
Golfo de
Guaymas 50 B2 Sonora, NW Mexico
Gubadag 122 C2 *Turkm.* Tel'man;
prev. Tel'mansk. Dashkhovuzskiy
Velayat, N Turkmenistan
Guben 94 D4 *var.* Wilhelm-Pieck-
Stadt. Brandenburg, E Germany
Gudara *see* Ghüdara
Gudaut'a 117 E1 NW Georgia
Guéret 90 C4 Creuse, C France
Guernsey 89 D8 UK *dependent
territory* NW Europe
Guerrero Negro 50 A2 Baja
California Sur, NW Mexico
Gui *see* Guangxi Zhuangzu Zizhiqu
Guiana *see* French Guiana
Guiana Highlands 62 D1 *var.*
Macizo de las Guayanas.
Mountain range N South America
Guidder *see* Guider
Guider 76 B4 *var.* Guidder. Nord,
N Cameroon
Guidimouni 75 G3 Zinder, S Niger
Guildford 89 D7 SE England, UK
Guilin 128 C6 *var.* Kuei-lin,
Kweilin. Guangxi Zhuangzu
Zizhiqu, S China
Guimarães 92 B2 *var.* Guimarães.
Braga, N Portugal
Guinea 74 C4 *var.* Guinée; *prev.*
French Guinea, People's
Revolutionary Republic of
Guinea. *Country* W Africa

Guinea 74

Official name Republic of Guinea
Formation 1958
Capital Conakry
Population 8.3 million / 87 people
per sq mile (34 people per sq km)
Total area 94,925 sq miles
(245,857 sq km)
Languages French, Fulani, Malinke,
Soussou
Religions Muslim 65%, Traditional
beliefs 33%, Christian 2%,
Ethnic mix Fila (Fulani) 30%,
Malinke 30%, Soussou 15%, Kissi
10%, other tribes 10%, other 25%
Government Multiparty republic
Currency Guinea franc = 100
centimes
Literacy rate 41.1%
Calorie consumption 2,353
kilocalories

Guinea Basin 69 A5 *undersea feature*
E Atlantic Ocean
Guinea-Bissau 74 B4 *Fr.* Guinée-
Bissau, *Port.* Guiné-Bissau; *prev.*
Portuguese Guinea. *Country*
W Africa

Guinea-Bissau 74

Official name Republic of
Guinea-Bissau
Formation 1974
Capital Bissau
Population 1.2 million / 86 people
per sq mile (33 people per sq km)
Total area 13,946 sq miles
(36,120 sq km)
Languages Portuguese Creole,
Fulani Balante, Malinke, Portuguese
Religions Indigenous beliefs 52%,
Muslim 40%, Christian 8%
Ethnic mix Balante 25%, Madinka
12%, Fula 20%, Mandyako 11%,
other 32%
Government Presidential
democracy
Currency CFA france = 100
centimes
Literacy rate 38.8%
Calorie consumption 2,333
kilocalories

Guinea, Gulf of 68 B4 *Fr.* Golfe de
Guinée. *Gulf* E Atlantic Ocean
Güiria 59 E1 Sucre, NE Venezuela
Guiyang 128 B6 *var.* Kuei-Yang,
Kuei-yang, Kueyang, Kweiyang;
prev. Kweichu. Guizhou, S China
Guizhou 128 B6 *var.* Guizhou Sheng,
Kuei-chou, Kweichow, Qian.
Guizhou Sheng *see* Guizhou
Gujarāt 134 C4 *var.* Gujerat. Admin.
region *state* W India
Gujerat *see* Gujarāt
Gujrānwāla 134 D2 Punjab,
NE Pakistan
Gujrāt 134 D2 Punjab, E Pakistan
Gulbarga 132 C1 Karnātaka, C India
Gulbene 106 D3 Ger. Alt-
Schwanenburg. Gulbene,
NE Latvia
Gulf, The 120 C4 *var.* Persian Gulf,
Ar. Khalīj al 'Arabī, *Per.* Khalīj-e
Fars. *Gulf* SE Asia
Guliston 123 E2 *Rus.* Gulistan.
Sirdaryo Wiloyati, E Uzbekistan
Gulja *see* Yining
Gulkana 36 D3 Alaska, USA
Gulu 73 B6 N Uganda
Gulyantsi 104 C1 Pleven,
N Bulgaria
Guma *see* Pishan
Gümülcine *see* Komotiní
Gümüljina *see* Komotiní
Gümüşane *see* Gümüşhane
Gümüşhane 117 E3 *var.* Gümüşane,
Gumushkhane. Gümüşhane,
NE Turkey
Gumushkhane *see* Gümüşhane
Güney Doğu Toroslar 117 E4
mountain range SE Turkey
Gunnbjørn Fjeld 82 D4 *var.*
Gunnbjörns Bjerge. *Mountain*
C Greenland
Gunnbjörns Bjerge *see* Gunnbjørn
Fjeld
Gunnedah 149 D6 New South
Wales, SE Australia
Gunnison 44 C5 Colorado, C USA
Gurbantünggüt Shamo 126 B2
desert W China
Gurgan *see* Gorgān
Guri, Embalse de 59 E2 *reservoir*
E Venezuela
Gurktaler Alpen 95 D7 *mountain
range* S Austria
Gürün 116 D3 Sivas, C Turkey
Gusau 75 G4 Zamfara, NW Nigeria
Gusev 106 B4 Ger. Gumbinnen.
Kaliningradskaya Oblast',
W Russian Federation
Gushgy 122 D4 *prev.* Kushka.
Maryyskiy Velayat,
S Turkmenistan

Gustavus 36 D4 Alaska, USA
Güstrow 94 C3 Mecklenburg-
Vorpommern, NE Germany
Gütersloh 94 B4 Nordrhein-
Westfalen, W Germany
Guwāhāti 135 G3 *prev.* Gauhāti.
Assam, NE India
Guyana 59 F3 *prev.* British Guiana.
Country N South America

Guyana 59

Official name Cooperative
Republic
of Guyana
Formation 1966
Capital Georgetown
Population 763,000 / 9 people
per sq mile (4 people per sq km)
Total area 83,000 sq miles
(214,970 sq km)
Languages English, English Creole,
Hindi, Tamil, Amerindian languages
Religions Christian 57%, Hindu
33%, Muslim 9%, other 1%
Ethnic mix East Indian 52%, Black
African 38%, other 10%
Government Presidential
democracy
Currency Guyana dollar = 100 cents
Literacy rate 98.5%
Calorie consumption 2,582
kilocalories

Guyane *see* French Guiana
Guymon 49 E1 Oklahoma, C USA
Güzelyurt *see* Mórfou
Gvardeysk 106 A4 Ger. Tapaiu.
Kaliningradskaya Oblast',
W Russian Federation
Gwādar 134 A3 *var.* Gwadur.
Baluchistān, SW Pakistan
Gwadur *see* Gwādar
Gwalior 134 D3 Madhya Pradesh,
C India
Gwanda 78 D3 Matabeleland South,
SW Zimbabwe
Gwy *see* Wye
Gyangzê 126 C5 Xizang Zizhiqu,
W China
Gyaring Co 126 C5 *lake* W China
Gympie 149 E5 Queensland,
E Australia
Gyomaendrőd 99 D7 Békés,
SE Hungary
Gyöngyös 99 D6 Heves,
NE Hungary
Győr 99 C6 Ger. Raab; *Lat.*
Arrabona. Győr-Moson-Sopron,
NW Hungary
Gýtheio 105 B6 *var.* Githio; *prev.*
Yithion. Pelopónnisos, S Greece
Gyumri 117 F2 *var.* Giumri, *Rus.*
Kumayri; *prev.* Aleksandropol',
Leninakan. W Armenia
Gyzylarbat 122 C2 *prev.* Kizyl-
Arvat. Balkanskiy Velayat,
W Turkmenistan

H

Haabai *see* Ha'apai Group
Haacht 87 C6 Vlaams Brabant,
C Belgium
Haaksbergen 86 E3 Overijssel,
E Netherlands
Ha'apai Group 145 F4 *var.* Haabai.
Island group C Tonga
Haapsalu 106 D2 Ger. Hapsal.
Läänemaa, W Estonia
Haarlem 86 C3 *prev.* Harlem.
Noord-Holland, W Netherlands
Haast 151 B6 West Coast, South
Island, NZ
Hachijō-jima 131 D6 *var.* Hatizyô
Zima. *Island* Izu-shotô,
SE Japan
Hachinohe 130 D3 Aomori,
Honshū, C Japan
Hadama *see* Nazrēt
Haddummati Atoll *see*
Hadhdhunmathi Atoll
Hadejia 75 G3 *river* N Nigeria
Hadejia 75 G4 Jigawa, N Nigeria
Hadera 119 A6 *var.* Khadera. Haifa,
C Israel

Hadhdhunmathi Atoll 132 A5 *var.*
Haddummati Atoll, Laamu Atoll.
Atoll S Maldives
Ha Đông 136 D3 *var.* Hadong. Ha
Tây, N Vietnam
Hadong *see* Ha Đông
Hạdramawt 121 C6 *Eng.*
Hadhramaut. *Mountain range*
S Yemen
Haerbin *see* Harbin
Haerhpin *see* Harbin
Hafren *see* Severn
Hagåtña 160 B1 *var.* Agana/Agaña.
Dependent territory capital (Guam),
NW Guam
Hagerstown 41 E4 Maryland,
NE USA
Ha Giang 136 D3 Ha Giang,
N Vietnam
Hagondange 90 D3 Moselle,
NE France
Haguenau 90 E3 Bas-Rhin,
NE France
Haicheng 128 D3 Liaoning,
NE China
Haidarabad *see* Hyderābād
Haifa *see* Hefa
Haifong *see* Hai Phong
Haikou 128 C7 *var.* Hai-k'ou,
Hoihow, *Fr.* Hoï-Hao. Hainan,
S China
Hai-k'ou *see* Haikou
Hā'il 120 B4 *off.* Mintaqah Hā'il.
Province N Saudi Arabia
Hai-la-erh *see* Hailar
Hailar 127 F1 *var.* Hai-la-erh; *prev.*
Hulun. Nei Mongol Zizhiqu,
N China
Hailuoto 84 D4 *Swe.* Karlö. *Island*
W Finland
Hainan 128 B7 *var.* Hainan Sheng,
Qiong. Admin. region *province*
S China
Hainan Dao 128 C7 *island* S China
Hainan Sheng *see* Hainan
Haines 36 D4 Alaska, USA
Hainichen 94 D4 Sachsen,
E Germany
Hai Phong 136 D3 *var.* Haifong,
Haiphong. N Vietnam
Haiphong *see* Hai Phong
Haiti 54 D3 C West Indies

Haiti 54

Official name Republic of Haiti
Formation 1804
Capital Port-au-Prince
Population 8.3 million / 775 people
per sq mile (299 people per sq km)
Total area 10,714 sq miles
(27,750 sq km)
Languages English, French Creole
Religions Roman Catholic 80%,
Protestant 16%, non-religious 1%,
other 3%
Ethnic mix Black African 95%,
Mulatto and European 5%
Government Multiparty republic
Currency Gourde = 100 centimes
Literacy rate 49.8%
Calorie consumption 2,056
kilocalories

Haiya 72 C3 Red Sea, NE Sudan
Hajdúhadház 99 D6 Hajdú-Bihar,
E Hungary
Hajine *see* Abū Hardān
Hajnówka 98 E3 Ger. Hermhausen.
Podlaskie, NE Poland
Hakodate 130 D3 Hokkaidō,
NE Japan
Halab 118 B2 Eng. Aleppo, *Fr.* Alep;
anc. Beroea. Halab, NW Syria
Halāniyāt, Juzur al 137 D6 *var.*
Jazā'ir Bin Ghalfān, *Eng.* Kuria
Muria Islands. *Island group*
S Oman
Halberstadt 94 C4 Sachsen-Anhalt,
C Germany
Halden 85 B6 *prev.* Fredrikshald.
Østfold, S Norway
Halfmoon Bay 151 A8 *var.* Oban.
Stewart Island, Southland, NZ
Halifax 39 F4 Nova Scotia,
SE Canada

Halkída *see* Chalkída
Halle 87 *B6 Fr.* Hal. Vlaams Brabant, C Belgium
Halle 94 *C4 var.* Halle an der Saale. Sachsen-Anhalt, C Germany
Halle an der Saale *see* Halle
Halle-Neustadt 94 *C4* Sachsen-Anhalt, C Germany
Halley 154 *B2 UK research station* Antarctica
Hall Islands 142 *B2 island group* C Micronesia
Halls Creek 146 *C3* Western Australia
Halmahera, Pulau 139 *F3 prev.* Djailolo, Gilolo, Jailolo. *Island* E Indonesia
Halmahera Sea 139 *F4 Ind.* Laut Halmahera. *Sea* E Indonesia
Halmstad 85 *B7* Halland, S Sweden
Hama *see* Ḥamāh
Hamada 131 *B6* Shimane, Honshū, SW Japan
Hamadán 120 *C3 anc.* Ecbatana. Hamadán, W Iran
Ḥamāh 118 *B3 var.* Hama; *anc.* Epiphania, *Bibl.* Hamath. Ḥamāh, W Syria
Hamamatsu 131 *D6 var.* Hamamatu. Shizuoka, Honshū, S Japan
Hamamatu *see* Hamamatsu
Hamar 85 *B5 prev.* Storhammer. Hedmark, S Norway
Hamath *see* Ḥamāh
Hamburg 94 *B3* Hamburg, N Germany
Ḥamḍ, Wādī al 136 *A4 dry watercourse* W Saudi Arabia
Hämeenlinna 85 *D5 Swe.* Tavastehus. Etelä-Suomi, S Finland
Hamersley Range 146 *A4 mountain range* Western Australia
Hamhŭng 129 *E3* C North Korea
Hami 126 *C3 var.* Ha-mi, Uigh. Kumul, Qomul. Xinjiang Uygur Zizhiqu, NW China
Ha-mi *see* Hami
Hamilton 42 *C2* Alabama, S USA
Hamilton 38 *D5* Ontario, S Canada
Hamilton 88 *C4* S Scotland, UK
Hamilton 150 *D3* Waikato, North Island, NZ
Ḥamīm, Wād̄ī al 87 *G2 river* NE Libya
Hamïs Musait *see* Khamïs Mushayt
Hamiton 42 *A5 dependent territory capital* (Bermuda) C Bermuda
Hamm 94 *B4 var.* Hamm in Westfalen. Nordrhein-Westfalen, W Germany
Hammada du Drâa *see* Dra, Hamada du
Hammamet, Golfe de 102 *D3 Ar.* Khalīj al Ḥammāmāt. *Gulf* NE Tunisia
Ḥammār, Hawr al 136 *C3 lake* SE Iraq
Hamm in Westfalen *see* Hamm
Hampden 151 *B7* Otago, South Island, NZ
Hampstead 89 *A7* SE England, UK
Hamrun 102 *B5* C Malta
Hânceşti *see* Hînceşti
Handan 128 *C4 var.* Han-tan. Hebei, E China
Haneda 130 *A2 international airport* (Tōkyō) Tōkyō, Honshū, S Japan
HaNegev 119 *A7 Eng.* Negev. *Desert* S Israel
Hanford 47 *C6* California, W USA
Hangayn Nuruu 126 *D2 mountain range* C Mongolia
Hang-chou *see* Hangzhou
Hangchow *see* Hangzhou
Hangö *see* Hanko
Hangzhou 128 *D5 var.* Hang-chou, Hangchow. Zhejiang, SE China
Hania *see* Chaniá
Hanka, Lake *see* Khanka, Lake
Hanko 85 *D6 Swe.* Hangö. Etelä-Suomi, SW Finland
Han-k'ou *see* Wuhan
Hankow *see* Wuhan
Hanmer Springs 151 *C5* Canterbury, South Island, NZ

Hannibal 45 *G4* Missouri, C USA
Hannover 94 *B3 Eng.* Hanover. Niedersachsen, NW Germany
Hanöbukten 85 *B7 bay* S Sweden
Ha Nôi 136 *D3 Eng.* Hanoi, *Fr.* Ha noï. *Country capital* (Vietnam) N Vietnam
Hanoi *see* Ha Nôi
Han Shui 127 *E4 river* C China
Han-tan *see* Handan
Hantsavichy 107 *B6 Pol.* Hancewicze, *Rus.* Gantsevichi. Brestskaya Voblasts', SW Belarus
Hanyang *see* Wuhan
Hanzhong 128 *B5* Shaanxi, C China
Hāora 135 *F4 prev.* Howrah. West Bengal, NE India
Haparanda 84 *D4* Norrbotten, N Sweden
Haradok 107 *E5 Rus.* Gorodok. Vitsyebskaya Voblasts' N, N Belarus
Haradzyets 107 *B6 Rus.* Gorodets. Brestskaya Voblasts', SW Belarus
Haramachi 130 *D4* Fukushima, Honshū, E Japan
Harany 107 *D5 Rus.* Gorany. Vitsyebskaya Voblasts', N Belarus
Harare 78 *D3 prev.* Salisbury. *Country capital* (Zimbabwe) Mashonaland East, NE Zimbabwe
Harbavichy 107 *E6 Rus.* Gorbovichi. Mahilyowskaya Voblasts', E Belarus
Harbel 74 *C5* W Liberia
Harbin 129 *E2 var.* Haerbin, Ha-erh-pin, Kharbin; *prev.* Haerhpin, Pingkiang, Pinkiang. Heilongjiang, NE China
Hardangerfjorden 85 *A6 fjord* S Norway
Hardangervidda 85 *A6 plateau* S Norway
Hardenberg 86 *E3* Overijssel, E Netherlands
Harelbeke 87 *A6 var.* Harlebeke. West-Vlaanderen, W Belgium
Harem *see* Ḥārim
Haren 86 *E2* Groningen, NE Netherlands
Härer 73 *D5* E Ethiopia
Hargeisa *see* Hargeysa
Hargeysa 73 *D5 var.* Hargeisa. Woqooyi Galbeed, NW Somalia
Hariana *see* Haryāna
Hari, Batang 138 *B4 prev.* Djambi. *River* Sumatera, W Indonesia
Ḥārim 118 *B2 var.* Harem. Idlib, W Syria
Harima-nada 131 *B6 sea* S Japan
Harīrūd *var.* Tedzhen, Turkm. Tejen. *River* Afghanistan/Iran *see also* Tedzhen
Harlan 45 *F3* Iowa, C USA
Harlebeke *see* Harelbeke
Harlingen 86 *D2 Fris.* Harns. Friesland, N Netherlands
Harlingen 49 *G5* Texas, SW USA
Harlow 89 *E6* E England, UK
Harney Basin 46 *B4 basin* Oregon, NW USA
Härnösand 85 *C5 var.* Hernösand. Västernorrland, C Sweden
Har Nuur 126 *C2 lake* NW Mongolia
Harper 74 *D5 var.* Cape Palmas. NE Liberia
Harricana 38 *D3 river* Quebec, SE Canada
Harris 88 *B3 physical region* NW Scotland, UK
Harrisburg 41 *E4 state capital* Pennsylvania, NE USA
Harrisonburg 41 *E4* Virginia, NE USA
Harrison, Cape 39 *F2 headland* Newfoundland and Labrador, E Canada
Harris Ridge *see* Lomonosov Ridge
Harrogate 89 *D5* N England, UK
Hârşova 108 *D5 prev.* Hîrşova. Constanţa, SE Romania
Harstad 84 *C2* Troms, N Norway
Hartford 41 *G3 state capital* Connecticut, NE USA
Hartlepool 89 *D5* N England, UK
Harunabad *see* Eslāmābād
Harwich 89 *E6* E England, UK

Haryāna 134 *D2 var.* Hariana. *Admin. region state* N India
Hasselt 87 *C6* Limburg, NE Belgium
Hassetché *see* Al Ḥasakah
Hastings 150 *E4* Hawke's Bay, North Island, NZ
Hastings 45 *E4* Nebraska, C USA
Hastings 89 *E7* SE England, UK
Haţeg 108 *B4 Ger.* Wallenthal, *Hung.* Hátszeg; *prev.* Hatzeg, Hötzing. Hunedoara, SW Romania
Hatizyō Zima *see* Hachijō-jima
Hattem 86 *D3* Gelderland, E Netherlands
Hatteras, Cape 43 *G1 headland* North Carolina, SE USA
Hatteras Plain 35 *D6 undersea feature* W Atlantic Ocean
Hattiesburg 42 *C3* Mississippi, S USA
Hatton Bank *see* Hatton Ridge
Hatton Ridge 80 *B2 var.* Hatton Bank. *Undersea feature* N Atlantic Ocean
Hat Yai 137 *C7 var.* Ban Hat Yai. Songkhla, SW Thailand
Haugesund 85 *A6* Rogaland, S Norway
Haukeligrend 85 *A6* Telemark, S Norway
Haukivesi 85 *E5 lake* SE Finland
Hauraki Gulf 150 *D2 gulf* North Island, NZ
Hauroko, Lake 151 *A7 lake* South Island, NZ
Haut Atlas 70 *B3 Eng.* High Atlas. *Mountain range* C Morocco
Hautes Fagnes 87 *D6 var.* Hohes Venn. *Mountain range* E Belgium
Haut Plateau du Dra *see* Dra, Hamada du
Hauts Plateaux 72 *D2 plateau* Algeria/Morocco
Hauzenberg 95 *D6* Bayern, SE Germany
Havana *see* La Habana
Havana 35 *D6* Illinois, N USA
Havant 89 *D7* S England, UK
Havelock 43 *F1* North Carolina, SE USA
Havelock North 150 *E4* Hawke's Bay, North Island, NZ
Haverfordwest 89 *C6* SW Wales, UK
Havíŕov 99 *C5* Ostravský Kraj, E Czech Republic
Havre 44 *C1* Montana, NW USA
Havre-St-Pierre 39 *F3* Quebec, E Canada
Hawaii 47 *B8 Haw.* Hawai'i. *Island* Hawaiian Islands, USA, C Pacific Ocean
Hawaii 47 *A8 off.* State of Hawaii; also known as Aloha State, Paradise of the Pacific. *State* USA, C Pacific Ocean
Hawaiian Islands 152 *D2 prev.* Sandwich Islands. *Island group* Hawaii, USA, C Pacific Ocean
Hawaiian Ridge 113 *H4 undersea feature* N Pacific Ocean
Hawash *see* Āwash
Hawea, Lake 151 *B6 lake* South Island, NZ
Hawera 150 *D4* Taranaki, North Island, NZ
Hawick 88 *C4* SE Scotland, UK
Hawke Bay 150 *E4 bay* North Island, NZ
Hawlēr *see* Arbīl
Hawthorne 47 *C6* Nevada, W USA
Hay 149 *C6* New South Wales, SE Australia
Hayes 38 *B2 river* Manitoba, C Canada
Hay River 37 *E4* Northwest Territories, W Canada
Hays 45 *E5* Kansas, C USA
Haysyn 108 *D3 Rus.* Gaysin. Vinnyts'ka Oblast', C Ukraine
Heard and McDonald Islands 141 *B7 Australian external territory* S Indian Ocean
Hearst 38 *C4* Ontario, S Canada
Heathrow 89 *A8 international airport* (London)SE England, UK
Hebei 128 *C4 var.* Hebei Sheng, Hopeh, Hopei, Ji; *prev.* Chihli. *Admin. region province* E China

Hebei Sheng *see* Hebei
Hebron 119 *A6 var.* Al Khalīl, El Khalil, *Heb.* Ḥevron; *anc.* Kiriath-Arba. S West Bank
Hebrus *see* Maritsa
Heemskerk 86 *C3* Noord-Holland, W Netherlands
Heerde 86 *D3* Gelderland, E Netherlands
Heerenveen 86 *D2 Fris.* It Hearrenfean. Friesland, N Netherlands
Heerhugowaard 86 *C2* Noord-Holland, NW Netherlands
Heerlen 87 *D6* Limburg, SE Netherlands
Heerwegen *see* Polkowice
Hefa 119 *A5 var.* Haifa; *hist.* Caiphas, *anc.* Sycaminum. Haifa, N Israel
Hefa, Mifraz 119 *A5 Eng.* Bay of Haifa. *Bay* N Israel
Hefei 128 *D5 var.* Hofei; *hist.* Luchow. Anhui, E China
Hegang 129 *E2* Heilongjiang, NE China
Hei *see* Heilongjiang
Heide 94 *B2* Schleswig-Holstein, N Germany
Heidelberg 95 *B5* Baden-Württemberg, SW Germany
Heidenheim *see* Heidenheim an der Brenz
Heidenheim an der Brenz 95 *B6 var.* Heidenheim. Baden-Württemberg, S Germany
Heilbronn 95 *B6* Baden-Württemberg, SW Germany
Heilongjiang 128 *D2 var.* Hei, Heilongjiang Sheng, Hei-lung-chiang, Heilungkiang. *Admin. region province* NE China
Heilongjiang Sheng *see* Heilongjiang
Heiloo 86 *C3* Noord-Holland, NW Netherlands
Hei-lung-chiang *see* Heilongjiang
Heilungkiang *see* Heilongjiang
Heimdal 85 *B5* Sør-Trøndelag, S Norway
Hekimhan 116 *D3* Malatya, C Turkey
Helena 44 *B2 state capital* Montana, NW USA
Helensville 150 *D2* Auckland, North Island, NZ
Helgoland Bay *see* Helgoländer Bucht
Helgoländer Bucht 94 *A2 var.* Helgoland Bay, Heligoland Bight. *Bay* NW Germany
Heligoland Bight *see* Helgoländer Bucht
Heliopolis *see* Baalbek
Hellevoetsluis 86 *B4* Zuid-Holland, SW Netherlands
Hellín 93 *E4* Castilla-La Mancha, C Spain
Helmand, Daryā-ye *var.* Rūd-e Hīrmand. *River* Afghanistan/Iran *see also* Hīrmand, Rūd-e
Helmond 87 *D5* Noord-Brabant, S Netherlands
Helsingborg 85 *B7 prev.* Hälsingborg. Skåne, S Sweden
Helsinki 85 *D6 Swe.* Helsingfors. *Country capital* (Finland) Etelä-Suomi, S Finland
Henan 128 *C5 var.* Henan Sheng, Honan, Yu. *Admin. region province* C China
Henan Sheng *see* Henan
Henderson 40 *B5* Kentucky, S USA
Henderson 47 *D7* Nevada, W USA
Henderson 49 *H3* Texas, SW USA
Hengchow *see* Hengyang
Hengduan Shan 128 *A5 mountain range* SW China
Hengelo 86 *E3* Overijssel, E Netherlands
Hengnan *see* Hengyang
Hengyang 128 *C6 var.* Hengnan, Hengchow; *prev.* Hengchow. Hunan, S China
Heng-yang *see* Hengyang
Heniches'k 109 *F4 Rus.* Genichesk. Khersons'ka Oblast', S Ukraine

Hennebont 90 A3 Morbihan, NW France

Henzada 136 B4 Irrawaddy, SW Myanmar

Herakleion *see* Irákleio

Herāt 122 D4 *var.* Herat; *anc.* Aria. Herāt, W Afghanistan

Herat *see* Herāt

Heredia 53 E4 Heredia, C Costa Rica

Hereford 49 E2 Texas, SW USA

Herford 94 B4 Nordrhein-Westfalen, NW Germany

Herk-de-Stad 87 C6 Limburg, NE Belgium

Hermansverk 85 A5 Sogn Og Fjordane, S Norway

Hermhausen *see* Hajnówka

Hermiston 46 C2 Oregon, NW USA

Hermon, Mount 119 B5 *Ar.* Jabal ash Shaykh. *Mountain* S Syria

Hermosillo 50 B2 Sonora, NW Mexico

Hermoupolis *see* Ermoúpoli

Hernösand *see* Härnösand

Herrera del Duque 92 D3 Extremadura, W Spain

Herselt 87 C5 Antwerpen, C Belgium

Herstal 87 D6 *Fr.* Héristal. Liège, E Belgium

Hessen 95 B5 *cultural region* C Germany

Hevron *see* Hebron

Heydebrech *see* Kędzierzyn-Kole

Heywood Islands 146 C3 *island group* Western Australia

Hibbing 45 F1 Minnesota, N USA

Hidalgo del Parral 50 C2 *var.* Parral. Chihuahua, N Mexico

Hida-sanmyaku 131 C5 *mountain range* Honshū, S Japan

Hierro 70 A3 *var.* Ferro. *Island* Islas Canarias, Spain, NE Atlantic Ocean

High Plains *see* Great Plains

High Point 43 E1 North Carolina, SE USA

High Veld *see* Great Karoo

Hiiumaa 106 C2 *Ger.* Dagden, *Swe.* Dagö. *Island* W Estonia

Hikurangi 150 D2 Northland, North Island, NZ

Hildesheim 94 B4 Niedersachsen, N Germany

Hilla *see* Al Ḥillah

Hillaby, Mount 55 G1 *mountain* N Barbados

Hillegom 86 C3 Zuid-Holland, W Netherlands

Hilo 47 B8 Hawaii, USA, C Pacific Ocean

Hilton Head Island 43 E2 South Carolina, SE USA

Hilversum 86 C3 Noord-Holland, C Netherlands

Himalaya *see* Himalayas

Himalayas 135 E2 *var.* Himalaya, *Chin.* Himalaya Shan. *Mountain range* S Asia

Himalaya Shan *see* Himalayas

Himeji 131 C6 *var.* Himezi. Hyōgo, Honshū, SW Japan

Himezi *see* Himeji

Hinçeşti 108 D4 *var.* Hânceşti; *prev.* Kotovsk. C Moldova

Hinchinbrook Island 148 D3 *island* Queensland, NE Australia

Hinds 151 C6 Canterbury, South Island, NZ

Hindu Kush 123 F4 *Per.* Hendū Kosh. *Mountain range* Afghanistan/Pakistan

Hinesville 43 E3 Georgia, SE USA

Hinnøya 84 C3 *island* C Norway

Hinson Bay 42 A5 *bay* W Bermuda

Hios *see* Chíos

Hirosaki 130 D3 Aomori, Honshū, C Japan

Hiroshima 131 B6 *var.* Hirosima. Hiroshima, Honshū, SW Japan

Hirosima *see* Hiroshima

Hirson 90 D3 Aisne, N France

Hispaniola 56 B1 *island* Dominion Republic/Haiti

Hitachi 131 D5 *var.* Hitati. Ibaraki, Honshū, S Japan

Hitati *see* Hitachi

Hitra 84 A4 *prev.* Hitteren. *Island* S Norway

Hjälmaren 85 C6 *Eng.* Lake Hjalmar. *Lake* C Sweden

Hjørring 85 B7 Nordjylland, N Denmark

Hkakabo Razi 136 B1 *mountain* Myanmar/China

Hlobyne 109 F2 *Rus.* Globino. Poltavs'ka Oblast', NE Ukraine

Hlukhiv 109 F1 *Rus.* Glukhov. Sums'ka Oblast', NE Ukraine

Hlybokaye 107 D5 *Rus.* Glubokoye. Vitsyebskaya Voblasts', N Belarus

Hoa Binh 136 D3 Hoa Binh, N Vietnam

Hoang Liên Son 136 D3 *mountain range* N Vietnam

Hobart 149 C8 *prev.* Hobarton, Hobart Town. *State capital* Tasmania, SE Australia

Hobbs 49 E3 New Mexico, SW USA

Hobro 85 A7 Nordjylland, N Denmark

Hô Chi Minh 136 E *var.* Ho Chi Minh City; *prev.* Saigon. S Vietnam

Ho Chi Minh City *see* Hô Chi Minh

Hódmezővásárhely 99 D7 Csongrád, SE Hungary

Hodna, Chott El 118 C4 *var.* Chott el-Hodna, *Ar.* Shatt al-Hodna. *Salt lake* N Algeria

Hodonín 99 C5 *Ger.* Göding. Brněnský Kraj, SE Czech Republic

Hoë Karoo *see* Great Karoo

Hof 95 C5 Bayern, SE Germany

Hofei *see* Hefei

Hōfu 131 B7 Yamaguchi, Honshū, SW Japan

Hofuf *see* Al Hufūf

Hogoley Islands *see* Chuuk Islands

Hohe Tauern 95 C7 *mountain range* W Austria

Hohhot 127 F3 *var.* Huhehot, Huhuohaote, *Mong.* Kukukhoto; *prev.* Kweisui, Kwesui. Nei Mongol Zizhiqu, N China

Hôi an 137 E5 *prev.* Faifo. Quang Nam-Đa Nẵng, C Vietnam

Hoï-Hao *see* Haikou

Hoihow *see* Haikou

Hokianga Harbour 150 C2 *inlet* SE Tasman Sea

Hokitika 151 B5 West Coast, South Island, NZ

Hokkaidō 130 C2 *prev.* Ezo, Yeso, Yezo. *Island* NE Japan

Hola Prystan' 109 E4 *Rus.* Golaya Pristan. Khersons'ka Oblast', S Ukraine

Holbrook 48 B2 Arizona, SW USA

Holetown 55 G1 *prev.* Jamestown. W Barbados

Holguín 54 C2 Holguín, SE Cuba

Hollabrunn 95 E6 Niederösterreich, NE Austria

Hollandia *see* Jayapura

Holly Springs 42 C1 Mississippi, S USA

Holman 37 E3 Victoria Island, Northwest Territories, N Canada

Holmsund 84 D4 Västerbotten, N Sweden

Holon 119 A6 *var.* Kholon. Tel Aviv, C Israel

Holovanivs'k 109 E3 *Rus.* Golovanevsk. Kirovohrads'ka Oblast', C Ukraine

Holstebro 85 A7 Ringkøbing, W Denmark

Holsteinborg *see* Sisimiut

Holsteinsborg *see* Sisimiut

Holstenborg *see* Sisimiut

Holstensborg *see* Sisimiut

Holyhead 89 C5 *Wel.* Caer Gybi. NW Wales, UK

Hombori 75 E3 Mopti, S Mali

Homs *see* Al Khums

Homs *see* Ḥimş

Homyel' 107 D7 *Rus.* Gomel'. Homyel'skaya Voblasts', SE Belarus

Honan *see* Henan

Honan *see* Luoyang

Hondo *see* Honshū

Hondo 49 F4 Texas, SW USA

Honduras 52 C2 *Country* Central America

Honduras 52

Official name	Republic of Honduras
Formation	1838
Capital	Tegucigalpa
Population	6.6 million / 153 people per sq mile (59 people per sq km)
Total area	43,278 sq miles (112,090 sq km)
Languages	Spanish, Black Carib, English Creole
Religions	Roman Catholic 97%, Protestant minority 3%
Ethnic mix	Mestizo 90%, Black African 5%, Amerindian 4%, White 1%
Government	Presidential democracy
Currency	Lempira = 100 centavos
Literacy rate	74.6%
Calorie consumption	2,395 kilocalories

Honduras, Gulf of 52 C2 *Sp.* Golfo de Honduras. *Gulf* W Caribbean Sea

Honefoss 85 B6 Buskerud, S Norway

Honey Lake 47 B5 *lake* California, W USA

Hon Gai *see* Hông Gai

Hongay *see* Hông Gai

Hông Gai 136 E3 *var.* Hon Gai, Hongay. Quang Ninh, N Vietnam

Hong Kong 128 A1 *Chin.* Xianggang. S China

Hong Kong Island 128 B2 *Chin.* Xianggang. *Island* S China

Honiara 144 C3 *country capital* (Solomon Islands) Guadalcanal, C Solomon Islands

Honjō 130 D4 *var.* Honzyô. Akita, Honshū, C Japan

Honolulu 47 A8 *admin capital* Oahu, Hawaii, USA, C Pacific Ocean

Honshū 131 E5 *var.* Hondo, Honsyû. *Island* SW Japan

Honsyû *see* Honshū

Honzyô *see* Honjō

Hoogeveen 86 D2 Drenthe, NE Netherlands

Hoogezand-Sappemeer 86 E2 Groningen, NE Netherlands

Hoorn 86 C2 Noord-Holland, NW Netherlands

Hopa 117 E2 Artvin, NE Turkey

Hope 36 C3 British Columbia, SW Canada

Hopedale 39 F2 Newfoundland and Labrador, NE Canada

Hopeh *see* Hebei

Hopei *see* Hebei

Hopkinsville 40 B5 Kentucky, S USA

Horasan 117 F3 Erzurum, NE Turkey

Horizon Deep 152 D4 *undersea feature* W Pacific Ocean

Horki 107 E6 *Rus.* Gorki. Mahilyowskaya Voblasts', E Belarus

Horlivka 109 G3 *Rom.* Adâncata, *Rus.* Gorlovka. Donets'ka Oblast', E Ukraine

Hormuz, Strait of 120 D4 *var.* Strait of Ormuz, *Per.* Tangeh-ye Hormoz. *Strait* Iran/Oman

Hornos, Cabo de 65 C8 *Eng.* Cape Horn. *Headland* S Chile

Hornsby 148 E1 New South Wales, SE Australia

Horodnya 109 E1 *Rus.* Gorodnya. Chernihivs'ka Oblast', NE Ukraine

Horodyshche 109 E2 *Rus.* Gorodishche. Cherkas'ka Oblast', C Ukraine

Horokok 108 B2 *Pol.* Gródek Jagielloński, *Rus.* Gorodok, Gorodok Yagellonski. L'vivs'ka Oblast', NW Ukraine

Horoshiri-dake 130 D2 *var.* Horosiri Dake. *Mountain* Hokkaidō, N Japan

Horosiri Dake *see* Horoshiri-dake

Horsburgh Atoll 132 A4 *atoll* N Maldives

Horseshoe Bay 42 A5 *bay* W Bermuda

Horseshoe Seamounts 80 A4 *undersea feature* E Atlantic Ocean

Horsham 149 B7 Victoria, SE Australia

Horst 87 D5 Limburg, SE Netherlands

Horten 85 B6 Vestfold, S Norway

Horyn' 107 B7 *Rus.* Goryn. *River* NW Ukraine

Hosingen 87 D7 Diekirch, NE Luxembourg

Hospitalet *see* L'Hospitalet de Llobregat

Hotan 126 B4 *var.* Khotan, *Chin.* Ho-t'ien. Xinjiang Uygur Zizhiqu, NW China

Ho-t'ien *see* Hotan

Hoting 84 C4 Jämtland, C Sweden

Hot Springs 42 B1 Arkansas, C USA

Houayxay 136 C3 *var.* Ban Houayxay, Ban Houei Sai. Bokèo, N Laos

Houghton 40 B1 Michigan, N USA

Houilles 91 B5 Yvelines, N France

Houlton 41 H1 Maine, NE USA

Houma 42 B3 Louisiana, S USA

Houston 49 H4 Texas, SW USA

Hovd 126 C2 *var.* Khovd. Hovd, W Mongolia

Hove 89 E7 SE England, UK

Hoverla, Hora 108 C3 *Rus.* Gora Goverla. *Mountain* W Ukraine

Hovsgol, Lake *see* Hövsgöl Nuur

Hövsgöl Nuur 126 D1 *var.* Lake Hovsgol. *Lake* N Mongolia

Howar, Wādi 72 A3 *var.* Ouadi Howa. *River* Chad/Sudan *see also* Howa, Ouadi

Hoy 88 C2 *island* N Scotland, UK

Hoyerswerda 94 D4 Sachsen, E Germany

Hradec Králové 99 B5 *Ger.* Königgrätz. Hradecký Kraj, N Czech Republic

Hrandzichy 107 B5 *Rus.* Grandichi. Hrodzyenskaya Voblasts', W Belarus

Hranice 99 C5 *Ger.* Mährisch-Weisskirchen. Olomoucký Kraj, E Czech Republic

Hrebinka 109 E2 *Rus.* Grebenka. Poltavs'ka Oblast', NE Ukraine

Hrodna 107 B5 *Pol.* Grodno. Hrodzyenskaya Voblasts', W Belarus

Hsia-men *see* Xiamen

Hsiang-t'an *see* Xiangtan

Hsi Chiang *see* Xi Jiang

Hsing-k'ai Hu *see* Khanka, Lake

Hsining *see* Xining

Hsinking *see* Changchun

Hsin-yang *see* Xinyang

Hsu-chou *see* Xuzhou

Huacho 60 C4 Lima, W Peru

Hua Hin *see* Ban Hua Hin

Huaihua 128 C5 Hunan, S China

Huailai 128 C3 *prev.* Shacheng. Hebei, E China

Huainan 128 D5 *var.* Huai-nan, Hwainan. Anhui, E China

Huai-nan *see* Huainan

Huajuapan 51 F5 *var.* Huajuapan de León. Oaxaca, SE Mexico

Huajuapan de León *see* Huajuapan

Hualapai Peak 48 A2 *mountain* Arizona, SW USA

Huallaga, Río 60 C3 *river* N Peru

Huambo 78 B2 *Port.* Nova Lisboa. Huambo, C Angola

Huancavelica 60 D4 Huancavelica, SW Peru

Huancayo 60 D3 Junín, C Peru

Huang He 128 C4 *var.* Yellow River. *River* C China

Huangshi 128 C5 *var.* Huang-shih, Hwangshih. Hubei, C China

Huang-shih *see* Huangshi

Huanta 60 D4 Ayacucho, C Peru

Huánuco 60 C3 Huánuco, C Peru
Huanuni 61 F4 Oruro, W Bolivia
Huaral 60 C4 Lima, W Peru
Huarás see Huaraz
Huaraz 60 C3 var. Huarás. Ancash,
W Peru
Huarmey 60 C3 Ancash, W Peru
Huatabampo 50 C2 Sonora,
NW Mexico
Hubli 124 B3 Karnātaka, SW India
Huddersfield 89 D5 N England,
UK
Hudiksvall 85 C5 Gävleborg,
C Sweden
Hudson Bay 37 G4 bay NE Canada
Hudson Strait 37 H3 Fr. Détroit
d'Hudson. Strait
Nunavut/Quebec, NE Canada
Hudur see Xuddur
Huê 136 E4 Thừa Thiên-Huê,
C Vietnam
Huehuetenango 52 A2
Huehuetenango, W Guatemala
Huelva 92 C4 anc. Onuba.
Andalucía, SW Spain
Huesca 93 F2 anc. Osca. Aragón,
NE Spain
Huéscar 93 E4 Andalucía, S Spain
Hughenden 148 C3 Queensland,
NE Australia
Hugo 49 G2 Oklahoma, C USA
Huhehot see Hohhot
Huhuohaote see Hohhot
Huíla Plateau 78 B2 plateau
S Angola
Huixtla 51 G5 Chiapas, SE Mexico
Hukui see Fukui
Hukuoka see Fukuoka
Hukusima see Fukushima
Hulingol 127 G2 prev. Huolin Gol.
Nei Mongol Zizhiqu, N China
Hull see Kingston upon Hull
Hull 38 D4 Quebec, SE Canada
Hulst 87 B5 Zeeland,
SW Netherlands
Hulun see Hailar
Hu-lun Ch'ih see Hulun Nur
Hulun Nur 127 F1 var. Hu-lun Ch'ih;
prev. Dalai Nor. lake NE China
Humaitá 62 D2 Amazonas, N Brazil
Humboldt River 47 C5 river
Nevada, W USA
Humphreys Peak 48 B1 mountain
Arizona, SW USA
Humpolec 99 B5 Ger. Gumpolds,
Humpoletz. Jihlavský Kraj,
C Czech Republic
Hunan 128 C6 var. Hunan Sheng,
Xiang. Admin. region province
S China
Hunan ShEng see Xiang
Hunedoara 108 B4 Ger. Eisenmarkt,
Hung. Vajdahunyad. Hunedoara,
SW Romania
Hünfeld 95 B5 Hessen, C Germany
Hungary 99 C6 Ger. Ungarn, Hung.
Magyarország, Rom. Ungaria, SCr.
Mađarska, Ukr. Uhorshchyna;
prev. Hungarian People's
Republic. Country C Europe

Hungary 99

Official name Republic of Hungary
Formation 1918
Capital Budapest
Population 9.9 million / 276 people
per sq mile (106 people per sq km)
Total area 35,919 sq miles
(93,030 sq km)
Languages Hungarian
Religions Roman Catholic 64%,
Calvinist 20%, non-religious 7%,
Lutheran 4%, other 5%
Ethnic mix Magyar 90%, German
2%, Romany 1%, Slovak 1%,
other 6%
Government Parliamentary
democracy
Currency Forint = 100 filler
Literacy rate 99%
Calorie consumption 3,458
kilocaloriesn

Hungary, Plain of see Great
Hungarian Plain

Hunter Island 149 B8 island
Tasmania, SE Australia
Huntington 40 D4 West Virginia,
NE USA
Huntington Beach 47 B8 California,
W USA
Huntly 150 D3 Waikato, North
Island, NZ
Huntsville 42 D1 Alabama, S USA
Huntsville 49 G3 Texas, SW USA
Hurghada 72 C2 var. Al Ghurdaqah,
Ghurdaqah. E Egypt
Huron 45 E3 South Dakota, N USA
Huron, Lake 40 D2 lake
Canada/USA
Hurukawa see Furukawa
Hurunui 151 C5 river South Island,
NZ
Húsavík 83 E4 Nordhurland Eystra,
NE Iceland
Husum 94 B2 Schleswig-Holstein,
N Germany
Hutchinson 45 E5 Kansas, C USA
Hutchinson Island 43 F4 island
Florida, SE USA
Huy 87 C6 Dut. Hoei, Hoey. Liège,
E Belgium
Huzi see Fuji
Hvannadalshnúkur 83 E5 mountain
S Iceland
Hvar 100 B4 It. Lesina; anc. Pharus.
Island S Croatia
Hwainan see Huainan
Hwange 78 D3 prev. Wankie.
Matabeleland North,
W Zimbabwe
Hwangshih see Huangshi
Hyargas Nuur 126 C2 lake
NW Mongolia
Hyderābād 134 D5 var. Haidarabad.
Andhra Pradesh, C India
Hyderābād 134 B3 var. Haidarabad.
Sind, SE Pakistan
Hyères 91 D6 Var, SE France
Hyères, Îles d' 91 D6 island group
S France
Hypanis see Kuban'
Hyrcania see Gorgān
Hyvinkää 85 D5 Swe. Hyvinge.
Etelä-Suomi, S Finland

I

Ialomiţa 108 C5 river SE Romania
Iaşi 108 D3 Ger. Jassy. Iaşi,
NE Romania
Ibadan 75 F5 Oyo, SW Nigeria
Ibagué 58 B3 Tolima, C Colombia
Ibar 100 D4 Alb. Ibër. River C Serbia
and Montenegro (Yugo.)
Ibarra 60 B1 var. San Miguel de
Ibarra. Imbabura, N Ecuador
Iberian Mountains see Ibérico,
Sistema
Iberian Peninsula 80 B4 physical
region Portugal/Spain
Iberian Plain 80 B4 undersea feature
E Atlantic Ocean
Ibérico, Sistema 93 E2 var.
Cordillera Ibérica, Eng. Iberian
Mountains. Mountain range
NE Spain
Ibiza see Eivissa
Ibo see Sassandra
Ica 60 D4 Ica, SW Peru
Içá see Putumayo, Río
Icaria see Ikaría
Içá, Rio 62 C2 var. Río Putumayo.
River NW South America see also
Putumayo, Río
Iceland 83 E4 Dan. Island, Icel.
Ísland. Country N Atlantic Ocean

Iceland 83

Official name Republic of Iceland
Formation 1944
Capital Reykjavik
Population 281,000 /7 people per
sq mile (3 people per sq km)
Total area 39,768 sq miles
(103,000 sq km)
Languages Icelandic
Religions Evangelical Lutheran
93%, non-religious 6%, other
Christian 1%

Iceland (continued)

Ethnic mix Icelandic 94%, Danish
1%, other 5%
Government Parliamentary
democracy
Currency Icelandic króna = 100
aurar
Literacy rate 99%
Calorie consumption 3,342
kilocalories

Iceland Basin 80 B1 undersea feature
N Atlantic Ocean
Icelandic Plateau see Iceland
Plateau
Iceland Plateau 172 B5 var.
Icelandic Plateau. Undersea feature
S Greenland Sea
Iconium see Konya
Idabel 49 H2 Oklahoma, C USA
Idaho 46 D3 off. State of Idaho; also
known as Gem of the Mountains,
Gem State. State NW USA
Idaho Falls 46 E3 Idaho, NW USA
Idensalmi see Iisalmi
Idfu 72 B2 var. Edfu. SE Egypt
Ídhra see Ýdra
Idi Amin, Lac see Edward, Lake
Idini 74 B2 Trarza, W Mauritania
Idlib 118 B3 Idlib, NW Syria
Idre 85 B5 Kopparberg, C Sweden
Iecava 106 C3 Bauska, S Latvia
Ieper 87 A6 Fr. Ypres. West-
Vlaanderen, W Belgium
Ierápetra 105 D8 Kríti, Greece,
E Mediterranean Sea
Ierisós see Ierissós
Ierissós 104 C4 var. Ierisós. Kentrikí
Makedonía, N Greece
Iferouâne 75 G2 Agadez, N Niger
Ifôghas, Adrar des 75 E2 var. Adrar
des Iforas. Mountain range NE Mali
Igarka 114 D3 Krasnoyarskiy Kray,
N Russian Federation
Iglesias 97 A5 Sardegna, Italy,
C Mediterranean Sea
Igloolik 37 G2 Nunavut,
N Canada
Igoumenítsa 104 A4 Ípeiros,
W Greece
Iguaçu, Rio 63 E4 Sp. Río Iguazú.
River Argentina/Brazil see also
Iguazú, Río
Iguaçu, Salto do 63 E4 Sp. Cataratas
del Iguazú; prev. Victoria Falls.
Waterfall Argentina/Brazil see also
Iguazú, Cataratas del
Iguala 51 E4 var. Iguala de la
Independencia. Guerrero, S Mexico
Iguala de la Independencia see
Iguala
Iguidi, 'Erg 70 C3 var. Erg Iguid.
Desert Algeria/Mauritania
Ihavandiffulu Atoll see
Ihavandippolhu Atoll
Ihavandippolhu Atoll 132 A3 var.
Ihavandiffulu Atoll. Atoll
N Maldives
Ihosy 79 F4 Fianarantsoa,
S Madagascar
Ijmuiden 86 C3 Noord-Holland, W
Netherlands
Iisalmi 84 E4 var. Idensalmi. Itä-
Suomi, C Finland
IJssel 86 D3 var. Yssel. River
Netherlands/Germany
IJsselmeer 86 C2 prev. Zuider Zee.
Lake N Netherlands
IJsselmuiden 86 D3 Overijssel,
E Netherlands
Ijzer 87 A6 river W Belgium
Ikaría 105 D6 var. Kariot, Nicaria,
Nikaria; anc. Icaria. Island
Dodekánisos, Greece, Aegean Sea
Ikela 77 D6 Equateur, C Dem. Rep.
Congo
Iki 131 A7 island SW Japan
Ilagan 139 E1 Luzon, N Philippines
Ilave 61 E4 Puno, S Peru
Iława 98 D3 Ger. Deutsch-Eylau.
Warmińsko-Mazurskie, NE
Poland
Ilebo 77 C6 prev. Port-Francqui.
Kasai Occidental, W Dem. Rep.
Congo

Île-de-France 90 C3 cultural region
N France
Îles de la Société see Société,
Archipel de la
Îles Tubuai see Australes, Îles
Ilfracombe 89 C7 SW England, UK
Ilha Caviana see Caviana de Fora,
Ilha
Ilha de Madeira see Madeira
Ilha do Corvo see Corvo
Ilha do Faial see Faial
Ilha do Pico see Pico
Ilha do Porto Santo see Porto Santo
Ilha Graciosa see Graciosa
Ilhas dos Açores see Azores
Ilha Terceira see Terceira
Ílhavo 92 B2 Aveiro, N Portugal
Ili 112 C3 Kaz. Ile, Rus. Reka Ili.
River China/Kazakhstan
Iliamna Lake 36 C3 lake Alaska,
USA
Ilici see Elche
Iligan 139 E2 off. Iligan City.
Mindanao, S Philippines
Illapel 64 B4 Coquimbo, C Chile
Illichivs'k 109 E4 Rus. Il'ichevsk.
Odes'ka Oblast', SW Ukraine
Illicis see Elche
Illinois 40 A4 off. State of Illinois;
also known as Prairie State,
Sucker State. State C USA
Illinois River 40 B4 river Illinois,
N USA
Ilo 61 E4 Moquegua, SW Peru
Iloilo 139 E2 off. Iloilo City. Panay
Island, C Philippines
Ilorin 75 F4 Kwara, W Nigeria
Îlots de Bass see Marotiri
Ilovlya 111 B6 Volgogradskaya
Oblast', SW Russian Federation
İluh see Batman
Il'yaly 122 C2 var. Yylanly.
Dashkhovuzskiy Velayat,
N Turkmenistan
Imatra 85 E5 Etelä-Suomi,
S Finland
Imbros see Gökçeada
İmişli 117 H3 Rus. Imishli.
C Azerbaijan
Imola 96 C3 Emilia-Romagna,
N Italy
Imperatriz 63 F2 Maranhão,
NE Brazil
Imperia 96 A3 Liguria, NW Italy
Impfondo 77 C5 La Likouala,
NE Congo
Imphāl 135 H3 Manipur, NE India
Imroz Adası see Gökçeada
Inagua Islands see Great Inagua
Inagua Islands see Little Inagua
Inarijärvi 84 D2 Lapp. Aanaarjävri,
Swe. Enareträsk. Lake N Finland
Inawashiro-ko 131 D5 var.
Inawasiro Ko. Lake Honshū,
C Japan
Inawasiro Ko see Inawashiro-ko
İncesu 116 D3 Kayseri, C Turkey
Inch'ŏn 129 E4 off. Inch'ŏn-
gwangyksi, Jap. Jinsen; prev.
Chemulpo. NW South Korea
Incudine, Monte 91 E7 mountain
Corse, France, C Mediterranean
Sea
Indefatigable Island see Santa
Cruz, Isla
Independence 45 F4 Missouri,
C USA
Independence Fjord 83 E1 fjord
N Greenland
Independence Mountains 46 C4
mountain range Nevada, W USA
India 124 B3 var. Indian Union,
Union of India, Hind. Bhārat.
Country S Asia

India 124

Official name Republic of India
Formation 1947
Capital New Delhi
Population 1.03 billion / 790 people
per sq mile (305 people per sq km)
Total area 1,269,339 sq miles
(3,287,590 sq km)
Languages Hindi, English, and 16
regional languages

India (continued)

Religions Hindu 83%, Muslim 11%, Christian 2%, Sikh 2%, other 2%
Ethnic mix Indo-Aryan 72%, Dravidian 25%, Mongoloid and other 3%
Government Parliamentary democracy
Currency Indian rupee = 100 paisa
Literacy rate 57.2%
Calorie consumption 2,428 kilocalories

Indiana 40 B4 off. State of Indiana; also known as The Hoosier State. *State* N USA
Indianapolis 40 C4 state capital Indiana, N USA
Indian Church 52 C1 Orange Walk, N Belize
Indian Desert see Thar Desert
Indianola 45 F4 Iowa, C USA
Indigirka 115 F2 river NE Russian Federation
Indija 100 D3 Hung. India; prev. Indjija. Serbia, N Serbia and Montenegro (Yugo.)
Indira Point 132 G3 headland Andaman and Nicobar Islands, India, NE Indian Ocean
Indomed Fracture Zone 141 B6 tectonic feature SW Indian Ocean
Indonesia 138 B4 Ind. Republik Indonesia; prev. Dutch East Indies, Netherlands East Indies, United States of Indonesia. Country SE Asia

Indonesia 138

Official name Republic of Indonesia
Formation 1949
Capital Jakarta
Population 214 million / 289 people per sq mile (111 people per sq km)
Total area 741,096 sq miles (1,919,440 sq km)
Languages Bahasa Indonesia, Javanese, Madurese, Sundanese, Dutch
Religions Muslim 87%, Protestant 6%, Roman Catholic 3%, other 4%
Ethnic mix Javanese 45%, Sundanese 14%, Coastal Malays 8%, Madurese 8%, other 25%
Government Multiparty republic
Currency Rupiah = 100 sen
Literacy rate 86.9%
Calorie consumption 2,902 kilocalories

Indore 134 D4 Madhya Pradesh, C India
Indus 134 C2 Chin. Yindu He; prev. Yin-tu Ho. River S Asia
Indus Cone see Indus Fan
Indus Fan 112 C5 var. Indus Cone. Undersea feature N Arabian Sea
Indus, Mouths of the 134 B4 delta S Pakistan
İnebolu 116 C2 Kastamonu, N Turkey
Ineu 108 A4 Hung. Borosjenő; prev. Inău. Arad, W Romania
Infiernillo, Presa del 51 E4 reservoir S Mexico
Inglewood 46 D2 California, W USA
Ingolstadt 95 C6 Bayern, S Germany
Inhambane 79 E4 Inhambane, SE Mozambique
Inhulets' 109 F3 Rus. Ingulets. Dnipropetrovs'ka Oblast', E Ukraine
I-ning see Yining
Inis see Ennis
Inis Ceithleann see Enniskillen
Inn 95 C6 river C Europe
Innaanganeq 82 C1 var. Kap York. Headland NW Greenland

Inner Hebrides 88 B4 island group W Scotland, UK
Inner Islands 79 H1 var. Central Group. Island group NE Seychelles
Inner Mongolia 127 F3 var. Nei Mongol, Eng. Inner Mongolia, Inner Mongolian Autonomous Region; prev. Nei Monggol Zizhiqu. Admin. region autonomous region N China
Inner Mongolian Autonomous Region see Inner Mongolia
Innisfail 148 D3 Queensland, NE Australia
Inniskilling see Enniskillen
Innsbruck see Innsbruck
Innsbruck 95 C7 var. Innsbruck. Tirol, W Austria
Inoucdjouac see Inukjuak
Inowrocław 98 C3 Ger. Hohensalza; prev. Inowrazlaw. Kujawski-pomorskie, C Poland
I-n-Salah 70 D3 var. In Salah. C Algeria
In Salah see I-n-Salah
Insula see Lille
Inta 110 E3 Respublika Komi, NW Russian Federation
International Falls 45 F1 Minnesota, N USA
Inukjuak 38 D2 var. Inoucdjouac; prev. Port Harrison. Quebec, NE Canada
Inuuvik see Inuvik
Inuvik 36 D3 var. Inuuvik. District capital Northwest Territories, NW Canada
Invercargill 151 A7 Southland, South Island, NZ
Inverness 88 C3 N Scotland, UK
Investigator Ridge 141 D5 undersea feature E Indian Ocean
Investigator Strait 149 B7 strait South Australia
Inyangani 78 D3 mountain NE Zimbabwe
Ioánnina 104 A4 var. Janina, Yannina. Ípeiros, W Greece
Iola 45 F5 Kansas, C USA
Ionia Basin see Ionian Basin
Ionian Basin 80 D5 var. Ionia Basin. Undersea feature Ionian Sea, C Mediterranean Sea
Ionian Islands see Iónioi Nísoi
Ionian Sea 103 E3 Gk. Iónio Pélagos, It. Mar Ionio. Sea C Mediterranean Sea
Iónioi Nísoi 105 A5 Eng. Ionian Islands. Island group W Greece
Íos 105 D6 var. Nio. Island Kykládes, Greece, Aegean Sea
Íos 105 D6 Íos, Kykládes, Greece, Aegean Sea
Iowa 45 F3 off. State of Iowa; also known as The Hawkeye State. State C USA
Iowa City 45 G3 Iowa, C USA
Iowa Falls 45 G3 Iowa, C USA
Ipel' 99 C6 var. Ipoly, Ger. Eipel. River Hungary/Slovakia
Ipiales 58 A4 Nariño, SW Colombia
Ipoh 138 B3 Perak, Peninsular Malaysia
Ipoly 99 C6 var. Ipel', Ger. Eipel. River Hungary/Slovakia
Ippy 76 C4 Ouaka, C Central African Republic
Ipswich 89 E6 hist. Gipeswic. E England, UK
Ipswich 149 E5 Queensland, E Australia
Iqaluit 37 H3 prev. Frobisher Bay. Baffin Island, Nunavut, NE Canada
Iquique 64 B1 Tarapacá, N Chile
Iquitos 60 C1 Loreto, N Peru
Irákleio 105 D7 var. Herakleion, Eng. Candia; prev. Iráklion. Kríti, Greece, E Mediterranean Sea
Iráklion see Irákleio
Iran 120 C3 prev. Persia. Country SW Asia

Iran 120

Official name Islamic Republic of Iran
Formation 1502
Capital Tehran
Population 71.4 million / 112 people per sq mile (43 people per sq km)
Total area 636,406 sq miles (1,648,293 sq km)
Languages Farsi, Azeri, Gilaki, Baluchi, Mazanderani, Kurdish, Arabic
Religions Shi'a Muslim 95%, Sunni Muslim 4%, other 1%
Ethnic mix Persian 50%, Azeri 24%, Lur and Bakhtiari 8%, Kurd 8%, other 10%
Government Islamic theocracy
Currency Iranian rial = 100 dinars
Literacy rate 76.8%
Calorie consumption 2,913 kilocalories

Iranian Plateau 120 D3 var. Plateau of Iran. plateau N Iran
Iran, Plateau of see Iranian Plateau
Irapuato 51 E4 Guanajuato, C Mexico
Iraq 120 B3 Ar. 'Irāq. Country SW Asia

Iraq 120

Official name Republic of Iraq
Formation 1932
Capital Baghdad
Population 23.6 million / 140 people per sq mile (54 people per sq km)
Total area 168,753 sq miles (437,072 sq km)
Languages Arabic, Kurdish, Armenian, Assyrian, Turkic languages
Religions Shi'a ithna Muslim 62%, Sunni Muslim 33%, other 5%
Ethnic mix Arab 79%, Kurdish 16%, Persian 3%, Turkman 2%
Government One-party republic
Currency Iraqi dinar = 1,000 fils
Literacy rate 55.9%
Calorie consumption 2,197 kilocalories

Irbid 119 B5 Irbid, N Jordan
Irbīl see Arbīl
Ireland 80 C3 Lat. Hibernia. Island Ireland/UK
Ireland, Republic of 89 A5 var. Ireland, Ir. Éire. Country NW Europe

Ireland 89

Official name Ireland
Formation 1922
Capital Dublin
Population 3.8 million / 140 people per sq mile (54 people per sq km)
Total area 27,135 sq miles (70,280 sq km)
Languages English, Irish Gaelic
Religions Roman Catholic 88%, Anglican 3%, other and non-religious 9%,
Ethnic mix Irish 95%, other 5%
Government Parliamentary democracy
Currency Euro (Punt until 2002)
Literacy rate 99%
Calorie consumption 3,613 kilocalories

Irian Barat see Papua
Irian Jaya see Papua
Irian, Teluk see Cenderawasih, Teluk
Iringa 73 C7 Iringa, C Tanzania
Iriomote-jima 130 A4 island Sakishima-shotō, SW Japan
Iriona 52 D2 Colón, NE Honduras

Irish Sea 89 C5 Ir. Muir Éireann. Sea C British Isles
Irkutsk 115 E4 Irkutskaya Oblast', S Russian Federation
Irminger Basin see Reykjanes Basin
Iroise 90 A3 sea NW France
Iron Mountain 40 B2 Michigan, N USA
Ironwood 40 B1 Michigan, N USA
Irrawaddy 136 B2 var. Ayeyarwady. River W Myanmar
Irrawaddy, Mouths of the 137 A5 delta SW Myanmar
Irtish see Irtysh
Irtysh 114 C4 var. Irtish, Kaz. Ertis. River C Asia
Irún 93 E1 País Vasco, N Spain
Iruña see Pamplona
Isabela, Isla 60 A5 var. Albemarle Island. Island Galapagos Islands, Ecuador, E Pacific Ocean
Isaccea 108 D4 Tulcea, E Romania
Isachsen 37 F1 Ellef Ringnes Island, Nunavut, N Canada
Ísafjördhur 83 E4 Vestfirdhir, NW Iceland
Isbarta see Isparta
Ise 131 C6 Mie, Honshū, SW Japan
Isère 91 D5 river E France
Isernia 97 D5 var. Æsernia. Molise, C Italy
Ise-wan 131 C6 bay S Japan
Isha Baydhabo see Baydhabo
Ishigaki-jima 130 A4 var. Isigaki Zima. Island Sakishima-shotō, SW Japan
Ishikari-wan 130 C2 bay Hokkaidō, NE Japan
Ishim 114 C4 Kaz. Esil. River Kazakhstan/Russian Federation
Ishim 114 C4 Tyumenskaya Oblast', C Russian Federation
Ishinomaki 130 D4 var. Isinomaki. Miyagi, Honshū, C Japan
Ishkoshim 123 F3 Rus. Ishkashim. S Tajikistan
Isigaki Zima see Ishigaki-jima
Isinomaki see Ishinomaki
Isiro 77 E5 Orientale, NE Dem. Rep. Congo
Iskăr see Iskūr
İskenderun 116 D4 Eng. Alexandretta. Hatay, S Turkey
İskenderun Körfezi 118 A2 Eng. Gulf of Alexandretta. Gulf S Turkey
Iskŭr 104 C2 var. Iskăr. River NW Bulgaria
Iskŭr, Yazovir 104 B2 prev. Yazovir Stalin. Reservoir W Bulgaria
Isla Cristina 92 C4 Andalucía, S Spain
Isla Gran Malvina see West Falkland
Islāmābād 134 C1 country capital (Pakistan) Federal Capital Territory Islāmābād, NE Pakistan
I-n-Sâkâne, 'Erg 75 E2 desert N Mali
Islas de los Galápagos see Galapagos Islands
Islas Malvinas see Falkland Islands
Islay 88 B4 island SW Scotland, UK
Isle 91 B5 river W France
Isle of Man 89 B5 UK crown dependency NW Europe
Ismailia see Ismâ'iliya
Ismâ'iliya 72 B1 var. Ismailia. N Egypt
Ismid see İzmit
Isna 72 B2 var. Esna. SE Egypt
Isoka 78 D1 Northern, NE Zambia
Isola Grossa see Dugi Otok
Isola Lunga see Dugi Otok
Isole Lipari see Eolie, Isole
Isparta 116 B4 var. Isbarta. SW Turkey
İspir 117 E3 Erzurum, NE Turkey
Israel 119 A7 var. Medinat Israel, Heb. Yisrael, Yisra'el. Country SW Asia

Israel 119

Official name State of Israel
Formation 1948
Capital Jerusalem

Israel (continued)

Population 6.2 million / 773 people per sq mile (305 people per sq km)
Total area 8,019 sq miles (20,770 sq km)
Languages Hebrew, Arabic, Yiddish, German, Russian, Polish, Romanian, Persian
Religions Jewish 82%, Muslim (mainly Sunni) 14%, other (including Druze) 4%
Ethnic mix Jewish 82%, other (mostly Arab) 18%
Government Parliamentary democracy
Currency Shekel = 100 agorot
Literacy rate 96%
Calorie consumption 3,562 kilocalories

Issiq Köl *see* Issyk-Kul', Ozero
Issoire 91 C5 Puy-de-Dôme, C France
Issyk-Kul', Ozero 123 G2 *var.* Issiq Köl, *Kir.* Ysyk-Köl. *Lake* E Kyrgyzstan
İstanbul 116 B2 *Bul.* Tsarigrad, *Eng.* Istanbul; *prev.* Constantinople, *anc.* Byzantium. İstanbul, NW Turkey
İstanbul Boğazı 116 B2 *var.* Bosporus Thracius, *Eng.* Bosphorus, Bosporus, *Turk.* Karadeniz Boğazı. *Strait* NW Turkey
Istra 100 A3 *Eng.* Istria, *Ger.* Istrien. *Cultural region* NW Croatia
Istra 96 D2 *Eng.* Istria. *Peninsula* NW Croatia
Itabuna 63 G3 Bahia, E Brazil
Itagüí 58 B3 Antioquia, W Colombia
Itaipú, Represa de 63 E4 *reservoir* Brazil/Paraguay
Itaituba 63 E2 Pará, NE Brazil

Italy 96

Official name Italian Republic
Formation 1861
Capital Rome
Population 57.5 million /494 people per sq mile (191 people per sq km)
Total area 116,305 sq miles (301,230 sq km)
Languages Italian, German, French, Rhaeto-Romanic, Sardinian
Religions Roman Catholic 83%, other and non-religious 17%
Ethnic mix Italian 94%, Sardinian 2%, other 4%
Government Parliamentary democracy
Currency Euro (Italian lira until 2002)
Literacy rate 98.4%
Calorie consumption 3,661 kilocalories

Italy 80 D4 Texas, SW USA
Iténez, Río *see* Guaporé, Rio
Ithaca 41 E3 New York, NE USA
Itoigawa 131 C5 Niigata, Honshū, C Japan
Itseqqortoormiit *see* Ittoqqortoormiit
Ittoqqortoormiit 83 E3 *var.* Itseqqortoormiit, *Dan.* Scoresbysund, *Eng.* Scoresby Sound. C Greenland
Iturup, Ostrov 130 E1 *island* Kuril'skiye Ostrova, SE Russian Federation
Itzehoe 94 B2 Schleswig-Holstein, N Germany
Ivalo 84 D2 *Lapp.* Avveel, Avvil. Lappi, N Finland
Ivanava 107 B7 Pol. Janów, Janów Poleski, *Rus.* Ivanovo. Brestskaya Voblasts', SW Belarus

Ivanhoe 149 C6 New South Wales, SE Australia
Ivano-Frankivs'k 108 C2 *Ger.* Stanislau, *Pol.* Stanisławów, *Rus.* Ivano-Frankovsk; *prev.* Stanislav. Ivano-Frankivs'ka Oblast', W Ukraine
Ivanovo 111 B5 Ivanovskaya Oblast', W Russian Federation
Ivatsevichy 107 B6 *Pol.* Iwacewicze, *Rus.* Ivantsevichi, Ivatsevichi. Brestskaya Voblasts', SW Belarus
Ivigtut *see* Ivittuut
Ivittuut 82 B4 *var.* Ivigtut. S Greenland
Iviza *see* Eivissa
Ivory Coast *see* Côte d'Ivoire
Ivujivik 38 D1 Quebec, NE Canada
Iwaki 131 D5 Fukushima, Honshū, N Japan
Iwakuni 131 B7 Yamaguchi, Honshū, SW Japan
Iwanai 130 C2 Hokkaidō, NE Japan
Iwate 130 D3 Iwate, Honshū, N Japan
Ixtapa 51 E5 Guerrero, S Mexico
Ixtepec 51 F5 Oaxaca, SE Mexico
Iyo-nada 131 B7 *sea* S Japan
Izabal, Lago de 52 B2 *prev.* Golfo Dulce. *Lake* E Guatemala
Īzad Khvāst 120 D3 Fārs, C Iran
Izegem 87 A6 *prev.* Iseghem. West-Vlaanderen, W Belgium
Izhevsk 111 D5 *prev.* Ustinov. Udmurtskaya Respublika, NW Russian Federation
Izmayil 108 D4 *Rus.* Izmail. Odes'ka Oblast', SW Ukraine
İzmir 116 A3 *prev.* Smyrna. İzmir, W Turkey
İzmit 116 B2 *var.* Ismid; *anc.* Astacus. Kocaeli, NW Turkey
İznik Gölü 116 B3 *lake* NW Turkey
Izu-hantō 131 D6 *peninsula* Honshū, S Japan
Izu Shichito *see* Izu-shotō
Izu-shotō 131 D6 *var.* Izu Shichito. *Island group* S Japan
Izvor 104 B2 Pernik, W Bulgaria
Izyaslav 108 C2 Khmel'nyts'ka Oblast', W Ukraine
Izyum 109 G2 Kharkivs'ka Oblast', E Ukraine

J

Jabal ash Shifā 120 A4 *desert* NW Saudi Arabia
Jabalpur 135 E4 *prev.* Jubbulpore. Madhya Pradesh, C India
Jabbūl, Sabkhat al 134 B2 *salt flat* NW Syria
Jablah 118 A3 *var.* Jeble, *Fr.* Djéblé. Al Lādhiqīyah, W Syria
Jaca 93 F1 Aragón, NE Spain
Jacaltenango 52 A2 Huehuetenango, W Guatemala
Jackson 42 B2 *state capital* Mississippi, S USA
Jackson 45 H5 Missouri, C USA
Jackson 42 C1 Tennessee, S USA
Jackson Head 151 A6 *headland* South Island, NZ
Jacksonville 43 E3 Florida, SE USA
Jacksonville 40 B4 Illinois, N USA
Jacksonville 43 F1 North Carolina, SE USA
Jacksonville 49 G3 Texas, SE USA
Jacmel 54 D3 *var.* Jaquemel. S Haiti
Jacobābād 134 B3 Sind, SE Pakistan
Jaén 92 D4 Andalucía, SW Spain
Jaén 60 B2 Cajamarca, N Peru
Jaffna 132 D3 Northern Province, N Sri Lanka
Jagannath *see* Puri
Jagdalpur 135 E5 Madhya Pradesh, C India
Jagdaqi 127 G1 Nei Mongol Zizhiqu, N China
Jagodina 100 D4 *prev.* Svetozarevo. Serbia, C Serbia and Montenegro (Yugo.)
Jahra *see* Al Jahrā'
Jaipur 134 D3 *prev.* Jeypore. Rājasthān, N India
Jaisalmer 134 C3 Rājasthān, NW India

Jajce 100 B3 Federacija Bosna I Hercegovina, W Bosnia and Herzegovina
Jakarta 138 C5 *prev.* Djakarta, *Dut.* Batavia. *Country capital* (Indonesia) Jawa, C Indonesia
Jakobstad 84 D4 Fin. Pietarsaari. Länsi-Suomi, W Finland
Jalālābād 123 F4 *var.* Jalalabad, Jelalabad. Nangarhār, E Afghanistan
Jalandhar 134 D2 *prev.* Jullundur. Punjab, N India
Jalapa *see* Xalapa
Jalapa 52 D3 Nueva Segovia, NW Nicaragua
Jalapa Enríquez *see* Xalapa
Jalpa 50 D4 Zacatecas, C Mexico
Jālū 71 G3 *var.* Jūlā. NE Libya
Jaluit Atoll 144 D2 *var.* Jālwōj. *Atoll* Ralik Chain, S Marshall Islands
Jālwōj *see* Jaluit Atoll
Jamaame 73 D6 *It.* Giamame; *prev.* Margherita. Jubbada Hoose, S Somalia
Jamaica 54 A4 *country* W West Indies

Jamaica 54

Official name Jamaica
Formation 1962
Capital Kingston
Population 2.6 million / 613 people per sq mile (237 people per sq km)
Total area 4,243 sq miles (10,990 sq km)
Languages English, English Creole
Religions Christian (Church of God, Baptist, Anglican, other Protestant) 55%, other and non-religious 45%
Ethnic mix Black African 75%, Mulatto 13%, European and Chinese 11%, Indian 1%
Government Parliamentary democracy
Currency Jamaican dollar = 100 cents
Literacy rate 86.8%
Calorie consumption 2,693 kilocalories

Jamaica 56 A1 *island* W West Indies
Jamaica Channel 54 D3 *channel* Haiti/Jamaica
Jamālpur 135 F3 Bihār, NE India
Jambi 138 B4 *var.* Telanaipura; *prev.* Djambi. Sumatera, W Indonesia
James Bay 38 C3 *bay* Ontario/Quebec, E Canada
James River 45 E2 *river* North Dakota/South Dakota, N USA
James River 41 E5 *river* Virginia, NE USA
Jamestown 41 E3 New York, NE USA
Jamestown 45 E2 North Dakota, N USA
Jammu 134 D2 *prev.* Jummoo. Jammu and Kashmir, NW India
Jammu and Kashmir 134 D1 *disputed region* India/Pakistan
Jāmnagar 134 C4 *prev.* Navanagar. Gujarāt, W India
Jamshedpur 135 F4 Bihār, NE India
Jamuna *see* Brahmaputra
Janaúba 63 F3 Minas Gerais, SE Brazil
Janesville 40 B3 Wisconsin, N USA
Janīn *see* Jenīn
Janina *see* Ioánnina
Jan Mayen 83 F4 *Norwegian dependency* N Atlantic Ocean
Jánoshalma 99 C7 *SCr.* Jankovac. Bács-Kiskun, S Hungary
Japan 130 C4 *var.* Nippon, *Jap.* Nihon. *Country* E Asia

Japan 130

Official name Japan
Formation 1590
Capital Tokyo
Population 127.3 million / 873

Japan (continued)

people per sq mile (337 people per sq km)
Total area 145,882 sq miles (377,835 sq km)
Languages Japanese, Korean, Chinese
Religions Shinto and Buddhist 76%, Buddhist 16%, other (including Christian) 8%
Ethnic mix Japanese 99%, other (mainly Korean) 1%
Government Parliamentary democracy
Currency Yen = 100 sen
Literacy rate 99%
Calorie consumption 2,762 kilocalories

Japan, Sea of 130 A4 *var.* East Sea, *Rus.* Yapanskoye More. *Sea* NW Pacific Ocean
Japan Trench 125 F1 *undersea feature* NW Pacific Ocean
Japiim 62 C2 *var.* Máncio Lima. Acre, W Brazil
Japurá, Rio 62 C2 *var.* Río Caquetá, Yapurá. *River* Brazil/Colombia *see also* Caquetá, Río
Jaqué 53 G5 Darién, SE Panama
Jaquemel *see* Jacmel
Jarablos *see* Jarābulus
Jarābulus 118 C2 *var.* Jarablos, Jerablus, *Fr.* Djérablous. Halab, N Syria
Jardines de la Reina, Archipiélago de los 54 B2 *island group* C Cuba
Jarocin 98 C4 Wielkopolskie, C Poland
Jarosław 99 E5 *Ger.* Jaroslau, *Rus.* Yaroslav. Podkarpackie, SE Poland
Jarqürghon 123 E3 *Rus.* Dzharkurgan. Surkhondaryo Wiloyati, S Uzbekistan
Jarvis Island 145 G2 *US unincorporated territory* C Pacific Ocean
Jasło 99 D5 Podkarpackie, SE Poland
Jastrzębie-Zdrój 99 C5 Śląskie, S Poland
Jataí 63 E3 Goiás, C Brazil
Játiva *see* Xàtiva
Jauf *see* Al Jawf
Jaunpiebalga 106 D3 Gulbene, NE Latvia
Jaunpur 135 E3 Uttar Pradesh, N India
Java 152 A3 *prev.* Djawa. *Island* C Indonesia
Javalambre 93 E3 *mountain* E Spain
Javari, Río 62 C2 *var.* Yavari. *River* Brazil/Peru
Java Sea 138 D4 *Ind.* Laut Jawa. *Sea* W Indonesia
Java Trench 124 D5 *var.* Sunda Trench. *Undersea feature* E Indian Ocean
Jawhar 73 D6 *var.* Jowhar, *It.* Giohar. Shabeellaha Dhexe, S Somalia
Jaya, Puncak 139 G4 *prev.* Puntjak Carstensz, Puntjak Sukarno. *Mountain* Papua, E Indonesia
Jayapura 139 H4 *var.* Djajapura, *Dut.* Hollandia; *prev.* Kotabaru, Sukarnapura. Papua, E Indonesia
Jazā'ir Bin Ghalfān *see* Halāniyāt, Juzur al
Jazīrat Jarbah *see* Jerba, Île de
Jazīreh-ye Qeshm *see* Qeshm
Jaz Mūrīān, Hāmūn-e 120 E4 *lake* SE Iran
Jebba 75 F4 Kwara, W Nigeria
Jebel esh Sharqi *see* Anti-Lebanon
Jebel Uweinat *see* 'Uwaynāt, Jabal al
Jeble *see* Jablah
Jędrzejów 98 D4 *Ger.* Endersdorf. Świętokrzyskie, C Poland

Jefferson City *45 G5 state capital* Missouri, C USA
Jega *75 F4* Kebbi, NW Nigeria
Jehol *see* Chengde
Jēkabpils *106 D4 Ger.* Jakobstadt. Jēkabpils, S Latvia
Jelalabad *see* Jalālābād
Jelenia Góra *98 B4 Ger.* Hirschberg, Hirschberg im Riesengebirge, Hirschberg in Riesengebirge, Hirschberg in Schlesien. Dolnośląskie, SW Poland
Jelgava *106 C3 Ger.* Mitau. Jelgava, C Latvia
Jemappes *87 B6* Hainaut, S Belgium
Jember *138 D5 prev.* Djember. Jawa, C Indonesia
Jena *94 C4* Thüringen, C Germany
Jenīn *119 A6 var.* Janīn, Jinīn; *anc.* Engannim. N West Bank
Jerablus *see* Jarābulus
Jerada *70 D2* NE Morocco
Jerba, Île de *71 F2 var.* Djerba, Jazīrat Jarbah. *Island* E Tunisia
Jérémie *54 D3* SW Haiti
Jerez *see* Jeréz de la Frontera
Jeréz de la Frontera *92 C5 var.* Jerez; *prev.* Xeres. Andalucía, SW Spain
Jeréz de los Caballeros *92 C4* Extremadura, W Spain
Jericho *119 B6 Ar.* Arīḥā, *Heb.* Yeriḥo. E West Bank
Jerid, Chott el 87 E2 var. Shaṭṭ al Jarīd. *Salt lake* SW Tunisia
Jersey *89 D8 UK dependent territory* NW Europe
Jerusalem *103 H4 Ar.* El Quds, *Heb.* Yerushalayim; *anc.* Hierosolyma. *Country capital* (Israel) Jerusalem, NE Israel
Jerusalem *112 A4* Admin. region *district* E Israel
Jesenice *95 D7 Ger.* Assling. NW Slovenia
Jessore *135 G4* Khulna, W Bangladesh
Jesús María *64 C3* Córdoba, C Argentina
Jhānsi *134 D3* Uttar Pradesh, N India
Jhelum *134 C2* Punjab, NE Pakistan
Ji *see* Hebei
Ji *see* Jilin
Jiangmen *128 C6* Guangdong, S China
Jiangsu *128 D4 var.* Chiang-su, Jiangsu Sheng, Kiangsu, Su. Admin. *region province* E China
Jiangsu Sheng *see* Jiangsu
Jiangxi *128 C6 var.* Chiang-hsi, Gan, Jiangxi Sheng, Kiangsi. Admin. region *province* S China
Jiangxi Sheng *see* Jiangxi
Jiaxing *128 D5* Zhejiang, SE China
Jiayi *see* Chiai
Jibuti *see* Djibouti
Jiddah *121 A5 Eng.* Jedda. Makkah, W Saudi Arabia
Jih-k'a-tse *see* Xigazê
Jihlava *99 B5 Ger.* Iglau, *Pol.* Igława. Jihlavský Kraj, C Czech Republic
Jilib *73 D6 It.* Gelib. Jubbada Dhexe, S Somalia
Jilin *128 D3 var.* Chi-lin, Girin, Ji, Jilin Sheng, Kirin. Admin. region *province* NE China
Jilin *129 E3 var.* Chi-lin, Girin, Kirin; *prev.* Yungki, Yunki. Jilin, NE China
Jilin Sheng *see* Jilin
Jīma *73 C5 var.* Jimma, *It.* Gimma. C Ethiopia
Jimbolia *108 A4 Ger.* Hatzfeld, *Hung.* Zsombolya. Timiş, W Romania
Jiménez *50 D2* Chihuahua, N Mexico
Jimma *see* Jīma
Jimsar *126 C3* Xinjiang Uygur Zizhiqu, NW China
Jin *see* Shanxi
Jin *see* Tianjin Shi
Jinan *128 C4 var.* Chinan, Chi-nan, Tsinan. Shandong, E China

Jingdezhen *128 C5* Jiangxi, S China
Jinghong *128 A6 var.* Yunjinghong. Yunnan, SW China
Jinhua *128 D5* Zhejiang, SE China
Jinīn *see* Jenīn
Jining *127 F3* Shandong, E China
Jinja *73 C6* S Uganda
Jinotega *52 D3* Jinotega, NW Nicaragua
Jinotepe *52 D3* Carazo, SW Nicaragua
Jinsha Jiang *128 A5 river* SW China
Jinzhou *128 D3 var.* Chin-chou, Chinchow; *prev.* Chinhsien. Liaoning, NE China
Jisr ash Shadadi *see* Ash Shadādah
Jiu *108 B5 Ger.* Schil, Schyl, *Hung.* Zsil, Zsily. *River* S Romania
Jiujiang *128 C5* Jiangxi, S China
Jixi *129 F2* Heilongjiang, NE China
Jīzān *121 B6 var.* Qīzān. Jīzān, SW Saudi Arabia
Jizzakh *123 E2 Rus.* Dzhizak. Jizzakh Wiloyati, C Uzbekistan
João Pessoa *63 G2 prev.* Paraíba. *State capital* Paraíba, E Brazil
Jo'burg *see* Johannesburg
Jo-ch'iang *see* Ruoqiang
Jodhpur *134 C3* Rājasthān, NW India
Joensuu *85 E5* Itä-Suomi, E Finland
Jõetsu *131 C5 var.* Zyôetu. Niigata, Honshū, C Japan
Johanna Island *see* Anjouan
Johannesburg *78 D4 var.* Egoli, Erautini, Gauteng, *abbrev.* Jo'burg. Gauteng, NE South Africa
John Day River *46 C3 river* Oregon, NW USA
John o'Groats *88 C2* N Scotland, UK
Johnston Atoll *143 E1 US* *unincorporated territory* C Pacific Ocean
Johor Baharu *see* Johor Bahru
Johor Bahru *138 B3 var.* Johor Baharu, Johore Bahru. Johor, Peninsular Malaysia
Johore Bahru *see* Johor Bahru
Johore Strait *138 A1 Mal.* Selat Johor. *Strait* Malaysia/Singapore
Joinville *see* Joinville
Joinville *63 E4 var.* Joinvile. Santa Catarina, S Brazil
Jokkmokk *84 C3* Norrbotten, N Sweden
Joliet *40 B3* Illinois, N USA
Jonava *106 B4 Ger.* Janow, *Pol.* Janów. Jonava, C Lithuania
Jonesboro *42 B1* Arkansas, C USA
Joniškis *106 B4 Ger.* Janischken. Joniškis, N Lithuania
Jönköping *85 B7* Jönköping, S Sweden
Jonquière *39 E4* Quebec, SE Canada
Joplin *45 F5* Missouri, C USA
Jordan *119 B5 Ar.* Urdunn, *Heb.* HaYarden. *River* SW Asia
Jordan *119 B6 Ar.* Al Mamlakah al Urdunīyah al Hāshimīyah, Al Urdunn; *prev.* Transjordan. *Country* SW Asia

Jordan 119

Official name Hashemite Kingdom of Jordan
Formation 1946
Capital Amman
Population 5.1 million /143 people per sq mile (55 people per sq km)
Total area 35,637 sq miles (92,300 sq km)
Languages Arabic
Religions Muslim (mainly Sunni) 92%, other (mostly Christian) 8%
Ethnic mix Arab 98% (Palestinian 40%), Armenian 1%, Circassian 1%
Government Constitutional monarchy
Currency Jordanian dinar = 1,000 fils
Literacy rate 89.2%
Calorie consumption 2,749 kilocalories

Jorhāt *135 H3* Assam, NE India
Jos *75 G4* Plateau, C Nigeria
Joseph Bonaparte Gulf *146 D2 gulf* N Australia
Jos Plateau *75 G4 plateau* C Nigeria
Jotunheimen *85 A5 mountain range* S Norway
Joŭnié *118 A4 var.* Junīyah. W Lebanon
Joure *86 D2 Fris.* De Jouwer. Friesland, N Netherlands
Joutseno *85 E5* Etelä-Suomi, S Finland
Jowhar *see* Jawhar
JStorm Thurmond Reservoir *see* Clark Hill Lake
Juan Aldama *50 D3* Zacatecas, C Mexico
Juan de Fuca, Strait of *46 A1 strait* Canada/USA
Juan Fernández, Islas *57 A6 Eng.* Juan Fernandez Islands. *Island group* W Chile
Juazeiro *63 G2 prev.* Joazeiro. Bahia, E Brazil
Juazeiro do Norte *63 G2* Ceará, E Brazil
Juba *73 D6 Amh.* Genalē Wenz, *It.* Guiba, Som. Ganaane, Webi Jubba. *River* Ethiopia/Somalia
Juba *73 B5 var.* Jūbā. Bahr el Gabel, S Sudan
Júcar *93 E3 var.* Jucar. *River* C Spain
Juchitán *51 F5 var.* Juchitán de Zaragosa. Oaxaca, SE Mexico
Juchitán de Zaragosa *see* Juchitán
Judayyidat Hāmir *120 B3* S Iraq
Judenburg *95 D7* Steiermark, C Austria
Juigalpa *52 D3* Chontales, S Nicaragua
Juiz de Fora *63 F4* Minas Gerais, SE Brazil
Jujuy *see* San Salvador de Jujuy
Jūlā *see* Jālū
Juliaca *61 E4* Puno, SE Peru
Juliana Top *59 G3 mountain* C Suriname
Jumilla *93 E4* Murcia, SE Spain
Jumporn *see* Chumphon
Junction City *45 F4* Kansas, C USA
Juneau *36 D4 state capital* Alaska, USA
Junín *64 C4* Buenos Aires, E Argentina
Junīyah *see* Joŭnié
Junkseylon *see* Phuket
Jur *73 B5 river* C Sudan
Jura *88 B4 island* SW Scotland, UK
Jura *95 A7 canton* NW Switzerland
Jura *90 D4 department* E France
Jurbarkas *106 B4 Ger.* Georgenburg, Jurburg. Jurbarkas, W Lithuania
Jūrmala *106 C3* Rīga, C Latvia
Juruá, Rio *62 C2 var.* Rio Yuruá. *River* Brazil/Peru
Juruena, Rio *62 D3 river* W Brazil
Jutiapa *52 B2* Jutiapa, S Guatemala
Juticalpa *52 D2* Olancho, C Honduras
Juventud, Isla de la *54 A2 var.* Isla de Pinos, *Eng.* Isle of Youth; *prev.* The Isle of the Pines. *Island* W Cuba
Južna Morava *101 E5 Ger.* Südliche Morava. *River* SE Serbia and Montenegro (Yugo.)
Juzur Qarqannah *see* Kerkenah, Îles de
Jwaneng *78 C4* Southern, SE Botswana
Jylland *85 A7 Eng.* Jutland. *Peninsula* W Denmark
Jyväskylä *85 D5* Länsi-Suomi, W Finland

K

K2 *126 A4 Chin.* Qogir Feng, *Eng.* Mount Godwin Austen. *Mountain* China/Pakistan
Kaafu Atoll *see* Male' Atoll
Kaaimanston *59 G3* Sipaliwini, N Suriname
Kaakhka *122 C3 var.* Kaka. Akhalskiy Velayat, S Turkmenistan

Kaala *see* Caála
Kaamanen *84 D2 Lapp.* Gámas. Lappi, N Finland
Kaapstad *see* Cape Town
Kaaresuvanto *84 C3 Lapp.* Gárassavon. Lappi, N Finland
Kabale *73 B6* SW Uganda
Kabinda *see* Cabinda
Kabinda *77 D7* Kasai Oriental, SE Dem. Rep. Congo
Kābol *see* Kābul
Kabompo *78 C2 river* W Zambia
Kābul *123 E4 var.* Kabul, *Per.* Kābol. *Country capital* (Afghanistan) Kābul, E Afghanistan
Kabul *see* Kābul
Kabwe *78 D2* Central, C Zambia
Kachchh, Gulf of *134 B4 var.* Gulf of Cutch, Gulf of Kutch. *Gulf* W India
Kachchh, Rann of *134 B4 var.* Rann of Kachh, Rann of Kutch. *Salt marsh* India/Pakistan
Kachh, Rann of *see* Kachchh, Rann of
Kadan Kyun *137 B5 prev.* King Island. *Island* Mergui Archipelago, S Myanmar
Kadavu *145 E4 prev.* Kandavu. *Island* S Fiji
Kadoma *78 D3 prev.* Gatooma. Mashonaland West, C Zimbabwe
Kadugli *72 B4* Southern Kordofan, S Sudan
Kaduna *75 G4* Kaduna, C Nigeria
Kadzhi-Say *123 G2 Kir.* Kajisay. Issyk-Kul'skaya Oblast', NE Kyrgyzstan
Kaédi *74 C3* Gorgol, S Mauritania
Kaffa *see* Feodosiya
Kafue *78 C2 river* C Zambia
Kafue *78 D2* Lusaka, SE Zambia
Kaga Bandoro *76 C4 prev.* Fort-Crampel. Nana-Grébizi, C Central African Republic
Kâghet *74 D1 var.* Karet. *Physical region* N Mauritania
Kagi *see* Chiai
Kagoshima *131 B8 var.* Kagosima. Kagoshima, Kyūshū, SW Japan
Kagoshima-wan *131 A8 bay* SW Japan
Kagosima *see* Kagoshima
Kahmard, Daryā-ye *123 E4 prev.* Darya-i-Surkhab. *River* NE Afghanistan
Kahraman Maraş *see* Kahramanmaraş
Kahramanmaraş *116 D4 var.* Kahraman Maraş, Maraş, Marash. Kahramanmaraş, S Turkey
Kaiapoi *151 C6* Canterbury, South Island, NZ
Kaifeng *128 C4* Henan, C China
Kai, Kepulauan *139 F4 prev.* Kei Islands. *Island group* Maluku, SE Indonesia
Kaikohe *150 C2* Northland, North Island, NZ
Kaikoura *151 C5* Canterbury, South Island, NZ
Kaikoura Peninsula *151 C5 peninsula* South Island, NZ
Kainji Lake *see* Kainji Reservoir
Kainji Reservoir *75 F4 var.* Kainji Lake. *Reservoir* W Nigeria
Kaipara Harbour *150 C2 harbour* North Island, NZ
Kairouan *71 E2 var.* Al Qayrawān. E Tunisia
Kaisaria *see* Kayseri
Kaiserslautern *95 A5* Rheinland-Pfalz, SW Germany
Kaišiadorys *107 B5* Kaišiadorys, S Lithuania
Kaitaia *150 C2* Northland, North Island, NZ
Kajaani *84 E4 Swe.* Kajana. Oulu, C Finland
Kaka *see* Kaakhka
Kake *36 D4* Kupreanof Island, Alaska, USA
Kakhovka *109 F4* Khersons'ka Oblast', S Ukraine

Kakhovs'ka Vodoskhovyshche 109 F4 *Rus.* Kakhovskoye Vodokhranilishche. *Reservoir* SE Ukraine
Kākināda 132 D1 *prev.* Cocanada. Andhra Pradesh, E India
Kaktovik 36 D2 Alaska, USA
Kalahari Desert 78 B4 *desert* Southern Africa
Kalamariá 104 B4 Kentrikí Makedonía, N Greece
Kalámata 105 B6 *prev.* Kalámai. Pelopónnisos, S Greece
Kalamazoo 40 C3 Michigan, N USA
Kalambaka *see* Kalampáka
Kálamos 105 C5 Attikí, C Greece
Kalampáka 104 B4 *var.* Kalambaka. Thessalía, C Greece
Kalanchak 109 F4 Khersons'ka Oblast', S Ukraine
Kalarash *see* Călăraşi
Kalasin 136 D4 *var.* Muang Kalasin. Kalasin, E Thailand
Kalāt 123 E5 *Per.* Qalāt. Zābul, S Afghanistan
Kālat 134 B2 *var.* Kelat, Khelat. Baluchistān, SW Pakistan
Kalbarri 147 A5 Western Australia
Kalecik 116 C3 Ankara, N Turkey
Kalemie 77 E6 *prev.* Albertville. Shaba, SE Dem. Rep. Congo
Kale Sultanie *see* Çanakkale
Kalgan *see* Zhangjiakou
Kalgoorlie 147 B6 Western Australia
Kalima 77 D6 Maniema, E Dem. Rep. Congo
Kalimantan 138 D4 *Eng.* Indonesian Borneo. *Geopolitical region* Borneo, C Indonesia
Kálimnos *see* Kálymnos
Kaliningrad 106 A4 Kaliningradskaya Oblast', W Russian Federation
Kaliningradskaya Oblast' 106 B4 *var.* Kaliningrad. Admin. region *province and enclave* W Russian Federation
Kalinkavichy 107 C7 *Rus.* Kalinkovichi. Homyel'skaya Voblasts', SE Belarus
Kalispell 44 B1 Montana, NW USA
Kalisz 98 C4 *Ger.* Kalisch, *Rus.* Kalish; *anc.* Calisia. Wielkopolskie, C Poland
Kalix 84 D4 Norrbotten, N Sweden
Kalixälven 84 D3 *river* N Sweden
Kallaste 106 E3 *Ger.* Krasnogor. Tartumaa, SE Estonia
Kallavesi 85 E5 *lake* SE Finland
Kalloní 105 D5 Lésvos, E Greece
Kalmar 85 C7 *var.* Calmar. Kalmar, S Sweden
Kalmthout 87 C5 Antwerpen, N Belgium
Kalpáki 104 A4 Ípeiros, W Greece
Kalpeni Island 132 B3 *island* Lakshadweep, India, N Indian Ocean
Kaluga 111 B5 Kaluzhskaya Oblast', W Russian Federation
Kalush 108 C2 *Pol.* Kałusz. Ivano-Frankivs'ka Oblast', W Ukraine
Kalutara 132 D4 Western Province, SW Sri Lanka
Kalvarija 107 B5 *Pol.* Kalwaria. Marijampolė, S Lithuania
Kalyān 134 C5 Mahārāshtra, W India
Kálymnos 105 D6 *var.* Kálimnos. *Island* Dodekánisos, Greece, Aegean Sea
Kama 110 D4 *river* NW Russian Federation
Kamarang 59 F3 W Guyana
Kamchatka *see* Kamchatka, Poluostrov
Kamchatka, Poluostrov 115 G3 *Eng.* Kamchatka. *Peninsula* E Russian Federation
Kamensk-Shakhtinskiy 111 B6 Rostovskaya Oblast', SW Russian Federation

Kamina 77 D7 Shaba, S Dem. Rep. Congo
Kamishli *see* Al Qāmishlī
Kamloops 37 E5 British Columbia, SW Canada
Kammu Seamount 152 C2 *undersea feature* N Pacific Ocean
Kampala 73 B6 *country capital* (Uganda) S Uganda
Kâmpóng Cham 137 D6 *prev.* Kompong Cham. Kâmpóng Cham, C Cambodia
Kâmpóng Chhnăng 137 D6 *prev.* Kompong. Kâmpóng Chhnăng, C Cambodia
Kâmpóng Saôm 137 D6 *prev.* Kompong Som, Sihanoukville. Kâmpóng Saôm, SW Cambodia
Kâmpóng Spoe 137 D6 *prev.* Kompong Speu. Kâmpóng Spœ, S Cambodia
Kâmpôt 137 D6 Kâmpôt, SW Cambodia
Kam"yanets'-Podil's'kyy 108 C3 *Rus.* Kamenets-Podol'skiy. Khmel'nyts'ka Oblast', W Ukraine
Kam"yanka-Dniprovs'ka 109 F3 *Rus.* Kamenka Dneprovskaya. Zaporiz'ka Oblast', SE Ukraine
Kamyshin 111 B6 Volgogradskaya Oblast', SW Russian Federation
Kanaky *see* New Caledonia
Kananga 77 D6 *prev.* Luluabourg. Kasai Occidental, S Dem. Rep. Congo
Kananur *see* Cannanore
Kanara *see* Karnātaka
Kanash 111 C5 Chuvashskaya Respublika, W Russian Federation
Kanazawa 131 C5 Ishikawa, Honshū, SW Japan
Kanbe 136 B4 Yangon, SW Myanmar
Kānchipuram 132 C2 *prev.* Conjeeveram. Tamil Nādu, SE India
Kandahār 123 E5 *Per.* Qandahār. Kandahār, S Afghanistan
Kandalakša *see* Kandalaksha
Kandalaksha 110 B2 *var.* Kandalakša, *Fin.* Kantalahti. Murmanskaya Oblast', NW Russian Federation
Kandangan 138 D4 Borneo, C Indonesia
Kandava 106 C3 *Ger.* Kandau. Tukums, W Latvia
Kandi 75 F4 N Benin
Kandy 132 D3 Central Province, C Sri Lanka
Kane Fracture Zone 66 B4 *tectonic feature* NW Atlantic Ocean
Kaneohe 47 A8 *Haw.* Kāne'ohe. Oahu, Hawaii, USA, C Pacific Ocean
Kangān 120 D4 Būshehr, S Iran
Kangaroo Island 149 A7 *island* South Australia
Kangertittivaq 83 E4 *Dan.* Scoresby Sund. *Fjord* E Greenland
Kangikajik 83 E4 *var.* Kap Brewster. *Headland* E Greenland
Kaniv 109 E2 *Rus.* Kanëv. Cherkas'ka Oblast', C Ukraine
Kaniv's'ke Vodoskhovyshche 109 E2 *Rus.* Kanevskoye Vodokhranilishche. *Reservoir* C Ukraine
Kanjiža 100 D2 *Ger.* Altkanischa, *Hung.* Magyarkanizsa, Ókanizsa; *prev.* Stara Kanjiža. Serbia, N Serbia and Montenegro (Yugo.)
Kankaanpää 85 D5 Länsi-Suomi, W Finland
Kankakee 40 B3 Illinois, N USA
Kankan 74 D4 Haute-Guinée, E Guinea
Kannur *see* Cannanore
Kano 75 G4 Kano, N Nigeria
Kānpur 135 E3 *Eng.* Cawnpore. Uttar Pradesh, N India
Kansas 49 F1 *off.* State of Kansas; also known as Jayhawker State, Sunflower State. *State* C USA
Kansas 45 F5 Kansas, C USA
Kansas City 45 F4 Kansas, C USA
Kansas City 45 F4 Missouri, C USA

Kansas River 45 F5 *river* Kansas, C USA
Kansk 115 E4 Krasnoyarskiy Kray, S Russian Federation
Kansu *see* Gansu
Kantalahti *see* Kandalaksha
Kántanos 105 C7 Kriti, Greece, E Mediterranean Sea
Kantemirovka 111 B6 Voronezhskaya Oblast', W Russian Federation
Kanton 145 F3 *var.* Abariringa, Canton Island; *prev.* Mary Island. *Atoll* Phoenix Islands, C Kiribati
Kanye 78 C4 Southern, SE Botswana
Kaohsiung 128 D6 *var.* Gaoxiong, *Jap.* Takao, Takow. S Taiwan
Kaolack 74 B3 *var.* Kaolak. W Senegal
Kaolak *see* Kaolack
Kaolan *see* Lanzhou
Kaoma 78 C2 Western, W Zambia
Kap Brewster *see* Kangikajik
Kapelle 87 B5 Zeeland, SW Netherlands
Kapellen 87 C5 Antwerpen, N Belgium
Kap Farvel *see* Uummannarsuaq
Kapka, Massif du 76 C2 *mountain range* E Chad
Kaplangky, Plato 122 C2 *ridge* Turkmenistan/Uzbekistan
Kapoeta 73 C5 Eastern Equatoria, SE Sudan
Kaposvár 99 C7 Somogy, SW Hungary
Kappeln 94 B2 Schleswig-Holstein, N Germany
Kapstad *see* Cape Town
Kaptsevichy 107 C7 *Rus.* Koptsevichi. Homyel'skaya Voblasts', SE Belarus
Kapuas, Sungai 138 C4 *prev.* Kapoeas. *River* Borneo, C Indonesia
Kapuskasing 38 C4 Ontario, S Canada
Kapyl' 107 C6 *Rus.* Kopyl'. Minskaya Voblasts', C Belarus
Kap York *see* Innaanganeq
Kara-Balta 123 F2 Chuyskaya Oblast', N Kyrgyzstan
Karabil', Vozvyshennost' 122 D3 *mountain range* S Turkmenistan
Karabük 116 C2 Karabük, NW Turkey
Karāchi 134 B3 Sind, SE Pakistan
Karadeniz *see* Black Sea
Karadeniz Boğazı *see* İstanbul Boğazı
Karaferiye *see* Véroia
Karaganda 114 C4 *Kaz.* Qaraghandy. Karaganda, C Kazakhstan
Karaginskiy, Ostrov 115 H2 *island* E Russian Federation
Karak *see* Al Karak
Kara-Kala 122 C3 *var.* Garrygala. Balkanskiy Velayat, W Turkmenistan
Karakax *see* Moyu
Karaklısse *see* Ağrı
Karakol 123 G2 *var.* Przheval'sk. Issyk-Kul'skaya Oblast', NE Kyrgyzstan
Karakol 123 G2 *var.* Karakolka. Issyk-Kul'skaya Oblast', NE Kyrgyzstan
Karakolka *see* Karakol
Karakoram Range 134 D1 *mountain range* C Asia
Karaköse *see* Ağrı
Kara Kum *see* Garagumy
Kara Kum Canal *see* Garagumskiy Kanal
Karakumskiy Kanal *see* Garagumskiy Kanal
Karamai *see* Karamay
Karaman 116 C4 Karaman, S Turkey
Karamay 126 B2 *var.* Karamai, Kelamayi, *prev.* K'o-la-ma-i. Xinjiang Uygur Zizhiqu, NW China
Karamea Bight 151 B5 *gulf* South Island, NZ

Karapelit 104 E1 *Rom.* Stejarul. Dobrich, NE Bulgaria
Kara-Say 123 G2 Issyk-Kul'skaya Oblast', NE Kyrgyzstan
Karasburg 78 B4 Karas, S Namibia
Kara Sea *see* Karskoye More
Karatau 114 C5 *Kaz.* Qarataū. Zhambyl, S Kazakhstan
Karavás 105 B7 Kýthira, S Greece
Karbalā' 120 B3 *var.* Kerbala, Kerbela. S Iraq
Kardhítsa *see* Karditsa
Karditsa 105 B5 *var.* Kardhítsa. Thessalía, C Greece
Kärdla 106 C2 *Ger.* Kertel. Hiiumaa, W Estonia
Karet *see* Kâghet
Kargi 116 C2 Çorum, N Turkey
Kargilik *see* Yecheng
Kariba 78 D2 Mashonaland West, N Zimbabwe
Kariba, Lake 78 D3 *reservoir* Zambia/Zimbabwe
Karibib 78 B3 Erongo, C Namibia
Karies *see* Karyés
Karigasniemi 84 D2 *Lapp.* Garegegasnjárga. Lappi, N Finland
Karimata, Selat 138 C4 *strait* W Indonesia
Karīmnagar 134 D5 Andhra Pradesh, C India
Karin 72 D4 Woqooyi Galbeed, N Somalia
Kariot *see* Ikaría
Karkiníts'ka Zatoka 109 E4 *Rus.* Karkinitskiy Zaliv. *Gulf* S Ukraine
Karkük *see* Kirkūk
Karlovac 100 B3 *Ger.* Karlstadt, *Hung.* Károlyváros. Karlovac, C Croatia
Karlovy Vary 99 A5 *Ger.* Karlsbad; *prev. Eng.* Carlsbad. Karlovarský Kraj, W Czech Republic
Karlskrona 85 C7 Blekinge, S Sweden
Karlsruhe 95 B6 *var.* Carlsruhe. Baden-Württemberg, SW Germany
Karlstad 85 B6 Värmland, C Sweden
Karnāl 134 D2 Haryāna, N India
Karnātaka 132 C1 *var.* Kanara; *prev.* Maisur, Mysore. Admin. region *state* W India
Karnobat 104 D2 Burgas, E Bulgaria
Karnul *see* Kurnool
Karpaten *see* Carpathian Mountains
Kárpathos 105 E7 *It.* Scarpanto; *anc.* Carpathos, Carpathus. *Island* SE Greece
Kárpathos 105 E7 Kárpathos, SE Greece
Karpaty *see* Carpathian Mountains
Karpenísi 105 B5 *prev.* Karpenísion. Stereá Ellás, C Greece
Kars 117 F2 *var.* Qars. Kars, NE Turkey
Kārsava 106 D4 *Ger.* Karsau; *prev. Rus.* Korsovka. Ludza, E Latvia
Karskiye Vorota, Proliv 110 E2 *Eng.* Kara Strait. *Strait* N Russian Federation
Karskoye More 114 D2 *Eng.* Kara Sea. *Sea* Arctic Ocean
Karyés 104 C4 *var.* Karies. Ágion Óros, N Greece
Kárystos 105 C6 *var.* Káristos. Évvoia, C Greece
Kasai 77 D6 *var.* Cassai, Kassai. *River* Angola/Dem. Rep. Congo
Kasaji 77 D7 Shaba, S Dem. Rep. Congo
Kasama 78 D1 Northern, N Zambia
Kāsargod 132 B2 Kerala, SW India
Kāshān 120 C3 Eşfahān, C Iran
Kashi 126 A3 *Chin.* Kaxgar, K'o-shih, *Uigh.* Kashgar. Xinjiang Uygur Zizhiqu, NW China
Kasongo 77 D6 Maniema, E Dem. Rep. Congo
Kasongo-Lunda 77 C7 Bandundu, SW Dem. Rep. Congo
Kásos 105 D7 *island* SE Greece
Kaspiysk 111 B8 Respublika Dagestan, SW Russian Federation

Kassai *see* Kasai
Kassala 72 *C4* Kassala, E Sudan
Kassel 94 *B4 prev.* Cassel. Hessen, C Germany
Kasserine 71 *E2 var.* Al Qaşrayn. W Tunisia
Kastamonu 116 *C2 var.* Castamoni, Kastamuni. Kastamonu, N Turkey
Kastamuni *see* Kastamonu
Kastaneá 104 *B4* Kentrikí Makedonía, N Greece
Kastéli 105 *C7* Kríti, Greece, E Mediterranean Sea
Kastoría 104 *B4* Dytikí Makedonía, N Greece
Kástro 105 *C6* Sífnos, Kykládes, Greece, Aegean Sea
Kastsyukovichi 107 *E7 Rus.* Kostyukovichi. Mahilyowskaya Voblasts', E Belarus
Kastsyukowka 107 *D7 Rus.* Kostyukovka. Homyel'skaya Voblasts', SE Belarus
Kasulu 73 *B7* Kigoma, W Tanzania
Kasumigaura 131 *D5 lake* Honshū, S Japan
Katahdin, Mount 41 *G1 mountain* Maine, NE USA
Katalla 36 *C3* Alaska, USA
Katana *see* Qaṭanā
Katanning 147 *B7* Western Australia
Katawaz *see* Zarghūn Shahr
Katchall Island 133 *F3 island* Nicobar Islands, India, NE Indian Ocean
Katerini 104 *B4* Kentrikí Makedonía, N Greece
Katha 136 *B2* Sagaing, N Myanmar
Katherine 148 *A2* Northern Territory, N Australia
Kathmandu 124 *C3 prev.* Kantipur. *Country capital* (Nepal) Central, C Nepal
Katikati 150 *D3* Bay of Plenty, North Island, NZ
Katima Mulilo 78 *C3* Caprivi, NE Namibia
Katiola 74 *D4* C Côte d'Ivoire
Káto Achaḯa 105 *B5 var.* Kato Ahaia, Káto Akhaía. Dytikí Ellás, S Greece
Kato Ahaia *see* Káto Achaḯa
Káto Akhaía *see* Káto Achaḯa
Katoúna 105 *A5* Dytikí Ellás, C Greece
Katowice 99 *C5 Ger.* Kattowitz. Śląskie, S Poland
Katsina 75 *G3* Katsina, N Nigeria
Kattaqŭrghon 123 *E2 Rus.* Kattakurgan. Samarqand Wiloyati, C Uzbekistan
Kattavía 105 *E7* Ródos, Dodekánisos, Greece, Aegean Sea
Kattegat 85 *B7 Dan.* Kattegatt. *Strait* N Europe
Kauai 47 *A7 Haw.* Kaua'i. *Island* Hawaiian Islands, Hawaii, USA, C Pacific Ocean
Kaufbeuren 95 *C6* Bayern, S Germany
Kaunas 106 *B4 var.* Kauen, *Pol.* Kowno; *prev. Rus.* Kovno. Kaunas, C Lithuania
Kavadarci 101 *E6* Turk. Kavadar. C FYR Macedonia
Kavajë 101 *L1* Tirana, W Albania
Kavála 104 *C3 prev.* Kaválla. Anatolikí Makedonía kai Thráki, NE Greece
Kāvali 132 *D2* Andhra Pradesh, E India
Kavango *see* Cubango
Kavaratti Island 132 *A3 island* Lakshadweep, India, N Indian Ocean
Kavarna 104 *E2* Dobrich, NE Bulgaria
Kavengo *see* Cubango
Kavīr, Dasht-e 120 *D3 var.* Great Salt Desert. *Salt pan* N Iran
Kavīr-e Lūt *see* Lūt, Dasht-e
Kawagoe 131 *D5* Saitama, Honshū, S Japan
Kawasaki 130 *A2* Kanagawa, Honshū, S Japan
Kawerau 150 *E3* Bay of Plenty, North Island, NZ

Kaya 75 *E3* C Burkina faso
Kayan 136 *B4* Yangon, SW Myanmar
Kayan, Sungai 138 *D3 prev.* Kajan. *River* Borneo, C Indonesia
Kayes 74 *C3* Kayes, W Mali
Kayseri 116 *D3 var.* Kaisaria; *anc.* Caesarea Mazaca, Mazaca. Kayseri, C Turkey
Kazach'ye 115 *F2* Respublika Sakha (Yakutiya), NE Russian Federation
Kazakhskiy Melkosopochnik 114 *C4 Eng.* Kazakh Uplands, Kirghiz Steppe, *Kaz.* Saryarqa. *Uplands* C Kazakhstan
Kazakhstan 114 *B4 var.* Kazakstan, *Kaz.* Qazaqstan, Qazaqstan Respublikasy; *prev.* Kazakh Soviet Socialist Republic, *Rus.* Kazakhskaya SSR. *Country* C Asia

Kazakhstan 114

Official name Republic of Kazakhstan
Formation 1991
Capital Astana
Population 16.1 million / 15 people per sq mile (6 people per sq km)
Total area 1,049,150 sq miles (2,717,300 sq km)
Languages Kazakh, Russian, German, Uighur, Korean
Religions Muslim (mainly Sunni) 50%, Russian Orthodox 13%, other 37%
Ethnic mix Kazakh 53%, Russian 30%, Ukranian 4%, German 2%, Tartar 2%, other 9%
Government Presidential democracy
Currency Tenge = 100 tein
Literacy rate 99%
Calorie consumption 2,991 kilocalories

Kazakh Uplands *see* Kazakhskiy Melkosopochnik
Kazan' 111 *C5* Respublika Tatarstan, W Russian Federation
Kazanlŭk 104 *D2 prev.* Kazanlik. Stara Zagora, C Bulgaria
Kazbegi *see* Kazbek
Kazbek 117 *F1 var.* Kazbegi, *Geor.* Mqinvartsveri. *Mountain* N Georgia
Kāzerūn 120 *D4* Fārs, S Iran
Kazvin *see* Qazvīn
Kéa 105 *C6 prev.* Kéos, *anc.* Ceos. *Island* Kykládes, Greece, Aegean Sea
Kéa 105 *C6* Kéa, Kykládes, Greece, Aegean Sea
Kea, Mauna 47 *B8 mountain* Hawaii, USA, C Pacific Ocean
Kéamu *see* Aneityum
Kearney 45 *E4* Nebraska, C USA
Keban Baraji 117 *E3 reservoir* C Turkey
Kebkabiya 72 *A4* Northern Darfur, W Sudan
Kebnekaise 84 *C3 mountain* N Sweden
Kecskemét 99 *D7* Bács-Kiskun, C Hungary
Kediri 138 *D5* Jawa, C Indonesia
Kędzierzyn-Kole 99 *C5 Ger.* Heydebrech. Opolskie, S Poland
Keelung *see* Chilung
Keetmanshoop 78 *B4* Karas, S Namibia
Kefallinía 105 *A5 var.* Kefaloniá. *Island* Iónioi Nísoi, Greece, C Mediterranean Sea
Kefallonía *see* Kefallinía
Kefe *see* Feodosiya
Kehl 95 *A6* Baden-Württemberg, SW Germany
Keila 106 *D2 Ger.* Kegel. Harjumaa, NW Estonia
Keïta 75 *F3* Tahoua, C Niger
Keitele 84 *D4 lake* C Finland
Keith 149 *B7* South Australia
Kēk-Art 123 *G2 prev.* Alaykel', Alay-Kuu. Oshskaya Oblast', SW Kyrgyzstan
Kékes 99 *C6 mountain* N Hungary

Kelamayi *see* Karamay
Kelang *see* Klang
Kelat *see* Kālat
Kelifskiy Uzboy 122 *D3 salt marsh* E Turkmenistan
Kelkit Çayı 117 *E3 river* N Turkey
Kelmė 106 *B4* Kelmė, C Lithuania
Kélo 76 *B4* Tandjilé, SW Chad
Kelowna 37 *E5* British Columbia, SW Canada
Kelso 46 *B2* Washington, NW USA
Keluang 138 *B3 var.* Kluang. Johor, Peninsular Malaysia
Kem' 110 *B3* Respublika Kareliya, NW Russian Federation
Kemah 117 *E3* Erzincan, E Turkey
Kemaman *see* Cukai
Kemerovo 114 *D4 prev.* Shcheglovsk. Kemerovskaya Oblast', C Russian Federation
Kemi 84 *D4* Lappi, NW Finland
Kemijärvi 84 *D3 Swe.* Kemiträsk. Lappi, N Finland
Kemijoki 84 *D3 river* NW Finland
Kemin 123 *G2 prev.* Bystrovka. Chuyskaya Oblast', N Kyrgyzstan
Kempele 84 *D4* Oulu, C Finland
Kempten 95 *B7* Bayern, S Germany
Kendal 89 *D5* NW England, UK
Kendari 139 *E4* Sulawesi, C Indonesia
Kenedy 49 *G4* Texas, SW USA
Kenema 74 *C4* SE Sierra Leone
Këneurgench 122 *C2 Turkm.* Köneürgench; *prev.* Kunya-Urgench. Dashkhovuzskiy Velayat, N Turkmenistan
Kenge 77 *C6* Bandundu, SW Dem. Rep. Congo
Keng Tung 136 *C3 var.* Kentung. Shan State, E Myanmar
Kénitra 70 *C2 prev.* Port-Lyautey. NW Morocco
Kennett 45 *H5* Missouri, C USA
Kennewick 46 *C2* Washington, NW USA
Kenora 38 *A3* Ontario, S Canada
Kenosha 40 *B3* Wisconsin, N USA
Kentau 114 *B5* Yuzhnyy Kazakhstan, S Kazakhstan
Kentucky 40 *C5 off.* Commonwealth of Kentucky; also known as The Bluegrass State. *State* C USA
Kentucky Lake 40 *B5 reservoir* Kentucky/Tennessee, S USA
Kentung *see* Keng Tung
Kenya 73 *C6 Country* E Africa

Kenya 73

Official name Republic of Kenya
Formation 1963
Capital Nairobi
Population 31.3 million / 139 people per sq mile (54 people per sq km)
Total area 224,961 sq miles (582,650 sq km)
Languages Kiswahili, English, Kikuyu, Luo, Kamba
Religions Christian 60%, Traditional beliefs 25%, Muslim 6%, other 9%
Ethnic mix Kikuyu 21%, Luhya 14%, Luo 13%, Kamba 11%, Kalenjin 11%, other 30%
Government Presidential democracy
Currency Kenya shilling = 100 cents
Literacy rate 82.4%
Calorie consumption 1,965 kilocalories

Keokuk 45 *G4* Iowa, C USA
Kępno 98 *C4* Wielkopolskie, C Poland
Keppel Island *see* Niuatoputapu
Kepulauan Sangihe *see* Sangir, Kepulauan
Kerak *see* Al Karak
Kerala 132 *C2 state* S India
Kerasunt *see* Giresun
Keratea *see* Keratéa
Keratéa 105 *C6 var.* Keratea. Attikí, C Greece
Kerbala *see* Karbalā'

Kerbela *see* Karbalā'
Kerch 109 *G5 Rus.* Kerch'.
Respublika Krym, SE Ukraine
Kerchens'ka Protska *see* Kerch Strait
Kerchenskiy Proliv *see* Kerch Strait
Kerch Strait 109 *G4 var.* Bosporus Cimmerius, Enikale Strait, *Rus.* Kerchenskiy Proliv, *Ukr.* Kerchens'ka Protska. *Strait* Black Sea/Sea of Azov
Kerguelen 141 *C7 island* C French Southern and Antarctic Territories
Kerguelen Plateau 141 *C7 undersea feature* S Indian Ocean
Kerí 105 *A6* Zákynthos, Iónioi Nísoi, Greece, C Mediterranean Sea
Kerikeri 150 *D2* Northland, North Island, NZ
Kerkenah, Îles de 102 *D4 var.* Kerkenna Islands, *Ar.* Juzur Qarqannah. *Island group* E Tunisia
Kerkenna Islands *see* Kerkenah, Îles de
Kerki 123 *D3* Lebapskiy Velayat, E Turkmenistan
Kérkira *see* Kérkyra
Kerkrade 87 *D6* Limburg, SE Netherlands
Kerkuk *see* Kirkūk
Kérkyra 104 *A4 var.* Kérkira, *Eng.* Corfu. *Island* Iónioi Nísoi, Greece, C Mediterranean Sea
Kermadec Islands 152 *C4 island group* NZ, SW Pacific Ocean
Kermadec Trench 143 *E4 undersea feature* SW Pacific Ocean
Kermān 120 *D3 var.* Kirman; *anc.* Carmana. Kermān, C Iran
Kermānshāh *see* Bākhtarān
Kerrville 49 *F4* Texas, SW USA
Kerulen 127 *E2 Chin.* Herlen He, *Mong.* Herlen Gol. *River* China/Mongolia
Kerýneia 102 *C5 var.* Girne, Kyrenia. N Cyprus
Kesennuma 130 *D4* Miyagi, Honshū, C Japan
Keszthely 99 *C7* Zala, SW Hungary
Ketchikan 36 *D4* Revillagigedo Island, Alaska, USA
Kętrzyn 98 *D2 Ger.* Rastenburg. Warmiusko-Mazurskie, NE Poland
Kettering 89 *D6* C England, UK
Kettering 40 *C4* Ohio, N USA
Keuruu 85 *D5* Länsi-Suomi, W Finland
Keweenaw Peninsula 40 *B1 peninsula* Michigan, N USA
Key Largo 43 *F5* Key Largo, Florida, SE USA
Key West 43 *E5* Florida Keys, Florida, SE USA
Khabarovsk 115 *G4* Khabarovskiy Kray, SE Russian Federation
Khadera *see* Ḥadera
Khairpur 134 *B3* Sind, SE Pakistan
Khalij al 'Aqabah *see* Aqaba, Gulf of
Khalij al 'Arabī *see* Gulf, The
Khalij-e Fars *see* Gulf, The
Khalkidhikí *see* Chalkidikí
Khalkís *see* Chalkída
Khambhāt, Gulf of 134 *C4 Eng.* Gulf of Cambay. *Gulf* W India
Khamīs Mushayt 121 *B6 var.* Hamīs Musait. 'Asīr, SW Saudi Arabia
Khānābād 123 *E3* Kunduz, NE Afghanistan
Khān al Baghdādī *see* Al Baghdādī
Khandwa 134 *D4* Madhya Pradesh, C India
Khanh *see* Soc Trăng
Khaniá *see* Chaniá
Khanka, Lake 129 *E2 var.* Hsing-k'ai Hu, Lake Hanka, *Chin.* Xingkai Hu, *Rus.* Ozero Khanka. *Lake* China/Russian Federation
Khanthabouli 136 *D4 prev.* Savannakhét. Savannakhét, S Laos
Khanty-Mansiysk 114 *C3 prev.* Ostyako-Voguls'k. Khanty-Mansiyskiy Avtonomnyy Okrug, C Russian Federation

Kragujevac 100 D4 Serbia, C Serbia and Montenegro (Yugo.)
Kra, Isthmus of 137 B6 *isthmus* Malaysia/Thailand
Kraków 99 D5 *Eng.* Cracow, *Ger.* Krakau; *anc.* Cracovia. Małopolskie, S Poland
Králāñh 137 D5 Siĕmréab, NW Cambodia
Kraljevo 100 D4 *prev.* Rankoviĉevo. Serbia, C Serbia and Montenegro (Yugo.)
Kramators'k 109 G3 *Rus.* Kramatorsk. Donets'ka Oblast', SE Ukraine
Kramfors 85 C5 Västernorrland, C Sweden
Kranéa 104 B4 Dytikí Makedonía, N Greece
Kranj 95 D7 *Ger.* Krainburg. NW Slovenia
Krāslava 106 D4 Krāslava, SE Latvia
Krasnaye 107 C5 *Rus.* Krasnoye. Minskaya Voblasts', C Belarus
Krasnoarmeysk 111 C6 Saratovskaya Oblast', W Russian Federation
Krasnodar 111 A7 *prev.* Ekaterinodar, Yekaterinodar. Krasnodarskiy Kray, SW Russian Federation
Krasnodon 109 H3 Luhans'ka Oblast', E Ukraine
Krasnohvardiys'ke 109 F4 *Rus.* Krasnogvardeyskoye. Respublika Krym, S Ukraine
Krasnokamensk 115 F4 Chitinskaya Oblast', S Russian Federation
Krasnokamsk 111 D5 Permskaya Oblast', W Russian Federation
Krasnoperekops'k 109 F4 *Rus.* Krasnoperekopsk. Respublika Krym, S Ukraine
Krasnovodskiy Zaliv 122 A2 *Turkm.* Krasnowodsk Aylagy. *Lake gulf* W Turkmenistan
Krasnoyarsk 114 D4 Krasnoyarskiy Kray, S Russian Federation
Krasnystaw 98 E4 *Rus.* Krasnostav. Lubelskie, E Poland
Krasnyy Kut 111 C6 Saratovskaya Oblast', W Russian Federation
Krasnyy Luch 109 H3 *prev.* Krindachevka. Luhans'ka Oblast', E Ukraine
Krāvanh, Chuŏr Phnum 137 C6 *Eng.* Cardamom Mountains, *Fr.* Chaîne des Cardamomes. *Mountain range* W Cambodia
Krefeld 94 A4 Nordrhein-Westfalen, W Germany
Kremenchuk 109 F2 *Rus.* Kremenchug. Poltavs'ka Oblast', NE Ukraine
Kremenchuts'ke Vodoskhovyshche 109 F2 *Eng.* Kremenchuk Reservoir, *Rus.* Kremenchugskoye Vodokhranilishche. *Reservoir* C Ukraine
Kremenets' 108 C2 *Pol.* Krzemieniec, *Rus.* Kremenets. Ternopil's'ka Oblast', W Ukraine
Kreminna 109 G2 *Rus.* Kremennaya. Luhans'ka Oblast', E Ukraine
Kresena *see* Kresna
Kresna 104 C3 *var.* Kresena. Blagoevgrad, SW Bulgaria
Kretikon Delagos *see* Kritikó Pélagos
Kretinga 106 B3 *Ger.* Krottingen. Kretinga, NW Lithuania
Krishna 132 C1 *prev.* Kistna. *River* C India
Krishnagiri 132 C2 Tamil Nādu, SE India
Kristiansand 85 A6 *var.* Christiansand. Vest-Agder, S Norway
Kristianstad 85 B7 Skåne, S Sweden
Kristiansund 84 A4 *var.* Christiansund. Møre og Romsdal, S Norway
Kríti 105 C7 *Eng.* Crete. *Island* Greece, Aegean Sea

Kritikó Pélagos 105 D7 *var.* Kretikon Delagos, *Eng.* Sea of Crete; *anc.* Mare Creticum. *Sea* Greece, Aegean Sea
Križevci 100 B2 *Ger.* Kreuz, *Hung.* Kőrös. Varaždin, NE Croatia
Krk 100 A3 *It.* Veglia; *anc.* Curieta. *Island* NW Croatia
Krolevets' 109 F1 *Rus.* Krolevets. Sums'ka Oblast', NE Ukraine
Kronach 95 C5 Bayern, E Germany
Kroonstad 78 D4 Free State, C South Africa
Kropotkin 111 A7 Krasnodarskiy Kray, SW Russian Federation
Krosno 99 D5 *Ger.* Krossen. Podkarpackie, SE Poland
Krosno Odrzańskie 98 B3 *Ger.* Crossen, Kreisstadt. Lubuskie, W Poland
Krško 95 E8 *Ger.* Gurkfeld; *prev.* Videm-Krško. E Slovenia
Kruhlaye 107 D6 *Rus.* Krugloye. Mahilyowskaya Voblasts', E Belarus
Kruja *see* Krujë
Krujë 101 C6 *var.* Kruja, *It.* Croia. Durrës, C Albania
Krummau *see* Český Krumlov
Krung Thep 137 C5 *var.* Krung Thep Mahanakhon, *Eng.* Bangkok. *Country capital* (Thailand) Bangkok, C Thailand
Krung Thep, Ao 137 C5 *var.* Bight of Bangkok. *Bay* S Thailand
Krung Thep Mahanakhon *see* Krung Thep
Krupki 107 D6 *Rus.* Krupki. Minskaya Voblasts', C Belarus
Krychaw 107 E7 *Rus.* Krichëv. Mahilyowskaya Voblasts', E Belarus
Krym *see* Crimea
Krymskaya Oblast' *see* Crimea
Kryms'ki Hory 109 F5 *mountain range* S Ukraine
Kryms'kyy Pivostriv 109 F5 *peninsula* S Ukraine
Krynica 99 D5 *Ger.* Tannenhof. Małopolskie, S Poland
Kryve Ozero 109 E3 Odes'ka Oblast', SW Ukraine
Kryvyy Rih 109 F3 *Rus.* Krivoy Rog. Dnipropetrovs'ka Oblast', SE Ukraine
Ksar al Kabir *see* Ksar-el-Kebir
Ksar al Soule *see* Er-Rachidia
Ksar-el-Kebir 70 C2 *var.* Alcázar, Ksar al Kabir, Ksar-el-Kébir, *Ar.* Al-Kasr al-Kebir, Al-Qsar al-Kbir, *Sp.* Alcazarquivir. NW Morocco
Ksar-el-Kébir *see* Ksar-el-Kebir
Kuala Dungun *see* Dungun
Kuala Lumpur 138 B3 *country capital* (Malaysia) Kuala Lumpur, Peninsular Malaysia
Kuala Terengganu 138 B3 *var.* Kuala Trengganu. Terengganu, Peninsular Malaysia
Kuala Trengganu *see* Kuala Terengganu
Kualatungkal 138 B4 Sumatera, W Indonesia
Kuang-chou *see* Guangzhou
Kuang-hsi *see* Guangxi Zhuangzu Zizhiqu
Kuang-tung *see* Guangdong
Kuang-yuan *see* Guangyuan
Kuantan 138 B3 Pahang, Peninsular Malaysia
Kuban' 109 G5 *var.* Hypanis. *River* SW Russian Federation
Kubango *see* Cubango
Kuching 138 C3 *prev.* Sarawak. Sarawak, East Malaysia
Küchnay Darweyshān 122 D5 Helmand, S Afghanistan
Kuçova *see* Kuçovë
Kuçovë 101 C6 *var.* Kuçova; *prev.* Qyteti Stalin. Berat, C Albania
Kudara *see* Ghūdara
Kudus 138 C5 *prev.* Koedoes. Jawa, C Indonesia
Kuei-chou *see* Guizhou
Kuei-lin *see* Guilin
Kuei-Yang *see* Guiyang
Kueyang *see* Guiyang

Kugluktuk 53 E3 *var.* Qurlurtuuq *prev.* Coppermine. Nunavut, NW Canada
Kuhmo 84 E4 Oulu, E Finland
Kühnö *see* Kihnu
Kuibyshev *see* Kuybyshevskoye Vodokhranilishche
Kuito 78 B2 *Port.* Silva Porto. Bié, C Angola
Kuji 130 D3 *var.* Kuzi. Iwate, Honshū, C Japan
Kukës 101 D5 *var.* Kukësi. Kukës, NE Albania
Kukësi *see* Kukës
Kukong *see* Shaoguan
Kukukhoto *see* Hohhot
Kula Kangri 135 G3 *var.* Kulhakangri. *Mountain* Bhutan/China
Kuldīga 106 B3 *Ger.* Goldingen. Kuldīga, W Latvia
Kuldja *see* Yining
Kulhakangri *see* Kula Kangri
Kullorsuaq 82 D2 *var.* Kuvdlorssuak. C Greenland
Kulmsee *see* Chełmża
Kŭlob 123 F3 *Rus.* Kulyab. SW Tajikistan
Kulu 116 D3 Konya, W Turkey
Kulunda Steppe 114 C4 *Kaz.* Qulyndy Zhazyghy, *Rus.* Kulundinskaya Ravnina. *Grassland* Kazakhstan/Russian Federation
Kum *see* Qom
Kuma 111 B7 *river* SW Russian Federation
Kumamoto 131 A7 Kumamoto, Kyūshū, SW Japan
Kumanovo 101 E5 *Turk.* Kumanova. N FYR Macedonia
Kumasi 75 E5 *prev.* Coomassie. C Ghana
Kumayri *see* Gyumri
Kumba 77 A5 Sud-Ouest, W Cameroon
Kumertau 106 D6 Respublika Bashkortostan, W Russian Federation
Kumo 75 G4 Gombe, E Nigeria
Kumon Range 136 B2 *mountain range* N Myanmar
Kumul *see* Hami
Kunashiri *see* Kunashir, Ostrov
Kunashir, Ostrov 130 E1 *var.* Kunashiri. *Island* Kuril'skiye Ostrova, SE Russian Federation
Kunda 106 E2 Lääne-Virumaa, NE Estonia
Kunduz 123 E3 *var.* Kondoz, Kondūz, Qondūz, *Per.* Kondūz. Kunduz, NE Afghanistan
Kuneitra *see* Al Qunayţirah
Kunene *see* Cunene
Kungsbacka 85 B7 Halland, S Sweden
Kungur 111 D5 Permskaya Oblast', NW Russian Federation
Kunlun Mountains *see* Kunlun Shan
Kunlun Shan 126 B4 *Eng.* Kunlun Mountains. *Mountain range* NW China
Kunming 128 B6 *var.* K'un-ming; *prev.* Yunnan. Yunnan, SW China
K'un-ming *see* Kunming
Kununurra 146 D3 Western Australia
Kuopio 85 E5 Itä-Suomi, C Finland
Kupang 139 E5 *prev.* Koepang. Timor, C Indonesia
Kup"yans'k 109 G2 *Rus.* Kupyansk. Kharkivs'ka Oblast', E Ukraine
Kura 117 H4 *Az.* Kür, *Geor.* Mtkvari, *Turk.* Kura Nehri. *River* SW Asia
Kurashiki 131 B6 *var.* Kurasiki. Okayama, Honshū, SW Japan
Kurasiki *see* Kurashiki
Kurdistan 117 F4 *cultural region* SW Asia
Kürdzhali 104 D3 *var.* Kirdzhali. Kürdzhali, S Bulgaria
Kure 131 B7 Hiroshima, Honshū, SW Japan
Küre Dağları 116 C2 *mountain range* N Turkey
Kuressaare 106 C2 *Ger.* Arensburg; *prev.* Kingissepp. Saaremaa, W Estonia

Kureyka 112 D2 *river* N Russian Federation
Kuria Muria Islands *see* Ḩalāniyāt, Juzur al
Kurile Islands *see* Kuril'skiye Ostrova
Kurile-Kamchatka Depression *see* Kurile Trench
Kurile Trench 113 F3 *var.* Kurile-Kamchatka Depression. *Undersea feature* NW Pacific Ocean
Kuril'sk 130 E1 Kuril'skiye Ostrova, Sakhalinskaya Oblats', SE Russian Federation
Kuril'skiye Ostrova 115 H4 *Eng.* Kurile Islands. *Island group* SE Russian Federation
Ku-ring-gai 148 E1 New South Wales, SE Australia
Kurnool 132 C1 *var.* Karnul. Andhra Pradesh, S India
Kursk 111 A6 Kurskaya Oblast', W Russian Federation
Kuršumlija 101 D5 Serbia, S Serbia and Montenegro (Yugo.)
Kuruktag 126 C3 *mountain range* NW China
Kurume 131 A7 Fukuoka, Kyūshū, SW Japan
Kurupukari 59 F3 C Guyana
Kurzeme 106 B3 *Eng.* Courland, *Ger.* Kurland. *Former province* W Latvia
Kushiro 130 D2 *var.* Kusiro. Hokkaidō, NE Japan
Kusiro *see* Kushiro
Kuskokwim Mountains 36 C3 *mountain range* Alaska, USA
Kuźnica 98 E2 Podlaskie, NE Poland
Kustanay *see* Kostanay
Küstence *see* Constanţa
Küstendje *see* Constanţa
Kütahya 116 B3 *prev.* Kutaia. Kütahya, W Turkey
Kutai *see* Mahakam, Sungai
K'ut'aisi 117 F2 W Georgia
Kūt al 'Amārah *see* Al Kūt
Kut al Imara *see* Al Kūt
Kutaradja *see* Bandaaceh
Kutaraja *see* Bandaaceh
Kutch, Gulf of *see* Kachchh, Gulf of
Kutch, Rann of *see* Kachchh, Rann of
Kutina 100 B3 Sisak-Moslavina, NE Croatia
Kutno 98 C3 Łódzkie, C Poland
Kuujjuaq 39 E2 *prev.* Fort-Chimo. Quebec, E Canada
Kuusamo 84 E3 Oulu, Finland
Kuvango *see* Cubango
Kuvdlorssuak *see* Kullorsuaq
Kuwait 120 C4 *var.* Dawlat al Kuwait, Koweit, Kuwait. *Country* SW Asia

Kuwait 120

Official name	State of Kuwait
Formation	1961
Capital	Kuwait City
Population	2 million / 291 people per sq mile (112 people per sq km)
Total area	6880 sq miles (17,820 sq km)
Languages	Arabic, English
Religions	Muslim (mainly Sunni) 85%, Christian, Hindu and other 15%
Ethnic mix	Kuwaiti 45%, other Arab 35%, South Asian 9%, Iranian 4%, other 7%
Government	Constitutional monarchy
Currency	Kuwaiti dinar = 1,000 fils
Literacy rate	82.6%
Calorie consumption	3,132 kilocalories

Kuwait *see* Al Kuwayt
Kuwait City *see* Al Kuwayt
Kuwajleen *see* Kwajalein Atoll
Kuwayt 120 C3 E Iraq

Kuybyshev Reservoir *see*
Kuybyshevskoye
Vodokhranilishche
Kuybyshevskoye
Vodokhranilishche *111 C5 var.*
Kuibyshev, *Eng.* Kuybyshev
Reservoir. *Reservoir* W Russian
Federation
Kuytun *126 B2* Xinjiang Uygur
Zizhiqu, NW China
Kuzi *see* Kuji
Kuznetsk *111 B6* Penzenskaya
Oblast', W Russian Federation
Kvaløya *84 C2 island* N Norway
Kvarnbergsvattnet *84 B4 var.*
Frostviken. *Lake* N Sweden
Kvarner *100 A3 var.* Carnaro, *It.*
Quarnero. *Gulf* W Croatia
Kvitøya *83 G1 island* NE Svalbard
Kwajalein Atoll *144 C1 var.*
Kuwajleen. *Atoll* Ralik Chain,
C Marshall Islands
Kwando *see* Cuando
Kwangchow *see* Guangzhou
Kwangju *129 E4 off.* Kwangju-
gwangyŏksi, *var.* Guangju,
Kwangchu, *Jap.* Kōshū. SW South
Korea
Kwango *77 C7 Port.* Cuango. *River*
Angola/Dem. Rep. Congo *see also*
Cuango
Kwango *see* Cuango
Kwangsi *see* Guangxi Zhuangzu
Zizhiqu
Kwangsi Chuang Autonomous
Region *see* Guangxi Zhuangzu
Zizhiqu
Kwangtung *see* Guangdong
Kwangyuan *see* Guangyuan
Kwanza *see* Cuanza
Kweichow *see* Guizhou
Kweichu *see* Guiyang
Kweilin *see* Guilin
Kweisui *see* Hohhot
Kweiyang *see* Guiyang
Kwekwe *78 D3 prev.* Que Que.
Midlands, C Zimbabwe
Kwesui *see* Hohhot
Kwidzyń *98 C2 Ger.* Marienwerder.
Pomorskie, N Poland
Kwigillingok *36 C3* Alaska, USA
Kwilu *77 C6 river* W Dem. Rep.
Congo
Kwito *see* Cuito
Kyabé *76 C4* Moyen-Chari, S Chad
Kyaikkami *137 B5 prev.* Amherst.
Mon State, S Myanmar
Kyaiklat *136 B4* Irrawaddy,
SW Myanmar
Kyaikto *136 B4* Mon State,
S Myanmar
Kyakhta *115 E5* Respublika
Buryatiya, S Russian Federation
Kyaukse *136 B3* Mandalay,
C Myanmar
Kyjov *99 C5 Ger.* Gaya. Brněnský
Kraj, SE Czech Republic
Kykládes *105 D6 var.* Kikládhes,
Eng. Cyclades. *Island group*
SE Greece
Kými *105 C5 prev.* Kími. Évvoia,
C Greece
Kyōto *131 C6* Kyōto, Honshū,
SW Japan
Kyparissía *105 B6 var.* Kiparissía.
Pelopónnisos, S Greece
Kyrá Panagía *105 C5 island* Vóreioi
Sporádes, Greece, Aegean Sea
Kyrenia *see* Kerýneia
Kyrgyzstan *123 F2 var.* Kirghizia;
prev. Kirgizskaya SSR, Kirghiz
SSR, Republic of Kyrgyzstan.
Country C Asia

Kyrgyzstan (continued)

Ethnic mix Kyrgyz 57%,
Russian 19%, Uzbek 13%,Tartar 2%,
Ukranian 2%, other 7%
Government Presidential
democracy
Currency Som = 100 teen
Literacy rate 97%
Calorie consumption 2,871
kilocalories

Kýthira *105 C7 var.* Kíthira, *It.*
Cerigo; *Lat.* Cythera. *Island*
S Greece
Kýthnos *105 C6 var.* Kíthnos,
Thermiá, *It.* Termia; *anc.* Cythnos.
Island Kykládes, Greece, Aegean
Sea
Kýthnos *105 C6* Kýthnos, Kykládes,
Greece, Aegean Sea
Kythréa *102 C5* N Cyprus
Kyūshū *131 B7 var.* Kyûsyû. *Island*
SW Japan
Kyushu-Palau Ridge *125 F3 var.*
Kyusyu-Palau Ridge. *Undersea*
feature W Pacific Ocean
Kyustendil *104 B2 anc.* Pautalia.
Kyustendil, W Bulgaria
Kyûsyû *see* Kyūshū
Kyusyu-Palau Ridge *see* Kyushu-
Palau Ridge
Kyyiv *109 E2 Eng.* Kiev, *Rus.* Kiyev.
Country capital (Ukraine)
Kyyivs'ka Oblast', N Ukraine
Kyyivs'ke Vodoskhovyshche *109*
E1 Eng. Kiev Reservoir, *Rus.*
Kiyevskoye Vodokhranilishche.
Reservoir N Ukraine
Kyzyl *114 D4* Respublika Tyva,
C Russian Federation
Kyzyl Kum *122 D2 var.* Kizil Kum,
Qizil Qum, Qizilqum. *Desert*
Kazakhstan/Uzbekistan
Kyzylorda *114 B5 var.* Kyzyl-orda,
Qizil Orda, *Kaz.* Qyzylorda; *prev.*
Perovsk. Kyzylorda, S Kazakhstan
Kyzyl-Suu *123 G2 var.* Pokrovka.
Issyk-Kul'skaya Oblast',
NE Kyrgyzstan
Kyzyl-orda *see* Kyzylorda

L

La Algaba *92 C4* Andalucía,
S Spain
Laamu Atoll *see* Hadhdhunmathi
Atoll
Laarne *87 B5* Oost-Vlaanderen,
NW Belgium
La Asunción *59 E1* Nueva Esparta,
NE Venezuela
Laâyoune *70 B3 var.* Aaiún.
Dependent territory capital (Western
Sahara) NW Western Sahara
la Baule-Escoublac *90 A4* Loire-
Atlantique, NW France
Labé *74 C4* Moyenne-Guinée,
NW Guinea
La Blanquilla *see* Blanquilla, Isla
Laborec *99 E5 Hung.* Laborca. *River*
E Slovakia
Labrador *39 F2 cultural region*
Newfoundland and Labrador,
SW Canada
Labrador Basin *34 E3 var.* Labrador
Sea Basin. *Undersea feature*
Labrador Sea
Labrador Sea *82 A4 sea*
NW Atlantic Ocean
Labrador Sea Basin *see* Labrador
Basin
Labutta *137 A5* Irrawaddy,
SW Myanmar
Laç *101 C6 var.* Laci. Lezhë,
C Albania
La Calera *64 B4* Valparaíso, C Chile
La Carolina *92 D4* Andalucía,
S Spain
Laccadive Islands *see* Lakshadweep
La Ceiba *52 D2* Atlántida,
N Honduras
Lachanás *104 B3* Kentrikí
Makedonía, N Greece
La Chaux-de-Fonds *95 A7*
Neuchâtel, W Switzerland

Lachlan River *149 C6 river* New
South Wales, SE Australia
Laci *see* Laç
la Ciotat *91 D6 anc.* Citharista.
Bouches-du-Rhône, SE France
La Concepción *58 C1* Zulia,
NW Venezuela
La Concepción *53 E5 var.*
Concepción. Chiriquí, W Panama
La Condamine *91 C8* NW Andorra
Laconia *41 G2* New Hampshire,
NE USA
La Crosse *40 A2* Wisconsin,
N USA
La Cruz *52 D4* Guanacaste,
NW Costa Rica
Lacus Asphaltites *see* Dead Sea
Ladoga, Lake *see* Ladozhskoye
Ozero
Ladozhskoye Ozero *110 B3 Eng.*
Lake Ladoga, *Fin.* Laatokka. *Lake*
NW Russian Federation
Ladysmith *40 B2* Wisconsin, N USA
Lae *144 B3* Morobe, W PNG
La Esperanza *52 C2* Intibucá,
SW Honduras
Lafayette *40 C4* Indiana, N USA
Lafayette *42 B3* Louisiana, S USA
La Fé *54 A2* Pinar del Río, W Cuba
Lafia *75 G4* Nassarawa, C Nigeria
la Flèche *90 B4* Sarthe, NW France
Lagdo, Lac de *76 B4 lake*
N Cameroon
Laghouat *70 D2* N Algeria
Lago dos Gansos *see* Goose Lake
Lago General Carrera *see* Buenos
Aires, Lago
Lago Nyassa *see* Nyasa, Lake
Lago Pampa Aullagas *see* Poopó,
Lago
Lagos *92 B5 anc.* Lacobriga. Faro,
S Portugal
Lagos *75 F5* Lagos, SW Nigeria
Lagos de Moreno *51 E4* Jalisco,
SW Mexico
Lagouira *70 A4* SW Western Sahara
La Grande *46 C3* Oregon, NW USA
La Guaira *66 B4* Distrito Federal,
N Venezuela
Laguna Merín *see* Mirim Lagoon
Lagunas *64 B1* Tarapacá, N Chile
Lagunillas *61 G4* Santa Cruz,
SE Bolivia
La Habana *54 B2 var.* Havana.
Country capital (Cuba) Ciudad de
La Habana, W Cuba
Lahat *138 B4* Sumatera,
W Indonesia
La Haye *see* 's-Gravenhage
Laholm *85 B7* Halland, S Sweden
Lahore *134 D2* Punjab, NE
Pakistan
Lahr *95 A6* Baden-Württemberg,
S Germany
Lahti *85 D5 Swe.* Lahtis. Etelä-
Suomi, S Finland
Laï *76 B4 prev.* Behagle, De Behagle.
Tandjilé, S Chad
Lai Châu *136 D3* Lai Châu,
N Vietnam
Laila *see* Laylá
La Junta *44 D5* Colorado, C USA
Lake Charles *42 A3* Louisiana,
S USA
Lake City *43 E3* Florida, SE USA
Lake District *89 C5 physical region*
NW England, UK
Lake Havasu City *48 A2* Arizona,
SW USA
Lake Jackson *49 H4* Texas, SW USA
Lakeland *43 E4* Florida, SE USA
Lakeside *47 C8* California, W USA
Lakewood *44 D4* Colorado, C USA
Lakhnau *see* Lucknow
Lakonikós Kólpos *105 B7 gulf*
S Greece
Laksely *84 D2* Finnmark,
N Norway
Lakshadweep *132 A3 Eng.*
Laccadive Islands. *Island group*
India, N Indian Ocean
la Laon *see* Laon
Lalibela *72 C4* N Ethiopia
La Libertad *52 B1* Petén,
N Guatemala
La Ligua *64 B4* Valparaíso, C Chile
Lalín *92 C1* Galicia, NW Spain

Lalitpur *135 F3* Central, C Nepal
La Louvière *87 B6* Hainaut,
S Belgium
La Maçana *see* La Massana
la Maddalena *96 A4* Sardegna, Italy,
C Mediterranean Sea
la Manche *see* English Channel
Lamar *44 D5* Colorado, C USA
La Marmora, Punta *97 A5 mountain*
Sardegna, Italy, C Mediterranean
Sea
La Massana *91 A8 var.* La Maçana.
W Andorra
Lambaréné *77 A6* Moyen-Ogooué,
W Gabon
Lamego *92 C2* Viseu, N Portugal
Lamesa *49 E3* Texas, SW USA
Lamezia *97 D6* Calabria, SE Italy
Lamía *105 B5* Stereá Ellás, C Greece
Lamoni *45 F4* Iowa, C USA
Lampang *136 C4 var.* Muang
Lampang. Lampang,
NW Thailand
Lámpeia *105 B6* Dytikí Ellás,
S Greece
Lanbi Kyun *137 B6 prev.* Sullivan
Island. *Island* Mergui Archipelago,
S Myanmar
Lancang Jiang *see* Mekong
Lancaster *47 C7* California, W USA
Lancaster *89 D5* NW England, UK
Lancaster *41 F4* Pennsylvania,
NE USA
Lancaster Sound *37 F2 sound*
Nunavut, N Canada
Lan-chou *see* Lanzhou
Lan-chow *see* Lanzhou
Landen *87 C6* Vlaams Brabant,
C Belgium
Lander *44 C3* Wyoming, C USA
Landerneau *90 A3* Finistère,
NW France
Landes *91 B5 department* SW France
Land's End *89 B8 headland*
SW England, UK
Landshut *95 C6* Bayern,
SE Germany
Langar *123 E2 Rus.* Lyangar.
Nawoiy Wiloyati, C Uzbekistan
Langfang *128 D4* Hebei, E China
Langkawi, Pulau *137 B7 island*
Peninsular Malaysia
Langres *90 D4* Haute-Marne,
N France
Langsa *138 A3* Sumatera,
W Indonesia
Lang Shan *127 E3 mountain range*
N China
Lang Son *136 D3 var.* Langson.
Lang Son, N Vietnam
Langson *see* Lang Son
Lang Suan *137 B6* Chumphon,
SW Thailand
Languedoc *91 C6 cultural region*
S France
Länkäran *117 H3 Rus.* Lenkoran'.
S Azerbaijan
Lansing *40 C3 state capital*
Michigan, N USA
Lanta, Ko *137 B7 island* S Thailand
Lantau Island *128 A2 Cant.* Tai Yue
Shan, *Chin.* Landao. *Island* Hong
Kong, S China
Lan-ts'ang Chiang *see* Mekong
Lanzarote *70 B3 island* Islas Canarias,
Spain, NE Atlantic Ocean
Lanzhou *128 B4 var.* Lan-chou,
Lanchow, Lan-chow; *prev.* Kaolan.
Gansu, C China
Lao Cai *136 D3* Lao Cai, N Vietnam
Laojunmiao *see* Yumen
Laon *90 D3 var.* la Laon; *anc.*
Laudunum. Aisne, N France
La Orchila, Isla *58 D1 island*
N Venezuela
La Oroya *60 C3* Junín, C Peru
Laos *136 D4 Country* SE Asia

Laos 136

Official name Lao People's
Democratic Republic
Formation 1953
Capital Vientiane
Population 5.4 million / 59 people
per sq mile (23 people per sq km)

Kyrgyzstan 123

Official name Kyrgyz Republic
Formation 1991
Capital Bishkek
Population 5 million /65 people
per sq mile (25 people per sq km)
Total area 76,641 sq miles
(198,500 sq km)
Languages Kyrgyz, Russian
Religions Muslim (mainly Sunni)
70%, Russian Orthodox 30%

Laos (continued)

Total area 91,428 sq miles
(236,800 sq km)
Languages Lao, Mon-Khmer,
Chinese, Vao, Vietnamese, French
Religions Buddhist 85%, other
(including Animist) 15%
Ethnic mix Lao Loum 66%, Lao
Theung 30%, Lao Soung 2%,
other 2%
Government One-party republic
Currency New kip = 100 cents
Literacy rate 48.7%
Calorie consumption 2,266
kilocalories

La Palma 70 A3 island Islas
Canarias, Spain, NE Atlantic
Ocean
La Palma 53 G5 Darién,
SE Panama
La Paz 61 F4 var. La Paz de
Ayacucho. Country capital
(Bolivia-legislative and
administrative capital) La Paz,
W Bolivia
La Paz 50 B3 Baja California Sur,
NW Mexico
La Paz, Bahía de 50 B3 bay
W Mexico
La Paz de Ayacucho see La Paz
La Perouse Strait 130 D1 Jap. Sōya-
kaikyō, Rus. Proliv Laperuza.
Strait Japan/Russian Federation
Lápithos 102 C5 NW Cyprus
Lapland 84 D3 Fin. Lappi, Swe.
Lappland. Cultural region N Europe
La Plata 64 D4 Buenos Aires,
E Argentina
Lappeenranta 85 E5 Swe.
Villmanstrand. Etelä-Suomi, S
Finland
Lappi see Lapland
Lappland see Lapland
Lapta see Lápithos
Laptev Sea see Laptevykh, More
Laptevykh, More 115 E2 Eng.
Laptev Sea. Sea Arctic Ocean
Lapua 85 D5 Swe. Lappo. Länsi-
Suomi, W Finland
La Puebla see La Pobla
Łapy 98 E3 Podlaskie
La Quiaca 64 C2 Jujuy,
N Argentina
L'Aquila 96 C4 var. Aquila, Aquila
degli Abruzzo. Abruzzo, C Italy
Laracha 92 B1 Galicia, NW Spain
Laramie 44 C4 Wyoming, C USA
Laramie Mountains 44 C3 mountain
range Wyoming, C USA
Laredo 93 E1 Cantabria, N Spain
Laredo 49 F5 Texas, SW USA
Largo, Cayo 54 B2 island W Cuba
Lario see Como, Lago di
La Rioja 93 E2 La Rioja,
NW Argentina
Lárisa 104 B4 var. Larissa. Thessalía,
C Greece
Larissa see Lárisa
Lārkāna 134 B3 var. Larkhana. Sind,
SE Pakistan
Larkana see Lārkāna
Larnaca see Lárnaka
Lárnaka 102 C5 var. Larnaca,
Larnax. SE Cyprus
Larnax see Lárnaka
la Rochelle 90 B4 anc. Rupella.
Charente-Maritime, W France
la Roche-sur-Yon 90 B4 prev.
Bourbon Vendée, Napoléon-
Vendée. Vendée, NW France
La Roda 93 E3 Castilla-La Mancha,
C Spain
La Romana 55 E3 E Dominican
Republic
Larvotto 91 C8 N Monaco
La-sa see Lhasa
Las Cabezas de San Juan 92 C5
Andalucía, S Spain
Las Cruces 48 D3 New Mexico,
SW USA
La See d'Urgel 93 G1 var. La Seu
d'Urgell, Seo de Urgel. Cataluña,
NE Spain

La Serena 64 B3 Coquimbo, C Chile
La Seu d'Urgell see La See d'Urgel
la Seyne-sur-Mer 91 D6 Var,
SE France
Lashio 136 B3 Shan State,
E Myanmar
Lashkar Gāh 122 D5 var. Lash-Kar-
Gar'. Helmand, S Afghanistan
Lash-Kar-Gar' see Lashkar Gāh
La Sila 97 D6 mountain range
SW Italy
La Sirena 52 D3 Región Autónoma
Atlántico Sur, E Nicaragua
Łask 98 C4 Łódzkie, C Poland
Las Lomitas 64 D2 Formosa,
N Argentina
La Solana 93 E4 Castilla-La
Mancha, C Spain
Las Palmas de Gran Canaria 70 A3
Gran Canaria, Islas Canarias,
Spain, NE Atlantic Ocean
La Spezia 96 B3 Liguria, NW Italy
Lassa see Lhasa
Las Tablas 53 F5 Los Santos,
S Panama
Las Tunas 54 C2 var. Victoria de las
Tunas. Las Tunas, E Cuba
Las Vegas 47 D7 Nevada, W USA
Latacunga 60 B1 Cotopaxi,
C Ecuador
la Teste 91 B5 Gironde, SW France
Latina 97 C5 prev. Littoria. Lazio,
C Italy
La Tortuga, Isla 59 E1 var. Isla
Tortuga. Island N Venezuela
La Tuque 39 E4 Quebec, SE Canada
Latvia 106 C3 Ger. Lettland, Latv.
Latvija, Latvijas Republika; prev.
Latvian SSR, Rus. Latviyskaya
SSR. Country NE Europe

Latvia 106

Official name Republic of Latvia
Formation 1991
Capital Riga
Population 2.4 million / 96 people
per sq mile (37 people per sq km)
Total area 24,938 sq miles
(64,589 sq km)
Languages Latvian, Russian
Religions Lutheran 55%, Roman
Catholic 24%, Russian Orthodox 9%,
other 12%
Ethnic mix Latvian 57%,
Russian 32%, Belarussian 4%,
Ukrainian 4%, Polish 2%, other 2%
Government Presidential democracy
Currency Lat = 100 santimi
Literacy rate 99%
Calorie consumption 2,855
kilocalories

Laudunum see Laon
Lauenburg see Lębork
Lauenburg in Pommern see Lębork
Lau Group 145 E4 island group E Fiji
Launceston 149 C8 Tasmania,
SE Australia
La Unión 93 F4 Murcia, SE Spain
La Unión 52 C2 Olancho,
C Honduras
Laurel 42 C3 Mississippi, S USA
Laurel 44 C2 Montana, NW USA
Laurentian Highlands see
Laurentian Mountains
Laurentian Mountains 39 E3 var.
Laurentian Highlands, Fr. Les
Laurentides. Plateau
Newfoundland and
Labrador/Quebec, Canada
Lauria 97 D6 Basilicata, S Italy
Laurinburg 43 F1 North Carolina,
SE USA
Lauru see Choiseul
Lausanne 95 A7 It. Losanna. Vaud,
SW Switzerland
Laut Banda see Banda Sea
Laut, Pulau 138 D4 prev. Laoet.
Island Borneo, C Indonesia
Laval 90 B3 Mayenne,
NW France
Laval 38 D4 Quebec, SE Canada
La Vega 55 E3 var. Concepción de la
Vega. C Dominican Republic
La Vila Joiosa see Villajoyosa

Lávrio 105 C6 prev. Lávrion. Attikí,
C Greece
Lawrence 41 G3 Massachusetts,
NE USA
Lawrenceburg 42 C1 Tennessee,
S USA
Lawton 49 F2 Oklahoma, C USA
La Yarada 61 E4 Tacna, SW Peru
Laylá 121 C5 var. Laila. Ar Riyāḍ,
C Saudi Arabia
Lazarev Sea 154 B1 sea Antarctica
Lázaro Cárdenas 51 E5 Michoacán
de Ocampo, SW Mexico
Læsø 85 B7 island N Denmark
Leamhcán see Lucan
Leamington 38 C5 Ontario, S Canada
Lebak 139 E3 Mindanao,
S Philippines
Lebanon 118 A4 Ar. Al Lubnān, Fr.
Liban. Country SW Asia

Lebanon 118

Official name Republic of Lebanon
Formation 1941
Capital Beirut
Population 3.6 million / 897 people
per sq mile (346 people per sq km)
Total area 4,015 sq miles
(10,400 sq km)
Languages Arabic, French,
Armenian, Assyrian
Religions Muslim 70%,
Christian 30%
Ethnic mix Arab 94%, Armenian
4%, other 2%
Government Multiparty republic
Currency Lebanese pound =
100 piastres
Literacy rate 86%
Calorie consumption 3,155
kilocalories

Lebanon 45 G5 Missouri, C USA
Lebanon 41 G2 New Hampshire,
NE USA
Lebanon 46 B3 Oregon, NW USA
Lebap 122 D2 Lebapskiy Velayat,
NE Turkmenistan
Lebedyn 109 F2 Rus. Lebedin.
Sums'ka Oblast', NE Ukraine
Lębork 98 C2 var. Lebórk, Ger.
Lauenburg, Lauenburg in
Pommern. Pomorskie,
N Poland
Lebrija 92 C5 Andalucía, S Spain
Lebu 65 A5 Bío Bío, C Chile
le Cannet 91 D6 Alpes-Maritimes,
SE France
Le Cap see Cap-Haïtien
Lecce 97 E6 Puglia, SE Italy
Lechainá 105 B6 var. Lehena,
Lekhainá. Dytikí Ellás,
S Greece
Leduc 37 E5 Alberta, SW Canada
Leech Lake 45 F2 lake Minnesota,
N USA
Leeds 89 D5 N England, UK
Leek 86 E2 Groningen,
NE Netherlands
Leer 94 A3 Niedersachsen,
NW Germany
Leeuwarden 86 D1 Fris. Ljouwert.
Friesland, N Netherlands
Leeuwin, Cape 142 A5 headland
Western Australia
Leeward Islands 55 G3 island group
E West Indies
Leeward Islands see Sotavento,
Ilhas de
Lefkáda 105 A5 It. Santa Maura;
prev. Levkás, anc. Leucas. Island
Iónioi Nísoi, Greece,
C Mediterranean Sea
Lefkáda 105 A5 prev. Levkás.
Lefkáda, Iónioi Nísoi, Greece,
C Mediterranean Sea
Lefká Óri 105 C7 mountain range
Kriti, Greece, E Mediterranean Sea
Lefkímmi 105 A5 var. Levkímmi.
Kérkyra, Iónioi Nísoi, Greece,
C Mediterranean Sea
Legaspi 139 E2 off. Legaspi City.
Luzon, N Philippines
Legnica 98 B4 Ger. Liegnitz.
Dolnośląskie

le Havre 90 B3 Eng. Havre; prev. le
Havre-de-Grâce. Seine-Maritime,
N France
Lehena see Lechainá
Leicester 89 D6 Lat. Batae
Coritanorum. C England, UK
Leiden 86 B3 prev. Leyden, anc.
Lugdunum Batavorum. Zuid-
Holland, W Netherlands
Leie 90 B2 Fr. Lys. River
Belgium/France
Leinster 89 B6 Ir. Cúige Laighean.
Cultural region E Ireland
Leipsoí 105 E6 island Dodekánisos,
Greece, Aegean Sea
Leipzig 94 C4 Pol. Lipsk; hist.
Leipsic, anc. Lipsia. Sachsen,
E Germany
Leiria 92 B3 anc. Collipo. Leiria,
C Portugal
Leirvik 85 A6 Hordaland,
S Norway
Lek 86 C4 river SW Netherlands
Lekhainá see Lechainá
Lekhchevo 104 C2 Montana,
NW Bulgaria
Leksand 85 C5 Kopparberg,
C Sweden
Lelystad 86 D3 Flevoland,
C Netherlands
le Mans 90 B3 Sarthe, NW France
Lemesós 102 C5 var. Limassol.
SW Cyprus
Lena 115 F3 river NE Russian
Federation
Lena Tablemount 141 B7 undersea
feature S Indian Ocean
Len Dao 128 C8 island S Spratly
Islands
Lengshuitan 128 C6 Hunan,
S China
Leninabad see Khūjand
Leninakan see Gyumri
Lenine 109 G5 Rus. Lenino.
Respublika Krym, S Ukraine
Leningorsk 114 D4 Kaz. Leningor.
Vostochnyy Kazakhstan,
E Kazakhstan
Leningrad see Sankt-Peterburg
Leningradskaya 154 B4 Russian
research station Antarctica
Leninobod see Khūjand
Leninpol' 123 F2 Talasskaya
Oblast', NW Kyrgyzstan
Lenti 99 B7 Zala, SW Hungary
Leoben 95 E7 Steiermark,
C Austria
León 51 E4 var. León de los
Aldamas. Guanajuato, C Mexico
León 92 D1 Castilla-León,
NW Spain
León 52 C3 León, NW Nicaragua
León de los Aldamas see León
Leonídi 105 B6 Pelopónnisos,
S Greece
Lepe 92 C4 Andalucía, S Spain
le Portel 90 C2 Pas-de-Calais,
N France
le Puy 91 C5 prev. le Puy-en-Velay,
hist. Anicium, Podium Anicensis.
Haute-Loire, C France
Léré 76 B4 Mayo-Kébbi, SW Chad
Lerma 92 D2 Castilla-León,
N Spain
Léros 105 D6 island Dodekánisos,
Greece, Aegean Sea
Lerrnayin Gharabakh see
Nagornyy Karabakh
Lerwick 88 D1 NE Scotland, UK
Lesbos see Lésvos
Les Cayes see Cayes
les Gonaïves see Gonaïves
Lesh see Lezhë
Leshan 128 B5 Sichuan, C China
les Herbiers 90 B4 Vendée,
NW France
Leshi see Lezhë
Leskovac 101 E5 Serbia, SE Serbia
and Montenegro (Yugo.)
Les Laurentides see Laurentian
Highlands
Lesotho 78 D4 prev. Basutoland.
Country S Africa

Lesotho 78

Official name Kingdom of Lesotho

Lesotho (continued)
Formation 1966
Capital Maseru
Population 2.1 million / 179 people per sq mile (69 people per sq km)
Total area 11,720 sq miles (30,355 sq km)
Languages English, Sesotho, Zulu
Religions Traditional beliefs 10% Christian 90%,
Ethnic mix Sotho 97%, European and Asian 3%
Government Constitutional monarchy
Currency Loti = 100 lisente
Literacy rate 83.3%
Calorie consumption 2,300 kilocalories

les Sables-d'Olonne 90 B4 Vendée, NW France
Lesser Antarctica 154 A3 var. West Antarctica. Physical region Antarctica
Lesser Antilles 55 G4 island group E West Indies
Lesser Caucasus 117 F2 Rus. Malyy Kavkaz. Mountain range SW Asia
Lesser Sunda Islands see Nusa Tenggara
Lésvos 116 A3 anc. Lesbos. Island E Greece
Leszno 98 B4 Ger. Lissa. Wielkopolskie, C Poland
Lethbridge 37 E5 Alberta, SW Canada
Lethem 59 F3 S Guyana
Leti, Kepulauan 139 F5 island group E Indonesia
Letpadan 136 B4 Pegu, SW Myanmar
Letsôk-aw Kyun 137 B6 var. Letsutan Island; prev. Domel Island. Island Mergui Archipelago, S Myanmar
Letsutan Island see Letsôk-aw Kyun
Leuven 87 C6 Fr. Louvain, Ger. Löwen. Vlaams Brabant, C Belgium
Leuze see Leuze-en-Hainaut
Leuze-en-Hainaut 87 B6 var. Leuze. Hainaut, SW Belgium
Levanger 84 B4 Nord-Trøndelag, C Norway
Levelland 49 E2 Texas, SW USA
Leverkusen 94 A4 Nordrhein-Westfalen, W Germany
Levice 99 C6 Ger. Lewentz, Lewenz, Hung. Léva. Nitriansky Kraj, SW Slovakia
Levin 150 D4 Manawatu-Wanganui, North Island, NZ
Levkímmi see Lefkímmi
Lewis, Isle of 88 B2 island NW Scotland, UK
Lewis Range 44 B1 mountain range Montana, NW USA
Lewiston 46 C2 Idaho, NW USA
Lewiston 41 G2 Maine, NE USA
Lewistown 44 C1 Montana, NW USA
Lexington 40 C5 Kentucky, S USA
Lexington 45 E4 Nebraska, C USA
Leyte 139 F2 island C Philippines
Leżajsk 99 E5 Podkarpackie, SE Poland
Lezha see Lezhë
Lezhë 101 C6 var. Lezha; prev. Lesh, Leshi. Lezhë, NW Albania
Lhasa 126 C5 var. La-sa, Lassa. Xizang Zizhiqu, W China
Lhaviyani Atoll see Faadhippolhu Atoll
Lhazê 126 C5 Xizang Zizhiqu, W China
L'Hospitalet de Llobregat 93 G2 var. Hospitalet. Cataluña, NE Spain
Liancourt Rocks 131 A5 Jap. Takeshima, Kor. Tok-Do. Island group Japan/South Korea
Lianyungang 128 D4 var. Xinpu. Jiangsu, E China

Liao see Liaoning
Liaodong Wan 127 G3 Eng. Gulf of Lantung, Gulf of Liaotung. Gulf NE China
Liao He 125 E1 river NE China
Liaoning 128 D3 var. Liao, Liaoning Sheng, Shengking; hist. Fengtien, Shenking. Admin. region province NE China
Liaoyuan 129 E3 var. Dongliao, Shuang-liao, Jap. Chengchiatun. Jilin, NE China
Liard see Fort Liard
Liban, Jebel 118 B4 Ar. Jabal al Gharbt, Jabal Lubnān, Eng. Mount Lebanon. Mountain range C Lebanon
Libby 44 A1 Montana, NW USA
Liberal 45 E5 Kansas, C USA
Liberec 98 B4 Ger. Reichenberg. Liberecký Kraj, N Czech Republic
Liberia 74 C5 Country W Africa

Liberia 74
Official name Republic of Liberia
Formation 1847
Capital Monrovia
Population 3.1 million / 72 people per sq mile (28 people per sq km)
Total area 43,000 sq miles (111,370 sq km)
Languages English, Kpelle, Vai, Bassa, Kru, Grebo, Kissi, Gola, Loma
Religions Christian 68%, Traditional beliefs 18%, Muslim 14%
Ethnic mix Indigenous tribes (16 main groups) 95%, Americo-Liberians 5%
Government Multiparty republic
Currency Liberian dollar = 100 cents
Literacy rate 54%
Calorie consumption 2,076 kilocalories

Liberia 52 D4 Guanacaste, NW Costa Rica
Libian Desert see Libyan Desert
Libourne 91 B5 Gironde, SW France
Libreville 77 A5 country capital (Gabon) Estuaire, NW Gabon
Libya 71 F3 Ar. Al Jamāhīrīyah al 'Arabīyah al Lībīyah ash Sha'bīyah al Ishtirākīyah; prev. Libyan Arab Republic. Country N Africa

Libya 71
Official name Great Socialist People's Libyan Arab Jamahariyah
Formation 1951
Capital Tripoli
Population 5.4 million /8 people per sq mile (3 people per sq km)
Total area 679,358 sq miles (1,759,540 sq km)
Languages Arabic, Tuareg
Religions Muslim (mainly Sunni) 97%, other 3%
Ethnic mix Arab and Berber 95%, other 5%
Government One-party state
Currency Libyan dinar = 1,000 dirhams
Literacy rate 80.1%
Calorie consumption 3,305 kilocalories

Libyan Desert 71 H4 var. Libian Desert, Ar. Aş Şahrā' al Lībīyah. Desert N Africa
Libyan Plateau 103 F4 var. Ad Diffah. Plateau Egypt/Libya
Lichtenfels 95 C5 Bayern, SE Germany
Lichtenvoorde 86 E4 Gelderland, E Netherlands
Lichuan 128 C5 Hubei, C China
Lida 107 B5 Rus. Lida. Hrodzyenskaya Voblasts', W Belarus

Lidköping 85 B6 Västra Götaland, S Sweden
Lidoríki 105 B5 prev. Lidhorikíon, Lidokhorikion. Stereá Ellás, C Greece
Lidzbark Warmiński 98 D2 Ger. Heilsberg. Warmińsko-Mazurskie, NE Poland
Liechtenstein 94 D1 Country C Europe

Liechtenstein 94
Official name Principality of Liechtenstein
Formation 1719
Capital Vaduz
Population 32,200/ 521 people per sq mile (201 people per sq km)
Total area 62 sq miles (160 sq km)
Languages German, Alemannish dialect, Italian
Religions Roman Catholic 81%, Protestant 7%, other 12%
Ethnic mix Liectensteiner 63%, Foreign residents 37%
Government Parliamentary democracy
Currency Swiss franc = 100 centimes
Literacy rate 99%
Calorie consumption not available

Liège 87 D6 Dut. Luik, Ger. Lüttich. Liège, E Belgium
Lienz 95 D7 Tirol, W Austria
Liepāja 106 B3 Ger. Libau. Liepāja, W Latvia
Liezen 95 D7 Steiermark, C Austria
Liffey 89 B6 river E Ireland
Lifou 144 D5 island Îles Loyauté, E New Caledonia
Liger see Loire
Ligure, Appennino 96 A2 Eng. Ligurian Mountains. Mountain range NW Italy
Ligurian Sea 96 A3 Fr. Mer Ligurienne, It. Mar Ligure. Sea N Mediterranean Sea
Lihue 47 A7 Haw. Līhu'e. Kauai, Hawaii, USA, C Pacific Ocean
Lihula 106 D2 Ger. Leal. Läänemaa, W Estonia
Likasi 77 D7 prev. Jadotville. Shaba, SE Dem. Rep. Congo
Liknes 85 A6 Vest-Agder, S Norway
Lille 90 C2 var. l'Isle, Dut. Rijssel, Flem. Ryssel; prev. Lisle, anc. Insula. Nord, N France
Lillehammer 85 B5 Oppland, S Norway
Lillestrøm 85 B6 Akershus, S Norway
Lilongwe 79 E2 country capital (Malawi) Central, W Malawi
Lima 60 C4 country capital (Peru) Lima, W Peru
Limanowa 99 D5 Małopolskie, S Poland
Limassol see Lemesós
Limerick 89 A6 Ir. Luimneach. SW Ireland
Límnos 103 F3 anc. Lemnos. Island E Greece
Limoges 91 C5 anc. Augustoritum Lemovicensium, Lemovices. Haute-Vienne, C France
Limón 53 E4 var. Puerto Limón. Limón, E Costa Rica
Limón 52 D2 Colón, NE Honduras
Limousin 91 C5 cultural region C France
Limoux 91 C6 Aude, S France
Limpopo 78 D3 var. Crocodile. River S Africa
Linares 92 D4 Andalucía, S Spain
Linares 64 B4 Maule, C Chile
Linares 51 E3 Nuevo León, NE Mexico
Linchuan 128 D5 var. Fuzhou. Jiangxi, S China
Lincoln 89 D5 anc. Lindum, Lindum Colonia. E England, UK

Lincoln 45 F4 state capital Nebraska, C USA
Lincoln 41 H2 Maine, NE USA
Lincoln Sea 34 D2 sea Arctic Ocean
Linden 59 F3 E Guyana
Líndhos see Líndos
Lindi 73 D8 Lindi, SE Tanzania
Líndos 105 E7 var. Líndhos. Ródos, Dodekánisos, Greece, Aegean Sea
Line Islands 145 G3 island group E Kiribati
Lingeh see Bandar-e Langeh
Lingen 94 A3 var. Lingen an der Ems. Niedersachsen, NW Germany
Lingen an der Ems see Lingen
Lingga, Kepulauan 138 B4 island group W Indonesia
Linköping 85 C6 Östergötland, S Sweden
Linz 95 D6 anc. Lentia. Oberösterreich, N Austria
Lion, Golfe du 91 C7 Eng. Gulf of Lion, Gulf of Lions; anc. Sinus Gallicus. Gulf S France
Lipari Islands see Eolie, Isole
Lipari, Isola 97 D6 island Isole Eolie, S Italy
Lipetsk 111 B5 Lipetskaya Oblast', W Russian Federation
Lipno 98 C3 Kujawsko-pomorskie, C Poland
Lipova 108 A4 Hung. Lippa. Arad, W Romania
Liqeni i Ohrit see Ohrid, Lake
Lira 73 B6 N Uganda
Lisala 77 C5 Equateur, N Dem. Rep. Congo
Lisboa 92 B4 Eng. Lisbon; anc. Felicitas Julia, Olisipo. Country capital (Portugal) Lisboa, W Portugal
Lisbon see Lisboa
Lisieux 90 B3 anc. Noviomagus. Calvados, N France
Liski 111 B6 prev. Georgiu-Dezh. Voronezhskaya Oblast', W Russian Federation
Lisle see Lille
l'Isle see Lille
Lismore 149 E5 Victoria, SE Australia
Lisse 86 C3 Zuid-Holland, W Netherlands
Litang 128 A5 Sichuan, C China
Litani, Nahr el 135 B5 var. Nahr al Litant. River C Lebanon
Lithgow 149 D6 New South Wales, SE Australia
Lithuania 106 B4 Ger. Litauen, Lith. Lietuva, Pol. Litwa, Rus. Litva; prev. Lithuanian SSR, Rus. Litovskaya SSR. Country NE Europe

Lithuania 106
Official name Republic of Lithuania
Formation 1991
Capital Vilnius
Population 3.7 million / 147 people per sq mile (57 peopleper sq km)
Total area 25,174 sq miles (65,200 sq km)
Languages Lithuanian, Russian
Religions Roman Catholic 83%, Protestant 5%, other 12%
Ethnic mix Lithuanian 80%, Russian 9%, Polish 7%, Belarussian 2%, other 2%
Government Parliamentary democracy
Currency Litas = 100 centas
Literacy rate 99%
Calorie consumption 3,040 kilocalories

Litóchoro 104 B4 var. Litohoro, Litókhoron. Kentriki Makedonía, N Greece
Litohoro see Litóchoro
Litókhoron see Litóchoro
Little Alföld 99 C6 Ger. Kleines Ungarisches Tiefland, Hung. Kisalföld, Slvk. Podunajská Rovina. Plain Hungary/Slovakia

Little Andaman *133 F2 island* Andaman Islands, India, NE Indian Ocean
Little Barrier Island *150 D2 island* N NZ
Little Bay *93 H5 bay* S Gibraltar
Little Cayman *54 B3 island* E Cayman Islands
Little Falls *45 F2* Minnesota, N USA
Littlefield *49 E2* Texas, SW USA
Little Inagua *54 D2 var.* Inagua Islands. *Island* S Bahamas
Little Minch, The *88 B3 strait* NW Scotland, UK
Little Missouri River *44 D2 river* NW USA
Little Nicobar *133 G3 island* Nicobar Islands, India, NE Indian Ocean
Little Rock *42 B1 state capital* Arkansas, C USA
Little Saint Bernard Pass *91 D5 Fr.* Col du Petit St-Bernard, *It.* Colle di Piccolo San Bernardo. *Pass* France/Italy
Little Sound *42 A5 bay* Bermuda, NW Atlantic Ocean
Littleton *44 D4* Colorado, C USA
Liu-chou *see* Liuzhou
Liuchow *see* Liuzhou
Liuzhou *128 C6 var.* Liu-chou, Liuchow. Guangxi Zhuangzu Zizhiqu, S China
Livanátes *105 B5 prev.* Livanátai. Stereá Ellás, C Greece
Līvāni *106 D4 Ger.* Lievenhof. Preiļi, SE Latvia
Liverpool *148 D2* New South Wales, SE Australia
Liverpool *39 F5* Nova Scotia, SE Canada
Liverpool *89 C5* NW England, UK
Livingston *44 B2* Montana, NW USA
Livingstone *78 C3 var.* Maramba. Southern, S Zambia
Livingstone *49 H3* Texas, SW USA
Livingstone Mountains *151 A7 mountain range* South Island, NZ
Livno *100 B4* Federacija Bosna I Hercegovina, SW Bosnia and Herzegovina
Livojoki *84 D4 river* C Finland
Livonia *40 D3* Michigan, N USA
Livorno *96 B3 Eng.* Leghorn. Toscana, C Italy
Lixoúri *105 A5 prev.* Lixoúrion. Kefallinía, Iónioi Nísoi, Greece, C Mediterranean Sea
Ljubljana *95 D7 Ger.* Laibach, *It.* Lubiana; *anc.* Aemona, Emona. *Country capital* (Slovenia) C Slovenia
Ljungby *85 B7* Kronoberg, S Sweden
Ljusdal *85 C5* Gävleborg, C Sweden
Ljusnan *85 C5 river* C Sweden
Llanelli *89 C6 prev.* Llanelly. SW Wales, UK
Llanes *92 D1* Asturias, N Spain
Llanos *58 D2 physical region* Colombia/Venezuela
Lleida *93 F2 Cast.* Lérida; *anc.* Ilerda. Cataluña, NE Spain
Lluchmayor *see* Llucmajor
Llucmajor *93 G3 var.* Lluchmayor. Mallorca, Spain, W Mediterranean Sea
Loaita Island *128 C8 island* W Spratly Islands
Loanda *see* Luanda
Lobatse *78 C4 var.* Lobatsi. Kgatleng, SE Botswana
Lobatsi *see* Lobatse
Löbau *94 D4* Sachsen, E Germany
Lobito *78 B2* Benguela, W Angola
Lob Nor *see* Lop Nur
Loburi *see* Lop Buri
Locarno *95 B8 Ger.* Luggarus. Ticino, S Switzerland
Lochem *86 E3* Gelderland, E Netherlands
Lockport *41 E3* New York, NE USA
Lodja *77 D6* Kasai Oriental, C Dem. Rep. Congo

Lodwar *73 C6* Rift Valley, NW Kenya
Łódź *98 D4 Rus.* Lodz. Łódzkie, C Poland
Loei *136 C4 var.* Loey, Muang Loei. Loei, C Thailand
Loey *see* Loei
Lofoten *84 B3 var.* Lofoten Islands. *Island group* C Norway
Lofoten Islands *see* Lofoten
Logan *44 B3* Utah, W USA
Logan, Mount *36 D3 mountain* Yukon Territory, W Canada
Logroño *93 E1 anc.* Vareia, *Lat.* Juliobriga. La Rioja, N Spain
Loibl Pass *95 D7 Ger.* Loiblpass, *Slvn.* Ljubelj. *Pass* Austria/Slovenia
Loi-kaw *136 B4* Kayah State, C Myanmar
Loire *90 B4 var.* Liger. *River* C France
Loja *60 B2* Loja, S Ecuador
Lokitaung *73 C5* Rift Valley, NW Kenya
Lokoja *75 G4* Kogi, C Nigeria
Loksa *106 E2 Ger.* Loxa. Harjumaa, NW Estonia
Lolland *85 B8 prev.* Laaland. *Island* S Denmark
Lom *104 C1 prev.* Lom-Palanka. Montana, NW Bulgaria
Lomami *77 D6 river* C Dem. Rep. Congo
Lomas *60 D4* Arequipa, SW Peru
Lomas de Zamora *64 D4* Buenos Aires, E Argentina
Lombardia *96 B2 cultural region* N Italy
Lombok, Pulau *138 D5 island* Nusa Tenggara, C Indonesia
Lomé *75 F5 country capital* (Togo) S Togo
Lomela *77 D6* Kasai Oriental, C Dem. Rep. Congo
Lommel *87 C5* Limburg, N Belgium
Lomond, Loch *88 B4 lake* C Scotland, UK
Lomonosov Ridge *155 B3 var.* Harris Ridge, *Rus.* Khrebet Lomonosova. *Undersea feature* Arctic Ocean
Lompoc *47 B7* California, W USA
Lom Sak *136 C4 var.* Muang Lom Sak. Phetchabun, C Thailand
Łomża *98 D3 off.* Województwo Łomżyńskie, *Rus.* Lomzha. Podlaskie, NE Poland
Loncoche *65 B5* Araucanía, C Chile
London *89 A7 anc.* Augusta, *Lat.* Londinium. *Country capital* (UK) SE England, UK
London *40 C5* Kentucky, S USA
London *38 C5* Ontario, S Canada
Londonderry *88 B4 var.* Derry, *Ir.* Doire. NW Northern Ireland, UK
Londonderry, Cape *146 C2 headland* Western Australia
Londrina *63 E4* Paraná, S Brazil
Longa, Proliv *115 G1 Eng.* Long Strait. *Strait* NE Russian Federation
Long Bay *43 F2 bay* North Carolina/South Carolina, E USA
Long Beach *47 C7* California, W USA
Longford *89 B5 Ir.* Longfort. C Ireland
Long Island *54 D2 island* C Bahamas
Long Island *41 G4 island* New York, NE USA
Long Island *see* Bermuda
Longlac *38 C3* Ontario, S Canada
Longmont *44 D4* Colorado, C USA
Longreach *148 C4* Queensland, E Australia
Long Strait *see* Longa, Proliv
Longview *49 H3* Texas, SW USA
Longview *46 B2* Washington, NW USA
Long Xuyên *137 D6 var.* Longxuyen. An Giang, S Vietnam
Longxuyen *see* Long Xuyên
Longyan *128 D6* Fujian, SE China

Longyearbyen *83 G2 dependent territory capital* (Svalbard) Spitsbergen, W Svalbard
Lons-le-Saunier *90 D4 anc.* Ledo Salinarius. Jura, E France
Lop Buri *137 C5 var.* Loburi. Lop Buri, C Thailand
Lop Nor *see* Lop Nur
Lop Nur *126 C3 var.* Lob Nor, Lop Nor, Lo-pu Po. *Seasonal lake* NW China
Loppersum *86 E1* Groningen, NE Netherlands
Lo-pu Po *see* Lop Nur
Lorca *93 E4 Ar.* Lurka; *anc.* Eliocroca, *Lat.* Illur co. Murcia, S Spain
Lord Howe Island *142 C4 island* E Australia
Lord Howe Rise *142 C4 undersea feature* SW Pacific Ocean
Loreto *50 B3* Baja California Sur, W Mexico
Lorient *90 A3 prev.* l'Orient. Morbihan, NW France
Lorn, Firth of *88 B4 inlet* W Scotland, UK
Loro Sae *see* East Timor
Lörrach *95 A7* Baden-Württemberg, S Germany
Lorraine *90 D3 cultural region* NE France
Los Alamos *48 C1* New Mexico, SW USA
Los Amates *52 B2* Izabal, E Guatemala
Los Angeles *47 C7* California, W USA
Los Ángeles *65 B5* Bío Bío, C Chile
Lošinj *100 A3 Ger.* Lussin, *It.* Lussino. *Island* W Croatia
Los Mochis *50 C3* Sinaloa, C Mexico
Los Roques, Islas *58 D1 island group* N Venezuela
Los Testigos, Isla *55 G5 island* NE Venezuela
Lost River Range *46 D3 mountain range* Idaho, C USA
Lot *91 B5 cultural region* C France
Lot *91 B5 river* S France
Lotagipi Swamp *73 C5 wetland* Kenya/Sudan
Louangnamtha *136 C3 var.* Luong Nam Tha. Louang Namtha, N Laos
Louangphabang *124 D3 var.* Louangphrabang, Luang Prabang. Louangphabang, N Laos
Louangphrabang *see* Louangphabang
Loudéac *90 A3* Côtes d'Armor, NW France
Loudi *128 C5* Hunan, S China
Louga *74 B3* NW Senegal
Louisiade Archipelago *144 B4 island group* SE PNG
Louisiana *42 A2 off.* State of Louisiana; also known as Creole State, Pelican State. *State* S USA
Louisville *40 C5* Kentucky, S USA
Louisville Ridge *143 F4 undersea feature* S Pacific Ocean
Loup River *45 E4 river* Nebraska, C USA
Lourdes *91 B6* Hautes-Pyrénées, S France
Louth *89 E5* E England, UK
Loutrá *104 C4* Kentrikí Makedonía, N Greece
Lóuva *78 C1* Lunda Norte, NE Angola
Louvain-la Neuve *87 C6* Wallon Brabant, C Belgium
Louviers *90 C3* Eure, N France
Lovech *104 C2* Lovech, N Bulgaria
Loveland *44 D4* Colorado, C USA
Lovosice *98 A4 Ger.* Lobositz. Ústecký Kraj, NW Czech Republic
Lowell *41 G3* Massachusetts, NE USA
Lower California *see* Baja California
Lower Hutt *151 D5* Wellington, North Island, NZ
Lower Lough Erne *89 A5 lake* SW Northern Ireland, UK

Lower Red Lake *45 F1 lake* Minnesota, N USA
Lower Tunguska *see* Nizhnyaya Tunguska
Lowestoft *89 E6* E England, UK
Lo-yang *see* Luoyang
Loyauté, Îles *144 D5 island group* S New Caledonia
Loyew *107 D8 Rus.* Loyev. Homyel'skaya Voblasts', SE Belarus
Loznica *100 C3* Serbia, W Serbia and Montenegro (Yugo.)
Lu *see* Shandong
Lualaba *77 D6 Fr.* Loualaba. *River* SE Dem. Rep. Congo
Luanda *78 A1 var.* Loanda, *Port.* São Paulo de Loanda. *Country capital* (Angola) Luanda, NW Angola
Luang Prabang *see* Louangphabang
Luang, Thale *137 C7 lagoon* S Thailand
Luangua, Rio *see* Luangwa
Luangwa *73 B8 var.* Aruângua, Rio Luangua. *River* Mozambique/Zambia
Luanshya *78 D2* Copperbelt, C Zambia
Luarca *92 C1* Asturias, N Spain
Lubaczów *99 E5 var.* Lúbaczów. Podkarpackie, SE Poland
Lubań *98 B4 var.* Koscian, *Ger.* Kosten. Dolnośląskie, SW Poland
Lubānas Ezers *see* Lubāns
Lubango *78 B2 Port.* Sá da Bandeira. Huíla, SW Angola
Lubāns *106 D4 var.* Lubānas Ezers. *Lake* E Latvia
Lubao *77 D6* Kasai Oriental, C Dem. Rep. Congo
Lübben *94 D4* Brandenburg, E Germany
Lübbenau *94 D4* Brandenburg, E Germany
Lubbock *49 E2* Texas, SW USA
Lübeck *94 C2* Schleswig-Holstein, N Germany
Lubelska, Wyżyna *98 E4 plateau* SE Poland
Lubin *98 B4 Ger.* Lüben. Dolnośląskie, W Poland
Lublin *98 E4 Rus.* Lyublin. Lubelskie, E Poland
Lubliniec *98 C4* Śląskie, S Poland
Lubny *109 F2* Poltavs'ka Oblast', NE Ukraine
Lubsko *98 B4 Ger.* Sommerfeld. Lubuskie, W Poland
Lubumbashi *77 E8 prev.* Élisabethville. Shaba, SE Dem. Rep. Congo
Lubutu *77 D6* Maniema, E Dem. Rep. Congo
Lucan *89 B5 Ir.* Leamhcán. E Ireland
Lucano, Appennino *97 D5 Eng.* Lucanian Mountains. *Mountain range* S Italy
Lucapa *78 C1 var.* Lukapa. Lunda Norte, NE Angola
Lucca *96 B3 anc.* Luca. Toscana, C Italy
Lucea *54 A4* W Jamaica
Lucena *139 E1 off.* Lucena City. Luzon, N Philippines
Lucena *92 D4* Andalucía, S Spain
Lučenec *99 D6 Ger.* Losontz, *Hung.* Losonc. Banskobystrický Kraj, C Slovakia
Luchow *see* Hefei
Lucknow *135 E3 var.* Lakhnau. Uttar Pradesh, N India
Lüda *see* Dalian
Luda Kamchiya *104 D2 river* E Bulgaria
Lüderitz *78 B4 prev.* Angra Pequena. Karas, SW Namibia
Ludhiāna *134 D2* Punjab, N India
Ludington *40 C2* Michigan, N USA
Ludus *108 B4 var.* Ludasch, *Hung.* Marosludas. Mureş, C Romania
Ludvika *85 C6* Kopparberg, C Sweden
Ludwiglust *94 C3* Mecklenburg-Vorpommern, N Germany

Ludwigsburg 95 B6 Baden-Württemberg, SW Germany
Ludwigsfelde 94 D3 Brandenburg, NE Germany
Ludwigshafen 95 B5 var. Ludwigshafen am Rhein. Rheinland-Pfalz, W Germany
Ludwigshafen am Rhein see Ludwigshafen
Ludza 106 D4 Ger. Ludsan. Ludza, E Latvia
Luebo 77 C6 Kasai Occidental, SW Dem. Rep. Congo
Luena 78 C2 var. Lwena, Port. Luso. Moxico, E Angola
Lufira 77 E7 river SE Dem. Rep. Congo
Lufkin 49 H3 Texas, SW USA
Luga 110 A4 Leningradskaya Oblast', NW Russian Federation
Lugano 95 B8 Ger. Lauis. Ticino, S Switzerland
Lugenda, Rio 79 E2 river N Mozambique
Lugo 92 C1 anc. Lugus Augusti. Galicia, NW Spain
Lugoj 108 A4 Ger. Lugosch, Hung. Lugos. Timiş, W Romania
Luhans'k 109 H3 Rus. Lugansk; prev. Voroshilovgrad. Luhans'ka Oblast', E Ukraine
Luimneach see Limerick
Lukapa see Lucapa
Lukenie 77 C6 river C Dem. Rep. Congo
Lukovit 104 C2 Lovech, NW Bulgaria
Łuków 98 E4 Ger. Bogendorf. Lubelskie, E Poland
Lukuga 77 D7 river SE Dem. Rep. Congo
Luleå 84 D4 Norrbotten, N Sweden
Luleälven 84 C3 river N Sweden
Lulonga 77 C5 river NW Dem. Rep. Congo
Lulua 77 D7 river S Dem. Rep. Congo
Lumbo 79 F2 Nampula, NE Mozambique
Lumsden 151 A7 Southland, South Island, NZ
Lund 85 B7 Skåne, S Sweden
Lüneburg 94 C3 Niedersachsen, N Germany
Lungkiang see Qiqihar
Lungué-Bungo 78 C2 var. Lungwebungu. River Angola/Zambia see also Lungwebungu
Lungwebungu see Lungué-Bungo
Luninets 107 B7 Pol. Łuniniec, Rus. Luninets. Brestskaya Voblasts', SW Belarus
Lunteren 86 D4 Gelderland, C Netherlands
Luong Nam Tha see Louangnamtha
Luoyang 128 C4 var. Honan, Lo-yang. Henan, C China
Lúrio 79 F2 Nampula, NE Mozambique
Lúrio, Rio 79 E2 river NE Mozambique
Lusaka 78 D2 country capital (Zambia) Lusaka, SE Zambia
Lushnja see Lushnjë
Lushnjë 101 C6 var. Lushnja. Fier, C Albania
Luso see Luena
Lūt, Dasht-e 120 D3 var. Kavīr-e Lūt. Desert E Iran
Luton 89 D6 SE England, UK
Lutselk'e 37 F4 prev. Snowdrift. Northwest Territories, W Canada
Luts'k 108 C1 Pol. Łuck, Rus. Lutsk. Volyns'ka Oblast', NW Ukraine
Lutzow-Holm Bay see Lützow Holmbukta
Lützow Holmbukta 154 C2 var. Lutzow-Holm Bay. Bay Antarctica
Luuq 73 D6 It. Lugh Ganana. Gedo, SW Somalia
Luvua 77 D7 river SE Dem. Rep. Congo
Luwego 73 C8 river S Tanzania

Luxembourg 87 D8 var. Lëtzebuerg, Luxemburg. Country NW Europe

Luxembourg 87

Official name Grand Duchy of Luxembourg
Formation 1867
Capital Luxembourg
Population 442,000/ 433 people per sq mile (171 people per sq km)
Total area 998 sq miles (2,586 sq km)
Languages French, German, Luxembourgish
Religions Roman Catholic 97%, other 3%
Ethnic mix Luxembourger 73%, Foreign residents 27%
Government Parliamentary democracy
Currency Euro (Luxembourg and Belgian Franc until 2002)
Literacy rate 99%
Calorie consumption 3,701 kilocalories

Luxembourg 87 D8 country capital (Luxembourg) Luxembourg, S Luxembourg
Luxor 72 B2 Ar. Al Uqsur. E Egypt
Luza 110 C4 Kirovskaya Oblast', NW Russian Federation
Luz, Costa de la 92 C5 coastal region SW Spain
Luzern 95 B7 Fr. Lucerne, It. Lucerna. Luzern, C Switzerland
Luzon 139 E1 island N Philippines
Luzon Strait 125 E3 strait Philippines/Taiwan
L'viv 108 B2 Ger. Lemberg, Pol. Lwów, Rus. L'vov. L'vivs'ka Oblast', W Ukraine
Lwena see Luena
Lyakhavichy 107 B6 Rus. Lyakhovichi. Brestskaya Voblasts', SW Belarus
Lycksele 84 C4 Västerbotten, N Sweden
Lycopolis see Asyût
Lyel'chytsy 107 C7 Rus. Lel'chitsy. Homyel'skaya Voblasts', SE Belarus
Lyepyel' 107 D5 Rus. Lepel'. Vitsyebskaya Voblasts', N Belarus
Lyme Bay 89 C7 bay S England, UK
Lynchburg 41 E5 Virginia, NE USA
Lynn Regis see King's Lynn
Lyon 91 D5 Eng. Lyons; anc. Lugdunum. Rhône, E France
Lyozna 107 E6 Rus. Liozno. Vitsyebskaya Voblasts', NE Belarus
Lypovets' 108 D2 Rus. Lipovets. Vinnyts'ka Oblast', C Ukraine
Lysychans'k 109 H3 Rus. Lisichansk. Luhans'ka Oblast', E Ukraine
Lyttelton 151 C6 Canterbury, South Island, NZ
Lyubotyn 109 G2 Rus. Lyubotin. Kharkivs'ka Oblast', E Ukraine
Lyulyakovo 104 E2 prev. Keremitlik. Burgas, E Bulgaria
Lyusina 107 B6 Rus. Lyusino. Brestskaya Voblasts', SW Belarus

M

Ma'ān 119 B7 Ma'ān, SW Jordan
Maardu 106 D2 Ger. Maart. Harjumaa, NW Estonia
Ma'aret-en-Nu'man see Ma'arrat an Nu'mān
Ma'arrat an Nu'mān 118 B3 var. Ma'aret-en-Nu'man, Fr. Maarret enn Naamâne. Idlib, NW Syria
Maarret enn Naamâne see Ma'arrat an Nu'mān
Maaseik 87 D5 prev. Maeseyck. Limburg, NE Belgium
Maastricht 87 D6 var. Maestricht; anc. Traietum ad Mosam, Traiectum Tungorum. Limburg, SE Netherlands

Macao 129 C6 Chin. Aomen, Port. Macao. S China
Macapá 63 E1 state capital Amapá, N Brazil
Macassar see Ujungpandang
MacCluer Gulf see Berau, Teluk
Macdonnell Ranges 146 D4 mountain range Northern Territory, C Australia
Macedonia, FYR 101 D6 var. Macedonia, Mac. Makedonija, abbrev. FYR Macedonia, FYROM. Country SE Europe

Macedonia 101

Official name Former Yugoslav Republic of Macedonia
Formation 1991
Capital Skopje
Population 2 million / 204 people per sq mile (79 people per sq km)
Total area 9,781 sq miles (25,333 sq km)
Languages Macedonian, Albania, Serbo-Croat
Religions Christian 74%, Muslim 26%
Ethnic mix Macedonian 67%, Albanian 23%, Turkish 4%, other 6%
Government Multiparty republic
Currency Macedonian denar = 100 deni
Literacy rate 94%
Calorie consumption 3,006 kilocalories

Maceió 63 G3 state capital Alagoas, E Brazil
Machachi 60 B1 Pichincha, C Ecuador
Machala 60 B2 El Oro, SW Ecuador
Machanga 79 E3 Sofala, E Mozambique
Machilipatnam 132 D1 var. Bandar Masulipatnam. Andhra Pradesh, E India
Machiques 58 C2 Zulia, NW Venezuela
Macías Nguema Biyogo see Bioco, Isla de
Măcin 108 D5 Tulcea, SE Romania
Macizo de las Guayanas see Guiana Highlands
Mackay 148 D4 Queensland, NE Australia
Mackay, Lake 146 C4 salt lake Northern Territory/Western Australia
Mackenzie 37 E3 river Northwest Territories, NW Canada
Mackenzie Bay 154 D3 bay Antarctica
Mackenzie Mountains 36 D3 mountain range Northwest Territories, NW Canada
Macleod, Lake 146 A4 lake Western Australia
Macomb 40 A4 Illinois, N USA
Macomer 97 A5 Sardegna, Italy, C Mediterranean Sea
Macon 42 D2 Georgia, SE USA
Macon 45 G4 Missouri, C USA
Mâcon 91 D5 anc. Matisco, Matisco Ædourum. Saône-et-Loire, C France
Macquarie Ridge 154 C5 undersea feature SW Pacific Ocean
Macuspana 51 G4 Tabasco, SE Mexico
Ma'dabā 119 B6 var. Mādabā, Madeba; anc. Medeba. 'Ammān, NW Jordan
Madagascar 79 F3 Malg. Madagasikara; prev. Malagasy Republic. Country W Indian Ocean

Madagascar 79

Official name Republic of Madagascar
Formation 1960
Capital Antananarivo
Population 16.4 million /72 people per sq mile (28 people per sq km)

Madagascar (continued)

Total area 226,656 sq miles (587,040 sq km)
Languages French, Malagasy
Religions Traditional beliefs 52%, Christian 41%, Muslim 7%
Ethnic mix Merina 26%, Betsileo 12%, Betsimisaraka 15%, other 47%
Government Presidential democracy
Currency Malagasy franc = 100 centimes
Literacy rate 66.5%
Calorie consumption 2,007 kilocalories

Madagascar 79 F3 island W Indian Ocean
Madagascar Basin 69 E7 undersea feature W Indian Ocean
Madagascar Plateau 69 E7 var. Madagascar Ridge, Madagascar Rise, Rus. Madagaskarskiy Khrebet. Undersea feature W Indian Ocean
Madagascar Ridge see Madagascar Plateau
Madagascar Rise see Madagascar Plateau
Madagaskarskiy Khrebet see Madagascar Plateau
Madang 144 B3 Madang, N PNG
Madanīyīn see Médenine
Made 86 C4 Noord-Brabant, S Netherlands
Madeba see Ma'dabā
Madeira 70 A2 var. Ilha de Madeira. Island Portugal, NE Atlantic Ocean
Madeira 70 A2 var. Madeira, Port. Arquipélago da Madeira. Island group Portugal, NE Atlantic Ocean
Madeira Plain 66 C3 undersea feature E Atlantic Ocean
Madeira, Rio 62 D2 Sp. Río Madera. River Bolivia/Brazil see also Madera, Río
Madeleine, Îles de la 39 F4 Eng. Magdalen Islands. Island group Quebec, E Canada
Madera 47 B6 California, W USA
Madhya Pradesh 135 E4 prev. Central Provinces and Berar. Admin. region state C India
Madīnat ath Thawrah 118 C2 var. Ath Thawrah. Ar Raqqah, N Syria Asia
Madison 40 B3 state capital Wisconsin, N USA
Madison 45 F3 South Dakota, N USA
Madiun 138 D5 prev. Madioen. Jawa, C Indonesia
Madona 106 D4 Ger. Modohn. Madona, E Latvia
Madras see Tamil Nādu
Madras see Chennai
Madre de Dios 56 B4 off. Departamento de Madre de Dios. Department E Peru
Madre de Dios, Río 61 E3 river Bolivia/Peru
Madre del Sur, Sierra 51 E5 mountain range S Mexico
Madre, Laguna 51 F3 lagoon NE Mexico
Madre, Laguna 49 G5 lake Texas, SW USA
Madre Occidental, Sierra 50 C3 var. Western Sierra Madre. Mountain range C Mexico
Madre Oriental, Sierra 51 E3 var. Eastern Sierra Madre. Mountain range C Mexico
Madrid 92 D3 country capital (Spain) Madrid, C Spain
Madurai 132 C3 prev. Madura, Mathurai. Tamil Nādu, S India
Madura, Pulau 138 D5 prev. Madoera. Island C Indonesia
Maebashi 131 D5 var. Maebasi, Mayebashi. Gunma, Honshū, S Japan
Maebasi see Maebashi

Mae Nam Khong see Mekong
Mae Nam Nan 136 C4 river NW Thailand
Mae Nam Yom 136 C4 river W Thailand
Maestricht see Maastricht
Maéwo 144 D4 prev. Aurora. Island C Vanuatu
Mafia 73 D7 island E Tanzania
Mafraq see Al Mafraq
Magadan 115 G3 Magadanskaya Oblast', E Russian Federation
Magangué 58 B2 Bolívar, N Colombia
Magdalena 56 A2 off. Departamento del Magdalena. Province N Colombia
Magdalena 61 F3 Beni, N Bolivia
Magdalena 50 B1 Sonora, NW Mexico
Magdalena, Isla 50 B3 island W Mexico
Magdalena, Río 58 B2 river C Colombia
Magdeburg 94 C4 Sachsen-Anhalt, C Germany
Magelang 138 C5 Jawa, C Indonesia
Magellan, Strait of 65 B8 Sp. Estrecho de Magallanes. Strait Argentina/Chile
Magerøy see Magerøya
Magerøya 84 D1 var. Magerøy. Island N Norway
Maggiore, Lake 96 B1 It. Lago Maggiore. Lake Italy/Switzerland
Maglaj 100 C3 Federacija Bosna I Hercegovina, N Bosnia and Herzegovina
Maglie 97 E6 Puglia, SE Italy
Magna 44 B4 Utah, W USA
Magnesia see Manisa
Magnitogorsk 114 B4 Chelyabinskaya Oblast', C Russian Federation
Magta' Lahjar 74 C3 var. Magta Lahjar, Magta' Lahjar, Magtá Lahjar. Brakna, SW Mauritania
Magway see Magwe
Magwe 136 A3 var. Magway. Magwe, W Myanmar
Mahajanga 79 F2 var. Majunga. Mahajanga, NW Madagascar
Mahakam, Sungai 138 D4 var. Koetai, Kutai. River Borneo, C Indonesia
Mahalapye 78 D3 var. Mahalatswe. Central, SE Botswana
Mahalatswe see Mahalapye
Mahān 120 D3 Kermān, E Iran
Mahānadi 135 F4 river E India
Mahārāshtra 134 D5 state W India
Mahbés see El Mahbas
Mahbūbnagar 134 D5 Andhra Pradesh, C India
Mahdia 71 F2 var. Al Mahdīyah, Mehdia. NE Tunisia
Mahé 79 H1 island Inner Islands, NE Seychelles
Mahia Peninsula 150 E4 peninsula North Island, NZ
Mahilyow 107 D6 Rus. Mogilëv. Mahilyowskaya Voblasts', E Belarus
Maḥmūd-e 'Erāqī see Maḥmūd-e Rāqī
Maḥmūd-e Rāqī 123 E4 var. Maḥmūd-e 'Erāqī. Kāpīsā, NE Afghanistan
Mahón 93 H3 Cat. Maó, Eng. Port Mahon; anc. Portus Magonis. Menorca, Spain, W Mediterranean Sea
Maicao 58 C1 La Guajira, N Colombia
Mai Ceu see Maych'ew
Mai Chio see Maych'ew
Maidstone 89 E7 SE England, UK
Maiduguri 75 H4 Borno, NE Nigeria
Maimāna see Meymaneh
Main 95 B5 river C Germany
Mai-Ndombe, Lac 77 C6 prev. Lac Léopold II. Lake W Dem. Rep. Congo
Maine 41 G2 off. State of Maine; also known as Lumber State, Pine Tree State. State NE USA

Maine 90 B3 cultural region NW France
Maine, Gulf of 41 H2 gulf NE USA
Main Island see Bermuda
Mainland 88 C2 island Orkney, N Scotland, UK
Mainland 88 D1 island Shetland, NE Scotland, UK
Mainz 95 B5 Fr. Mayence. Rheinland-Pfalz, SW Germany
Maio 74 A3 var. Mayo. Island Ilhas de Sotavento, SE Cape Verde
Maisur see Karnātaka
Maisur see Mysore
Maizhokunggar 126 C5 Xizang Zizhiqu, W China
Maíz, Islas del 53 E3 var. Corn Islands. Island group SE Nicaragua
Mājro see Majuro Atoll
Majunga see Mahajanga
Majuro Atoll 144 D2 var. Mājro. Atoll Ratak Chain, SE Marshall Islands
Makale see Mek'elē
Makarov Basin 155 B3 undersea feature Arctic Ocean
Makarska 100 B4 It. Macarsca. Split-Dalmacija, SE Croatia
Makasar see Ujungpandang
Makassar see Ujungpandang
Makassar Strait 138 D4 Ind. Selat Makasar. Strait C Indonesia
Makay 79 F3 var. Massif du Makay. Mountain range SW Madagascar
Makeni 74 C4 C Sierra Leone
Makhachkala 114 A4 prev. Petrovsk-Port. Respublika Dagestan, SW Russian Federation
Makin 144 D2 prev. Pitt Island. Atoll Tungaru, W Kiribati
Makira see San Cristobal
Makiyivka 109 G3 Rus. Makeyevka; prev. Dmitriyevsk. Donets'ka Oblast', E Ukraine
Makkah 121 A5 Eng. Mecca. Makkah, W Saudi Arabia
Makkovik 39 F2 Newfoundland and Labrador, NE Canada
Makó 99 D7 Rom. Macău. Csongrád, SE Hungary
Makoua 77 B5 Cuvette, C Congo
Makran Coast 120 E4 coastal region SE Iran
Makrany 107 A6 Rus. Mokrany. Brestskaya Voblasts', SW Belarus
Mākū 120 B2 Āẕarbāyjān-e Bākhtarī, NW Iran
Makurdi 75 G4 Benue, C Nigeria
Mala see Malaita
Malabār Coast 132 B3 coast SW India
Malabo 98 C2 Ger. Marienburg, Marienburg in Westpreussen. Pomorskie, N Poland prev. Santa Isabel. Country capital (Equatorial Guinea) Isla de Bioco, NW Equatorial Guinea
Malacca see Melaka
Malacca, Strait of 138 B3 Ind. Selat Malaka. Strait Indonesia/Malaysia
Malacky 99 C6 Hung. Malacka. Bratislavský Kraj, W Slovakia
Maladzyechna 107 C5 Pol. Molodeczno, Rus. Molodechno. Minskaya Voblasts', C Belarus
Málaga 92 D5 anc. Malaca. Andalucía, S Spain
Malagarasi River 73 B7 river W Tanzania
Malaita 144 C3 var. Mala. Island N Solomon Islands
Malakal 73 B5 Upper Nile, S Sudan
Malakula see Malekula
Malang 138 D5 Jawa, C Indonesia
Malange see Malanje
Malanje 78 B1 var. Malange. Malanje, NW Angola
Mālaren 85 C6 lake C Sweden
Malatya 117 E4 anc. Melitene. Malatya, SE Turkey
Mala Vyska 109 E3 Rus. Malaya Viska. Kirovohrads'ka Oblast', S Ukraine

Malawi 79 E1 prev. Nyasaland, Nyasaland Protectorate. Country S Africa

Malawi 79

Official name Republic of Malawi
Formation 1964
Capital Lilongwe
Population 11.6 million / 254 people per sq mile (98 people per sq km)
Total area 45,745 sq miles (118,480 sq km)
Languages English, Chewa, Lomwe, Yao, Ngoni
Religions Protestant 55%, Roman Catholic 20%, Muslim 20%, other 5%
Ethnic mix Bantu 99%, other 1%
Government Multiparty democracy
Currency Malawi kwacha = 100 tambala
Literacy rate 60.1%
Calorie consumption 2,181 kilocalories

Malawi, Lake see Nyasa, Lake
Malay Peninsula 124 D4 peninsula Malaysia/Thailand
Malaysia 138 B3 var. Federation of Malaysia; prev. the separate territories of Federation of Malaya, Sarawak and Sabah (North Borneo) and Singapore. Country SE Asia

Malaysia 138

Official name Federation of Malaysia
Formation 1963
Capital Kuala Lumpur
Population 22.6 million / 178 people per sq mile (69 people per sq km)
Total area 127,316 sq miles (329,750 sq km)
Languages English, Bahasa Malaysia, Malay, Chinese, Tamil
Religions Muslim 53%, Buddhist 19%, Chinese faiths 12%, other 16%
Ethnic mix Malay 48%, Chinese 29%, Indigenous tribes 12%, other 11%
Government Presidential democracy
Currency Ringgit = 100 cents
Literacy rate 87.5%
Calorie consumption 2,919 kilocalories

Malaysia, Federation of see Malaysia
Malbork 98 C2 Ger. Marienburg, Marienburg in Westpreussen. Pomorskie, N Poland
Malchin 94 C3 Mecklenburg-Vorpommern, N Germany
Malden 45 H5 Missouri, C USA
Malden Island 145 G3 prev. Independence Island. Atoll E Kiribati
Maldives 132 A4 Country N Indian Ocean

Maldives 132

Official name Republic of Maldives
Formation 1965
Capital Malé
Population 300,000 / 2,590 people per sq mile (1,000 people per sq km)
Total area 116 sq miles (300 sq km)
Languages Dhivehi (Maldivian),
Religions Sunni Muslim 100%
Ethnic mix Mixed Arab, Sinhalese, Malay 100%
Government Non-party democracy
Currency Rufiyaa (Maldivian rupee) = 100 laari
Literacy rate 96.4%
Calorie consumption 2,592 kilocalories

Male' 132 B4 Male' Atoll, C Maldives
Male' Atoll 132 B4 var. Kaafu Atoll. Atoll C Maldives
Malekula 144 D4 var. Malakula; prev. Mallicolo. Island W Vanuatu
Malesína 105 C5 Stereá Ellás, E Greece
Malheur Lake 46 C3 lake Oregon, NW USA
Mali 75 E3 Fr. République du Mali; prev. French Sudan, Sudanese Republic. Country W Africa

Mali 75

Official name Republic of Mali
Formation 1960
Capital Bamako
Population 11.7 million / 24 people per sq mile (9 people per sq km)
Total area 478,764 sq miles (1,240,000 sq km)
Languages French, Bambara, Fulani, Senufo, Soninké
Religions Muslim (mainly Sunni) 80%, Traditional beliefs 18%, other 2%
Ethnic mix Bambara 32%, Fula 14%, Senufu 12%, Soninka 9%, other 33%
Government Multiparty democracy
Currency CFA franc = 100 centimes
Literacy rate 41.4%
Calorie consumption 2,403 kilocalories

Malik, Wadi al see Milk, Wadi el
Mali Kyun 137 B5 var. Tavoy Island. Island Mergui Archipelago, S Myanmar
Malindi 73 D7 Coast, SE Kenya
Malko Tŭrnovo 104 E3 Burgas, E Bulgaria
Mallaig 88 B3 N Scotland, UK
Mallicolo see Malekula
Mallorca 93 G3 Eng. Majorca; anc. Baleares Major. Island Islas Baleares, Spain, W Mediterranean Sea
Malmberget 84 C3 Norrbotten, N Sweden
Malmédy 87 D6 Liège, E Belgium
Malmö 85 B7 Skåne, S Sweden
Maloelap see Maloelap Atoll
Maloelap Atoll 144 D1 var. Maloelap. Atoll E Marshall Islands
Małopolska 98 D4 plateau S Poland
Malozemel'skaya Tundra 110 D3 physical region NW Russian Federation
Malta 97 C8 Country C Mediterranean Sea

Malta 97

Official name Republic of Malta
Formation 1964
Capital Valletta
Population 392,000 / 3,213 people per sq mile (1,241 people per sq km)
Total area 122 sq miles (316 sq km)
Languages Maltese, English
Religions Roman Catholic 98%, other and non-religious 2%
Ethnic mix Maltese (mixed Arab, Sicilian, Norman, Spanish, Italian, English) 96%, other 4%
Government Parliamentary democracy
Currency Maltese lira = 100 cents
Literacy rate 92.1%
Calorie consumption 3,543 kilocalories

Malta 97 C8 island Malta, C Mediterranean Sea
Malta 44 C1 Montana, NW USA
Malta 106 D4 Rēzekne, SE Latvia
Malta Channel 97 C8 It. Canale di Malta. Strait Italy/Malta
Maluku 139 F4 Dut. Molukken, Eng. Moluccas; prev. Spice Islands. Island group E Indonesia

Malung 85 B6 Kopparberg,
C Sweden
Malyn 108 D2 Rus. Malin.
Zhytomyrs'ka Oblast', N Ukraine
Mamberamo, Sungai 139 H4 river
Papua, E Indonesia
Mambij see Manbij
Mamonovo 106 A4 Ger.
Heiligenbeil. Kaliningradskaya
Oblast', W Russian Federation
Mamoré, Rio 61 F3 river
Bolivia/Brazil
Mamou 74 C4 Moyenne-Guinée,
W Guinea
Mamoudzou 79 F2 dependent
territory capital (Mayotte)
C Mayotte
Mamuno 78 C3 Ghanzi,
W Botswana
Manacor 93 G3 Mallorca, Spain,
W Mediterranean Sea
Manado 139 F3 prev. Menado.
Sulawesi, C Indonesia
Managua 52 D3 country capital
(Nicaragua) Managua,
W Nicaragua
Managua, Lago de 52 C3 var.
Xolotlán. Lake W Nicaragua
Manakara 79 G4 Fianarantsoa,
SE Madagascar
Manama see Al Manāmah
Mananjary 79 G3 Fianarantsoa,
SE Madagascar
Manapouri, Lake 151 A7 lake South
Island, NZ
Manar see Mannar
Manas, Gora 123 E2 mountain
Kyrgyzstan/Uzbekistan
Manaus 62 D2 prev. Manáos. State
capital Amazonas, NW Brazil
Manavgat 116 B4 Antalya,
SW Turkey
Manbij 118 C2 var. Mambij, Fr.
Membidj. Ḥalab, N Syria
Manchester 89 D5 Lat. Mancunium.
NW England,
UK
Manchester 41 G3 New Hampshire,
NE USA
Man-chou-li see Manzhouli
Manchuria 125 E1 cultural region
NE China
Máncio Lima see Japiim
Mand see Mand, Rūd-e
Mandalay 136 B3 Mandalay,
C Myanmar
Mandan 45 E2 North Dakota,
N USA
Mandeville 54 B5 C Jamaica
Mándra 105 C6 Attikí, C Greece
Mand, Rūd-e 120 D4 var. Mand.
River S Iran
Mandurah 147 A6 Western
Australia
Manduria 97 E5 Puglia, SE Italy
Mandya 132 C2 Karnātaka, C India
Manfredonia 97 D5 Puglia, SE Italy
Mangai 77 C6 Bandundu, W Dem.
Rep. Congo
Mangaia 145 G5 island group S Cook
Islands
Mangalia 108 D5 anc. Callatis.
Constanţa, SE Romania
Mangalmé 76 C3 Guéra, SE Chad
Mangalore 132 B2 Karnātaka,
W India
Mangaung see Bloemfontein
Mango see Sansanné-Mango
Mangoky 79 F3 river
W Madagascar
Manhattan 45 F4 Kansas, C USA
Manicouagan, Réservoir 38 D3 lake
Quebec, E Canada
Manihiki 145 G4 atoll N Cook
Islands
Manihiki Plateau 143 E3 undersea
feature C Pacific Ocean
Maniitsoq 82 C3 var. Manîtsoq,
Dan. Sukkertoppen. S Greenland
Manila 139 E1 off. City of Manila.
Country capital (Philippines)
Luzon, N Philippines
Manisa 116 A3 var. Manissa; prev.
Saruhan, anc. Magnesia. Manisa,
W Turkey
Manissa see Manisa
Manitoba 37 F5 province S Canada

Manitoba, Lake 37 F5 lake
Manitoba, S Canada
Manitoulin Island 38 C4 island
Ontario, S Canada
Manîtsoq see Maniitsoq
Manizales 58 B3 Caldas,
W Colombia
Manjimup 147 A7 Western
Australia
Mankato 45 F3 Minnesota, N USA
Manlleu 93 G2 Cataluña, NE Spain
Manly 148 E1 New South Wales,
SE Australia
Manmād 134 C5 Mahārāshtra,
W India
Mannar 132 C3 var. Manar.
Northern Province, NW Sri Lanka
Mannar, Gulf of 132 C3 gulf
India/Sri Lanka
Mannheim 95 B5 Baden-
Württemberg, SW Germany
Manono 77 E7 Shaba, SE Dem. Rep.
Congo
Manosque 91 D6 Alpes-de-Haute-
Provence, SE France
Manra 145 F3 prev. Sydney Island.
Atoll Phoenix Islands, C Kiribati
Mansa 78 D2 prev. Fort Rosebery.
Luapula, N Zambia
Mansel Island 37 G3 island
Nunavut, NE Canada
Mansfield 40 D4 Ohio, N USA
Manta 60 A2 Manabí, W Ecuador
Manteca 47 B6 California, W USA
Mantova 96 B2 Eng. Mantua, Fr.
Mantoue. Lombardia, NW Italy
Manuae 145 G4 island S Cook Islands
Manurewa 150 D3 var. Manukau.
Auckland, North Island, NZ
Manzanares 93 E3 Castilla-La
Mancha, C Spain
Manzanillo 50 D4 Colima,
SW Mexico
Manzanillo 54 C3 Granma, E Cuba
Manzhouli 127 F1 var. Man-chou-li.
Nei Mongol Zizhiqu, N China
Mao 76 B3 Kanem, W Chad
Maoke, Pegunungan 139 H4 Dut.
Sneeuw-gebergte, Eng. Snow
Mountains. Mountain range
Papua, E Indonesia
Maoming 128 C6 Guangdong,
S China
Mapmaker Seamounts 125 H2
undersea feature N Pacific Ocean
Maputo 78 D4 prev. Lourenço
Marques. Country capital
(Mozambique) Maputo,
S Mozambique
Marabá 63 F2 Pará, NE Brazil
Maracaibo 58 C1 Zulia,
NW Venezuela
Maracaibo, Lago de 58 C2 var. Lake
Maracaibo. Inlet NW Venezuela
Maracaibo, Lake see Maracaibo,
Lago de
Maracay 58 D2 Aragua,
N Venezuela
Marada see Marādah
Marādah 71 G3 var. Marada.
N Libya
Maradi 75 G3 Maradi, S Niger
Maragha see Marāgheh
Marāgheh 120 C2 var. Maragha.
Āžarbāyjān-e Khāvarī, NW Iran
Marajó, Baía de 63 F1 bay N Brazil
Marajó, Ilha de 63 E1 island
N Brazil
Marakesh see Marrakech
Maramba see Livingstone
Maranhão 63 F2 off. Estado do
Maranhão. State E Brazil
Marañón, Río 60 B2 river N Peru
Maraş see Kahramanmaraş
Marash see Kahramanmaraş
Marathon 38 C4 Ontario, S Canada
Marathónas 105 C5 prev. Marathón.
Attikí, C Greece
Marbella 92 D5 Andalucía,
S Spain
Marble Bar 146 B4 Western
Australia
Marburg an der Lahn 94 B4 hist.
Marburg. Hessen, W Germany
March see Morava
Marche 91 C5 cultural region
C France

Marche 96 C3 cultural region
E Italy
Marche-en-Famenne 87 C7
Luxembourg, SE Belgium
Marchena, Isla 60 B5 var. Bindloe
Island. Island Galapagos Islands,
Ecuador, E Pacific Ocean
Mar Chiquita, Laguna 64 C3 lake
C Argentina
Marcounda see Markounda
Mardān 134 C1 North-West Frontier
Province, N Pakistan
Mar del Plata 65 D5 Buenos Aires,
E Argentina
Mardin 117 E4 Mardin, SE Turkey
Maré 144 D5 island Îles Loyauté,
E New Caledonia
Marea Neagrã see Black Sea
Mare Creticum see Kritikó Pélagos
Mareeba 148 D3 Queensland,
NE Australia
Margarita, Isla de 59 E1 island
N Venezuela
Margate 89 E7 prev. Mergate.
SE England, UK
Marghita 108 B3 Hung. Margitta.
Bihor, NW Romania
Marhanets' 109 F3 Rus. Marganets.
Dnipropetrovs'ka Oblast',
E Ukraine
María Cleofas, Isla 50 C4 island
C Mexico
Maria Island 149 C8 island
Tasmania, SE Australia
María Madre, Isla 50 C4 island
C Mexico
María Magdalena, Isla 50 C4 island
C Mexico
Mariana Trench 125 G4 undersea
feature W Pacific Ocean
Mariánské Lázně 99 A5 Ger.
Marienbad. Karlovarský Kraj,
W Czech Republic
Marías, Islas 50 C4 island group
C Mexico
Maribor 95 E7 Ger. Marburg.
NE Slovenia
Marica see Maritsa
Maridi 73 B5 Western Equatoria,
SW Sudan
Marie Byrd Land 154 A3 physical
region Antarctica
Marie-Galante 55 G4 var. Ceyre to
the Caribs. Island SE
Guadeloupe
Mariental 78 B4 Hardap,
SW Namibia
Mariestad 85 B6 Västra Götaland,
S Sweden
Marietta 42 D2 Georgia, SE USA
Marijampolé 106 B4 prev.
Kapsukas. Marijampolé,
S Lithuania
Marília 63 E4 São Paulo, S Brazil
Marín 92 B1 Galicia, NW Spain
Mar''ina Horka 107 C6 Rus.
Mar'ina Gorka. Minskaya
Voblasts', C Belarus
Maringá 63 E4 Paraná, S Brazil
Marion 45 G3 Iowa, C USA
Marion 40 D4 Ohio, N USA
Marion, Lake 43 E2 reservoir South
Carolina, SE USA
Mariscal Estigarribia 64 D2
Boquerón, NW Paraguay
Maritsa 104 D3 var. Marica, Gk.
Évros, Turk. Meriç; anc. Hebrus.
River SW Europe see also
Évros/Meriç
Maritzburg see Pietermaritzburg
Mariupol' 109 G4 prev. Zhdanov.
Donets'ka Oblast', SE Ukraine
Marka 73 D6 var. Merca.
Shabeellaha Hoose, S Somalia
Markham, Mount 154 B4 mountain
Antarctica
Markounda 76 C4 var. Marcounda.
Ouham, NW Central African
Republic
Marktredwitz 95 C5 Bayern,
E Germany
Marlborough 148 D4 Queensland,
E Australia
Marmande 91 B5 anc. Marmanda.
Lot-et-Garonne, SW France
Marmara Denizi 116 A2 Eng. Sea of
Marmara. Sea NW Turkey

Marmara, Sea of see Marmara
Denizi
Marmaris 116 A4 Muğla,
SW Turkey
Marne 90 C3 cultural region
N France
Marne 90 D3 river N France
Maro 76 C4 Moyen-Chari, S Chad
Maroantsetra 79 G2 Toamasina,
NE Madagascar
Maromokotro 79 G2 mountain
N Madagascar
Maroni River 59 G3 Dut. Marowijne.
River French Guiana/Suriname
Maros see Mureş
Marosch see Mureş
Marotiri 143 F4 var. Îlots de Bass,
Morotiri. Island group Îles
Australes, SW French Polynesia
Maroua 76 B3 Extrême-Nord,
N Cameroon
Marquesas Fracture Zone 153 E3
tectonic feature E Pacific Ocean
Marquesas Islands 153 E3 island
group N French Polynesia
Marquette 40 B1 Michigan, N USA
Marrakech 70 C2 var. Marakesh,
Eng. Marrakesh; prev. Morocco.
W Morocco
Marrakesh see Marrakech
Marrawah 149 C8 Tasmania,
SE Australia
Marree 149 B5 South Australia
Marsá al Burayqah 71 G3 var.
Al Burayqah. N Libya
Marsabit 73 C6 Eastern, N Kenya
Marsala 97 B7 anc. Lilybaeum.
Sicilia, Italy, C Mediterranean Sea
Marsberg 94 B4 Nordrhein-
Westfalen, W Germany
Marseille 91 D6 Eng. Marseilles;
anc. Massilia. Bouches-du-Rhône,
SE France
Marshall 45 F2 Minnesota, N USA
Marshall 49 H2 Texas, SW USA
Marshall Islands 144 C1 Country
W Pacific Ocean

Marshall Islands 144

Official name Republic of the
Marshall Islands
Formation 1986
Capital Majuro
Population 68,100 / 973 people
per sq mile (376 people per sq km)
Total area 70 sq miles (181 sq km)
Languages Marshallese, English,
Japanese, German
Religions Protestant 90%, Roman
Catholic 8%, other 2%
Ethnic mix Micronesian 97%,
other 3%
Government Parliamentary
democracy
Currency US dollar = 100 cents
Literacy rate 91%
Calorie consumption not available

Marshall Seamounts 125 H3
undersea feature N Pacific Ocean
Marsh Harbour 54 C1 Great Abaco,
W Bahamas
Martaban 136 B4 var. Moktama.
Mon State, S Myanmar
Martha's Vineyard 41 G3 island
Massachusetts, NE USA
Martigues 91 D6 Bouches-du-
Rhône, SE France
Martin 99 C5 Ger. Sankt Martin,
Hung. Turócszentmárton; prev.
Turčiansky Svätý Martin. Žilinský
Kraj, N Slovakia
Martinique 55 G4 French overseas
department E West Indies
Martinique Channel see
Martinique Passage
Martinique Passage 55 G4 var.
Dominica Channel, Martinique
Channel. Channel
Dominica/Martinique
Marton 150 D4 Manawatu-
Wanganui, North Island, NZ
Martos 92 D4 Andalucía, S Spain
Marungu 77 E7 mountain range
SE Dem. Rep. Congo

Mary 122 D3 *prev.* Merv. Maryyskiy Velayat, S Turkmenistan
Maryborough *see* Portlaoise
Maryborough 149 D4 Queensland, E Australia
Mary Island *see* Kanton
Maryland 41 E5 *off.* State of Maryland; also known as America in Miniature, Cockade State, Free State, Old Line State. *State* NE USA
Maryland 42 D1 Tennessee, S USA
Maryville 45 F4 Missouri, C USA
Masai Steppe 73 C7 *grassland* NW Tanzania
Masaka 73 B6 SW Uganda
Masalli 117 H3 *Rus.* Masally. S Azerbaijan
Masasi 73 C8 Mtwara, SE Tanzania
Masawa *see* Massawa
Masaya 52 D3 Masaya, W Nicaragua
Mascarene Basin 141 B5 *undersea feature* W Indian Ocean
Mascarene Islands 79 H4 *island group* W Indian Ocean
Mascarene Plain 141 B5 *undersea feature* W Indian Ocean
Mascarene Plateau 141 B5 *undersea feature* W Indian Ocean
Maseru 78 D4 *country capital* (Lesotho) W Lesotho
Mashhad 120 E2 *var.* Meshed. Khorāsān, NE Iran
Mas-ha 119 D7 W Bank
Masindi 73 B6 W Uganda
Masīra *see* Maşīrah, Jazīrat
Masira, Gulf of *see* Maşīrah, Khalīj
Maşīrah, Jazīrat 121 E5 *var.* Masīra. *Island* E Oman
Maşīrah, Khalīj 121 E5 *var.* Gulf of Masira. *Bay* E Oman
Masis *see* Büyükağrı Dağı
Maskat *see* Masqaţ
Mason City 45 F3 Iowa, C USA
Masqaţ 121 E5 *var.* Maskat, *Eng.* Muscat. *Country capital* (Oman) NE Oman
Massa 96 B3 Toscana, C Italy
Massachusetts 41 G3 *off.* Commonwealth of Massachusetts; also known as Bay State, Old Bay State, Old Colony State. *State* NE USA
Massawa 72 C4 *var.* Masawa, *Amh.* Mits'iwa. E Eritrea
Massenya 76 B3 Chari-Baguirmi, SW Chad
Massif Central 91 C5 *plateau* C France
Massif du Makay *see* Makay
Massoukou *see* Franceville
Masterton 151 D5 Wellington, North Island, NZ
Masty 107 B5 *Rus.* Mosty. Hrodzyenskaya Voblasts', W Belarus
Masuda 131 B6 Shimane, Honshū, SW Japan
Masuku *see* Franceville
Masvingo 78 D3 *prev.* Fort Victoria, Nyanda, Victoria. Masvingo, SE Zimbabwe
Maşyāf 118 B3 *Fr.* Misiaf. Ḥamāh, C Syria
Matadi 77 B6 Bas-Zaïre, W Dem. Rep. Congo
Matagalpa 52 D3 Matagalpa, C Nicaragua
Matale 132 D3 Central Province, C Sri Lanka
Matam 74 C3 NE Senegal
Matamata 150 D3 Waikato, North Island, NZ
Matamoros 50 D3 Coahuila de Zaragoza, NE Mexico
Matamoros 51 E2 Tamaulipas, C Mexico
Matane 39 E4 Quebec, SE Canada
Matanzas 54 B2 Matanzas, NW Cuba
Matara 132 D4 Southern Province, S Sri Lanka
Mataram 138 D5 Pulau Lombok, C Indonesia
Mataró 93 G2 *anc.* Illuro. Cataluña, E Spain
Mataura 151 B7 *river* South Island, NZ

Mataura 151 B7 Southland, South Island, NZ
Mata Uta *see* Matā'utu
Matā'utu 145 E4 *var.* Mata Uta. *Dependent territory capital* (Wallis and Futuna) Île Uvea, Wallis and Futuna
Matera 97 E5 Basilicata, S Italy
Matías Romero 51 F5 Oaxaca, SE Mexico
Mato Grosso 63 E4 *prev.* Vila Bela da Santissima Trindade. Mato Grosso, W Brazil
Mato Grosso do Sul 63 E4 *off.* Estado de Mato Grosso do Sul. *State* S Brazil
Mato Grosso, Planalto de 56 C4 *plateau* C Brazil
Matosinhos 92 B2 *prev.* Matozinhos. Porto, NW Portugal
Matsue 131 B6 *var.* Matsuye, Matue. Shimane, Honshū, SW Japan
Matsumoto 131 C5 *var.* Matumoto. Nagano, Honshū, S Japan
Matsuyama 131 B7 *var.* Matuyama. Ehime, Shikoku, SW Japan
Matsuye *see* Matsue
Matterhorn 95 A8 *It.* Monte Cervino. *Mountain* Italy/Switzerland *see also* Cervino, Monte
Matthews Ridge 59 F2 N Guyana
Matthew Town 54 D2 Great Inagua, S Bahamas
Matucana 60 C4 Lima, W Peru
Matue *see* Matsue
Matumoto *see* Matsumoto
Maturín 59 E2 Monagas, NE Venezuela
Matuyama *see* Matsuyama
Mau 135 E3 *var.* Maunāth Bhanjan. Uttar Pradesh, N India
Maui 47 B8 *island* Hawaii, USA, C Pacific Ocean
Maulmain *see* Moulmein
Maun 78 C3 Ngamiland, C Botswana
Maunāth Bhanjan *see* Mau
Mauren 94 E1 NE Liechtenstein
Mauritania 74 C2 *Ar.* Mūrītānīyah. *Country* W Africa

Mauritania 74

Official name Islamic Republic of Mauritania
Formation 1960
Capital Nouakchott
Population 2.7 million / 7 people per sq mile (3 people per sq km)
Total area 397,953 sq miles (1,030,700 sq km)
Languages Hassaniyah Arabic, French, Wolof
Religions Muslim (Sunni) 100%
Ethnic mix Maure 81%, Wolof 7%, Tukolor 5%, Soninka 3%, other 4%
Government Multiparty republic
Currency Ouguiya = 5 khoums
Literacy rate 42.3%
Calorie consumption 2,638 kilocalories

Mauritius 79 H3 *Fr.* Maurice. *Country* W Indian Ocean

Mauritius 79

Official name Mauritius
Formation 1968
Capital Port Louis
Population 1.2 million / 1,671 people per sq mile (645 people per sq km)
Total area 718 sq miles (1,860 sq km)
Languages English, French, French Creole, Hindi, Urdu, Tamil, Chinese
Religions Hindu 52%, Muslim 17%, Roman Catholic 26%, other 5%
Ethnic mix Indo-Mauritian 68%, Creole 27%, Sino-Mauritian 3%, Franco-Mauritian 2%
Government Parliamentary democracy

Mauritius (continued)

Currency Mauritian rupee = 100 cents
Literacy rate 84.6%
Calorie consumption 2,985 kilocalories

Mauritius 141 B5 *island* W Indian Ocean
Mawlamyine *see* Moulmein
Mawson 154 D2 *Australian research station* Antarctica
Maya 52 B1 *river* E Russian Federation
Mayadin *see* Al Mayādīn
Mayaguana 54 D2 *island* SE Bahamas
Mayaguana Passage 54 D2 *passage* SE Bahamas
Mayagüez 55 F3 W Puerto Rico
Mayamey 120 D2 Semnān, N Iran
Maya Mountains 52 B2 *Sp.* Montañas Mayas. *Mountain range* Belize/Guatemala
Maych'ew 72 C4 *var.* Mai Chio, *It.* Mai Ceu. N Ethiopia
Maydān Shahr 123 E4 Wardag, E Afghanistan
Mayebashi *see* Maebashi
Mayfield 151 B6 Canterbury, South Island, NZ
Maykop 111 A7 Respublika Adygeya, SW Russian Federation
Maymana *see* Meymaneh
Maymyo 136 B3 Mandalay, C Myanmar
Mayo *see* Maio
Mayor Island 150 D3 *island* NE NZ
Mayor Pablo Lagerenza *see* Capitán Pablo Lagerenza
Mayotte 79 F2 *French territorial collectivity* E Africa
May Pen 54 B5 C Jamaica
Mazabuka 78 D2 Southern, S Zambia
Mazaca *see* Kayseri
Mazār-i Sharīf 123 E3 *var.* Mazār-i Sharif. Balkh, N Afghanistan
Mazār-i Sharif *see* Mazār-e Sharīf
Mazatlán 50 C3 Sinaloa, C Mexico
Mažeikiai 106 B3 Mažeikiai, NW Lithuania
Mazirbe 106 C2 Talsi, NW Latvia
Mazra'a *see* Al Mazra'ah
Mazury 98 D3 *physical region* NE Poland
Mazyr 107 C7 *Rus.* Mozyr'. Homyel'skaya Voblasts', SE Belarus
Mbabane 78 D4 *country capital* (Swaziland) NW Swaziland
Mbacké *see* Mbaïki
M'Baïki *see* Mbaïki
Mbaïki 77 C5 *var.* M'Baïki. Lobaye, SW Central African Republic
Mbaké 74 B3 *var.* Mbacké. W Senegal
Mbala 78 D1 *prev.* Abercorn. Northern, NE Zambia
Mbale 73 C6 E Uganda
Mbandaka 77 C5 *prev.* Coquilhatville. Equateur, NW Dem. Rep. Congo
M'Banza Congo 78 B1 *var.* Mbanza Congo; *prev.* São Salvador, São Salvador do Congo. Zaire, NW Angola
Mbanza-Ngungu 77 B6 Bas-Zaïre, W Dem. Rep. Congo
Mbarara 73 B6 SW Uganda
Mbé 76 B4 Nord, N Cameroon
Mbeya 73 C7 Mbeya, SW Tanzania
Mbomou *see* Bomu
M'Bomu *see* Bomu
Mbour 74 B3 W Senegal
Mbuji-Mayi 77 D7 *prev.* Bakwanga. Kasai Oriental, S Dem. Rep. Congo
McAlester 49 G2 Oklahoma, C USA
McAllen 49 G5 Texas, SW USA
McCamey 49 E3 Texas, SW USA
McClintock Channel 37 F2 *channel* Nunavut, N Canada
McComb 42 B3 Mississippi, S USA

McCook 45 E4 Nebraska, C USA
McKean Island 145 E3 *island* Phoenix Islands, C Kiribati
McKinley, Mount 36 C3 *var.* Denali. *Mountain* Alaska, USA
McKinley Park 36 C3 Alaska, USA
McMinnville 46 B3 Oregon, NW USA
McMurdo Base 154 B4 *US research station* Antarctica
McPherson *see* Fort McPherson
McPherson 45 E5 Kansas, C USA
Mdantsane 78 D5 Eastern Cape, SE South Africa
Mead, Lake 47 D6 *reservoir* Arizona/Nevada, W USA
Meghālaya 113 G3 *state*, NE India
Mecca *see* Makkah
Mechelen 87 C5 *Eng.* Mechlin, *Fr.* Malines. Antwerpen, C Belgium
Mecklenburger Bucht 94 C2 *bay* N Germany
Mecsek 99 C7 *mountain range* SW Hungary
Medan 138 B3 Sumatera, E Indonesia
Medeba *see* Ma'dabā
Medellín 58 B3 Antioquia, NW Colombia
Médenine 71 F2 *var.* Madanīyīn. SE Tunisia
Medford 46 B4 Oregon, NW USA
Medgidia 108 D5 Constanţa, SE Romania
Mediaş 108 B4 *Ger.* Mediasch, *Hung.* Medgyes. Sibiu, C Romania
Medicine Hat 37 F5 Alberta, SW Canada
Medinaceli 93 E2 Castilla-León, N Spain
Medina del Campo 92 D2 Castilla-León, N Spain
Mediterranean Sea 102 D3 *Fr.* Mer Méditerranée. *Sea* Africa/Asia/Europe
Médoc 91 B5 *cultural region* SW France
Medvezh'yegorsk 110 B3 Respublika Kareliya, NW Russian Federation
Meekatharra 147 B5 Western Australia
Meemu Atoll *see* Mulaku Atoll
Meerssen 87 D6 *var.* Mersen. Limburg, SE Netherlands
Meerut 134 D2 Uttar Pradesh, N India
Mehdia *see* Mahdia
Meheso *see* Mī'ēso
Me Hka *see* Nmai Hka
Mehrīz 120 D3 Yazd, C Iran
Mehtar Lām *see* Mehtarlām
Mehtarlām 123 F4 *var.* Mehtar Lām, Meterlam, Methariam, Metharlam. Laghmān, E Afghanistan
Meiktila 136 B3 Mandalay, C Myanmar
Mejillones 64 B2 Antofagasta, N Chile
Mek'elē 72 C4 *var.* Makale. N Ethiopia
Mékhé 74 B3 NW Senegal
Mekong 124 D3 *var.* Lan-ts'ang Chiang, *Cam.* Mékôngk, *Chin.* Lancang Jiang, *Lao.* Mènam Khong, *Th.* Mae Nam Khong, *Tib.* Dza Chu, *Vtn.* Sông Tiên Giang. *River* SE Asia
Mékôngk *see* Mekong
Mekong, Mouths of the 137 E6 *delta* S Vietnam
Melaka 138 B3 *var.* Malacca. Melaka, Peninsular Malaysia
Melanesia 144 D3 *island group* W Pacific Ocean
Melanesian Basin 142 C2 *undersea feature* W Pacific Ocean
Melbourne 149 C7 *state capital* Victoria, SE Australia
Melbourne 43 E4 Florida, SE USA
Melghir, Chott 71 E2 *var.* Chott Melrhir. *Salt lake* E Algeria
Melilla 80 B5 *anc.* Rusaddir, Russadir. Melilla, Spain, N Africa
Melilla 70 D2 *enclave* Spain, N Africa
Melita 37 F5 Manitoba, S Canada

Melitopol' 109 F4 Zaporiz'ka Oblast', SE Ukraine
Melle 87 B5 Oost-Vlaanderen, NW Belgium
Mellerud 85 B6 Västra Götaland, S Sweden
Mellieha 102 B5 E Malta
Mellizo Sur, Cerro 65 A7 *mountain* S Chile
Melo 64 E4 Cerro Largo, NE Uruguay
Melsungen 94 B4 Hessen, C Germany
Melun 90 C3 *anc.* Melodunum. Seine-et-Marne, N France
Melville Island 146 D2 *island* Northern Territory, N Australia
Melville Island 37 E2 *island* Parry Islands, Northwest Territories/Nunavut, NW Canada
Melville, Lake 39 F2 *lake* Newfoundland and Labrador, E Canada
Melville Peninsula 37 G3 *peninsula* Northwest Territories, NE Canada
Membidj *see* Manbij
Memmingen 95 B6 Bayern, S Germany
Memphis 42 C1 Tennessee, S USA
Ménaka 75 F3 Goa, E Mali
Menaldum 86 D1 Fris. Menaam. Friesland, N Netherlands
Mènam Khong *see* Mekong
Mendaña Fracture Zone 153 F4 *tectonic feature* E Pacific Ocean
Mende 91 C5 *anc.* Mimatum. Lozère, S France
Mendeleyev Ridge 155 B2 *undersea feature* Arctic Ocean
Mendocino Fracture Zone 152 D2 *tectonic feature* NE Pacific Ocean
Mendoza 64 B4 Mendoza, W Argentina
Menemen 116 A3 İzmir, W Turkey
Menengiyn Tal 127 F2 *plain* E Mongolia
Menongue 78 B2 *var.* Vila Serpa Pinto, *Port.* Serpa Pinto. Cuando Cubango, C Angola
Menorca 93 H3 Eng. N Africa
Mentawai, Kepulauan 138 A4 *island group* W Indonesia
Meppel 86 D2 Drenthe, NE Netherlands
Merano 96 C1 Ger. Meran. Trentino-Alto Adige, N Italy
Merca *see* Marka
Mercedes *see* Villa Mercedes
Mercedes 64 D3 Corrientes, NE Argentina
Mercedes 64 D4 Soriano, SW Uruguay
Meredith, Lake 49 E1 *reservoir* Texas, SW USA
Merefa 109 G2 Kharkivs'ka Oblast', E Ukraine
Mergui 137 B6 Tenasserim, S Myanmar
Mergui Archipelago 137 B6 *island group* S Myanmar
Meriç *see* Maritsa
Mérida 92 C4 *anc.* Augusta Emerita. Extremadura, W Spain
Mérida 58 C2 Mérida, W Venezuela
Mérida 51 H3 Yucatán, SW Mexico
Meridian 42 C2 Mississippi, S USA
Mérignac 91 B5 Gironde, SW France
Merkinė 107 B5 Varėna, S Lithuania
Merowe 72 B3 *desert* W Sudan
Merredin 147 B6 Western Australia
Mersen *see* Meerssen
Mersey 89 D5 *river* NW England, UK
Mersin 116 C4 İçel, S Turkey
Mērsrags 106 C3 Talsi, NW Latvia

Meru 73 C6 Eastern, C Kenya
Merzifon 116 D2 Amasya, N Turkey
Merzig 95 A5 Saarland, SW Germany
Mesa 48 B2 Arizona, SW USA
Meshed *see* Mashhad
Mesopotamia 57 C5 *var.* Mesopotamia Argentina. *Physical region* NE Argentina
Mesopotamia Argentina *see* Mesopotamia
Messalo, Rio 79 E2 *var.* Mualo. *River* NE Mozambique
Messana *see* Messina
Messene *see* Messina
Messina 97 D7 *var.* Messana, Messene; *anc.* Zancle. Sicilia, Italy, C Mediterranean Sea
Messina 78 D3 Northern, NE South Africa
Messina, Stretto di 97 D7 Eng. Strait of Messina. *Strait* SW Italy
Messíni 105 B6 Pelopónnisos, S Greece
Mestghanem *see* Mostaganem
Mestia 117 F1 *var.* Mestiya. N Georgia
Mestiya *see* Mestia
Mestre 96 C2 Veneto, NE Italy
Meta 56 B2 *off.* Departamento del Meta. *Province* C Colombia
Metairie 42 B3 Louisiana, S USA
Metán 64 C2 Salta, N Argentina
Metapán 52 B2 Santa Ana, NW El Salvador
Meta, Río 58 D3 *river* Colombia/Venezuela
Meterlam *see* Mehtarlām
Methariam *see* Mehtarlām
Metharlam *see* Mehtarlām
Metković 100 B4 Dubrovnik-Neretva, SE Croatia
Métsovo 104 B4 prev. Métsovon. Ípeiros, C Greece
Metz 90 D3 *anc.* Divodurum Mediomatricum, Mediomatrica, Metis. Moselle, NE France
Meulaboh 138 A3 Sumatera, W Indonesia
Meuse 87 C6 *Dut.* Maas. *River* W Europe *see also* Maas
Meuse 90 D3 *department* NE France
Mexcala, Río *see* Balsas, Río
Mexicali 50 A1 Baja California, NW Mexico
Mexico 50 C3 *var.* Méjico, México, *Sp.* Estados Unidos Mexicanos. *Country* N Central America

Mexico 50

Official name United States of Mexico
Formation 1836
Capital Mexico City
Population 100.4 million / 132 people per sq mile (51 people per sq km)
Total area 761,602 sq miles (1,972,550 sq km)
Languages Spanish, Nahuatl, Mayan, Zapotec, Mixtec, Otomi, Totonac, Tzotzil, Tzeltal
Religions Roman Catholic 95%, Protestant 1%, other 4%
Ethnic mix Mestizo 55%, Amerindian 20%, European 16%, other 9%
Government Presidential democracy
Currency Mexican peso = 100 centavos
Literacy rate 91.3%
Calorie consumption 3,165 kilocalories

Mexico 45 G4 Missouri, C USA
México 51 E4 *var.* Ciudad de México, Eng. Mexico City. *Country capital* (Mexico) México, C Mexico
Mexico City *see* México
Mexico, Gulf of 51 F2 *Sp.* Golfo de México. *Gulf* W Atlantic Ocean

Meyadine *see* Al Mayādīn
Meymaneh 122 D3 *var.* Maimāna, Maymana. Fāryāb, NW Afghanistan
Mezen' 110 D3 *river* NW Russian Federation
Mezőtúr 99 D7 Jász-Nagykun-Szolnok, E Hungary
Mgarr 102 A5 Gozo, N Malta
Miahuatlán 51 F5 *var.* Miahuatlán de Porfirio Díaz. Oaxaca, SE Mexico
Miahuatlán de Porfirio Díaz *see* Miahuatlán
Miami 43 F5 Florida, SE USA
Miami 49 G1 Oklahoma, C USA
Miami Beach 43 F5 Florida, SE USA
Miāneh 120 C2 *var.* Miyāneh. Āžarbāyjān-e Khāvarī, NW Iran
Mianyang 128 B5 Sichuan, C China
Miastko 98 C2 Ger. Rummelsburg in Pommern. Pomorskie, N Poland
Mi Chai *see* Nong Khai
Michalovce 99 E5 Ger. Grossmichel, Hung. Nagymihály. Košický Kraj, E Slovakia
Michigan 40 C1 *off.* State of Michigan; also known as Great Lakes State, Lake State, Wolverine State. *State* N USA
Michigan, Lake 40 C2 *lake* N USA
Michurinsk 111 B5 Tambovskaya Oblast', W Russian Federation
Micoud 55 F2 SE Saint Lucia
Micronesia 144 B1 Country W Pacific Ocean

Micronesia 144

Official name Federated States of Micronesia
Formation 1986
Capital Palikir (Pohnpei island)
Population 2500 / 490 people per sq mile (189 people per sq km)
Total area 271 sq miles (702 sq km)
Languages English, Trukese, Pohnpeian, Mortlockese, Losrean
Religions Roman Catholic 50%, Protestant 48%, other 2%
Ethnic mix Micronesian 100%
Government Non-party democracy
Currency US dollar = 100 cents
Literacy rate 89%
Calorie consumption not available

Micronesia 144 C1 *island group* W Pacific Ocean
Mid-Atlantic Cordillera *see* Mid-Atlantic Ridge
Mid-Atlantic Ridge 66 C3 *var.* Mid-Atlantic Cordillera, Mid-Atlantic Rise, Mid-Atlantic Swell. *Undersea feature* Atlantic Ocean
Mid-Atlantic Rise *see* Mid-Atlantic Ridge
Mid-Atlantic Swell *see* Mid-Atlantic Ridge
Middelburg 87 B5 Zeeland, SW Netherlands
Middelharnis 86 B4 Zuid-Holland, SW Netherlands
Middelkerke 87 A5 West-Vlaanderen, W Belgium
Middle America Trench 35 B7 *undersea feature* E Pacific Ocean
Middle Andaman 133 F2 *island* Andaman Islands, India, NE Indian Ocean
Middlesboro 42 C5 Kentucky, S USA
Middlesbrough 89 D5 N England, UK
Middletown 41 F4 New Jersey, NE USA
Middletown 41 F3 New York, NE USA
Mid-Indian Basin 141 C5 *undersea feature* N Indian Ocean
Mid-Indian Ridge 141 C5 *var.* Central Indian Ridge. *Undersea feature* C Indian Ocean
Midland 40 C3 Michigan, N USA
Midland 38 D5 Ontario, S Canada

Midland 49 E3 Texas, SW USA
Mid-Pacific Mountains 152 C2 *var.* Mid-Pacific Seamounts. *Undersea feature* NW Pacific Ocean
Mid-Pacific Seamounts *see* Mid-Pacific Mountains
Midway Islands 152 D2 US *territory* C Pacific Ocean
Miechów 99 D5 Małopolskie, S Poland
Międzyrzec Podlaski 98 E3 Lubelskie, E Poland
Międzyrzecz 98 B3 Ger. Meseritz. Lubuskie, W Poland
Mielec 99 D5 Podkarpackie, SE Poland
Miercurea-Ciuc 108 C4 Ger. Szeklerburg, Hung. Csíkszereda. Harghita, C Romania
Mieres del Camín *see* Mieres del Camino
Mieres del Camino 108 D1 *var.* Mieres del Camín. Asturias, NW Spain
Mieresch *see* Mureş
Mi'ēso 73 D5 *var.* Meheso, Miesso. C Ethiopia
Miesso *see* Mi'ēso
Miguel Asua 50 D3 *var.* Miguel Auza. Zacatecas, C Mexico
Miguel Auza *see* Miguel Asua
Mijdrecht 86 C3 Utrecht, C Netherlands
Mikashevichy 107 C7 Pol. Mikaszewicze, *Rus.* Mikashevichi. Brestskaya Voblasts', SW Belarus
Mikhaylovka 111 B6 Volgogradskaya Oblast', SW Russian Federation
Míkonos *see* Mýkonos
Mikre 104 C2 Lovech, N Bulgaria
Mikun' 110 D4 Respublika Komi, NW Russian Federation
Mikuni-sanmyaku 131 D5 *mountain range* Honshū, N Japan
Mikura-jima 131 D6 *island* E Japan
Milagro 60 B2 Guayas, SW Ecuador
Milan *see* Milano
Milange 79 E2 Zambézia, NE Mozambique
Milano 96 B2 Eng. Milan, Ger. Mailand; *anc.* Mediolanum. Lombardia, N Italy
Milas 116 A4 Muğla, SW Turkey
Milashavichy 107 C7 Rus. Milashevichi. Homyel'skaya Voblasts', SE Belarus
Mildura 149 C6 Victoria, SE Australia
Mile *see* Mili Atoll
Miles 149 D5 Queensland, E Australia
Miles City 44 C2 Montana, NW USA
Milford Haven 89 C6 prev. Milford. SW Wales, UK
Milford Sound 151 A6 *inlet* South Island, NZ
Milford Sound 151 A6 Southland, South Island, NZ
Mili Atoll 144 D2 *var.* Mile. *Atoll* Ratak Chain, SE Marshall Islands
Mil'kovo 115 H3 Kamchatskaya Oblast', E Russian Federation
Milk River 44 C1 *river* Montana, NW USA
Milk River 37 E5 Alberta, SW Canada
Milk, Wadi el 88 B4 *var.* Wadi al Malik. *River* C Sudan
Milledgeville 43 E2 Georgia, SE USA
Mille Lacs Lake 45 F2 *lake* Minnesota, N USA
Millennium Island 160 C8 prev. Caroline Island, Thornton Island. *Atoll* Line Islands, E Kiribati
Millerovo 111 B6 Rostovskaya Oblast', SW Russian Federation
Mílos 105 C7 *island* Kykládes, Greece, Aegean Sea
Milos 105 C6 Mílos, Kykládes, Greece, Aegean Sea
Milton 151 B7 Otago, South Island, NZ
Milton Keynes 89 D6 SE England, UK
Milwaukee 40 B3 Wisconsin, N USA
Min *see* Fujian
Mīnā' Qābūs 140 B3 NE Oman

Minas Gerais 63 F3 off. Estado de Minas Gerais. *State* E Brazil
Minatitlán 51 F4 Veracruz-Llave, E Mexico
Minbu 136 A3 Magwe, W Myanmar
Minch, The 88 B3 var. North Minch. *Strait* NW Scotland, UK
Mindanao 139 F2 *island* S Philippines
Mindanao Sea *see* Bohol Sea
Mindello 95 C6 Bayern, S Germany
Mindello *see* Mindelo
Mindelo 74 A2 var. Mindello; *prev.* Porto Grande. São Vicente, N Cape Verde
Minden 94 B4 anc. Minthun. Nordrhein-Westfalen, NW Germany
Mindoro 139 E2 *island* N Philippines
Mindoro Strait 139 E2 *strait* W Philippines
Mineral Wells 49 F2 Texas, SW USA
Mingäçevir 117 G2 *Rus.* Mingechaur, Mingechevir. C Azerbaijan
Mingāora 134 C1 var. Mingora, Mongora. North-West Frontier Province, N Pakistan
Mingora *see* Mingāora
Minho 92 B2 *former province* N Portugal
Minho, Rio 92 B2 Sp. Miño. *river* Portugal/Spain *see also* Miño
Minicoy Island 132 B3 *island* SW India
Minius *see* Miño
Minna 75 G4 Niger, C Nigeria
Minneapolis 45 F2 Minnesota, N USA
Minnesota 45 F2 off. State of Minnesota; also known as Gopher State, New England of the West, North Star State. *State* N USA
Miño 92 B2 var. Mino, Minius, Port. Rio Minho. *river* Portugal/Spain *see also* Minho, Rio
Mino *see* Miño
Minot 45 E1 North Dakota, N USA
Minsk 107 C6 *country capital* (Belarus) Minskaya Voblasts', C Belarus
Minskaya Wzvyshsha 107 C6 *mountain range* C Belarus
Minsk Mazowiecki 98 D3 var. Nowo-Minsk. Mazowieckie, C Poland
Minto, Lac 38 D2 *lake* Quebec, C Canada
Minya *see* El Minya
Miraflores 50 C3 Baja California Sur, W Mexico
Miranda de Ebro 93 E1 La Rioja, N Spain
Miri 138 D3 Sarawak, East Malaysia
Mirim Lagoon 63 E5 var. Lake Mirim, *Sp.* Laguna Merín. *Lagoon* Brazil/Uruguay
Mirim, Lake *see* Mirim Lagoon
Mírina *see* Mýrina
Mīrjāveh 120 E4 Sīstān va Balūchestān, SE Iran
Mirny 154 C3 *Russian research station* Antarctica
Mirnyy 115 F3 Respublika Sakha (Yakutiya), NE Russian Federation
Mīrpur Khās 134 B3 Sind, SE Pakistan
Mirtóo Pélagos 105 C6 Eng. Mirtoan Sea; *anc.* Myrtoum Mare. *Sea* S Greece
Miskito Coast *see* Mosquito Coast
Miskitos, Cayos 53 E2 *island group* NE Nicaragua
Miskolc 99 D6 Borsod-Abaúj-Zemplén, NE Hungary
Misool, Pulau 139 F4 *island* Maluku, E Indonesia
Miṣrātah 71 F2 var. Misurata. NW Libya
Mission 49 G5 Texas, SW USA
Mississippi 42 B2 off. State of Mississippi; also known as Bayou State, Magnolia State. *State* SE USA

Mississippi Delta 42 B4 *delta* Louisiana, S USA
Mississippi River 35 C6 *river* C USA
Missoula 44 B1 Montana, NW USA
Missouri 45 F5 off. State of Missouri; also known as Bullion State, Show Me State. *State* C USA
Missouri River 45 E3 *river* C USA
Mistassini, Lac 38 D3 *lake* Quebec, SE Canada
Mistelbach an der Zaya 95 E6 Niederösterreich, NE Austria
Misti, Volcán 61 E4 *mountain* S Peru
Misurata *see* Miṣrātah
Mitchell 149 D5 Queensland, E Australia
Mitchell 45 E3 South Dakota, N USA
Mitchell, Mount 43 E1 *mountain* North Carolina, SE USA
Mitchell River 148 C2 *river* Queensland, NE Australia
Mi Tho *see* My Tho
Mitilíni *see* Mytilíni
Mito 131 D5 Ibaraki, Honshū, S Japan
Mits'iwa *see* Massawa
Mitspe Ramon *see* Mizpé Ramon
Mitú 58 C4 Vaupés, SE Colombia
Mitumba, Monts 77 E7 var. Chaîne des Mitumba, Mitumba Range. *Mountain range* SE Dem. Rep. Congo
Mitumba Range *see* Mitumba, Monts
Miyako 130 D4 Iwate, Honshū, C Japan
Miyako-jima 131 D6 *island* Sakishima-shotō, SW Japan
Miyakonojō 131 B8 var. Miyakonzyô. Miyazaki, Kyūshū, SW Japan
Miyakonzyô *see* Miyakonojō
Miyāneh *see* Miāneh
Miyazaki 131 B8 Miyazaki, Kyūshū, SW Japan
Mizil 108 C5 Prahova, SE Romania
Miziya 104 C1 Vratsa, NW Bulgaria
Mizpé Ramon 119 A7 var. Mitspe Ramon, Southern, S Israel
Mjøsa 85 B6 var. Mjøsen. *Lake* S Norway
Mjøsen *see* Mjøsa
Mladenovac 100 D4 Serbia, C Serbia and Montenegro (Yugo.)
Mława 98 D3 Mazowieckie, C Poland
Mljet 101 B5 It. Meleda; *anc.* Melita. *Island* S Croatia
Mmabatho 78 C4 North-West, N South Africa
Moab 44 B5 Utah, W USA
Moab, Kir of *see* Al Karak
Moa Island 148 C1 *island* Queensland, NE Australia
Moanda 77 B6 var. Mouanda. Haut-Ogooué, SE Gabon
Moba 77 E7 Shaba, E Dem. Rep. Congo
Mobay *see* Montego Bay
Mobaye 77 C5 Basse-Kotto, S Central African Republic
Moberly 45 G4 Missouri, C USA
Mobile 42 C3 Alabama, S USA
Mobutu Sese Seko, Lac *see* Albert, Lake
Mochudi 78 C4 Kgatleng, SE Botswana
Mocímboa da Praia 79 F2 var. Vila de Mocímboa da Praia. Cabo Delgado, N Mozambique
Môco 78 B2 var. Morro de Môco. *Mountain* W Angola
Mocoa 58 A4 Putumayo, SW Colombia
Mocuba 79 E3 Zambézia, NE Mozambique
Modena 96 B3 anc. Mutina. Emilia-Romagna, N Italy
Modesto 47 B6 California, W USA
Modica 97 C7 anc. Motyca. Sicilia, Italy, C Mediterranean Sea
Modimolle 56 D4 var. Nylstroom, NE South Africa
Modriča 100 C3 Republika Srpska, N Bosnia and Herzegovina
Moe 149 C7 Victoria, SE Australia
Moero, Lac *see* Mweru, Lake

Mogadishu *see* Muqdisho
Mogilno 98 C3 Kujawski-pomorskie, C Poland
Mohammedia 70 C2 prev. Fédala. NW Morocco
Mohave, Lake 47 D7 *reservoir* Arizona/Nevada, W USA
Mohawk River 41 F3 *river* New York, NE USA
Mohéli 79 F2 var. Mwali, Mohilla, Mohila, Fr. Moili. *Island* S Comoros
Mohila *see* Mohéli
Mohilla *see* Mohéli
Mohns Ridge 83 F3 *undersea feature* Greenland Sea/Norwegian Sea
Moho 61 E4 Puno, SW Peru
Mohoro 73 C7 Pwani, E Tanzania
Mohyliv-Podil's'kyy 108 D3 Rus. Mogilev-Podol'skiy. Vinnyts'ka Oblast', C Ukraine
Moi 85 A6 Rogaland, S Norway
Moili *see* Mohéli
Mo i Rana 84 C3 Nordland, C Norway
Mõisaküla 106 D3 Ger. Moiseküll. Viljandimaa, S Estonia
Moissac 91 B6 Tarn-et-Garonne, S France
Mojácar 93 E5 Andalucía, S Spain
Mojave Desert 47 D7 *plain* California, W USA
Moktama *see* Martaban
Mol 87 C5 prev. Moll. Antwerpen, N Belgium
Moldavia *see* Moldova
Moldavian SSR/Moldavskaya SSR *see* Moldova
Molde 85 A5 Møre og Romsdal, S Norway
Moldo-Too, Khrebet 123 G2 prev. Khrebet Moldotau. *Mountain range* C Kyrgyzstan
Moldova 108 D3 var. Moldavia; prev. Moldavian SSR, Rus. Moldavskaya SSR. *Country* SE Europe

Moldova 108

Official name Republic of Moldova
Formation 1991
Capital Chisinau
Population 4.3 million / 329 people per sq mile (127 people per sq km)
Total area 13,067 sq miles (33,843 sq km)
Languages Romanian, Moldovan, Russian
Religions Eastern Orthodox 98%, Jewish 2%
Ethnic mix Moldovan 65%, Ukranian 14%, Russian 13%, Gagauzi 4%, other 4%
Government Parliamentary democracy
Currency Moldovan leu = 100 bani
Literacy rate 99%
Calorie consumption 2,764 kilocalories

Moldova Nouă 108 A4 Ger. Neumoldowa, Hung. Ujmoldova. Caraş-Severin, SW Romania
Moldoveanul *see* Vârful Moldoveanu
Molfetta 97 E5 Puglia, SE Italy
Mollendo 61 E4 Arequipa, SW Peru
Mölndal 85 B7 Västra Götaland, S Sweden
Molochans'k 109 G4 Rus. Molochansk. Zaporiz'ka Oblast', SE Ukraine
Molodezhnaya 154 C2 *Russian research station* Antarctica
Molokai 47 B8 Haw. Moloka'i. *Island* Hawaii, USA, C Pacific Ocean
Molokai Fracture Zone 153 E2 *tectonic feature* NE Pacific Ocean
Molopo 78 C4 *seasonal river* Botswana/South Africa
Mólos 105 B5 Stereá Ellás, C Greece
Moluccas *see* Maluku
Molucca Sea 139 F4 Ind. Laut Maluku. *Sea* E Indonesia
Mombasa 73 D7 *international airport* Coast, SE Kenya

Mombasa 73 D7 Coast, SE Kenya
Mombetsu *see* Monbetsu
Momchilgrad 104 D3 prev. Mastanli. Kŭrdzhali, S Bulgaria
Møn 85 B8 prev. Möen. *Island* SE Denmark
Monaco 91 E6 *Country* W Europe

Monaco 91

Official name Principality of Monaco
Formation 1861
Capital Monaco
Population 31,700 / 42,104 people per sq mile (16,256 people per sq km)
Total area 0.75 sq miles (1.95 sq km)
Languages French, Italian, Monégasque, English
Religions Roman Catholic, 89%, Protestant 6%, other 5%
Ethnic mix French 47%, Monégasque 17%, Italian 16%, other 20%
Government Constitutional monarchy
Currency Euro (French franc until 2002)
Literacy rate 99%
Calorie consumption not available

Monaco 91 C7 var. Monaco-Ville; anc. Monoecus. *Country capital* (Monaco) S Monaco
Monaco, Port de 91 C8 *bay* S Monaco
Monaco-Ville *see* Monaco
Monahans 49 E3 Texas, SW USA
Mona, Isla 55 E3 *island* W Puerto Rico
Mona Passage 55 E3 Sp. Canal de la Mona. *Channel* Dominican Republic/Puerto Rico
Monbetsu 130 D2 var. Mombetsu, Monbetu. Hokkaidō, NE Japan
Monbetu *see* Monbetsu
Moncalieri 96 A2 Piemonte, NW Italy
Monchegorsk 110 C2 Murmanskaya Oblast', NW Russian Federation
Monclova 50 D2 Coahuila de Zaragoza, NE Mexico
Moncton 39 F4 New Brunswick, SE Canada
Mondovi 96 A2 Piemonte, NW Italy
Monfalcone 96 D2 Friuli-Venezia Giulia, NE Italy
Monforte 92 C1 Galicia, NW Spain
Mongo 76 C3 Guéra, C Chad
Mongolia 126 C2 Mong. Mongol Uls. *Country* E Asia

Mongolia 126

Official name Mongolia
Formation 1924
Capital Ulan Bator
Population 2.6 million / 4 people per sq mile (2 people per sq km)
Total area 604,247 sq miles (1,565,000 sq km)
Languages Khalkha Mongolian, Kazakh, Chinese, Russian
Religions Tibetan Buddhist 96%, Muslim 4%
Ethnic mix Mongol 90%, Kazakh 4%, Chinese 2%, Russian 2%, other 2%
Government Multiparty republic
Currency Tugrik (togrog) = 100 möngös
Literacy rate 99%
Calorie consumption 1,981 kilocalories

Mongolia, Plateau of 124 D1 *plateau* E Mongolia
Mongora *see* Mingāora
Mongu 78 C2 Western, W Zambia
Monkchester *see* Newcastle upon Tyne
Monkey Bay 79 E2 Southern, SE Malawi

Monkey River *see* Monkey River Town
Monkey River Town 52 *C2 var.* Monkey River. Toledo, SE Belize
Monoecus *see* Monaco
Mono Lake 47 *C6 lake* California, W USA
Monóvar 93 *F4* País Valenciano, E Spain
Monroe 42 *B2* Louisiana, S USA
Monrovia 74 *C5 country capital* (Liberia) W Liberia
Mons 87 *B6 Dut.* Bergen. Hainaut, S Belgium
Monselice 96 *C2* Veneto, NE Italy
Montagnes Rocheuses *see* Rocky Mountains
Montana 44 *B1 off.* State of Montana; also known as Mountain State, Treasure State. *State* NW USA
Montana 104 *C2 prev.* Ferdinand, Mikhaylovgrad. Montana, NW Bulgaria
Montargis 90 *C4* Loiret, C France
Montauban 91 *B6* Tarn-et-Garonne, S France
Montbéliard 90 *D4* Doubs, E France
Mont Cenis, Col du 91 *D5 pass* E France
Mont-de-Marsan 91 *B6* Landes, SW France
Monteagudo 61 *G4* Chuquisaca, S Bolivia
Monte-Carlo 91 *C8* NE Monaco
Monte Caseros 64 *D3* Corrientes, NE Argentina
Monte Cristi 54 *D3 var.* San Fernando de Monte Cristi. NW Dominican Republic
Montegiardino 96 *E2* SE San Marino
Montego Bay 54 *A4 var.* Mobay. W Jamaica
Montélimar 91 *D5 anc.* Acunum Acusio, Montilium Adhemari. Drôme, E France
Montemorelos 51 *E3* Nuevo León, NE Mexico
Montenegro 101 *C5 Serb.* Crna Gora. Admin. region *republic* SW Serbia and Montenegro (Yugo.)
Monte Patria 64 *B3* Coquimbo, N Chile
Monterey *see* Monterrey
Monterey 47 *B6* California, W USA
Monterey Bay 47 *A6 bay* California, W USA
Montería 58 *B2* Córdoba, NW Colombia
Montero 61 *G4* Santa Cruz, C Bolivia
Monterrey 51 *E3 var.* Monterey. Nuevo León, NE Mexico
Montes Claros 63 *F3* Minas Gerais, SE Brazil
Montevideo 64 *D4 country capital* (Uruguay) Montevideo, S Uruguay
Montevideo 45 *F2* Minnesota, N USA
Montgenèvre, Col de 91 *D5 pass* France/Italy
Montgomery 42 *D2 state capital* Alabama, S USA
Monthey 95 *A7* Valais, SW Switzerland
Montluçon 90 *C4* Allier, C France
Montoro 92 *D4* Andalucía, S Spain
Montpelier 41 *G2 state capital* Vermont, NE USA
Montpellier 91 *C6* Hérault, S France
Montréal 39 *E4 Eng.* Montreal. Quebec, SE Canada
Montrose 44 *C5* Colorado, C USA
Montrose 88 *D3* E Scotland, UK
Montserrat 55 *G3 var.* Emerald Isle. *UK dependent territory* E West Indies
Monywa 136 *B3* Sagaing, C Myanmar
Monza 96 *B2* Lombardia, N Italy
Monze 78 *D2* Southern, S Zambia

Monzón 93 *F2* Aragón, NE Spain
Moonie 149 *D5* Queensland, E Australia
Moora 147 *A6* Western Australia
Moore 49 *G1* Oklahoma, C USA
Moore, Lake 147 *B6 lake* Western Australia
Moorhead 45 *F2* Minnesota, N USA
Moose 38 *C3 river* Ontario, S Canada
Moosehead Lake 41 *G1 lake* Maine, NE USA
Moosonee 38 *C3* Ontario, SE Canada
Mopti 75 *E3* Mopti, C Mali
Moquegua 61 *E4* Moquegua, SE Peru
Mora 85 *C5* Kopparberg, C Sweden
Morales 52 *C2* Izabal, E Guatemala
Morant Bay 54 *B5* E Jamaica
Moratalla 93 *E4* Murcia, SE Spain
Morava 99 *C5 var.* March. *River* C Europe *see also* March
Morava *see* Velika Morava
Moravia 99 *B5* Iowa, C USA
Moray Firth 88 *C3 inlet* N Scotland, UK
Morea *see* Pelopónnisos
Moreau River 44 *D2 river* South Dakota, N USA
Moree 149 *D5* New South Wales, SE Australia
Morelia 51 *E4* Michoacán de Ocampo, S Mexico
Morena, Sierra 92 *C4 mountain range* S Spain
Moreni 108 *C5* Dâmbovița, S Romania
Mórfou 102 *C5* W Cyprus
Morgan City 42 *B3* Louisiana, S USA
Morghāb, Daryā-ye 122 *D3 var.* Murgab, Murghab, *Turkm.* Murgap Deryasy. *River* Afghanistan/Turkmenistan *see also* Murgab
Morioka 130 *D4* Iwate, Honshū, C Japan
Morlaix 90 *A3* Finistère, NW France
Mornington Abyssal Plain 67 *A7 undersea feature* SE Pacific Ocean
Mornington Island 148 *B2 island* Wellesley Islands, Queensland, N Australia
Morocco 70 *B3 Ar.* Al Mamlakah. *Country* N Africa

Morocco 70

Official name Kingdom of Morocco
Formation 1956
Capital Rabat
Population 30.4 million / 176 people per sq mile (68 people per sq km)
Total area 172,316 sq miles (446,300 sq km)
Languages Arabic, Berber (Shluh, Tamazight, Riffian), French, Spanish
Religions Muslim 99%, other 1%
Ethnic mix Arab 70%, Berber 29%, European 1%
Government Constitutional monarchy
Currency Moroccan dirham = 100 centimes
Literacy rate 48.9%
Calorie consumption 2,964 kilocalories

Morocco *see* Marrakech
Morogoro 73 *C7* Morogoro, E Tanzania
Moro Gulf 139 *E3 gulf* S Philippines
Morón 54 *C2* Ciego de Ávila, C Cuba
Mörön 126 *D2* Hövsgöl, N Mongolia
Morondava 79 *F3* Toliara, W Madagascar
Moroni 79 *F2 country capital* (Comoros) Grande Comore, NW Comoros
Morotai, Pulau 139 *F3 island* Maluku, E Indonesia

Morotiri *see* Marotiri
Morrinsville 150 *D3* Waikato, North Island, NZ
Morris 45 *F2* Minnesota, N USA
Morris Jesup, Kap 83 *E1 headland* N Greenland
Morro de Môco *see* Môco
Morvan 90 *D4 physical region* C France
Moscow *see* Moskva
Moscow 46 *C2* Idaho, NW USA
Mosel 95 *A5 Fr.* Moselle. *River* W Europe *see also* Moselle
Moselle 87 *E8 Ger.* Mosel. *River* W Europe *see also* Mosel
Moselle 90 *D3 department* NE France
Mosgiel 151 *B7* Otago, South Island, NZ
Moshi 73 *C7* Kilimanjaro, NE Tanzania
Mosjøen 84 *B4* Nordland, C Norway
Moskva 111 *B5 Eng.* Moscow. *Country capital* (Russian Federation) Gorod Moskva, W Russian Federation
Moskva 123 *E3 Rus.* Moskovskiy; *prev.* Chubek. SW Tajikistan
Mosonmagyaróvár 99 *C6 Ger.* Wieselburg-Ungarisch-Altenburg; *prev.* Moson and Magyaróvár, *Ger.* Wieselburg and Ungarisch-Altenburg. Győr-Moson-Sopron, NW Hungary
Mosquito Coast 53 *E3 var.* Miskito Coast. *Coastal region* E Nicaragua
Mosquitos, Golfo de los 53 *F4 Eng.* Mosquito Gulf. *Gulf* N Panama
Moss 85 *B6* Østfold, S Norway
Mosselbaai 78 *C7 var.* Mosselbai, *Eng.* Mossel Bay. Western Cape, SW South Africa
Mossendjo 77 *B6* Le Niari, SW Congo
Mossoró 63 *G2* Rio Grande do Norte, NE Brazil
Most 98 *A4 Ger.* Brüx. Ústecký Kraj, NW Czech Republic
Mosta 102 *B5 var.* Musta. C Malta
Mostaganem 70 *D2 var.* Mestghanem. NW Algeria
Mostar 100 *C4* Federacija Bosna I Hercegovina, S Bosnia and Herzegovina
Mosul *see* Al Mawşil
Mota del Cuervo 93 *E3* Castilla-La Mancha, C Spain
Motagua, Río 52 *B2 river* Guatemala/Honduras
Motril 92 *D5* Andalucía, S Spain
Motru 108 *B4* Gorj, SW Romania
Motueka 151 *C5* Tasman, South Island, NZ
Motul 51 *H3 var.* Motul de Felipe Carrillo Puerto. Yucatán, SE Mexico
Motul de Felipe Carrillo Puerto *see* Motul
Mouanda *see* Moanda
Mouhoun *see* Black Volta
Mouila 77 *A6* Ngounié, C Gabon
Mould Bay 37 *E2* Prince Patrick Island, Northwest Territories/Nunavut, N Canada
Moulins 90 *C4* Allier, C France
Moulmein 136 *B4 var.* Maulmain, Mawlamyine. Mon State, S Myanmar
Moundou 76 *B4* Logone-Occidental, SW Chad
Moŭng Roessei 137 *D5* Bătdâmbâng, W Cambodia
Moun Hou *see* Black Volta
Mountain Home 42 *B1* Arkansas, C USA
Mount Ara *see* Büyükağrı Dağı
Mount Cook 151 *B6* Canterbury, South Island, NZ
Mount Desert Island 41 *H2 island* Maine, NE USA
Mount Fuji *see* Fuji-san
Mount Gambier 149 *B7* South Australia
Mount Isa 148 *B3* Queensland, C Australia
Mount Magnet 147 *B5* Western Australia

Mount Pleasant 45 *G4* Iowa, C USA
Mount Pleasant 40 *C3* Michigan, N USA
Mount Vernon 40 *B5* Illinois, N USA
Mount Vernon 46 *B1* Washington, NW USA
Mourdi, Dépression du 76 *C2 desert lowland* Chad/Sudan
Mouscron 87 *A6 Dut.* Moeskroen. Hainaut, W Belgium
Mouse River *see* Souris River
Moussoro 76 *B3* Kanem, W Chad
Moyen Atlas 70 *C2 Eng.* Middle Atlas. *Mountain range* N Morocco
Moyobamba 60 *B2* San Martín, NW Peru
Moyu 126 *B3 var.* Karakax. Xinjiang Uygur Zizhiqu, NW China
Moyynkum, Peski 123 *F1 Kaz.* Moyynqum. *Desert* S Kazakhstan
Mozambique 79 *E3 prev.* People's Republic of Mozambique, Portuguese East Africa. *Country* S Africa

Mozambique 79

Official name Republic of Mozambique
Formation 1975
Capital Maputo
Population 18.6 million / 60 people per sq mile (23 people per sq km)
Total area 309,494 sq miles (801,590 sq km)
Languages Portuguese, Makua, Tsonga, Sena, Lomwe
Religions Traditional beliefs 60%, Christian 30%, Muslim 10%
Ethnic mix Makua Lomwe 47%, Tsonga 23%, Malawi 12%, Shona 11%, Yao 4%, other 3%
Government Multiparty republic
Currency Metical = 100 centavos
Literacy rate 44%
Calorie consumption 1,927 kilocalories

Mozambique Basin *see* Natal Basin
Mozambique Channel 79 *E3 Fr.* Canal de Mozambique, *Mal.* Lakandranon' i Mozambika. *Strait* W Indian Ocean
Mozambique Plateau 69 *D7 var.* Mozambique Rise. *Undersea feature* SW Indian Ocean
Mozambique Rise *see* Mozambique Plateau
Mpama 77 *B6 river* C Congo
Mpika 78 *D2* Northern, NE Zambia
Mqinvartsveri *see* Kazbek
Mragowo 98 *D2 Ger.* Sensburg. Olsztyn, NE Poland
Mtwara 73 *D8* Mtwara, SE Tanzania
Mualo *see* Messalo, Rio
Muang Chiang Rai *see* Chiang Rai
Muang Kalasin *see* Kalasin
Muang Không 137 *D5* Champasak, S Laos
Muang Khôngxédôn 137 *D5 var.* Khong Sedone. Salavan, S Laos
Muang Khon Kaen *see* Khon Kaen
Muang Lampang *see* Lampang
Muang Loei *see* Loei
Muang Lom Sak *see* Lom Sak
Muang Nakhon Sawan *see* Nakhon Sawan
Muang Namo 136 *C3* Oudômxai, N Laos
Muang Nan *see* Nan
Muang Phalan 136 *C3 var.* Muang Phalane. Savannakhét, S Laos
Muang Phalane *see* Muang Phalan
Muang Phayao *see* Phayao
Muang Phitsanulok *see* Phitsanulok
Muang Phrae *see* Phrae
Muang Roi Et *see* Roi Et
Muang Sakon Nakhon *see* Sakon Nakhon
Muang Samut Prakan *see* Samut Prakan
Muang Sing 136 *C3* Louang Namtha, N Laos

Muang Ubon *see* Ubon Ratchathani
Muar 138 B3 *var.* Bandar Maharani.
  Johor, Peninsular Malaysia
Mucojo 79 F2 Cabo Delgado,
  N Mozambique
Mudanjiang 129 E3 *var.* Mu-tan-
  chiang. Heilongjiang, NE China
Mudon 137 B5 Mon State,
  S Myanmar
Muenchen *see* Munich
Muenster *see* Münster
Mufulira 78 D2 Copperbelt,
  C Zambia
Mughla *see* Muğla
Muğla 116 A4 *var.* Mughla. Muğla,
  SW Turkey
Mūḥ, Sabkhat al 134 C3 *lake*
  C Syria
Muir Éireann *see* Irish Sea
Muisne 60 A1 Esmeraldas,
  NW Ecuador
Mukacheve 108 B3 *Hung.* Munkács,
  Rus. Mukachevo. Zakarpats'ka
  Oblast', W Ukraine
Mukalla *see* Al Mukallā
Mula 93 E4 Murcia, SE Spain
Mulaku Atoll 132 B4 *var.* Meemu
  Atoll. *Atoll* C Maldives
Muleshoe 49 E2 Texas, SW USA
Mulhacén 93 E5 *var.* Cerro de
  Mulhacén. *Mountain* S Spain
Mulhouse 90 E4 Ger. Mülhausen.
  Haut-Rhin, NE France
Muller, Pegunungan 138 D4 *Dut.*
  Müller-gerbergte. *Mountain range*
  Borneo, C Indonesia
Müllheim 95 A6 Baden-
  Württemberg, SW Germany
Mull, Isle of 88 B4 *island*
  W Scotland, UK
Mulongo 77 D2 Shaba, SE Dem.
  Rep. Congo
Multan 134 C2 Punjab, E Pakistan
Mumbai 134 C5 *prev.* Bombay.
  Mahārāshtra, W India
Munamägi *see* Suur Munamägi
München 95 C5 Bayern,
  E Germany
Muncie 40 C4 Indiana, N USA
Mungbere 77 E5 Orientale,
  NE Dem. Rep. Congo
Mu Nggava *see* Rennell
Munich 80 D4 *var.* Muenchen,
  Bayern, SE Germany
Munkhafaḍ al Qaṭṭārah *see*
  Qaṭṭāra, Monkhafad el
Munster 89 A6 *Ir.* Cúige Mumhan.
  Cultural region S Ireland
Münster 94 A4 *var.* Muenster,
  Münster in Westfalen. Nordrhein-
  Westfalen, W Germany
Münster in Westfalen *see* Münster
Muong Xiang Ngeun 136 C4 *var.*
  Xieng Ngeun. Louangphabang,
  N Laos
Muonio 84 D3 Lappi,
  N Finland
Muonioälv 84 D3 *river*
  Finland/Sweden
Muqāṭ 119 C5 Al Mafraq,
  E Jordan
Muqdisho 73 D6 Eng. Mogadishu,
  It. Mogadiscio. *Country capital*
  (Somalia) Banaadir, S Somalia
Mur 95 E7 SCr. Mura. *River*
  C Europe
Muradiye 117 F3 Van, E Turkey
Murapara *see* Murupara
Murata 96 E2 S San Marino
Murchison River 147 A5 *river*
  Western Australia
Murcia 93 E4 *cultural region*
  SE Spain
Murcia 93 F4 Murcia, SE Spain
Mureş 108 A4 *var.* Maros, Mureşul,
  Ger. Marosch, Mieresch. *River*
  Hungary/Romania *see also* Maros
Mureşul *see* Mureş
Murfreesboro 42 D1 Tennessee,
  S USA
Murgab 122 D3 *prev.* Murgap.
  Maryyskiy Velayat,
  S Turkmenistan
Murgab 122 D3 *var.* Murghab, Pash.
  Daryā-ye Morghāb, *Turkm.*
  Murgap Deryasy. *River*
  Afghanistan/Turkmenistan *see*
  also Morghāb, Daryā-ye

Murgap *see* Murgab
Murgap Deryasy *see* Morghāb,
  Daryā-ye/Murgab
Murghab *see* Morghāb, Daryā-
  ye/Murgab
Murghob 123 F3 *Rus.* Murgab.
  SE Tajikistan
Murgon 149 E5 Queensland,
  E Australia
Müritz 94 C3 *var.* Müritzee. *Lake*
  NE Germany
Müritzee *see* Müritz
Murmansk 110 C2 Murmanskaya
  Oblast', NW Russian Federation
Murmashi 110 C2 Murmanskaya
  Oblast', NW Russian Federation
Murom 111 B5 Vladimirskaya
  Oblast', W Russian Federation
Muroran 130 D3 Hokkaidō,
  NE Japan
Muros 92 B1 Galicia, NW Spain
Murray Fracture Zone 153 E2
  tectonic feature NE Pacific Ocean
Murray Range *see* Murray Ridge
Murray Ridge 112 C5 *var.* Murray
  Range. *Undersea feature* N Arabian
  Sea
Murray River 149 B6 *river*
  SE Australia
Murrumbidgee River 149 C6 *river*
  New South Wales, SE Australia
Murska Sobota 95 E7 Ger. Olsnitz.
  NE Slovenia
Murupara 150 E3 *var.* Murapara.
  Bay of Plenty, North Island, NZ
Murviedro *see* Sagunto
Murwāra 135 E4 Madhya Pradesh,
  N India
Murwillumbah 149 E5 New South
  Wales, SE Australia
Murzuq, Idhān 71 F4 *var.* Edeyin
  Murzuq. *Desert* SW Libya
Mürzzuschlag 95 E7 Steiermark,
  E Austria
Muş 117 F3 *var.* Mush. Muş,
  E Turkey
Mûsa, Gebel 72 C2 *mountain*
  NE Egypt
Musala 104 B3 *mountain* W Bulgaria
Muscat *see* Masqaţ
Muscatine 45 G3 Iowa, C USA
Musgrave Ranges 147 D5 *mountain
  range* South Australia
Mush *see* Muş
Muskegon 40 C3 Michigan,
  N USA
Muskogee 49 G1 Oklahoma,
  C USA
Musoma 73 C6 Mara, N Tanzania
Musta *see* Mosta
Musters, Lago 65 B6 *lake*
  S Argentina
Muswellbrook 149 D6 New South
  Wales, SE Australia
Mut 116 C4 İçel, S Turkey
Mu-tan-chiang *see* Mudanjiang
Mutare 78 D3 *var.* Mutari; *prev.*
  Umtali. Manicaland, E Zimbabwe
Mutari *see* Mutare
Mutsu-wan 130 D3 *bay* N Japan
Muttonbird Islands 151 A8 *island
  group* SW NZ
Mu Us Shamo 127 E3 *var.* Ordos
  Desert. N China
Muy Muy 52 D3 Matagalpa,
  C Nicaragua
Müynoq 122 C1 *Rus.* Muynak.
  Qoraqalpoghiston Respublikasi,
  NW Uzbekistan
Mužlja 100 D3 *Hung.* Felsőmuzslya;
  prev. Gornja Mužlja. Serbia,
  N Serbia and
  Montenegro (Yugo.)
Mwali *see* Mohéli
Mwanza 73 B6 Mwanza,
  NW Tanzania
Mweka 77 C6 Kasai Occidental,
  C Dem. Rep. Congo
Mwene-Ditu 77 D7 Kasai Oriental,
  S Dem. Rep. Congo
Mweru, Lake 77 D7 *var.* Lac Moero.
  Lake Congo (Zaire)/Zambia
Mweru Wantipa, Lake 77 E7 *lake*
  N Zambia
Myadzyel 107 C5 Pol. Miadzioł
  Nowy, *Rus.* Myadel'. Minskaya
  Voblasts', N Belarus

Myanmar 136 A3 *var.* Burma.
  Country SE Asia

Myanmar (Burma) 136

Official name Union of Myanmar
Formation 1948
Capital Rangoon (Yangoon)
Population 48.4 million / 185 people
  per sq mile (71 people per sq km)
Total area 261,969 sq miles
  (678,500 sq km)
Languages Burmese, Karen, Shan,
  Chin, Kachin, Mon, Palaung, Wa
Religions Buddhist 87%, Christian
  6%, Muslim 4%, Hindu 1%, other 2%
Ethnic mix Burman (Bamah) 68%,
  Shan 9%, Karen 6%, Rakhine 4%,
  other 13%
Government Military-based regime
Currency Kyat = 100 pyas
Literacy rate 84.7%
Calorie consumption 2,842
  kilocalories

Myanaung 136 B4 Irrawaddy,
  SW Myanmar
Myaungmya 136 A4 Irrawaddy,
  SW Myanmar
Myerkulavichy 107 D7 *Rus.*
  Merkulovichi. Homyel'skaya
  Voblasts', SE Belarus
Myingyan 136 B3 Mandalay,
  C Myanmar
Myitkyina 136 B2 Kachin State,
  N Myanmar
Mykolayiv 109 E4 *Rus.* Nikolayev.
  Mykolayivs'ka Oblast', S Ukraine
Mýkonos 105 D6 *var.* Míkonos. *Island*
  Kyklades, Greece, Aegean Sea
Myrhorod 109 F2 *Rus.* Mirgorod.
  Poltavs'ka Oblast', NE Ukraine
Mýrina 104 D4 *var.* Mírina. Limnos,
  SE Greece
Myrtle Beach 43 F2 South Carolina,
  SE USA
Mýrtos 105 D8 Kríti, Greece,
  E Mediterranean Sea
Myślibórz 98 B3
  Zachodniopomorskie, NW Poland
Mysore 132 C2 *var.* Maisur.
  Karnātaka, W India
Mysore *see* Karnātaka
My Tho 137 E6 *var.* Mi Tho. Tiên
  Giang, S Vietnam
Mytilene *see* Mytilíni
Mytilíni 105 D5 *var.* Mitilíni; *anc.*
  Mytilene. Lésvos, E Greece
Mzuzu 79 E2 Northern, N Malawi

N

Naberezhnyye Chelny 111 D5 *prev.*
  Brezhnev. Respublika Tatarstan,
  W Russian Federation
Nablus 119 A6 *var.* Nābulus, *Heb.*
  Shekhem; *anc.* Neapolis, *Bibl.*
  Shechem. N West Bank
Nābulus *see* Nablus
Nacala 79 F2 Nampula,
  NE Mozambique
Nada *see* Danzhou
Nadi 145 E4 *prev.* Nandi. Viti Levu,
  W Fiji
Nadur 102 A5 Gozo, N Malta
Nadvirna 108 C3 Pol. Nadwórna,
  Rus. Nadvornaya. Ivano-
  Frankivs'ka Oblast', W Ukraine
Nadvoitsy 110 B3 Respublika
  Kareliya, NW Russian Federation
Nadym 114 C3 Yamalo-Nenetskiy
  Avtonomnyy Okrug, N Russian
  Federation
Náfpaktos 105 B5 *var.* Návpaktos.
  Dytikí Ellás, C Greece
Náfplio 105 B6 *prev.* Návplion.
  Pelopónnisos, S Greece
Naga 139 E2 *off.* Naga City; *prev.*
  Nueva Caceres. Luzon,
  N Philippines
Nagano 131 C5 Nagano, Honshū,
  S Japan
Nagaoka 131 D5 Niigata, Honshū,
  C Japan
Nagara Pathom *see* Nakhon
  Pathom

Nagara Sridharmaraj *see* Nakhon
  Si Thammarat
Nagara Svarga *see* Nakhon Sawan
Nagasaki 131 A7 Nagasaki,
  Kyūshū, SW Japan
Nagato 131 A7 Yamaguchi, Honshū,
  SW Japan
Nāgercoil 132 C3 Tamil Nādu,
  SE India
**Nagorno-Karabakhskaya
  Avtonomnaya Oblast** *see*
  Nagornyy Karabakh
Nagornyy Karabakh 117 G3 *var.*
  Nagorno-Karabakhskaya
  Avtonomnaya Oblast , *Arm.*
  Lerrnayin Gharabakh, *Az.* Dağliq
  Qarabağ. *Former autonomous region*
  SW Azerbaijan
Nagoya 131 C6 Aichi, Honshū,
  SW Japan
Nāgpur 134 D4 Mahārāshtra,
  C India
Nagqu 126 C5 Chin. Na-ch'ii; *prev.*
  Hei-ho. Xizang Zizhiqu, W China
Nagykálló 99 E6 Szabolcs-Szatmár-
  Bereg, E Hungary
Nagykanizsa 99 C7 Ger.
  Grosskanizsa. Zala, SW Hungary
Nagykőrös 99 D7 Pest, C Hungary
Nagyszentmiklós *see* Sânnicolau
  Mare
Naha 130 A3 Okinawa, Okinawa,
  SW Japan
Nahariya *see* Nahariyya
Nahariyya 119 A5 *var.* Nahariya.
  Northern, N Israel
Nahr al 'Aşī *see* Orantes
Nahr al Litant *see* Lītani, Nahr el
Nahr an Nīl *see* Nile
Nahr el Aassi *see* Orantes
Nahuel Huapi, Lago 65 B5 *lake*
  W Argentina
Nā'īn 120 D3 Eşfahān, C Iran
Nain 39 F2 Newfoundland and
  Labrador, NE Canada
Nairobi 69 E5 *country capital*
  (Kenya) Nairobi Area, S Kenya
Nairobi 73 C6 *international airport*
  Nairobi Area, S Kenya
Najaf *see* An Najaf
Najima *see* Fukuoka
Najin 129 E3 NE North Korea
Najrān 121 B6 *var.* Abā as Su'ūd.
  Najrān, S Saudi Arabia
Nakambé *see* White Volta
Nakamura 131 B7 Kōchi, Shikoku,
  SW Japan
Nakatsugawa 131 C6 *var.*
  Nakatugawa. Gifu, Honshū,
  SW Japan
Nakatugawa *see* Nakatsugawa
Nakhodka 115 G5 Primorskiy Kray,
  SE Russian Federation
Nakhon Pathom 137 C5 *var.* Nagara
  Pathom, Nakorn Pathom. Nakhon
  Pathom, W Thailand
Nakhon Ratchasima 137 C5 *var.*
  Khorat, Korat. Nakhon
  Ratchasima, E Thailand
Nakhon Sawan 137 C5 *var.* Muang
  Nakhon Sawan, Nagara Svarga.
  Nakhon Sawan, W Thailand
Nakhon Si Thammarat 137 C7 *var.*
  Nagara Sridharmaraj, Nakhon
  Sithamnaraj. Nakhon Si
  Thammarat, SW Thailand
Nakhon Sithamnaraj *see* Nakhon
  Si Thammarat
Nakorn Pathom *see* Nakhon Pathom
Nakuru 73 C6 Rift Valley, SW Kenya
Nal'chik 111 B8 Kabardino-
  Balkarskaya Respublika,
  SW Russian Federation
Nālūt 71 F2 NW Libya
Namakan Lake 40 A1 lake
  Canada/USA
Namangan 123 F2 Namangan
  Wiloyati, E Uzbekistan
Nambala 78 D2 Central, C Zambia
Nam Co 126 C5 *lake* W China
Nam Đinh 136 D3 Nam Ha,
  N Vietnam
Namib Desert 78 B3 *desert*
  W Namibia
Namibe 78 A2 Port. Moçâmedes,
  Mossâmedes. Namibe,
  SW Angola

Namibia 78 B3 var. South West
Africa, Afr. Suidwes-Afrika, Ger.
Deutsch-Südwestafrika; prev.
German Southwest Africa, South-
West Africa. Country S Africa

Namibia 78

Official name Republic of Namibia
Formation 1990
Capital Windhoek
Population 1.8 million / 6 people
per sq mile (2 people per sq km)
Total area 318,694 sq miles
(825,418 sq km)
Languages English, Ovambo,
Kavango, Bergdama, German,
Afrikaans
Religions Christian 90%, other 10%
Ethnic mix Ovambo 50%, other
tribes 16%, Kavango 9%, Herero 8%,
Damara 8%, other 9%
Government Parliamentary
democracy
Currency Namibian dollar = 100
cents
Literacy rate 82%
Calorie consumption 2,649
kilocalories

Namo see Namu Atoll
Nam Ou 136 C3 river N Laos
Nampa 46 D3 Idaho, NW USA
Nampula 79 E2 Nampula,
NE Mozambique
Namsos 84 B4 Nord-Trøndelag,
C Norway
Nam Tha 136 C4 river N Laos
Namu Atoll 144 D2 var. Namo.
Atoll Ralik Chain, C Marshall
Islands
Namur 87 C6 Dut. Namen. Namur,
SE Belgium
Namyit Island 128 C8 island
S Spratly Islands
Nan 136 C4 var. Muang Nan. Nan,
NW Thailand
Nanaimo 36 D5 Vancouver Island,
British Columbia, SW Canada
Nanchang 128 C5 var. Nan-ch'ang,
Nanch'ang-hsien. Jiangxi, S China
Nanch'ang-hsien see Nanchang
Nan-ching see Nanjing
Nancy 90 D3 Meurthe-et-Moselle,
NE France
Nandaime 52 D3 Granada,
SW Nicaragua
Nānded 134 D5 Mahārāshtra,
C India
Nandyāl 132 C1 Andhra Pradesh,
E India
Nanjing 128 D5 var. Nan-ching,
Nanking; prev. Chianning, Chian-
ning, Kiang-ning. Jiangsu,
E China
Nanking see Nanjing
Nanning 128 B6 var. Nan-ning; prev.
Yung-ning. Guangxi Zhuangzu
Zizhiqu, S China
Nan-ning see Nanning
Nanortalik 82 C5 S Greenland
Nanpan Jiang 136 D2 river S China
Nanping 128 D6 var. Nan-p'ing;
prev. Yenping. Fujian, SE China
Nansei-Shotō 130 A2 var. Ryukyu
Islands. Island group SW Japan
Nansei Syotō Trench see Ryukyu
Trench
Nansen Basin 155 C4 undersea
feature Arctic Ocean
Nansen Cordillera 155 B3 var.
Arctic-Mid Oceanic Ridge,
Nansen Ridge. Undersea feature
Arctic Ocean
Nansen Ridge see Nansen
Cordillera
Nanterre 90 D1 Hauts-de-Seine,
N France
Nantes 90 B4 Bret. Naoned; anc.
Condivincum, Namnetes. Loire-
Atlantique, NW France
Nantucket Island 41 G3 island
Massachusetts, NE USA
Nanumaga 145 E3 var. Nanumanga.
Atoll NW Tuvalu
Nanumanga see Nanumaga

Nanumea Atoll 145 E3 atoll
NW Tuvalu
Nanyang 128 C5 var. Nan-yang.
Henan, C China
Napa 47 B6 California, W USA
Napier 150 E4 Hawke's Bay, North
Island, NZ
Naples 80 D5 anc. Neapolis.
Campania, S Italy
Naples 43 E5 Florida, SE USA
Napo 56 A3 province NE Ecuador
Napo, Río 60 C1 river
Ecuador/Peru
Naracoorte 149 B7 South Australia
Naradhivas see Narathiwat
Narathiwat 137 C7 var. Naradhivas.
Narathiwat, SW Thailand
Narbada see Narmada
Narbonne 91 C6 anc. Narbo
Martius. Aude, S France
Narborough Island see Fernandina,
Isla
Nares Abyssal Plain see Nares Plain
Nares Plain 35 E6 var. Nares
Abyssal Plain. Undersea feature
NW Atlantic Ocean
Nares Strait 82 D1 Dan. Nares
Stræde. Strait Canada/Greenland
Narew 98 E3 river E Poland
Narmada 124 B3 var. Narbada. River
C India
Narowlya 107 C8 Rus. Narovlja.
Homyel'skaya Voblasts',
SE Belarus
Närpes 85 D5 Fin. Närpiö. Länsi-
Suomi, W Finland
Narrabri 149 D6 New South Wales,
SE Australia
Narrogin 147 B6 Western Australia
Narva 106 E2 prev. Narova. River
Estonia/Russian Federation
Narva 106 E2 Ida-Virumaa,
NE Estonia
Narva Bay 106 E2 Est. Narva Laht,
Ger. Narwa-Bucht, Rus. Narvskiy
Zaliv. Bay Estonia/Russian
Federation
Narva Reservoir 106 E2 Est. Narva
Veehoidla, Rus. Narvskoye
Vodokhranilishche. Reservoir
Estonia/Russian Federation
Narvik 84 C3 Nordland, C Norway
Nar'yan-Mar 110 D3 prev.
Beloshchel'ye, Dzerzhinskiy.
Nenetskiy Avtonomnyy Okrug,
NW Russian Federation
Naryn 123 G2 Narynskaya Oblast',
C Kyrgyzstan
Năsăud 108 B3 Ger. Nussdorf,
Hung. Naszód. Bistrița-Năsăud,
N Romania
Nase see Naze
Nāshik 134 C5 prev. Nāsik.
Mahārāshtra, W India
Nashua 41 G3 New Hampshire,
NE USA
Nashville 42 C1 state capital
Tennessee, S USA
Näsijärvi 85 D5 lake SW Finland
Nāsiri see Ahvāz
Nasiriya see An Nāşirīyah
Nassau 54 C1 country capital
(Bahamas) New Providence,
N Bahamas
Nasser, Lake 72 B3 var. Buhayrat
Nasir, Buḩayrat Nāşir, Buheiret
Nâsir. Lake Egypt/Sudan
Nata 78 C3 Central, NE Botswana
Natal 63 G2 Rio Grande do Norte,
E Brazil
Natal Basin 141 A6 var.
Mozambique Basin. Undersea
feature W Indian Ocean
Natanya see Netanya
Natchez 42 B3 Mississippi, S USA
Natchitoches 42 A2 Louisiana,
S USA
Nathanya see Netanya
Natitingou 75 F4 NW Benin
Natsrat see Nazaret
Natuna Islands 124 D4 island group
W Indonesia
Naturaliste Plateau 141 E6 undersea
feature E Indian Ocean
Naugard see Nowogard
Naujamiestis 106 C4 Panevėžys,
C Lithuania

Nauru 144 D2 prev. Pleasant Island.
Country W Pacific Ocean

Nauru 144

Official name Republic of Nauru
Formation 1968
Capital No official capital
Population 11,800 / 1,455 people
per sq mile (562 people per sq km)
Total area 8 sq miles (21 sq km)
Languages Nauruan, English,
Kiribati, Chinese, Tuvaluan
Religions Nauruan Congregational
Church 60%, Roman Catholic 35,
other 5%
Ethnic mix Nauruan 62%, other
Pacific islanders 25%, Chinese and
Vietnamese 8%, European 5%
Government Non-party democracy
Currency Australian dollar = 100
cents
Literacy rate 99%
Calorie consumption not available

Nauta 60 C2 Loreto, N Peru
Navahrudak 107 C6 Pol.
Nowogródek, Rus. Novogrudok.
Hrodzyenskaya Voblasts',
W Belarus
Navapolatsk 107 D5 Rus.
Novopolotsk. Vitsyebskaya
Voblasts', N Belarus
Navarra 93 E2 cultural region
N Spain
Navassa Island 54 C3 US
unincorporated territory C West
Indies
Navojoa 50 C2 Sonora, NW Mexico
Navolat see Navolato
Navolato 66 C3 var. Navolat.
Sinaloa, C Mexico
Návpaktos see Náfpaktos
Nawabashah see Nawābshāh
Nawābshāh 134 B3 var.
Nawabashah. Sind, S Pakistan
Nawoiy 123 E2 Rus. Navoi. Nawoiy
Wiloyati, C Uzbekistan
Naxçıvan 117 C3 Rus.
Nakhichevan'. SW Azerbaijan
Náxos 105 D6 var. Naxos. Náxos,
Kykládes, Greece, Aegean Sea
Náxos 105 D6 island Kykládes,
Greece, Aegean Sea
Nayoro 130 D2 Hokkaidō,
NE Japan
Nazca 60 D4 Ica, S Peru
Nazca Ridge 57 A5 undersea feature
E Pacific Ocean
Naze 130 B3 var. Nase. Kagoshima,
Amami-ōshima, SW Japan
Nazerat 119 A5 var. Natsrat, Ar. En
Nazira, Eng. Nazareth. Northern,
N Israel
Nazilli 116 A4 Aydın, SW Turkey
Nazrēt 73 C5 var. Adama, Hadama.
C Ethiopia
N'Dalatando 78 B1 Port. Salazar,
Vila Salazar. Cuanza Norte,
NW Angola
Ndélé 76 C4 Bamingui-Bangoran,
N Central African Republic
Ndendé 77 B6 Ngounié, S Gabon
Ndindi 77 A6 Nyanga, S Gabon
Ndjamena 76 B3 var. N'Djamena;
prev. Fort-Lamy. Country capital
(Chad) Chari-Baguirmi,
W Chad
Ndjolé 77 A5 Moyen-Ogooué,
W Gabon
Ndola 78 D2 Copperbelt, C Zambia
Neagh, Lough 89 B5 lake
E Northern Ireland, UK
Néa Moudania 104 C4 var. Néa
Moudhaniá. Kentrikí Makedonía,
N Greece
Néa Moudhaniá see Néa Moudania
Neápoli 104 B4 prev. Neápolis.
Dytikí Makedonía, N Greece
Neápoli 105 D8 Kríti, Greece,
E Mediterranean Sea
Neápoli 105 C7 Pelopónnisos,
S Greece
Neapolis see Nablus
Near Islands 36 A2 island group
Aleutian Islands, Alaska, USA

Néa Zíchni 104 C3 var. Néa Zíkhni;
prev. Néa Zíkhna. Kentrikí
Makedonía, NE Greece
Néa Zíkhna see Néa Zíchni
Néa Zíkhni see Néa Zíchni
Nebaj 52 B2 Quiché, W Guatemala
Nebitdag 122 B2 Balkanskiy
Velayat, W Turkmenistan
Neblina, Pico da 62 C1 mountain
NW Brazil
Nebraska 44 D4 off. State of
Nebraska; also known as
Blackwater State, Cornhusker
State, Tree Planters State. State
C USA
Nebraska City 45 F4 Nebraska,
C USA
Neches River 49 H3 river Texas,
SW USA
Neckar 95 B6 river SW Germany
Necochea 65 D5 Buenos Aires,
E Argentina
Neder Rijn 86 D4 Eng. Lower
Rhine. River C Netherlands
Nederweert 87 D5 Limburg,
SE Netherlands
Neede 86 E3 Gelderland,
E Netherlands
Neerpelt 87 D5 Limburg,
NE Belgium
Neftekamsk 111 D5 Respublika
Bashkortostan, W Russian
Federation
Negēlē 73 D5 var. Negelli, It.
Neghelli. C Ethiopia
Negelli see Negēlē
Neghelli see Negēlē
Negomane 79 E2 var. Negomano.
Cabo Delgado, N Mozambique
Negomano see Negomane
Negombo 132 C3 Western Province,
SW Sri Lanka
Negotin 100 E4 Serbia, E Serbia and
Montenegro (Yugo.)
Negra, Punta 60 A3 headland
NW Peru
Negreşti-Oaş 108 B3 Hung.
Avasfelsőfalu; prev. Negreşti. Satu
Mare, NE Romania
Negro, Río 65 C5 river E Argentina
Negro, Río 62 D1 river N South
America
Negro, Río 64 D4 river
Brazil/Uruguay
Negros 139 E2 island C Philippines
Nehbandān 120 E3 Khorāsān, E Iran
Neijiang 128 B5 Sichuan, C China
Nei Monggol Zizhiqu see Inner
Mongolia
Nei Mongol see Inner Mongolia
Neiva 58 B3 Huila, S Colombia
Nellore 132 D2 Andhra Pradesh,
E India
Nelson 37 G4 river Manitoba,
C Canada
Nelson 151 C5 Nelson, South
Island, NZ
Néma 74 D3 Hodh ech Chargui,
SE Mauritania
Neman 106 A4 Bel. Nyoman, Ger.
Memel, Lith. Nemunas, Pol.
Niemen, Rus. Neman. River
NE Europe
Neman 106 B4 Ger. Ragnit.
Kaliningradskaya Oblast',
W Russian Federation
Neméa 105 B6 Pelopónnisos,
S Greece
Nemours 90 C3 Seine-et-Marne,
N France
Nemuro 130 E2 Hokkaidō,
NE Japan
Neochóri 105 B5 Dytikí Ellás,
C Greece
Nepal 135 E3 Country S Asia

Nepal 135

Official name Kingdom of Nepal
Formation 1769
Capital Kathmandu
Population 23.6 million / 434
people per sq mile (168 people per
sq km)
Total area 54,363 sq miles
(140,800 sq km)

Nepal (continued)

Languages Nepali, Maithili,Bhojpuri
Religions Hindu 90%, Buddhist 5%, Muslim 3%, other 2%
Ethnic mix Nepalese 52%, Maithili 11%, Tibeto-Burmese 10%, Bhojpuri 8%, other 19%
Government Constitutional monarchy
Currency Nepalese rupee = 100 paisa
Literacy rate 41.5%
Calorie consumption 2,436 kilocalories

Nereta 106 C4 Aizkraukle, S Latvia
Neretva 100 C4 *river* Bosnia and Herzegovina/Croatia
Neringa 106 A3 *Ger.* Nidden; *prev.* Nida. Neringa, SW Lithuania
Neris 107 C5 *Bel.* Viliya, *Pol.* Wilia; *prev. Pol.* Wilja. *River* Belarus/Lithuania
Nerva 92 C4 Andalucía, S Spain
Neryungri 115 F4 Respublika Sakha (Yakutiya), NE Russian Federation
Neskaupstadhur 83 E5 Austurland, E Iceland
Ness, Loch 88 C3 *lake* N Scotland, UK
Néstos 104 C3 *Bul.* Mesta, *Turk.* Kara Su. *River* Bulgaria/Greece *see also* Mesta
Netanya 119 A6 *var.* Natanya, Nathanya. Central, C Israel
Netherlands 86 C3 *var.* Holland, *Dut.* Koninkrijk der Nederlanden, Nederland. *Country* NW Europe

Netherlands 86

Official name Kingdom of the Netherlands
Formation 1648
Capital Amsterdam, The Hague
Population 16.2 million / 1,010 people per sq mile (390 people per sq km)
Total area 16,033 sq miles (41,526 sq km)
Languages Dutch, Frisian
Religions Roman Catholic 36%, Protestant 27%, Muslim 3%, other 34%
Ethnic mix Dutch 82%, other 18%
Government Parliamentary democracy   **Currency** Euro (Netherlands guilder until 2002)
Literacy rate 99%
Calorie consumption 3,294 kilocalories

Netherlands Antilles 55 E5 *prev.* Dutch West Indies. *Dutch autonomous region* S Caribbean Sea
Netherlands New Guinea *see* Papua
Nettilling Lake 37 G3 *lake* Baffin Island, Nunavut, N Canada
Neubrandenburg 94 D3 Mecklenburg-Vorpommern, NE Germany
Neuchâtel 95 A7 *Ger.* Neuenburg. Neuchâtel, W Switzerland
Neuchâtel, Lac de 47 *Ger.* Neuenburger See. *Lake* W Switzerland
Neufchâteau 87 D8 Luxembourg, SE Belgium
Neumünster 94 B2 Schleswig-Holstein, N Germany
Neunkirchen 95 A5 Saarland, SW Germany
Neuquén 65 B5 Neuquén, SE Argentina
Neuruppin 94 C3 Brandenburg, NE Germany
Neusalz an der Oder *see* Nowa Sól
Neusiedler See 95 E6 *Hung.* Fertő. *Lake* Austria/Hungary

Neustadt an der Weinstrasse 95 B5 *prev.* Neustadt an der Haardt, *hist.* Niewenstat, *anc.* Nova Civitas. Rheinland-Pfalz, SW Germany
Neustrelitz 94 D3 Mecklenburg-Vorpommern, NE Germany
Neu-Ulm 95 B6 Bayern, S Germany
Neuwied 95 A5 Rheinland-Pfalz, W Germany
Neuzen *see* Terneuzen
Nevada 47 C5 *off.* State of Nevada; *also known as* Battle Born State, Sagebrush State, Silver State. *State* W USA
Nevada, Sierra 92 D5 *mountain range* S Spain
Nevers 90 C4 *anc.* Noviodunum. Nièvre, C France
Neves 76 E2 São Tomé, S Sao Tome and Principe
Nevinnomyssk 111 B7 Stavropol'skiy Kray, SW Russian Federation
Nevşehir 116 C3 *var.* Nevshehr. Nevşehir, C Turkey
Nevshehr *see* Nevşehir
Newala 73 C8 Mtwara, SE Tanzania
New Albany 40 C5 Indiana, N USA
New Amsterdam 59 G3 E Guyana
Newark 41 F4 New Jersey, NE USA
New Bedford 41 G3 Massachusetts, NE USA
Newberg 46 B3 Oregon, NW USA
New Bern 43 F1 North Carolina, SE USA
New Braunfels 49 G4 Texas, SW USA
Newbridge 89 B6 *Ir.* An Droichead Nua. C Ireland
New Britain 144 B3 *island* E PNG
New Brunswick 39 E4 *Fr.* Nouveau-Brunswick. *Province* SE Canada
New Caledonia 144 D4 *var.* Kanaky, *Fr.* Nouvelle-Calédonie. *French overseas territory* SW Pacific Ocean
New Caledonia 144 C5 *island* SW Pacific Ocean
New Caledonia Basin 142 C4 *undersea feature* W Pacific Ocean
Newcastle *see* Newcastle upon Tyne
Newcastle 149 D6 New South Wales, SE Australia
Newcastle upon Tyne 88 D4 *var.* Newcastle; *hist.* Monkchester, *Lat.* Pons Aelii. NE England, UK
New Delhi 134 D3 *country capital* (India) Delhi, N India
Newfoundland 39 G3 *Fr.* Terre-Neuve. *Island* Newfoundland, SE Canada
Newfoundland 39 F2 *Fr.* Terre Neuve. *Province* SE Canada
Newfoundland Basin 86 B3 *undersea feature* NW Atlantic Ocean
New Georgia Islands 144 C3 *island group* W Solomon Islands
New Glasgow 39 F4 Nova Scotia, SE Canada
New Goa *see* Pānji
New Guinea 144 A3 *Dut.* Nieuw Guinea, *Ind.* Irian. *Island* Indonesia/PNG
New Hampshire 41 F2 *off.* State of New Hampshire; *also known as* The Granite State. *State* NE USA
New Haven 41 G3 Connecticut, NE USA
New Iberia 42 B3 Louisiana, S USA
New Ireland 144 C3 *island* NE PNG
New Jersey 41 F4 *off.* State of New Jersey; *also known as* The Garden State. *State* NE USA
Newman 146 B4 Western Australia
Newmarket 89 E6 E England, UK
New Mexico 48 C2 *off.* State of New Mexico; *also known as* Land of Enchantment, Sunshine State. *State* SW USA
New Orleans 42 B3 Louisiana, S USA
New Plymouth 150 C4 Taranaki, North Island, NZ
Newport 40 C4 Kentucky, S USA

Newport 89 D7 S England, UK
Newport 89 C7 SE Wales, UK
Newport 41 G2 Vermont, NE USA
Newport News 41 F5 Virginia, NE USA
New Providence 54 C1 *island* N Bahamas
Newquay 89 C7 SW England, UK
Newry 89 B5 *Ir.* An tIúr. SE Northern Ireland, UK
New Sarum *see* Salisbury
New Siberian Islands *see* Novosibirskiye Ostrova
New South Wales 149 C6 *state* SE Australia
Newton 45 G3 Iowa, C USA
Newtownabbey 89 B5 *Ir.* Baile na Mainistreach. E Northern Ireland, UK
New Ulm 45 F2 Minnesota, N USA
New York 41 F4 New York, NE USA
New York 41 F3 *state* NE USA
New Zealand 150 A4 *abbrev.* NZ. *Country* SW Pacific Ocean

New Zealand 150

Official name Dominion of New Zealand
Formation 1947
Capital Wellington
Population 3.8 million /37 people per sq mile (14 people per sq km)
Total area 103,737 sq miles (268,680 sqkm)
Languages English, Maori
Religions Methodist 24%, Presbyterian 18%, non-religious 16%, Roman Catholic 15%, Methodist 5%, other 22%
Ethnic mix European 77%, Maori 12%, Pacific Islanders 5%, other 6%
Government Parliamentary democracy
Currency New Zealand dollar = 100 cents
Literacy rate 99%
Calorie consumption 3252 kilocalories

Neyveli 132 C2 Tamil Nādu, SE India
Ngangzê Co 126 B5 *lake* W China
Ngaoundéré 76 B4 *var.* N'Gaoundéré. Adamaoua, N Cameroon
N'Giva 78 B3 *var.* Ondjiva, *Port.* Vila Pereira de Eça. Cunene, S Angola
Ngo 77 B6 Plateaux, SE Congo
Ngoko 77 B5 *river* Cameroon/Congo
Ngourti 75 H3 Diffa, E Niger
Nguigmi 75 H4 *var.* N'Guigmi. Diffa, SE Niger
Nguru 75 G3 Yobe, NE Nigeria
Nha Trang 137 E6 Khanh Hoa, S Vietnam
Niagara Falls 40 D3 *waterfall* Canada/USA
Niagara Falls 41 E3 New York, NE USA
Niagara Falls 38 D5 Ontario, S Canada
Niamey 75 F3 *country capital* (Niger) Niamey, SW Niger
Niangay, Lac 75 E3 *lake* E Mali
Nia-Nia 77 E5 Orientale, NE Dem. Rep. Congo
Nias, Pulau 138 A3 *island* W Indonesia
Nicaragua 52 D3 *Country* Central America

Nicaragua 52

Official name Republic of Nicaragua
Formation 1838
Capital Managua
Population 5.2 million /104 people per sq mile (40 people per sq km)
Total area 49,998 sq miles (129,494 sq km)

Nicaragua 52

Languages Spanish, English Creole, 40%, Traditional beliefs 10%
Ethnic mix Hausa 21%, Yoruba 21%, Ibo 18%, Fulani 11%, other 29%
Government Multiparty republic
Currency Naira = 100 kobo
Literacy rate 63.9%
Calorie consumption 2,850 kilocalories

Nicaragua, Lago de 52 D4 *var.* Cocibolca, Gran Lago, *Eng.* Lake Nicaragua. *Lake* S Nicaragua
Nicaragua, Lake *see* Nicaragua, Lago de
Nicaria *see* Ikaría
Nice 91 D6 *It.* Nizza; *anc.* Nicaea. Alpes-Maritimes, SE France
Nicephorium *see* Ar Raqqah
Nicholas II Land *see* Severnaya Zemlya
Nicholls Town 54 C1 Andros Island, NW Bahamas
Nicobar Islands 124 B4 *island group* India, E Indian Ocean
Nicosa 102 C5 Gk. Lefkosía, *Turk.* Lefkoşa. *Country capital* (Cyprus) C Cyprus
Nicoya 52 D4 Guanacaste, W Costa Rica
Nicoya, Golfo de 52 D5 *gulf* W Costa Rica
Nicoya, Península de 52 D4 *peninsula* NW Costa Rica
Nidzica 98 D3 *Ger.* Niedenburg. Warmińsko-Mazurskie, NE Poland
Niedere Tauern 99 A6 *mountain range* C Austria
Nieuw Amsterdam 59 G3 Commewijne, NE Suriname
Nieuw-Bergen 86 D4 Limburg, SE Netherlands
Nieuwegein 86 C4 Utrecht, C Netherlands
Nieuw Nickerie 59 G3 Nickerie, NW Suriname
Niğde 116 C4 Niğde, C Turkey
Niger 75 F3 *Country* W Africa

Niger 75

Official name Republic of Niger
Formation 1960
Capital Niamey
Population 11.2 million / 23 people per sq mile (9 people per sq km)
Total area 489,189 sq miles (1,267,000 sq km)
Languages French, Hausa, Djerma
Religions Muslim 85%, Traditional beliefs 14%, other 1%
Ethnic mix Hausa 54%, Djerma and Songhai 21%, Fulani 10%, Tuareg 9%, other 6%
Government Multiparty republic
Currency CFA franc = 100 centimes
Literacy rate 15.9%
Calorie consumption 2,089 kilocalories

Niger 75 F4 *river* W Africa
Nigeria 75 F4 *Country* W Africa

Nigeria 75

Official name Federal Republic of Nigeria
Formation 1960
Capital Abuja
Population 116.9 million / 328 people per sq mile (127 people per sq km)
Total area 356,667 sq miles (923,768 sq km)
Languages English, Hausa, Yoruba, Ibo
Religions Muslim 50%, Christian 40%, Traditional beliefs 10%
Ethnic mix Hausa 21%, Yoruba 21%, Ibo 18%, Fulani 11%, other 29%
Government Multiparty republic
Currency Naira = 100 kobo

Nigeria (continued)

Literacy rate 63.9%
Calorie consumption 2,850 kilocalories

Niger, Mouths of the 75 F5 *delta* S Nigeria
Nihon *see* Japan
Niigata 131 D5 Niigata, Honshū, C Japan
Niihama 131 B7 Ehime, Shikoku, SW Japan
Niihau 47 A7 *island* Hawaii, USA, C Pacific Ocean
Nii-jima 131 D6 *island* E Japan
Nijkerk 86 D3 Gelderland, C Netherlands
Nijlen 87 C5 Antwerpen, N Belgium
Nijmegen 86 D4 *Ger.* Nimwegen; *anc.* Noviomagus. Gelderland, SE Netherlands
Nikaria *see* Ikaría
Nikel' 110 C2 Murmanskaya Oblast', NW Russian Federation
Nikiniki 139 E5 Timor, S Indonesia
Nikopol' 109 F3 Pleven, N Bulgaria
Nikšić 101 C5 Montenegro, SW Serbia and Montenegro (Yugo.)
Nikumaroro 145 E3 *prev.* Gardner Island, Kemins Island. *Atoll* Phoenix Islands, C Kiribati
Nikunau 145 E3 *var.* Nukunau; *prev.* Byron Island. *Atoll* Tungaru, W Kiribati
Nile 68 D3 *Ar.* Nahr an Nīl. *River* N Africa
Nile 72 B2 *former province* NW Uganda
Nile Delta 72 B1 *delta* N Egypt
Nîmes 91 C6 *anc.* Nemausus, Nismes. Gard, S France
Nine Degree Channel 132 B3 *channel* India/Maldives
Ninetyeast Ridge 141 D5 *undersea feature* E Indian Ocean
Ninety Mile Beach 150 C1 *beach* North Island, NZ
Ningbo 128 D5 *var.* Ning-po, Yin-hsien; *prev.* Ninghsien. Zhejiang, SE China
Ninghsien *see* Ningbo
Ning-po *see* Ningbo
Ningxia 128 B4 *off.* Ningxia Huizu Zizhiqu, *var.* Ning-hsia, Ningsia, *Eng.* Ningsia Hui, Ningsia Hui Autonomous Region. Admin. region *autonomous region* N China
Ningxia Huizu Zizhiqu *see* Ningxia
Nio *see* Íos
Niobrara River 45 E3 *river* Nebraska/Wyoming, C USA
Nioro 74 D3 *var.* Nioro du Sahel. Kayes, W Mali
Nioro du Sahel *see* Nioro
Niort 90 B4 Deux-Sèvres, W France
Nipigon 38 B4 Ontario, S Canada
Nipigon, Lake 38 B3 *lake* Ontario, S Canada
Nippon *see* Japan
Niš 101 E5 *Eng.* Nish, *Ger.* Nisch; *anc.* Naissus. Serbia, SE Serbia and Montenegro (Yugo.)
Niṣab 120 B4 Al Ḥudūd ash Shamālīyah, N Saudi Arabia
Nisibin *see* Nusaybin
Nisiros *see* Nísyros
Nisko 98 E4 Podkarpackie, SE Poland
Nísyros 105 E7 *var.* Nisiros. *Island* Dodekánisos, Greece, Aegean Sea
Nitra 99 C6 *Ger.* Neutra, *Hung.* Nyitra. *River* W Slovakia
Nitra 99 C6 *Ger.* Neutra, *Hung.* Nyitra. Nitriansky Kraj, SW Slovakia
Niuatobutabu *see* Niuatoputapu
Niuatoputapu 145 E4 *var.* Niuatobutabu; *prev.* Keppel Island. *Island* N Tonga

Niue 145 F4 *self-governing territory in free association with NZ* S Pacific Ocean
Niulakita 145 E3 *var.* Nurakita. *Atoll* S Tuvalu
Niutao 145 E3 *atoll* NW Tuvalu
Nivernais 90 C4 *cultural region* C France
Nizāmābād 134 D5 Andhra Pradesh, C India
Nizhnekamsk 111 C5 Respublika Tatarstan, W Russian Federation
Nizhnevartovsk 114 D3 Khanty-Mansiyskiy Avtonomnyy Okrug, C Russian Federation
Nizhniy Novgorod 111 C5 *prev.* Gor'kiy. Nizhegorodskaya Oblast', W Russian Federation
Nizhniy Odes 110 D4 Respublika Komi, NW Russian Federation
Nizhnyaya Tunguska 115 E3 *Eng.* Lower Tunguska. *River* N Russian Federation
Nizhyn 109 E1 *Rus.* Nezhin. Chernihivs'ka Oblast', NE Ukraine
Njazidja *see* Grande Comore
Njombe 73 C8 Iringa, S Tanzania
Nkayi 77 B6 *prev.* Jacob. La Bouenza, S Congo
Nkongsamba 76 A4 *var.* N'Kongsamba. Littoral, W Cameroon
Nmai Hka 136 B2 *var.* Me Hka. *River* N Myanmar
Nobeoka 131 B7 Miyazaki, Kyūshū, SW Japan
Noboribetsu 130 D3 *var.* Noboribetu. Hokkaidō, NE Japan
Noboribetu *see* Noboribetsu
Nogales 48 B3 Arizona, SW USA
Nogales 50 B1 Sonora, NW Mexico
Nogal Valley *see* Dooxo Nugaaleed
Nokia 85 D5 Länsi-Suomi, W Finland
Nokou 76 B3 Kanem, W Chad
Nola 77 B5 Sangha-Mbaéré, SW Central African Republic
Nolinsk 111 C5 Kirovskaya Oblast', NW Russian Federation
Nongkaya *see* Nong Khai
Nong Khai 136 C4 *var.* Mi Chai, Nongkaya. Nong Khai, E Thailand
Nonouti 144 D2 *prev.* Sydenham Island. *Atoll* Tungaru, W Kiribati
Noord-Beveland 86 B4 *var.* North Beveland. *Island* SW Netherlands
Noordwijk aan Zee 86 C3 Zuid-Holland, W Netherlands
Nora 85 C6 Örebro, C Sweden
Norak 123 E3 *Rus.* Nurek. W Tajikistan
Nord 83 F1 N Greenland
Nordaustlandet 83 G1 *island* NE Svalbard
Norden 94 A3 Niedersachsen, NW Germany
Norderstedt 94 B3 Schleswig-Holstein, N Germany
Nordfriesische Inseln *see* North Frisian Islands
Nordhausen 94 C4 Thüringen, C Germany
Nordhorn 94 A3 Niedersachsen, NW Germany
Nordkapp 84 D1 *Eng.* North Cape. *Headland* N Norway
Norfolk 45 E3 Nebraska, C USA
Norfolk 41 F5 Virginia, NE USA
Norfolk Island 142 D4 *Australian external territory* SW Pacific Ocean
Norfolk Ridge 142 D4 *undersea feature* W Pacific Ocean
Norias 49 C5 Texas, SW USA
Noril'sk 114 D3 Taymyrskiy (Dolgano-Nenetskiy) Avtonomnyy Okrug, N Russian Federation
Norman 49 G1 Oklahoma, USA
Normandie 90 B3 *Eng.* Normandy. *Cultural region* N France
Normandy *see* Normandie
Normanton 148 C3 Queensland, NE Australia

Norrköping 85 C6 Östergötland, S Sweden
Norrtälje 85 C6 Stockholm, C Sweden
Norseman 147 B6 Western Australia
North Albanian Alps 101 C5 *Alb.* Bjeshkët e Namuna, *SCr.* Prokletije. *Mountain range* Albania/Serbia and Montenegro (Yugo.)
Northallerton 89 D5 N England, UK
North America 34 *continent*
Northampton 89 D6 C England, UK
North Andaman 133 F2 *island* Andaman Islands, India, NE Indian Ocean
North Australian Basin 141 E5 *Fr.* Bassin Nord de l' Australie. *Undersea feature* E Indian Ocean
North Bay 38 D4 Ontario, S Canada
North Beveland *see* Noord-Beveland
North Cape 66 D1 *headland* New Ireland, NE PNG
North Cape 150 C1 *headland* North Island, NZ
North Cape *see* Nordkapp
North Carolina 43 E1 *off.* State of North Carolina; also known as Old North State, Tar Heel State, Turpentine State. *State* SE USA
North Channel 40 D2 *lake channel* Canada/USA
North Charleston 43 F2 South Carolina, SE USA
North Dakota 44 D2 *off.* State of North Dakota; also known as Flickertail State, Peace Garden State, Sioux State. *State* N USA
Northeast Providence Channel 54 C1 *channel* N Bahamas
Northeim 94 B4 Niedersachsen, C Germany
Northern Cook Islands 145 F4 *island group* N Cook Islands
Northern Cyprus, Turkish Republic of 102 D5 *disputed region* N Cyprus
Northern Dvina *see* Severnaya Dvina
Northern Ireland 88 B4 *var.* The Six Counties. *Political division* UK
Northern Mariana Islands 142 B1 *US commonwealth territory* W Pacific Ocean
Northern Sporades *see* Vóreioi Sporádes
Northern Territory 144 A5 *territory* N Australia
North European Plain 81 E3 *plain* N Europe
Northfield 45 F2 Minnesota, N USA
North Fiji Basin 142 D3 *undersea feature* N Coral Sea
North Frisian Islands 94 B2 *var.* Nordfriesische Inseln. *Island group* N Germany
North Huvadhu Atoll 132 B5 *var.* Gaafu Alifu Atoll. *Atoll* S Maldives
North Island 150 B2 *island* N NZ
North Korea 129 E3 *Kor.* Chosŏn-minjujuŭi-inmin-kanghwaguk. *Country* E Asia

North Korea 129

Official name Democratic People's Republic of Korea
Formation 1948
Capital Pyongyang
Population 22.4 million /481 people per sq mile (186 people per sq km)
Total area 46,540 sq miles (120,540 sq km)
Languages Korean, Chinese
Religions Atheist 100%
Ethnic mix Korean 100%
Government One-party republic
Currency N Korean won = 100 chon
Literacy rate 95%
Calorie consumption 2,185 kilocalories

North Little Rock 42 B1 Arkansas, C USA
North Minch *see* Minch, The
North Mole 93 G4 *harbour wall* NW Gibraltar
North Platte 45 E4 Nebraska, C USA
North Platte River 44 D4 *river* C USA
North Pole 155 B3 *pole* Arctic Ocean
North Saskatchewan 37 F5 *river* Alberta/Saskatchewan, S Canada
North Sea 78 D2 *Dan.* Nordsøen, *Dut.* Noordzee, *Fr.* Mer du Nord, *Ger.* Nordsee, *Nor.* Nordsjøen; *prev.* German Ocean, *Lat.* Mare Germanicum. *Sea* NW Europe
North Siberian Lowland *see* Severo-Sibirskaya Nizmennost'
North Siberian Plain *see* Severo-Sibirskaya Nizmennost'
North Taranaki Bight 150 C3 *gulf* North Island, NZ
North Uist 88 B3 *island* NW Scotland, UK
Northwest Atlantic Mid-Ocean Canyon 34 E4 *undersea feature* N Atlantic Ocean
North West Highlands 88 C3 *mountain range* N Scotland, UK
Northwest Pacific Basin 113 G4 *undersea feature* NW Pacific Ocean
Northwest Providence Channel 54 C1 *channel* N Bahamas
Northwest Territories 37 E3 *Fr.* Territoires du Nord-Ouest. *Territory* NW Canada (the eastern part is now the territory of Nunavut)
Northwind Plain 155 B2 *undersea feature* Arctic Ocean
Norton Sound 36 C2 *inlet* Alaska, USA
Norway 85 A5 *Nor.* Norge. *Country* N Europe

Norway 85

Official name Kingdom of Norway
Formation 1905
Capital Oslo
Population 4.5 million /36 people per sq mile (14 people per sq km)
Total area 125,181 sq miles (324,220 sq km)
Languages Norwegian, Sami
Religions Evangelical Lutheran 89%, Roman Catholic 1%, other and non-religious 10%
Ethnic mix Norwegian 93%, Sami 1%, other 6%
Government Parliamentary democracy
Currency Norwegian krone = 100 ore
Literacy rate 99%
Calorie consumption 3,414 kilocalories

Norwegian Basin 83 F4 *undersea feature* NW Norwegian Sea
Norwegian Sea 83 F4 *Nor.* Norske Havet. *Sea* NE Atlantic Ocean
Norwich 89 E6 E England, UK
Noshiro 130 D4 *var.* Nosiro; *prev.* Noshirominato. Akita, Honshū, C Japan
Noshirominato *see* Noshiro
Nosiro *see* Noshiro
Nosivka 109 E1 *Rus.* Nosovka. Chernihivs'ka Oblast', NE Ukraine
Noṣratābād 120 E3 Sīstān va Balūchestān, E Iran
Nossob 78 C4 *river* E Namibia
Noteć 98 C3 *var.* Netze. *River* NW Poland
Nóties Sporádes *see* Dodekánisos
Nottingham 89 D6 C England, UK
Nouâdhibou 74 B2 *prev.* Port-Étienne. Dakhlet Nouâdhibou, W Mauritania
Nouakchott 74 B2 *country capital* (Mauritania) Nouakchott District, SW Mauritania
Nouméa 144 C5 *dependent territory capital* (New Caledonia) Province Sud, S New Caledonia

Nouvelle-Calédonie *see* New Caledonia
Nova Gorica 95 D8 W Slovenia
Nova Gradiška 100 C3 *Ger.* Neugradisk, *Hung.* Újgradiska. Brod-Posavina, NE Croatia
Nova Iguaçu 63 F4 Rio de Janeiro, SE Brazil
Novara 96 B2 *anc.* Novaria. Piemonte, NW Italy
Nova Scotia 39 F4 *Fr.* Nouvelle Écosse. *Province* SE Canada
Nova Scotia 35 E5 *physical region* SE Canada
Novaya Sibir', Ostrov 115 F1 *island* Novosibirskiye Ostrova, NE Russian Federation
Novaya Zemlya 110 D1 *island group* N Russian Federation
Novaya Zemlya Trench *see* East Novaya Zemlya Trench
Novgorod 110 B4 Novgorodskaya Oblast', W Russian Federation
Novi Grad *see* Bosanski Novi
Novi Iskŭr 104 C2 Sofiya-Grad, W Bulgaria
Novi Pazar 101 D5 *Turk.* Yenipazar. Shumen, NE Bulgaria
Novi Sad 100 D3 *Ger.* Neusatz, *Hung.* Újvidék. Serbia, N Serbia and Montenegro (Yugo.)
Novoazovs'k 109 G4 *Rus.* Novoazovsk. Donets'ka Oblast', E Ukraine
Novocheboksarsk 111 C5 Chuvashskaya Respublika, W Russian Federation
Novocherkassk 111 B7 Rostovskaya Oblast', SW Russian Federation
Novodvinsk 110 C3 Arkhangel'skaya Oblast', NW Russian Federation
Novohrad-Volyns'kyy 108 D2 *Rus.* Novograd-Volynskiy. Zhytomyrs'ka Oblast', N Ukraine
Novokazalinsk *see* Ayteke Bi
Novokuznetsk 114 D4 *prev.* Stalinsk. Kemerovskaya Oblast', S Russian Federation
Novolazarevskaya 154 C2 *Russian research station* Antarctica
Novo Mesto 95 E8 *Ger.* Rudolfswert; *prev. Ger.* Neustadtl. SE Slovenia
Novomoskovs'k 109 F3 *Rus.* Novomoskovsk. Dnipropetrovs'ka Oblast', E Ukraine
Novomoskovsk 111 B5 Tul'skaya Oblast', W Russian Federation
Novorossiysk 111 A7 Krasnodarskiy Kray, SW Russian Federation
Novoshakhtinsk 111 B6 Rostovskaya Oblast', SW Russian Federation
Novosibirsk 114 D4 Novosibirskaya Oblast', C Russian Federation
Novosibirskiye Ostrova 115 F1 *Eng.* New Siberian Islands. *Island group* N Russian Federation
Novotroitsk 111 D6 Orenburgskaya Oblast', W Russian Federation
Novotroyits'ke 109 F4 *Rus.* Novotroitskoye. Khersons'ka Oblast', S Ukraine
Novovolyns'k 108 C1 *Rus.* Novovolynsk. Volyns'ka Oblast', NW Ukraine
Novy Dvor 107 B6 *Rus.* Novvy Dvor. Hrodzyenskaya Voblasts', W Belarus
Novyy Buh 109 E3 *Rus.* Novyy Bug. Mykolayivs'ka Oblast', S Ukraine
Novyy Uzen' *see* Zhanaözen
Nowa Sól 98 B4 *var.* Nowasól, *Ger.* Neusalz an der Oder. Lubuskie, W Poland
Nowogard 98 B2 *var.* Nowógard, *Ger.* Naugard. Zachodniopomorskie, NW Poland
Nowógard *see* Nowogard
Nowo-Minsk *see* Miusk Mazowiecki
Nowy Dwór Mazowiecki 98 D3 Mazowieckie, C Poland

Nowy Sącz 99 D5 *Ger.* Neu Sandec. Małopolskie, S Poland
Nowy Tomyśl 98 B3 *var.* Nowy Tomyśl. Wielkopolskie, C Poland
Noyon 90 C3 Oise, N France
Nsanje 79 E3 Southern, S Malawi
Nsawam 75 E5 SE Ghana
Ntomba, Lac 77 C6 *var.* Lac Tumba. *Lake* NW Dem. Rep. Congo
Nubian Desert 72 B3 *desert* NE Sudan
Nu'eima 119 E7 E West Bank
Nueva Gerona 54 B2 Isla de la Juventud, S Cuba
Nueva Rosita 50 D2 Coahuila de Zaragoza, NE Mexico
Nuevitas 54 C2 Camagüey, E Cuba
Nuevo, Bajo 53 G1 *island* NW Colombia
Nuevo Casas Grandes 50 C1 Chihuahua, N Mexico
Nuevo, Golfo 65 C6 *gulf* S Argentina
Nuevo Laredo 51 E2 Tamaulipas, NE Mexico
Nui Atoll 145 E3 *atoll* W Tuvalu
Nûk *see* Nuuk
Nuku'alofa 145 E5 *country capital* (Tonga) Tongatapu, S Tonga
Nukufetau Atoll 145 E3 *atoll* C Tuvalu
Nukulaelae Atoll 145 E3 *var.* Nukulailai. *Atoll* E Tuvalu
Nukulailai *see* Nukulaelae Atoll
Nukunau *see* Nikunau
Nukunonu Atoll 145 E3 *island* C Tokelau
Nukus 122 C2 Qoraqalpoghiston Respublikasi, W Uzbekistan
Nullarbor Plain 147 C6 *plateau* South Australia/Western Australia
Nunap Isua 98 B5 *var.* Uummannarsuaq, *Dan.* Kap Farvel, *Eng.* Cape Farewell. *Headland* S Greenland
Nunavut 37 F3 *territory* N Canada
Nuneaton 89 D6 C England, UK
Nunivak Island 36 B2 *island* Alaska, USA
Nunspeet 86 D3 Gelderland, E Netherlands
Nuoro 97 A5 Sardegna, Italy, C Mediterranean Sea
Nuquí 58 A3 Chocó, W Colombia
Nurakita *see* Niulakita
Nuremberg *see* Nürnberg
Nurmes 84 E4 Itä-Suomi, E Finland
Nürnberg 95 C5 *Eng.* Nuremberg. Bayern, S Germany
Nurota 123 E2 *Rus.* Nurata. Nawoiy Wiloyati, C Uzbekistan
Nusa Tenggara 139 E5 *Eng.* Lesser Sunda Islands. East Timor / C Indonesia
Nusaybin 117 F4 *var.* Nisibin. Manisa, SE Turkey
Nuuk 82 C4 *var.* Nûk, *Dan.* Godthaab, Godthåb. *Dependent territory capital* (Greenland) SW Greenland
Nyagan' 114 C3 Khanty-Mansiyskiy Avtonomnyy Okrug, N Russian Federation
Nyaingêntanglha Shan 126 C5 *mountain range* W China
Nyala 72 A4 Southern Darfur, W Sudan
Nyamapanda 78 D3 Mashonaland East, NE Zimbabwe
Nyamtumbo 73 C8 Ruvuma, S Tanzania
Nyandoma 110 C4 Arkhangel'skaya Oblast', NW Russian Federation
Nyantakara 73 B7 Kagera, NW Tanzania
Nyasa, Lake 79 E2 *var.* Lake Malawi; *prev.* Lago Nyassa. *Lake* E Africa
Nyasvizh 107 C6 *Pol.* Nieśwież, *Rus.* Nesvizh. Minskaya Voblasts', C Belarus
Nyaunglebin 136 B4 Pegu, SW Myanmar
Nyeri 73 C6 Central, C Kenya
Nyima 126 C5 Xizang Zizhiqu, W China

Nyíregyháza 99 D6 Szabolcs-Szatmár-Bereg, NE Hungary
Nykøbing 85 B8 Storstrøm, SE Denmark
Nyköping 85 C6 Södermanland, S Sweden
Nylstroom *see* Modimolle
Nyngan 149 D6 New South Wales, SE Australia
Nyurba 115 F3 Respublika Sakha (Yakutiya), NE Russian Federation
Nyzhn'ohirs'kyy 109 F4 *Rus.* Nizhnegorskiy. Respublika Krym, S Ukraine
Nzega 73 C7 Tabora, C Tanzania
Nzérékoré 74 D4 Guinée-Forestière, SE Guinea
Nzwani *see* Anjouan

O

Oahu 47 A7 *Haw.* O'ahu. *Island* Hawaii, USA, C Pacific Ocean
Oak Harbor 46 B1 Washington, NW USA
Oakland 47 B6 California, W USA
Oamaru 151 B7 Otago, South Island, NZ
Oaxaca 51 F5 *var.* Oaxaca de Juárez; *prev.* Antequera. Oaxaca, SE Mexico
Oaxaca de Juárez *see* Oaxaca
Ob' 112 C2 *river* C Russian Federation
Obal' 107 D5 *Rus.* Obol'. Vitsyebskaya Voblasts', N Belarus
Oban *see* Halfmoon Bay
Oban 88 C4 W Scotland, UK
Obando *see* Puerto Inírida
Obeliai 106 C4 Rokiškis, NE Lithuania
Oberhollabrunn *see* Tulln
Ob, Gulf of *see* Obskaya Guba
Obihiro 130 D2 Hokkaidō, NE Japan
Obo 76 D4 Haut-Mbomou, E Central African Republic
Obock 72 D4 E Djibouti
Oborniki 98 C3 Wielkopolskie, C Poland
Obskaya Guba 114 D3 *Eng.* Gulf of Ob'. *Gulf* N Russian Federation
Ob' Tablemount 141 B7 *undersea feature* S Indian Ocean
Ocala 43 E4 Florida, SE USA
Ocaña 92 D3 Castilla-La Mancha, C Spain
Ocaña 58 B2 Norte de Santander, N Colombia
O Carballiño 108 C1 *var* Carballiño. Gallicia, NW Spain
Occidental, Cordillera 61 E4 *mountain range* W South America
Occidental, Cordillera 58 B2 *mountain range* W Colombia
Occidental, Cordillera 60 D4 *mountain range* W Peru
Ocean Falls 36 D5 British Columbia, SW Canada
Ocean Island *see* Banaba
Oceanside 47 C8 California, W USA
Ochakiv 109 E4 *Rus.* Ochakov. Mykolayivs'ka Oblast', S Ukraine
Och'amch'ire 117 E2 *Rus.* Ochamchira. W Georgia
Ocho Rios 54 B4 C Jamaica
Ochrida, Lake *see* Ohrid, Lake
Ocotal 52 D3 Nueva Segovia, NW Nicaragua
Ocozocuautla 51 G5 Chiapas, SE Mexico
Ocú 53 F5 Herrera, S Panama
Ödate 130 D3 Akita, Honshū, C Japan
Oddur *see* Xuddur
Ödemiş 116 A4 Izmir, SW Turkey
Odense 85 B7 Fyn, C Denmark
Oder 80 B3 *Cz./Pol.* Odra. *River* C Europe
Oderhaff *see* Szczeciński, Zalew
Odesa 109 E4 *Rus.* Odessa. Odes'ka Oblast', SW Ukraine
Odessa 49 E3 Texas, SW USA
Odienné 74 D4 NW Côte d'Ivoire
Ödöngk 137 D6 Kâmpóng Spoe, S Cambodia

Odoorn 86 E2 Drenthe, NE Netherlands
Of 117 E2 Trabzon, NE Turkey
Ofanto 97 D5 *river* S Italy
Offenbach *see* Offenbach am Main. Hessen, W Germany
Offenbach am Main *see* Offenbach
Offenburg 95 B6 Baden-Württemberg, SW Germany
Ogaden 73 D5 *Som.* Ogaadeen. *Plateau* Ethiopia/Somalia
Ōgaki 131 C6 Gifu, Honshū, SW Japan
Ogallala 44 D4 Nebraska, C USA
Ogbomosho 75 F4 Oyo, W Nigeria
Ogden 44 B4 Utah, W USA
Ogdensburg 41 F2 New York, NE USA
Ogulin 100 A3 Karlovac, NW Croatia
Ohio 40 C4 *off.* State of Ohio; also known as The Buckeye State. *State* N USA
Ohio River 40 C4 *river* N USA
Ohrid 101 D6 *Turk.* Ochrida, Ohri. SW FYR Macedonia
Ohrid, Lake 101 D6 *var.* Lake Ochrida, *Alb.* Liqeni i Ohrit, *Mac.* Ohridsko Ezero. *Lake* Albania/FYR Macedonia
Ohridsko Ezero *see* Ohrid, Lake
Ohura 150 D3 Manawatu-Wanganui, North Island, NZ
Oirschot 87 C5 Noord-Brabant, S Netherlands
Oise 90 C3 *river* N France
Oistins 55 G2 S Barbados
Ōita 131 B7 Ōita, Kyūshū, SW Japan
Ojinaga 50 D2 Chihuahua, N Mexico
Ojos del Salado, Cerro 64 B3 *mountain* W Argentina
Okaihau 150 C2 Northland, North Island, NZ
Okāra 134 C2 Punjab, E Pakistan
Okavanggo *see* Cubango
Okavango *see* Cubango
Okavango 78 C3 *district* NW Namibia
Okavango Delta 78 C3 *wetland* N Botswana
Okayama 131 B6 Okayama, Honshū, SW Japan
Okazaki 131 C6 Aichi, Honshū, C Japan
Okeechobee, Lake 43 E4 *lake* Florida, SE USA
Okefenokee Swamp 43 E3 *wetland* Georgia, SE USA
Okhotsk 115 G3 Khabarovskiy Kray, E Russian Federation
Okhotskoye More 115 G3 *sea* NW Pacific Ocean
Okhotsk, Sea of 113 F3 *sea* NW Pacific Ocean
Okhtyrka 109 F2 *Rus.* Akhtyrka. Sums'ka Oblast', NE Ukraine
Oki-guntō *see* Oki-shotō
Okinawa 130 A3 *island* Okinawa, SW Japan
Okinawa-shotō 130 A3 *island group* SW Japan
Oki-shotō 131 B6 *var.* Oki-guntō. *Island group* SW Japan
Oklahoma 49 F2 *off.* State of Oklahoma; also known as The Sooner State. *State* C USA
Oklahoma City 49 G1 *state capital* Oklahoma, C USA
Okmulgee 49 G1 Oklahoma, C USA
Oko, Wadi 72 C3 *river* NE Sudan
Oktyabr'skiy 111 D6 Volgogradskaya Oblast', SW Russian Federation
Oktyabr'skoy Revolyutsii, Ostrov 115 E2 *Eng.* October Revolution Island. *Island* Severnaya Zemlya, N Russian Federation
Okulovka *see* Uglovka
Okushiri-tō 130 C3 *var.* Okusiri Tô. *Island* NE Japan
Okusiri Tô *see* Okushiri-tō
Öland 85 C7 *island* S Sweden
Olavarría 65 D5 Buenos Aires, E Argentina
Oława 98 C4 *Ger.* Ohlau. Dolnośląskie, SW Poland

Olbia 97 A5 *prev.* Terranova
Pausania. Sardegna, Italy,
C Mediterranean Sea
Oldebroek 86 D3 Gelderland,
E Netherlands
Oldenburg 94 B3 Niedersachsen,
NW Germany
Oldenburg 94 C2 Schleswig-
Holstein, N Germany
Oldenzaal 86 E3 Overijssel,
E Netherlands
Old Harbour 54 B5 C Jamaica
Olëkma 115 F4 *river* C Russian
Federation
Olëkminsk 115 F3 Respublika
Sakha (Yakutiya), NE Russian
Federation
Oleksandrovka 109 E3 *Rus.*
Aleksandrovka. Kirovohrads'ka
Oblast', C Ukraine
Oleksandriya 109 F3 *Rus.*
Aleksandriya. Kirovohrads'ka
Oblast', C Ukraine
Olenegorsk 110 C2 Murmanskaya
Oblast', NW Russian Federation
Olenëk 115 E3 Respublika Sakha
(Yakutiya), NE Russian Federation
Olenëk 115 E3 *river* NE Russian
Federation
Oléron, Île d' 91 A5 *island* W France
Olevs'k 108 D1 *Rus.* Olevsk.
Zhytomyrs'ka Oblast', N Ukraine
Ölgiy 126 C2 Bayan-Ölgiy,
W Mongolia
Olhão 92 B5 Faro, S Portugal
Olifa 78 B3 Kunene, NW Namibia
Ólimbos *see* Ólympos
Olimpo *see* Fuerte Olimpo
Oliva 93 F4 País Valenciano, E Spain
Olivet 90 C4 Loiret, C France
Olmaliq 123 E2 *Rus.* Almalyk.
Toshkent Wiloyati, E Uzbekistan
Olomouc 99 C5 *Ger.* Olmütz, *Pol.*
Ołomuniec. Olomoucký Kraj,
E Czech Republic
Olonets 110 B3 Respublika
Kareliya, NW Russian Federation
Olovyannaya 115 F4 Chitinskaya
Oblast', S Russian Federation
Olpe 94 B4 Nordrhein-Westfalen,
W Germany
Olsztyn 98 D2 *Ger.* Allenstein.
Warmińsko-Mazurskie, NE
Poland
Olt 108 B5 *var.* Oltul, *Ger.* Alt. *River*
S Romania
Olteniţa 108 C5 *prev. Eng.* Oltenitsa,
anc. Constantiola. Călăraşi,
SE Romania
Oltul *see* Olt
Olvera 92 D5 Andalucía,
S Spain
Olympia 46 B2 *state capital*
Washington, NW USA
Olympic Mountains 46 A2 *mountain
range* Washington, NW USA
Ólympos 104 B4 *var.* Ólimbos, *Eng.*
Mount Olympus. *Mountain*
N Greece
Olympus, Mount *see* Ólympos
Omagh 89 B5 *Ir.* An Ómaigh.
W Northern Ireland, UK
Omaha 45 F4 Nebraska, C USA
Oman 121 D6 *Ar.* Salţanat 'Umān;
prev. Muscat and Oman. *Country*
SW Asia

Oman 121

Official name Sultanate of Oman
Formation 1951
Capital Muscat
Population 2.6 million / 32 people
per sq mile (12 people per sq km)
Total area 82,031 sq miles
(212,460 sq km)
Languages Arabic, Baluchi
Religions Ibadi Muslim 75%,
other Muslim and Hindu 25%
Ethnic mix Arab 88%, Baluch 4%,
Persian 3%, Indian and Pakistani
3%, African 2%
Government Monarchy
Currency Omani rial = 1,000 baizas
Literacy rate 71.8%
Calorie consumption not available

Oman, Gulf of 120 E4 *Ar.* Khalīj
'Umān. *Gulf* N Arabian Sea
Omboué 77 A6 Ogooué-Maritime,
W Gabon
Omdurman 72 B4 *var.* Umm
Durmān. Khartoum, C Sudan
Ometepe, Isla de 52 D4 *island*
S Nicaragua
Ommen 86 E3 Overijssel,
E Netherlands
Omsk 114 C4 Omskaya Oblast',
C Russian Federation
Ōmuta 131 A7 Fukuoka, Kyūshū,
SW Japan
Onda 93 F3 País Valenciano, E Spain
Ondjiva *see* N'Giva
Öndörhaan 127 E2 Hentiy,
E Mongolia
Onega 110 B4 *river* NW Russian
Federation
Onega 110 C3 Arkhangel'skaya
Oblast', NW Russian Federation
Onega, Lake *see* Onezhskoye
Ozero
Onex 95 A7 Genève,
SW Switzerland
Onezhskoye Ozero 110 B4 *Eng.*
Lake Onega. *Lake* NW Russian
Federation
Ongole 132 D1 Andhra Pradesh,
E India
Onitsha 75 G5 Anambra, S Nigeria
Onon Gol 127 E2 *river* N Mongolia
Ononte *see* Orantes
Onslow 146 A4 Western Australia
Onslow Bay 43 F1 *bay* North
Carolina, E USA
Ontario 38 B3 *province* S Canada
Ontario, Lake 41 E3 *lake*
Canada / USA
Onteniente *see* Ontinyent
Ontinyent 93 F4 *var.* Onteniente.
País Valenciano, E Spain
Ontong Java Rise 125 H4 *undersea
feature* W Pacific Ocean
Oostakker 87 B5 Oost-Vlaanderen,
NW Belgium
Oostburg 87 B5 Zeeland,
SW Netherlands
Oostende 87 A5 *Eng.* Ostend, *Fr.*
Ostende. West-Vlaanderen,
NW Belgium
Oosterbeek 86 D4 Gelderland,
SE Netherlands
Oosterhout 86 C4 Noord-Brabant,
S Netherlands
Opatija 100 A2 *It.* Abbazia.
Primorje-Gorski Kotar, NW Croatia
Opava 99 C5 *Ger.* Troppau.
Ostravský Kraj, E Czech Republic
Opelika 42 D2 Alabama, S USA
Opelousas 42 B3 Louisiana, S USA
Opmeer 86 C2 Noord-Holland,
NW Netherlands
Opochka 110 A4 Pskovskaya
Oblast', W Russian Federation
Opole 98 C4 *Ger.* Oppeln. Opolskie,
S Poland
Opotiki 150 E3 Bay of Plenty, North
Island, NZ
Oppidum Ubiorum *see* Köln
Oqtosh 123 E2 *Rus.* Aktash.
Samarqand Wiloyati, C Uzbekistan
Oradea 108 B3 *prev.* Oradea Mare,
Ger. Grosswardein, *Hung.*
Nagyvárad. Bihor, NW Romania
Orahovac 101 D5 Alb. Rahovec.
Serbia, S Serbia and Montenegro
(Yugo.)
Oran 70 D2 *var.* Ouahran, Wahran.
NW Algeria
Orange 91 D6 *anc.* Arausio.
Vaucluse, SE France
Orange 149 D6 New South Wales,
SE Australia
Orangeburg 43 E2 South Carolina,
SE USA
Orange Cone *see* Orange Fan
Orange Fan 69 C7 *var.* Orange
Cone. *Undersea feature* SW Indian
Ocean
Orange Mouth *see* Oranjemund
Orangemund *see* Oranjemund
Orange River 78 B4 *Afr.*
Oranjerivier. *River* S Africa
Orange Walk 52 C1 Orange Walk,
N Belize

Oranienburg 94 D3 Brandenburg,
NE Germany
Oranjemund 78 B4 *var.*
Orangemund; *prev.* Orange
Mouth. Karas, SW Namibia
Oranjestad 55 E5 *dependent territory
capital* (Aruba) W Aruba
Orantes 118 B3 *var.* Ononte, *Ar.*
Nahr el Aassi, Nahr al 'Aşī. *River*
SW Asia
Oraviţa 108 A4 *Ger.* Orawitza,
Hung. Oravicabánya. Caraş-
Severin, SW Romania
Orbetello 96 B4 Toscana, C Italy
Orcadas 154 A1 *Argentinian research
station* South Orkney Islands,
Antarctica
Orchard Homes 44 B1 Montana,
NW USA
Ordino 91 A8 NW Andorra
Ordos Desert *see* Mu Us Shamo
Ordu 116 D2 *anc.* Cotyora. Ordu,
N Turkey
Ordzhonikidze 109 F3
Dnipropetrovs'ka Oblast',
E Ukraine
Orealla 59 G3 E Guyana
Örebro 85 C6 Örebro, C Sweden
Oregon 46 B3 *off.* State of Oregon;
also known as Beaver State,
Sunset State, Valentine State,
Webfoot State. *State* NW USA
Oregon City 46 B3 Oregon,
NW USA
Orël 111 B5 Orlovskaya Oblast',
W Russian Federation
Orem 44 B4 Utah, W USA
Orenburg 111 D6 *prev.* Chkalov.
Orenburgskaya Oblast',
W Russian Federation
Orense *see* Ourense
Oreor 144 A2 *var.* Koror. *Country
capital* (Palau) Oreor, N Palau
Orestiáda 104 D3 *prev.* Orestiás.
Anatolikí Makedonía kai Thráki,
NE Greece
Organ Peak 48 D3 *mountain* New
Mexico, SW USA
Orgeyev *see* Orhei
Orhei 108 D3 *var.* Orheiu, *Rus.*
Orgeyev. N Moldova
Orheiu *see* Orhei
Oriental, Cordillera 60 D3 *mountain
range* Bolivia / Peru
Oriental, Cordillera 61 F4 *mountain
range* C Bolivia
Oriental, Cordillera 58 B3 *mountain
range* C Colombia
Orihuela 93 F4 País Valenciano,
E Spain
Orikhiv 109 G3 *Rus.* Orekhov.
Zaporiz'ka Oblast', SE Ukraine
Orinoco, Río 59 E2 *river*
Colombia / Venezuela
Orissa 135 F4 *state* NE India
Orissaare 106 C2 *Ger.* Orissaar.
Saaremaa, W Estonia
Oristano 97 A5 Sardegna, Italy,
C Mediterranean Sea
Orito 58 A4 Putumayo,
SW Colombia
Orizaba, Volcán Pico de 35 C7 *var.*
Citlaltépetl. *Mountain* S Mexico
Orkney *see* Orkney Islands
Orkney Islands 88 C2 *var.* Orkney,
Orkneys. *Island group* N Scotland,
UK
Orkneys *see* Orkney Islands
Orlando 43 E4 Florida, SE USA
Orléanais 90 C4 *cultural region*
C France
Orléans 90 C4 *anc.* Aurelianum.
Loiret, C France
Orléansville *see* Chlef
Orly 90 E2 *international airport*
(Paris) Essonne, N France
Orlya 107 B6 *Rus.* Orlya.
Hrodzyenskaya Voblasts',
W Belarus
Ormuz, Strait of *see* Hormuz, Strait
of
Örnsköldsvik 85 C5
Västernorrland, C Sweden
Oromocto 39 F4 New Brunswick,
SE Canada
Orona 145 F3 *prev.* Hull Island. *Atoll*
Phoenix Islands, C Kiribati

Orosirá Rodhópis *see* Rhodope
Mountains
Orpington 89 B8 SE England, UK
Orsha 107 E6 *Rus.* Orsha.
Vitsyebskaya Voblasts', NE Belarus
Orsk 114 B4 Orenburgskaya
Oblast', W Russian Federation
Orşova 108 A4 *Ger.* Orschowa,
Hung. Orsova. Mehedinţi,
SW Romania
Orthez 91 B6 Pyrénées-Atlantiques,
SW France
Ortona 96 D4 Abruzzo, C Italy
Oruba *see* Aruba
Oruro 61 F4 Oruro, W Bolivia
Ōsaka 131 C6 *hist.* Naniwa. Ōsaka,
Honshū, SW Japan
Osa, Península de 53 E5 *peninsula*
S Costa Rica
Osborn Plateau 141 D5 *undersea
feature* E Indian Ocean
Osh 123 F2 Oshskaya Oblast',
SW Kyrgyzstan
Oshawa 38 D5 Ontario, SE Canada
Oshikango 78 B3 Ohangwena,
N Namibia
Ō-shima 131 D6 *island* S Japan
Oshkosh 40 B2 Wisconsin, N USA
Osijek 100 C3 *prev.* Osiek, Osjek,
Ger. Esseg, *Hung.* Eszék. Osijek-
Baranja, E Croatia
Oskaloosa 45 G4 Iowa, C USA
Oskarshamn 85 C7 Kalmar,
S Sweden
Oskil 109 G2 *Rus.* Oskol. *River*
Russian Federation / Ukraine
Oslo 85 B6 *prev.* Christiania,
Kristiania. *Country capital*
(Norway) Oslo, S Norway
Osmaniye 116 D4 Osmaniye,
admin. region *province* S Turkey
Osnabrück 94 A3 Niedersachsen,
NW Germany
Osogov Mountains 120 B3 *var.*
Osogovske Planine, Osogovski
Planina, *Mac.* Osogovski Planini.
mountain range Bulgaria / FYR,
Macedonia
**Osogovske Planine/Osogovski
Planina/Osogovski Planini** *see*
Osogov Mountains
Osorno 65 B5 Los Lagos, C Chile
Oss 86 D4 Noord-Brabant,
S Netherlands
Ossa, Serra d' 92 C4 *mountain range*
SE Portugal
Ossora 115 H2 Koryakskiy
Avtonomnyy Okrug, E Russian
Federation
Ostend *see* Oostende
Ostende *see* Oostende
Oster 109 E1 Chernihivs'ka Oblast',
N Ukraine
Östersund 85 C5 Jämtland,
C Sweden
Ostfriesische Inseln 94 A3 *Eng.*
East Frisian Islands. *Island group*
NW Germany
Ostiglia 96 C2 Lombardia, N Italy
Ostrava 99 C5 Ostravský Kraj,
E Czech Republic
Ostróda 98 D3 *Ger.* Osterode,
Osterode in Ostpreussen.
Warmińsko-Mazurskie, NE Poland
Ostrołęka 98 D3 *Ger.* Wiesenhof,
Rus. Ostrolenka. Mazowieckie, C
Poland
Ostrov 110 A4 *Latv.* Austrava.
Karlovarský Kraj, W Czech
Republic
Ostrovets *see* Ostrowiec
Świętokrzyski
Ostrów *see* Ostrów Wielkopolski
Ostrowiec *see* Ostrowiec
Świętokrzyski
Ostrowiec Świętokrzyski 98 D4
var. Ostrowiec, *Rus.* Ostrovets.
Świętokrzyskie, C Poland
Ostrów Mazowiecka 98 D3 *var.*
Ostrów Mazowiecki.
Mazowieckie, C Poland
Ostrów Mazowiecki *see* Ostrów
Mazowiecka
Ostrowo *see* Ostrów Wielkopolski
Ostrów Wielkopolski 98 C4 *var.*
Ostrów, *Ger.* Ostrowo.
Wielkopolskie, C Poland

Osum *see* Osumit, Lumi i
Ōsumi-shotō 131 A8 *island group*
SW Japan
Osumit, Lumi i 101 D7 *var.* Osum.
River SE Albania
Osuna 92 D4 Andalucía, S Spain
Oswego 41 F2 New York, NE USA
Otago Peninsula 151 B7 *peninsula*
South Island, NZ
Otaki 150 D4 Wellington, North
Island, NZ
Otaru 130 C2 Hokkaidō, NE Japan
Otavalo 60 B1 Imbabura,
N Ecuador
Otavi 78 B3 Otjozondjupa,
N Namibia
Oţelu Roşu 108 B4 *Ger.*
Ferdinandsberg, *Hung.*
Nándorhgy. Caras-Severin,
SW Romania
Otepää 106 D3 *Ger.* Odenpäh.
Valgamaa, SE Estonia
Oti 75 E4 *river* W Africa
Otira 151 C6 West Coast, South
Island, NZ
Otjiwarongo 78 B3 Otjozondjupa,
N Namibia
Otorohanga 150 D3 Waikato, North
Island, NZ
Otranto, Strait of 101 C6 *It.* Canale
d'Otranto. *Strait* Albania/Italy
Otrokovice 99 C5 *Ger.* Otrokowitz.
Zlínský Kraj, E Czech Republic
Ōtsu 131 C6 *var.* Ōtu. Shiga,
Honshū, SW Japan
Ottawa 41 E2 *Fr.* Outaouais. Admin.
region *river* Ontario/Quebec,
SE Canada
Ottawa 38 D5 *country capital*
(Canada) Ontario, SE Canada
Ottawa 40 B3 Illinois, N USA
Ottawa 45 F5 Kansas, C USA
Ottawa Islands 38 C1 *island group*
Northwest Territories, C Canada
Ottignies 87 C6 Wallon Brabant,
C Belgium
Ottumwa 45 G4 Iowa, C USA
Ōtu *see* Ōtsu
Ouachita Mountains 42 A1
mountain range
Arkansas/Oklahoma, C USA
Ouachita River 42 B2 *river*
Arkansas/Louisiana, C USA
Ouadi Howa *see* Howar, Wādi
Ouagadougou 75 E4 *var.*
Wagadugu. *Country capital*
(Burkina Faso) C Burkina Faso
Ouahigouya 75 E3 NW Burkina
faso
Ouahran *see* Oran
Oualâta *see* Oualāta
Oualāta 74 D3 *var.* Oualata. Hodh
ech Chargui, SE Mauritania
Ouanary 59 H3 E French Guiana
Ouanda Djallé 76 D4 Vakaga,
NE Central African Republic
Ouarâne 74 D2 *desert* C Mauritania
Ouargla 71 E2 *var.* Wargla.
NE Algeria
Ouarzazate 70 C3 S Morocco
Oubangui *see* Ubangi
Oubangui-Chari *see* Central
African Republic
Ouessant, Île d' 90 A3 *Eng.* Ushant.
Island NW France
Ouésso 77 B5 La Sangha,
NW Congo
Oujda 70 D2 *Ar.* Oudjda, Ujda.
NE Morocco
Oujeft 74 C2 Adrar, C Mauritania
Oulu 84 D4 *Swe.* Uleåborg. Oulu,
C Finland
Oulujärvi 84 D4 *Swe.* Uleträsk. *Lake*
C Finland
Oulujoki 84 D4 *Swe.* Uleälv. *River*
C Finland
Ounianga Kébir 76 C2 Borkou-
Ennedi-Tibesti, N Chad
Oup *see* Auob
Oupeye 87 D6 Liège, E Belgium
Our 87 D6 *river* NW Europe
Ourense 92 C1 *var.* Cast. Orense;
Lat. Aurium. Galicia, NW Spain
Ourique 92 B4 Beja, S Portugal
Ourthe 87 D7 *river* E Belgium
Ouse 89 D5 *river* N England, UK

Outer Hebrides 88 B3 *var.* Western
Isles. *Island group* NW Scotland,
UK
Outer Islands 79 G1 *island group*
SW Seychelles
Outes 92 B1 Galicia, NW Spain
Ouvéa 144 D5 *island* Îles Loyauté,
NE New Caledonia
Ouyen 149 C6 Victoria, SE Australia
Ovalle 64 B3 Coquimbo, N Chile
Ovar 92 B2 Aveiro, N Portugal
Overflakkee 86 B4 *island*
SW Netherlands
Overijse 87 C6 Vlaams Brabant,
C Belgium
Oviedo 92 C1 *anc.* Asturias.
Asturias, NW Spain
Ovruch 108 D1 Zhytomyrs'ka
Oblast', N Ukraine
Owando 77 B5 *prev.* Fort-Rousset.
Cuvette, C Congo
Owase 131 C6 Mie, Honshū,
SW Japan
Owatonna 45 F3 Minnesota, N USA
Owen Fracture Zone 140 B4 *tectonic
feature* W Arabian Sea
Owen, Mount 151 C5 *mountain*
South Island, NZ
Owensboro 40 B5 Kentucky, S USA
Owen Stanley Range 144 B3
mountain range S PNG
Owerri 75 G5 Imo, S Nigeria
Owo 75 F5 Ondo, SW Nigeria
Owyhee River 46 C4 *river*
Idaho/Oregon, NW USA
Oxford 89 D6 *Lat.* Oxonia.
S England, UK
Oxford 151 C6 Canterbury, South
Island, NZ
Oxkutzcab 51 H4 Yucatán,
SE Mexico
Oxnard 47 B7 California, W USA
Oyama 131 D5 Tochigi, Honshū,
S Japan
Oyem 77 B5 Woleu-Ntem, N Gabon
Oyo 77 B6 Cuvette, C Congo
Oyo 75 F4 Oyo, W Nigeria
Ozark 42 D3 Alabama, S USA
Ozark Plateau 45 G5 *plain*
Arkansas/Missouri, C USA
Ozarks, Lake of the 45 F5 *reservoir*
Missouri, C USA
Ozbourn Seamount 152 D4
undersea feature W Pacific Ocean
Ózd 99 D6 Borsod-Abaúj-Zemplén,
NE Hungary
Ozero Khanka *see* Khanka, Lake
Ozero Ubsu-Nur *see* Uvs Nuur
Ozieri 97 A5 Sardegna, Italy,
C Mediterranean Sea

P

Paamiut 82 B4 *var.* Pâmiut, *Dan.*
Frederikshåb. S Greenland
Pa-an 136 B4 Karen State, S Myanmar
Pabianice 98 C4 Lodz, C Poland
Pabna 135 G4 Rajshahi,
W Bangladesh
Pachuca 51 E4 *var.* Pachuca de Soto.
Hidalgo, C Mexico
Pachuca de Soto *see* Pachuca
Pacific-Antarctic Ridge 154 B5
undersea feature S Pacific Ocean
Pacific Ocean 152 D3 *ocean*
Padalung *see* Phatthalung
Padang 138 B4 Sumatera,
W Indonesia
Paderborn 94 B4 Nordrhein-
Westfalen, NW Germany
Padma *see* Brahmaputra
Padova 96 C2 *Eng.* Padua; *anc.*
Patavium. Veneto, NE Italy
Padre Island 49 G5 *island* Texas,
SW USA
Padua *see* Padova
Paducah 40 B5 Kentucky, S USA
Paeroa 150 D3 Waikato, North
Island, NZ
Páfos 102 C5 *var.* Paphos.
W Cyprus
Pag 100 A3 *It.* Pago. *Island* Zadar
SW Croatia
Page 48 B1 Arizona, SW USA
Pago Pago 145 F4 *dependent territory
capital* (American Samoa) Tutuila,
W American Samoa

Pahiatua 150 D4 Manawatu-
Wanganui, North Island, NZ
Pahsien *see* Chongqing
Paide 106 D2 *Ger.* Weissenstein.
Järvamaa, N Estonia
Paihia 150 D2 Northland, North
Island, NZ
Päijänne 85 D5 *lake* S Finland
Paine, Cerro 65 A7 *mountain* S Chile
Painted Desert 48 B1 *desert*
Arizona, SW USA
Paisley 88 C4 W Scotland, UK
País Valenciano 93 F3 *cultural region*
NE Spain
País Vasco 93 E1 *cultural region*
N Spain
Paita 60 B3 Piura, NW Peru
Pakanbaru *see* Pekanbaru
Pakaraima Mountains 59 E3 *var.*
Serra Pacaraim, Sierra Pacaraima.
Mountain range N South America
Pakistan 134 A2 *var.* Islami
Jamhuriya e Pakistan. *Country* S Asia

Pakistan 134

Official name Islamic Republic of
Pakistan
Formation 1947
Capital Islamabad
Population 145 million / 467 people
per sq mile (180 people per sq km)
Total area 310,401 sq miles
(803,940 sq km)
Languages Urdu, Punjabi, Sindhi
Religions Sunni Muslim 77%, Shi'a
Muslim 20%, Hindu 2%,
Christian 1%
Ethnic mix Punjabi 50%, Sindhi
15%, Pashto 15%, Mohajir 8%,
other 12%
Government Military-based regime
Currency Pakistani rupee = 100
paisa
Literacy rate 46.1%
Calorie consumption 2,452
kilocalories

Paknam *see* Samut Prakan
Pakokku 136 A3 Magwe,
C Myanmar
Pak Phanang 137 C7 *var.* Ban Pak
Phanang. Nakhon Si Thammarat,
SW Thailand
Pakruojis 106 C4 Pakruojis,
N Lithuania
Paks 99 C7 Tolna, S Hungary
Paksé *see* Pakxé
Pakxé 137 D5 *var.* Paksé.
Champasak, S Laos
Palafrugell 93 G2 Cataluña, NE Spain
Palagruža 101 B5 *It.* Pelagosa. *Island*
SW Croatia
Palaiá Epídavros 105 C6
Peloponnisos, S Greece
Palaiseau 90 D2 Essonne, N France
Palamós 93 G2 Cataluña, NE Spain
Palamuse 106 E2 *Ger.* Sankt-
Bartholomäi. Jõgevamaa,
E Estonia
Pālanpur 134 C4 Gujarāt, W India
Palapye 78 D3 Central,
SE Botswana
Palau 144 A2 *var.* Belau. *Country*
W Pacific Ocean

Palau 144

Official name Republic of Palau
Formation 1994
Capital Koror
Population 19,100 / 108 people per
sq mile (42 people per sq km)
Total area 177 sq miles (458 sq km)
Languages Palauan, English,
Japanese, Angaur, Tobi,
Sonsorolese
Religions Christian 66%,
Modekngei 34%
Ethnic mix Micronesian 87%,
Filipino 8%, Chinese 5%
Government Non-party democracy
Currency US dollar = 100 cents
Literacy rate 92%
Calorie consumption not available

Palawan 139 E2 *island*
W Philippines
Palawan Passage 138 D2 *passage*
W Philippines
Paldiski 106 D2 *prev.* Baltiski, *Eng.*
Baltic Port, *Ger.* Baltischport.
Harjumaa, NW Estonia
Palembang 138 B4 Sumatera,
W Indonesia
Palencia 92 D2 *anc.* Palantia,
Pallantia. Castilla-León,
NW Spain
Palermo 97 C7 Fr. Palerme; *anc.*
Panhormus, Panormus. Sicilia,
Italy, C Mediterranean Sea
Pāli 134 C3 Rājasthān, N India
Palikir 144 C2 *country capital*
(Micronesia) Pohnpei,
E Micronesia
Palimé *see* Kpalimé
Palioúri, Akrotírio 104 C4 *var.* Akra
Kanestron. *Headland* N Greece
Palk Strait 132 C3 *strait* India/Sri
Lanka
Palliser, Cape 151 D5 *headland*
North Island, NZ
Palma 93 G3 *var.* Palma de
Mallorca. Mallorca, Spain,
W Mediterranean Sea
Palma del Río 92 D4 Andalucía,
S Spain
Palma de Mallorca *see* Palma
Palmar Sur 53 E5 Puntarenas,
SE Costa Rica
Palma Soriano 54 C3 Santiago de
Cuba, E Cuba
Palm Beach 148 E1 New South
Wales, SE Australia
Palmer 154 A2 *US research station*
Antarctica
Palmer Land 154 A3 *physical region*
Antarctica
Palmerston 145 F4 *island* S Cook
Islands
Palmerston North 150 D4
Manawatu-Wanganui, North
Island, NZ
Palmi 97 D7 Calabria, SW Italy
Palmira 58 B3 Valle del Cauca,
W Colombia
Palm Springs 47 D7 California,
W USA
Palmyra *see* Tudmur
Palmyra Atoll 145 G2 *US privately
owned unincorporated territory*
C Pacific Ocean
Palo Alto 47 B6 California, W USA
Palu 139 E4 *prev.* Paloe. Sulawesi,
C Indonesia
Pamiers 91 B6 Ariège, S France
Pamir *var.* Daryā-ye Pāmīr, *Taj.*
Dar"yoi Pomir. *River*
Afghanistan/Tajikistan *see also*
Pāmīr, Daryā-ye
Pamirs 123 F3 Pash. Daryā-ye
Pāmīr, *Rus.* Pamir. *Mountain range*
C Asia
Pâmiut *see* Paamiut
Pamlico Sound 43 G1 *sound* North
Carolina, SE USA
Pampa 49 E1 Texas, SW USA
Pampas 64 C4 *plain* C Argentina
Pamplona 93 E1 Basq. Iruña; *prev.*
Pampeluna, *anc.* Pompaelo.
Navarra, N Spain
Pamplona 58 C2 Norte de
Santander, N Colombia
Panaji *see* Pānji
Panama 53 G5 *Country* Central
America

Panama 53

Official name Republic of Panama
Formation 1903
Capital Panama City
Population 2.9 million / 96 people
per sq mile (37 people per sq km)
Total area 30,193 sq miles
(78,200 sq km)
Languages Spanish, English Creole,
Amerindian languages, Chibchan
Religions Roman Catholic 86%,
Protestant 6%, other 8%
Ethnic mix Mestizo 60%, White
14%, Black 12%, Amerindian 8%,
Asian 4%, other 2%

Panama (continued)

Government Presidential democracy
Currency Balboa = 100 centesimos
Literacy rate 91.9%
Calorie consumption 2,488 kilocalories

Panamá 53 G4 *var.* Ciudad de Panamá, *Eng.* Panama City. *Country capital* (Panama) Panamá, C Panama
Panama Basin 35 C8 *undersea feature* E Pacific Ocean
Panama Canal 53 F4 *canal* E Panama
Panama City *see* Panamá
Panama City 42 D3 Florida, SE USA
Panamá, Golfo de 53 G5 *var.* Gulf of Panama. *Gulf* S Panama
Panama, Gulf of *see* Panamá, Golfo de
Panamá, Isthmus of *see* Panamá, Istmo de
Panamá, Istmo de 53 G4 *Eng.* Isthmus of Panama; *prev.* Isthmus of Darien. *Isthmus* E Panama
Panay Island 139 E2 *island* C Philippines
Pančevo 100 D3 *Ger.* Pantschowa, *Hung.* Pancsova. Serbia, N Serbia and Montenegro (Yugo.)
Paneas *see* Bāniyās
Panevėžys 106 C4 Panevėžys, C Lithuania
Pangim *see* Pānji
Pangkalpinang 138 C4 Pulau Bangka, W Indonesia
Panjim *see* Pānji
Pānji 132 B1 *var.* Pangim, Panaji, Panjim, New Goa. Goa, W India
Pánormos 105 C7 Kriti, Greece, E Mediterranean Sea
Pantanal 63 E3 *var.* Pantanalmato-Grossense. *Swamp* SW Brazil
Pantanalmato-Grossense *see* Pantanal
Pantelleria, Isola di 97 B7 *island* SW Italy
Pánuco 51 E3 Veracruz-Llave, E Mexico
Pao-chi *see* Baoji
Paoki *see* Baoji
Paola 102 B5 E Malta
Pao-shan *see* Baoshan
Pao-t'ou *see* Baotou
Paotow *see* Baotou
Papagayo, Golfo de 52 C4 *gulf* NW Costa Rica
Papakura 150 D3 Auckland, North Island, NZ
Papantla 51 F4 *var.* Papantla de Olarte. Veracruz-Llave, E Mexico
Papantla de Olarte *see* Papantla
Papeete 145 H4 *dependent territory capital* (French Polynesia) Tahiti, W French Polynesia
Paphos *see* Páfos
Papilė 106 B3 Akmenė, NW Lithuania
Papillion 45 F4 Nebraska, C USA
Papua 139 H4 *var.* Irian Barat, Irian Jaya, West Irian, West New Guinea, West Papua; *prev.* Dutch New Guinea, Netherlands New Guinea. Admin. region *province* E Indonesia
Papua, Gulf of 144 B3 *gulf* S PNG
Papua New Guinea 144 B3 *prev.* Territory of Papua and New Guinea, *abbrev.* PNG. *Country* NW Melanesia

Papua New Guinea 144

Official name Independent State of Papua New Guinea
Formation 1975
Capital Port Moresby
Population 5.2 million / 29 people per sq mile (11 people per sq km)
Total area 178,703 sq miles (462,840 sq km)

Papua New Guinea (continued)

Languages English, Pidgin English, Papuan, Motu, c.750 native languages
Religions Protestant 60%, Roman Catholic 37%, other 3%
Ethnic mix Melanesian and mixed 100%
Government Multiparty republic
Currency Kina = 100 toea
Literacy rate 63.9%
Calorie consumption 2,175 kilocalories

Papuk 100 C3 *mountain range* NE Croatia
Pará 63 E2 *off.* Estado do Pará. *State* NE Brazil
Pará *see* Belém
Paracel Islands 125 E3 *disputed territory* SE Asia
Paraćin 100 D4 Serbia, C Serbia and Montenegro (Yugo.)
Paragua, Río 59 E3 *river* SE Venezuela
Paraguay 64 D2 *var.* Río Paraguay. *River* C South America
Paraguay 64 C2 *country* C South America

Paraguay 64

Official name Republic of Paraguay
Formation 1811
Capital Asunción
Population 5.6 million /36 people per sq mile (14 people per sq km)
Total area 157,046 sq miles (406,750 sq km)
Languages Spanish, Guaraní
Religions Roman Catholic 96%, Protestant (including Mennonite) 4%
Ethnic mix Mestizo 90%, Amerindian 2%, other 8%
Government Presidential democracy
Currency Guaraní = 100 centimos
Literacy rate 93.3%
Calorie consumption 2,533 kilocalories

Paraguay, Río *see* Paraguay
Paraíba 63 G2 *off.* Estado da Paraíba; *prev.* Parahiba, Parahyba. *State* E Brazil
Parakou 75 F4 C Benin
Paramaribo 59 G3 *country capital* (Suriname) Paramaribo, N Suriname
Paramushir, Ostrov 115 H3 *island* SE Russian Federation
Paraná 63 E5 *off.* Estado do Paraná. *State* S Brazil
Paraná 57 C5 *var.* Alto Paraná. *River* C South America
Paraná 63 E4 Entre Ríos, E Argentina
Paranéstio 104 C3 Anatolikí Makedonía kai Thráki, NE Greece
Paraparaumu 151 D5 Wellington, North Island, NZ
Parchim 94 C3 Mecklenburg-Vorpommern, N Germany
Parczew 98 E4 Lubelskie, E Poland
Pardubice 95 B5 *Ger.* Pardubitz. Pardubický Kraj, C Czech Republic
Parechcha 107 B5 *Rus.* Porech'ye. Hrodzyenskaya Voblasts', NE Belarus
Parecis, Chapada dos 62 D3 *var.* Serra dos Parecis. *Mountain range* W Brazil
Parepare 139 E4 Sulawesi, C Indonesia
Párga 105 A5 Ípeiros, W Greece
Paria, Golfo de *see* Paria, Gulf of
Paria, Gulf of 59 E1 *var.* Golfo de Paria. *Gulf* Trinidad and Tobago/Venezuela
Parika 59 F2 NE Guyana

Paris 90 D1 *anc.* Lutetia, Lutetia Parisiorum, Parisii. *Country capital* (France) Paris, N France
Paris 49 G2 Texas, SW USA
Parkersburg 40 D4 West Virginia, NE USA
Parkes 149 D6 New South Wales, SE Australia
Parma 96 B2 Emilia-Romagna, N Italy
Parnahyba *see* Parnaíba
Parnaíba 63 F2 *var.* Parnahyba. Piauí, E Brazil
Pärnu 106 D2 *Ger.* Pernau, *Latv.* Pērnava; *prev. Rus.* Pernov. Pärnumaa, SW Estonia
Pärnu 106 D2 *var.* Parnu Jõgi, *Ger.* Pernau. *River* SW Estonia
Pärnu-Jaagupi 106 D2 *Ger.* Sankt-Jakobi. Pärnumaa, SW Estonia
Parnu Jõgi *see* Pärnu
Pärnu Laht 106 D2 *Ger.* Pernauer Bucht. *Bay* SW Estonia
Páros 105 C6 *island* Kykládes, Greece, Aegean Sea
Páros 105 D6 Páros, Kykládes, Greece, Aegean Sea
Parral *see* Hidalgo del Parral
Parral 64 B4 Maule, C Chile
Parramatta 148 D1 New South Wales, SE Australia
Parras 50 D3 *var.* Parras de la Fuente. Coahuila de Zaragoza, NE Mexico
Parras de la Fuente *see* Parras
Parsons 45 F5 Kansas, C USA
Pasadena 47 C7 California, W USA
Pasadena 49 H4 Texas, SW USA
Pașcani 108 C3 *Hung.* Páskán. Iași, NE Romania
Pasco 46 C2 Washington, NW USA
Pas de Calais *see* Dover, Strait of
Pasewalk 94 D3 Mecklenburg-Vorpommern, NE Germany
Pasinler 117 F3 Erzurum, NE Turkey
Pasłęk 98 D2 *Ger.* Preußisch Holland. Warmińsko-Mazurskie, NE Poland
Pasni 134 A3 Baluchistān, SW Pakistan
Paso de Indios 65 B6 Chubut, S Argentina
Passau 95 D6 Bayern, SE Germany
Passo del Brennero *see* Brenner Pass
Passo Fundo 63 E5 Rio Grande do Sul, S Brazil
Pastavy 107 C5 *Pol.* Postawy, *Rus.* Postavy. Vitsyebskaya Voblasts', NW Belarus
Pastaza, Río 60 B2 *river* Ecuador/Peru
Pasto 58 A4 Nariño, SW Colombia
Pasvalys 106 C4 Pasvalys, N Lithuania
Patagonia 57 B7 *physical region* Argentina/Chile
Patalung *see* Phatthalung
Patani *see* Pattani
Patavium *see* Padova
Patea 150 D4 Taranaki, North Island, NZ
Paterson 41 F3 New Jersey, NE USA
Pátmos 105 D6 *island* Dodekánisos, Greece, Aegean Sea
Patna 135 F3 *var.* Azimabad. Bihār, N India
Patnos 117 F3 Ağrı, E Turkey
Patos, Lagoa dos 63 E5 *lagoon* S Brazil
Pátra 105 B5 *Eng.* Patras; *prev.* Pátrai. Dytikí Ellás, S Greece
Pattani 137 C7 *var.* Patani. Pattani, SW Thailand
Pattaya 137 C5 Chon Buri, S Thailand
Patuca, Río 52 D2 *river* E Honduras
Pau 91 B6 Pyrénées-Atlantiques, SW France
Paulatuk 37 E3 Northwest Territories, NW Canada
Paungde 136 B4 Pegu, C Myanmar
Pavia 96 B2 *anc.* Ticinum. Lombardia, N Italy
Pāvilosta 106 B3 Liepāja, W Latvia

Pavlikeni 104 D2 Veliko Tŭrnovo, N Bulgaria
Pavlodar 114 C4 Pavlodar, NE Kazakhstan
Pavlohrad 109 G3 *Rus.* Pavlograd. Dnipropetrovs'ka Oblast', E Ukraine
Pawn 136 B3 *river* C Myanmar
Paxoí 105 A5 *island* Iónioi Nísoi, Greece, C Mediterranean Sea
Payo Obispo *see* Chetumal
Paysandú 64 D4 Paysandú, W Uruguay
Pazar 117 E2 Rize, NE Turkey
Pazardzhik 104 C3 *prev.* Tatar Pazardzhik. Pazardzhik, C Bulgaria
Pearl River 42 B3 *river* Louisiana/Mississippi, S USA
Pearsall 49 F4 Texas, SW USA
Peć 101 D5 *Alb.* Pejë, *Turk.* Ipek. Serbia, S Serbia and Montenegro (Yugo.)
Pechora 110 D3 *river* NW Russian Federation
Pechora 110 D3 Respublika Komi, NW Russian Federation
Pechorskoye More 110 D2 *Eng.* Pechora Sea. *Sea* NW Russian Federation
Pecos 49 E3 Texas, SW USA
Pecos River 49 E3 *river* New Mexico/Texas, SW USA
Pécs 99 C7 *Ger.* Fünfkirchen; *Lat.* Sopianae. Baranya, SW Hungary
Pedra Lume 74 A3 Sal, NE Cape Verde
Pedro Cays 54 C3 *island group* S Jamaica
Pedro Juan Caballero 64 D2 Amambay, E Paraguay
Peer 87 D5 Limburg, NE Belgium
Pegasus Bay 151 C6 *bay* South Island, NZ
Pegu 136 B4 *var.* Bago. Pegu, SW Myanmar
Pehuajó 64 C4 Buenos Aires, E Argentina
Pei-ching *see* Beijing
Peine 94 B3 Niedersachsen, C Germany
Pei-p'ing *see* Beijing
Peipus, Lake 93 E3 *Est.* Peipsi Järv, *Ger.* Peipus-See, *Rus.* Chudskoye Ozero. *Lake* Estonia/Russian Federation
Peiraías 105 C6 *prev.* Piraiévs, *Eng.* Piraeus. Attikí, C Greece
Pèk 136 D4 *var.* Xieng Khouang; *prev.* Xiangkhoang. Xiangkhoang, N Laos
Pekalongan 138 C4 Jawa, C Indonesia
Pekanbaru 138 B3 *var.* Pakanbaru. Sumatera, W Indonesia
Pekin 40 B4 Illinois, N USA
Peking *see* Beijing
Pelagie, Isole 97 B8 *island group* SW Italy
Pelly Bay 37 G3 Nunavut, N Canada
Peloponnese *see* Pelopónnisos
Peloponnesus *see* Pelopónnisos
Pelopónnisos 105 B6 *var.* Morea, *Eng.* Peloponnese; *anc.* Peloponnesus. *Peninsula* S Greece
Pematangsiantar 138 B3 Sumatera, W Indonesia
Pemba 79 F2 *prev.* Port Amelia, Porto Amélia. Cabo Delgado, NE Mozambique
Pemba 73 D7 *island* E Tanzania
Pembroke 38 D4 Ontario, SE Canada
Penang *see* George Town
Penang *see* Pinang, Pulau
Penas, Golfo de 65 A7 *gulf* S Chile
Penderma *see* Bandırma
Pendleton 46 C3 Oregon, NW USA
Pend Oreille, Lake 46 D2 *lake* Idaho, NW USA
Peneius *see* Pineiós
Peng-pu *see* Bengbu
Peniche 92 B3 Leiria, W Portugal
Péninsule de la Gaspésie *see* Gaspé, Péninsule de

227

Pennine Alps 95 A8 *Fr.* Alpes Pennines, *It.* Alpi Pennine; *Lat.* Alpes Penninae. *Mountain range* Italy/Switzerland
Pennine Chain *see* Pennines
Pennines 89 D5 *var.* Pennine Chain. *Mountain range* N England, UK
Pennsylvania 40 D3 *off.* Commonwealth of Pennsylvania; also known as The Keystone State. *State* NE USA
Penobscot River 41 G2 *river* Maine, NE USA
Penong 149 A6 South Australia
Penonomé 53 F5 Coclé, C Panama
Penrhyn 145 G3 *atoll* N Cook Islands
Penrhyn Basin 143 F3 *undersea feature* C Pacific Ocean
Penrith 148 D1 New South Wales, SE Australia
Penrith 89 D5 NW England, UK
Pensacola 42 C3 Florida, SE USA
Pentecost 144 D4 *Fr.* Pentecôte. *Island* C Vanuatu
Penza 111 C6 Penzenskaya Oblast', W Russian Federation
Penzance 89 C7 SW England, UK
Peoria 40 B4 Illinois, N USA
Perchtoldsdorf 95 E6 Niederösterreich, NE Austria
Percival Lakes 146 C4 *lakes* Western Australia
Perdido, Monte 93 F1 *mountain* NE Spain
Perece Vela Basin *see* West Mariana Basin
Pereira 58 B3 Risaralda, W Colombia
Pergamino 64 C4 Buenos Aires, E Argentina
Périgueux 91 C5 *anc.* Vesuna. Dordogne, SW France
Perito Moreno 65 B6 Santa Cruz, S Argentina
Perlas, Archipiélago de las 53 G5 *Eng.* Pearl Islands. *Island group* SE Panama
Perlas, Laguna de 53 E3 *Eng.* Pearl Lagoon. *Lagoon* E Nicaragua
Perleberg 94 C3 Brandenburg, N Germany
Perm' 114 C3 *prev.* Molotov. Permskaya Oblast', NW Russian Federation
Pernambuco 63 G2 *off.* Estado de Pernambuco. *State* E Brazil
Pernambuco Abyssal Plain *see* Pernambuco Plain
Pernambuco Plain 67 C5 *var.* Pernambuco Abyssal Plain. *Undersea feature* E Atlantic Ocean
Pernau *see* Pärnu
Pernik 104 B2 *prev.* Dimitrovo. Pernik, W Bulgaria
Perote 51 F4 Veracruz-Llave, E Mexico
Perovsk *see* Kyzylorda
Perpignan 91 C6 Pyrénées-Orientales, S France
Perryton 49 F1 Texas, SW USA
Perryville 45 H5 Missouri, C USA
Persian Gulf *see* Gulf, The
Perth 147 A6 *state capital* Western Australia
Perth 88 C4 C Scotland, UK
Perth Basin 141 E6 *undersea feature* SE Indian Ocean
Peru 60 C3 *Country* W South America

Peru 60

Official name Republic of Peru
Formation 1824
Capital Lima
Population 26.1 million / 53 people per sq mile (20 people per sq km)
Total area 496,223 sq miles (1,285,220 sq km)
Languages Spanish, Quechua, Aymará
Religions Roman Catholic 95%, other 5%
Ethnic mix Amerindian 54%, Mestizo 32%, White 12%, other 2%
Government Presidential democracy

Peru (continued)

Currency New sol = 100 centimos
Literacy rate 89.9%
Calorie consumption 2,624 kilocalories

Peru *see* Beru
Peru Basin 67 A5 *undersea feature* E Pacific Ocean
Peru-Chile Trench 56 A4 *undersea feature* E Pacific Ocean
Perugia 96 C4 *Fr.* Pérouse; *anc.* Perusia. Umbria, C Italy
Péruwelz 87 B6 Hainaut, SW Belgium
Pervomays'k 109 E3 *prev.* Ol'viopol'. Mykolayivs'ka Oblast', S Ukraine
Pervyy Kuril'skiy Proliv 115 H3 *strait* E Russian Federation
Pesaro 96 C3 *anc.* Pisaurum. Marche, C Italy
Pescara 96 D4 *anc.* Aternum, Ostia Aterni. Abruzzo, C Italy
Peshāwar 134 C1 North-West Frontier Province, N Pakistan
Peshkopi 101 C6 *var.* Peshkopia, Peshkopija. Dibër, NE Albania
Peshkopia *see* Peshkopi
Peshkopija *see* Peshkopi
Peski Karakumy *see* Garagumy
Pessac 91 B5 Gironde, SW France
Petach-Tikva *see* Petaẖ Tiqwa
Petaẖ Tiqwa *see* Petaẖ Tiqwa
Petaẖ Tiqwa 119 A6 *var.* Petach-Tikva, Petaẖ Tiqva, Petakh Tikva. Tel Aviv, C Israel
Petakh Tikva *see* Petaẖ Tiqwa
Pétange 87 D8 Luxembourg, SW Luxembourg
Petchaburi *see* Phetchaburi
Peterborough 89 E6 *prev.* Medeshamstede. E England, UK
Peterborough 38 D5 Ontario, SE Canada
Peterborough 149 B6 South Australia
Peterhead 88 D3 NE Scotland, UK
Peter I Island 154 A3 *Norwegian dependency* Antarctica
Petermann Bjerg 83 E3 *mountain* C Greenland
Petersburg 41 E5 Virginia, NE USA
Peters Mine 59 F3 *var.* Peter's Mine. N Guyana
Peto 51 H4 Yucatán, SE Mexico
Petoskey 40 C2 Michigan, N USA
Petra *see* Wādī Mūsā
Petrich 104 C3 Blagoevgrad, SW Bulgaria
Petrinja 100 B3 Sisak-Moslavina, C Croatia
Petrodvorets 110 A4 *Fin.* Pietarhovi. Leningradskaya Oblast', NW Russian Federation
Petrograd *see* Sankt-Peterburg
Petropavlovsk 114 C4 *Kaz.* Petropavl. Severnyy Kazakhstan, N Kazakhstan
Petropavlovsk-Kamchatskiy 115 H3 Kamchatskaya Oblast', E Russian Federation
Petroşani 108 B4 *var.* Petroşeni, *Ger.* Petroschen, *Hung.* Petrozsény. Hunedoara, W Romania
Petroschen *see* Petroşani
Petroşeni *see* Petroşani
Petrozavodsk 114 B2 *Fin.* Petroskoi. Respublika Kareliya, NW Russian Federation
Pevek 115 G1 Chukotskiy Avtonomnyy Okrug, NE Russian Federation
Pezinok 99 C6 *Ger.* Bösing, *Hung.* Bazin. Bratislavský Kraj, W Slovakia
Pforzheim 95 B6 Baden-Württemberg, SW Germany
Pfungstadt 95 B5 Hessen, W Germany
Phangan, Ko 137 C6 *island* SW Thailand

Phang-Nga 137 B7 *var.* Pang-Nga, Phangnga. Phangnga, SW Thailand
Phangnga *see* Phang-Nga
Phanom Dang Raek *see* Dângrêk, Chuŏr Phnum
Phanom Dong Rak *see* Dângrêk, Chuŏr Phnum
Phan Rang *see* Phan Rang-Thap Cham
Phan Rang-Thap Cham 137 E6 *var.* Phanrang, Phan Rang, Phan Rang Thap Cham. Ninh Thuận, S Vietnam
Phan Thiết 137 E6 Bình Thuận, S Vietnam
Pharnacia *see* Giresun
Phatthalung 137 C7 *var.* Padalung, Patalung. Phatthalung, SW Thailand
Phayao 136 C4 *var.* Muang Phayao. Phayao, NW Thailand
Phenix City 42 D2 Alabama, S USA
Phet Buri *see* Phetchaburi
Phetchaburi 137 C5 *var.* Bejraburi, Petchaburi, Phet Buri. Phetchaburi, SW Thailand
Philadelphia *see* 'Ammān
Philadelphia 41 F4 Pennsylvania, NE USA
Philippine Basin 125 F3 *undersea feature* W Pacific Ocean
Philippines 139 E1 *Country* SE Asia

Philippines 139

Official name Republic of the Philippines
Formation 1946
Capital Manila
Population 77.1 million / 666 people per sq mile (257 people per sq km)
Total area 115,830 sq miles (300,000 sq km)
Languages Filipino, English, Cebuano
Religions Roman Catholic 83%, Protestant 9%, Muslim 5%, other 3%
Ethnic mix Filipino 50%, Indonesian and Polynesian 30%, other 20%
Government Presidential democracy
Currency Peso = 100 centavos
Literacy rate 95.3%
Calorie consumption 2,379 kilocalories

Philippines 139 E1 *island group* W Pacific Ocean
Philippine Sea 125 F3 *sea* W Pacific Ocean
Philippine Trench 142 A1 *undersea feature* W Philippine Sea
Phitsanulok 136 C4 *var.* Bisnulok, Muang Phitsanulok, Pitsanulok. Phitsanulok, C Thailand
Phlórina *see* Flórina
Phnom Penh *see* Phnum Penh
Phnum Penh 137 D6 *var.* Phnom Penh. *Country capital* (Cambodia) Phnum Penh, S Cambodia
Phoenix 48 B2 *state capital* Arizona, SW USA
Phoenix Islands 145 E3 *island group* C Kiribati
Phôngsali 136 C3 *var.* Phong Saly. Phôngsali, N Laos
Phong Saly *see* Phôngsali
Phrae 136 C4 *var.* Muang Phrae, Prae. Phrae, NW Thailand
Phra Nakhon Si Ayutthaya *see* Ayutthaya
Phra Thong, Ko 137 B6 *island* SW Thailand
Phuket 137 B7 *var.* Bhuket, Puket, *Mal.* Ujung Salang; *prev.* Junkseylon, Salang. Phuket, SW Thailand
Phuket, Ko 137 B7 *island* SW Thailand
Phumĭ Kâmpóng Trâbêk 137 D5 Kâmpóng Chhnăng, N Cambodia
Phumĭ Sâmraông 137 D5 Poŭthĭsăt, NW Cambodia

Phu Vinh *see* Tra Vinh
Piacenza 96 B2 *Fr.* Paisance; *anc.* Placentia. Emilia-Romagna, N Italy
Piatra-Neamţ 108 C4 *Hung.* Karácsonkő. Neamţ, NE Romania
Piauí 63 F2 *off.* Estado do Piauí; *prev.* Piauhy. *State* E Brazil
Picardie 90 C3 *Eng.* Picardy. *Cultural region* N France
Pichilemu 64 B4 Libertador, C Chile
Pico 92 A5 *var.* Ilha do Pico. *Island* Azores, Portugal, NE Atlantic Ocean
Picos 63 F2 Piauí, E Brazil
Picton 151 C5 Marlborough, South Island, NZ
Piedras Negras 51 E2 *var.* Ciudad Porfirio Díaz. Coahuila de Zaragoza, NE Mexico
Pielinen 84 E4 *var.* Pielisjärvi. *Lake* E Finland
Pielisjärvi *see* Pielinen
Piemonte 96 A2 *Eng.* Piedmont. *Cultural region* NW Italy
Pierre 45 E3 *state capital* South Dakota, N USA
Piešt'any 99 C6 *Ger.* Pistyan, *Hung.* Pöstyén. Trnavský Kraj, W Slovakia
Pietermaritzburg 78 C5 *var.* Maritzburg. KwaZulu/Natal, E South Africa
Pietersburg *see* Polokwane
Pigs, Bay of *see* Cochinos, Bahía de
Pijijiapán 51 G5 Chiapas, SE Mexico
Pikes Peak 44 C5 *mountain* Colorado, C USA
Pikeville 40 D5 Kentucky, S USA
Pikinni *see* Bikini Atoll
Piła 98 B3 *Ger.* Schneidemühl. Wielkopolskie, C Poland
Pilar 64 D3 *var.* Villa del Pilar. Neembucú, S Paraguay
Pilcomayo 57 C5 *river* C South America
Pilos *see* Pýlos
Pinang *see* George Town
Pinang, Pulau 138 B3 *var.* Penang, Pinang; *prev.* Prince of Wales Island. *Island* Peninsular Malaysia
Pinar del Río 54 A2 Pinar del Río, W Cuba
Píndhos *see* Píndos
Píndhos Óros *see* Píndos
Píndos 104 A4 *var.* Píndhos Óros, *Eng.* Pindus Mountains; *prev.* Píndhos. *Mountain range* C Greece
Pindus Mountains *see* Píndos
Pine Bluff 42 B2 Arkansas, C USA
Pine Creek 146 D2 Northern Territory, N Australia
Pinega 110 C3 *river* NW Russian Federation
Pineiós 104 B4 *var.* Piniós; *anc.* Peneius. *River* C Greece
Pineland 49 H3 Texas, SW USA
Pines, The Isle of the *see* Juventud, Isla de la
Pingdingshan 128 C4 Henan, C China
Pingkiang *see* Harbin
Ping, Mae Nam 136 B4 *river* W Thailand
Piniós *see* Pineiós
Pinkiang *see* Harbin
Pínnes, Akrotírio 104 C4 *headland* N Greece
Pinos, Isla de *see* Juventud, Isla de la
Pinotepa Nacional 51 F5 *var.* Santiago Pinotepa Nacional. Oaxaca, SE Mexico
Pinsk 107 B7 *Pol.* Pińsk. SW Belarus
Pinta, Isla 60 A5 *var.* Abingdon. *Island* Galapagos Islands, Ecuador, E Pacific Ocean
Piombino 96 B3 Toscana, C Italy
Pioneer Mountains 46 D3 *mountain range* Montana, N USA
Pionerskiy 106 A4 *Ger.* Neukuhren. Kaliningradskaya Oblast', W Russian Federation
Piotrków Trybunalski 98 D4 *Ger.* Petrikau, *Rus.* Petrovkov. Łódzkie, C Poland

Piraeus *see* Peiraiás
Pírgos *see* Pýrgos
Piripiri 63 F2 Piauí, E Brazil
Pirna 94 D4 Sachsen, E Germany
Pirot 101 E5 Serbia, SE Serbia and
Montenegro (Yugo.)
Pisa 96 B3 *var.* Pisae. Toscana,
C Italy
Pisae *see* Pisa
Pisco 60 D4 Ica, SW Peru
Písek 99 A5 Budějovicky Kraj,
S Czech Republic
Pishan 126 A3 *var.* Guma. Xinjiang
Uygur Zizhiqu, NW China
Pishpek *see* Bishkek
Pistoia 96 B3 *anc.* Pistoria, Pistoriæ.
Toscana, C Italy
Pisz 98 D3 *Ger.* Johannisburg.
Warminsko-Mazurskie,
NE Poland
Pita 74 C4 Moyenne-Guinée,
NW Guinea
Pitalito 58 B4 Huila, S Colombia
Pitcairn Island 143 G4 *island*
S Pitcairn Islands
Pitcairn Islands 143 G4 UK
dependent territory C Pacific Ocean
Piteå 84 D4 Norrbotten, N Sweden
Pitești 108 B5 Argeș, S Romania
Pitsanulok *see* Phitsanulok
Pittsburg 45 F5 Kansas, C USA
Pittsburgh 41 E4 Pennsylvania,
NE USA
Pittsfield 41 F3 Massachusetts,
NE USA
Piura 60 B2 Piura, NW Peru
Pivdennyy Buh 109 E3 *Rus.*
Yuzhnyy Bug. *River* S Ukraine
Placetas 54 B2 Villa Clara,
C Cuba
Plainview 49 E2 Texas, SW USA
Planeta Rica 58 B2 Córdoba,
NW Colombia
Planken 94 E1 C Liechtenstein
Plano 49 G2 Texas, SW USA
Plasencia 92 C3 Extremadura,
W Spain
Plata, Río de la 64 D4 *var.* River
Plate. *Estuary* Argentina/Uruguay
Plateau du Bemaraha *see* Bemaraha
Platinum 36 C3 Alaska, USA
Plattensee *see* Balaton
Platte River 45 E4 *river* Nebraska,
C USA
Plattsburgh 41 F2 New York,
NE USA
Plauen 95 C5 *var.* Plauen im
Vogtland. Sachsen, E Germany
Plauen im Vogtland *see* Plauen
Plavinas 106 D4 *Ger.*
Stockmannshof. Aizkraukle,
S Latvia
Plây Cu 137 E5 *var.* Pleiku. Gia Lai,
C Vietnam
Pleiku *see* Plây Cu
Plenty, Bay of 150 E3 *bay* North
Island, NZ
Plérin 90 A3 Côtes d'Armor,
NW France
Plesetsk 110 C3 Arkhangel'skaya
Oblast', NW Russian Federation
Pleszew 98 C4 Wielkopolskie,
C Poland
Pleven 104 C2 *prev.* Plevna. Pleven,
N Bulgaria
Pljevlja 100 C4 *var.* Plevlja, Plevlje.
Montenegro, N Serbia and
Montenegro (Yugo.)
Ploče 100 B4 *It.* Plocce; *prev.*
Kardeljevo. Dubrovnik-Neretva,
SE Croatia
Płock 98 D3 *Ger.* Plozk.
Mazowieckie, C Poland
Plöcken Pass 95 C7 *Ger.*
Plöckenpass, *It.* Passo di Monte
Croce Carnico. *Pass* SW Austria
Ploiești 108 C5 *prev.* Ploești.
Prahova, SE Romania
Plomári 105 D5 *prev.* Plomárion.
Lésvos, E Greece
Płońsk 98 D3 Mazowieckie,
C Poland
Plovdiv 104 C3 *prev.* Eumolpias,
anc. Evmolpia, Philippopolis, *Lat.*
Trimontium. Plovdiv, C Bulgaria
Plungė 106 B3 Plungė,
W Lithuania

Plyeshchanitsy 107 D5 *Rus.*
Pleshchenitsy. Minskaya Voblasts',
N Belarus
Plymouth 55 G3 *dependent territory
capital* (Montserrat)
SW Montserrat
Plymouth 89 C7 SW England, UK
Plzeň 99 A5 *Ger.* Pilsen, *Pol.* Pilzno.
Plzeňský Kraj, W Czech Republic
Po 80 D4 *river* N Italy
Pobeda Peak *see* Pobedy, Pik
Pobedy, Pik 126 B3 *var.* Pobeda
Peak, *Chin.* Tomur Feng. *Mountain*
China/Kyrgyzstan *see also* Tomur
Feng
Pocahontas 42 B1 Arkansas, C USA
Pocatello 46 E4 Idaho, NW USA
Pochinok 111 A5 Smolenskaya
Oblast', W Russian Federation
Pocking 95 D6 Bayern, SE Germany
Poděbrady 99 B5 *Ger.* Podiebrad.
Středočesky Kraj, C Czech
Republic
Podgorica 101 C5 *prev.* Titograd.
Montenegro, SW Serbia and
Montenegro (Yugo.)
Podil's'ka Vysochina 108 D3 *Rus.*
Podol'skaya Vozvyshennost'.
Mountain range SW Ukraine
Podkarpackie admin. region
province SE Poland
Podol'sk 111 B5 Moskovskaya
Oblast', W Russian Federation
Podravska Slatina *see* Slatina
Podujevo 101 D5 Serbia, S Serbia
and Montenegro (Yugo.)
Po, Foci del 96 C2 *var.* Bocche del
Po. *River* NE Italy
Pogradec 101 D6 *var.* Pogradeci.
Korçë, SE Albania
Pogradeci *see* Pogradec
Pohnpei 144 C2 *prev.* Ponape
Ascension Island. *Island*
E Micronesia
Poinsett, Cape 154 D4 *headland*
Antarctica
Pointe-à-Pitre 55 G3 Grande Terre,
C Guadeloupe
Pointe-Noire 77 B6 Le Kouilou,
S Congo
Point Lay 36 C2 Alaska, USA
Poitiers 90 B4 *prev.* Poictiers, *anc.*
Limonum. Vienne, W France
Poitou 90 B4 *cultural region*
W France
Pokhara 135 E3 Western, C Nepal
Pokrovs'ke 109 G3 *Rus.*
Pokrovskoye. Dnipropetrovs'ka
Oblast', E Ukraine
Pola de Lena 92 D1 Asturias,
N Spain
Poland 98 *var.* Polish Republic,
Pol. Polska, Rzeczpospolita
Polska; *prev. Pol.* Polska
Rzeczpospolita Ludowa, Polish
People's Republic. *Country*
C Europe

Poland 98

Official name Republic of Poland
Formation 1918
Capital Warsaw
Population 38.6 million / 320 people
per sq mile (123 peopleper sq km)
Total area 120,728 sq miles
(312,685 sq km)
Languages Polish
Religions Roman Catholic 93%,
Eastern Orthodox 2%, other
and non-religious 5%
Ethnic mix Polish 98%, German 1%,
other 1%
Government Parliamentary
democracy
Currency Zloty = 100 groszy
Literacy rate 99%
Calorie consumption 3,376
kilocalories

Poland 81 E3 Kiritimati, E Kiribati
Polatlı 116 C3 Ankara, C Turkey
Polatsk 107 D5 *Rus.* Polotsk.
Vitsyebskaya Voblasts', N Belarus
Pol-e Khomrī 123 E4 *var.* Pul-i-
Khumri. Baghlān, NE Afghanistan

Poli *see* Pólis
Polikastro *see* Polýkastro
Políkastron *see* Polýkastro
Polikrayshte 104 D2 Veliko
Tŭrnovo, N Bulgaria
Pólis 102 C5 *var.* Poli. W Cyprus
Polkowice 98 B4 *Ger.* Heerwegen.
Dolnośląskie, SW Poland
Pollença 93 G3 *var.* Pollensa.
Mallorca, Spain, W Mediterranean
Sea
Pollensa *see* Pollença
Polohy 109 G3 *Rus.* Pologi.
Zaporiz'ka Oblast', SE Ukraine
Polokwane 56 D4 *Var.* Pietersburg,
NE South Africa
Polonne 108 D2 *Rus.* Polonnoye.
Khmel'nyts'ka Oblast', N
NW Ukraine
Polsko Kosovo 104 D2 Ruse,
N Bulgaria
Poltava 109 F2 Poltavs'ka Oblast',
NE Ukraine
Põlva 106 E3 *Ger.* Pölwe. Põlvamaa,
SE Estonia
Polyarnyy 110 C2 Murmanskaya
Oblast', NW Russian Federation
Polýkastro 104 B3 *var.* Polikastro;
prev. Polikastron. Kentrikí
Makedonía, N Greece
Polynesia 143 F4 *island group*
C Pacific Ocean
Pomeranian Bay 94 D2 *Ger.*
Pommersche Bucht, *Pol.* Zatoka
Pomorska. *Bay* Germany/Poland
Pomorskiy Proliv 110 D2 *strait*
NW Russian Federation
Pompano Beach 43 F5 Florida,
SE USA
Ponca City 49 G1 Oklahoma, C USA
Ponce 55 F3 C Puerto Rico
Pondicherry 132 C2 *var.*
Puducherri, *Fr.* Pondichéry.
Pondicherry, SE India
Pondichéry *see* Pondicherry
Ponferrada 92 C1 Castilla-León,
NW Spain
Poniatowa 98 E4 Lublin, E Poland
Pons Aelii *see* Newcastle upon
Tyne
Ponta Delgada 92 B5 São Miguel,
Azores, Portugal, NE Atlantic
Ocean
Ponta Grossa 63 E4 Paraná, S Brazil
Pontarlier 90 D4 Doubs, E France
Ponteareas 92 B2 Galicia,
NW Spain
Ponte da Barca 92 B2 Viana do
Castelo, N Portugal
Pontevedra 92 B1 *anc.* Pons Vetus.
Galicia, NW Spain
Pontiac 40 D3 Michigan, N USA
Pontianak 138 C4 Borneo,
C Indonesia
Pontivy 90 A3 Morbihan,
NW France
Pontoise 90 C3 *anc.* Briva Isarae,
Cergy-Pontoise, Pontisarae. Val-
d'Oise, N France
Ponziane, Isole 97 C5 *island* C Italy
Poole 89 D7 S England, UK
Poopó, Lago 61 F4 *var.* Lago Pampa
Aullagas. *Lake* W Bolivia
Popayán 58 B4 Cauca,
SW Colombia
Poperinge 87 A6 West-Vlaanderen,
W Belgium
Poplar Bluff 45 G5 Missouri,
C USA
Popocatépetl 51 E4 *volcano*
S Mexico
Poprad 99 D5 *Ger.* Deutschendorf,
Hung. Poprád. Prešovský Kraj,
E Slovakia
Poprad 99 D5 *Ger.* Popper, *Hung.*
Poprád. *River* Poland/Slovakia
Porbandar 134 B4 Gujarāt, W India
Porcupine Plain 80 B3 *undersea
feature* E Atlantic Ocean
Pordenone 96 C2 *anc.* Portenau.
Friuli-Venezia Giulia, NE Italy
Poreč 100 A2 *It.* Parenzo. Istra,
NW Croatia
Pori 85 D5 *Swe.* Björneborg. Länsi-
Suomi, W Finland
Porirua 151 D5 Wellington, North
Island, NZ

Porkhov 110 A4 Pskovskaya
Oblast', W Russian Federation
Porlamar 59 E1 Nueva Esparta,
NE Venezuela
Póros 105 A5 Kefallinía, Iónioi
Nísoi, Greece, C Mediterranean
Sea
Póros 105 C6 Póros, S Greece
Porsangen 84 D2 *fjord* N Norway
Porsgrunn 85 B6 Telemark,
S Norway
Portachuelo 61 G4 Santa Cruz,
C Bolivia
Portadown 89 B5 *Ir.* Port An
Dúnáin. S Northern Ireland, UK
Portalegre 92 C3 *anc.* Ammaia,
Amoea. Portalegre, E Portugal
Port Alexander 36 D4 Baranof
Island, Alaska, USA
Port Alfred 78 D5 Eastern Cape,
S South Africa
Port An Dúnáin *see* Portadown
Port Angeles 46 B1 Washington,
NW USA
Port Antonio 54 B5 NE Jamaica
Port Arthur 49 H4 Texas, SW USA
Port Augusta 149 B6 South
Australia
Port-au-Prince 54 D3 *country capital*
(Haiti) C Haiti
Port-au-Prince 35 D7 *international
airport* E Haiti
Port Blair 133 F2 Andaman and
Nicobar Islands, SE India
Port Charlotte 43 E4 Florida,
SE USA
Port d'Envalira 91 B8 E Andorra
Port Douglas 148 D3 Queensland,
NE Australia
Port Elizabeth 78 C5 Eastern Cape,
S South Africa
Porterville 47 C7 California, W USA
Port-Gentil 77 A6 Ogooué-
Maritime, W Gabon
Port Harcourt 75 G5 Rivers,
S Nigeria
Port Hardy 36 D5 Vancouver
Island, British Columbia,
SW Canada
Port Harrison *see* Inukjuak
Port Hedland 146 B4 Western
Australia
Port Huron 40 D3 Michigan, N USA
Portimão 92 B4 *var.* Vila Nova de
Portimão. Faro, S Portugal
Port Jackson 148 E1 *harbour* New
South Wales, SE Australia
Port Láirge *see* Waterford
Portland 41 G2 Maine, NE USA
Portland 46 B3 Oregon, NW USA
Portland 49 G4 Texas, SW USA
Portland 149 B7 Victoria,
SE Australia
Portland Bight 54 B5 *bay* S Jamaica
Portlaoighise *see* Portlaoise
Portlaoise 89 B6 *Ir.* Portlaoighise;
prev. Maryborough. C Ireland
Port Lavaca 49 G4 Texas, SW USA
Port Lincoln 149 A6 South Australia
Port Louis 79 H3 *country capital*
(Mauritius) NW Mauritius
Port Macquarie 149 E6 New South
Wales, SE Australia
Portmore 54 B5 C Jamaica
Port Moresby 144 B3 *country capital*
(PNG) Central/National Capital
District, SW PNG
Port Musgrave 149 B9 *bay*
Queensland, N Australia
Port Natal *see* Durban
Porto 92 B2 *Eng.* Oporto; *anc.* Portus
Cale. Porto, NW Portugal
Porto Alegre 63 E5 *var.* Porto
Alegre. *State capital* Rio Grande
do Sul, S Brazil
Porto Alegre 76 E2 São Tomé, S Sao
Tome and Principe
Porto Bello *see* Portobelo
Portobelo 53 G4 *var.* Porto Bello,
Puerto Bello. Colón, N Panama
Port O'Connor 49 G4 Texas,
SW USA
Porto Edda *see* Sarandë
Portoferraio 96 B4 Toscana, C Italy
Port-of-Spain 55 H5 *country capital*
(Trinidad and Tobago) Trinidad,
Trinidad and Tobago

Porto Grande *see* Mindelo
Portogruaro *96 C2* Veneto, NE Italy
Porto-Novo *75 F5 country capital* (Benin) S Benin
Porto Santo *70 A2 var.* Ilha do Porto Santo. *Island* Madeira, Portugal, NE Atlantic Ocean
Porto Torres *97 A5* Sardegna, Italy, C Mediterranean Sea
Porto Velho *62 D2 var.* Velho. *State capital* Rondônia, W Brazil
Portoviejo *60 A2 var.* Puertoviejo. Manabí, W Ecuador
Port Pirie *149 B6* South Australia
Port Said *72 B1 Ar.* Būr Sa'īd. N Egypt
Portsmouth *41 G3* New Hampshire, NE USA
Portsmouth *40 D4* Ohio, N USA
Portsmouth *89 D7* S England, UK
Portsmouth *41 F5* Virginia, NE USA
Port Stanley *see* Stanley
Port Sudan *72 C3* Red Sea, NE Sudan
Port Swettenham *see* Klang
Port Talbot *89 C7* S Wales, UK
Portugal *92 B3 Country* SW Europe

Portugal 92

Official name Republic of Portugal
Formation 1139
Capital Lisbon
Population 10 million / 280 people per sq mile (108 people per sq km)
Total area 35,672 sq miles (92,391 sq km)
Languages Portuguese
Religions Roman Catholic 97%, Protestant 1%, other 2%
Ethnic mix Portuguese 98%, African and other 2%
Government Parliamentary democracy
Currency Euro (Portuguese escudo until 2002)
Literacy rate 92.3%
Calorie consumption 3,716 kilocalories

Portuguese Timor *see* East Timor
Port-Vila *144 D4 var.* Vila. *Country capital* (Vanuatu) Éfaté, C Vanuatu
Porvenir *65 B8* Magallanes, S Chile
Porvenir *61 E3* Pando, NW Bolivia
Porvoo *85 E6 Swe.* Borgå. Etelä-Suomi, S Finland
Posadas *64 D3* Misiones, NE Argentina
Poschega *see* Požega
Posterholt *87 D5* Limburg, SE Netherlands
Postojna *95 D8 Ger.* Adelsberg, *It.* Postumia. SW Slovenia
Potamós *105 C7* Antikýthira, S Greece
Potenza *97 D5 anc.* Potentia. Basilicata, S Italy
P'ot'i *117 F2* W Georgia
Potiskum *75 G4* Yobe, NE Nigeria
Potomac River *41 E5 river* NE USA
Potosí *61 F4* Potosí, S Bolivia
Potsdam *94 D3* Brandenburg, NE Germany
Potwar Plateau *134 C2 plateau* NE Pakistan
Poŭthĭsăt *137 D6 prev.* Pursat. Poŭthĭsăt, W Cambodia
Po Valley *96 C2 It.* Valle del Po. *Valley* N Italy
Považská Bystrica *99 C5 Ger.* Waagbistritz, *Hung.* Vágbeszterce. Trenčiansky Kraj, W Slovakia
Poverty Bay *150 E4 inlet* North Island, NZ
Póvoa de Varzim *92 B2* Porto, NW Portugal
Powder River *44 D2 river* Montana/Wyoming, NW USA
Powell *44 C2* Wyoming, C USA
Powell, Lake *44 B5 lake* Utah, W USA
Požarevac *100 D4 Ger.* Passarowitz. Serbia, NE Serbia and Montenegro (Yugo.)

Poza Rica *51 F4 var.* Poza Rica de Hidalgo. Veracruz-Llave, E Mexico
Poza Rica de Hidalgo *see* Poza Rica
Požega *100 D4 prev.* Slavonska Požega. *Ger.* Poschega, *Hung.* Pozsega. Požega-Slavonija, NE Croatia
Pozega *see* Požega
Poznań *98 C3 Ger.* Posen, Posnania. Wielkopolskie, C Poland
Pozoblanco *92 D4* Andalucía, S Spain
Pozzallo *97 C8* Sicilia, Italy, C Mediterranean Sea
Prachatice *99 A5 Ger.* Prachatitz. Budějovický Kraj, S Czech Republic
Prado del Ganso *see* Goose Green
Prae *see* Phrae
Prague *80 D3* Oklahoma, C USA
Praha *99 A5 Eng.* Prague, *Ger.* Prag, *Pol.* Praga. *Country capital* (Czech Republic) Středočeský Kraj, NW Czech Republic
Praia *74 A3 country capital* (Cape Verde) Santiago, S Cape Verde
Prato *96 B3* Toscana, C Italy
Pratt *45 E5* Kansas, C USA
Prattville *42 D2* Alabama, S USA
Pravda *104 D1 prev.* Dogrular. Silistra, NE Bulgaria
Pravia *92 C1* Asturias, N Spain
Prenzlau *94 D3* Brandenburg, NE Germany
Přerov *99 C5 Ger.* Prerau. Olomoucký Kraj, E Czech Republic
Presa de la Amistad *see* Amistad Reservoir
Preschau *see* Prešov
Prescott *48 B2* Arizona, SW USA
Preševo *101 D5* Serbia, SE Serbia and Montenegro (Yugo.)
Presidente Epitácio *63 E4* São Paulo, S Brazil
Prešov *99 D5 var.* Preschau, *Ger.* Eperies, *Hung.* Eperjes. Prešovský Kraj, E Slovakia
Prespa, Lake *101 D6 Alb.* Liqen i Prespës, *Gk.* Limni Megáli Préspa, Limni Prespa, *Mac.* Prespansko Ezero, *Serb.* Prespansko Jezero. *Lake* SE Europe
Presque Isle *41 H1* Maine, NE USA
Preston *89 D5* NW England, UK
Prestwick *88 C4* W Scotland, UK
Pretoria *78 D4 var.* Epitoli, Tshwane. *Country capital(South Africa-administrative capital)* Gauteng, NE South Africa
Préveza *105 A5* Ípeiros, W Greece
Pribilof Islands *36 A3 island group* Alaska, USA
Priboj *100 C4* Serbia, W Serbia and Montenegro (Yugo.)
Price *44 B4* Utah, W USA
Prichard *42 C3* Alabama, S USA
Priekulė *106 B3 Ger.* Prökuls. Gargždai, W Lithuania
Prienai *107 B5 Pol.* Preny. Prienai, S Lithuania
Prieska *78 C4* Northern Cape, C South Africa
Prijedor *100 B3* Republika Srpska, NW Bosnia and Herzegovina
Prijepolje *100 D4* Serbia, W Serbia and Montenegro (Yugo.)
Prilep *101 D6 Turk.* Perlepe. S FYR Macedonia
Primorsk *106 A4 Ger.* Fischhausen. Kaliningradskaya Oblast', W Russian Federation
Primorsko *104 E2 prev.* Keupriya. Burgas, E Bulgaria
Prince Albert *37 F5* Saskatchewan, S Canada
Prince Edward Island *39 F4 Fr.* Île-du Prince-Édouard. *Province* SE Canada
Prince Edward Islands *69 E8 island group* S South Africa
Prince George *37 E5* British Columbia, SW Canada
Prince of Wales Island *37 F2 island* Queen Elizabeth Islands, Nunavut, NW Canada

Prince of Wales Island *148 B1 island* Queensland, E Australia
Prince Patrick Island *37 E2 island* Parry Islands, Northwest Territories, NW Canada
Prince Rupert *36 D4* British Columbia, SW Canada
Prince's Island *see* Príncipe
Princess Charlotte Bay *148 C2 bay* Queensland, NE Australia
Princess Elizabeth Land *154 C3 physical region* Antarctica
Príncipe *77 A5 var.* Príncipe Island, *Eng.* Prince's Island. *Island* N Sao Tome and Principe
Príncipe Island *see* Príncipe
Prinzapolka *53 E3* Región Autónoma Atlántico Norte, NE Nicaragua
Pripet *107 C7 Bel.* Prypyats', *Ukr.* Pryp''yat'. *River* Belarus/Ukraine
Pripet Marshes *107 B7 wetland* Belarus/Ukraine
Priština *101 D5 Alb.* Prishtinë. Serbia, S Serbia and Montenegro (Yugo.)
Privas *91 D5* Ardèche, E France
Prizren *101 D5 Alb.* Prizreni. Serbia, S Serbia and Montenegro (Yugo.)
Probolinggo *138 D5* Jawa, C Indonesia
Progreso *51 H3* Yucatán, SE Mexico
Prokhladnyy *111 B8* Kabardino-Balkarskaya Respublika, SW Russian Federation
Prokuplje *101 D5* Serbia, SE Serbia and Montenegro (Yugo.)
Prome *136 B4 var.* Pyè. Pegu, C Myanmar
Promyshlennyy *110 E3* Respublika Komi, NW Russian Federation
Prostějov *99 C5 Ger.* Prossnitz, *Pol.* Prościejów. Olomoucký Kraj, E Czech Republic
Provence *91 D6 cultural region* SE France
Providence *see* Fort Providence
Providence *41 G3 state capital* Rhode Island, NE USA
Providencia, Isla de *53 F3 island* NW Colombia
Provideniya *172 B1* Chukotskiy Avtonomnyy Okrug, NE Russian Federation
Provo *44 B4* Utah, W USA
Prudhoe Bay *36 D2* Alaska, USA
Prusa *see* Bursa
Pruszków *98 D3 Ger.* Kaltdorf. Mazowieckie, C Poland
Prut *108 D4 Ger.* Pruth. *River* E Europe
Pruzhany *107 B6 Pol.* Pružana. Brestskaya Voblasts', SW Belarus
Prydz Bay *154 D3 bay* Antarctica
Pryluky *109 E2 Rus.* Priluki. Chernihivs'ka Oblast', NE Ukraine
Prymors'k *109 G4 Rus.* Primorsk; *prev.* Primorskoye. Zaporiz'ka Oblast', SE Ukraine
Przemyśl *99 E5 Rus.* Peremyshl. Podkarpackie, SE Poland
Psará *105 D5 island* E Greece
Psël *109 F2 river* Russian Federation/Ukraine
Pskov *114 B2 Ger.* Pleskau, *Latv.* Pleskava. Pskovskaya Oblast', W Russian Federation
Pskov, Lake *114 B3 Est.* Pihkva Järv, *Ger.* Pleskauer See, *Rus.* Pskovskoye Ozero. *Lake* Estonia/Russian Federation
Ptich *107 C7 Rus.* Ptich'. *River* SE Belarus
Ptich *107 C7 Rus.* Ptich'. Homyel'skaya Voblasts', SE Belarus
Ptuj *95 E7 Ger.* Pettau; *anc.* Poetovio. NE Slovenia
Pucallpa *60 C3* Ucayali, C Peru
Puck *98 C2* Pomorskie, N Poland
Pudasjärvi *84 D4* Oulu, C Finland
Puducherri *see* Pondicherry
Puebla *51 F4 var.* Puebla de Zaragoza. Puebla, S Mexico
Puebla de Zaragoza *see* Puebla
Pueblo *44 D5* Colorado, C USA

Puerto Acosta *61 E4* La Paz, W Bolivia
Puerto Aisén *65 B6* Aisén, S Chile
Puerto Ángel *51 F5* Oaxaca, SE Mexico
Puerto Argentino *see* Stanley
Puerto Ayacucho *58 D3* Amazonas, SW Venezuela
Puerto Baquerizo Moreno *60 B5 var.* Baquerizo Moreno. Galapagos Islands, Ecuador, E Pacific Ocean
Puerto Barrios *52 C2* Izabal, E Guatemala
Puerto Bello *see* Portobelo
Puerto Berrío *58 B2* Antioquia, C Colombia
Puerto Cabello *58 D1* Carabobo, N Venezuela
Puerto Cabezas *53 E2 var.* Bilwi. Región Autónoma Atlántico Norte, NE Nicaragua
Puerto Carreño *58 D3* Vichada, E Colombia
Puerto Cortés *52 C2* Cortés, NW Honduras
Puerto Cumarebo *58 C1* Falcón, N Venezuela
Puerto Deseado *65 C7* Santa Cruz, SE Argentina
Puerto Escondido *51 F5* Oaxaca, SE Mexico
Puerto Francisco de Orellana *60 B1 var.* Coca. Napo, N Ecuador
Puerto Gallegos *see* Río Gallegos
Puerto Inírida *58 D3 var.* Obando. Guainía, E Colombia
Puerto La Cruz *59 E1* Anzoátegui, NE Venezuela
Puerto Lempira *53 E2* Gracias a Dios, E Honduras
Puerto Limón *see* Limón
Puertollano *92 D4* Castilla-La Mancha, C Spain
Puerto López *58 C1* La Guajira, N Colombia
Puerto Maldonado *61 E3* Madre de Dios, E Peru
Puerto México *see* Coatzacoalcos
Puerto Montt *65 B5* Los Lagos, C Chile
Puerto Natales *65 B7* Magallanes, S Chile
Puerto Obaldía *53 H5* San Blas, NE Panama
Puerto Plata *55 E3 var.* San Felipe de Puerto Plata. N Dominican Republic
Puerto Princesa *139 E2 off.* Puerto Princesa City. Palawan, W Philippines
Puerto Rico *55 F3 off.* Commonwealth of Puerto Rico; *prev.* Porto Rico. *US commonwealth territory* C West Indies
Puerto Rico *56 B1 island* C West Indies
Puerto Rico Trench *56 B1 undersea feature* NE Caribbean Sea
Puerto San José *see* San José
Puerto San Julián *65 B7 var.* San Julián. Santa Cruz, SE Argentina
Puerto Suárez *61 H4* Santa Cruz, E Bolivia
Puerto Vallarta *50 D4* Jalisco, SW Mexico
Puerto Varas *65 B5* Los Lagos, C Chile
Puerto Viejo *53 E4* Heredia, NE Costa Rica
Puertoviejo *see* Portoviejo
Puget Sound *46 B1 sound* Washington, NW USA
Puglia *97 E5 Eng.* Apulia. *Cultural region* SE Italy
Pukaki, Lake *151 B6 lake* South Island, NZ
Pukekohe *150 D3* Auckland, North Island, NZ
Puket *see* Phuket
Pukhovichi *107 C6 Rus.* Pukhovichi. Minskaya Voblasts', C Belarus
Pula *100 A3 It.* Pola; *prev.* Pulj. Istra, NW Croatia
Pulaski *40 D5* Virginia, NE USA
Pulau Butung *see* Buton, Pulau

Puławy 98 D4 Ger. Neu Amerika.
Lublin, E Poland
Pul-i-Khumri see Pol-e Khomrī
Pullman 46 C2 Washington,
NW USA
Pułtusk 98 D3 Mazowieckie,
C Poland
Puná, Isla 60 A2 island SW Ecuador
Pune 134 C5 prev. Poona.
Mahārāshtra, W India
Punjab 134 C2 prev. West Punjab,
Western Punjab. Province
E Pakistan
Puno 61 E4 Puno, SE Peru
Punta Alta 65 C5 Buenos Aires,
E Argentina
Punta Arenas 65 B8 prev.
Magallanes. Magallanes, S Chile
Punta Gorda 53 E4 Región
Autónoma Atlántico Sur,
SE Nicaragua
Punta Gorda 52 C2 Toledo, SE Belize
Puntarenas 52 D4 Puntarenas,
W Costa Rica
Punto Fijo 58 C1 Falcón,
N Venezuela
Pupuya, Nevado 61 E4 mountain
W Bolivia
Puri 135 F5 var. Jagannath. Orissa,
E India
Puriramya see Buriram
Purmerend 86 C3 Noord-Holland,
C Netherlands
Purus, Río 62 C2 Sp. Río Purús.
River Brazil/Peru
Pusan 129 E4 off. Pusan-
gwangyŏksi, var. Busan, Jap.
Fusan. SE South Korea
Püspökladány 99 D6 Hajdú-Bihar,
E Hungary
Putorana Mountains see Putorana,
Plato
Putorana, Plato 114 D3 var. Gory
Putorana, Eng. Putorana
Mountains. Mountain range
N Russian Federation
Puttalam 132 C3 North Western
Province, W Sri Lanka
Puttgarden 94 C2 Schleswig-
Holstein, N Germany
Putumayo, Río 58 B5 var. Río Içá.
River NW South America see also
Içá, Río
Putumayo, Río see Içá, Rio
Puurmani 106 D2 Ger. Talkhof.
Jõgevamaa, E Estonia
Pyatigorsk 111 B7 Stavropol'skiy
Kray, SW Russian Federation
P"yatykhatky 109 F3 Rus.
Pyatikhatki. Dnipropetrovs'ka
Oblast', E Ukraine
Pyè see Prome
Pyetrykaw 107 C7 Rus. Petrikov.
Homyel'skaya Voblasts',
SE Belarus
Pyinmana 136 B4 Mandalay,
C Myanmar
Pýlos 105 B6 var. Pilos.
Pelopónnisos, S Greece
P'yŏngyang 129 E4 var.
P'yŏngyang-si, Eng. Pyongyang.
Country capital (North Korea)
SW North Korea
P'yŏngyang-si see P'yŏngyang
Pyramid Lake 47 C5 lake Nevada,
W USA
Pyrenees 102 B2 Fr. Pyrénées, Sp.
Pirineos; anc. Pyrenaei Montes.
Mountain range SW Europe
Pýrgos 105 B6 var. Pírgos. Dytikí
Ellás, S Greece
Pyryatyn 109 E2 Rus. Piryatin.
Poltavs'ka Oblast', NE Ukraine
Pyrzyce 98 B3 Ger. Pyritz.
Zachodniopomorskie, NW Poland
Pyu 136 B4 Pegu, C Myanmar
Pyuntaza 136 B4 Pegu,
SW Myanmar

Q

Qā' al Jafr 119 C7 lake S Jordan
Qaanaaq 82 D1 var. Qânâq, Dan.
Thule. N Greenland
Qabātiya 119 E6 N West Bank
Qābis see Gabès
Qacentina see Constantine

Qafşah see Gafsa
Qagan Us see Dulan
Qahremānshahr see Bākhtarān
Qaidam Pendi 126 C4 basin C China
Qal'aikhum 123 F3 Rus.
Kalaikhum. S Tajikistan
Qal'at Bīshah 121 B5 'Asīr,
SW Saudi Arabia
Qalqīlya 119 D6 N West Bank
Qamdo 126 D5 Xizang Zizhiqu,
W China
Qamishly see Al Qāmishlī
Qânâq see Qaanaaq
Qaqortoq 82 C4 Dan. Julianehåb.
S Greenland
Qara Qum see Garagumy
Qarkilik see Ruoqiang
Qarokŭl 123 F3 Rus. Karakul'.
E Tajikistan
Qars see Kars
Qarshi 123 E3 Rus. Karshi; prev.
Bek-Budi. Qashqadaryo Wiloyati,
S Uzbekistan
Qasigianguit see Qasigiannguit
Qasigiannguit 82 C3 var.
Qasigianguit, Dan. Christianshåb.
C Greenland
Qasr Farâfra 72 B2 W Egypt
Qaţanā 119 B5 var. Katana.
Dimashq, S Syria
Qatar 120 C4 Ar. Dawlat Qaţar.
Country SW Asia

Qatar 120

Official name State of Qatar
Formation 1971
Capital Doha
Population 575,000 / 130 people
per sq mile (50 people per sq km)
Total area 4,416 sq miles
(11,437 sq km)
Languages Arabic
Religions Muslim (mainly Sunni)
95%, other 5%
Ethnic mix Arab 40%, Pakistani
18%, Indian 18%, Iranian 10%,
other 14%
Government Monarchy
Currency Qatar riyal = 100 dirhams
Literacy rate 81.2%
Calorie consumption not available

Qattara Depression see Qaţţâra,
Monkhafad el
Qaţţâra, Monkhafad el 88 A1 var.
Munkhafad al Qaţţārah, Eng.
Qattara Depression. Desert
NW Egypt
Qazimämmäd 117 H3 Rus. Kazi
Magomed. SE Azerbaijan
Qazvīn 120 C2 var. Kazvin. Qazvin,
N Iran
Qena 72 B2 var. Qinā; anc. Caene,
Caenepolis. E Egypt
Qeqertarssuaq see Qeqertarsuaq
Qeqertarsuaq 82 C3 var.
Qeqertarssuaq, Dan. Godhavn.
S Greenland
Qeqertarsuaq 82 C3 island
W Greenland
Qeqertarsuup Tunua 82 C3 Dan.
Disko Bugt. Inlet W Greenland
Qerveh see Qorveh
Qeshm 120 D4 var. Jazīreh-ye
Qeshm, Qeshm Island. Island S Iran
Qeshm Island see Qeshm
Qian see Guizhou
Qilian Shan 126 D3 var. Kilien
Mountains. Mountain range
N China
Qimusseriarsuaq 82 C2 Dan.
Melville Bugt, Eng. Melville Bay.
Bay NW Greenland
Qinā see Qena
Qing see Qinghai
Qingdao 128 D4 var. Ching-Tao,
Ch'ing-tao, Tsingtao, Tsintao, Ger.
Tsingtau. Shandong, E China
Qinghai 126 C4 var. Chinghai, Koko
Nor, Qing, Qinghai Sheng,
Tsinghai. Admin. region province
C China
Qinghai Hu 126 D4 var. Ch'ing Hai,
Tsing Hai, Mong. Koko Nor. lake
C China

Qinghai Sheng see Qinghai
Qingzang Gaoyuan 126 B4 var.
Xizang Gaoyuan, Eng. Plateau of
Tibet. Plateau W China
Qinhuangdao 128 D3 Hebei, E China
Qinzhou 128 B6 Guangxi
Zhuangzu Zizhiqu, S China
Qiong see Hainan
Qiqihar 128 D2 var. Ch'i-ch'i-ha-
erh, Tsitsihar; prev. Lungkiang.
Heilongjiang, NE China
Qira 126 B4 Xinjiang Uygur
Zizhiqu, NW China
Qitai 126 C3 Xinjiang Uygur
Zizhiqu, NW China
Qīzān see Jīzān
Qizil Orda see Kyzylorda
Qizil Qum see Kyzyl Kum
Qizilrabot 123 G3 Rus. Kyzylrabot.
SE Tajikistan
Qom 120 C3 var. Kum, Qum. Qom,
N Iran
Qomul see Hami
Qondūz see Kunduz
Qorveh 120 C3 var. Qerveh,
Qurveh. Kordestān, W Iran
Qostanay see Kostanay
Qoubaïyât 118 B4 var. Al Qubayyāt.
N Lebanon
Qoussantina see Constantine
Quang Ngai 137 B5 var. Quangngai,
Quang Nghia. Quang Ngai,
C Vietnam
Quangngai see Quang Ngai
Quang Nghia see Quang Ngai
Quanzhou 128 D6 var. Ch'uan-
chou, Tsinkiang; prev. Chin-
chiang. Fujian, SE China
Quanzhou 128 C6 Guangxi
Zhuangzu Zizhiqu, S China
Qu'Appelle 37 F5 river
Saskatchewan, S Canada
Quarles, Pegunungan 139 E4
mountain range Sulawesi,
C Indonesia
Quarnero see Kvarner
Quartu Sant' Elena 97 A6 Sardegna,
Italy, C Mediterranean Sea
Quba 117 H2 Rus. Kuba.
N Azerbaijan
Qubba see Ba'qūbah
Québec 39 E4 var. Quebec. Quebec,
SE Canada
Quebec 38 D3 var. Quebec. Admin.
region province SE Canada
Queen Charlotte Islands 36 C5 Fr.
Îles de la Reine-Charlotte. Island
group British Columbia,
SW Canada
Queen Charlotte Sound 36 C5 sea
area British Columbia, W Canada
Queen Elizabeth Islands 37 F2 Fr.
Îles de la Reine-Élisabeth. Island
group Northwest
Territories/Nunavut, N Canada
Queensland 148 B4 state
N Australia
Queenstown 78 D5 Eastern Cape,
S South Africa
Queenstown 151 B7 Otago, South
Island, NZ
Quelimane 79 E3 var. Kilimane,
Kilmain, Quilimane. Zambézia,
NE Mozambique
Quepos 53 E4 Puntarenas, S Costa
Rica
Querétaro 51 E4 Querétaro de
Arteaga, C Mexico
Quesada 53 E4 var. Ciudad
Quesada, San Carlos. Alajuela,
N Costa Rica
Quetta 134 B2 Baluchistān,
SW Pakistan
Quetzalcoalco see Coatzacoalcos
Quetzaltenango see Quezaltenango
Quezaltenango 52 A2 var.
Quetzaltenango. Quezaltenango,
W Guatemala
Quibdó 58 A3 Chocó, W Colombia
Quilimane see Quelimane
Quillabamba 60 D3 Cusco, C Peru
Quilon 132 C3 var. Kolam, Kollam.
Kerala, SW India
Quimper 90 A3 anc. Quimper
Corentin. Finistère, NW France
Quimperlé 90 A3 Finistère,
NW France

Quincy 40 A4 Illinois, N USA
Qui Nhon see Quy Nhon
Quissico 79 E4 Inhambane,
S Mozambique
Quito 60 B1 country capital
(Ecuador) Pichincha, N Ecuador
Qullai Garmo see Kommunizm,
Qullai
Qum see Qom
Qunaytra see Al Qunayţirah
Qŭqon 123 F2 var. Khokand, Rus.
Kokand. Farghona Wiloyati,
E Uzbekistan
Qurein see Al Kuwayt
Qŭrghonteppa 123 E3 Rus. Kurgan-
Tyube. SW Tajikistan
Qurlurtuuq see Kugluktuk
Qurveh see Qorveh
Qusayr see Al Quşayr
Quy Nhon 137 E5 var. Quinhon,
Qui Nhon. Binh Dinh, C Vietnam
Qyteti Stalin see Kuçovë
Qyzylorda see Kyzylorda

R

Raab 100 B1 Hung. Rába. River
Austria/Hungary see also Rába
Raahe 84 D4 Swe. Brahestad. Oulu,
W Finland
Raalte 86 D3 Overijssel,
E Netherlands
Raamsdonksveer 86 C4 Noord-
Brabant, S Netherlands
Raasiku 106 D2 Ger. Rasik.
Harjumaa, NW Estonia
Rába 99 B7 Ger. Raab. River
Austria/Hungary see also Raab
Rabat 70 C2 var. al Dar al Baida.
Country capital (Morocco)
NW Morocco
Rabat see Victoria
Rabat 102 B5 W Malta
Rabbah Ammon see 'Ammān
Rabbath Ammon see 'Ammān
Rabinal 52 B2 Baja Verapaz,
C Guatemala
Rabka 99 D5 Małopolskie,
S Poland
Râbniţa see Rîbniţa
Rabyanāh, Ramlat 71 G4 var.
Rebiana Sand Sea, şaḥrā'
Rabyanāh. Desert SE Libya
Race, Cape 39 H3 headland
Newfoundland, Newfoundland
and Labrador, E Canada
Rach Gia 137 D6 Kiên Giang,
S Vietnam
Rach Gia, Vinh 137 D6 bay
S Vietnam
Racine 40 B3 Wisconsin, N USA
Rădăuţi 108 C3 Ger. Radautz, Hung.
Rádóc. Suceava, N Romania
Radom 98 D4 Mazowieckie,
C Poland
Radomsko 98 D4 Rus.
Novoradomsk. Łódzkie, C Poland
Radomyshl' 108 D2 Zhytomyrs'ka
Oblast', N Ukraine
Radoviš 101 E6 prev. Radoviše.
E FYR Macedonia
Radviliškis 106 B4 Radviliškis,
N Lithuania
Radzyń Podlaski 98 E4 Lubelskie,
E Poland
Rae-Edzo see Edzo
Raetihi 150 D4 Manawatu-
Wanganui, North Island, NZ
Rafa see Rafah
Rafaela 64 C3 Santa Fe,
E Argentina
Rafah 119 A7 var. Rafa, Rafaḥ, Heb.
Rafiaḥ, Raphiah. SW Gaza Strip
Rafaḥ see Rafah
Rafḥah 120 B4 Al Ḥudūd ash
Shamālīyah, N Saudi Arabia
Rafiah see Rafah
Raga 73 A5 Western Bahr el Ghazal,
SW Sudan
Ragged Island Range 54 C2 island
group S Bahamas
Ragusa 97 C7 Sicilia, Italy,
C Mediterranean Sea
Rahachow 107 D7 Rus. Rogachëv.
Homyel'skaya Voblasts',
SE Belarus
Rahaeng see Tak

Rahaṭ, Ḥarrat *121 B5 lavaflow*
 W Saudi Arabia
Rahīmyār Khān *134 C3* Punjab,
 SE Pakistan
Raiatea *145 G4 island* Îles Sous le
 Vent, W French Polynesia
Rāichūr *132 C1* Karnātaka, C India
Rainier, Mount *34 A4 volcano*
 Washington, NW USA
Rainy Lake *38 A4 lake*
 Canada/USA
Raipur *135 E4* Madhya Pradesh,
 C India
Rājahmundry *135 E5* Andhra
 Pradesh, E India
Rajang *see* Rajang, Batang
Rajang, Batang *138 D3 var.* Rajang.
 River East Malaysia
Rājapālaiyam *132 C3* Tamil Nādu,
 SE India
Rājasthān *134 C3 state* NW India
Rājkot *134 C4* Gujarāt, W India
Rāj Nāndgaon *135 E4* Madhya
 Pradesh, C India
Rajshahi *135 G3 prev.* Rampur
 Boalia. Rajshahi, W Bangladesh
Rakahanga *145 F3 atoll* N Cook
 Islands
Rakaia *151 B6 river* South Island, NZ
Rakka *see* Ar Raqqah
Rakke *106 E2* Lääne-Virumaa,
 NE Estonia
Rakvere *106 E2 Ger.* Wesenberg.
 Lääne-Virumaa, N Estonia
Ralik Chain *144 D1 island group*
 Ralik Chain, W Marshall Islands
Ramadi *see* Ar Ramādī
Ramlat Ahl Wahībah *see* Wahībah,
 Ramlat Āl
Ramlat Al Wahaybah *see* Wahībah,
 Ramlat Āl
Râmnicu Sărat *108 C4 prev.*
 Râmnicul-Sărat, Rîmnicu-Sărat.
 Buzău, E Romania
Râmnicu Vâlcea *108 B4 prev.*
 Rîmnicu Vîlcea. Vâlcea,
 C Romania
Ramree Island *136 A4 island*
 W Myanmar
Ramtha *see* Ar Ramthā
Rancagua *64 B4* Libertador,
 C Chile
Rānchi *135 F4* Bihār, N India
Randers *85 B7* Århus, C Denmark
Rangiora *151 C6* Canterbury, South
 Island, NZ
Rangitikei *150 D4 river* North
 Island, NZ
Rangoon *see* Yangon
Rangpur *135 G3* Rajshahi,
 N Bangladesh
Rankin Inlet *37 G3* Nunavut,
 C Canada
Ranong *137 B6* Ranong,
 SW Thailand
Rapa Nui *see* Easter Island
Raphiah *see* Rafah
Rapid City *44 D3* South Dakota,
 N USA
Räpina *106 E3 Ger.* Rappin.
 Põlvamaa, SE Estonia
Rapla *106 D2 Ger.* Rappel.
 Raplamaa, NW Estonia
Rarotonga *145 G5 island* S Cook
 Islands, C Pacific Ocean
Ras al ʿAin *see* Raʾs al ʿAyn
Raʾs al ʿAyn *118 D1 var.* Ras al ʿAin.
 Al Ḥasakah, N Syria
Raʾs an Naqb *119 B7* Maʿān,
 S Jordan
Raseiniai *106 B4* Raseiniai,
 C Lithuania
Ras Hafun *see* Xaafuun, Raas
Rasht *120 C2 var.* Resht. Gīlān,
 NW Iran
Râşnov *108 C4 prev.* Rîşno,
 Rozsnyó, *Hung.* Barcarozsnyó.
 Braşov, C Romania
Ratak Chain *144 D1 island group*
 Ratak Chain, E Marshall Islands
Ratan *85 C5* Jämtland, C Sweden
Rat Buri *see* Ratchaburi
Ratchaburi *137 C5 var.* Rat Buri.
 Ratchaburi, W Thailand
Rastenburg *see* Kętrzyn
Rat Islands *36 A2 island group*
 Aleutian Islands, Alaska, USA

Ratlām *134 D4 prev.* Rutlam.
 Madhya Pradesh, C India
Ratnapura *132 D4* Sabaragamuwa
 Province, S Sri Lanka
Raton *48 D1* New Mexico, SW USA
Rättvik *85 C5* Kopparberg,
 C Sweden
Raudhatain *see* Ar Rawḍatayn
Raufarhöfn *83 E4* Norðhurland
 Eystra, NE Iceland
Raukawa *see* Cook Strait
Raukumara Range *150 E3 mountain
 range* North Island, NZ
Rāulakela *151 F4 var.* Rāurkela, *prev.*
 Rourkela. Orissa, E India
Rauma *85 D5 Swe.* Raumo. Länsi-
 Suomi, W Finland
Raurkela *see* Raulakela
Ravenna *96 C3* Emilia-Romagna,
 N Italy
Rāvi *134 C2 river* India/Pakistan
Rāwalpindi *134 C1* Punjab,
 NE Pakistan
Rawa Mazowiecka *98 D4* Łódzkie,
 C Poland
Rawicz *98 C4 Ger.* Rawitsch.
 Wielkopolskie, C Poland
Rawlins *44 C3* Wyoming, C USA
Rawson *65 C6* Chubut,
 SE Argentina
Rayak *118 B4 var.* Rayaq, Riyāq.
 E Lebanon
Rayaq *see* Rayak
Rayleigh *43 F1 state capital* North
 Carolina, SE USA
Rayong *137 C5* Rayong, S Thailand
Razāzah, Buḩayrat ar *120 B3 var.*
 Baḩr al Milḩ. *Lake* C Iraq
Razgrad *104 D2* Razgrad,
 N Bulgaria
Razim, Lacul *108 D5 prev.* Lacul
 Razelm. *Lagoon* NW Black Sea
Reading *41 F4* Pennsylvania,
 NE USA
Reading *89 D7* S England, UK
Realicó *64 C4* La Pampa,
 C Argentina
Reäng Kesei *137 D5* Bătdâmbâng,
 W Cambodia
Rebecca, Lake *147 C6 lake* Western
 Australia
Rebiana Sand Sea *see* Rabyanāh,
 Ramlat
Rebun-tō *130 C2 island* NE Japan
Rechytsa *107 D7 Rus.* Rechitsa.
 Brestskaya Voblastsʾ, SW Belarus
Recife *63 G2 prev.* Pernambuco.
 State capital Pernambuco, E Brazil
Recklinghausen *94 A4* Nordrhein-
 Westfalen, W Germany
Recogne *87 C7* Luxembourg,
 SE Belgium
Reconquista *64 D3* Santa Fe,
 C Argentina
Red Deer *37 E5* Alberta, SW Canada
Redding *47 B5* California, W USA
Redon *90 B4* Ille-et-Vilaine,
 NW France
Red River *136 C2 var.* Yuan, *Chin.*
 Yuan Jiang, *Vtn.* Sông Hông Hà.
 River China/Vietnam
Red River *45 E1 river* Canada/USA
Red River *42 B3 river* Louisiana,
 S USA
Red River *35 C6 river* S USA
Red Sea *72 C3 anc.* Sinus Arabicus.
 Sea Africa/Asia
Red Wing *45 G2* Minnesota, N USA
Reefton *151 C5* West Coast, South
 Island, NZ
Reese River *47 C5 river* Nevada,
 W USA
Refahiye *117 E3* Erzincan, C Turkey
Regensburg *95 C6 Eng.* Ratisbon,
 Fr. Ratisbonne; *hist.* Ratisbona,
 anc. Castra Regina, Reginum.
 Bayern, SE Germany
Regenstauf *95 C6* Bayern,
 SE Germany
Reggane *70 D3 C* Algeria
Reggio *see* Reggio nellʾ Emilia
Reggio Calabria *see* Reggio di
 Calabria
Reggio di Calabria *97 D7 var.*
 Reggio Calabria, *Gk.* Rhegion; *anc.*
 Regium, Rhegium. Calabria,
 SW Italy

Reggio Emilia *see* Reggio nellʾ
 Emilia
Reggio nellʾ Emilia *96 B2 var.*
 Reggio Emilia, *abbrev.* Reggio; *anc.*
 Regium Lepidum. Emilia-
 Romagna, N Italy
Reghin *108 C4 Ger.* Sächsisch-Reen,
 Hung. Szászrégen; *prev.* Reghinul
 Săsesc, *Ger.* Sächsisch-Regen.
 Mureş, C Romania
Regina *37 F5* Saskatchewan,
 S Canada
Registan *see* Rīgestān
Regium *see* Reggio di Calabria
Regium Lepidum *see* Reggio nellʾ
 Emilia
Rehoboth *see* Reḥovot
Rehoboth *78 B3* Hardap,
 C Namibia
Reḥovot *119 A6 var.* Rehoboth,
 Rehovoth, Rekhovot. Central,
 C Israel
Rehovoth *see* Reḥovot
Reid *147 D6* Western Australia
Reikjavik *see* Reykjavík
Ré, Île de *90 A4 island* W France
Reims *90 D3 Eng.* Rheims; *anc.*
 Durocortorum, Remi. Marne,
 N France
Reindeer Lake *37 F4 lake*
 Manitoba/Saskatchewan,
 C Canada
Reinga, Cape *150 C1 headland* North
 Island, NZ
Reinosa *92 D1* Cantabria, N Spain
Rekhovot *see* Reḥovot
Reliance *37 F4* Northwest
 Territories, C Canada
Rendina *see* Rentína
Rendsburg *94 B2* Schleswig-
 Holstein, N Germany
Rengat *138 B4* Sumatera,
 W Indonesia
Reni *108 D4* Odesʾka Oblastʾ,
 SW Ukraine
Rennell *144 C4 var.* Mu Nggava.
 Island S Solomon Islands
Rennes *90 B3 Bret.* Roazon; *anc.*
 Condate. Ille-et-Vilaine,
 NW France
Reno *47 C5* Nevada, W USA
Renqiu *128 C4* Hebei, E China
Rentína *105 B5 var.* Rendina.
 Thessalía, C Greece
Republika Srpska *Admin. region
 republic* Bosnia and Herzegovina
République Centrafricaine *see*
 Central African Republic
Repulse Bay *37 G3* Nunavut,
 N Canada
Resht *see* Rasht
Resistencia *64 D3* Chaco,
 NE Argentina
Reşiţa *108 A4 Ger.* Reschitza, *Hung.*
 Resicabánya. Caraş-Severin,
 W Romania
Resolute *37 F2* Cornwallis Island,
 Nunavut, N Canada
Resolution Island *39 E1 island*
 Northwest Territories, NE Canada
Resolution Island *151 A7 island*
 SW NZ
Réunion *79 H4 off.* La Réunion.
 French overseas department
 W Indian Ocean
Réunion *141 B5 island* W Indian
 Ocean
Reus *93 F2* Cataluña, E Spain
Reutlingen *95 B6* Baden-
 Württemberg, S Germany
Reuver *87 D5* Limburg,
 SE Netherlands
Revillagigedo Islands *see*
 Revillagigedo, Islas
Revillagigedo, Islas *50 B5 Eng.*
 Revillagigedo Islands. *Island group*
 W Mexico
Rexburg *46 E3* Idaho, NW USA
Reyes *61 F3* Beni, NW Bolivia
Rey, Isla del *53 G5 island*
 Archipiélago de las Perlas,
 SE Panama
Reykjanes Basin *82 C5 var.*
 Irminger Basin. *Undersea feature*
 N Atlantic Ocean
Reykjanes Ridge *80 A1 undersea
 feature* N Atlantic Ocean

Reykjavík *83 E5 var.* Reikjavik.
 Country capital (Iceland)
 Höfuðhborgarsvaedhi, W Iceland
Reynosa *51 E2* Tamaulipas,
 C Mexico
Rezé *90 A4* Loire-Atlantique,
 NW France
Rēzekne *106 D4 Ger.* Rositten; *prev.*
 Rus. Rezhitsa. Rēzekne, SE Latvia
Rezovo *104 E3 Turk.* Rezve. Burgas,
 E Bulgaria
Rhegion *see* Reggio di Calabria
Rhegium *see* Reggio di Calabria
Rhein *see* Rhine
Rheine *94 A3 var.* Rheine in
 Westfalen. Nordrhein-Westfalen,
 NW Germany
Rheine in Westfalen *see* Rheine
Rheinisches Schiefergebirge *95 A5
 var.* Rhine State Uplands, *Eng.*
 Rhenish Slate Mountains.
 Mountain range W Germany
Rhenish Slate Mountains *see*
 Rheinisches Schiefergebirge
Rhine *80 D4 Dut.* Rijn, *Fr.* Rhin, *Ger.*
 Rhein. *River* W Europe
Rhinelander *40 B2* Wisconsin,
 N USA
Rhine State Uplands *see*
 Rheinisches Schiefergebirge
Rho *96 B2* Lombardia, N Italy
Rhode Island *41 G3 off.* State of
 Rhode Island and Providence
 Plantations; also known as Little
 Rhody, Ocean State. *State* NE USA
Rhodes *see* Ródos
Rhodope Mountains *104 C3 var.*
 Rodhópi Óri, *Bul.* Rhodope
 Planina, Rodopi, *Gk.* Orosirá
 Rodhópis, *Turk.* Dospad Dagh.
 Mountain range Bulgaria/Greece
Rhodope Planina *see* Rhodope
 Mountains
Rhodos *see* Ródos
Rhône *91 D6 river*
 France/Switzerland
Rhône *91 D6 department* E France
Rhum *88 B3 var.* Rum. *Island*
 W Scotland, UK
Ribble *89 D5 river* NW England, UK
Ribeira *92 B1* Galicia, NW Spain
Ribeirão Preto *63 F4* São Paulo,
 S Brazil
Riberalta *61 F2* Beni, N Bolivia
Ribnița *108 D3 var.* Rābnița, *Rus.*
 Rybnitsa. NE Moldova
Rice Lake *40 A2* Wisconsin, N USA
Richard Toll *74 B3* N Senegal
Richfield *44 B4* Utah, W USA
Richland *46 C2* Washington,
 NW USA
Richmond *41 E5 state capital*
 Virginia, NE USA
Richmond *40 C5* Kentucky, S USA
Richmond *151 C5* Tasman, South
 Island, NZ
Richmond Range *151 C5 mountain
 range* South Island, NZ
Ricobayo, Embalse de *92 C2
 reservoir* NW Spain
Ridgecrest *47 C7* California,
 W USA
Ried *see* Ried im Innkreis
Ried im Innkreis *95 D6 var.* Ried.
 Oberösterreich, NW Austria
Riemst *87 D6* Limburg, NE Belgium
Riesa *94 D4* Sachsen, E Germany
Rift Valley *see* Great Rift Valley
Rīga *106 C3 Eng.* Riga. *Country
 capital* (Latvia) Riga, C Latvia
Riga, Gulf of *106 C3 Est.* Liivi Laht,
 Ger. Rigaer Bucht, *Latv.* Rīgas
 Jūras Līcis, *Rus.* Rizhskiy Zaliv;
 prev. est. Riia Laht. *Gulf*
 Estonia/Latvia
Rīgān *120 E4* Kermān, SE Iran
Rīgestān *122 D5 var.* Registan.
 Desert region S Afghanistan
Riihimäki *85 D5* Etelä-Suomi,
 S Finland
Rijeka *100 A2 Ger.* Sankt Veit am
 Flaum, *It.* Fiume, *Slvn.* Reka; *anc.*
 Tarsatica. Primorje-Gorski Kotar,
 NW Croatia
Rijssel *see* Lille
Rijssen *86 E3* Overijssel,
 E Netherlands

Rimah, Wādī ar 120 B4 var. Wādī ar
Rummah. *Dry watercourse* C Saudi
Arabia
Rimini 96 C3 anc. Ariminum.
Emilia-Romagna, N Italy
Rimouski 39 E4 Quebec,
SE Canada
Ringebu 85 B5 Oppland, S Norway
Ringkøbing Fjord 85 A7 *fjord*
W Denmark
Ringvassøya 84 C2 *island* N Norway
Rio *see* Rio de Janeiro
Riobamba 60 B1 Chimborazo,
C Ecuador
Rio Branco 56 B3 *state capital* Acre,
W Brazil
Río Bravo 51 E2 Tamaulipas,
C Mexico
Río Cuarto 64 C4 Córdoba,
C Argentina
Rio de Janeiro 63 F4 var. Rio. *State
capital* Rio de Janeiro, SE Brazil
Río Gallegos 65 B7 var. Gallegos,
Puerto Gallegos. Santa Cruz,
S Argentina
Rio Grande 63 E5 var. São Pedro do
Rio Grande do Sul. Rio Grande do
Sul, S Brazil
Río Grande 50 D3 Zacatecas,
C Mexico
Rio Grande do Norte 63 G2 *off.*
Estado do Rio Grande do Norte.
State E Brazil
Rio Grande do Sul 63 E5 *off.* Estado
do Rio Grande do Sul. *State*
S Brazil
Rio Grande Plateau *see* Rio Grande
Rise
Rio Grande Rise 57 E6 var. Rio
Grande Plateau. *Undersea feature*
SW Atlantic Ocean
Ríohacha 58 B1 La Guajira,
N Colombia
Río Lagartos 51 H3 Yucatán,
SE Mexico
Riom 91 C5 anc. Ricomagus. Puy-
de-Dôme, C France
Río San Juan 53 E4 *department*
S Nicaragua
Rioverde *see* Río Verde
Río Verde 51 E4 var. Rioverde. San
Luis Potosí, C Mexico
Ripoll 93 G2 Cataluña, NE Spain
Rishiri-tō 130 C2 var. Risiri Tō.
Island NE Japan
Risiri Tō *see* Rishiri-tō
Risti 106 D2 Ger. Kreuz. Läänemaa,
W Estonia
Rivas 52 D4 Rivas, SW Nicaragua
Rivera 64 D1 Rivera, NE
Uruguay
River Falls 40 A2 Wisconsin,
N USA
River Plate *see* Plata, Río de la
Riverside 47 C7 California, W USA
Riverton 151 A7 Southland, South
Island, NZ
Riverton 44 C3 Wyoming, C USA
Rivière-du-Loup 39 E4 Quebec,
SE Canada
Rivne 108 C2 Pol. Równe, Rus.
Rovno. Rivnens'ka Oblast',
NW Ukraine
Rivoli 96 A2 Piemonte, NW Italy
Riyadh *see* Ar Riyāḍ
Riyāq *see* Rayak
Rize 117 E2 Rize, NE Turkey
Rizhao 128 D4 Shandong, E China
Rkîz 74 C3 Trarza, W Mauritania
Road Town 55 F3 *dependent territory
capital* (British Virgin Islands)
Tortola, C British Virgin Islands
Roanne 91 C5 anc. Rodunma. Loire,
E France
Roanoke 41 E5 Virginia, NE USA
Roanoke River 43 F1 *river* North
Carolina/Virginia, SE USA
Roatán 52 C2 var. Coxen Hole.
Coxin Hole. Islas de la Bahía,
N Honduras
Robbie Ridge 143 E3 *undersea
feature* W Pacific Ocean
Robert Williams *see* Caála
Robinson Range 147 B5 *mountain
range* Western Australia
Robson, Mount 37 E5 *mountain*
British Columbia, SW Canada

Robstown 49 G4 Texas, SW USA
Roca Partida, Isla 50 B5 *island*
W Mexico
Rocas, Atol das 63 G2 *island*
E Brazil
Rochefort 90 B4 var. Rochefort sur
Mer. Charente-Maritime, W France
Rochefort 87 C7 Namur, SE Belgium
Rochefort sur Mer *see* Rochefort
Rochester 45 G3 Minnesota, N USA
Rochester 41 G2 New Hampshire,
NE USA
Rochester 41 E3 New York, NE USA
Rockall Bank 80 B2 *undersea feature*
N Atlantic Ocean
Rockall Trough 80 B2 *undersea
feature* N Atlantic Ocean
Rockdale 148 E2 New South Wales,
SE Australia
Rockford 40 B3 Illinois, N USA
Rockhampton 148 D4 Queensland,
E Australia
Rock Hill 43 E1 South Carolina,
SE USA
Rockies *see* Rocky Mountains
Rockingham 147 A6 Western
Australia
Rock Island 40 B3 Illinois, N USA
Rock Sound 54 C1 Eleuthera Island,
C Bahamas
Rock Springs 44 C3 Wyoming,
C USA
Rockstone 59 F3 C Guyana
Rocky Mount 43 F1 North Carolina,
SE USA
Rocky Mountains 34 B4 var.
Rockies, Fr. Montagnes
Rocheuses. *Mountain range*
Canada/USA
Roden 86 E2 Drenthe,
NE Netherlands
Rodez 91 C5 anc. Segodunum.
Aveyron, S France
Rodhópi Óri *see* Rhodope
Mountains
Ródhos *see* Ródos
Rodi *see* Ródos
Rodopi *see* Rhodope Mountains
Ródos 105 E7 var. Ródhos, Eng.
Rhodes, It. Rodi; anc. Rhodus.
Island Dodekánisos, Greece,
Aegean Sea
Roermond 87 D5 Limburg,
SE Netherlands
Roeselare 87 A6 Fr. Roulers; prev.
Rousselaere. West-Vlaanderen,
W Belgium
Rogatica 100 C4 Republika Srpska,
SE Bosnia and Herzegovina
Rogers 42 A1 Arkansas, C USA
Roger Simpson Island *see*
Abemama
Roi Ed *see* Roi Et
Roi Et 137 D5 var. Muang Roi Et,
Roi Ed. Roi Et, E Thailand
Roja 106 C2 Talsi, NW Latvia
Rokiškis 106 C4 Rokiškis,
NE Lithuania
Rokycany 99 A5 Ger. Rokytzan.
Plzeňský Kraj, W Czech Republic
Rokytzan *see* Rokycany
Rôlas, Ilha das 76 E2 *island* S Sao
Tome and Principe
Rolla 45 G5 Missouri, C USA
Roma 96 C4 Eng. Rome. *Country
capital* (Italy) Lazio, C Italy
Roma 149 D5 Queensland,
E Australia
Roman 108 C4 Hung. Románvásár.
Neamţ, NE Romania
Roman 104 C2 Vratsa, NW Bulgaria
Romania 108 B4 Bul. Rumŭniya,
Ger. Rumänien, Hung. Románia,
Rom. România, SCr. Rumunjska,
Ukr. Rumuniya; prev. Republica
Socialistă România, Roumania,
Rumania, Socialist Republic of
Romania, Rom. România. *Country*
SE Europe

Romania 108

Official name Romania
Formation 1878
Capital Bucharest
Population 21.7 million / 237

Romania (continued)

Population 21.7 million / 237
people per sq mile (91 people
per sq km)
Total area 91,699 sq miles
(237,500 sq km)
Languages Romanian, Hungarian,
German, Romany
Religions Romanian Orthodox 87%,
Roman Catholic 5%, other 8%
Ethnic mix Romanian 89%, Magyar
9%, Romany 1%, other 1%
Government Multiparty republic
Currency Romanian Leu = 100 bani
Literacy rate 98.1%
Calorie consumption 3,274
kilocalories

Rome *see* Roma
Rome 42 D2 Georgia, SE USA
Romny 109 F2 Sums'ka Oblast',
NE Ukraine
Rømø 85 A7 Ger. Röm. *Island*
SW Denmark
Roncador, Serra do 56 D4 *mountain
range* C Brazil
Ronda 92 D5 Andalucía, S Spain
Rondônia 62 D3 *off.* Estado de
Rondônia; prev. Território de
Rondônia. *State* W Brazil
Rondonópolis 63 E3 Mato Grosso,
W Brazil
Rongelap Atoll 144 D1 var. Rōṇḷap.
Atoll Ralik Chain, NW Marshall
Islands
Rõngu 106 D3 Ger. Ringen.
Tartumaa, SE Estonia
Rōṇḷap *see* Rongelap Atoll
Rønne 85 B8 Bornholm,
E Denmark
Ronne Ice Shelf 154 A3 *ice shelf*
Antarctica
Roosendaal 87 C5 Noord-Brabant,
S Netherlands
Roosevelt Island 154 B4 *island*
Antarctica
Roraima 62 D1 *off.* Estado de
Roraima; prev. Território do Rio
Branco, Território de Roraima.
State N Brazil
Roraima, Mount 59 E3 *mountain*
N South America
Røros 85 B5 Sør-Trøndelag,
S Norway
Rosa, Lake 54 D2 *lake* Great Inagua,
S Bahamas
Rosario 64 D2 San Pedro,
C Paraguay
Rosario 64 D4 Santa Fe,
C Argentina
Rosarito 50 A1 Baja California,
NW Mexico
Roscommon 40 C2 Michigan,
N USA
Roseau 55 G4 prev. Charlotte Town.
Country capital (Dominica)
SW Dominica
Roseburg 46 B4 Oregon, NW USA
Rosenberg 49 G4 Texas, SW USA
Rosengarten 94 B3 Niedersachsen,
N Germany
Rosenheim 95 C6 Bayern,
S Germany
Rosia 93 H5 W Gibraltar
Rosia Bay 93 H5 *bay* SW Gibraltar
Roşiori de Vede 108 B5 Teleorman,
S Romania
Roslavl' 111 A5 Smolenskaya
Oblast', W Russian Federation
Rosmalen 86 C4 Noord-Brabant,
S Netherlands
Ross 151 B6 West Coast, South
Island, NZ
Rossano 97 E6 anc. Roscianum.
Calabria, SW Italy
Ross Ice Shelf 154 B4 *ice shelf*
Antarctica
Rosso 74 B3 Trarza, SW Mauritania
Rossosh' 111 B6 Voronezhskaya
Oblast', W Russian Federation
Ross Sea 154 B4 *sea* Antarctica
Rostak *see* Ar Rustāq
Rostock 94 C2 Mecklenburg-
Vorpommern, NE Germany
Rostov *see* Rostov-na-Donu

Rostov-na-Donu 111 B7 var. Rostov,
Eng. Rostov-on-Don. Rostovskaya
Oblast', SW Russian Federation
Rostov-on-Don *see* Rostov-na-
Donu
Roswell 48 D2 New Mexico,
SW USA
Rota 144 B1 *island* S Northern
Mariana Islands
Rothera 154 A2 *UK research station*
Antarctica
Rotorua 150 D3 Bay of Plenty,
North Island, NZ
Rotorua, Lake 150 D3 *lake* North
Island, NZ
Rotterdam 86 C4 Zuid-Holland,
SW Netherlands
Rottweil 95 B6 Baden-
Württemberg, S Germany
Rotuma 145 E4 *island* NW Fiji
Roubaix 90 C2 Nord, N France
Rouen 90 C3 anc. Rotomagus.
Seine-Maritime, N France
Round Rock 49 G3 Texas, SW USA
Rourkela *see* Rāulakela
Roussillon 91 C6 *cultural region*
S France
Rouyn-Noranda 38 D4 Quebec,
SE Canada
Rovaniemi 84 D3 Lappi,
N Finland
Rovigo 96 C2 Veneto, NE Italy
Rovinj 100 A3 It. Rovigno. Istra,
NW Croatia
Rovuma, Rio 79 F2 var. Ruvuma.
River Mozambique/Tanzania *see
also* Ruvuma
Rovuma, Rio *see* Ruvuma
Roxas City 139 E2 Panay Island,
C Philippines
Royale, Isle 40 B1 *island* Michigan,
N USA
Royan 91 B5 Charente-Maritime,
W France
Rozdol'ne 109 F4 Rus. Razdolnoye.
Respublika Krym, S Ukraine
Rožňava 99 D6 Ger. Rosenau,
Hung. Rozsnyó. Košický Kraj,
E Slovakia
Ruapehu, Mount 150 D4 *mountain*
North Island, NZ
Ruapuke Island 151 B8 *island*
SW NZ
Ruatoria 150 E3 Gisborne, North
Island, NZ
Ruawai 150 D2 Northland, North
Island, NZ
Rubizhne 109 H3 Rus. Rubezhnoye.
Luhans'ka Oblast', E Ukraine
Ruby Mountains 47 D5 *mountain
range* Nevada, W USA
Rucava 106 B3 Liepāja, SW Latvia
Rūd-e Hīrmand *see* Helmand,
Daryā-ye
Rūdişkės 107 B5 Trakai,
S Lithuania
Rudnik 104 E2 Varna, E Bulgaria
Rudny *see* Rudnyy
Rudnyy 114 C4 var. Rudny.
Kostanay, N Kazakhstan
Rudolf, Lake *see* Turkana, Lake
Rudolfswert *see* Novo Mesto
Rudzyensk 107 C6 Rus. Rudensk.
Minskaya Voblasts', C Belarus
Rufiji 73 C7 *river* E Tanzania
Rufino 64 C4 Santa Fe, C Argentina
Rugāji 106 D4 Balvi, E Latvia
Rügen 94 D2 *headland*
NE Germany
Ruggell 94 E1 N Liechtenstein
Ruhnu 106 C2 var. Ruhnu Saar, Swe.
Runö. *Island* SW Estonia
Ruhnu Saar *see* Ruhnu
Rūjiena 106 D3 Est. Ruhja, Ger.
Rujen. Valmiera, N Latvia
Rukwa, Lake 73 B7 *lake*
SE Tanzania
Rum *see* Rhum
Ruma 100 D3 Serbia, N Serbia and
Montenegro (Yugo.)
Rum Cay 54 D2 *island* C Bahamas
Rumia 98 C2 Pomorskie, N Poland
Rummah, Wādī ar *see* Rimah,
Wādī ar

Runanga 151 B5 West Coast, South Island, NZ
Runaway Bay 54 B4 C Jamaica
Rundu 78 C3 *var.* Runtu. Okavango, NE Namibia
Runö *see* Ruhnu
Runtu *see* Rundu
Ruoqiang 126 C3 *var.* Jo-ch'iang, *Uigh.* Charkhlik, Charkhliq, Qarkilik. Xinjiang Uygur Zizhiqu, NW China
Rupea 108 C4 *Ger.* Reps, *Hung.* Kőhalom; *prev.* Cohalm. Braşov, C Romania
Rupel 87 B5 *river* N Belgium
Rupert, Rivière de 38 D3 *river* Quebec, C Canada
Ruschuk *see* Ruse
Ruşçuk *see* Ruse
Ruse 104 D1 *var.* Ruschuk, Rustchuk, *Turk.* Ruşçuk. Ruse, N Bulgaria
Rus Krymskaya ASSR *see* Crimea
Russellville 42 A1 Arkansas, C USA
Russian Federation 112 D2 *var.* Russia, *Latv.* Krievija, *Rus.* Rossiyskaya Federatsiya. *Country* Asia/Europe

Russian Federation 112

Official name Russian Federation
Formation 1991
Capital Moscow
Population 144.7 million / 22 people per sq mile (8 people per sq km)
Total area 6,592,735 sq miles (17,075,200 sq km)
Languages Russian
Religions Russian Orthodox 75%, other 25%
Ethnic mix Russian 82%, Tatar 4%, Ukranian 3%, Chavash 1%, other 10%
Government Presidential democracy
Currency Rouble = 100 kopeks
Literacy rate 99%
Calorie consumption 2,917 kilocalories

Rustaq *see* Ar Rustāq
Rust'avi 117 G2 SE Georgia
Rustchuk *see* Ruse
Ruston 42 B2 Louisiana, S USA
Rutanzige I M, Lake *see* Edward, Lake
Rutba *see* Ar Ruţbah
Rutland 41 F2 Vermont, NE USA
Rutog 126 A4 *var.* Rutok. Xizang Zizhiqu, W China
Rutok *see* Rutog
Ruvuma 69 E5 *var.* Rio Rovuma. *River* Mozambique/Tanzania *see also* Rovuma, Rio
Ruvuma *see* Rovuma, Rio
Ruwenzori 77 E5 *mountain range* Uganda/Dem. Rep. Congo
Ruzhany 107 B6 *Rus.* Ruzhany. Brestskaya Voblasts', SW Belarus
Ružomberok 99 C5 *Ger.* Rosenberg, *Hung.* Rózsahegy. Žilinsky Kraj, N Slovakia
Rwanda 73 B6 *prev.* Ruanda. *Country* C Africa

Rwanda 73

Official name Republic of Rwanda
Formation 1962
Capital Kigali
Population 7.9 million / 777 people per sq mile (300 people per sq km)
Total area 10,169 sq miles (26,338 sq km)
Languages French, Kinyarwanda, Kiswahili, English
Religions Roman Catholic 65%, Traditional beliefs 25%, Protestant 9%, Muslim 1%
Ethnic mix Hutu 90%, Tutsi 9%, other (including Twa) 1%

Rwanda (continued)

Government Transitional regime
Currency Rwanda franc = 100 centimes
Literacy rate 66.8%
Calorie consumption 2,2077 kilocalories

Ryazan' 111 B5 Ryazanskaya Oblast', W Russian Federation
Rybinsk 110 B4 *prev.* Andropov. Yaroslavskaya Oblast', W Russian Federation
Rybnik 99 C5 Śląskie, S Poland
Rybnitsa *see* Rîbniţa
Ryde 148 E1 New South Wales, SE Australia
Ryki 98 D4 Lublin, E Poland
Rypin 98 C3 Kujawsko-pomorskie, C Poland
Ryssel *see* Lille
Rysy 99 C5 *mountain* S Poland
Ryukyu Islands 125 E3 *island group* SW Japan
Ryukyu Trench 125 F3 *var.* Nansei Syotō Trench. *Undersea feature* S East China Sea
Rzeszów 99 E5 Podkarpackie, SE Poland
Rzhev 110 B4 Tverskaya Oblast', W Russian Federation

S

Saale 94 C4 *river* C Germany
Saalfeld 95 C5 *var.* Saalfeld an der Saale. Thüringen, C Germany
Saalfeld an der Saale *see* Saalfeld
Saarbrücken 95 A6 *Fr.* Sarrebruck. Saarland, SW Germany
Sääre 106 C2 *var.* Sjar. Saaremaa, W Estonia
Saaremaa 106 C2 *Ger.* Oesel, Ösel; *prev.* Saare. *Island* W Estonia
Saariselkä 84 D2 *Lapp.* Suoločielgi. Lappi, N Finland
Sab' Ābār 118 C4 *var.* Sab'a Biyar, Sa'b Bi'ār. Ḥimş, C Syria
Sab'a Biyar *see* Sab' Ābār
Šabac 100 D3 Serbia, W Serbia and Montenegro (Yugo.)
Sabadell 93 G2 Cataluña, E Spain
Sabah 138 D3 *cultural region* Borneo, SE Asia
Sabanalarga 58 B1 Atlántico, N Colombia
Sabaneta 58 C1 Falcón, N Venezuela
Sab'atayn, Ramlat as 121 C6 *desert* C Yemen
Sabaya 61 F4 Oruro, S Bolivia
Sa'b Bi'ār *see* Sab' Ābār
Sabinas 51 E2 Coahuila de Zaragoza, NE Mexico
Sabinas Hidalgo 51 E2 Nuevo León, NE Mexico
Sabine River 49 H3 *river* Louisiana/Texas, SW USA
Sabkha *see* As Sabkhah
Sable, Cape 43 E5 *headland* Florida, SE USA
Sable Island 39 G4 *island* Nova Scotia, SE Canada
Şabyā 121 B6 Jīzān, SW Saudi Arabia
Sabzawar *see* Sabzevār
Sabzevār 120 D2 *var.* Sabzawar. Khorāsān, NE Iran
Sachsen 94 D4 *Eng.* Saxony, *Fr.* Saxe. *State* E Germany
Sachs Harbour 37 E2 Banks Island, Northwest Territories, N Canada
Sacramento 47 B5 *state capital* California, W USA
Sacramento Mountains 48 D2 *mountain range* New Mexico, SW USA
Sacramento River 47 B5 *river* California, W USA

Sacramento Valley 47 B5 *valley* California, W USA
Şa'dah 121 B6 NW Yemen
Sado 131 C5 *var.* Sadoga-shima. *Island* C Japan
Sadoga-shima *see* Sado
Safad *see* Zefat
Safed *see* Zefat
Säffle 85 B6 Värmland, C Sweden
Safford 48 C3 Arizona, SW USA
Safi 70 B2 W Morocco
Safid Kūh, Selseleh-ye 122 D4 *Eng.* Paropamisus Range. *Mountain range* W Afghanistan
Sagaing 136 B3 Sagaing, C Myanmar
Sagami-nada 131 D6 *inlet* SW Japan
Sagan *see* Żagań
Sāgar 134 D4 *prev.* Saugor. Madhya Pradesh, C India
Saghez *see* Saqqez
Saginaw 40 C3 Michigan, N USA
Saginaw Bay 40 D2 *lake bay* Michigan, N USA
Sagua la Grande 54 B2 Villa Clara, C Cuba
Sagunt *see* Sagunto
Sagunto 93 F3 *var.* Sagunt, *Ar.* Murviedro; *anc.* Saguntum. País Valenciano, E Spain
Saguntum *see* Sagunto
Sahara 68 B3 *desert* Libya/Algeria
Sahara el Gharbîya 72 B2 *var.* Aş Şaḥrā' al Gharbīyah, *Eng.* Western Desert. *Desert* C Egypt
Saharan Atlas *see* Atlas Saharien
Sahel 74 D3 *physical region* C Africa
Sāḥiliyah, Jibāl as 118 B3 *mountain range* NW Syria
Sāḥiwāl 134 C2 *prev.* Montgomery. Punjab, E Pakistan
şaḥrā' Rabyanāh *see* Rabyanāh, Ramlat
Saïda 119 A5 *var.* Şaydā, Sayida; *anc.* Sidon. W Lebanon
Saidpur 135 G3 *var.* Syedpur. Rajshahi, NW Bangladesh
Saigon *see* Hồ Chí Minh
Sai Hun *see* Syr Darya
Saimaa 85 E5 *lake* SE Finland
St Albans 89 E6 *anc.* Verulamium. E England, UK
Saint Albans 40 D5 West Virginia, NE USA
St Andrews 88 C4 E Scotland, UK
Saint Anna Trough *see* Svyataya Anna Trough
St.Ann's Bay 54 B4 C Jamaica
St.Anthony 39 G3 Newfoundland, Newfoundland and Labrador, SE Canada
Saint Augustine 43 E3 Florida, SE USA
St Austell 89 C7 SW England, UK
St-Brieuc 90 A3 Côtes d'Armor, NW France
St. Catharines 38 D5 Ontario, S Canada
St-Chamond 91 D5 Loire, E France
St.Clair, Lake 40 D3 *Fr.* Lac à L'Eau Claire. Lake Canada/USA
St-Claude 91 D5 *anc.* Condate. Jura, E France
Saint Cloud 45 F2 Minnesota, N USA
St Croix 55 F3 *island* S Virgin Islands (US)
Saint Croix River 40 A2 *river* Minnesota/Wisconsin, N USA
St David's Island 42 B5 *island* E Bermuda
St-Denis 79 G4 *dependent territory capital* (Réunion) NW Réunion
St-Dié 90 E4 Vosges, NE France
St-Égrève 91 D5 Isère, E France
Saintes 91 B5 *anc.* Mediolanum. Charente-Maritime, W France
St-Étienne 91 D5 Loire, E France
St-Flour 91 C5 Cantal, C France
Saint Gall *see* Sankt Gallen
St-Gaudens 91 B6 Haute-Garonne, S France
St George 42 B4 N Bermuda
Saint George 149 D5 Queensland, E Australia
Saint George 44 A5 Utah, W USA
St.George's 55 G5 *country capital* (Grenada) SW Grenada

St-Georges 59 H3 E French Guiana
St-Georges 39 E4 Quebec, SE Canada
St George's Channel 89 B6 *channel* Ireland/Wales, UK
St George's Island 42 B4 *island* E Bermuda
Saint Helena 69 B6 UK *dependent territory* C Atlantic Ocean
St.Helena Bay 78 B5 *bay* SW South Africa
St Helier 89 D8 *dependent territory capital* (Jersey) S Jersey, Channel Islands
Saint Ignace 40 C2 Michigan, N USA
St-Jean, Lac 39 E4 *lake* Quebec, SE Canada
Saint Joe River 46 D2 *river* Idaho, NW USA
Saint John 41 H1 *river* Canada/USA
Saint John 39 F4 New Brunswick, SE Canada
St John's 55 G3 *country capital* (Antigua and Barbuda) Antigua, Antigua and Barbuda
St.John's 39 H3 Newfoundland, Newfoundland and Labrador, E Canada
Saint Joseph 45 F4 Missouri, C USA
St Julian's 102 B5 N Malta
St Kilda 88 A3 *island* NW Scotland, UK
Saint Kitts and Nevis 55 F3 *var.* Saint Christopher-Nevis. *Country* E West Indies

Saint Kitts & Nevis 55

Official name Federation of Saint Christopher and Nevis
Formation 1983
Capital Basseterre
Population 41,000 / 407 people per sq mile (157 people per sq km)
Total area 101 sq miles (261 sq km)
Languages English, English Creole
Religions Anglican 33%, Methodist 29%, Moravian 9%, Roman Catholic 7%, other 22%
Ethnic mix Black 94%, Mixed 3%, Other and Amerindian 2%, other 1%
Government Parliamentary democracy
Currency Eastern Caribbean dollar = 100 cents
Literacy rate 90%
Calorie consumption 2,685 kilocalories

St-Laurent-du-Maroni 59 H3 *var.* St-Laurent. NW French Guiana
St.Lawrence 39 E4 *Fr.* Fleuve St-Laurent. *River* Canada/USA
St.Lawrence, Gulf of 39 F3 *gulf* NW Atlantic Ocean
Saint Lawrence Island 36 B2 *island* Alaska, USA
St-Lô 90 B3 *anc.* Briovera, Laudus. Manche, N France
St-Louis 90 E4 Haut-Rhin, NE France
Saint Louis 45 G4 Missouri, C USA
Saint Louis 74 B3 NW Senegal
Saint Lucia 55 E1 *country* SE West Indies

Saint Lucia 55

Official name Saint Lucia
Formation 1979
Capital Castries
Population 156,300 / 653 people per sq mile (252 people per sq km)
Total area 239 sq miles (620 sq km)
Languages English, French Creole
Religions Roman Catholic 90%, other 10%
Ethnic mix Black 90%, Mulatto 6%, Asian 3%, White 1%
Government Parliamentary democracy
Currency Eastern Caribbean dollar = 100 cents

Saint Lucia (continued)

Literacy rate 82%
Calorie consumption 2,838 kilocalories

Saint Lucia Channel 55 H4 *channel* Martinique/Saint Lucia
St-Malo 90 B3 Ille-et-Vilaine, NW France
St-Malo, Golfe de 90 A3 *gulf* NW France
St Matthew's Island *see* Zadetkyi Kyun
St.Matthias Group 144 B3 *island group* NE PNG
St-Maur-des-Fossés 90 E2 Val-de-Marne, N France
St.Moritz 95 B7 *Ger.* Sankt Moritz, *Rmsch.* San Murezzan. Graubünden, SE Switzerland
St-Nazaire 90 A4 Loire-Atlantique, NW France
St-Omer 90 C2 Pas-de-Calais, N France
Saint Paul 45 F2 *state capital* Minnesota, N USA
St-Paul, Île 141 C6 *var.* St.Paul Island. *Island* NE French Southern and Antarctic Territories
St Peter Port 89 D8 *dependent territory capital* (Guernsey) C Guernsey, Channel Islands
Saint Petersburg *see* Sankt-Peterburg
Saint Petersburg 43 E4 Florida, SE USA
St-Pierre and Miquelon 35 E5 *Fr.* Îles St-Pierre et Miquelon. *French territorial collectivity* NE North America
St-Quentin 90 C3 Aisne, N France
Saint Vincent 55 G4 *island* N Saint Vincent and the Grenadines
Saint Vincent and the Grenadines 55 H4 *country* SE West Indies

Saint Vincent & The Grenadines 55

Official name Saint Vincent and the Grenadines
Formation 1979
Capital Kingston
Population 115,500 / 769 people per sq mile (297 people per sq km)
Total area 150 sq miles (389 sq km)
Languages English, English Creole
Religions Anglican 42%, Methodist 20%, Roman Catholic 19%, other 19%
Ethnic mix Black 66%, Mulatto 19%, Asian 6%, White 4%, other 5%
Government Parliamentary democracy
Currency Eastern Caribbean dollar = 100 cents
Literacy rate 82%
Calorie consumption 2,579 kilocalories

Saint Vincent Passage 55 H4 *passage* Saint Lucia/Saint Vincent and the Grenadines
Saipan 142 B1 *island country capital* (Northern Mariana Islands) S Northern Mariana Islands
Sajama, Nevado 61 F4 *mountain* W Bolivia
Sájószentpéter 99 D6 Borsod-Abaúj-Zemplén, NE Hungary
Sakākah 120 B4 Al Jawf, NW Saudi Arabia
Sakakawea, Lake 44 D1 *reservoir* North Dakota, N USA
Sakata 130 D4 Yamagata, Honshū, C Japan
Sakhalin *see* Sakhalin, Ostrov
Sakhalin, Ostrov 115 G4 *var.* Sakhalin. *Island* SE Russian Federation
Sakhon Nakhon *see* Sakon Nakhon
Şäki 117 G2 *Rus.* Sheki; *prev.* Nukha. NW Azerbaijan

Sakishima-shotō 130 A3 *var.* Sakisima Syotö. *Island group* SW Japan
Sakisima Syotö *see* Sakishima-shotō
Sakiz *see* Saqqez
Sakiz-Adasi *see* Chíos
Sakon Nakhon 136 D4 *var.* Muang Sakon Nakhon, Sakhon Nakhon. Sakon Nakhon, E Thailand
Saky 109 F5 *Rus.* Saki. Respublika Krym, S Ukraine
Sal 74 A3 *island* Ilhas de Barlavento, NE Cape Verde
Sala 85 C6 Västmanland, C Sweden
Salacgrīva 106 C3 Est. Salatsi. Limbaži, N Latvia
Sala Consilina 97 D5 Campania, S Italy
Salado, Río 64 C3 *river* C Argentina
Salado, Río 62 D5 *river* E Argentina
Şalālah 121 D6 SW Oman
Salamá 52 B2 Baja Verapaz, C Guatemala
Salamanca 92 D2 *anc.* Helmantica, Salmantica. Castilla-León, NW Spain
Salamanca 64 B4 Coquimbo, C Chile
Salamīyah 118 B3 *var.* As Salamīyah. Ḥamāh, W Syria
Salang *see* Phuket
Salantai 106 B3 Kretinga, NW Lithuania
Salavan 137 D5 *var.* Saravan, Saravane. Salavan, S Laos
Salavat 111 D6 Respublika Bashkortostan, W Russian Federation
Sala y Gomez 153 F4 *island* Chile, E Pacific Ocean
Sala y Gomez Fracture Zone *see* Sala y Gomez Ridge
Sala y Gomez Ridge 153 G4 *var.* Sala y Gomez Fracture Zone. *Tectonic feature* SE Pacific Ocean
Šalčininkai 107 C5 Šalčininkai, SE Lithuania
Saldus 106 B3 *Ger.* Frauenburg. Saldus, W Latvia
Sale 149 C7 Victoria, SE Australia
Salé 70 C2 NW Morocco
Salekhard 114 D3 *prev.* Obdorsk. Yamalo-Nenetskiy Avtonomnyy Okrug, N Russian Federation
Salem 46 B3 *state capital* Oregon, NW USA
Salem 132 C2 Tamil Nādu, SE India
Salerno 97 D5 *anc.* Salernum. Campania, S Italy
Salerno, Golfo di 97 C5 *Eng.* Gulf of Salerno. *Gulf* S Italy
Salihorsk 107 C7 *Rus.* Soligorsk. Minskaya Voblasts', S Belarus
Salima 79 E2 Central, C Malawi
Salina 45 F5 Kansas, C USA
Salina Cruz 51 F5 Oaxaca, SE Mexico
Salinas 47 B6 California, W USA
Salinas 60 A2 Guayas, W Ecuador
Salisbury 89 D7 *var.* New Sarum. S England, UK
Sallyana *see* Salyan
Salmon River 46 D3 *river* Idaho, NW USA
Salmon River Mountains 46 D3 *mountain range* Idaho, NW USA
Salo 85 D6 Länsi-Suomi, W Finland
Salon-de-Provence 91 D6 Bouches-du-Rhône, SE France
Salonta 108 A3 *Hung.* Nagyszalonta. Bihor, W Romania
Sal'sk 111 B7 Rostovskaya Oblast', SW Russian Federation
Salt *see* As Salṭ
Salta 64 C2 Salta, NW Argentina
Saltash 89 C7 SW England, UK
Saltillo 51 E3 Coahuila de Zaragoza, NE Mexico
Salt Lake City 44 B4 *state capital* Utah, W USA
Salto 64 D4 Salto, N Uruguay
Salton Sea 47 D8 *lake* California, W USA
Salvador 63 G3 *prev.* São Salvador. Bahia, E Brazil
Salween 124 C2 *Bur.* Thanlwin, *Chin.* Nu Chiang, Nu Jiang. *River* SE Asia

Salyan 135 E3 *var.* Sallyana. Mid Western, W Nepal
Salzburg 95 D6 *anc.* Juvavum. Salzburg, N Austria
Salzgitter 94 C4 *prev.* Watenstedt-Salzgitter. Niedersachsen, C Germany
Salzwedel 94 C3 Sachsen-Anhalt, N Germany
Šamac *see* Bosanski Šamac
Samakhixai 137 E5 *var.* Attapu, Attopeu. Attapu, S Laos
Samalayuca 50 C1 Chihuahua, N Mexico
Samar 139 F2 *island* C Philippines
Samara 114 B3 *prev.* Kuybyshev. Samarskaya Oblast', W Russian Federation
Samarang *see* Semarang
Samarinda 138 D4 Borneo, C Indonesia
Samarqand 123 E2 *Rus.* Samarkand. Samrqand Wiloyati, C Uzbekistan
Samawa *see* As Samāwah
Sambalpur 135 F4 Orissa, E India
Sambava 79 G2 Antsiraňana, NE Madagascar
Sambir 108 B2 *Rus.* Sambor. L'vivs'ka Oblast', NW Ukraine
Sambre 90 D2 *river* Belgium/France
Samfya 78 D2 Luapula, N Zambia
Saminatal 94 E2 *valley* Austria/Liechtenstein
Samnān *see* Semnān
Sam Neua *see* Xam Nua
Samoa 145 E4 *var.* Sāmoa; *prev.* Western Samoa. *Country* W Polynesia

Samoa 145

Official name Independent State of Samoa
Formation 1962
Capital Apia
Population 159,000 / 144 people per sq mile (56 people per sq km)
Total area 1,104 sq miles (2,860 sq km)
Languages Samoan, English
Religions Christian 99%, other 1%
Ethnic mix Polynesian 90%, Euronesian 9%, other 1%
Government Parliamentary democracy
Currency Tala = 100 sene
Literacy rate 80.2%
Calorie consumption not available

Samoa Basin 143 E3 *undersea feature* W Pacific Ocean
Samobor 100 A2 Zagreb, N Croatia
Sámos 105 E6 *prev.* Limín Vathéos. Sámos, Dodekánisos, Greece, Aegean Sea
Sámos 105 D6 *island* Dodekánisos, Greece, Aegean Sea
Samosch *see* Someş
Samothráki 104 C4 *anc.* Samothrace. *Island* NE Greece
Samothráki 104 D4 Samothráki, NE Greece
Sampit 138 C4 Borneo, C Indonesia
Samsun 116 D2 *anc.* Amisus. Samsun, N Turkey
Samtredia 117 F2 W Georgia
Samui, Ko 137 C6 *island* SW Thailand
Samut Prakan 137 C5 *var.* Muang Samut Prakan, Paknam. Samut Prakan, C Thailand
San 99 E5 *river* SE Poland
San 74 D3 Ségou, C Mali
Şan'ā' 121 B6 *Eng.* Sana. *Country capital* (Yemen) W Yemen
Sana 100 B3 *river* NW Bosnia and Herzegovina
Sana *see* Şan'ā'
Sanae 154 B2 *South African research station* Antarctica
Sanaga 77 B5 *river* C Cameroon
San Ambrosio, Isla 57 A5 *Eng.* San Ambrosio Island. *Island* W Chile
Sanandaj 120 C3 *prev.* Sinneh. Kordestān, W Iran

San Andrés, Isla de 53 F3 *island* NW Colombia
San Andrés Tuxtla 51 F4 *var.* Tuxtla. Veracruz-Llave, E Mexico
San Angelo 49 F3 Texas, SW USA
San Antonio 49 F4 Texas, SW USA
San Antonio 52 B2 Toledo, S Belize
San Antonio 64 B4 Valparaíso, C Chile
San Antonio Oeste 65 C5 Río Negro, E Argentina
San Antonio River 49 G4 *river* Texas, SW USA
Sanāw 121 C6 *var.* Sanaw. NE Yemen
San Benedicto, Isla 50 B4 *island* W Mexico
San Benito 52 B1 Petén, N Guatemala
San Benito 49 G5 Texas, SW USA
San Bernardino 47 C7 California, W USA
San Blas 50 C3 Sinaloa, C Mexico
San Blas, Cape 42 D3 *headland* Florida, SE USA
San Blas, Cordillera de 53 G4 *mountain range* NE Panama
San Carlos *see* Quesada
San Carlos 48 B2 Arizona, SW USA
San Carlos 52 D4 Río San Juan, S Nicaragua
San Carlos de Bariloche 65 B5 Río Negro, SW Argentina
San Carlos del Zulia 58 C2 Zulia, W Venezuela
San Clemente Island 47 B8 *island* Channel Islands, California, W USA
San Cristóbal 144 C4 *var.* Makira. *Island* SE Solomon Islands
San Cristóbal *see* San Cristóbal de Las Casas
San Cristóbal 58 C2 Táchira, W Venezuela
San Cristóbal de Las Casas 51 G5 *var.* San Cristóbal. Chiapas, SE Mexico
San Cristóbal, Isla 60 B5 *var.* Chatham Island. *Island* Galapagos Islands, Ecuador, E Pacific Ocean
Sancti Spíritus 54 B2 Sancti Spíritus, C Cuba
Sandakan 138 D3 Sabah, East Malaysia
Sandanski 104 C3 *prev.* Sveti Vrach. Blagoevgrad, SW Bulgaria
Sanday 88 D2 *island* NE Scotland, UK
Sanders 48 C2 Arizona, SW USA
Sand Hills 44 D3 *mountain range* Nebraska, C USA
San Diego 47 C8 California, W USA
Sandnes 85 A6 Rogaland, S Norway
Sandomierz 98 D4 *Rus.* Sandomir. Świętokrzyskie, C Poland
Sandoway 136 A4 Arakan State, W Myanmar
Sandpoint 46 C1 Idaho, NW USA
Sand Springs 49 G1 Oklahoma, C USA
Sandusky 40 D3 Ohio, N USA
Sandvika 85 A6 Akershus, S Norway
Sandviken 85 C6 Gävleborg, C Sweden
Sandy Bay 93 H5 *bay* E Gibraltar
Sandy City 44 B4 Utah, W USA
Sandy Lake 38 B3 *lake* Ontario, C Canada
San Esteban 52 D2 Olancho, C Honduras
San Felipe 58 D1 Yaracuy, NW Venezuela
San Felipe de Puerto Plata *see* Puerto Plata
San Félix, Isla 57 A5 *Eng.* San Felix Island. *Island* W Chile
San Fernando 92 C5 *prev.* Isla de León. Andalucía, S Spain
San Fernando 58 D2 *var.* San Fernando de Apure. Apure, C Venezuela
San Fernando 46 D1 California, W USA
San Fernando 55 H5 Trinidad, Trinidad and Tobago

San Fernando de Apure see San
Fernando
**San Fernando del Valle de
Catamarca** 64 C3 var. Catamarca.
Catamarca, NW Argentina
San Fernando de Monte Cristi see
Monte Cristi
San Francisco 47 B6 California,
W USA
San Francisco del Oro 50 C2
Chihuahua, N Mexico
San Francisco de Macorís 55 E3
C Dominican Republic
San Gabriel 60 B1 Carchi,
N Ecuador
San Gabriel Mountains 46 E1
mountain range California, W USA
Sangir, Kepulauan 139 F3 var.
Kepulauan Sangihe. Island group
N Indonesia
Sāngli 132 B1 Mahārāshtra,
W India
Sangmélima 77 B5 Sud,
S Cameroon
Sangre de Cristo Mountains 48 D1
mountain range Colorado/New
Mexico, C USA
San Ignacio 52 B1 prev. Cayo,
El Cayo. Cayo, W Belize
San Ignacio 50 B2 Baja California
Sur, W Mexico
San Ignacio 61 F3 Beni, N Bolivia
San Joaquin Valley 47 B7 valley
California, W USA
San Jorge, Golfo 65 C6 var. Gulf of
San Jorge. Gulf S Argentina
San Jorge, Gulf of see San Jorge,
Golfo
San José 52 B1 San José del Guaviare
San José 47 B6 California, W USA
San José 52 B3 var. Puerto San José.
Escuintla, S Guatemala
San José 61 G3 var. San José de
Chiquitos. Santa Cruz, E Bolivia
San José 53 E4 country capital (Costa
Rica) San José, C Costa Rica
San José de Chiquitos see San José
San José de Cúcuta see Cúcuta
San José del Guaviare 58 C4 var.
San José. Guaviare, S Colombia
San Juan 55 F3 dependent territory
capital (Puerto Rico) NE Puerto
Rico
San Juan see San Juan de los
Morros
San Juan 64 B4 San Juan,
W Argentina
San Juan Bautista 64 D3 Misiones,
S Paraguay
San Juan Bautista Tuxtepec see
Tuxtepec
San Juan de Alicante 93 F4 País
Valenciano, E Spain
San Juan del Norte 53 E4 var.
Greytown. Río San Juan,
SE Nicaragua
San Juan de los Morros 58 D2 var.
San Juan. Guárico, N Venezuela
San Juanito, Isla 50 C4 island
C Mexico
San Juan Mountains 48 D1
mountain range Colorado, C USA
San Juan River 48 C1 river
Colorado/Utah, W USA
San Julián see Puerto San Julián
Sankt Gallen 95 B7 var. St.Gallen,
Eng. Saint Gall, Fr. St-Gall. Sankt
Gallen, NE Switzerland
Sankt-Peterburg 110 B4 prev.
Leningrad, Petrograd, Eng. Saint
Petersburg, Fin. Pietari.
Leningradskaya Oblast',
NW Russian Federation
Sankt Pölten 95 E6
Niederösterreich, N Austria
Sankuru 77 D6 river C Dem. Rep.
Congo
Şanlıurfa 117 E4 prev. Sanli Urfa,
Urfa, anc. Edessa. Şanlıurfa,
S Turkey
San Lorenzo 60 A1 Esmeraldas,
N Ecuador
San Lorenzo 61 G5 Tarija, S Bolivia
San Lorenzo, Isla 60 C4 island
W Peru
Sanlúcar de Barrameda 92 C5
Andalucía, S Spain

San Luis 50 A1 var. San Luis Río
Colorado. Sonora, NW Mexico
San Luis 52 B2 Petén,
NE Guatemala
San Luis 64 C4 San Luis,
C Argentina
San Luis Obispo 47 B7 California,
W USA
San Luis Potosí 51 E3 San Luis
Potosí, C Mexico
San Luis Río Colorado see San
Luis
San Marcos 52 A2 San Marcos,
W Guatemala
San Marcos 49 G4 Texas, SW USA
San Marino 96 D1 Country
S Europe

San Marino 96

Official name Republic of San
Marino
Formation 1631
Capital San Marino
Population 26,900 / 1,138 people
per sq mile (440 people per sq km)
Total area 24 sq miles (61 sq km)
Languages Italian
Religions Roman Catholic 93%,
other and non-religious 7%
Ethnic mix Sammarinese 80%,
Italian 19%, other 1%
Government Parliamentary
democracy
Currency Euro (Lira until 2002)
Literacy rate 99%
Calorie consumption not available

San Marino 96 E1 country capital
(San Marino) C San Marino
San Martín 154 A2 Argentinian
research station Antarctica
San Mateo 59 E2 Anzoátegui,
NE Venezuela
San Matías 61 H3 Santa Cruz,
E Bolivia
San Matías, Golfo 65 C5 var. Gulf
of San Matías. Gulf E Argentina
San Matías, Gulf of see San Matías,
Golfo
Sanmenxia 128 C4 var. Shan Xian.
Henan, C China
Sânmiclăuş Mare see Sânnicolau
Mare
San Miguel 50 D2 Coahuila de
Zaragoza, N Mexico
San Miguel 52 C3 San Miguel,
SE El Salvador
San Miguel de Ibarra see Ibarra
San Miguel de Tucumán 64 C3 var.
Tucumán. Tucumán, N Argentina
San Miguelito 53 G4 Panamá,
C Panama
San Miguel, Río 61 G3 river E Bolivia
Sannär see Sennar
Sânnicolaul-Mare see Sânnicolau
Mare
Sânnicolau Mare 108 A4 var.
Sânnicolaul-Mare, Hung.
Nagyszentmiklós; prev.
Sânmiclăuş Mare, Sînnicolau
Mare. Timiş, W Romania
Sanok 99 E5 Podkarpackie,
SE Poland
San Pablo 61 F5 Potosí, S Bolivia
San Pedro 50 D3 var. San Pedro de
las Colonias. Coahuila de
Zaragoza, NE Mexico
San Pedro 52 C1 Corozal, NE Belize
San-Pédro 74 D5 S Côte d'Ivoire
San Pedro de la Cueva 50 C2
Sonora, NW Mexico
San Pedro de las Colonias see San
Pedro
San Pedro de Lloc 60 B3 La
Libertad, NW Peru
San Pedro Mártir, Sierra 50 A1
mountain range NW Mexico
San Pedro Sula 52 C2 Cortés,
NW Honduras
San Rafael 64 B4 Mendoza,
W Argentina
San Rafael Mountains 47 C7
mountain range California, W USA
San Ramón de la Nueva Orán 64
C2 Salta, N Argentina

San Remo 96 A3 Liguria, NW Italy
San Salvador 52 B3 country capital
(El Salvador) San Salvador,
SW El Salvador
San Salvador de Jujuy 64 C2 var.
Jujuy. Jujuy, N Argentina
San Salvador, Isla 60 A4 prev.
Watlings Island. Island E Bahamas
Sansanné-Mango 75 E4 var. Mango.
N Togo
Sansepolcro 96 C3 Toscana, C Italy
San Severo 97 D5 Puglia, SE Italy
Santa Ana 61 F3 Beni, N Bolivia
Santa Ana 46 D2 California, W USA
Santa Ana 52 B3 Santa Ana,
NW El Salvador
Santa Ana Mountains 46 E2
mountain range California, W USA
Santa Barbara 47 C7 California,
W USA
Santa Barbara 50 C2 Chihuahua,
N Mexico
Santa Catalina Island 47 B8 island
Channel Islands, California,
W USA
Santa Catarina 63 E5 off. Estado de
Santa Catarina. State S Brazil
Santa Clara 54 B2 Villa Clara,
C Cuba
Santa Clarita 46 D1 California,
W USA
Santa Comba 92 B1 Galicia,
NW Spain
Santa Cruz 61 G4 var. Santa Cruz de
la Sierra. Santa Cruz, C Bolivia
Santa Cruz 47 B6 California, W USA
Santa Cruz 76 D2 São Tomé, C Sao
Tome and Principe
Santa Cruz Barillas see Barillas
Santa Cruz de la Sierra see Santa
Cruz
Santa Cruz del Quiché 52 B2
Quiché, W Guatemala
Santa Cruz de Tenerife 70 A3
Tenerife, Islas Canarias, Spain,
NE Atlantic Ocean
Santa Cruz, Isla 60 B5 var.
Indefatigable Island, Isla Chávez.
Island Galapagos Islands,
Ecuador, E Pacific Ocean
Santa Cruz Islands 144 D3 island
group E Solomon Islands
Santa Cruz, Río 65 B7 river
S Argentina
Santa Elena 52 B1 Cayo, W Belize
Santa Fe 48 D1 state capital New
Mexico, SW USA
Santa Fe 64 C4 Santa Fe, C Argentina
Santa Genoveva 50 B3 mountain
W Mexico
Santa Isabel 144 C3 var. Bughotu.
Island N Solomon Islands
Santa Lucia Range 47 B7 mountain
range California, W USA
Santa Margarita, Isla 50 B3 island
W Mexico
Santa Maria 92 A5 island Azores,
Portugal, NE Atlantic Ocean
Santa Maria 47 B7 California,
W USA
Santa Maria 63 E5 Rio Grande do
Sul, S Brazil
Santa María, Isla 60 A5 var. Isla
Floreana, Charles Island. Island
Galapagos Islands, Ecuador,
E Pacific Ocean
Santa Marta 58 B1 Magdalena,
N Colombia
Santa Monica 46 D1 California,
W USA
Santana 76 E2 São Tomé, S Sao
Tome and Principe
Santander 92 D1 Cantabria,
N Spain
Santanilla, Islas 53 E1 Eng. Swan
Islands. Island NE Honduras
Santarém 92 B3 anc. Scalabis.
Santarém, W Portugal
Santarém 63 E2 Pará, N Brazil
Santa Rosa see Santa Rosa de
Copán
Santa Rosa 47 B6 California,
W USA
Santa Rosa 64 C4 La Pampa,
C Argentina
Santa Rosa de Copán 52 C2 var.
Santa Rosa. Copán, W Honduras

Santa Rosa Island 47 B8 island
California, W USA
Sant Carles de la Ràpida see Sant
Carles de la Ràpita
Sant Carles de la Ràpita 93 F3 var.
Sant Carles de la Rápida.
Cataluña, NE Spain
Santiago 64 B4 var. Gran Santiago.
Country capital (Chile) Santiago,
C Chile
Santiago 92 B1 var. Santiago de
Compostela, Eng. Compostella;
anc. Campus Stellae. Galicia,
NW Spain
Santiago 55 E3 var. Santiago de los
Caballeros. N Dominican
Republic
Santiago 74 A3 var. São Tiago. Island
Ilhas de Sotavento, S Cape Verde
Santiago see Santiago de Cuba
Santiago de Compostela see
Santiago
Santiago de Cuba 54 C3 var.
Santiago. Santiago de Cuba,
E Cuba
Santiago de Guayaquil see
Guayaquil
Santiago del Estero 64 C3 Santiago
del Estero, C Argentina
Santiago de los Caballeros see
Santiago
Santiago Pinotepa Nacional see
Pinotepa Nacional
Santiago, Río 60 B2 river N Peru
Santi Quaranta see Sarandë
Santissima Trinidad see Chilung
Sant Julià de Lòria 91 A8
SW Andorra
Santo see Espiritu Santo
Santo Antão 74 A2 island Ilhas de
Barlavento, N Cape Verde
Santo António 76 E1 Príncipe,
N Sao Tome and Principe
Santo Domingo 55 D3 prev. Ciudad
Trujillo. Country capital
(Dominican Republic)
SE Dominican Republic
Santo Domingo de los Colorados
60 B1 Pichincha, NW Ecuador
Santo Domingo Tehuantepec see
Tehuantepec
Santos 63 F4 São Paulo, S Brazil
Santos Plateau 57 D5 undersea
feature SW Atlantic Ocean
Santo Tomé 64 D3 Corrientes,
NE Argentina
San Valentín, Cerro 65 A6 mountain
S Chile
San Vicente 52 C3 San Vicente,
C El Salvador
São Francisco, Rio 63 F3 river
E Brazil
Sao Hill 73 C7 Iringa,
S Tanzania
São João da Madeira 92 B2 Aveiro,
N Portugal
São Jorge 92 A5 island Azores,
Portugal, NE Atlantic Ocean
São Luís 63 F2 state capital
Maranhão, NE Brazil
São Mandol see São Manuel, Rio
São Manuel, Rio 63 E3 var. São
Mandol, Teles Pirés. River C Brazil
São Marcos, Baía de 63 F1 bay
N Brazil
São Miguel 92 A5 island Azores,
Portugal, NE Atlantic Ocean
Saona, Isla 55 E3 island
SE Dominican Republic
Saône 91 D5 river E France
São Nicolau 74 A3 Eng. Saint
Nicholas. Island Ilhas de
Barlavento, N Cape Verde
São Paulo 63 E4 off. Estado de São
Paulo. State S Brazil
São Paulo 63 E4 state capital São
Paulo, S Brazil
São Paulo de Loanda see Luanda
São Pedro do Rio Grande do Sul
see Rio Grande
São Roque, Cabo de 63 G2 headland
E Brazil
São Salvador see M'Banza Congo
São Salvador do Congo see
M'Banza Congo
São Tiago see Santiago

São Tomé *76 E2 Eng.* Saint Thomas. *Island* S Sao Tome and Principe
São Tomé *77 A5 country capital* (Sao Tome and Principe) São Tomé, S Sao Tome and Principe
Sao Tome and Principe *76 D1 Country* E Atlantic Ocean

Sao Tome & Principe 76

Official name Democratic Republic of São Tomé and Príncipe
Formation 1975
Capital São Tomé
Population 159,900 / 414 people per sq mile (160 people per sq km)
Total area 386 sq miles (1,001 sq km)
Languages Portuguese, Portuguese Creole
Religions Roman Catholic 84%, other Christian 16%
Ethnic mix Black 90%, Portuguese and Creole 10%
Government Multiparty republic
Currency Dobra = 100 centimos
Literacy rate 75%
Calorie consumption 2,390 kilocalories

São Tomé, Pico de *76 D2 mountain* São Tomé, S Sao Tome and Principe
São Vicente, Cabo de *92 B5 Eng.* Cape Saint Vincent, *Port.* Cabo de São Vicente. *Headland* S Portugal
São Vincente *74 A3 Eng.* Saint Vincent. *Island* Ilhas de Barlavento, N Cape Verde
Sápai *see* Sápes
Sapele *75 F5* Delta, S Nigeria
Sápes *104 D3 var.* Sápai. Anatolikí Makedonía kai Thráki, NE Greece
Sapir *see* Sappir
Sa Pobla *93 G3 var.* La Puebla. Mallorca, Spain, W Mediterranean Sea
Sappir *119 B7 var.* Sapir. Southern, S Israel
Sapporo *130 D2* Hokkaidō, NE Japan
Sapri *97 D6* Campania, S Italy
Sapulpa *49 G1* Oklahoma, C USA
Saqqez *120 C2 var.* Saghez, Saqi, Saqqiz. Kordestān, NW Iran
Saqqiz *see* Saqqez
Sara Buri *137 C5 var.* Saraburi. Saraburi, C Thailand
Saragt *see* Serakhs
Saraguro *60 B2* Loja, S Ecuador
Sarajevo *100 C4 country capital* (Bosnia and Herzegovina). Federacija Bosna I Hercegovina, SE Bosnia and Herzegovina
Sarakhs *120 E2* Khorāsān, NE Iran
Saraktash *111 D6* Orenburgskaya Oblast', W Russian Federation
Saran' *114 C4 Kaz.* Saran. Karaganda, C Kazakhstan
Saranda *see* Sarandë
Sarandë *101 C7 var.* Saranda, *It.* Porto Edda; *prev.* Santi Quaranta. Vlorë, S Albania
Saransk *111 C5* Respublika Mordoviya, W Russian Federation
Sarasota *43 E4* Florida, SE USA
Saratov *114 B3* Saratovskaya Oblast', W Russian Federation
Saravan *see* Salavan
Saravane *see* Salavan
Sarawak *138 D3 cultural region* Borneo, SE Asia
Sarawak and Sabah (North Borneo) and Singapore *see* Malaysia
Sarcelles *90 D1* Val-d'Oise, N France
Sardegna *97 A5 Eng.* Sardinia. *Island* Italy, C Mediterranean Sea
Sardinia *see* Sardegna
Sarera, Teluk *see* Cenderawasih, Teluk
Sargasso Sea *66 B4 sea* W Atlantic Ocean
Sargodha *134 C2* Punjab, NE Pakistan

Sarh *76 C4 prev.* Fort-Archambault. Moyen-Chari, S Chad
Sārī *120 D2 var.* Sari, Sāri. Māzandarān, N Iran
Saría *105 E7 island* SE Greece
Sarıkamış *117 F3* Kars, NE Turkey
Sarikol Range *123 G3 Rus.* Sarykol'skiy Khrebet. *Mountain range* China/Tajikistan
Sark *89 D8 Fr.* Sercq. *Island* Channel Islands
Şarkışla *116 D3* Sivas, C Turkey
Sarmiento *65 B6* Chubut, S Argentina
Sarnia *38 C5* Ontario, S Canada
Sarny *108 C1* Rivnens'ka Oblast', NW Ukraine
Sarochyna *107 D5 Rus.* Sorochino. Vitsyebskaya Voblasts', N Belarus
Sarpsborg *85 B6* Østfold, S Norway
Sartène *91 E7* Corse, France, C Mediterranean Sea
Sarthe *90 B4 cultural region* N France
Sárti *104 C4* Kentrikí Makedonía, N Greece
Saruhan *see* Manisa
Saryesik-Atyrau, Peski *123 G1 desert* E Kazakhstan
Sary-Tash *123 F2* Oshskaya Oblast', SW Kyrgyzstan
Sasebo *131 A7* Nagasaki, Kyūshū, SW Japan
Saskatchewan *37 F5 river* Manitoba/Saskatchewan, C Canada
Saskatchewan *37 F5 province* SW Canada
Saskatoon *37 F5* Saskatchewan, S Canada
Sasovo *111 B5* Ryazanskaya Oblast', W Russian Federation
Sassandra *74 D5 var.* Ibo, Sassandra Fleuve. *River* S Côte d'Ivoire
Sassandra *74 D5* S Côte d'Ivoire
Sassandra Fleuve *see* Sassandra
Sassari *97 A5* Sardegna, Italy, C Mediterranean Sea
Sassenheim *86 C3* Zuid-Holland, W Netherlands
Sassnitz *94 D2* Mecklenburg-Vorpommern, NE Germany
Sátoraljaújhely *99 D6* Borsod-Abaúj-Zemplén, NE Hungary
Sātpura Range *134 D4 mountain range* C India
Satsunan-shotō *130 A3 var.* Satunan Syotō. *Island group* SW Japan
Sattanen *84 D3* Lappi, NE Finland
Satu Mare *108 B3 Ger.* Sathmar, *Hung.* Szatmárrémeti. Satu Mare, NW Romania
Satunan Syotō *see* Satsunan-shotō
Saudi Arabia *121 B5 Ar.* Al 'Arabīyah as Su'ūdīyah, Al Mamlakah al 'Arabīyah as Su'ūdīyah. *Country* SW Asia

Saudi Arabia 121

Official name Kingdom of Saudi Arabia
Formation 1932
Capital Riyadh
Population 21 million / 28 people per sq mile (11 people per sq km)
Total area 756,981 sq miles (1,960,582 sq km)
Languages Arabic
Religions Sunni Muslim 85%, Shi'a Muslim 15%
Ethnic mix Arab 90%, Afro-Asian 10%
Government Monarchy
Currency Saudi riyal = 100 malalah
Literacy rate 77%
Calorie consumption 2,875 kilocalories

Sauer *see* Sûre
Saulkrasti *106 C3* Rīga, C Latvia
Sault Sainte Marie *40 C1* Michigan, N USA

Sault Ste.Marie *38 C4* Ontario, S Canada
Saumur *90 B4* Maine-et-Loire, NW France
Saurimo *78 C1 Port.* Henrique de Carvalho, Vila Henrique de Carvalho. Lunda Sul, NE Angola
Sava *100 B3 Eng.* Save, *Ger.* Sau, *Hung.* Száva. *River* SE Europe
Sava *107 E6 Rus.* Sava. Mahilyowskaya Voblasts', E Belarus
Savá *52 D2* Colón, N Honduras
Savai'i *145 E4 island* NW Samoa
Savannah *43 E2* Georgia, SE USA
Savannah River *43 E2 river* Georgia/South Carolina, SE USA
Savanna-La-Mar *54 A5* W Jamaica
Save, Rio *79 E3 var.* Rio Sabi. *River* Mozambique/Zimbabwe
Saverne *90 E3 var.* Zabern; *anc.* Tres Tabernae. Bas-Rhin, NE France
Savigliano *96 A2* Piemonte, NW Italy
Savigsivik *see* Savissivik
Savinski *see* Savinskiy
Savinskiy *110 C3 var.* Savinski. Arkhangel'skaya Oblast', NW Russian Federation
Savissivik *82 D1 var.* Savigsivik. N Greenland
Savoie *91 D5 cultural region* E France
Savona *96 A2* Liguria, NW Italy
Savu Sea *139 E5 Ind.* Laut Sawu. *Sea* S Indonesia
Sawakin *see* Suakin
Sawdirī *see* Sodiri
Sawhāj *see* Sohâg
Şawqirah *121 D6 var.* Suqrah. S Oman
Sayanskiy Khrebet *112 D3 mountain range* S Russian Federation
Sayat *122 D3* Lebapskiy Velayat, E Turkmenistan
Sayaxché *52 B2* Petén, N Guatemala
Şaydā *see* Saïda
Sayhūt *121 D6* E Yemen
Sayida *see* Saïda
Saynshand *127 E2* Dornogovĭ, SE Mongolia
Sayre *41 E3* Pennsylvania, NE USA
Say'ūn *121 C6 var.* Saywūn. C Yemen
Saywūn *see* Say'ūn
Scandinavia *66 D2 geophysical region* NW Europe
Scarborough *89 D5* N England, UK
Schaan *94 E1* W Liechtenstein
Schaerbeek *87 C6* Brussels, C Belgium
Schaffhausen *95 B7 Fr.* Schaffhouse. Schaffhausen, N Switzerland
Schagen *86 C2* Noord-Holland, NW Netherlands
Schebschi Mountains *see* Shebshi Mountains
Scheessel *94 B3* Niedersachsen, NW Germany
Schefferville *39 E2* Quebec, E Canada
Scheldt *87 B5 Dut.* Schelde, *Fr.* Escaut. *River* W Europe
Schell Creek Range *47 D5 mountain range* Nevada, W USA
Schenectady *41 F3* New York, NE USA
Schertz *49 G4* Texas, SW USA
Schiermonnikoog *86 D1 Fris.* Skiermûntseach. *Island* Waddeneilanden, N Netherlands
Schijndel *86 D4* Noord-Brabant, S Netherlands
Schiltigheim *90 E3* Bas-Rhin, NE France
Schleswig *94 B2* Schleswig-Holstein, N Germany
Schleswig-Holstein *94 B2 cultural region* N Germany
Schönebeck *94 C4* Sachsen-Anhalt, C Germany
Schooten *see* Schoten
Schoten *87 C5 var.* Schooten. Antwerpen, N Belgium

Schouwen *86 B4 island* SW Netherlands
Schwabenalb *see* Schwäbische Alb
Schwäbische Alb *95 B6 var.* Schwabenalb, *Eng.* Swabian Jura. *Mountain range* S Germany
Schwandorf *95 C5* Bayern, SE Germany
Schwarzwald *95 B6 Eng.* Black Forest. *Mountain range* SW Germany
Schwaz *95 C7* Tirol, W Austria
Schweinfurt *95 B5* Bayern, SE Germany
Schwerin *94 C3* Mecklenburg-Vorpommern, N Germany
Schwiz *see* Schwyz
Schwyz *95 B7 var.* Schwiz. Schwyz, C Switzerland
Scilly, Isles of *89 B8 island group* SW England, UK
Scio *see* Chíos
Scoresby Sound *see* Ittoqqortoormiit
Scoresbysund *see* Ittoqqortoormiit
Scotia Sea *57 C8 sea* SW Atlantic Ocean
Scotland *88 C3 national region* UK
Scott Base *154 B4* NZ research station Antarctica
Scott Island *154 B5 island* Antarctica
Scottsbluff *44 D3* Nebraska, C USA
Scottsboro *42 D1* Alabama, S USA
Scottsdale *48 B2* Arizona, SW USA
Scranton *41 F3* Pennsylvania, NE USA
Scupi *see* Skopje
Scutari *see* Shkodër
Scutari, Lake *101 C5 Alb.* Liqeni i Shkodrës, SCr. Skadarsko Jezero. *Lake* Albania/Serbia and Montenegro (Yugo.)
Scyros *see* Skýros
Searcy *42 B1* Arkansas, C USA
Seattle *46 B2* Washington, NW USA
Sébaco *52 D3* Matagalpa, W Nicaragua
Sebastián Vizcaíno, Bahía *50 A2 bay* NW Mexico
Sechura, Bahía de *60 A3 bay* NW Peru
Secunderābād *134 D5 var.* Sikandarabad. Andhra Pradesh, C India
Sedan *90 D3* Ardennes, N France
Seddon *151 D5* Marlborough, South Island, NZ
Seddonville *151 C5* West Coast, South Island, NZ
Sédhiou *74 B3* SW Senegal
Sedona *48 B2* Arizona, SW USA
Seesen *94 B4* Niedersachsen, C Germany
Segestica *see* Sisak
Segezha *110 B3* Respublika Kareliya, NW Russian Federation
Ségou *74 D3 var.* Segu. Ségou, C Mali
Segovia *92 D2* Castilla-León, C Spain
Segoviao Wangkí *see* Coco, Río
Segu *see* Ségou
Séguédine *75 H2* Agadez, NE Niger
Seguin *49 G4* Texas, SW USA
Segura *93 E4 river* S Spain
Seinäjoki *85 D5 Swe.* Östermyra. Länsi-Suomi, W Finland
Seine *90 D1 river* N France
Seine, Baie de la *90 B3 bay* N France
Sekondi *see* Sekondi-Takoradi
Sekondi-Takoradi *75 E5 var.* Sekondi. S Ghana
Selat Balabac *see* Balabac Strait
Selenga *127 E1 Mong.* Selenge Mörön. *River* Mongolia/Russian Federation
Sélestat *90 E4 Ger.* Schlettstadt. Bas-Rhin, NE France
Selfoss *83 E5* Sudhurland, SW Iceland
Sélibabi *74 C3 var.* Sélibaby. Guidimaka, S Mauritania
Sélibaby *see* Sélibabi
Selma *42 C2* Alabama, S USA
Selma *47 C6* California, W USA
Selway River *46 D2 river* Idaho, NW USA

237

Selwyn Range 148 B3 *mountain range* Queensland, C Australia
Selzaete *see* Zelzate
Semarang 138 C5 *var.* Samarang. Jawa, C Indonesia
Sembé 77 B5 La Sangha, NW Congo
Semey *see* Semipalatinsk
Seminole 49 E3 Texas, SW USA
Seminole, Lake 42 D3 *reservoir* Florida/Georgia, SE USA
Semipalatinsk 114 D4 *Kaz.* Semey. Vostochnyy kazakhstan, E Kazakhstan
Semnān 120 D3 *var.* Samnān. Semnān, N Iran
Semois 87 C8 *river* SE Belgium
Sendai 131 A8 Kagoshima, Kyūshū, SW Japan
Sendai 130 D4 Miyagi, Honshū, C Japan
Sendai-wan 131 A8 *bay* E Japan
Senec 99 C6 *Ger.* Wartberg, *Hung.* Szenc; *prev.* Szempcz. Bratislavský Kraj, W Slovakia
Senegal 74 C3 *Fr.* Sénégal. *River* W Africa
Senegal 74 B3 *Fr.* Sénégal. *Country* W Africa

Senegal 74

Official name Republic of Senegal
Formation 1960
Capital Dakar
Population 9.7 million / 128 people per sq mile (49 people per sq km)
Total area 75,749 sq miles (196,190 sq km)
Languages French, Wolof, Fulani, Serer, Diola, Malinke, Soninke, Arabic
Religions Sunni Muslim 90%, Christian (mainly Roman Catholic) 5%, Traditional beliefs 5%
Ethnic mix Wolof 44%, Serer 15%, Fula 12%, Diola 5%, Malinke 4%, other 20%
Government Presidential democracy
Currency CFA franc = 100 centimes
Literacy rate 37.4%
Calorie consumption 2,257 kilocalories

Senftenberg 94 D4 Brandenburg, E Germany
Senica 99 C6 *Ger.* Senitz, *Hung.* Szenice. Trnavský Kraj, W Slovakia
Senj 100 A3 *Ger.* Zengg, *It.* Segna; *anc.* Senia. Lika-Senj, NW Croatia
Senja 84 C2 *prev.* Senjen. *Island* N Norway
Senkaku-shotō 130 A3 *island group* SW Japan
Senlis 90 C3 Oise, N France
Sennar 72 C4 *var.* Sannār. Sinnar, C Sudan
Sens 90 C3 *anc.* Agendicum, Senones. Yonne, C France
Senta 100 D3 *Hung.* Zenta. Serbia, N Serbia and Montenegro (Yugo.)
Seo de Urgel *see* La Seo d'Urgel
Seoul *see* Sŏul
Sept-Îles 39 E3 Quebec, SE Canada
Seraing 87 D6 Liège, E Belgium
Serakhs 122 D3 *var.* Saragt. Akhalskiy Velayat, S Turkmenistan
Seram, Pulau 139 F4 *var.* Serang, *Eng.* Ceram. *Island* Maluku, E Indonesia
Serang *see* Seram, Pulau
Serang 138 C5 Jawa, C Indonesia
Serasan, Selat 138 C3 *strait* Indonesia/Malaysia
Serbia 100 D4 *Ger.* Serbien, *Serb.* Srbija. Admin. region *province* Serbia and Montenegro (Yugo.)
Serbia and Montenegro (Yugo.) 100 D4 SCr. Jugoslavija, Savezna Republika Jugoslavija. *Country* SE Europe

Serbia and Montenegro (Yugo.) 100

Official name Serbia and Montenegro
Formation 1992
Capital Belgrade
Population 10.5 million / 266 people per sq mile (103 people per sq km)
Total area 39,449 sq miles (102,173 sq km)
Languages Serbo-Croat, Albanian, Hungarian
Religions Eastern Orthodox 65, Muslim 19%, Roman Catholic 4%, other 12%
Ethnic mix Serb 62%, Albanian 17%, Montenegrin 5%, other 16%
Government Multiparty republic
Currency Dinar (Euro widely used in Montenegro)
Literacy rate 93.3%
Calorie consumption 2,570 kilocalories

Serdica *see* Sofiya
Seremban 138 B3 Negeri Sembilan, Peninsular Malaysia
Serenje 78 D2 Central, E Zambia
Seres *see* Sérres
Seret *see* Siret
Sereth *see* Siret
Sérifos 105 C6 *anc.* Seriphos. *Island* Kykládes, Greece, Aegean Sea
Serov 114 C3 Sverdlovskaya Oblast', C Russian Federation
Serowe 78 D3 Central, SE Botswana
Serpa Pinto *see* Menongue
Serpent's Mouth, The 59 F2 *Sp.* Boca de la Serpiente. *Strait* Trinidad and Tobago/Venezuela
Serpukhov 111 B5 Moskovskaya Oblast', W Russian Federation
Serra dos Parecis *see* Parecis, Chapada dos
Sérrai *see* Sérres
Serrana, Cayo de 53 F2 *island group* NW Colombia
Serranilla, Cayo de 53 F2 *island group* NW Colombia
Serra Pacaraim *see* Pakaraima Mountains
Serra Tumucumaque *see* Tumuc Humac Mountains
Serravalle 96 E1 N San Marino
Sérres 104 C3 *var.* Seres; *prev.* Sérrai. Kentrikí Makedonía, NE Greece
Sert *see* Siirt
Sesto San Giovanni 96 B2 Lombardia, N Italy
Sesvete 100 B2 Zagreb, N Croatia
Setabis *see* Xátiva
Sète 91 C6 *prev.* Cette. Hérault, S France
Setesdal 85 A6 *valley* S Norway
Sétif 71 E2 *var.* Stif. N Algeria
Setté Cama 77 A6 Ogooué-Maritime, SW Gabon
Setúbal 92 B4 *Eng.* Saint Ubes, Saint Yves. Setúbal, W Portugal
Setúbal, Baía de 92 B4 *bay* W Portugal
Seul, Lac 38 B3 *lake* Ontario, S Canada
Sevan 117 G2 C Armenia
Sevana Lich 117 G3 *Eng.* Lake Sevan, *Rus.* Ozero Sevan. *Lake* E Armenia
Sevastopol' 109 F5 *Eng.* Sebastopol. Respublika Krym, S Ukraine
Severn 89 D6 *Wel.* Hafren. *River* England/Wales, UK
Severn 38 C2 *river* Ontario, S Canada
Severnaya Dvina 110 C4 *var.* Northern Dvina. *River* NW Russian Federation
Severnaya Zemlya 115 E2 *var.* Nicholas II Land. *Island group* N Russian Federation
Severnyy 110 E3 Respublika Komi, NW Russian Federation
Severodvinsk 110 C4 *prev.* Molotov, Sudostroy. Arkhangel'skaya Oblast', NW Russian Federation

Severomorsk 110 C2 Murmanskaya Oblast', NW Russian Federation
Severo-Sibirskaya Nizmennost' 115 E2 *var.* North Siberian Plain, *Eng.* North Siberian Lowland. *Lowlands* N Russian Federation
Seversky Donets *see* Donets
Sevier Lake 44 A4 *lake* Utah, W USA
Sevilla 92 C4 *Eng.* Seville; *anc.* Hispalis. Andalucía, SW Spain
Seville *see* Sevilla
Sevlievo 104 D2 Gabrovo, N Bulgaria
Seychelles 79 G1 *Country* W Indian Ocean

Seychelles 79

Official name Republic of the Seychelles
Formation 1976
Capital Victoria
Population 79,300 / 451 people per sq mile (174 people per sq km)
Total area 176 sq miles (455 sq km)
Languages French Creole (Seselwa), English, French
Religions Roman Catholic 90%, Anglican 8%, other 2%
Ethnic mix Creole 89%, Indian 5%, Chinese 2%, other 4%
Government Multiparty republic
Currency Seychelles rupee = 100 cents
Literacy rate 84%
Calorie consumption 2,432 kilocalories

Seydhisfjördhur 83 E5 Austurland, E Iceland
Seydi 122 D2 *prev.* Neftezavodsk. Lebapskiy Velayat, E Turkmenistan
Seyhan *see* Adana
Sfákia 105 C8 Kríti, Greece, E Mediterranean Sea
Sfântu Gheorghe 108 C4 *Ger.* Sankt-Georgen, *Hung.* Sepsiszentgyörgy; *prev.* Şepsi-Sângeorz, Sfîntu Gheorghe. Covasna, C Romania
Sfax 71 F2 *Ar.* Şafāqis. E Tunisia
's-Gravenhage 86 B4 *var.* Den Haag, *Eng.* The Hague, *Fr.* La Haye. *Country capital* (Netherlands-seat of government) Zuid-Holland, W Netherlands
's-Gravenzande 86 B4 Zuid-Holland, W Netherlands
Shaan *see* Shaanxi
Shaanxi 128 B5 *var.* Shaan, Shaanxi Sheng, Shan-hsi, Shenshi, Shensi. Admin. region *province* C China
Shaanxi Sheng *see* Shaanxi
Shache 126 A3 *var.* Yarkant. Xinjiang Uygur Zizhiqu, NW China
Shackleton Ice Shelf 154 D3 *ice shelf* Antarctica
Shaddādī *see* Ash Shadādāh
Shāhābād *see* Eslāmābād
Shahjahanabad *see* Delhi
Shahr-e Kord 120 C3 *var.* Shahr Kord. Chahār Maḥall va Bakhtiārī, C Iran
Shahr Kord *see* Shahr-e Kord
Shāhrūd 120 D2 *prev.* Emāmrūd, Emāmshahr. Semnān, N Iran
Shandī *see* Shendi
Shandong 128 D4 *var.* Lu, Shandong Sheng, Shantung. Admin. region *province* E China
Shandong Sheng *see* Shandong
Shanghai 128 D5 *var.* Shang-hai. Shanghai Shi, E China
Shang-hai *see* Shanghai
Shangrao 128 D5 Jiangxi, S China
Shan-hsi *see* Shaanxi
Shan-hsi *see* Shanxi
Shannon 89 A6 *Ir.* na tSionainn. *River* W Ireland
Shan Plateau 136 B3 *plateau* E Myanmar
Shansi *see* Shanxi
Shantarskiye Ostrova 115 G3 *Eng.* Shantar Islands. *Island group* E Russian Federation

Shantou 128 D6 *var.* Shan-t'ou, Swatow. Guangdong, S China
Shantung *see* Shandong
Shanxi 128 C4 *var.* Jin, Shan-hsi, Shansi, Shanxi Sheng. Admin. region *province* C China
Shan Xian *see* Sanmenxia
Shanxi Sheng *see* Shanxi
Shaoguan 128 C6 *var.* Shao-kuan, *Cant.* Kukong; *prev.* Ch'u-chiang. Guangdong, S China
Shao-kuan *see* Shaoguan
Shaqrā *see* Shuqrah
Shaqrā' 120 B4 Ar Riyāḍ, C Saudi Arabia
Shar 130 D5 *var.* Charsk. Vostochnyy Kazakhstan, E Kazakhstan
Shari *see* Chari
Shari 130 D2 Hokkaidō, NE Japan
Shark Bay 147 A5 *bay* Western Australia
Shashe 78 D3 *var.* Shashi. *River* Botswana/Zimbabwe
Shashi *see* Shashe
Shatskiy Rise 125 G1 *undersea feature* N Pacific Ocean
Shatt al-Hodna *see* Hodna, Chott El
Shaṭṭ al Jarīd *see* Jarīd, Chott el
Shawnee 49 G1 Oklahoma, C USA
Shchadryn 107 D7 *Rus.* Shchedrin. Homyel'skaya Voblasts', SE Belarus
Shchëkino 111 B5 Tul'skaya Oblast', W Russian Federation
Shchors 109 E1 Chernihivs'ka Oblast', N Ukraine
Shchuchinsk 114 C4 *prev.* Shchuchye. Severnyy kazakhstan, N Kazakhstan
Shchuchyn 107 B5 *Pol.* Szczuczyn Nowogródzki, *Rus.* Shchuchin. Hrodzyenskaya Voblasts', W Belarus
Shebekino 111 A6 Belgorodskaya Oblast', W Russian Federation
Shebeli 73 D5 *Amh.* Wabē Shebelē Wenz, *It.* Scebeli, *Som.* Webi Shabeelle. *River* Ethiopia/Somalia
Sheberghān 123 E3 *var.* Shibarghān, Shiberghan, Shiberghān. Jowzjān, N Afghanistan
Sheboygan 40 B2 Wisconsin, N USA
Shebshi Mountains 76 A4 *var.* Schebschi Mountains. *Mountain range* E Nigeria
Shechem *see* Nablus
Shedadi *see* Ash Shadādah
Sheffield 89 D5 N England, UK
Shekhem *see* Nablus
Shelby 44 B1 Montana, NW USA
Sheldon 45 F3 Iowa, C USA
Shelekhov Gulf *see* Shelikhova, Zaliv
Shelikhova, Zaliv 115 G2 *Eng.* Shelekhov Gulf. *Gulf* E Russian Federation
Shendi 72 C4 *var.* Shandī. River Nile, NE Sudan
Shengking *see* Liaoning
Shenking *see* Liaoning
Shenshi *see* Shaanxi
Shensi *see* Shaanxi
Shenyang 128 D3 *Chin.* Shen-yang, *Eng.* Moukden, Mukden; *prev.* Fengtien. Liaoning, NE China
Shepetivka 108 D2 *Rus.* Shepetovka. Khmel'nyts'ka Oblast', NW Ukraine
Shepparton 149 C7 Victoria, SE Australia
Sherbrooke 39 E4 Quebec, SE Canada
Shereik 72 C3 River Nile, N Sudan
Sheridan 44 C2 Wyoming, C USA
Sherman 49 G2 Texas, SW USA
's-Hertogenbosch 86 D4 *Fr.* Bois-le-Duc, *Ger.* Herzogenbusch. Noord-Brabant, S Netherlands
Shetland Islands 88 D1 *island group* NE Scotland, UK
Shibarghān *see* Sheberghān
Shiberghan *see* Sheberghān
Shibetsu 130 D2 *var.* Sibetu. Hokkaidō, NE Japan

Shibh Jazīrat Sīnā' *see* Sinai
Shibushi-wan 131 B8 *bay* SW Japan
Shigatse *see* Xigazê
Shih-chia-chuang *see* Shijiazhuang
Shihezi 126 C2 Xinjiang Uygur Zizhiqu, NW China
Shihmen *see* Shijiazhuang
Shijiazhuang 128 C4 *var.* Shih-chia-chuang; *prev.* Shihmen. Hebei, E China
Shikārpur 134 B3 Sind, S Pakistan
Shikoku 131 C7 *var.* Sikoku. *Island* SW Japan
Shikoku Basin 125 F2 *var.* Sikoku Basin. *Undersea feature* N Philippine Sea
Shikotan, Ostrov 130 E2 *Jap.* Shikotan-tō. *Island* NE Russian Federation
Shilabo 73 D5 E Ethiopia
Shiliguri 135 F3 *prev.* Siliguri. West Bengal, NE India
Shilka 115 F4 *river* S Russian Federation
Shilong 113 G3 E India
Shimbir Berris *see* Shimbiris
Shimbiris 72 E4 *var.* Shimbir Berris. *Mountain* N Somalia
Shimoga 132 C2 Karnātaka, W India
Shimonoseki 131 A7 *var.* Simonoseki; *hist.* Akamagaseki, Bakan. Yamaguchi, Honshū, SW Japan
Shinano-gawa 131 C5 *var.* Sinano Gawa. *River* Honshū, C Japan
Shīndand 122 D4 Farāh, W Afghanistan
Shingū 131 C6 *var.* Singû. Wakayama, Honshū, SW Japan
Shinjō 130 D4 *var.* Sinzyô. Yamagata, Honshū, C Japan
Shinyanga 73 C7 Shinyanga, NW Tanzania
Shiprock 48 C1 New Mexico, SW USA
Shīrāz 120 D4 *var.* Shīrāz. Fārs, S Iran
Shivpuri 134 D3 Madhya Pradesh, C India
Shizugawa 130 D4 Miyagi, Honshū, NE Japan
Shizuoka 131 D6 *var.* Sizuoka. Shizuoka, Honshū, S Japan
Shklow 107 D6 *Rus.* Shklov. Mahilyowskaya Voblasts', E Belarus
Shkodër 101 C5 *var.* Shkodra, *It.* Scutari, *SCr.* Skadar. Shkodër, NW Albania
Shkodra *see* Shkodër
Shkumbi, Lumi i 101 C6 *var.* Shkumbî, Shkumbin. *River* C Albania
Shkumbî *see* Shkumbin, Lumi i
Shkumbin *see* Shkumbin, Lumi i
Sholāpur *see* Solāpur
Shostka 109 F1 Sums'ka Oblast', NE Ukraine
Show Low 48 B2 Arizona, SW USA
Shpola 109 E3 Cherkas'ka Oblast', N Ukraine
Shreveport 42 A2 Louisiana, S USA
Shrewsbury 89 D6 *hist.* Scrobesbyrig'. W England, UK
Shu 114 C5 *Kaz.* Shū. Zhambyl, SE Kazakhstan
Shuang-liao *see* Liaoyuan
Shumagin Islands 36 B3 *island group* Alaska, USA
Shumen 104 D2 Shumen, NE Bulgaria
Shumilina 107 E5 *Rus.* Shumilino. Vitsyebskaya Voblasts', NE Belarus
Shuqrah 121 B7 *var.* Shaqrā. SW Yemen
Shwebo 136 B3 Sagaing, C Myanmar
Shyichy 107 C7 *Rus.* Shiichi. Homyel'skaya Voblasts', SE Belarus
Shymkent 114 B5 *prev.* Chimkent. Yuzhnyy Kazakhstan, S Kazakhstan
Shyshchytsy 107 C6 *Rus.* Shishchitsy. Minskaya Voblasts', C Belarus
Si *see* Syr Darya
Siam, Gulf of *see* Thailand, Gulf of

Sian *see* Xi'an
Siang *see* Brahmaputra
Siangtan *see* Xiangtan
Šiauliai 106 B4 *Ger.* Schaulen.
Šiauliai, N Lithuania
Sibay 111 D6 Respublika Bashkortostan, W Russian Federation
Šibenik 116 B4 *It.* Sebenico. Šibenik-Knin, S Croatia
Siberia *see* Sibir'
Siberut, Pulau 138 A4 *prev.* Siberoet. *Island* Kepulauan Mentawai, W Indonesia
Sibetu *see* Shibetsu
Sibi 134 B2 Baluchistān, SW Pakistan
Sibir' 115 E3 *var.* Siberia. *Physical region* NE Russian Federation
Sibiti 77 B6 La Lékoumou, S Congo
Sibiu 108 B4 *Ger.* Hermannstadt, *Hung.* Nagyszeben. Sibiu, C Romania
Sibolga 138 B3 Sumatera, W Indonesia
Sibu 138 D3 Sarawak, East Malaysia
Sibut 76 C4 *prev.* Fort-Sibut. Kémo, S Central African Republic
Sibuyan Sea 139 E2 *sea* C Philippines
Sichon 137 C6 *var.* Ban Sichon, Si Chon. Nakhon Si Thammarat, SW Thailand
Sichuan 128 B5 *var.* Chuan, Sichuan Sheng, Ssu-ch'uan, Szechuan, Szechwan. Admin. region *province* C China
Sichuan Pendi 128 B5 *depression* C China
Sichuan Sheng *see* Sichuan
Sicilia 97 C7 *Eng.* Sicily; *anc.* Trinacria. *Island* Italy, C Mediterranean Sea
Sicilian Channel *see* Sicily, Strait of
Sicily *see* Sicilia
Sicily, Strait of 97 B7 *var.* Sicilian Channel. *Strait* C Mediterranean Sea
Sicuani 61 E4 Cusco, S Peru
Sidári 104 A4 Kérkyra, Iónioi Nísoi, Greece, C Mediterranean Sea
Sidas 138 C4 Borneo, C Indonesia
Siderno 97 D7 Calabria, SW Italy
Sîdi Barrâni 72 A1 NW Egypt
Sidi Bel Abbès 70 D2 *var.* Sidi bel Abbès, Sidi-Bel-Abbès. NW Algeria
Sidirókastro 104 C3 *prev.* Sidhirókastron. Kentrikí Makedonía, NE Greece
Sidley, Mount 154 B4 *mountain* Antarctica
Sidney 44 D1 Montana, NW USA
Sidney 44 D3 Nebraska, C USA
Sidney 40 C4 Ohio, N USA
Sidon *see* Saïda
Sidra *see* Surt
Siedlce 98 E3 *Ger.* Sedlez, *Rus.* Sesdlets. Mazowieckie, C Poland
Siegen 94 B4 Nordrhein-Westfalen, W Germany
Siemiatycze 98 E3 Podlaskie, NE Poland
Siena 96 B3 *Fr.* Sienne; *anc.* Saena Julia. Toscana, C Italy
Sieradz 98 C4 Łódzkie, C Poland
Sierpc 98 D3 Mazowieckie, C Poland
Sierra de Soconusco *see* Sierra Madre
Sierra Leone 74 C4 *Country* W Africa

Sierra Leone 74

Official name Republic of Sierra Leone
Formation 1961
Capital Freetown
Population 4.6 million / 166 people per sq mile (64 people per sq km)
Total area 27,699 sq miles (71,740 sq km)
Languages English, Mende, Temne, Krio
Religions Traditional beliefs 30%, Muslim 30%, Christian 10%, other 30%

Sierra Leone (continued)

Ethnic mix Mende 35%, Temne 32%, Limba 8%, Kuranko 4%, other 21%
Government Multiparty republic
Currency Leone = 100 cents
Literacy rate 36.3%
Calorie consumption 1,863 kilocalories

Sierra Leone Basin 66 C4 *undersea feature* E Atlantic Ocean
Sierra Leone Ridge *see* Sierra Leone Rise
Sierra Leone Rise 66 C4 *var.* Sierra Leone Ridge, Sierra Leone Schwelle. *Undersea feature* E Atlantic Ocean
Sierra Leone Schwelle *see* Sierra Leone Rise
Sierra Madre 52 B2 *var.* Sierra de Soconusco. *Mountain range* Guatemala/Mexico
Sierra Madre *see* Madre Occidental, Sierra
Sierra Nevada 47 C6 *mountain range* W USA
Sierra Pacaraima *see* Pakaraima Mountains
Sierra Vieja 48 D3 *mountain range* Texas, SW USA
Sierra Vista 48 B3 Arizona, SW USA
Sífnos 105 C6 *anc.* Siphnos. *Island* Kykládes, Greece, Aegean Sea
Sigli 138 A3 Sumatera, W Indonesia
Siglufjördhur 83 E4 Nordhurland Vestra, N Iceland
Signal Peak 48 A2 *mountain* Arizona, SW USA
Signan *see* Xi'an
Signy 154 A2 *UK research station* South Orkney Islands, Antarctica
Siguatepeque 52 C2 Comayagua, W Honduras
Siguiri 74 D4 Haute-Guinée, NE Guinea
Siilinjärvi 84 E4 Itä-Suomi, C Finland
Siirt 117 F4 *var.* Sert; *anc.* Tigranocerta. Siirt, SE Turkey
Sikandarabad *see* Secunderābād
Sikasso 74 D4 Sikasso, S Mali
Sikeston 45 H5 Missouri, C USA
Sikhote-Alin', Khrebet 115 G4 *mountain range* SE Russian Federation
Siking *see* Xi'an
Siklós 99 C7 Baranya, SW Hungary
Sikoku *see* Shikoku
Sikoku Basin *see* Shikoku Basin
Šilalė 106 B4 Šilalė, W Lithuania
Silchar 135 G3 Assam, NE India
Silesia 98 B4 *physical region* SW Poland
Silifke 116 C4 *anc.* Seleucia. İçel, S Turkey
Siling Co 126 C5 *lake* W China
Silinhot *see* Xilinhot
Silistra 104 E1 *var.* Silistria; *anc.* Durostorum. Silistra, NE Bulgaria
Silistria *see* Silistra
Sillamäe 106 E2 *Ger.* Sillamäggi. Ida-Virumaa, NE Estonia
Šilutė 106 B4 *Ger.* Heydekrug. Šilutė, W Lithuania
Silvan 117 F4 Diyarbakır, SE Turkey
Silverek 117 E4 Şanlıurfa, SE Turkey
Simangang *see* Sri Aman
Simanichy 107 C7 *Rus.* Simonichi. Homyel'skaya Voblasts', SE Belarus
Simav 116 A3 Kütahya, W Turkey
Simav Çayı 116 A3 *river* NW Turkey
Simeto 97 C7 *river* Sicilia, Italy, C Mediterranean Sea
Simeulue, Pulau 138 A3 *island* NW Indonesia
Simferopol' 109 F5 Respublika Krym, S Ukraine
Simitli 104 C3 Blagoevgrad, SW Bulgaria

Şimleu Silvaniei 108 B3 *Hung.* Szilágysomlyó; *prev.* Şimlăul Silvaniei, Şimleul Silvaniei. Sălaj, NW Romania
Simonoseki *see* Shimonoseki
Simpelveld 87 D6 Limburg, SE Netherlands
Simplon Pass 95 B8 *pass* S Switzerland
Simpson *see* Fort Simpson
Simpson Desert 148 B4 *desert* Northern Territory/South Australia
Sīnā' *see* Sinai
Sinai 72 C2 *var.* Sinai Peninsula, *Ar.* Shibh Jazīrat Sīnā', Sīnā'. *Physical region* NE Egypt
Sinaia 108 C4 Prahova, SE Romania
Sinai Peninsula *see* Sinai
Sinano Gawa *see* Shinano-gawa
Sincelejo 58 B2 Sucre, NW Colombia
Sind 134 B3 *var.* Sindh. Admin. region *province* SE Pakistan
Sindelfingen 95 B6 Baden-Württemberg, SW Germany
Sindh *see* Sind
Sindi 106 D2 *Ger.* Zintenhof. Pärnumaa, SW Estonia
Sines 92 B4 Setúbal, S Portugal
Singan *see* Xi'an
Singapore 138 A1 *Country* SE Asia

Singapore 138

Official name Republic of Singapore
Formation 1965
Capital Singapore
Population 4.1 million / 16,400 people per sq mile (6,332 people per sq km)
Total area 250 sq miles (648 sq km)
Languages Malay, English, Mandarin, Tamil
Religions Buddhist 55%, Taoism 22%, Muslim 16%, Hindu, Christian, Sikh 7%
Ethnic mix Chinese 77%, Malay 14%, Indian 8%, other 1%
Government Parliamentary democracy
Currency Singapore dollar = 100 cents
Literacy rate 92.4%
Calorie consumption not available

Singapore 138 B3 *country capital* (Singapore) S Singapore
Singen 95 B6 Baden-Württemberg, S Germany
Singida 73 C7 Singida, C Tanzania
Singkang 139 E4 Sulawesi, C Indonesia
Singkawang 138 C3 Borneo, C Indonesia
Singora *see* Songkhla
Singû *see* Shingū
Sining *see* Xining
Siniscola 97 A5 Sardegna, Italy, C Mediterranean Sea
Sinj 100 B4 Split-Dalmacija, SE Croatia
Sinkiang *see* Xinjiang Uygur Zizhiqu
Sinkiang Uighur Autonomous Region *see* Xinjiang Uygur Zizhiqu
Sinnamarie *see* Sinnamary
Sinnamary 59 H3 *var.* Sinnamarie. N French Guiana
Sînnicolau Mare *see* Sânnicolau Mare
Sinoie, Lacul 108 D5 *prev.* Lacul Sinoe. *Lagoon* SE Romania
Sinop 116 D2 *anc.* Sinope. Sinop, N Turkey
Sinsheim 95 B6 Baden-Württemberg, SW Germany
Sint Maarten 55 G3 *Eng.* Saint Martin. *Island* N Netherlands Antilles
Sint-Michielsgestel 86 C4 Noord-Brabant, S Netherlands

Sint-Niklaas 87 B5 Fr. Saint-Nicolas. Oost-Vlaanderen, N Belgium
Sint-Pieters-Leeuw 87 B6 Vlaams Brabant, C Belgium
Sintra 92 B3 prev. Cintra. Lisboa, W Portugal
Sinujiif 73 E5 Nugaal, NE Somalia
Sinus Aelaniticus see Aqaba, Gulf of
Sinyang see Xinyang
Sinzyō see Shinjō
Sion 95 A7 Ger. Sitten; anc. Sedunum. Valais, SW Switzerland
Sioux City 45 F3 Iowa, C USA
Sioux Falls 45 F3 South Dakota, N USA
Siping 128 D3 var. Ssu-p'ing, Szeping; prev. Ssu-p'ing-chieh. Jilin, NE China
Siple, Mount 154 A4 mountain Siple Island, Antarctica
Siquirres 53 E4 Limón, E Costa Rica
Siracusa 97 D7 Eng. Syracuse. Sicilia, Italy, C Mediterranean Sea
Sir Darya see Syr Darya
Sir Edward Pellew Group 148 B2 island group Northern Territory, NE Australia
Siret 108 C3 var. Siretul, Ger. Sereth, Rus. Seret, Ukr. Siret. River Romania/Ukraine
Siret see Siret
Siretul see Siret
Sirikit Reservoir 136 C4 lake N Thailand
Sīrjān 120 D4 prev. Sa'īdābād. Kermān, S Iran
Sirna see Sýrna
Şırnak 117 F4 Şırnak, SE Turkey
Síros see Sýros
Sirte see Surt
Sirte, Gulf of see Surt, Khalīj
Sisak 100 B3 var. Siscia, Ger. Sissek, Hung. Sziszek; anc. Segestica. Sisak-Moslavina, C Croatia
Siscia see Sisak
Sisimiut 82 C3 var. Holsteinborg, Holsteinsborg, Holstenborg, Holstensborg. S Greenland
Sissek see Sisak
Sistema Penibético see Béticos, Sistemas
Siteía 105 D8 var. Sitía. Kríti, Greece, E Mediterranean Sea
Sitges 93 G2 Cataluña, NE Spain
Sitía see Siteía
Sittang 136 B4 var. Sittoung. River S Myanmar
Sittard 87 D5 Limburg, SE Netherlands
Sittoung see Sittang
Sittwe 136 A3 var. Akyab. Arakan State, W Myanmar
Siuna 52 D3 Región Autónoma Atlántico Norte, NE Nicaragua
Siut see Asyūt
Sivas 116 D3 anc. Sebastia, Sebaste. Sivas, C Turkey
Sivers'kyy Donets' see Donets
Siwa 72 A2 var. Siwah. NW Egypt
Sīwah see Siwa
Six-Fours-les-Plages 91 D6 Var, SE France
Siyäzän 117 H2 Rus. Siazan'. NE Azerbaijan
Sizuoka see Shizuoka
Sjar see Sääre
Sjælland 85 Eng. Zealand, Ger. Seeland. Island E Denmark
Sjenica 101 D5 Turk. Seniça. Serbia, SW Serbia and Montenegro (Yugo.)
Skadar see Shkodër
Skagerak see Skagerrak
Skagerrak 85 A6 var. Skagerak. Channel N Europe
Skagit River 46 B1 river Washington, NW USA
Skalka 84 C3 lake N Sweden
Skarżysko-Kamienna 98 D4 Świętokrzyskie, C Poland
Skaudvilė 106 B4 Tauragė, SW Lithuania
Skegness 89 E6 E England, UK
Skellefteå 84 D4 Västerbotten, N Sweden

Skellefteälven 84 C4 river N Sweden
Ski 85 B6 Akershus, S Norway
Skíathos 105 C5 Skíathos, Vóreioi Sporádes, Greece, Aegean Sea
Skidal' 107 B5 Rus. Skidel'. Hrodzyenskaya Voblasts', W Belarus
Skierniewice 98 D3 Lodzkie, C Poland
Skiftet 106 C1 Fin. Kihti. Strait Gulf of Bothnia/Gulf of Finland
Skíros see Skýros
Skópelos 105 C5 Skópelos, Vóreioi Sporádes, Greece, Aegean Sea
Skopje 101 D6 var. Üsküb, Turk. Üsküp; prev. Skoplje, anc. Scupi. Country capital (FYR Macedonia) N FYR Macedonia
Skoplje see Skopje
Skovorodino 115 F4 Amurskaya Oblast', SE Russian Federation
Skuodas 106 B3 Ger. Schoden, Pol. Szkudy. Skuodas, NW Lithuania
Skye, Isle of 88 B3 island NW Scotland, UK
Skýros 105 C5 var. Skíros. Skýros, Vóreioi Sporádes, Greece, Aegean Sea
Skýros 105 C5 var. Skíros; anc. Scyros. Island Vóreioi Sporádes, Greece, Aegean Sea
Slagelse 85 B7 Vestsjælland, E Denmark
Slatina 108 B5 Olt, S Romania
Slatina 100 C3 Hung. Szlatina, prev. Podravska Slatina. Virovtica-Podravina, NE Croatia
Slavonska Požega see Požega
Slavonski Brod 100 C3 Ger. Brod, Hung. Bród; prev. Brod, Brod na Savi. Brod-Posavina, NE Croatia
Slavuta 108 C2 Khmel'nyts'ka Oblast', NW Ukraine
Slawharad 107 E7 Rus. Slavgorod. Mahilyowskaya Voblasts', E Belarus
Sławno 98 C2 Zachodniopomorskie, NW Poland
Sléibhte Chill Mhantáin see Wicklow Mountains
Slēmānī see As Sulaymānīyah
Sliema 102 B5 N Malta
Sligeach see Sligo
Sligo 89 A5 Ir. Sligeach. NW Ireland
Sliven 104 D2 var. Slivno. Sliven, C Bulgaria
Slivnitsa 104 B2 Sofiya, W Bulgaria
Slivno see Sliven
Slobozia 108 C5 Ialomița, SE Romania
Slonim 107 B6 Pol. Słonim, Rus. Slonim. Hrodzyenskaya Voblasts', W Belarus
Slovakia 99 C6 Ger. Slowakei, Hung. Szlovákia, Slvk. Slovensko. Country C Europe

Slovakia 99

Official name Slovak Republic
Formation 1993
Capital Bratislava
Population 5.4 million / 286 people per sq mile (111 people per sq km)
Total area 18,859 sq miles (48,845 sq km)
Languages Slovak, Hungarian, Czech
Religions Roman Catholic 60%, Atheist 10%, Protestant 8%, Orthodox 4%, other 18%
Ethnic mix Slovak 85%, Magyar 11%, Romany 1%, Czech 1%, other 2%
Government Parliamentary democracy
Currency Koruna = 100 halierov
Literacy rate 99%
Calorie consumption 3,133 kilocalories

Slovak Ore Mountains see Slovenské rudohorie

Slovenia 95 D8 Ger. Slowenien, Slvn. Slovenija. Country SE Europe

Slovenia 95

Official name Republic of Slovenia
Formation 1991
Capital Ljubljana
Population 2 million /256 people per sq mile (99 people per sq km)
Total area 7820 sq miles (20,253 sq km)
Languages Slovene, Serbo-Croat
Religions Roman Catholic 96%, Muslim 1%, other 3%
Ethnic mix Slovene 88%, Croat 3%, Serb 2%, Muslim 1%, other 6%
Government Parliamentary democracy
Currency Tolar = 100 stotins
Literacy rate 99%
Calorie consumption 3,168 kilocalories

Slovenské rudohorie 99 D6 Eng. Slovak Ore Mountains, Ger. Slowakisches Erzgebirge, Ungarisches Erzgebirge. Mountain range C Slovakia
Slov"yans'k 109 G3 Rus. Slavyansk. Donets'ka Oblast', E Ukraine
Slowakisches Erzgebirge see Slovenské rudohorie
Słubice 98 B3 Ger. Frankfurt. Lubuskie, W Poland
Sluch 108 D1 river NW Ukraine
Słupsk 98 C2 Ger. Stolp. Pomorskie, N Poland
Slutsk 107 C6 Rus. Slutsk. Minskaya Voblasts', S Belarus
Smallwood Reservoir 39 F2 lake Newfoundland and Labrador, S Canada
Smara 70 B3 var. Es Semara. N Western Sahara
Smarhon' 107 C5 Pol. Smorgonie, Rus. Smorgon'. Hrodzyenskaya Voblasts', W Belarus
Smederevo 100 D4 Ger. Semendria. Serbia, N Serbia and Montenegro (Yugo.)
Smederevska Palanka 100 D4 Serbia, C Serbia and Montenegro (Yugo.)
Smila 109 E2 Rus. Smela. Cherkas'ka Oblast', C Ukraine
Smiltene 106 D3 Ger. Smilten. Valka, N Latvia
Smola 84 A4 island W Norway
Smolensk 111 A5 Smolenskaya Oblast', W Russian Federation
Snake 34 B4 island W Norway
Snake River 46 C3 river NW USA
Snake River Plain 46 D4 plain Idaho, NW USA
Sneek 86 D2 Friesland, N Netherlands
Snežka 98 B4 Ger. Schneekoppe. Mountain N Czech Republic
Śniardwy, Jezioro 111 D2 Ger. Spirdingsee. Lake NE Poland
Snína 99 E5 Hung. Szinna. Prešovský Kraj, E Slovakia
Snowdonia 89 C6 mountain range NW Wales, UK
Snyder 49 F3 Texas, SW USA
Sobradinho, Represa de 63 F2 var. Barragem de Sobradinho. Reservoir E Brazil
Sochi 111 A7 Krasnodarskiy Kray, SW Russian Federation
Société, Archipel de la 145 G4 var. Archipel de Tahiti, Îles de la Société, Eng. Society Islands. Island group W French Polynesia
Society Islands see Société, Archipel de la
Socorro 48 D2 New Mexico, SW USA
Socorro, Isla 50 B5 island W Mexico
Socotra see Suqutrā
Soc Trăng 137 D6 var. Khanh. Soc Trăng, S Vietnam
Socuéllamos 93 E3 Castilla-La Mancha, C Spain

Sodankylä 84 D3 Lappi, N Finland
Sodari see Sodiri
Söderhamn 85 C5 Gävleborg, C Sweden
Södertälje 85 C6 Stockholm, C Sweden
Sodiri 72 B4 var. Sawdirī, Sodari. Northern Kordofan, C Sudan
Sofia see Sofiya
Sofiya 104 C2 var. Sophia, Eng. Sofia; Lat. Serdica. Country capital (Bulgaria) Sofiya-Grad, W Bulgaria
Sogamoso 58 B3 Boyacá, C Colombia
Sognefjorden 85 A5 fjord NE North Sea
Sohâg 72 B2 var. Sawhāj, Suliag. C Egypt
Sohar see Şuḩār
Sohm Plain 66 B3 undersea feature NW Atlantic Ocean
Sohrau see Żory
Sokal' 108 C2 Rus. Sokal. L'vivs'ka Oblast', NW Ukraine
Söke 116 A4 Aydın, SW Turkey
Sokhumi 117 E1 Rus. Sukhumi. NW Georgia
Sokodé 75 F4 C Togo
Sokol 110 C4 Vologodskaya Oblast', NW Russian Federation
Sokółka 98 E3 Białystok, NE Poland
Sokolov 99 A5 Ger. Falkenau an der Eger; prev. Falknov nad Ohří. Karlovarský Kraj, W Czech Republic
Sokone 74 B3 W Senegal
Sokoto 75 F4 river NW Nigeria
Sokoto 75 F3 Sokoto, NW Nigeria
Sokotra see Suquṭrā
Solāpur 124 B3 var. Sholāpur. Mahārāshtra, W India
Solca 108 C3 Ger. Solka. Suceava, N Romania
Sol, Costa del 92 D5 coastal region S Spain
Soldeu 91 B7 NE Andorra
Solec Kujawski 98 C3 Kujawski-pomorskie, C Poland
Soledad, Isla see East Falkland
Soledad 58 B1 Anzoátegui, NE Venezuela
Solikamsk 114 C3 Permskaya Oblast', NW Russian Federation
Sol'-Iletsk 111 D6 Orenburgskaya Oblast', W Russian Federation
Solingen 94 A4 Nordrhein-Westfalen, W Germany
Sollentuna 85 C6 Stockholm, C Sweden
Solok 138 B4 Sumatera, W Indonesia
Solomon Islands 144 C3 prev. British Solomon Islands Protectorate. Country W Pacific Ocean

Solomon Islands 144

Official name Solomon Islands
Formation 1978
Capital Honiara
Population 463,000 / 42 people per sq mile (16 people per sq km)
Total area 10,985 sq miles (28,450 sq km)
Languages English, Pidgin English, Melanesian Pidgin
Religions Anglican 34%, Roman Catholic 19%, South Seas Evangelical Church 17%, Methodist 11%, other 19%
Ethnic mix Melanesian 94%, other 6%
Government Parliamentary democracy
Currency Solomon Islands dollar = 100 cents
Literacy rate 62%
Calorie consumption 2,277 kilocalories

Solomon Islands 144 C3 island group PNG/Solomon Islands

Solomon Sea *144 B3 sea* W Pacific Ocean
Soltau *94 B3* Niedersachsen, NW Germany
Sol'tsy *110 A4* Novgorodskaya Oblast', W Russian Federation
Solwezi *78 D2* North Western, NW Zambia
Sōma *130 D4* Fukushima, Honshū, C Japan
Somalia *73 D5 Som.* Jamuuriyada Demuqraadiga Soomaaliyeed, Soomaaliya; *prev.* Italian Somaliland, Somaliland Protectorate. *Country* E Africa

Somalia 73

Official name Somali
Formation 1960
Capital Mogadishu
Population 9.2 million / 37 people per sq mile (14 people per sq km)
Total area 246,199 sq miles (637,657 sq km)
Languages Arabic, Somali, English, Italian
Religions Sunni Muslim 98%, other 2%
Ethnic mix Somali 85%, other 15%
Government Transitional regime
Currency Somali shilling = 100 cents
Literacy rate 24.1%
Calorie consumption 1,628 kilocalorie

Somali Basin *69 E5 undersea feature* W Indian Ocean
Sombor *100 C3 Hung.* Zombor. Serbia, NW Serbia and Montenegro (Yugo.)
Someren *87 D5* Noord-Brabant, SE Netherlands
Somerset *42 A5 var.* Somerset Village. W Bermuda
Somerset *40 C5* Kentucky, S USA
Somerset Island *37 F2 island* Queen Elizabeth Islands, Nunavut, NW Canada
Somerset Island *42 A5 island* W Bermuda
Somerset Village *see* Somerset
Somers Islands *see* Bermuda
Somerton *48 A2* Arizona, SW USA
Someş *108 B3 var.* Somesch, Someşul, Szamos, *Ger.* Samosch. *River* Hungary/Romania
Somesch *see* Someş
Someşul *see* Someş
Somme *90 C2 river* N France
Somotillo *52 C3* Chinandega, NW Nicaragua
Somoto *52 D3* Madriz, NW Nicaragua
Songea *73 C8* Ruvuma, S Tanzania
Sông Hông Hà *see* Red River
Songkhla *137 C7 var.* Songkla, *Mal.* Singora. Songkhla, SW Thailand
Songkla *see* Songkhla
Sông Srepok *see* Srêpôk, Tônle
Sông Tiên Giang *see* Mekong
Sonoran Desert *48 A3 var.* Desierto de Altar. *Desert* Mexico/USA *see also* Altar, Desierto de
Sonsonate *52 B3* Sonsonate, W El Salvador
Soochow *see* Suzhou
Sop Hao *136 D3* Houaphan, N Laos
Sophia *see* Sofiya
Sopot *98 C2 Ger.* Zoppot. Plovdiv, C Bulgaria
Sopron *99 B6 Ger.* Ödenburg. Győr-Moson-Sopron, NW Hungary
Sorgues *91 D6* Vaucluse, SE France
Sorgun *116 D3* Yozgat, C Turkey
Soria *93 E2* Castilla-León, N Spain
Soroca *108 D3 Rus.* Soroki. N Moldova
Sorong *139 F4* Papua, E Indonesia
Sørøy *see* Sørøya
Sørøya *84 C2 var.* Sørøy. *Island* N Norway
Sortavala *110 B3* Respublika Kareliya, NW Russian Federation

Sotavento, Ilhas de *74 A3 var.* Leeward Islands. *Island group* S Cape Verde
Sotkamo *84 E4* Oulu, C Finland
Souanké *77 B5* La Sangha, NW Congo
Soueida *see* As Suwaydā'
Souflí *104 D3 prev.* Souflíon. Anatolikí Makedonía kai Thráki, NE Greece
Soufrière *55 F2 volcano* S Dominica
Soukhné *see* As Sukhnah
Sŏul *129 E4 off.* Sŏul-t'ŭkpyŏlsi, *Eng.* Seoul, *Jap.* Keijō; *prev.* Kyŏngsŏng. *Country capital* (South Korea) NW South Korea
Soûr *119 A5 var.* Şūr; *anc.* Tyre. SW Lebanon
Souris River *45 E1 var.* Mouse River. *River* Canada/USA
Sourpi *105 B5* Thessalía, C Greece
Sousse *71 F2 var.* Sūsah. NE Tunisia
South Africa *78 C4 Afr.* Suid-Afrika. *Country* S Africa

South Africa 78

Official name Republic of South Africa
Formation 1934
Capital Pretoria (administrative)
Population 43.8 million / 93 people per sq mile (36 people per sq km)
Total area 471,008 sq miles (1,219,912 sq km)
Languages Afrikaans, English, 9 other African languages
Religions Black Independent 17%, Duthc reformed 11%, Roman Catholic 8%, Methodist 6%, other 58%
Ethnic mix Zulu 23%, other Black 38%, White 16%, Mixed 10%, other 13%
Government Parliamentary democracy
Currency Rand = 100 cents
Literacy rate 85.3%
Calorie consumption 2,886 kilocalorie

South America *56 continent*
Southampton *89 D7 hist.* Hamwih, *Lat.* Clausentum. S England, UK
Southampton Island *37 G3 island* Nunavut, NE Canada
South Andaman *133 F2 island* Andaman Islands, India, NE Indian Ocean
South Australia *149 A5 state* S Australia
South Australian Basin *142 B5 undersea feature* SW Indian Ocean
South Bend *40 C3* Indiana, N USA
South Beveland *see* Zuid-Beveland
South Bruny Island *149 C8 island* Tasmania, SE Australia
South Carolina *43 E2 off.* State of South Carolina; also known as The Palmetto State. *State* SE USA
South China Basin *125 E4 undersea feature* SW South China Sea
South China Sea *124 D4 Chin.* Nan Hai, *Ind.* Laut Cina Selatan, *Vtn.* Biên Đông. *Sea* SE Asia
South Dakota *44 D2 off.* State of South Dakota; also known as The Coyote State, Sunshine State. *State* N USA
Southeast Indian Ridge *141 D7 undersea feature* Indian Ocean/Pacific Ocean
Southeast Pacific Basin *153 E5 var.* Belling Hausen Mulde. *Undersea feature* SE Pacific Ocean
South East Point *149 C7 headland* Victoria, S Australia
Southend-on-Sea *89 E6* E England, UK
Southern Alps *151 B6 mountain range* South Island, NZ
Southern Cook Islands *145 F4 island group* S Cook Islands

Southern Cross *147 B6* Western Australia
Southern Indian Lake *37 F4 lake* Manitoba, C Canada
Southern Ocean *67 B7 ocean*
Southern Uplands *88 C4 mountain range* S Scotland, UK
South Fiji Basin *142 D4 undersea feature* S Pacific Ocean
South Geomagnetic Pole *154 B3 pole* Antarctica
South Georgia *57 D8 island* South Georgia and the South Sandwich Islands, SW Atlantic Ocean
South Goulburn Island *146 E2 island* Northern Territory, N Australia
South Huvadhu Atoll *132 A5 var.* Gaafu Dhaalu Atoll. *Atoll* S Maldives
South Indian Basin *141 D7 undersea feature* Indian Ocean/Pacific Ocean
South Island *151 C6 island* S NZ
South Korea *129 E4 Kor.* Taehan Min'guk. *Country* E Asia

South Korea 129

Official name Republic of Korea
Formation 1948
Capital Seoul
Population 47.1 million / 1,239 people per sq mile (478 people per sq km)
Total area 38,023 sq miles (98,480 sq km)
Languages Korean, Chinese
Religions Mahayana Buddhist 47%, Protestant 38%, Roman Catholic 11%, Confucian 3%, other 1%
Ethnic mix Korean 100%
Government Presidential democracy
Currency Korean won = 100 chon
Literacy rate 97.8%
Calorie consumption 3,093 kilocalories

South Lake Tahoe *47 C5* California, W USA
South Orkney Islands *154 A2 island group* Antarctica
South Ossetia *117 F2 former autonomous region* SW Georgia
South Pacific Basin *see* Southwest Pacific Basin
South Platte River *44 D4 river* Colorado/Nebraska, C USA
South Pole *154 B3 pole* Antarctica
South Sandwich Islands *57 D8 island group* SE South Georgia and South Sandwich Islands
South Sandwich Trench *57 E8 undersea feature* SW Atlantic Ocean
South Shetland Islands *154 A2 island group* Antarctica
South Shields *88 D4* NE England, UK
South Sioux City *45 F3* Nebraska, C USA
South Taranaki Bight *150 C4 bight* SE Tasman Sea
South Tasmania Plateau *see* Tasman Plateau
South Uist *88 B3 island* NW Scotland, UK
South West Cape *151 A8 headland* Stewart Island, NZ
Southwest Indian Ocean Ridge *see* Southwest Indian Ridge
Southwest Indian Ridge *141 B6 var.* Southwest Indian Ocean Ridge. *Undersea feature* SW Indian Ocean
Southwest Pacific Basin *143 E4 var.* South Pacific Basin. *Undersea feature* SE Pacific Ocean
Sovereign Base Area *102 C5 UK military installation* E Cyprus
Sovereign Base Area *102 C5 UK military installation* S Cyprus
Soweto *78 D4* Gauteng, NE South Africa
Spain *92 D3 Sp.* España; *anc.* Hispania, Iberia, *Lat.* Hispana. *Country* SW Europe

Spain 92

Official name Kingdom of Spain
Formation 1492
Capital Madrid
Population 39.9 million / 205 people per sq mile (79 people per sq km)
Total area 194,896 sq miles (504,782 sq km)
Languages Spanish, Catalan, Galician, Basque
Religions Roman Catholic 96%, other 4%
Ethnic mix Castilian Spanish 72%, Catalan 17%, Galician 6%, other 5%
Government Parliamentary democracy
Currency Euro (pesata until 2002)
Literacy rate 97.7%
Calorie consumption 3,352 kilocalories

Spanish Town *54 B5 hist.* St.Iago de la Vega. C Jamaica
Sparks *47 C5* Nevada, W USA
Spartanburg *43 E1* South Carolina, SE USA
Spárti *105 B6 Eng.* Sparta. Pelopónnisos, S Greece
Spearfish *44 D2* South Dakota, N USA
Speightstown *55 G1* NW Barbados
Spencer *45 F3* Iowa, C USA
Spencer Gulf *149 B6 gulf* South Australia
Spey *88 C3 river* NE Scotland, UK
Spiess Seamount *67 C7 undersea feature* S Atlantic Ocean
Spijkenisse *86 B4* Zuid-Holland, SW Netherlands
Spíli *105 C8* Kríti, Greece, E Mediterranean Sea
Spīn Būldak *123 E5* Kandahār, S Afghanistan
Spirdingsee *see* Śniardwg, Jezioro
Spitsbergen *83 F2 island* NW Svalbard
Split *100 B4 It.* Spalato. Split-Dalmacija, S Croatia
Špoģi *106 D4* Daugvapils, SE Latvia
Spokane *46 C2* Washington, NW USA
Spratly Islands *138 B2 Chin.* Nansha Qundao. *Disputed territory* SE Asia
Spree *94 D4 river* E Germany
Springfield *40 B4 state capital* Illinois, N USA
Springfield *41 G3* Massachusetts, NE USA
Springfield *45 G5* Missouri, C USA
Springfield *40 C4* Ohio, N USA
Springfield *46 B3* Oregon, NW USA
Spring Garden *59 F2* NE Guyana
Spring Hill *43 E4* Florida, SE USA
Springs Junction *151 C5* West Coast, South Island, NZ
Springsure *148 D4* Queensland, E Australia
Spruce Knob *41 E4 mountain* West Virginia, NE USA
Srbinje *see* Foča
Srbobran *see* Donji Vakuf
Srebrenica *100 C4* Republika Srpska, E Bosnia and Herzegovina
Sredets *104 E2 prev.* Grudovo. Burgas, E Bulgaria
Sredets *104 D2 prev.* Syulemeshlii. Stara Zagora, C Bulgaria
Srednerusskaya Vozvyshennost' *109 G1 Eng.* Central Russian Upland. *Mountain range* W Russian Federation
Srednesibirskoye Ploskogor'ye *114 D3 var.* Central Siberian Uplands, *Eng.* Central Siberian Plateau. *Mountain range* N Russian Federation
Sremska Mitrovica *100 C3 prev.* Mitrovica, *Ger.* Mitrowitz. Serbia, NW Serbia and Montenegro(Yugo.)

Srêpôk, Tônle *137 E5 var.*
Sông Srepok. *River*
Cambodia/Vietnam
Sri Aman *138 C3 var.* Bandar Sri
Aman, Simanggang. Borneo, East
Malaysia
Sri Jayawardanapura *132 D3 var.*
Sri Jayawardenepura; *prev.*
Kotte. Western Province, W Sri
Lanka
Sri Jayawardenepura *see* Sri
Jayawardanapura
Srikákulam *135 F5* Andhra
Pradesh, E India
Sri Lanka *132 D3 prev.* Ceylon.
Country S Asia

Sri Lanka 132

Official name Democratic Socialist
Republic of Sri Lanka
Formation 1948
Capital Colombo
Population 19.1 million / 754
people per sq mile (291 people per
sq km)
Total area 25,332 sq miles
(65,610 sq km)
Languages Sinhalese, Tamil,
English
Religions Buddhist 69%, Hindu
15%, Christian 8%, Muslim 8%
Ethnic mix Sinhalese 74%, Tamil
18%, Moor 7%, other 1%
Government Presidential
democracy
Currency Sri Lanka rupee = 100
cents
Literacy rate 91.7%
Calorie consumption 2,405
kilocalories

Srpska, Republika *100 B3* Admin.
region *republic* NE Bosnia and
Herzegovina
Srinagarind Reservoir *137 C5 lake*
W Thailand
Ssu-ch'uan *see* Sichuan
Ssu-p'ing *see* Siping
Ssu-p'ing-chieh *see* Siping
Stabroek *87 B5* Antwerpen,
N Belgium
Stade *94 B3* Niedersachsen,
NW Germany
Stadskanaal *86 E2* Groningen,
NE Netherlands
Stafford *89 D6* C England, UK
Staicele *106 D3* Limbaži, N Latvia
Stakhanov *109 H3* Luhans'ka
Oblast', E Ukraine
Stalinabad *see* Dushanbe
Stalingrad *see* Volgograd
Stalinobod *see* Dushanbe
Stalin Peak *see* Kommunizm,
Qullai
Stalowa Wola *98 E4* Podkarpackie,
SE Poland
Stamford *41 F3* Connecticut, NE USA
Stampalia *see* Astypálaia
Stanley *65 D7 var.* Port Stanley,
Puerto Argentino. *Dependent
territory capital* (Falkland Islands)
East Falkland, Falkland Islands
Stanovoy Khrebet *113 E3 mountain
range* SE Russian Federation
Stanthorpe *149 D5* Queensland,
E Australia
Staphorst *86 D2* Overijssel,
E Netherlands
Starachowice *98 D4*
Świętokrzyskie, C Poland
Stara Pazova *100 D3 Ger.* Altpasua,
Hung. Ópazova. Serbia, N Serbia
and Montenegro (Yugo.)
Stara Zagora *104 D2 Lat.* Augusta
Trajana. Stara Zagora, C Bulgaria
Starbuck Island *145 G3 prev.*
Volunteer Island. E Kiribati
Stargard Szczeciński *98 B3 Ger.*
Stargard in Pommern.
Zachodniopomorskie, NW Poland
Starobil'sk *109 H2 Rus.*
Luhans'ka Oblast',
E Ukraine
Starobyn *107 C7 Rus.* Starobin.
Minskaya Voblasts', S Belarus

Starogard Pomorskiei *98 C2 Ger.*
Preussisch-Stargard. Pomorskie,
N Poland
Starokostyantyniv *108 D2 Rus.*
Starokonstantinov. Khmel'nyts'ka
Oblast', NW Ukraine
Starominskaya *111 A7*
Krasnodarskiy Kray, SW Russian
Federation
Staryya Darohi *107 C6 Rus.* Staryye
Dorogi. Minskaya Voblasts',
S Belarus
Staryy Oskol *111 B6* Belgorodskaya
Oblast', W Russian Federation
State College *41 E4* Pennsylvania,
NE USA
Statesboro *43 E2* Georgia, SE USA
Staunton *41 E5* Virginia, NE USA
Stavanger *85 A6* Rogaland,
S Norway
Stavers Island *see* Vostok Island
Stavropol' *111 B7 prev.*
Voroshilovsk. Stavropol'skiy Kray,
SW Russian Federation
Steamboat Springs *44 C4* Colorado,
C USA
Steenwijk *86 D2* Overijssel,
N Netherlands
Steier *see* Steyr
Steinkjer *84 B4* Nord-Trøndelag,
C Norway
Stendal *94 C3* Sachsen-Anhalt,
C Germany
Stephenville *49 F3* Texas, SW USA
Sterling *44 D2* Colorado, C USA
Sterling *40 B3* Illinois, N USA
Sterlitamak *114 B3* Respublika
Bashkortostan, W Russian
Federation
Stettiner Haff *see* Szczeciński,
Zalew
Stevenage *89 E6* E England, UK
Stevens Point *40 B2* Wisconsin,
N USA
Stewart Island *151 A8 island* S NZ
Steyr *95 D6 var.* Steier.
Oberösterreich, N Austria
St-Gall *see* Sankt Gallen
StGallen *see* Sankt Gallen
Stif *see* Sétif
Stillwater *49 G1* Oklahoma, C USA
Stirling *88 C4* C Scotland, UK
Stjørdal *84 B4* Nord-Trøndelag,
C Norway
St-Laurent *see* St-Laurent-du-
Maroni
Stockach *95 B6* Baden-
Württemberg, S Germany
Stockholm *85 C6 country capital*
(Sweden) Stockholm, C Sweden
Stockton *47 B6* California, W USA
Stockton Plateau *49 E4 plain* Texas,
SW USA
Stœng Trêng *137 D5 prev.* Stung
Treng. Stœng Trêng,
NE Cambodia
Stoke *see* Stoke-on-Trent
Stoke-on-Trent *89 D6 var.* Stoke.
C England, UK
Stómio *105 B4* Thessalía, C Greece
Stony Tunguska *112 D2 river*
C Russian Federation
Store Bælt *see* Storebælt
Storebælt *85 B8 var.* Store Bælt, *Eng.*
Great Belt, Storebelt. *Channel*
Baltic Sea/Kattegat
Storebelt *see* Storebælt
Støren *85 B5* Sør-Trøndelag,
S Norway
Storfjorden *83 G2 fjord* S Norway
Stornoway *88 B2* NW Scotland,
UK
Storsjön *85 B5 lake* C Sweden
Storuman *84 C4 lake* N Sweden
Storuman *84 C4* Västerbotten,
N Sweden
Stowbtsy *107 C6 Pol.* Stolbce, *Rus.*
Stolbtsy. Minskaya Voblasts',
C Belarus
St.Paul Island *see* St-Paul, Île
St-Pierre and Miquelon *39 G4 Fr.*
Îles St-Pierre et Miquelon. *French
territorial collectivity* NE North
America

Strabane *89 B5 Ir.* An Srath Bán.
W Northern Ireland, UK
Strakonice *99 A5 Ger.* Strakonitz.
Budějovický Kraj, S Czech
Republic
Stralsund *94 D2* Mecklenburg-
Vorpommern, NE Germany
Stranraer *89 C5* S Scotland,
UK
Strasbourg *90 E3 Ger.* Strassburg;
anc. Argentoratum. Bas-Rhin,
NE France
Strășeni *108 D3 var.* Strasheny.
C Moldova
Strasheny *see* Strășeni
Stratford *150 D4* Taranaki, North
Island, NZ
Strathfield *148 E2* New South
Wales, SE Australia
Straubing *95 C6* Bayern,
SE Germany
Strehaia *108 B5* Mehedinți,
SW Romania
Strelka *114 D4* Krasnoyarskiy Kray,
C Russian Federation
Strofilía *see* Strofyliá
Strofyliá *105 C5 var.* Strofilia.
Évvoia, C Greece
Stromboli, Isola *97 D6 island* Isole
Eolie, S Italy
Stromeferry *88 C3* N Scotland, UK
Strömstad *85 B6* Västra Götaland,
S Sweden
Strömsund *84 C4* Jämtland,
C Sweden
Struga *101 D6* SW FYR Macedonia
Strumica *101 E6* E FYR Macedonia
Strumyani *104 C3* Blagoevgrad,
SW Bulgaria
Strymónas *104 C3 Bul.* Struma.
River Bulgaria/Greece *see also*
Struma
Stryy *108 B2* L'vivs'ka Oblast',
NW Ukraine
Studholme *151 B6* Canterbury,
South Island, NZ
Sturgis *44 D3* South Dakota, N USA
Stuttgart *95 B6* Baden-
Württemberg, SW Germany
Stykkishólmur *83 E4* Vesturland,
W Iceland
Styr *108 C1 Rus.* Styr'. *River*
Belarus/Ukraine
Su *see* Jiangsu
Suakin *72 C3 var.* Sawakin. Red Sea,
NE Sudan
Subačius *106 C4* Kupiškis,
NE Lithuania
Subaykhān *118 E3* Dayr az Zawr,
E Syria
Subotica *100 D2 Ger.* Maria-
Theresiopel, *Hung.* Szabadka.
Serbia, N Serbia and Montenegro
(Yugo.)
Suceava *108 C3 Ger.* Suczawa,
Hung. Szucsava. Suceava,
NE Romania
Su-chou *see* Suzhou
Suchow *see* Xuzhou
Sucre *61 F4 hist.* Chuquisaca, La
Plata. *Country capital* (Bolivia-legal
capital) Chuquisaca, S Bolivia
Sudan *72 A4 Ar.* Jumhuriyat as-
Sudan; *prev.* Anglo-Egyptian
Sudan. *country* N Africa

Sudan 72

Official name Republic of the
Sudan
Formation 1956
Capital Khartoum
Population 31.8 million / 33 people
per sq mile (13 people per sq km)
Total area 967,493 sq miles
(2,505,810 sq km)
Languages Arabic, Dinka, Nuer,
Zande, Nubian, Beja, Bari, Fur,
Shilluk, Lotuko
Religions Muslim (mainly Sunni)
70%, Traditional beliefs 20%,
other 10%
Ethnic mix Arab 40%, Tribal 30%,
Dinka and Beja 7%, other 23%

Sudan (continued)

Government Presidential regime
Currency Sudanese pound or dinar
= 100 piastres
Literacy rate 58%
Calorie consumption 2,348
kilocalories

Sudbury *38 C4* Ontario, S Canada
Sudd *73 B5 swamp region*
S Sudan
Sudeten *98 B4 var.* Sudetes, Sudetic
Mountains, *Cz./Pol.* Sudety.
Mountain range Czech
Republic/Poland
Sudetes *see* Sudeten
Sudetic Mountains *see* Sudeten
Sudety *see* Sudeten
Südkarpaten *see* Carpații
Meridionali
Sue *73 B5 river* S Sudan
Sueca *93 F3* País Valenciano,
E Spain
Sue Wood Bay *42 B5 bay*
W Bermuda
Suez *72 B1 Ar.* As Suways,
El Suweis. NE Egypt
Suez Canal *72 B1 Ar.* Qanāt as
Suways. *Canal* NE Egypt
Suez, Gulf of *72 B2 Ar.* Khalīj as
Suways. *Gulf* NE Egypt
Suğla Gölü *116 C4 lake* SW Turkey
Şuḥār *121 D5 var.* Sohar.
N Oman
Sühbaatar *127 E1* Selenge,
N Mongolia
Suhl *95 C5* Thüringen, C Germany
Suixi *128 C6* Guangdong,
S China
Sujāwal *134 B3* Sind, SE Pakistan
Sukabumi *138 C5 prev.* Soekaboemi.
Jawa, C Indonesia
Sukagawa *131 D5* Fukushima,
Honshū, C Japan
Sukarnapura *see* Jayapura
Sukhne *see* As Sukhnah
Sukhona *110 C4 var.* Tot'ma. *River*
NW Russian Federation
Sukkertoppen *see* Maniitsoq
Sukkur *134 B3* Sind, SE Pakistan
Sukumo *131 B7* Kōchi, Shikoku,
SW Japan
Sulaimaniya *see* As Sulaymānīyah
Sulaimān Range *134 C2 mountain
range* C Pakistan
Sula, Kepulauan *139 E4 island
group* C Indonesia
Sulawesi *139 E4 Eng.* Celebes.
Island C Indonesia
Sulechów *98 B3 Ger.* Züllichau.
Lubuskie, W Poland
Suliag *see* Sohâg
Sullana *60 B2* Piura, NW Peru
Sulphur Springs *49 G2* Texas,
SW USA
Sulu Archipelago *139 E3 island
group* SW Philippines
Sulu Sea *139 E2 Ind.* Laut Sulu. *Sea*
SW Philippines
Sulyukta *123 E2 Kir.* Sülüktü.
Oshskaya Oblast', SW
Kyrgyzstan
Sumatera *137 B8 Eng.* Sumatra.
Island W Indonesia
Sumatra *see* Sumatera
Sumba, Pulau *139 E5 Eng.*
Sandalwood Island; *prev.* Soemba.
Island Nusa Tenggara,
C Indonesia
Sumba, Selat *139 E5 strait* Nusa
Tenggara, S Indonesia
Sumbawanga *73 B7* Rukwa,
W Tanzania
Sumbe *78 B2 prev.* N'Gunza, *Port.*
Novo Redondo. Cuanza Sul,
W Angola
Sumeih *73 B5* Southern Darfur,
S Sudan
Summer Lake *46 B4 lake* Oregon,
NW USA
Summit *93 H5 mountain*
C Gibraltar

Sumqayıt *117 H2 Rus.* Sumgait.
E Azerbaijan
Sumy *109 F2* Sums'ka Oblast',
NE Ukraine
Sunbury *149 C7* Victoria,
SE Australia
Sunda Islands *see* Greater Sunda
Islands
Sunda, Selat *138 B5 strait*
Jawa/Sumatera, SW Indonesia
Sunda Trench *see* Java Trench
Sunderland *88 D4 var.* Wearmouth.
NE England, UK
Sundsvall *85 C5* Västernorrland,
C Sweden
Sungaipenuh *138 B4 prev.*
Soengaipenoeh. Sumatera,
W Indonesia
Sunnyvale *47 A6* California,
W USA
Suntar *115 F3* Respublika Sakha
(Yakutiya), NE Russian
Federation
Sunyani *75 E5* W Ghana
Suomussalmi *84 E4* Oulu,
E Finland
Suŏng *137 D6* Kâmpóng Cham,
C Cambodia
Suoyarvi *110 B3* Respublika
Kareliya, NW Russian Federation
Supe *60 C3* Lima, W Peru
Superior *40 A1* Wisconsin, N USA
Superior, Lake *40 B1 Fr.* Lac
Supérieur. *Lake* Canada/USA
Suqrah *see* Şawqirah
Suquţrā *121 C7 var.* Sokotra, *Eng.*
Socotra. *Island* SE Yemen
Şūr *see* Soûr
Şūr *121 E5* NE Oman
Surabaya *138 D5 prev.* Soerabaja,
Surabaja. Jawa, C Indonesia
Surakarta *138 C5 Eng.* Solo; *prev.*
Soerakarta. Jawa, S Indonesia
Šurany *99 C6 Hung.* Nagysurány.
Nitriansky Kraj, SW Slovakia
Sūrat *134 C4* Gujarāt, W India
Suratdhani *see* Surat Thani
Surat Thani *137 C6 var.* Suratdhani.
Surat Thani, SW Thailand
Surazh *107 E5 Rus.* Surazh.
Vitsyebskaya Voblasts',
NE Belarus
Surdulica *101 E5* Serbia, SE Serbia
and Montenegro (Yugo.)
Sûre *87 D7 var.* Sauer. *River*
W Europe *see also* Sauer
Surendranagar *134 C4* Gujarāt,
W India
Surfers Paradise *149 E5*
Queensland, E Australia
Surgut *114 D3* Khanty-Mansiyskiy
Avtonomnyy Okrug, C Russian
Federation
Surin *137 D5* Surin, E Thailand
Surinam *see* Suriname
Suriname *59 G3 var.* Surinam; *prev.*
Dutch Guiana, Netherlands
Guiana. *Country* N S America

Suriname 59

Official name Republic of Suriname
Formation 1975
Capital Paramaribo
Population 419,000 / 7 people
per sq mile (3 people per sq km)
Total area 63,039 sq miles
(163,270 sq km)
Languages Dutch, Sranan,
Saramaccan, Javanese, Sarnami
Hindi, Chinese
Religions Christian 48%, Hindu
27%, Muslim 20%, other 5%
Ethnic mix South Asian 34%, Creole
34%, Javanese 18%, Black 9%,
other 5%
Government Parliamentary
democracy
Currency Suriname guilder = 100
cents
Literacy rate 94.2%
Calorie consumption 2,652
kilocalories

Surkhob *123 F3 river*
C Tajikistan
Surt *71 G2 var.* Sidra, Sirte.
N Libya
Surt, Khalīj *71 F2 Eng.* Gulf of
Sidra, Gulf of Sirti, Sidra. *Gulf*
N Libya
Surtsey *83 E5 island* S Iceland
Suruga-wan *131 D6 bay*
SE Japan
Susa *96 A2* Piemonte, NE Italy
Sūsah *see* Sousse
Susanville *47 B5* California,
W USA
Susitna *36 C3* Alaska, USA
Susteren *87 D5* Limburg,
SE Netherlands
Susuman *115 G3* Magadanskaya
Oblast', E Russian Federation
Sutherland *148 E2* New South
Wales, SE Australia
Sutlej *134 C2 river* India/Pakistan
Suur Munamägi *106 D3 var.*
Munamägi, *Ger.* Eier-Berg.
Mountain SE Estonia
Suur Väin *106 C2 Ger.* Grosser
Sund. *Strait* W Estonia
Suva *145 E4 country capital* (Fiji) Viti
Levu, W Fiji
Suwałki *98 E2 Lith.* Suvalkai, *Rus.*
Suvalki. Podlaskie, NE Poland
Şuwār *see* Aş Şuwār
Suzhou *128 D5 var.* Soochow, Su-
chou, Suchow; *prev.* Wuhsien.
Jiangsu, E China
Svalbard *83 E1 Norwegian
dependency* Arctic Ocean
Svartisen *84 C3 glacier*
C Norway
Svay Riěng *137 D6* Svay Riěng,
S Cambodia
Sveg *85 B5* Jämtland,
C Sweden
Svenstavik *85 C5* Jämtland,
C Sweden
Svetlograd *111 B7* Stavropol'skiy
Kray, SW Russian Federation
Svilengrad *104 D3 prev.* Mustafa-
Pasha. Khaskovo, S Bulgaria
Svitlovods'k *109 F3 Rus.*
Svetlovodsk. Kirovohrads'ka
Oblast', C Ukraine
Svobodnyy *115 G4* Amurskaya
Oblast', SE Russian
Federation
Svyataya Anna Trough *172 C4 var.*
Saint Anna Trough. *Undersea
feature* N Kara Sea
Svyetlahorsk *107 D7 Rus.*
Svetlogorsk. Homyel'skaya
Voblasts', SE Belarus
Swabian Jura *see* Schwäbische Alb
Swakopmund *78 B3* Erongo,
W Namibia
Swansea *89 C7 Wel.* Abertawe.
S Wales, UK
Swarzędz *98 C3* Wielkopolskie,
C Poland
Swatow *see* Shantou
Swaziland *78 D4 Country* S Africa

Swaziland 78

Official name Kingdom of
Swaziland
Formation 1968
Capital Mbabane
Population 938,000 / 140 people
per sq mile (54 people per sq km)
Total area 6,704 sq miles
(17,363 sq km)
Languages Siswati, English, Zulu,
Tsonga
Religions Christian 60%,
Traditional beliefs 40%
Ethnic mix Swazi 97%, other 3%
Government Constitutional
monarchy
Currency Lilangeni = 100 cents
Literacy rate 79.6%
Calorie consumption 2,620
kilocalories

Sweden *84 B4 Swe.* Sverige. *Country*
N Europe

Sweden 84

Official name Kingdom of Sweden
Formation 1523
Capital Stockholm
Population 8.8 million /
51 people per sq mile (20 people
per sq km)
Total area 173,731 sq miles
(449,964 sq km)
Languages Swedish, Finnish,
Sami
Religions Evangelical Lutheran
89%, Roman Catholic 2%, other 9%
Ethnic mix Swedish 91%, Finnish
and Sami 3%, other European 6%
Government Parliamentary
democracy
Currency Swedish krona = 100 ore
Literacy rate 99%
Calorie consumption 3,109
kilocalories

Swed Ormsö *see* Vormsi
Sweetwater *49 F3* Texas,
SW USA
Świdnica *98 B4 Ger.* Schweidnitz.
Wałbrzych, SW Poland
Świdwin *98 B2 Ger.* Schivelbein.
Zachodniopomorskie, NW Poland
Świebodzice *98 B4 Ger.* Freiburg in
Schlesien, Swiebodzice.
Wałbrzych, SW Poland
Świebodzin *98 B3 Ger.* Schwiebus.
Lubuskie, W Poland
Świecie *98 C3 Ger.* Schwertberg.
Kujawski-pomorskie, C Poland
Swindon *89 D7* S England, UK
Świnoujście *98 B2 Ger.*
Swinemünde.
Zachodniopomorskie, NW Poland
Switzerland *95 A7 Fr.* La Suisse,
Ger. Schweiz, *It.* Svizzera; *anc.*
Helvetia. *Country* C Europe

Switzerland 95

Official name Swiss Confederation
Formation 1291
Capital Bern
Population 7.2 million / 469 people
per sq mile (174 people per sq km)
Total area 15,942 sq miles
(41,290 sq km)
Languages German, French, Italian,
Swiss German, Romansch
Religions Roman Catholic 46%,
Protestant 40%, other 14%
Ethnic mix German 65%, French
18%, Italian 10%, Romansh 1%,
other 6%
Government Parliamentary
democracy
Currency Swiss franc = 100
centimes
Literacy rate 99%
Calorie consumption 3,293
kilocalories

Sycaminum *see* Hefa
Sydney *148 D1 state capital* New
South Wales, SE Australia
Sydney *39 G4* Cape Breton Island,
Nova Scotia, SE Canada
Syedpur *see* Saidpur
Syemyezhava *107 C6 Rus.*
Semezhevo. Minskaya Voblasts',
C Belarus
Syene *see* Aswân
Syeverodonets'k *109 H3 Rus.*
Severodonetsk. Luhans'ka
Oblast', E Ukraine
Syktyvkar *110 D4 prev.* Ust'-
Sysol'sk. Respublika Komi,
NW Russian Federation
Sylhet *135 G3* Chittagong,
NE Bangladesh
Synel'nykove *109 G3*
Dnipropetrovs'ka Oblast',
E Ukraine

Syowa *154 C2 Japanese research
station* Antarctica
Syracuse *41 E3* New York, NE USA
Syrdariya *see* Syr Darya
Syr Darya *114 B4 var.* Sai Hun, Sir
Darya, Syrdarya, *Kaz.* Syrdariya,
Rus. Syrdar'ya, *Uzb.* Sirdaryo; *anc.*
Jaxartes. *River* C Asia
Syria *118 B3 var.* Siria, Syrie, *Ar.* Al-
Jumhūrīyah al-'Arabīyah as-
Sūrīyah, Sūrīya. *Country* SW Asia

Syria 118

Official name Syrian Arab Republic
Formation 1941
Capital Damascus
Population 16.6 million / 232
people per sq mile (90 people
per sq km)
Total area 71,498 sq miles
(185,180 sq km)
Languages Arabic, French, Kurdish
Religions Sunni Muslim 74%, other
Muslim 16%, Christian 10%
Ethnic mix Arab 89%, Kurdish 6%,
Armenian, Turkmen, Circassian 2%,
other 3%
Government One-party republic
Currency Syrian pound = 100
piastres
Literacy rate 74.5%
Calorie consumption 3,038
kilocalories

Syrian Desert *119 D5 Ar.*
Al Hamad, Bādiyat ash Shām.
Desert SW Asia
Sýrna *105 E7 var.* Sirna. *Island*
Kykládes, Greece, Aegean Sea
Sýros *105 C6 var.* Síros. *Island*
Kykládes, Greece, Aegean Sea
Syvash, Zatoka *109 F4 Rus.* Zaliv
Syvash. *Inlet* S Ukraine
Syzran' *111 C6* Samarskaya Oblast',
W Russian Federation
Szamos *see* Someş
Szamotuły *98 B3* Wielkopolskie,
C Poland
Szczecin *98 B3 Eng./Ger.* Stettin.
Zachodniopomorskie, NW Poland
Szczecinek *98 B2 Ger.* Neustettin.
Zachodniopomorskie, NW Poland
Szczeciński, Zalew *98 A2 var.*
Stettiner Haff, *Ger.* Oderhaff. *Bay*
Germany/Poland
Szczytno *98 D3 Ger.* Ortelsburg.
Olsztyn, NE Poland
Szechuan *see* Sichuan
Szechwan *see* Sichuan
Szeged *99 D7 Ger.* Szegedin, *Rom.*
Seghedin. Csongrád, SE Hungary
Székesfehérvár *99 C6 Ger.*
Stuhlweissenberg; *anc.* Alba
Regia. Fejér, W Hungary
Szekszárd *99 C7* Tolna, S Hungary
Szenttamás *see* Srbobran
Szeping *see* Siping
Sziszek *see* Sisak
Szlatina *see* Slatina
Szolnok *99 D6* Jász-Nagykun-
Szolnok, C Hungary
Szombathely *99 B6 Ger.*
Steinamanger; *anc.* Sabaria,
Savaria. Vas, W Hungary
Szprotawa *98 B4 Ger.* Sprottau.
Lubuskie, W Poland

T

Table Rock Lake *49 G1 reservoir*
Arkansas/Missouri, C USA
Tábor *99 B5* Budějovický Kraj,
S Czech Republic
Tabora *73 B7* Tabora, W Tanzania
Tabrīz *120 C2 var.* Tebriz; *anc.*
Tauris. Āžarbāyjān-e Khāvarī,
NW Iran
Tabuaeran *145 G2 prev.* Fanning
Island. *Atoll* Line Islands,
E Kiribati
Tabūk *120 A4* Tabūk, NW Saudi
Arabia

Täby *85 C6* Stockholm, C Sweden
Tachov *99 A5 Ger.* Tachau. Plzeňský Kraj, W Czech Republic
Tacloban *139 F2 off.* Tacloban City. Leyte, C Philippines
Tacna *61 E4* Tacna, SE Peru
Tacoma *46 B2* Washington, NW USA
Tacuarembó *64 D4 prev.* San Fructuoso. Tacuarembó, C Uruguay
Tademaït, Plateau du *70 D3 plateau* C Algeria
Tadmor *see* Tudmur
Tadmur *see* Tudmur
Tādpatri *132 C2* Andhra Pradesh, E India
Taegu *129 E4 off.* Taegu-gwangyŏksi, *var.* Daegu, *Jap.* Taikyū. SE South Korea
Taejŏn *129 E4 off.* Taejŏn-gwangyŏksi, *Jap.* Taiden. C South Korea
Tafassâsset, Ténéré du *75 G2 desert* N Niger
Tafila *see* Aṭ Ṭafīlah
Taganrog *111 A7* Rostovskaya Oblast', SW Russian Federation
Taganrog, Gulf of *109 G4 Rus.* Taganrogskiy Zaliv, *Ukr.* Tahanroz'ka Zatoka. *Gulf* Russian Federation/Ukraine
Taguatinga *63 F3* Tocantins, C Brazil
Tagus *92 C3 Port.* Rio Tejo, *Sp.* Río Tajo. *River* Portugal/Spain
Tagus Plain *80 A4 undersea feature* E Atlantic Ocean
Tahat *71 E4 mountain* SE Algeria
Tahiti *145 H4 island* Îles du Vent, W French Polynesia
Tahlequah *49 G1* Oklahoma, C USA
Tahoe, Lake *47 B5 lake* California/Nevada, W USA
Tahoua *75 F3* Tahoua, W Niger
T'aichung *128 D6 Jap.* Taichū; *prev.* Taiwan. C Taiwan
Taieri *151 B7 river* South Island, NZ
Taihape *150 D4* Manawatu-Wanganui, North Island, NZ
Tailem Bend *149 B7* South Australia
T'ainan *128 D6 Jap.* Tainan; *prev.* Dainan. S Taiwan
T'aipei *128 D6 Jap.* Taihoku; *prev.* Daihoku. *Country capital* (Taiwan) N Taiwan
Taiping *138 B3* Perak, Peninsular Malaysia
Taiwan *128 D6 var.* Formosa, Formo'sa. *Country* E Asia

Taiwan 128

Official name Republic of China (Taiwan)
Formation 1949
Capital Taipei
Population 22.2 million / 1,598 people per sq mile (617 people per sq km)
Total area 13,892 sq miles (35,980 sq km)
Languages Mandarin Chinese, Amoy Chinese, Hakka Chinese
Religions Buddhist, Confucian, Taoist 93%, Christian 5%, other 2%
Ethnic mix Indigenous Chinese 84%, Mainland Chinese 14%, Aborigine 2%
Government Multiparty republic
Currency Taiwan dollar = 100 cents
Literacy rate 94%
Calorie consumption not available

T'aiwan Haihsia *see* Taiwan Strait
Taiwan Haixia *see* Taiwan Strait
Taiwan Strait *128 D6 var.* Formosa Strait, *Chin.* T'aiwan Haihsia, Taiwan Haixia. *Strait* China/Taiwan
Taiyuan *128 C4 prev.* T'ai-yuan, T'ai-yüan; Yangku. Shanxi, C China

Ta'izz *121 B7* SW Yemen
Tajikistan *123 E3 Rus.* Tadzhikistan, *Taj.* Jumhurii Tojikiston; *prev.* Tajik S.S.R. *Country* C Asia

Tajikistan 123

Official name Republic of Tajikistan
Formation 1991
Capital Dushanbe
Population 6.1 million / 110 people per sq mile (43 people per sq km)
Total area 55,251 sq miles (143,100 sq km)
Languages Tajik, Russian
Religions Sunni Muslim 80%, Shi'a Muslim 5%, other 15%
Ethnic mix Tajik 62%, Uzbek 24%, Russian 8%, Tatar 1%, Kyrgyz 1%, other 4%
Government Multiparty republic
Currency Somoni
Literacy rate 99%
Calorie consumption 1720 kilocalories

Tak *136 C4 var.* Rahaeng. Tak, W Thailand
Takao *see* Kaohsiung
Takaoka *131 C5* Toyama, Honshū, SW Japan
Takapuna *150 D2* Auckland, North Island, NZ
Takhiatosh *122 C2 Rus.* Takhiatash. Qoraqalpog'iston Respublikasi, W Uzbekistan
Takhtakŭpir *122 D1 Rus.* Takhtakupyr. Qoraqalpog'iston Respublikasi, NW Uzbekistan
Takikawa *130 D2* Hokkaidō, NE Japan
Takla Makan Desert *see* Taklimakan Shamo
Taklimakan Shamo *126 B3 Eng.* Takla Makan Desert. *Desert* NW China
Takow *see* Kaohsiung
Takutea *145 G4 island* S Cook Islands
Talachyn *107 D6 Rus.* Tolochin. Vitsyebskaya Voblasts', NE Belarus
Talamanca, Cordillera de *53 E5 mountain range* S Costa Rica
Talara *60 B2* Piura, NW Peru
Talas *123 F2* Talasskaya Oblast', NW Kyrgyzstan
Talaud, Kepulauan *139 F3 island group* E Indonesia
Talavera de la Reina *92 D3 anc.* Caesarobriga, Talabriga. Castilla-La Mancha, C Spain
Talca *64 B4* Maule, C Chile
Talcahuano *65 B5* Bío Bío, C Chile
Taldykorgan *114 C5 Kaz.* Taldyqorghan; *prev.* Taldy-Kurgan. Almaty, SE Kazakhstan
Taldy-Kurgan/Taldyqorghan *see* Taldykorgan
Ta-lien *see* Dalian
Taliq-an *see* Tāloqān
Tal'ka *107 C6 Rus.* Tal'ka. Minskaya Voblasts', C Belarus
Tallahassee *42 D3 prev.* Muskogean. *State capital* Florida, SE USA
Tall al Abyaḍ *see* At Tall al Abyaḍ
Tallinn *106 D2 Ger.* Reval, *Rus.* Tallin; *prev.* Revel. *Country capital* (Estonia) Harjumaa, NW Estonia
Tall Kalakh *118 B4 var.* Tell Kalakh. Ḥimṣ, C Syria
Tallulah *42 B2* Louisiana, S USA
Talnakh *114 D3* Taymyrskiy (Dolgano-Nenetskiy) Avtonomnyy Okrug, N Russian Federation
Tal'ne *109 E3 Rus.* Tal'noye. Cherkas'ka Oblast', C Ukraine
Taloga *49 F1* Oklahoma, C USA
Tāloqān *123 E3 var.* Taliq-an. Takhār, NE Afghanistan

Talsi *106 C3 Ger.* Talsen. Talsi, NW Latvia
Taltal *64 B2* Antofagasta, N Chile
Talvik *84 D2* Finnmark, N Norway
Tamabo, Banjaran *138 D3 mountain range* East Malaysia
Tamale *75 E4* C Ghana
Tamana *145 E3 prev.* Rotcher Island. *Atoll* Tungaru, W Kiribati
Tamanrasset *71 E4 var.* Tamenghest. S Algeria
Tamar *89 C7 river* SW England, UK
Tamar *see* Tudmur
Tamatave *see* Toamasina
Tamazunchale *51 E4* San Luis Potosí, C Mexico
Tambacounda *74 C3* SE Senegal
Tambov *111 B6* Tambovskaya Oblast', W Russian Federation
Tambura *73 B5* Western Equatoria, SW Sudan
Tamchaket *see* Tâmchekkeṭ
Tâmchekkeṭ *74 C3 var.* Tamchaket. Hodh el Gharbi, S Mauritania
Tamenghest *see* Tamanrasset
Tamiahua, Laguna de *51 F4 lagoon* E Mexico
Tamil Nādu *132 C3 prev.* Madras. *State* SE India
Tam Ky *137 E5* Quang Nam-Đa Nâng, C Vietnam
Tampa *43 E4* Florida, SE USA
Tampa Bay *43 E4 bay* Florida, SE USA
Tampere *85 D5 Swe.* Tammerfors. Länsi-Suomi, W Finland
Tampico *51 E3* Tamaulipas, C Mexico
Tamworth *149 D6* New South Wales, SE Australia
Tana *84 D2 var.* Tenojoki, *Fin.* Teno, *Lapp.* Dealnu. *River* Finland/Norway *see also* Teno
Tana *84 D2* Finnmark, N Norway
Tanabe *131 C7* Wakayama, Honshū, SW Japan
T'ana Hāyk' *72 C4 Eng.* Lake Tana. *Lake* NW Ethiopia
Tanais *see* Don
Tanami Desert *146 D3 desert* Northern Territory, N Australia
Ţāndārei *108 D5* Ialomiţa, SE Romania
Tandil *65 D5* Buenos Aires, E Argentina
Tanega-shima *131 B8 island* Nansei-shotō, SW Japan
Tane Range *136 B4 Bur.* Tanen Taunggyi. *Mountain range* W Thailand
Tanezrouft *70 D4 desert* Algeria/Mali
Ţanf, Jabal aṭ *118 D4 mountain* SE Syria
Tanga *69 E5* Tanga, E Tanzania
Tanga *73 C7 region* E Tanzania
Tanganyika, Lake *73 B7 lake* E Africa
Tangeh-ye Hormoz *see* Hormuz, Strait of
Tanger *70 C2 var.* Tangiers, Tangier, *Fr./Ger.* Tangerk, *Sp.* Tánger; *anc.* Tingis. NW Morocco
Tangerk *see* Tanger
Tangiers *see* Tanger
Tangla Range *see* Tanggula Shan
Tangra Yumco *126 B5 var.* Tangro Tso. *Lake* W China
Tangro Tso *see* Tangra Yumco
Tangshan *128 D3 var.* T'ang-shan. Hebei, E China
T'ang-shan *see* Tangshan
Tanimbar, Kepulauan *139 F5 island group* Maluku, E Indonesia
Tanna *144 D5* island S Vanuatu
Tannenhof *see* Krynica
Tan-Tan *70 B3* SW Morocco
Tan-tung *see* Dandong

Tanzania *73 C7 Swa.* Jamhuri ya Muungano wa Tanzania; *prev.* German East Africa, Tanganyika and Zanzibar. *Country* E Africa

Tanzania 73

Official name United Republic of Tanzania
Formation 1961
Capital Dodoma
Population 36 million / 99 people per sq mile (38 people per sq km)
Total area 364,898 sq miles (945,087 sq km)
Languages English, Kiswahili, Sukuma
Religions Muslim 33%, Christian 33%, Traditional beliefs 30%, other 4%
Ethnic mix Native African (over 120 tribes) 99%, European and Asian 1%
Government Presidential democracy
Currency Tanzanian shilling = 100 cents
Literacy rate 75.8%
Calorie consumption 1,906 kilocalories

Taoudenit *see* Taoudenni
Taoudenni *75 E2 var.* Taoudenit. Tombouctou, N Mali
Tapa *106 E2 Ger.* Taps. Lääne-Virumaa, NE Estonia
Tapachula *51 G5* Chiapas, SE Mexico
Tapajós, Rio *63 E2 var.* Tapajóz. *River* NW Brazil
Tapajóz *see* Tapajós, Rio
Ţarābulus *71 F2 var.* Ţarābulus al Gharb, *Eng.* Tripoli.*Country capital* (Libya) NW Libya
Ţarābulus *see* Tripoli
Ţarābulus al Gharb *see* Ţarābulus
Ţarābulus ash Shām *see* Tripoli
Taraclia *108 D4 Rus.* Tarakliya. S Moldova
Taranaki, Mount *150 C4 var.* Egmont, Mount. *Mountain* North Island, NZ
Tarancón *93 E3* Castilla-La Mancha, C Spain
Taranto *97 E6 var.* Tarentum. Puglia, SE Italy
Taranto, Golfo di *97 E6 Eng.* Gulf of Taranto. *Gulf* S Italy
Tarapoto *60 C2* San Martín, N Peru
Tarare *91 D5* Rhône, E France
Tarascon *91 D6* Bouches-du-Rhône, SE France
Tarawa *144 D2 atoll* Tungaru, W Kiribati
Taraz *114 C5 prev.* Aulie Ata, Auliye-Ata, Dzhambul, Zhambyl. Zhambyl, S Kazakhstan
Tarazona *93 E2* Aragón, NE Spain
Tarbes *91 B6 anc.* Bigorra. Hautes-Pyrénées, S France
Tarcoola *149 A6* South Australia
Taree *149 D6* New South Wales, SE Australia
Tarentum *see* Taranto
Târgovişte *108 C5 prev.* Tîrgovişte. Dâmboviţa, S Romania
Târgu Jiu *108 B4 prev.* Tîrgu Jiu. Gorj, W Romania
Târgul-Neamţ *see* Târgu-Neamţ
Târgu Mures *108 B4 prev.* Oşorhei, Tîrgu Mures, *Ger.* Neumarkt, *Hung.* Marosvásárhely. Mures, C Romania
Târgu-Neamţ *108 C3 var.* Târgul-Neamţ; *prev.* Tîrgu-Neamţ. Neamţ, NE Romania
Târgu Ocna *108 C4 Hung.* Aknavásár; *prev.* Tîrgu Ocna. Bacău, E Romania
Târgu Secuiesc *108 C4 Ger.* Neumarkt, Szekler Neumarkt, *Hung.* Kézdivásárhely; *prev.* Chezdi-Oşorheiu, Târgul-Săcuiesc, Tîrgu Secuiesc. Covasna, E Romania

Tarija 61 G5 Tarija, S Bolivia
Tarīm 121 C6 C Yemen
Tarim Basin 124 C2 basin
NW China
Tarim He 126 B3 river NW China
Tarma 60 C3 Junín, C Peru
Tarn 91 C6 cultural region S France
Tarn 91 C6 river S France
Tarnobrzeg 98 D4 Podkarpackie,
SE Poland
Tarnów 99 D5 Małopolskie,
S Poland
Tarragona 93 G2 anc. Tarraco.
Cataluña, E Spain
Tàrrega 93 F2 var. Tarrega.
Cataluña, NE Spain
Tarsus 116 C4 İçel, S Turkey
Tartu 106 D3 Ger. Dorpat; prev. Rus.
Yurev, Yur'yev. Tartumaa,
SE Estonia
Ţarţūs 118 A3 Fr. Tartouss; anc.
Tortosa. Ţarţūs, W Syria
Ta Ru Tao, Ko 137 B7 island
S Thailand
Tarvisio 96 D2 Friuli-Venezia
Giulia, NE Italy
Tashi Chho Dzong see Thimphu
Tashkent see Toshkent
Tash-Kumyr 123 F2 Kir. Tash-
Kömür. Dzhalal-Abadskaya
Oblast', W Kyrgyzstan
Tashqurghan see Kholm
Tasikmalaya 138 C5 prev.
Tasikmalaja. Jawa, C Indonesia
Tasman Basin 142 C5 var. East
Australian Basin. Undersea feature
S Tasman Sea
Tasman Bay 151 C5 inlet South
Island, NZ
Tasmania 149 B8 prev. Van
Diemen's Land. State SE Australia
Tasmania 152 B4 island SE Australia
Tasman Plateau 142 C5 var. South
Tasmania Plateau. Undersea feature
SW Tasman Sea
Tasman Sea 142 C5 sea SW Pacific
Ocean
Tassili-n-Ajjer 71 E4 plateau
E Algeria
Tatabánya 99 C6 Komárom-
Esztergom, NW Hungary
Tathlīth 121 B5 'Asīr, S Saudi
Arabia
Tatra Mountains 99 D5 Ger. Tatra,
Hung. Tátra, Pol./Slvk. Tatry.
Mountain range Poland/Slovakia
Ta-t'ung see Datong
Tatvan 117 F3 Bitlis, SE Turkey
Ta'ū 145 F4 var. Tau. Island Manua
Islands, E American Samoa
Tau see Ta'ū
Taukum, Peski 123 G1 desert
SE Kazakhstan
Taumarunui 150 D4 Manawatu-
Wanganui, North Island, NZ
Taungdwingyi 136 B3 Magwe,
C Myanmar
Taunggyi 136 B3 Shan State,
C Myanmar
Taunton 89 C7 SW England, UK
Taupo 150 D3 Waikato, North
Island, NZ
Taupo, Lake 150 D3 lake North
Island, NZ
Taurage 106 B4 Ger. Tauroggen.
Tauragė, SW Lithuania
Tauranga 150 D3 Bay of Plenty,
North Island, NZ
Tauris see Tabrīz
Tavas 116 B4 Denizli, SW Turkey
Tavira 92 C5 Faro, S Portugal
Tavoy 137 B5 var. Dawei.
Tenasserim, S Myanmar
Tavoy Island see Mali Kyun
Tawakoni, Lake 49 G2 reservoir
Texas, SW USA
Tawau 138 D3 Sabah, East Malaysia
Ţawkar see Tokar
Tawzar see Tozeur
Taxco 51 E4 var. Taxco de Alarcón.
Guerrero, S Mexico
Taxco de Alarcón see Taxco
Tay 88 C3 river C Scotland, UK

Taylor 49 G3 Texas, SW USA
Taymā' 120 A4 Tabūk, NW Saudi
Arabia
Taymyr, Ozero 115 E2 lake
N Russian Federation
Taymyr, Poluostrov 115 E2
peninsula N Russian Federation
Taz 114 D3 river N Russian
Federation
T'bilisi 117 G2 Eng. Tiflis. Country
capital (Georgia) SE Georgia
T'bilisi 112 B4 international airport
S Georgia
Tchien see Zwedru
Tchongking see Chongqing
Tczew 98 C2 Ger. Dirschau.
Pomorskie, N Poland
Te Anau 151 A7 Southland, South
Island, NZ
Te Anau, Lake 151 A7 lake South
Island, NZ
Teapa 51 G4 Tabasco, SE Mexico
Teate see Chieti
Tebingtinggi 138 B3 Sumatera,
N Indonesia
Tebriz see Tabrīz
Techirghiol 108 D5 Constanţa,
SE Romania
Tecomán 50 D4 Colima, SW Mexico
Tecpan 51 E5 var. Tecpan de
Galeana. Guerrero, S Mexico
Tecpan de Galeana see Tecpan
Tecuci 108 C4 Galaţi, E Romania
Tedzhen 122 C3 Turkm. Tejen.
Akhalskiy Velayat,
S Turkmenistan
Tedzhen see Harīrūd
Tees 89 D5 river N England, UK
Tefé 62 D2 Amazonas, N Brazil
Tegal 138 C4 Jawa, C Indonesia
Tegelen 87 D5 Limburg,
SE Netherlands
Tegucigalpa 52 C3 country capital
(Honduras) Francisco Morazán,
SW Honduras
Teheran see Tehrān
Tehrān 120 C3 var. Teheran. Country
capital (Iran) Tehrān, N Iran
Tehuacán 51 F4 Puebla, S Mexico
Tehuantepec 51 F5 var. Santo
Domingo Tehuantepec. Oaxaca,
SE Mexico
Tehuantepec, Golfo de 51 F5 var.
Gulf of Tehuantepec. Gulf
S Mexico
Tehuantepec, Gulf of see
Tehuantepec, Golfo de
Tehuantepec, Isthmus of see
Tehuantepec, Istmo de
Tehuantepec, Istmo de 51 F5 var.
Isthmus of Tehuantepec. Isthmus
SE Mexico
Tejen see Harīrūd
Te Kao 150 C1 Northland, North
Island, NZ
Tekax 51 H4 var. Tekax de Álvaro
Obregón. Yucatán, SE Mexico
Tekax de Álvaro Obregón see
Tekax
Tekeli 114 C5 Almaty,
SE Kazakhstan
Tekirdağ 116 A2 It. Rodosto; anc.
Bisanthe, Raidestos, Rhaedestus.
Tekirdağ, NW Turkey
Te Kuiti 150 D3 Waikato, North
Island, NZ
Tela 52 C2 Atlántida,
NW Honduras
Telanaipura see Jambi
Tel Aviv-Jaffa see Tel Aviv-Yafo
Tel Aviv-Yafo 119 A6 var. Tel
Aviv-Jaffa. Tel Aviv, C Israel
Teles Pirés see São Manuel, Rio
Telish 104 C2 prev. Azizie. Pleven,
NW Bulgaria
Tell Abiad see At Tall al Abyaḍ
Tell Abyad see At Tall al Abyaḍ
Tell Kalakh see Tall Kalakh
Tell Shedadi see Ash Shadādah
Telšiai 106 B3 Ger. Telschen. Telšiai,
NW Lithuania
Teluk Irian see Cenderawasih,
Teluk

Teluk Serera see Cenderawasih,
Teluk
Temerin 100 D3 Serbia, N Serbia
and Montenegro (Yugo.)
Temirtau 114 C4 prev.
Samarkandski, Samarkandskoye.
Karaganda, C Kazakhstan
Tempio Pausania 97 A5 Sardegna,
Italy, C Mediterranean Sea
Temple 49 G3 Texas, SW USA
Temuco 65 B5 Araucanía, C Chile
Temuka 151 B6 Canterbury, South
Island, NZ
Tenasserim 137 B6 Tenasserim,
S Myanmar
Ténenkou 74 D3 Mopti, C Mali
Ténéré 75 G3 physical region C Niger
Tenerife 70 A3 island Islas Canarias,
Spain, NE Atlantic Ocean
Tengger Shamo 127 E3 desert
N China
Tengréla 74 D4 var. Tingréla.
N Côte d'Ivoire
Tenkodogo 75 E4 S Burkina faso
Tennant Creek 148 A3 Northern
Territory, C Australia
Tennessee 42 C1 off. State of
Tennessee; also known as The
Volunteer State. State SE USA
Tennessee River 42 C1 river S USA
Teno see Tana
Tenojoki see Tana
Tepelena see Tepelenë
Tepelenë 101 C7 var. Tepelena, It.
Tepeleni. Gjirokastër, S Albania
Tepeleni see Tepelenë
Tepic 50 D4 Nayarit, C Mexico
Teplice 98 A4 Ger. Teplitz; prev.
Teplice-Šanov, Teplitz-Schönau.
Ústecký Kraj, NW Czech Republic
Tequila 50 D4 Jalisco, SW Mexico
Teraina 145 G2 prev. Washington
Island. Atoll Line Islands,
E Kiribati
Teramo 96 C4 anc. Interamna.
Abruzzo, C Italy
Tercan 117 E3 Erzincan, NE Turkey
Terceira 92 A5 var. Ilha Terceira.
Island Azores, Portugal,
NE Atlantic Ocean
Teresina 63 F2 var. Therezina. State
capital Piauí, NE Brazil
Termia see Kýthnos
Términos, Laguna de 51 G4 lagoon
SE Mexico
Termiz 123 E3 Rus. Termez.
Surkhondaryo Wiloyati,
S Uzbekistan
Termoli 96 D4 Molise, C Italy
Terneuzen 87 B5 var. Neuzen.
Zeeland, SW Netherlands
Terni 96 C4 anc. Interamna Nahars.
Umbria, C Italy
Ternopil' 108 C2 Pol. Tarnopol, Rus.
Ternopol'. Ternopil's'ka Oblast',
W Ukraine
Terracina 97 C5 Lazio, C Italy
Terrassa 93 G2 Cast. Tarrasa.
Cataluña, E Spain
Terre Adélie 154 C4 disputed region
SE Antarctica
Terre Haute 40 B4 Indiana, N USA
Territoire du Yukon see Yukon
Territory
Terschelling 86 C1 Fris. Skylge.
Island Waddeneilanden,
N Netherlands
Teruel 93 F3 anc. Turba. Aragón,
E Spain
Tervel 104 E1 prev. Kurtbunar, Rom.
Curtbunar. Dobrich, NE Bulgaria
Tervueren see Tervuren
Tervuren 87 C6 var. Tervueren.
Vlaams Brabant, C Belgium
Teseney 72 C4 var. Tesseneï.
W Eritrea
Tessalit 75 E2 Kidal, NE Mali
Tessaoua 75 G3 Maradi, S Niger
Tessenderlo 87 C5 Limburg,
NE Belgium
Tesseneï see Teseney
Testigos, Islas los 59 E1 island group
N Venezuela

Tete 79 E2 Tete, NW Mozambique
Teterow 94 C3 Mecklenburg-
Vorpommern, NE Germany
Tétouan 70 C2 var. Tetouan, Tetuán.
N Morocco
Tetovo 101 D5 Alb. Tetova, Tetovë,
Turk. Kalkandelen. Razgrad,
N Bulgaria
Tetuán see Tétouan
Tevere 96 C4 Eng. Tiber. River
C Italy
Teverya 119 B5 var. Tiberias, Tverya.
Northern, N Israel
Te Waewae Bay 151 A7 bay South
Island, NZ
Texarkana 42 A2 Arkansas, C USA
Texarkana 49 H2 Texas, SW USA
Texas 49 F3 off. State of Texas; also
known as The Lone Star State.
State S USA
Texas City 49 H4 Texas, SW USA
Texel 86 C2 island Waddeneilanden,
NW Netherlands
Texoma, Lake 49 G2 reservoir
Oklahoma/Texas, C USA
Teziutlán 51 F4 Puebla, S Mexico
Thaa Atoll see Kolhumadulu Atoll
Thai Binh 136 D3 Thai Binh,
N Vietnam
Thailand 137 C5 Th. Prathet Thai;
prev. Siam. Country SE Asia

Thailand 137

Official name Kingdom of Thailand
Formation 1238
Capital Bangkok
Population 63.6 million /
322 people per sq mile (124 people
per sq km)
Total area 197,254 sq miles
(510,890 sq km)
Languages Thai, Chinese, Malay,
Khmer, Mon, Karen, Miao
Religions Buddhist 95%, Muslim
3%, Christian 1%, other 1%
Ethnic mix Thai 83%, Chinese 12%,
Malay 3%, Khmer and other 2%
Government Parliamentary
democracy
Currency Baht = 100 stangs
Literacy rate 95.5%
Calorie consumption 2,506
kilocalories

Thailand, Gulf of 137 C6 var. Gulf
of Siam, Th. Ao Thai, Vtn. Vinh
Thai Lan. Gulf SE Asia
Thai Nguyên 136 D3 Bắc Thai,
N Vietnam
Thakhèk 136 D4 prev. Muang
Khammouan. Khammouan,
C Laos
Thamarīd see Thamarīt
Thamarīt 121 D6 var. Thamarīd,
Thumrayt. SW Oman
Thames 89 B8 river S England, UK
Thames 150 D3 Waikato, North
Island, NZ
Thanh Hoa 136 D3 Vinh Phu,
N Vietnam
Thanintari Taungdan see
Bilauktaung Range
Thar Desert 134 C3 var. Great
Indian Desert, Indian Desert.
Desert India/Pakistan
Tharthār, Buḩayrat ath 120 B3 lake
C Iraq
Thásos 104 C4 island E Greece
Thásos 104 C4 Thásos, E Greece
Thaton 136 B4 Mon State,
S Myanmar
Thayetmyo 136 A4 Magwe,
C Myanmar
The Crane 55 H2 var. Crane.
S Barbados
The Dalles 46 B3 Oregon,
NW USA
The Flatts Village see Flatts Village
The Hague see 's-Gravenhage
Theodosia see Feodosiya
The Pas 37 F5 Manitoba, C Canada
Therezina see Teresina

Thérma 105 D6 Ikaría, Dodekánisos, Greece, Aegean Sea
Thermaïkós Kólpos 104 B4 Eng. Thermaic Gulf; anc. Thermaicus Sinus. Gulf N Greece
Thermiá see Kýthnos
Thérmo 105 B5 Dytiki Ellás, C Greece
The Rock 93 H4 E Gibraltar
The Six Counties see Northern Ireland
Thessaloníki 104 C3 Eng. Salonica, Salonika, SCr. Solun, Turk. Selânik. Kentrikí Makedonía, N Greece
The Valley 55 G3 dependent territory capital (Anguilla) E Anguilla
The Village 49 G1 Oklahoma, C USA
Thiamis see Thýamis
Thibet see Xizang Zizhiqu
Thief River Falls 45 F1 Minnesota, N USA
Thienen see Tienen
Thiers 91 C5 Puy-de-Dôme, C France
Thiès 74 B3 W Senegal
Thimbu see Thimphu
Thimphu 135 G3 var. Thimbu; prev. Tashi Chho Dzong. Country capital (Bhutan) W Bhutan
Thionville 90 D3 Ger. Diedenhofen. Moselle, NE France
Thíra 105 D7 prev. Santorin, Santoríni, anc. Thera. Island Kykládes, Greece, Aegean Sea
Thíra 105 D7 Thíra, Kykládes, Greece, Aegean Sea
Thiruvananthapuram see Trivandrum
Thitu Island 128 C8 island NW Spratly Islands
Tholen 86 B4 island SW Netherlands
Thomasville 42 D3 Georgia, SE USA
Thompson 37 F4 Manitoba, C Canada
Thonon-les-Bains 91 D5 Haute-Savoie, E France
Thorláskhöfn 83 E5 Sudhurland, SW Iceland
Thornton Island see Millennium Island
Thouars 90 B4 Deux-Sèvres, W France
Thracian Sea 104 D4 Gk. Thrakikó Pélagos; anc. Thracium Mare. Sea Greece/Turkey
Three Kings Islands 150 C1 island group N NZ
Thrissur see Trichūr
Thuin 87 B7 Hainaut, S Belgium
Thule see Qaanaaq
Thumrayt see Thamarīt
Thun 95 A7 Fr. Thoune. Bern, W Switzerland
Thunder Bay 38 B4 Ontario, S Canada
Thuner See 95 A7 lake C Switzerland
Thung Song 137 C7 var. Cha Mai. Nakhon Si Thammarat, SW Thailand
Thurso 88 C2 N Scotland, UK
Thýamis 104 A4 var. Thiamis. River W Greece
Tianjin 128 D4 var. Tientsin. Tianjin Shi, E China
Tianjin see Tianjin Shi
Tianjin Shi 128 D4 var. Jin, Tianjin, T'ien-ching, Tientsin. Admin. region municipality E China
Tianshui 128 B4 Gansu, C China
Tiba see Chiba
Tiberias see Teverya
Tiberias, Lake 119 B5 var. Chinnereth, Sea of Bahr Tabariya, Sea of Galilee, Ar. Bahrat Tabariya, Heb. Yam Kinneret. Lake N Israel
Tibesti 76 C2 var. Tibesti Massif, Ar. Tîbistî. Mountain range N Africa

Tibesti Massif see Tibesti
Tibet see Xizang Zizhiqu
Tibetan Autonomous Region see Xizang Zizhiqu
Tibet, Plateau of see Qingzang Gaoyuan
Tibistî see Tibesti
Tibnī see At Tibnī
Tiburón, Isla 50 B2 var. Isla del Tiburón. Isla NW Mexico
Tiburón, Isla del see Tiburón, Isla
Tichît 74 D2 var. Tichitt. Tagant, C Mauritania
Tichitt see Tichît
Ticul 51 H3 Yucatán, SE Mexico
Tidjikdja see Tidjikja
Tidjikja 74 C2 var. Tidjikdja; prev. Fort-Cappolani. Tagant, C Mauritania
T'ien-ching see Tianjin Shi
Tienen 87 C6 var. Thienen, Fr. Tirlemont. Vlaams Brabant, C Belgium
Tien Shan 126 B3 Chin. Thian Shan, Tian Shan, Rus. Tyan'-Shan'. Mountain range C Asia
Tientsin see Tianjin Shi
Tierp 85 C6 Uppsala, C Sweden
Tierra del Fuego 65 B8 off. Provincia de la Tierra del Fuego. Admin. region province S Argentina
Tierra del Fuego 57 B8 island Argentina/Chile
Tifton 42 D3 Georgia, SE USA
Tifu 139 F4 Pulau Buru, E Indonesia
Tighina 108 D4 Rus. Bendery; prev. Bender. E Moldova
Tigranocerta see Siirt
Tigris 120 B2 Ar. Dijlah, Turk. Dicle. River Iraq/Turkey
Tiguentourine 71 E3 E Algeria
Ti-hua see Ürümqi
Tihwa see Ürümqi
Tijuana 50 A1 Baja California, NW Mexico
Tikhoretsk 111 A7 Krasnodarskiy Kray, SW Russian Federation
Tikhvin 110 B4 Leningradskaya Oblast', NW Russian Federation
Tiki Basin 143 G3 undersea feature S Pacific Ocean
Tiksi 115 F2 Respublika Sakha (Yakutiya), NE Russian Federation
Tilburg 86 C4 Noord-Brabant, S Netherlands
Tilimsen see Tlemcen
Tillabéri 75 F3 var. Tillabéry. Tillabéri, W Niger
Tillabéry see Tillabéri
Tílos 105 E7 island Dodekánisos, Greece, Aegean Sea
Timanskiy Kryazh 110 D3 Eng. Timan Ridge. Ridge NW Russian Federation
Timaru 151 B6 Canterbury, South Island, NZ
Timbaki see Tympáki
Timbákion see Tympáki
Timbedgha 74 D3 var. Timbédra. Hodh ech Chargui, SE Mauritania
Timbédra see Timbedgha
Timbuktu see Tombouctou
Timiş 108 A4 river W Romania
Timişoara 108 A4 Ger. Temeschwar, Temeswar, Hung. Temesvár; prev. Temeschburg. Timiş, W Romania
Timmins 38 C4 Ontario, S Canada
Timor 125 F5 island Nusa Tenggara, East Timor/Indonesia
Timor Timur see East Timor
Timor Sea 125 F5 sea E Indian Ocean
Timor Trench see Timor Trough
Timor Trough 125 F5 var. Timor Trench. Undersea feature NE Timor Sea
Timrå 85 C5 Västernorrland, C Sweden
Tindouf 70 C3 W Algeria
Tineo 92 C1 Asturias, N Spain
Tingis |MM see Tanger

Tingo María 60 C3 Huánuco, C Peru
Tingréla see Tengréla
Tinhosa Grande 76 E2 island N Sao Tome and Principe
Tinhosa Pequena 76 E1 island N Sao Tome and Principe
Tinian 144 B1 island N Northern Mariana Islands
Tínos 105 D6 anc. Tenos. Island Kykládes, Greece, Aegean Sea
Tínos 105 D6 Tínos, Kykládes, Greece, Aegean Sea
Tip 101 E6 Papua, E Indonesia
Tipitapa 52 D3 Managua, W Nicaragua
Tip Top Mountain 38 C4 mountain Ontario, S Canada
Tirana see Tiranë
Tiranë 101 C6 var. Tirana. Country capital (Albania) Tiranë, C Albania
Tiraspol 108 D4 Rus. Tiraspol'. E Moldova
Tiree 88 B3 island W Scotland, UK
Tîrgu-Neamţ see Târgu-Neamţ
Tirlemont see Tienen
Tírnavos see Týrnavos
Tirol 95 C7 cultural region Austria/Italy
Tiruchchirāppalli 132 C3 prev. Trichinopoly. Tamil Nādu, SE India
Tiruppattūr 132 C2 Tamil Nādu, SE India
Tisza 103 F1 Ger. Theiss, Rom./Slvn./SCr. Tisa, Rus. Tissa, Ukr. Tysa. River SE Europe see also Tisa
Tiszakécske 99 D7 Bács-Kiskun, C Hungary
Titano, Monte 96 E1 mountain C San Marino
Titicaca, Lake 61 E4 lake Bolivia/Peru
Titose see Chitose
Titu 108 C5 Dâmboviţa, S Romania
Titule 77 D5 Orientale, N Dem. Rep. Congo
Tiverton 89 C7 SW England, UK
Tivoli 96 C4 anc. Tiber. Lazio, C Italy
Tizimín 51 H3 Yucatán, SE Mexico
Tizi Ouzou 71 E1 var. Tizi-Ouzou. N Algeria
Tiznit 70 B3 SW Morocco
Tlaquepaque 50 D4 Jalisco, C Mexico
Tlascala see Tlaxcala
Tlaxcala 51 F4 var. Tlascala, Tlaxcala de Xicohténcatl. Tlaxcala, C Mexico
Tlaxcala de Xicohténcatl see Tlaxcala
Tlemcen 70 D2 var. Tilimsen, Tlemsen. NW Algeria
Tlemsen see Tlemcen
Toamasina 79 G3 var. Tamatave. Toamasina, E Madagascar
Toba, Danau 138 B3 lake Sumatera, W Indonesia
Tobago 55 H5 island NE Trinidad and Tobago
Tobol 114 C4 Kaz. Tobyl. River Kazakhstan/Russian Federation
Tobol'sk 114 C3 Tyumenskaya Oblast', C Russian Federation
Tocantins 63 E3 off. Estado do Tocantins. State C Brazil
Tocantins, Rio 63 F2 river N Brazil
Tocoa 52 D2 Colón, N Honduras
Tocopilla 64 B2 Antofagasta, N Chile
Todi 96 C4 Umbria, C Italy
Todos os Santos, Baía de 63 G3 bay E Brazil
Toetoes Bay 151 B8 bay South Island, NZ
Tofua 145 E4 island Ha'apai Group, C Tonga
Togo 75 E4 French Togoland. Country W Africa

Togo 75

Official name Republic of Togo
Formation 1960
Capital Lomé
Population 4.7 million / 214 people per sq mile (83 people per sq km)
Total area 21,925 sq miles (56,785 sq km) **Languages** French, Ewe, Kabye, Gurma
Religions Traditional beliefs 50%, Christian 35%, Muslim 15%
Ethnic mix Ewe 46%, other African 53%, European 1%
Government Presidential regime
Currency CFA franc = 100 centimes
Literacy rate 57.3%
Calorie consumption 2,329 kilocalories

Tokanui 151 B7 Southland, South Island, NZ
Tokar 72 C3 var. Ţawkar. Red Sea, NE Sudan
Tokat 116 D3 Tokat, N Turkey
Tokelau 145 E3 NZ overseas territory W Polynesia
Tokio see Tōkyō
Tokmak 123 G2 Kir. Tokmok. Chuyskaya Oblast', N Kyrgyzstan
Tokmak 109 G4 var. Velykyy Tokmak. Zaporiz'ka Oblast', SE Ukraine
Tokoroa 150 D3 Waikato, North Island, NZ
Tokounou 74 C4 Haute-Guinée, C Guinea
Tokushima 131 C6 var. Tokusima. Tokushima, Shikoku, SW Japan
Tokusima see Tokushima
Tōkyō 130 A1 var. Tokio. Country capital (Japan) Tōkyō, Honshū, S Japan
Tōkyō Bay 130 A2 bay SW Japan
Toledo 92 D3 anc. Toletum. Castilla-La Mancha, C Spain
Toledo 40 D3 Ohio, N USA
Toledo Bend Reservoir 49 G3 reservoir Louisiana/Texas, SW USA
Toliara 79 F4 var. Toliary; prev. Tuléar. Toliara, SW Madagascar
Toliary see Toliara
Tolmin 95 D7 Ger. Tolmein, It. Tolmino. W Slovenia
Tolna 99 C7 Ger. Tolnau. Tolna, S Hungary
Tolosa 93 E1 País Vasco, N Spain
Toluca 51 E4 var. Toluca de Lerdo. México, S Mexico
Toluca de Lerdo see Toluca
Tol'yatti 111 C6 prev. Stavropol'. Samarskaya Oblast', W Russian Federation
Tomah 40 B2 Wisconsin, N USA
Tomakomai 130 D2 Hokkaidō, NE Japan
Tomar 92 B3 Santarém, W Portugal
Tomaschow see Tomaszów Mazowiecki
Tomaszów see Tomaszów Mazowiecki
Tomaszów Lubelski 98 E4 Ger. Tomaschow. Lubelskie, E Poland
Tomaszów Mazowiecka see Tomaszów Mazowiecki
Tomaszów Mazowiecki 98 D4 var. Tomaszów Mazowiecka; prev. Tomaszów, Ger. Tomaschow. Łódzkie, C Poland
Tombigbee River 42 C3 river Alabama/Mississippi, S USA
Tombouctou 75 E3 Eng. Timbuktu. Tombouctou, N Mali
Tombua 78 A2 Port. Porto Alexandre. Namibe, SW Angola
Tomelloso 93 E3 Castilla-La Mancha, C Spain
Tomini, Gulf of 139 E4 var. Teluk Tomini; prev. Teluk Gorontalo. Bay Sulawesi, C Indonesia

Tomini, Teluk see Tomini, Gulf of
Tomsk 114 D4 Tomskaya Oblast',
C Russian Federation
Tomur Feng see Pobedy, Pik
Tonga 145 E4 var. Friendly Islands.
Country SW Pacific Ocean

Tonga 145

Official name Kingdom of Tonga
Formation 1970
Capital Nuku'alofa
Population 102,200 / 354 people
per sq mile (137 people per sq km)
Total area 289 sq miles (748 sq km)
Languages Tongan, English
Religions Free Wesleyan 64%,
Roman Catholic 15%, Other 21%
Ethnic mix Polynesian 99%, other
Pacific groups and European 1%
Government Monarchy
Currency Pa'anga (Tongan dollar) =
100 seniti
Literacy rate 98.5%
Calorie consumption not available

Tongatapu 145 E5 island Tongatapu
Group, S Tonga
Tonga Trench 143 E3 undersea
feature S Pacific Ocean
Tongchuan 128 C4 Shaanxi,
C China
Tongeren 87 D6 Fr. Tongres.
Limburg, NE Belgium
Tongking, Gulf of 128 B7 Chin.
Beibu Wan, Vtn. Vinh Bắc Bộ. Gulf
China/Vietnam
Tongliao 127 G2 Nei Mongol
Zizhiqu, N China
Tongshan see Xuzhou
Tongtian He 126 C4 river C China
Tonj 73 B5 Warab, SW Sudan
Tônlé Sap 137 D5 Eng. Great Lake.
Lake W Cambodia
Tonopah 47 C6 Nevada, W USA
Tonyezh 107 C7 Rus. Tonezh.
Homyel'skaya Voblasts',
SE Belarus
Tooele 44 B4 Utah, W USA
Toowoomba 149 E5 Queensland,
E Australia
Topeka 45 F4 state capital Kansas,
C USA
Topliţa 108 C3 Ger. Töplitz, Hung.
Maroshévíz; prev. Topliţa Română,
Hung. Oláh-Toplicza, Toplicza.
Harghita, C Romania
Topoľčany 99 C6 Hung.
Nagytapolcsány. Nitriansky Kraj,
SW Slovakia
Topolovgrad 104 D3 prev. Kavakli.
Khaskovo, S Bulgaria
Top Springs Roadhouse 146 D3
Northern Territory, N Australia
Torez 109 H3 Donets'ka Oblast',
SE Ukraine
Torgau 94 D4 Sachsen, E Germany
Torhout 87 A5 West-Vlaanderen,
W Belgium
Torino 96 A2 Eng. Turin. Piemonte,
NW Italy
Tornacum see Tournai
Torneälven see Tornionjoki
Torneträsk 84 C3 lake N Sweden
Tornio 84 D4 Swe. Torneå. Lappi,
NW Finland
Torniojoki see Tornionjoki
Tornionjoki 84 D3 var. Torniojoki,
Swe. Torneälven. River
Finland/Sweden
Toro 92 D2 Castilla-León, N Spain
Toronto 38 D5 Ontario, S Canada
Toros Dağları 116 C4 Eng. Taurus
Mountains. Mountain range
S Turkey
Torquay 89 C7 SW England, UK
Torrance 46 D2 California, W USA
Torre, Alto da 92 B3 mountain
C Portugal
Torre del Greco 97 D5 Campania,
S Italy
Torrejón de Ardoz 93 E3 Madrid,
C Spain

Torrelavega 92 D1 Cantabria,
N Spain
Torrens, Lake 149 A6 salt lake South
Australia
Torrent see Torrente
Torrent de l'Horta see Torrente
Torrente 93 F3 var. Torrent, Torrent
de l'Horta. País Valenciano,
E Spain
Torreón 50 D3 Coahuila de
Zaragoza, NE Mexico
Torres Strait 148 C1 strait
Australia/PNG
Torres Vedras 92 B3 Lisboa,
C Portugal
Torrington 44 D3 Wyoming, C USA
Tórshavn 83 F5 Dan. Thorshavn.
Dependent territory capital (Faeroe
Islands) N Faeroe Islands
Tortoise Islands see Galapagos
Islands
Tortosa 93 F2 anc. Dertosa.
Cataluña, E Spain
Tortue, Montagne 59 H3 mountain
range C French Guiana
Tortuga, Isla see La Tortuga, Isla
Toruń 98 C3 Ger. Thorn. Kujawskie-
pomorskie, C Poland
Tõrva 106 D3 Ger. Törwa.
Valgamaa, S Estonia
Torzhok 110 B4 Tverskaya Oblast',
W Russian Federation
Tosa-wan 131 B7 bay SW Japan
Toscana 96 B3 Eng. Tuscany.
Cultural region C Italy
Toscano, Arcipelago 96 B4 Eng.
Tuscan Archipelago. Island group
C Italy
Toshkent 123 E2 Eng./Rus.
Tashkent. Country capital
(Uzbekistan) Toshkent Wiloyati,
E Uzbekistan
Totana 93 E4 Murcia, SE Spain
Tot'ma see Sukhona
Totness 59 G3 Coronie, N Suriname
Tottori 131 B6 Tottori, Honshū,
SW Japan
Touâjîl 74 C2 Tiris Zemmour,
N Mauritania
Touggourt 71 E2 NE Algeria
Toukoto 74 C3 Kayes, W Mali
Toul 90 D3 Meurthe-et-Moselle,
NE France
Toulon 91 D6 anc. Telo Martius,
Tilio Martius. Var, SE France
Toulouse 91 B6 anc. Tolosa. Haute-
Garonne, S France
Toungoo 136 B4 Pegu, C Myanmar
Touraine 90 B4 cultural region
C France
Tourcoing 90 C2 Nord, N France
Tournai 87 A6 var. Tournay, Dut.
Doornik; anc. Tornacum. Hainaut,
SW Belgium
Tournay see Tournai
Tours 90 B4 anc. Caesarodunum,
Turoni. Indre-et-Loire, C France
Tovarkovskiy 111 B5 Tul'skaya
Oblast', W Russian Federation
Tower Island see Genovesa, Isla
Townsville 148 D3 Queensland,
NE Australia
Towraghoudī 122 D4 Herāt,
NW Afghanistan
Towson 41 F4 Maryland, NE USA
Towuti, Danau 139 E4 Dut. Towoeti
Meer. Lake Sulawesi, C Indonesia
Toyama 131 C5 Toyama, Honshū,
SW Japan
Toyama-wan 131 B5 bay W Japan
Toyota 131 C6 Aichi, Honshū,
SW Japan
Tozeur 71 E2 var. Tawzar. W Tunisia
Trâblous see Tripoli
Trabzon 117 E2 Eng. Trebizond; anc.
Trapezus. Trabzon, NE Turkey
Traiectum Tungorum see
Maastricht
Traietum ad Mosam see Maastricht
Traiskirchen 95 E6
Niederösterreich, NE Austria
Trakai 107 C5 Ger. Traken, Pol.
Troki. Trakai, SE Lithuania

Tralee 89 A6 Ir. Trá Lí. SW Ireland
Trá Lí see Tralee
Tralles see Aydın
Trang 137 C7 Trang, S Thailand
Transantarctic Mountains 154 B3
mountain range Antarctica
Transsylvanische Alpen see
Carpaţii Meridionali
Transylvania 108 B4 Eng. Ardeal,
Transilvania, Ger. Siebenbürgen,
Hung. Erdély. Cultural region
NW Romania
Transylvanian Alps see Carpaţii
Meridionali
Trapani 97 B7 anc. Drepanum.
Sicilia, Italy, C Mediterranean Sea
Trăpeăng Vêng 137 D5 Kâmpóng
Thum, C Cambodia
Traralgon 149 C7 Victoria,
SE Australia
Trasimeno, Lago C4 Eng. Lake of
Perugia, Ger. Trasimenischersee.
Lake C Italy
Traverse City 40 C2 Michigan,
N USA
Tra Vinh 137 D6 var. Phu Vinh. Tra
Vinh, S Vietnam
Travis, Lake 49 F3 reservoir Texas,
SW USA
Travnik 100 C4 Federacija Bosna I
Hercegovina, C Bosnia and
Herzegovina
Trbovlje 95 E7 Ger. Trifail. C Slovenia
Třebíč 99 B5 Ger. Trebitsch.
Jíhlavský Kraj, C Czech Republic
Trebinje 101 C5 Republika Srpska,
S Bosnia and Herzegovina
Trebišov 99 D6 Hung. Tőketerebes.
Košický Kraj, E Slovakia
Trélazé 90 B4 Maine-et-Loire,
NW France
Trelew 65 C6 Chubut, SE Argentina
Tremelo 87 C5 Vlaams Brabant,
C Belgium
Trenčín 99 C5 Ger. Trentschin,
Hung. Trencsén. Trenčiansky Kraj,
W Slovakia
Trenque Lauquen 64 C4 Buenos
Aires, E Argentina
Trento 96 C2 Eng. Trent, Ger. Trient;
anc.Tridentum. Trentino-Alto
Adige, N Italy
Trenton 41 F4 state capital New
Jersey, NE USA
Tres Arroyos 65 D5 Buenos Aires,
E Argentina
Treskavica 100 C4 mountain range
SE Bosnia and Herzegovina
Tres Tabernae see Saverne
Treviso 96 C2 anc. Tarvisium.
Veneto, NE Italy
Trichūr 132 C3 var. Thrissur. Kerala,
SW India
Trier 95 A5 Eng. Treves, Fr. Trèves;
anc. Augusta Treverorum.
Rheinland-Pfalz, SW Germany
Triesen 94 E2 SW Liechtenstein
Triesenberg 94 E2
SW Liechtenstein
Trieste 96 D2 Slvn. Trst. Friuli-
Venezia Giulia, NE Italy
Tríkala 104 B4 prev. Trikkala.
Thessalía, C Greece
Trincomalee 132 D3 var. Trinkomali.
Eastern Province, NE Sri Lanka
Trindade, Ilha da 67 C5 island
Brazil, W Atlantic Ocean
Trinidad 55 H5 island C Trinidad
and Tobago
Trinidad 61 F3 Beni, N Bolivia
Trinidad 44 D5 Colorado, C USA
Trinidad 64 D3 Flores, S Uruguay
Trinidad and Tobago 55 H5 Country
SE West Indies

Trinidad & Tobago 55

Official name Republic of Trinidad
and Tobago
Formation 1962
Capital Port-of-Spain
Population 1.3 million / 657 people
per sq mile (254 people per sq km)

Trinidad & Tobago (continued)

Total area 1980 sq miles
(5,128 sq km)
Languages English, English Creole,
Hindi. French, Spanish
Religions Christian 61%, Hindu
24%, other and non-religious 15%
Ethnic mix Asian 40%, Black 40%,
Mixed 19%, White and Chinese 1%
Government Parliamentary
democracy
Currency Trinidad and Tobago
dollar = 100 cents
Literacy rate 93.8%
Calorie consumption 2,777
kilocalories

Trinité, Montagnes de la 59 H3
mountain range C French Guiana
Trinity River 49 G3 river Texas,
SW USA
Trinkomali see Trincomalee
Tripoli 118 B4 var. Ţarābulus,
Ţarābulus ash Shām, Trâblous;
anc. Tripolis. N Lebanon
Tripoli see Ţarābulus
Trípoli 105 B6 prev. Trípolis.
Pelopónnisos, S Greece
Tripolis see Tripoli
Tristan da Cunha 69 B7 dependency
of Saint Helena SE Atlantic Ocean
Triton Island 128 B7 island S Paracel
Islands
Trivandrum 132 C3 var.
Thiruvananthapuram. Kerala,
SW India
Trnava 99 C6 Ger. Tyrnau, Hung.
Nagyszombat. Trnavský Kraj,
W Slovakia
Trogir 100 B4 It. Traù. Split-
Dalmacija, S Croatia
Troglav 100 B4 mountain Bosnia and
Herzegovina/Croatia
Trois-Rivières 39 E4 Quebec,
SE Canada
Trollhättan 85 B6 Västra Götaland,
S Sweden
Tromsø 84 C2 Fin. Tromssa. Troms,
N Norway
Trondheim 84 B4 Ger. Drontheim;
prev. Nidaros, Trondhjem. Sør-
Trøndelag, S Norway
Trondheimsfjorden 84 B4 fjord
S Norway
Troódos 102 C5 var. Troodos
Mountains. Mountain range
C Cyprus
Troodos Mountains see Troódos
Troy 42 D3 Alabama, S USA
Troy 41 F3 New York, NE USA
Troyan 104 C2 Lovech, N Bulgaria
Troyes 90 D3 anc. Augustobona
Tricassium. Aube, N France
Trstenik 100 E4 Serbia, C Serbia
and Montenegro (Yugo.)
Trujillo 52 D2 Colón, NE Honduras
Trujillo 92 C3 Extremadura,
W Spain
Trujillo 60 B3 La Libertad,
NW Peru
Truk Islands see Chuuk Islands
Trŭn 104 B2 Pernik, W Bulgaria
Truro 39 F4 Nova Scotia, SE Canada
Truro 89 C7 SW England, UK
Trzcianka 98 B3 Ger. Schönlanke.
Wielkopolskie, C Poland
Trzebnica 98 C4 Ger. Trebnitz.
Dolnośląskie, SW Poland
Tsalka 117 F2 S Georgia
Tsamkong see Zhanjiang
Tsangpo see Brahmaputra
Tsarevo 104 E2 prev. Michurin.
Burgas, E Bulgaria
Tsaritsyn see Volgograd
Tsefat see Zefat
Tsetserleg 126 D2 Arhangay,
C Mongolia
Tsevat see Zefat
Tshela 77 B6 Bas-Zaïre, W Dem.
Rep. Congo
Tshikapa 77 C7 Kasai Occidental,
SW Dem. Rep. Congo

247

Tshuapa 77 D6 *river* C Dem. Rep.
Congo
Tshwane *see* Pretoria
Tsinan *see* Jinan
Tsing Hai *see* Qinghai Hu
Tsingtao *see* Qingdao
Tsingtau *see* Qingdao
Tsinkiang *see* Quanzhou
Tsintao *see* Qingdao
Tsitsihar *see* Qiqihar
Tsu 131 C6 *var.* Tu. Mie, Honshū,
SW Japan
Tsugaru-kaikyō 130 C3 *strait*
N Japan
Tsumeb 78 B3 Otjikoto, N Namibia
Tsuruga 131 D6 *var.* Turuga. Fukui,
Honshū, SW Japan
Tsuruoka 130 D4 *var.* Turuoka.
Yamagata, Honshū, C Japan
Tsushima 131 A7 *var.* Tsushima-tō,
Tusima. *Island group* SW Japan
Tsushima-tō *see* Tsushima
Tsyerakhowka 107 D8 *Rus.*
Terekhovka. Homyel'skaya
Voblasts', SE Belarus
Tsyurupyns'k 109 E4 *Rus.*
Tsyurupinsk. Khersons'ka Oblast',
S Ukraine
Tu *see* Tsu
Tuamotu Fracture Zone 143 H3
tectonic feature E Pacific Ocean
Tuamotu, Îles 145 H4 *var.* Archipel
des Tuamotu, Dangerous
Archipelago, Tuamotu Islands.
Island group N French Polynesia
Tuamotu Islands *see* Tuamotu, Îles
Tuapi 53 E2 Región Autónoma
Atlántico Norte, NE Nicaragua
Tuapse 111 A7 Krasnodarskiy Kray,
SW Russian Federation
Tuba City 48 B1 Arizona, SW USA
Tubbergen 86 E3 Overijssel,
E Netherlands
Tubize 87 B6 *Dut.* Tubeke. Wallon
Brabant, C Belgium
Tubmanburg 74 C5 NW Liberia
Ţubruq 71 H2 *Eng.* Tobruk, *It.*
Tobruch. NE Libya
Tubuai Islands *see* Australes,
Îles
Tucker's Town 42 B5 E Bermuda
Tucson 48 B3 Arizona, SW USA
Tucumán *see* San Miguel de
Tucumán
Tucumcari 49 E2 New Mexico,
SW USA
Tucupita 59 E2 Delta Amacuro,
NE Venezuela
Tucuruí, Represa de 63 F2 *reservoir*
NE Brazil
Tudela 93 E2 *Basq.* Tutera; *anc.*
Tutela. Navarra, N Spain
Tudmur 118 C3 *var.* Tadmur, Tamar,
Gk. Palmyra; *Bibl.* Tadmor. Ḥimş,
C Syria
Tuguegarao 139 E1 Luzon,
N Philippines
Tuktoyaktuk 37 E3 Northwest
Territories, NW Canada
Tukums 106 C3 *Ger.* Tuckum.
Tukums, W Latvia
Tula 111 B5 Tul'skaya Oblast',
W Russian Federation
Tulancingo 51 E4 Hidalgo,
C Mexico
Tulare Lake Bed 47 C7 *salt flat*
California, W USA
Tulcán 60 B1 Carchi, N Ecuador
Tulcea 108 D5 Tulcea, E Romania
Tul'chyn 108 D3 *Rus.* Tul'chin.
Vinnyts'ka Oblast', C Ukraine
Tuléar *see* Toliara
Tulia 49 E2 Texas, SW USA
Tulle 91 C5 *anc.* Tutela. Corrèze,
C France
Tulln 95 E6 *var.* Oberhollabrunn.
Niederösterreich,
NE Austria
Tully 148 D3 Queensland,
NE Australia
Tulsa 49 G1 Oklahoma, C USA
Tuluá 58 B3 Valle del Cauca,
W Colombia

Tulun 115 E4 Irkutskaya Oblast',
S Russian Federation
Tumaco 58 A4 Nariño,
SW Colombia
Tumba, Lac *see* Ntomba, Lac
Tumbes 60 A2 Tumbes, NW Peru
Tumkūr 132 C2 Karnātaka,
W India
Tumuc Humac Mountains 63 E1
var. Serra Tumucumaque.
Mountain range N South America
Tunduru 73 C8 Ruvuma, S Tanzania
Tundzha 104 D3 *Turk.* Tunca Nehri.
River Bulgaria / Turkey *see also*
Tunca Nehri
Tungabhadra Reservoir 132 C2 *lake*
S India
Tungaru 145 E2 *prev.* Gilbert
Islands. *Island group* W Kiribati
T'ung-shan *see* Xuzhou
Tungsten 36 D4 Northwest
Territories, W Canada
Tung-t'ing Hu *see* Dongting Hu
Tunis 71 E1 *var.* Tūnis. *Country*
capital (Tunisia) NE Tunisia
Tūnis *see* Tunis
Tunis, Golfe de 102 D3 *Ar.* Khalīj
Tūnis. *Gulf* NE Tunisia
Tunisia 71 F2 *Ar.* Al Jumhūrīyah at
Tūnisīyah, *Fr.* République
Tunisienne. *Country* N Africa

Tunisia 71

Official name Republic of Tunisia
Formation 1956
Capital Tunis
Population 9.6 million / 152 people
per sq mile (59 people per sq km)
Total area 63,170 sq miles
(163,610 sq km)
Languages Arabic, French
Religions Muslim (mainly Sunni)
98%, Christian 1%, Jewish 1%
Ethnic mix Arab and Berber 98%,
European 1%, other 1%
Government Presidential
democracy
Currency Tunisian dinar =
1,000 millimes
Literacy rate 71%
Calorie consumption 3,299
kilocalories

Tunja 58 B3 Boyacá, C Colombia
Tuong Buong *see* T,ong Đ,ong
Tupelo 42 C2 Mississippi, S USA
Tupiza 61 G5 Potosí, S Bolivia
Turabah 121 B5 Makkah, W Saudi
Arabia
Turangi 150 D4 Waikato, North
Island, NZ
Turan Lowland 122 C2 *var.* Turan
Plain, *Kaz.* Turan Oypaty, *Rus.*
Turanskaya Nizmennost', *Turk.*
Turan Pesligi, *Uzb.* Turon
Pasttekisligi. *Plain* C Asia
Turan Oypaty *see* Turan
Lowland
Turan Pesligi *see* Turan Lowland
Turan Plain *see* Turan Lowland
Turanskaya Nizmennost' *see* Turan
Lowland
Ţurayf 120 A3 Al Ḥudūd ash
Shamālīyah, NW Saudi Arabia
Turbat 134 A3 Baluchistān,
SW Pakistan
Turda 108 B4 *Ger.* Thorenburg,
Hung. Torda. Cluj, NW
Romania
Turek 98 C3 Wielkopolskie, C
Poland
Turfan *see* Turpan
Turin *see* Torino
Turkana, Lake 89 C6 *var.* Lake
Rudolph. *Lake* N Kenya
**Turkish Republic of Northern
Cyprus** 102 D5 *Ger.* Dependent
territory, *disputed territory.*
Cyprus
Turkestan 114 B5 *Kaz.* Türkistan.
Yuzhnyy Kazakhstan,
S Kazakhstan

Turkey 116 B3 *Turk.* Türkiye
Cumhuriyeti. *Country* SW Asia

Turkey 116

Official name Republic of Turkey
Formation 1923
Capital Ankara
Population 67.6 million / 224
people per sq mile (87 people
per sq km)
Total area 301,382 sq miles
(780,580 sq km)
Languages Turkish, Kurdish,
Arabic, Circassian, Armenian, Greek,
Georgian
Religions Muslim (mainly Sunni)
99%, other 1%
Ethnic mix Turkish 70%, Kurdish
20%, Arab 2%, other 8%
Government Parliamentary
democracy
Currency Turkish lira = 100 krural
Literacy rate 85.1%
Calorie consumption 3,416
kilocalories

Turkmenbashi 122 B2 *prev.*
Krasnovodsk. Balkanskiy Velayat,
W Turkmenistan
Turkmenistan 122 B2 *prev.*
Turkmenskaya Soviet Socialist
Republic. *Country* C Asia

Turkmenistan 122

Official name Turkmenistan
Formation 1991
Capital Ashgabat
Population 4.8 million /
25 people per sq mile (10 people
per sq km)
Total area 188,455 sq miles
(488,100 sq km)
Languages Turkmen, Uzbek,
Russian
Religions Sunni Muslim 87%,
Eastern Orthodox 11%, other 2%
Ethnic mix Turkmen 73%, Russian
10%, Uzbek 9%, Kazakh 2%, Tatar
1%, other 5%
Government One-party state
Currency Manat = 100 tenge
Literacy rate 98%
Calorie consumption 2,675
kilocalories

Turkmenskiy Zaliv 122 B2 *Turkm.*
Türkmen Aylagy. *Lake gulf*
W Turkmenistan
Turks and Caicos Islands 55 E2 *UK*
dependent territory N West Indies
Turlock 47 B6 California, W USA
Turnagain, Cape 150 D4 *headland*
North Island, NZ
Turnhout 87 C5 Antwerpen,
N Belgium
Turnov 98 B4 *Ger.* Turnau.
Liberecký Kraj, N Czech Republic
Turnu Măgurele 108 B5 *var.* Turnu-
Măgurele. Teleorman, S Romania
Turon Pasttekisligi *see* Turan
Lowland
Turpan 126 C3 *var.* Turfan. Xinjiang
Uygur Zizhiqu, NW China
Turpan Pendi 126 C3 *Eng.* Turpan
Depression. *Depression* NW China
Türtkül 122 D2 *Rus.* Turtkul'; *prev.*
Petroaleksandrovsk.
Qoraqalpoghiston Respublikasi,
W Uzbekistan
Turuga *see* Tsuruga
Turuoka *see* Tsuruoka
Tuscaloosa 42 C2 Alabama, S USA
Tusima *see* Tsushima
Tuticorin 132 C3 Tamil Nādu,
SE India
Tutrakan 104 D1 Silistra,
NE Bulgaria
Tutuila 145 F4 *island* W American
Samoa
Tuvalu 145 E3 *prev.* Ellice Islands.
Country SW Pacific Ocean

Tuvalu 145

Official name Tuvalu
Formation 1978
Capital Fongafale, on Funafuti Atoll
Population 10,800 / 1,076 people
per sq mile (415 people per sq km)
Total area 10 sq miles (26 sq km)
Languages English, Tuvaluan,
Kiribati
Religions Church of Tuvalu 97%,
Seventh-day Adventist 1%, Baha'i
1%, other 1%
Ethnic mix Polynesian 96%,
other 4%
Government Non-party democracy
Currency Australian dollar and
Tuvaluan dollar = 100 cents
Literacy rate 95%
Calorie consumption not available

Ţuwayq, Jabal 121 C5 *mountain*
range C Saudi Arabia
Tuxpán 51 F4 *var.* Tuxpán de
Rodríguez Cano. Veracruz-Llave,
E Mexico
Tuxpan 50 D4 Jalisco, C Mexico
Tuxpan 50 D4 Nayarit, C Mexico
Tuxpán de Rodríguez Cano *see*
Tuxpán
Tuxtepec 51 F4 *var.* San Juan Bautista
Tuxtepec. Oaxaca, S Mexico
Tuxtla 51 G5 *var.* Tuxtla Gutiérrez.
Chiapas, SE Mexico
Tuxtla *see* San Andrés Tuxtla
Tuxtla Gutiérrez *see* Tuxtla
Tuy Hoa 137 E5 Phu Yên, S Vietnam
Tuz Gölü 116 C3 *lake* C Turkey
Tuzla 100 C3 Federacija Bosna I
Hercegovina, NE Bosnia and
Herzegovina
Tver' 110 B4 *prev.* Kalinin. Tverskaya
Oblast', W Russian Federation
Tverya *see* Teverya
Twin Falls 46 D4 Idaho, NW USA
Tychy 99 D5 *Ger.* Tichau. Śląskie,
S Poland
Tyler 49 G3 Texas, SW USA
Tympáki 105 C8 *var.* Timbaki; *prev.*
Timbákion. Kriti, Greece,
E Mediterranean Sea
Tynda 115 F4 Amurskaya Oblast',
SE Russian Federation
Tyne 88 D4 *river* N England, UK
Tŷôsi *see* Chōshi
Tyre *see* Soûr
Týrnavos 104 B4 *var.* Tirnavos.
Thessalía, C Greece
Tyrrhenian Sea 97 B6 *It.* Mare
Tirreno. *Sea* N Mediterranean Sea
Tyumen' 114 C3 Tyumenskaya
Oblast', C Russian Federation
Tyup 123 G2 *Kir.* Tüp. Issyk-
Kul'skaya Oblast', NE Kyrgyzstan
Tywyn 89 C6 W Wales, UK
Tzekung *see* Zigong
T,ong Đ,ong 136 D4 *var.* Tuong
Buong. Nghê An, N Vietnam

U

Uanle Uen *see* Wanlaweyn
Uaupés, Rio *see* Vaupés, Río
Ubangi 77 C5 *Fr.* Oubangui. *River*
C Africa
Ubangi-Shari *see* Central African
Republic
Ube 131 B7 Yamaguchi, Honshū,
SW Japan
Ubeda 93 E4 Andalucía, S Spain
Uberaba 63 F4 Minas Gerais,
SE Brazil
Uberlândia 63 F4 Minas Gerais,
SE Brazil
Ubol Rajadhani *see* Ubon
Ratchathani
Ubol Ratchathani *see* Ubon
Ratchathani
Ubon Ratchathani 137 D5 *var.*
Muang Ubon, Ubol Rajadhani,
Ubol Ratchathani, Udon
Ratchathani. Ubon Ratchathani,
E Thailand

Ubrique 92 D5 Andalucía, S Spain
Ucayali, Río 60 D3 *river* C Peru
Uchiura-wan 130 D3 *bay* NW Pacific Ocean
Uchquduq 122 D2 *Rus.* Uchkuduk. Nawoiy Wiloyati, N Uzbekistan
Uchtagan, Peski 122 C2 *Turkm.* Uchtagan Gumy. *Desert* NW Turkmenistan
Udaipur 134 C3 *prev.* Oodeypore. Rājasthān, N India
Uddevalla 85 B6 Västra Götaland, S Sweden
Udine 96 D2 *anc.* Utina. Friuli-Venezia Giulia, NE Italy
Udintsev Fracture Zone 154 A5 *tectonic feature* S Pacific Ocean
Udipi *see* Udupi
Udon Ratchathani *see* Ubon Ratchathani
Udon Thani 136 C4 *var.* Ban Mak Khaeng, Udorndhani. Udon Thani, N Thailand
Udorndhani *see* Udon Thani
Udupi 132 B2 *var.* Udipi. Karnātaka, SW India
Uele 77 D5 *var.* Welle. *River* NE Dem. Rep. Congo
Uelzen 94 C3 Niedersachsen, N Germany
Ufa 111 D6 Respublika Bashkortostan, W Russian Federation
Ugāle 106 C2 Ventspils, NW Latvia
Uganda 73 B6 *Country* E Africa

Uganda 73

Official name Republic of Uganda
Formation 1962
Capital Kampala
Population 24 million / 263 people per sq mile (102 people per sq km)
Total area 91,135 sq miles (236,040 sq km)
Languages English, Nkole, Luganda
Religions Roman Catholic 38%, Protestant 33%, Traditional beliefs 13%, Muslim (mainly Sunni) 5%, other 11%
Ethnic mix Bantu Tribes 50%, other 50%
Government Non-party democracy
Currency New Uganda shilling = 100 cents
Literacy rate 67.1%
Calorie consumption 2,359 kilocalories

Uglovka 110 B4 *var.* Okulovka. Novgorodskaya Oblast', W Russian Federation
Uhuru Peak *see* Kilimanjaro
Uíge 78 B1 *Port.* Carmona, Vila Marechal Carmona. Uíge, NW Angola
Uinta Mountains 44 B4 *mountain range* Utah, W USA
Uitenhage 78 C5 Eastern Cape, S South Africa
Uithoorn 86 C3 Noord-Holland, C Netherlands
Ujelang Atoll 144 C1 *var.* Wujlān. *Atoll* Ralik Chain, W Marshall Islands
Ujungpandang 139 E4 *var.* Macassar, Makassar; *prev.* Makasar. Sulawesi, C Indonesia
Ujung Salang *see* Phuket
Ukhta 114 C3 Respublika Komi, NW Russian Federation
Ukiah 47 B5 California, W USA
Ukmergé 106 C4 *Pol.* Wiłkomierz. Ukmergé, C Lithuania
Ukraine 108 C2 *Ukr.* Ukrayina; *prev.* Ukrainian Soviet Socialist Republic, Ukrainskaya S.S.R. *Country* SE Europe

Ukraine 108

Official name Ukraine
Formation 1991

Ukraine (continued)

Official name Ukraine
Formation 1991
Capital Kiev
Population 48.4 million / 208 people per sq mile (80 people per sq km)
Total area 223,089 sq miles (603,700 sq km)
Languages Ukrainian, Russian, Tartar
Religions Christian (mainly Ukrainian Orthodox) 95%, Jewish 1%, other 4%
Ethnic mix Ukrainian 73%, Russian 22%, Jewish 1%, other 4%
Government Presidential democracy
Currency Hryvnia = 100 kopiykas
Literacy rate 99%
Calorie consumption 2,871 kilocalories

Ulaanbaatar 127 E2 *Eng.* Ulan Bator. *Country capital* (Mongolia) Töv, C Mongolia
Ulaangom 126 C2 Uvs, NW Mongolia
Ulan Bator *see* Ulaanbaatar
Ulanhad *see* Chifeng
Ulan-Ude 115 E4 *prev.* Verkhneudinsk. Respublika Buryatiya, S Russian Federation
Ulft 86 E4 Gelderland, E Netherlands
Ullapool 88 C3 N Scotland, UK
Ulm 95 B6 Baden-Württemberg, S Germany
Ulsan 129 E4 *Jap.* Urusan. SE South Korea
Ulster 89 B5 *cultural region* N Ireland
Ulungur Hu 126 B2 *lake* NW China
Uluru 147 D5 *var.* Ayers Rock. *Rocky outcrop* Northern Territory, C Australia
Ulyanivka 109 E3 *Rus.* Ul'yanovka. Kirovohrads'ka Oblast', C Ukraine
Ul'yanovsk 111 C5 *prev.* Simbirsk. Ul'yanovskaya Oblast', W Russian Federation
Uman' 109 E3 *Rus.* Uman. Cherkas'ka Oblast', C Ukraine
Umán 51 H3 Yucatán, SE Mexico
Umanak *see* Uummannaq
Umanaq *see* Uummannaq
Umbro-Marchigiano, Appennino 96 C3 *Eng.* Umbrian-Machigian Mountains. *Mountain range* C Italy
Umeå 84 C4 Västerbotten, N Sweden
Umeälven 84 C4 *river* N Sweden
Umiat 36 D2 Alaska, USA
Umm Buru 72 A4 Western Darfur, W Sudan
Umm Durmān *see* Omdurman
Umm Ruwaba 72 C4 *var.* Umm Ruwābah, Um Ruwāba. Northern Kordofan, C Sudan
Umm Ruwābah *see* Umm Ruwaba
Umnak Island 36 A3 *island* Aleutian Islands, Alaska, USA
Um Ruwāba *see* Umm Ruwaba
Umtali *see* Mutare
Umtata 78 D5 Eastern Cape, SE South Africa
Una 100 B3 *river* Bosnia and Herzegovina/Croatia
Unac 100 B3 *river* W Bosnia and Herzegovina
Unalaska Island 36 A3 *island* Aleutian Islands, Alaska, USA
'Unayzah 120 B4 *var.* Anaiza. Al Qaşīm, C Saudi Arabia
Uncía 61 F4 Potosí, C Bolivia
Uncompahgre Peak 44 B5 *mountain* Colorado, C USA
Ungarisches Erzgebirge *see* Slovenské rudohorie
Ungava Bay 39 E1 *bay* Quebec, E Canada
Ungava, Péninsule d' 38 D1 *peninsula* Quebec, SE Canada

Ungheni 108 D3 *Rus.* Ungeny. W Moldova
Unimak Island 36 B3 *island* Aleutian Islands, Alaska, USA
Union 43 E1 South Carolina, SE USA
Union City Tennessee, S USA
United Arab Emirates 121 C5 *Ar.* Al Imārāt al 'Arabīyah al Muttaḥidah, *abbrev.* UAE; *prev.* Trucial States. *Country* SW Asia

United Arab Emirates 121

Official name United Arab Emirates
Formation 1971
Capital Abu Dhabi
Population 2.7 million / 84 people per sq mile (33 people per sq km)
Total area 32,000 sq miles (82,880 sq km)
Languages Arabic, Farsi, English, Indian and Pakistani languages
Religions Muslim (mainly Sunni) 96%, Christian, Hindu and other 4%
Ethnic mix Asian 60%, Emirian 25%, other Arab 12%, European 3%
Government Monarchy
Currency UAE dirham = 100 fils
Literacy rate 75.6%
Calorie consumption 3,192 kilocalories

United Kingdom 89 B5 *abbrev.* UK. *Country* NW Europe

United Kingdom 89

Official name United Kingdom of Great Britain and Northern Ireland
Formation 1707
Capital London
Population 59.5 million / 629 people per sq mile (243 people per sq km)
Total area 94,525 sq miles (244,820 sq km)
Languages English, Welsh, Scottish
Religions Anglican 47%, Presbyterian 4%, Roman Catholic 9%, other 40%
Ethnic mix English 80%, Scottish 9%, Northern Irish 3%, Welsh 3%, other 5%
Government Parliamentary democracy
Currency Pound sterling = 100 pence
Literacy rate 99%
Calorie consumption 3,334 kilocalories

United States of America 35 B5 *var.* America, The States, *abbrev.* U.S., USA. *Country*

United States of America 35

Official name United States of America
Formation 1776
Capital Washington DC
Population 281.4 million /76 people per sq mile (29 people per sq km)
Total area 3,717,792 sq miles (9,629,091 sq km)
Languages English, Spanish, Italian, German, French, Polish, Chinese, Greek
Religions Protestant 61%, Roman Catholic 25%, Jewish 2%, other 12%
Ethnic mix White (including Hispanic) 81%, Native American 2%, Asia 4%, Black American African 13%
Government Presidential democracy
Currency US dollar = 100 cents
Literacy rate 99%
Calorie consumption 3,772 kilocalories

Unst 88 D1 *island* NE Scotland, UK
Ünye 116 D2 Ordu, W Turkey
Upala 52 D4 Alajuela, NW Costa Rica
Upata 59 E2 Bolívar, E Venezuela
Upemba, Lac 77 D7 *lake* SE Dem. Rep. Congo
Upernavik 82 C2 *var.* Upernivik. C Greenland
Upernivik *see* Upernavik
Upington 78 C4 Northern Cape, W South Africa
Upolu 145 F4 *island* SE Samoa
Upper Klamath Lake 46 A4 *lake* Oregon, NW USA
Upper Lough Erne 89 A5 *lake* SW Northern Ireland, UK
Upper Red Lake 45 F1 *lake* Minnesota, N USA
Uppsala 85 C6 Uppsala, C Sweden
Ural 112 B3 *Kaz.* Zayyq. *River* Kazakhstan/Russian Federation
Ural Mountains *see* Ural'skiye Gory
Ural'sk 114 B3 *Kaz.* Oral. Zapadnyy Kazakhstan, NW Kazakhstan
Ural'skiye Gory 114 C3 *var.* Ural'skiy Khrebet, *Eng.* Ural Mountains. *Mountain range* Kazakhstan/Russian Federation
Ural'skiy Khrebet *see* Ural'skiye Gory
Uraricoera 62 D1 Roraima, N Brazil
Urbandale 45 F3 Iowa, C USA
Uren' 111 C5 Nizhegorodskaya Oblast', W Russian Federation
Urganch 122 D2 *Rus.* Urgench; *prev.* Novo-Urgench. Khorazm Wiloyati, W Uzbekistan
Urgut 123 E3 Samarqand Wiloyati, C Uzbekistan
Uroševac 101 D5 *Alb.* Ferizaj. Serbia, S Serbia and Montenegro (Yugo.)
Üroteppa 123 E2 *Rus.* Ura-Tyube. NW Tajikistan
Uruapan 51 E4 *var.* Uruapan del Progreso. Michoacán de Ocampo, SW Mexico
Uruapan del Progreso *see* Uruapan
Uruguai, Río *see* Uruguay
Uruguay 64 D4 *prev.* La Banda Oriental. *Country* E South America

Uruguay 64

Official name Eastern Republic of Uruguay
Formation 1828
Capital Montevideo
Population 3.4 million /50 people per sq mile (19 people per sq km)
Total area 68,039 sq miles (176,220 sqkm)
Languages Spanish
Religions Roman Catholic 66%, non-religious 30%, Jewish 2%, Protestant 2%
Ethnic mix White 90%, other 10%
Government Presidential democracy
Currency Uruguayan peso = 100 centimes
Literacy rate 97.8%
Calorie consumption 2,879 kilocalories

Uruguay 64 D3 *var.* Rio Uruguai, Río Uruguay. *River* E South America
Uruguay, Río *see* Uruguay
Urumchi *see* Ürümqi
Urumqi *see* Ürümqi
Ürümqi 126 C3 *var.* Tihwa, Urumchi, Urumqi, Urumtsi, Wu-lu-k'o-mu-shi, Wu-lu-mu-ch'i; *prev.* Tihua. *Autonomous region capital* Xinjiang Uygur Zizhiqu, NW China
Urumtsi *see* Ürümqi

Urup, Ostrov *115 H4 island*
Kuril'skiye Ostrova, SE Russian
Federation
Urziceni *108 C5* Ialomiţa,
SE Romania
Usa *110 E3 river* NW Russian
Federation
Uşak *116 B3 prev.* Ushak. Uşak,
W Turkey
Ushuaia *65 B8* Tierra del Fuego,
S Argentina
Usinsk *110 E3* Respublika Komi,
NW Russian Federation
Üsküb *see* Skopje
Üsküp *see* Skopje
Usmas Ezers *106 B3 lake* NW Latvia
Usol'ye-Sibirskoye *115 E4*
Irkutskaya Oblast', C Russian
Federation
Ussel *91 C5* Corrèze, C France
Ussuriysk *115 G5 prev.* Nikol'sk,
Nikol'sk-Ussuriyskiy, Voroshilov.
Primorskiy Kray, SE
Ustica, Isola d' *97 B6 island* S Italy
Ust'-Ilimsk *115 E4* Irkutskaya
Oblast', C Russian Federation
Ústí nad Labem *98 A4 Ger.* Aussig.
Ústecký Kraj, NW Czech Republic
Ustka *98 C2 Ger.* Stolpmünde.
Pomorskie, N Poland
Ust'-Kamchatsk *115 H2*
Kamchatskaya Oblast', E Russian
Federation
Ust'-Kamenogorsk *114 D5 Kaz.*
Öskemen. Vostochnyy
Kazakhstan, E Kazakhstan
Ust'-Kut *115 E4* Irkutskaya Oblast',
C Russian Federation
Ust'-Olenëk *115 E3* Respublika
Sakha (Yakutiya), NE Russian
Federation
Ustrzyki Dolne *99 E5*
Podkarpackie, SE Poland
Ust Urt *see* Ustyurt Plateau
Ustyurt Plateau *122 B1 var.* Ust Urt,
Uzb. Ustyurt Platosi. *Plateau*
Kazakhstan/Uzbekistan
Ustyurt Platosi *see* Ustyurt Plateau
Usulután *52 C3* Usulután,
SE El Salvador
Usumacinta, Río *52 B1 river*
Guatemala/Mexico
Utah *48 A1 off.* State of Utah; also
known as Beehive State, Mormon
State. *State* W USA
Utah Lake *44 B4 lake* Utah, W USA
Utena *106 C4* Utena, E Lithuania
Utica *41 F3* New York, NE USA
Utrecht *86 C4 Lat.* Trajectum ad
Rhenum. Utrecht, C Netherlands
Utsunomiya *131 D5 var.*
Utunomiya. Tochigi, Honshū,
S Japan
Uttar Pradesh *135 E3 prev.* United
Provinces, United Provinces of
Agra and Oudh. *State* N India
Utunomiya *see* Utsunomiya
Uulu *106 D2* Pärnumaa,
SW Estonia
Uummannaq *82 C3 var.* Umanak,
Umanaq. C Greenland
Uummannarsuaq *see* Nunap Isua
Uvalde *49 F4* Texas, SW USA
Uvarovichy *107 D7 Rus.* Uvarovichi.
Homyel'skaya Voblasts',
SE Belarus
Uvea, Île *145 E4 island* N Wallis and
Futuna
Uvs Nuur *126 C1 var.* Ozero Ubsu-
Nur. *Lake* Mongolia/Russian
Federation
'Uwaynāt, Jabal al *88 A3 var.* Jebel
Uweinat. *Mountain* Libya/Sudan
Uyo *75 G5* Akwa Ibom, S Nigeria
Uyuni *61 F5* Potosí, W Bolivia
Uzbekistan *122 D2 Country* C Asia

Uzbekistan *122*

Official name Republic of
Uzbekistan
Formation 1991
Capital Tashkent

Uzbekistan (continued)

Population 25.3 million / 146
people per sq mile (57 people
per sq km)
Total area 172,741 sq miles
(447,400 sq km)
Languages Uzbek, Russian
Religions Sunni Muslim 88%,
Eastern Orthodox 9%, other 3%
Ethnic mix Uzbek 71%, Russian 8%,
Tajik 5%, Kazakh 4%, other 12%
Government Presidential
democracy
Currency Som = 100 teen
Literacy rate 88.9%
Calorie consumption 2,317
kilocalories

Uzhhorod *108 B2 Rus.* Uzhgorod;
prev. Ungvár. Zakarpats'ka
Oblast', W Ukraine
Užice *100 D4 prev.* Titovo Užice.
Serbia, W Serbia and Montenegro
(Yugo.)

V

Vaal *78 D4 river* C South Africa
Vaals *87 D6* Limburg,
SE Netherlands
Vaasa *85 D5 Swe.* Vasa; *prev.*
Nikolainkaupunki. Länsi-Suomi,
W Finland
Vaassen *86 D3* Gelderland,
E Netherlands
Vác *99 C6 Ger.* Waitzen. Pest,
N Hungary
Vadodara *134 C4 prev.* Baroda.
Gujarāt, W India
Vaduz *94 E2 country capital*
(Liechtenstein) W Liechtenstein
Váh *99 C5 Ger.* Waag, *Hung.* Vág.
River W Slovakia
Väinameri *106 C2 prev.* Muhu Väin,
Ger. Moon-Sund. *Sea* E Baltic Sea
Valachia *see* Wallachia
Valday *110 B4* Novgorodskaya
Oblast', W Russian Federation
Valdecañas, Embalse de *92 D3*
reservoir W Spain
Valdepeñas *93 E4* Castilla-La
Mancha, C Spain
Valdés, Península *65 C6 peninsula*
SE Argentina
Valdez *36 C3* Alaska, USA
Valdia *see* Weldiya
Valdivia *65 B5* Los Lagos, C Chile
Val-d'Or *38 D4* Quebec, SE Canada
Valdosta *43 E3* Georgia, SE USA
Valence *91 D5 anc.* Valentia, Valentia
Julia, Ventia. Drôme, E France
Valencia *46 D1* California, W USA
Valencia *58 D1* Carabobo,
N Venezuela
Valencia *93 F3* País Valenciano,
E Spain
Valencia, Golfo de *93 F3 var.* Gulf
of Valencia. *Gulf* E Spain
Valencia, Gulf of *see* Valencia,
Golfo de
Valenciennes *90 D2* Nord,
N France
Valera *58 C2* Trujillo,
NW Venezuela
Valga *106 D3 Ger.* Walk, *Latv.* Valka.
Valgamaa, S Estonia
Valira *91 A8 river* Andorra/Spain
Valjevo *100 C4* Serbia, W Serbia
and Montenegro (Yugo.)
Valjok *see* Válljohka
Valka *106 D3 Ger.* Walk. Valka,
N Latvia
Valkenswaard *87 D5* Noord-
Brabant, S Netherlands
Valladolid *92 D2* Castilla-León,
NW Spain
Valladolid *51 H3* Yucatán,
SE Mexico
Vall d'Uxó *93 F3* País Valenciano,
E Spain
Valle de La Pascua *58 D2* Guárico,
N Venezuela

Valledupar *58 B1* Cesar,
N Colombia
Vallejo *47 B6* California, W USA
Vallenar *64 B3* Atacama, N Chile
Valletta *97 C8 prev.* Valetta. *Country*
capital (Malta) E Malta
Valley City *45 E2* North Dakota,
N USA
Válljohka *84 D2 var.* Valjok.
Finnmark, N Norway
Valls *93 G2* Cataluña, NE Spain
Valmiera *106 D3 Est.* Volmari, *Ger.*
Wolmar. Valmiera, N Latvia
Valozhyn *107 C5 Pol.* Wołożyn, *Rus.*
Volozhin. Minskaya Voblasts',
C Belarus
Valparaíso *40 C3* Indiana, N USA
Valparaíso *64 B4* Valparaíso,
C Chile
Valverde del Camino *92 C4*
Andalucía, S Spain
Van *117 F3* Van, E Turkey
Vanadzor *117 F2 prev.* Kirovakan.
N Armenia
Vancouver *36 D5* British Columbia,
SW Canada
Vancouver *46 B3* Washington,
NW USA
Vancouver Island *36 D5 island*
British Columbia, SW Canada
Van Diemen Gulf *146 D2 gulf*
Northern Territory, N Australia
Vänern *85 B6 Eng.* Lake Vaner; *prev.*
Lake Vener. *Lake* S Sweden
Vangaindrano *79 G4* Fianarantsoa,
SE Madagascar
Van Gölü *117 F3 Eng.* Lake Van;
anc. Thospitis. *Salt lake* E Turkey
Van Horn *48 D3* Texas, SW USA
Van, Lake *see* Van Gölü
Vannes *90 A3 anc.* Dariorigum.
Morbihan, NW France
Vantaa *85 D6 Swe.* Vanda. Etelä-
Suomi, S Finland
Vanua Levu *145 E4 island* N Fiji
Vanuatu *144 C4 prev.* New
Hebrides. *Country* SW Pacific
Ocean

Vanuatu *144*

Official name Republic of Vanuatu
Formation 1980
Capital Port Vila
Population 200,000 / 42 people per
sq mile (16 people per sq km)
Total area 4,710 sq miles
(12,200 sq km)
Languages Bislama, English, French
Religions Presbyterian 37%,
Anglican 15%, Roman Catholic 15%,
Indigenous beliefs 8%, Seventh-day
Adventist 6%, other 19%
Ethnic mix Melanesian 94%,
Polynesian 3%, other 3%
Government Parliamentary
democracy
Currency Vatu = 100 centimes
Literacy rate 64%
Calorie consumption 2,587
kilocalories

Van Wert *40 C4* Ohio, N USA
Varakļani *106 D4* Madona,
C Latvia
Vārānasi *135 E3 prev.* Banaras,
Benares, *hist.* Kasi. Uttar Pradesh,
N India
Varangerfjorden *84 E2 fjord*
N Norway
Varangerhalvøya *84 D2 peninsula*
N Norway
Varannó *see* Vranov nad Topl'ou
Varaždin *100 B2 Ger.* Warasdin,
Hung. Varasd. Varaždin,
N Croatia
Varberg *85 B7* Halland, S Sweden
Vardar *101 E6 Gk.* Axiós. *River* FYR
Macedonia/Greece *see also* Axiós
Varde *85 A7* Ribe, W Denmark
Varēna *107 B5 Pol.* Orany. Varēna,
S Lithuania
Varese *96 B2* Lombardia, N Italy

Vârful Moldoveanu *108 B4 var.*
Moldoveanul; *prev.* Vîrful
Moldoveanu. *Mountain*
C Romania
Varkaus *85 E5* Itä-Suomi,
C Finland
Varna *104 E2 prev.* Stalin, *anc.*
Odessus. Varna, E Bulgaria
Varnenski Zaliv *104 E2 prev.*
Stalinski Zaliv. *Bay* E Bulgaria
Vasiliki *105 A5* Lefkáda, Iónioi
Nísoi, Greece, C Mediterranean
Sea
Vasilishki *107 B5 Pol.* Wasiliszki,
Rus. Vasilishki. Hrodzyenskaya
Voblasts', W Belarus
Vaslui *108 D4* Vaslui, C Romania
Västerås *85 C6* Västmanland,
C Sweden
Vasyl'kiv *109 E2 Rus.* Vasil'kov.
Kyyivs'ka Oblast', N Ukraine
Vaté *see* Efate
Vatican City *97 A7 Country*
S Europe

Vatican City *97*

Official name State of the
Vatican City
Formation 1929
Capital Vatican City
Population 524 /3,082 people per
sq mile (1,191 people per sq km)
Total area 0.17 sq miles (0.44 sq km)
Languages Italian, Latin
Religions Roman Catholic 100%
Ethnic mix The current pope is
Polish, ending nearly 500 years of
Italian popes. Cardinals are from
many nationalities, but Italians form
the largest group. Most of the
resident lay persons are Italian.
Government Papal state
Currency Euro (Lira until 2002)
Literacy rate 99%
Calorie consumption not available

Vatnajökull *83 E5 glacier* SE Iceland
Vättern *85 B6 Eng.* Lake Vatter; *prev.*
Lake Vetter. *Lake* S Sweden
Vaughn *48 D2* New Mexico,
SW USA
Vaupés *65 A8 var.* Rio Uaupés.
River Brazil/Colombia *see also*
Uaupés, Rio
Vava'u Group *145 E4 island group*
N Tonga
Vavuniya *132 D3* Northern
Province, N Sri Lanka
Vawkavysk *107 B6 Pol.*
Wołkowysk, *Rus.* Volkovysk.
Hrodzyenskaya Voblasts',
W Belarus
Växjö *85 C7 var.* Vexiö. Kronoberg,
S Sweden
Vaygach, Ostrov *110 E2 island*
NW Russian Federation
Veendam *86 E2* Groningen,
NE Netherlands
Veenendaal *86 D4* Utrecht,
C Netherlands
Vega *84 B4 island* C Norway
Veisiejai *107 B5* Lazdijai,
S Lithuania
Vejer de la Frontera *92 C5*
Andalucía, S Spain
Veldhoven *87 D5* Noord-Brabant,
S Netherlands
Velebit *100 A3 mountain range*
C Croatia
Velenje *95 E7 Ger.* Wöllan.
N Slovenia
Veles *101 E6 Turk.* Köprülü. C FYR
Macedonia
Velho *see* Porto Velho
Velika Morava *100 D4 var.* Glavn'a
Morava, Morava, *Ger.* Grosse
Morava. *River* C Serbia and
Montenegro (Yugo.)
Velikaya *113 G2 river* NE Russian
Federation
Velikiye Luki *110 A4* Pskovskaya
Oblast', W Russian Federation

Veliko Tŭrnovo 104 D2 prev.
Tirnovo, Trnovo, Tŭrnovo. Veliko
Tŭrnovo, N Bulgaria
Velingrad 104 C3 Pazardzhik,
C Bulgaria
Vel'ký Krtíš 99 D6 Banskobystrický
Kraj, C Slovakia
Vellore 132 C2 Tamil Nādu,
SE India
Velobriga see Viana do Castelo
Velsen see Velsen-Noord
Velsen-Noord 86 C3 var. Velsen.
Noord-Holland, W Netherlands
Vel'sk 110 C4 var. Velsk.
Arkhangel'skaya Oblast',
NW Russian Federation
Velsk see Vel'sk
Velvendos see Velvendós
Velvendós 104 B4 var. Velvendos.
Dytikí Makedonía, N Greece
Velykyy Tokmak see Tokmak
Vendôme 90 C4 Loir-et-Cher,
C France
Venezia 96 C2 Eng. Venice, Fr.
Venise, Ger. Venedig; anc.Venetia.
Veneto, NE Italy
Venezuela 58 D2 prev. Estados
Unidos de Venezuela, United
States of Venezuela. Country
N South America

Venezuela 58

Official name Bolivarian Republic
of Venezuela
Formation 1830
Capital Caracas
Population 24.6 million /70 people
per sq mile (27 people per sq km)
Total area 352,143 sq miles
(912,050 sq km)
Languages Spanish, Amerindian
languages
Religions Roman Catholic 89%,
Protestant and other 11%
Ethnic mix Mestizo 69%, White
20%, Black 9%, Amerindian 2%
Government Presidential
democracy
Currency Bolívar = 100 centimos
Literacy rate 92.6%
Calorie consumption 2,256
kilocalories

Venezuela, Golfo de 58 C1 Eng.
Gulf of Maracaibo, Gulf of
Venezuela. Gulf NW Venezuela
Venezuelan Basin 56 B1 undersea
feature E Caribbean Sea
Venice see Venezia
Venice 42 C4 Louisiana, S USA
Venice, Gulf of 96 C2 It. Golfo di
Venezia, Slvn. Beneški Zaliv. Gulf
N Adriatic Sea
Venlo 87 D5 prev. Venloo. Limburg,
SE Netherlands
Venta 106 B3 Ger. Windau. River
Latvia/Lithuania
Ventimiglia 96 A3 Liguria,
NW Italy
Ventspils 106 B2 Ger. Windau.
Ventspils, NW Latvia
Vera 64 D3 Santa Fe, C Argentina
Veracruz 51 F4 var. Veracruz Llave.
Veracruz-Llave, E Mexico
Veracruz Llave see Veracruz
Vercelli 96 A2 anc. Vercellae.
Piemonte, NW Italy
Verdalsøra 84 B4 Nord-Trøndelag,
C Norway
Verde, Costa 92 D1 coastal region
N Spain
Verden 94 B3 Niedersachsen,
NW Germany
Veria see Véroia
Verkhoyanskiy Khrebet 115 F3
mountain range NE Russian
Federation
Vermillion 45 F3 South Dakota,
N USA
Vermont 41 F2 off. State of Vermont;
also known as The Green
Mountain State. State NE USA

Vernal 44 B4 Utah, W USA
Vernon 49 F2 Texas, SW USA
Véroia 104 B4 var. Veria, Vérroia,
Turk. Karaferiye. Kentrikí
Makedonía, N Greece
Verona 96 C2 Veneto, NE Italy
Vérroia see Véroia
Versailles 90 D1 Yvelines,
N France
Verviers 87 D6 Liège, E Belgium
Vesdre 87 D6 river E Belgium
Veselinovo 104 D2 Shumen,
NE Bulgaria
Vesoul 90 D4 anc. Vesulium,
Vesulum. Haute-Saône, E France
Vesterålen 84 B2 island group
N Norway
Vestfjorden 84 C3 fjord C Norway
Vestmannaeyjar 83 E5 Sudhurland,
S Iceland
Vesuvio 97 D5 Eng. Vesuvius.
Volcano S Italy
Veszprém 99 C7 Ger. Veszprim.
Veszprém, W Hungary
Vetrino 104 E2 Varna, E Bulgaria
Veurne 87 A5 var. Furnes. West-
Vlaanderen, W Belgium
Vexiö see Växjö
Viacha 61 F4 La Paz, W Bolivia
Viana do Castelo 92 B2 var. Viana do
Castelo
Viana do Castelo 92 B2 var. Viana
de Castelo; anc. Velobriga. Viana
do Castelo, NW Portugal
Vianen 86 C4 Zuid-Holland,
C Netherlands
Viangchan 136 C4 Eng./Fr.
Vientiane. Country capital (Laos)
C Laos
Viangphoukha 136 C3 var. Vieng
Pou Kha. Louang Namtha,
N Laos
Viareggio 96 B3 Toscana, C Italy
Viborg 85 A7 Viborg,
NW Denmark
Vic 93 G2 var. Vich; anc. Ausa, Vicus
Ausonensis. Cataluña, NE Spain
Vicenza 96 C2 anc. Vicentia. Veneto,
NE Italy
Vich see Vic
Vichy 91 C5 Allier, C France
Vicksburg 42 B2 Mississippi, S USA
Victoria 102 A5 var. Rabat. Gozo,
NW Malta
Victoria 79 H1 country capital
(Seychelles) Mahé, SW Seychelles
Victoria 49 G4 Texas, SW USA
Victoria 36 D5 Vancouver Island,
British Columbia, SW Canada
Victoria 149 C7 state SE Australia
Victoria Bank see Vitória
Seamount
Victoria de Durango see Durango
Victoria de las Tunas see Las Tunas
Victoria Falls 78 C2 waterfall
Zambia/Zimbabwe
Victoria Falls 78 C3 Matabeleland
North, W Zimbabwe
Victoria Island 37 F3 island
Northwest Territories/Nunavut,
NW Canada
Victoria, Lake 73 B6 var. Victoria
Nyanza. Lake E Africa
Victoria Land 154 C4 physical region
Antarctica
Victoria Nyanza see Victoria, Lake
Victoria River 146 D3 river
Northern Territory, N Australia
Victorville 47 C7 California, W
USA
Vicus Ausonensis see Vic
Vidalia 43 E2 Georgia, SE USA
Vidin 104 B1 anc. Bononia. Vidin,
NW Bulgaria
Vidzy 107 C5 Rus. Vidzy.
Vitsyebskaya Voblasts',
NW Belarus
Viedma 65 C5 Río Negro,
E Argentina
Vieng Pou Kha see Viangphoukha
Vienna see Wien
Vienne 91 D5 anc. Vienna. Isère,
E France

Vienne 90 B4 river W France
Vientiane see Viangchan
Vierzon 90 C4 Cher, C France
Viesīte 106 C4 Ger. Eckengraf.
Jēkabpils, S Latvia
Vietnam 136 D4 Vtn. Công Hoa Xa
Hôi Chu Nghia Viêt Nam.
Country SE Asia

Vietnam 136

Official name Socialist Republic
of Vietnam
Formation 1976
Capital Hanoi
Population 79.2 million / 622
people per sq mile (240 people per
sq km)
Total area 127,243 sq miles
(329,560 sq km)
Languages Vietnamese, Chinese,
Thai, Khmer, Muong, Nung, Miao,
Yao
Religions Buddhist 55%, Christian
7%, other and non-religious 38%
Ethnic mix Vietnamese 88%,
Chinese 4%, Thai 2%, other 6%
Government One-party republic
Currency Dông = 10 hao = 100 xu
Literacy rate 93.4%
Calorie consumption 2,583
kilocalories

Vietri see Viêt Tri
Viêt Tri 136 D3 var. Vietri. Vinh
Phu, N Vietnam
Vieux Fort 55 F2 S Saint Lucia
Vigo 92 B2 Galicia, NW Spain
Vijayawāda 132 D1 prev. Bezwada.
Andhra Pradesh, SE India
Vijosa see Vjosës, Lumi i
Vijosë see Vjosës, Lumi i
Vila see Port-Vila
Vila Artur de Paiva see Cubango
Vila da Ponte see Cubango
Vila de Mocímboa da Praia see
Mocímboa da Praia
Vila do Conde 92 B2 Porto,
NW Portugal
Vila do Zumbo 78 D2 prev. Vila do
Zumbu, Zumbo. Tete,
NW Mozambique
Vilafranca del Penedés 93 G2 var.
Villafranca del Panadés. Cataluña,
NE Spain
Vila General Machado see
Camacupa
Viļaka 106 D4 Ger. Marienhausen.
Balvi, NE Latvia
Vilalba 92 C1 Galicia, NW Spain
Vila Nova de Gaia 92 B2 Porto,
NW Portugal
Vila Nova de Portimão see
Portimão
Vila Pereira de Eça see N'Giva
Vila Real 92 C2 var. Vila Rial. Vila
Real, N Portugal
Vila Rial see Vila Real
Vila Robert Williams see Caála
Vila Serpa Pinto see Menongue
Vilhelmina 84 C4 Västerbotten,
N Sweden
Vilhena 62 D3 Rondônia, W Brazil
Vilia 105 C5 Attikí, C Greece
Viliya 107 C5 Lith. Neris, Rus.
Viliya. River W Belarus
Viljandi 106 D2 Ger. Fellin.
Viljandimaa, S Estonia
Vilkaviškis 106 B4 Pol.
Wyłkowyszki. Vilkaviškis,
SW Lithuania
Villa Acuña 50 D2 var. Cuidad
Acuña. Coahuila de Zaragoza, NE
Mexico
Villa Bella 61 F2 Beni, N Bolivia
Villacarrillo 93 E4 Andalucía,
S Spain
Villa Cecilia see Ciudad Madero
Villach 95 D7 Slvn. Beljak. Kärnten,
S Austria
Villacidro 97 A5 Sardegna, Italy,
C Mediterranean Sea
Villa Concepción see Concepción

Villa del Pilar see Pilar
Villafranca de los Barros 92 C4
Extremadura, W Spain
Villafranca del Panadés see
Vilafranca del Penedés
Villahermosa 51 G4 prev. San Juan
Bautista. Tabasco, SE Mexico
Villajoyosa 93 F4 var. La Vila Jojosa.
País Valenciano, E Spain
Villa María 64 C4 Córdoba,
C Argentina
Villa Martín 61 F5 Potosí,
SW Bolivia
Villa Mercedes 64 C4 prev.
Mercedes. San Luis,
C Argentina
Villanueva 50 D3 Zacatecas,
C Mexico
Villanueva de la Serena 92 C3
Extremadura, W Spain
Villanueva de los Infantes 93 E4
Castilla-La Mancha, C Spain
Villarrica 64 D2 Guairá,
SE Paraguay
Villavicencio 58 B3 Meta,
C Colombia
Villaviciosa 92 D1 Asturias,
N Spain
Villazón 61 G5 Potosí, S Bolivia
Villena 93 F4 País Valenciano,
E Spain
Villeurbanne 91 D5 Rhône,
E France
Villingen-Schwenningen 95 B6
Baden-Württemberg, S Germany
Vilnius 107 C5 Pol. Wilno, Ger.
Wilna; prev. Rus. Vilna. Country
capital (Lithuania) Vilnius,
SE Lithuania
Vil'shanka 109 E3 Rus. Olshanka.
Kirovohrads'ka Oblast',
C Ukraine
Vilvoorde 87 C6 Fr. Vilvorde.
Vlaams Brabant, C Belgium
Vilyeyka 107 C5 Pol. Wilejka, Rus.
Vileyka. Minskaya Voblasts',
NW Belarus
Vilyuy 115 F3 river NE Russian
Federation
Viña del Mar 64 B4 Valparaíso,
C Chile
Vinaròs 93 F3 País Valenciano,
E Spain
Vincennes 40 B4 Indiana, N USA
Vindhya Mountains see Vindhya
Range
Vindhya Range 134 D4 var.
Vindhya Mountains. Mountain
range N India
Vineland 41 F4 New Jersey,
NE USA
Vinh 136 D4 Nghê An, N Vietnam
Vinh Loi see Bac Liêu
Vinh Thai Lan see Thailand,
Gulf of
Vinishte 104 C2 Montana,
NW Bulgaria
Vinita 49 G1 Oklahoma, C USA
Vinkovci 100 C3 Ger. Winkowitz,
Hung. Vinkovcze. Vukovar-Srijem,
E Croatia
Vinnytsya 108 D2 Rus. Vinnitsa.
Vinnyts'ka Oblast', C Ukraine
Vinson Massif 154 A3 mountain
Antarctica
Viranşehir 117 E4 Şanlıurfa,
SE Turkey
Vîrful Moldoveanu see Vârful
Moldoveanu
Virginia 41 E5 off. Commonwealth
of Virginia; also known as Mother
of Presidents, Mother of States,
Old Dominion. State NE USA
Virginia 49 G1 Minnesota, N USA
Virginia Beach 41 F5 Virginia,
NE USA
Virgin Islands see British Virgin
Islands
Virgin Islands (US) 55 F3 var.
Virgin Islands of the United
States; prev. Danish West Indies.
US unincorporated territory E West
Indies

Virgin Islands of the United States
see Virgin Islands (US)
Viröchey 137 E5 Rôtânôkiri,
NE Cambodia
Virovitica 100 C2 Ger. Virovititz,
Hung. Verőcze; *prev. Ger.*
Werowitz. Virovitica-Podravina,
NE Croatia
Virton 87 D8 Luxembourg,
SE Belgium
Virtsu 106 D2 Ger. Werder.
Läänemaa, W Estonia
Vis 100 B4 *It.* Lissa; *anc.* Issa. *Island*
S Croatia
Vis *see* Fish
Visaginas 106 C4 *prev.* Sniečkus.
Ignalina, E Lithuania
Visākhapatnam 135 E5 Andhra
Pradesh, SE India
Visalia 47 C6 California, W USA
Visby 85 C7 Ger. Wisby. Gotland,
SE Sweden
Viscount Melville Sound 37 F2
prev. Melville Sound. *Sound*
Northwest Territories/Nunavut,
N Canada
Visé 87 D6 Liège, E Belgium
Viseu 92 C2 *prev.* Vizeu. Viseu,
N Portugal
Visoko 100 C4 Federacija Bosna I
Hercegovina, C Bosnia and
Herzegovina
Vistula *see* Wisła
Vistula Lagoon 98 C2 Ger. Frisches
Haff, *Pol.* Zalew Wiślany, *Rus.*
Vislinskiy Zaliv. *Lagoon*
Poland/Russian Federation
Viterbo 96 C4 *anc.* Vicus Elbii.
Lazio, C Italy
Viti Levu 145 E4 *island* W Fiji
Vitim 115 F4 *river* C Russian
Federation
Vitoria *see* Vitoria-Gasteiz
Vitória 63 F4 Espírito Santo,
SE Brazil
Vitoria Bank *see* Vitória Seamount
Vitória da Conquista 63 F3 Bahia,
E Brazil
Vitoria-Gasteiz 93 E1 *var.* Vitoria,
Eng. Vittoria. País Vasco, N Spain
Vitória Seamount 67 B5 *var.*
Victoria Bank, Vitoria Bank.
Undersea feature C Atlantic Ocean
Vitré 90 B3 Ille-et-Vilaine,
NW France
Vitsyebsk 107 E5 Rus. Vitebsk.
Vitsyebskaya Voblasts',
NE Belarus
Vittoria *see* Vitoria-Gasteiz
Vittoria 97 C7 Sicilia, Italy,
C Mediterranean Sea
Vizianagaram 135 E5 *var.*
Vizianagram. Andhra Pradesh,
E India
Vizianagram *see* Vizianagaram
Vjosës, Lumi i 101 C7 *var.* Vijosa,
Vijosë, *Gk.* Aóos. *River*
Albania/Greece *see also* Aóos
Vlaardingen 86 B4 Zuid-Holland,
SW Netherlands
Vladikavkaz 111 B8 *prev.*
Dzaudzhikau, Ordzhonikidze.
Severnaya Osetiya-Alaniya,
SW Russian Federation
Vladimir 111 B5 Vladimirskaya
Oblast', W Russian Federation
Vladivostok 115 G5 Primorskiy
Kray, SE Russian Federation
Vlagtwedde 86 E2 Groningen,
NE Netherlands
Vlasotince 101 E5 Serbia, SE Serbia
and Montenegro (Yugo.)
Vlieland 86 C1 Fris. Flylân. *Island*
Waddeneilanden, N Netherlands
Vlijmen 86 C4 Noord-Brabant,
S Netherlands
Vlissingen 87 B5 Eng. Flushing, Fr.
Flessingue. Zeeland,
SW Netherlands
Vlorë 101 C7 *prev.* Vlonë, *It.* Valona,
Vlora. Vlorë, SW Albania
Vöcklabruck 95 D6 Oberösterreich,
NW Austria

Vohimena, Tanjona 79 F4 Fr. Cap
Sainte Marie. *Headland*
S Madagascar
Voiron 91 D5 Isère, E France
Vojvodina 100 D3 Ger. Wojwodina.
Region N Serbia and Montenegro
(Yugo.)
Volcán de Chiriquí *see* Barú,
Volcán
Volga 111 B7 *river* NW Russian
Federation
Volga Uplands 81 G3 *Russ.*
Privolzhskaya Vozvyshennost'
mountain range W Russian
Federation
Volgodonsk 111 B7 Rostovskaya
Oblast', SW Russian Federation
Volgograd 111 B7 *prev.* Stalingrad,
Tsaritsyn. Volgogradskaya
Oblast', SW Russian Federation
Volkhov 110 B4 Leningradskaya
Oblast', NW Russian Federation
Volnovakha 109 G3 Donets'ka
Oblast', SE Ukraine
Volodymyr-Volyns'kyy 108 C1 Pol.
Włodzimierz, *Rus.* Vladimir-
Volynskiy. Volyns'ka Oblast',
NW Ukraine
Vologda 110 B4 Vologodskaya
Oblast', W Russian Federation
Vólos 105 B5 Thessalía, C Greece
Vol'sk 111 C6 Saratovskaya Oblast',
W Russian Federation
Volta 75 E5 *river* SE Ghana
Volta Blanche *see* White Volta
Volta, Lake 75 E5 *reservoir*
SE Ghana
Volta Noire *see* Black Volta
Volturno 97 D5 *river* S Italy
Volzhskiy 111 B6 Volgogradskaya
Oblast', SW Russian Federation
Võnnu 106 E3 Ger. Wendau.
Tartumaa, SE Estonia
Voorst 86 D3 Gelderland,
E Netherlands
Voranava 107 C5 Pol. Werenów, *Rus.*
Voronovo. Hrodzyenskaya
Voblasts', W Belarus
Vorderrhein 95 B7 *river*
SE Switzerland
Vóreioi Sporádes 105 C5 *var.* Vórioi
Sporádhes, *Eng.* Northern
Sporades. *Island group* E Greece
Vórioi Sporádhes *see* Vóreioi
Sporádes
Vorkuta 114 C2 Respublika Komi,
NW Russian Federation
Vormsi 106 C2 *var.* Vormsi Saar, *Ger.*
Worms, Swed. Ormsö. *Island*
W Estonia
Vormsi Saar *see* Vormsi
Voronezh 111 B6 Voronezhskaya
Oblast', W Russian Federation
Võru 106 D3 Ger. Werro. Võrumaa,
SE Estonia
Vosges 90 E4 *mountain range*
NE France
Vostochno-Sibirskoye More 115 F1
Eng. East Siberian Sea. *Sea* Arctic
Ocean
Vostok Island *see* Vostok Island
Vostok 154 C3 *Russian research
station* Antarctica
Vostok Island 145 G3 *var.* Vostok
Island; *prev.* Stavers Island. *Island*
Line Islands, SE Kiribati
Voznesens'k 109 E3 *Rus.*
Voznesensk. Mykolayivs'ka
Oblast', S Ukraine
Vrangelya, Ostrov 115 F1 Eng.
Wrangel Island. *Island* NE Russian
Federation
Vranje 101 E5 Serbia, SE Serbia and
Montenegro (Yugo.)
Vranov *see* Vranov nad Topľou
Vranov nad Topľou 99 D5 *var.*
Vranov, *Hung.* Varannó.
Prešovský kraj, E Slovakia
Vratsa 104 C2 Vratsa, NW Bulgaria
Vrbas 100 C3 *river* N Bosnia and
Herzegovina
Vrbas 100 C3 Serbia, NW Serbia
and Montenegro (Yugo.)

Vsetín 99 C5 Ger. Wsetin. Zlínský
Kraj, E Czech Republic
Vučitrn 101 D5 Serbia, S Serbia and
Montenegro (Yugo.)
Vukovar 100 C3 Hung. Vukóvár.
Vukovar-Srijem, E Croatia
Vulcano, Isola 97 C7 *island* Isole
Eolie, S Italy
Vung Tau 137 E6 *prev. Fr.* Cape
Saint Jacques, Cap Saint-Jacques.
Ba Ria-Vung Tau, S Vietnam
Vyatka 111 C5 *river* NW Russian
Federation
Vyborg 110 B3 Fin. Viipuri.
Leningradskaya Oblast',
NW Russian Federation
Vyerkhnyadzvinsk 107 D5 Rus.
Verkhnedvinsk. Vitsyebskaya
Voblasts', N Belarus
Vyetryna 107 D5 Rus. Vetrino.
Vitsyebskaya Voblasts', N Belarus
Vynohradiv 108 B3 Cz. Sevluš,
Hung. Nagyszőllős, *Rus.*
Vinogradov; *prev.* Sevlyush.
Zakarpats'ka Oblast', W Ukraine

W

Wa 75 E4 NW Ghana
Waal 86 C4 *river* S Netherlands
Wabash 40 C4 Indiana, N USA
Wabash River 40 B5 *river* N USA
Waco 49 G3 Texas, SW USA
Waddān 71 F3 NW Libya
Waddeneilanden 86 C1 Eng. West
Frisian Islands. *Island group*
N Netherlands
Waddenzee 86 C1 *var.* Wadden Zee.
Sea SE North Sea
Waddington, Mount 36 D5
mountain British Columbia,
SW Canada
Wādī as Sīr 119 B6 *var.* Wadi es Sir.
'Ammān, NW Jordan
Wadi es Sir *see* Wādī as Sīr
Wadi Halfa 72 B3 *var.* Wādī Ḥalfā'.
Northern, N Sudan
Wādī Mūsā 119 B7 *var.* Petra.
Ma'ān, S Jordan
Wad Madanī *see* Wad Medani
Wad Medani 72 C4 *var.* Wad
Madanī. Gezira, C Sudan
Waflia 139 F4 Pulau Buru,
E Indonesia
Wagadugu *see* Ouagadougou
Wagga Wagga 149 C7 New South
Wales, SE Australia
Wagin 147 B7 Western Australia
Wāh 134 C1 Punjab, NE Pakistan
Wahai 139 F4 Pulau Seram,
E Indonesia
Wahiawa 47 A8 Haw. Wahiawā.
Oahu, Hawaii, USA, C Pacific
Ocean
Wahībah, Ramlat Āl 121 E5 *var.*
Ramlat Ahl Wahībah, Ramlat
Al Wahaybah, *Eng.* Wahibah
Sands. *Desert* N Oman
Wahibah Sands *see* Wahībah,
Ramlat Āl
Wahpeton 45 F2 North Dakota,
N USA
Wahran *see* Oran
Waiau 151 A7 *river* South Island,
NZ
Waigeo, Pulau 139 G4 *island*
Maluku, E Indonesia
Waikaremoana, Lake 150 E4 *lake*
North Island, NZ
Wailuku 47 B8 Maui, Hawaii, USA,
C Pacific Ocean
Waimate 151 B6 Canterbury, South
Island, NZ
Waiouru 150 D4 Manawatu-
Wanganui, North Island, NZ
Waipara 151 C6 Canterbury, South
Island, NZ
Waipawa 150 E4 Hawke's Bay,
North Island, NZ
Waipukurau 150 E4 Hawke's Bay,
North Island, NZ
Wairau 151 C5 *river*
South Island, NZ

Wairoa 150 D2 *river* North Island,
NZ
Wairoa 150 E4 Hawke's Bay, North
Island, NZ
Waitaki 151 B6 *river* South Island,
NZ
Waitara 150 D4 Taranaki, North
Island, NZ
Waiuku 150 D3 Auckland, North
Island, NZ
Wakasa-wan 131 C6 *bay* C Japan
Wakatipu, Lake 151 A7 *lake* South
Island, NZ
Wakayama 131 C6 Wakayama,
Honshū, SW Japan
Wake Island 142 D1 *atoll*
NW Pacific Ocean
Wake Island 152 C2 US
unincorporated territory NW Pacific
Ocean
Wakkanai 130 C1 Hokkaidō,
NE Japan
Walachei *see* Wallachia
Walachia *see* Wallachia
Wałbrzych 98 B4 Ger. Waldenburg,
Waldenburg in Schlesien.
Dolnośląskie, SW Poland
Walcourt 87 C7 Namur, S Belgium
Wałcz 98 B3 Ger. Deutsch Krone.
Zachodniopomorskie, NW Poland
Waldia *see* Weldiya
Wales 89 C6 Wel. Cymru. *National
region* UK
Wales 36 C2 Alaska, USA
Wales Island, Prince of *see* Pinang,
Pulau
Walgett 149 D5 New South Wales,
SE Australia
Walker Lake 47 C5 *lake* Nevada,
W USA
Wallachia 108 B5 *var.* Walachia, Ger.
Walachei, Rom. Valachia. *Cultural
region* S Romania
Walla Walla 46 C2 Washington,
NW USA
Wallis and Futuna 145 E4 Fr.
Territoire de Wallis et Futuna.
French overseas territory C Pacific
Ocean
Walnut Ridge 42 B1 Arkansas,
C USA
Walthamstow 89 B7 SE England,
UK
Walvis Bay 78 A4 Afr. Walvisbaai.
Erongo, NW Namibia
Walvish Ridge *see* Walvis Ridge
Walvis Ridge 69 B7 *var.* Walvish
Ridge. *Undersea feature* E Atlantic
Ocean
Wan *see* Anhui
Wanaka 151 B6 Otago, South
Island, NZ
Wanaka, Lake 151 A6 *lake* South
Island, NZ
Wanchuan *see* Zhangjiakou
Wandel Sea 83 E1 *sea* Arctic Ocean
Wandsworth 89 A8 SE England,
UK
Wanganui 150 D4 Manawatu-
Wanganui, North Island, NZ
Wangaratta 149 C7 Victoria,
SE Australia
Wanki, Río *see* Coco, Río
Wanlaweyn 73 D6 *var.* Wanle Weyn,
It. Uanle Uen. Shabeellaha Hoose,
SW Somalia
Wanle Weyn *see* Wanlaweyn
Wanxian 128 B5 Chongqing,
C China
Warangal 135 E5 Andhra Pradesh,
C India
Warburg 94 B4 Nordrhein-
Westfalen, W Germany
Ware 37 E4 British Columbia,
W Canada
Waremme 87 C6 Liège, E Belgium
Waren 94 C3 Mecklenburg-
Vorpommern, NE Germany
Wargla *see* Ouargla
Warkworth 150 D2 Auckland,
North Island, NZ
Warnemünde 94 C2 Mecklenburg-
Vorpommern, NE Germany

Warner 49 G1 Oklahoma, C USA
Warnes 61 G4 Santa Cruz, C Bolivia
Warrego River 149 C5 *seasonal river* New South Wales/Queensland, E Australia
Warren 40 D3 Michigan, N USA
Warren 40 D3 Ohio, N USA
Warren 41 E3 Pennsylvania, NE USA
Warri 75 F5 Delta, S Nigeria
Warrnambool 149 B7 Victoria, SE Australia
Warsaw *see* Mazowieckie
Warszawa 98 D3 *Eng.* Warsaw, *Ger.* Warschau, *Rus.* Varshava. *Country capital* (Poland) Mazowieckie, C Poland
Warta 98 B3 *Ger.* Warthe. *River* W Poland
Warwick 149 E5 Queensland, E Australia
Washington 44 A2 *off.* State of Washington; also known as Chinook State, Evergreen State. *State* NW USA
Washington DC 41 E4 *country capital* (USA) District of Columbia, NE USA
Washington, Mount 41 G2 *mountain* New Hampshire, NE USA
Wash, The 89 E6 *inlet* E England, UK
Waspam 53 E2 *var.* Waspán. Región Autónoma Atlántico Norte, NE Nicaragua
Waspán *see* Waspam
Watampone 139 E4 *var.* Bone. Sulawesi, C Indonesia
Waterbury 41 F3 Connecticut, NE USA
Waterford 89 B6 *Ir.* Port Láirge. S Ireland
Waterloo 45 G3 Iowa, C USA
Watertown 41 F2 New York, NE USA
Watertown 45 F2 South Dakota, N USA
Waterville 41 G2 Maine, NE USA
Watford 89 A7 SE England, UK
Watsa 77 E5 Orientale, NE Dem. Rep. Congo
Watts Bar Lake *reservoir* Tennessee, S USA
Wau 73 B5 *var.* Wāw. Western Bahr el Ghazal, S Sudan
Waukegan 40 B3 Illinois, N USA
Waukesha 40 B3 Wisconsin, N USA
Wausau 40 B2 Wisconsin, N USA
Waverly 45 G3 Iowa, C USA
Wavre 87 C6 Wallon Brabant, C Belgium
Wāw *see* Wau
Wawa 38 C4 Ontario, S Canada
Waycross 43 E3 Georgia, SE USA
Wearmouth *see* Sunderland
Webster City 45 F3 Iowa, C USA
Weddell Plain 154 A2 *undersea feature* SW Atlantic Ocean
Weddell Sea 154 A2 *sea* SW Atlantic Ocean
Weener 94 A3 Niedersachsen, NW Germany
Weert 87 D5 Limburg, SE Netherlands
Weesp 86 C3 Noord-Holland, C Netherlands
Węgorzewo 98 D2 *Ger.* Angerburg. Warmińsko-Mazurskie, NE Poland
Weimar 94 C4 Thüringen, C Germany
Weissenburg 95 C6 Bayern, SE Germany
Weiswampach 87 D7 Diekirch, N Luxembourg
Wejherowo 98 C2 Pomorskie, NW Poland
Welchman Hall 55 G1 C Barbados
Weldiya 72 C4 *var.* Waldia, *It.* Valdia. N Ethiopia
Welkom 78 D4 Free State, C South Africa
Welle *see* Uele

Wellesley Islands 148 B2 *island group* Queensland, N Australia
Wellington 151 D5 *country capital* (NZ) Wellington, North Island, NZ
Wellington *see* Wellington, Isla
Wellington 45 F5 Kansas, C USA
Wellington, Isla 65 A7 *var.* Wellington. *Island* S Chile
Wells 46 D4 Nevada, W USA
Wellsford 150 D2 Auckland, North Island, NZ
Wells, Lake 147 C5 *lake* Western Australia
Wels 95 D6 *anc.* Ovilava. Oberösterreich, N Austria
Wembley 89 A8 SE England, UK
Wemmel 87 B6 Vlaams Brabant, C Belgium
Wenatchee 46 B2 Washington, NW USA
Wenchi 75 E4 W Ghana
Wen-chou *see* Wenzhou
Wenchow *see* Wenzhou
Wenmen Island *see* Wolf, Isla
Wenzhou 128 D5 *var.* Wen-chou, Wenchow. Zhejiang, SE China
Werda 78 C4 Kgalagadi, S Botswana
Werkendam 86 C4 Noord-Brabant, S Netherlands
Weser 94 B3 *river* NW Germany
Wessel Islands 148 B1 *island group* Northern Territory, N Australia
West Antarctica *see* Lesser Antarctica
West Bank 119 A6 *disputed region* SW Asia
West Bend 40 B3 Wisconsin, N USA
West Bengal 135 F4 *state* NE India
West Cape 151 A7 *headland* South Island, NZ
West Des Moines 45 F3 Iowa, C USA
Westerland 94 B2 Schleswig-Holstein, N Germany
Western Australia 146 B4 *state* W Australia
Western Desert *see* Sahara el Gharbîya
Western Dvina 85 E7 *Bel.* Dzvina, *Ger.* Düna, *Latv.* Daugava, *Rus.* Zapadnaya Dvina. *River* W Europe
Western Ghats 134 C5 *mountain range* SW India
Western Isles *see* Outer Hebrides
Western Sahara 70 B3 UK *disputed territory* N Africa
Western Samoa *see* Samoa
Westerschelde 87 B5 *Eng.* Western Scheldt; *prev.* Honte. *Inlet* S North Sea
West Falkland 65 C7 *var.* Isla Gran Malvina. *Island* W Falkland Islands
West Fargo 45 F2 North Dakota, N USA
West Irian *see* Papua
West Mariana Basin 142 B1 *var.* Perece Vela Basin. *Undersea feature* W Pacific Ocean
West Memphis 42 B1 Arkansas, C USA
West New Guinea *see* Papua
West Papua *see* Papua
Weston-super-Mare 89 D7 SW England, UK
West Palm Beach 43 F4 Florida, SE USA
Westport 151 C5 West Coast, South Island, NZ
West River *see* Xi Jiang
West Siberian Plain *see* Zapadno-Sibirskaya Ravnina
West Virginia 40 D4 *off.* State of West Virginia; also known as The Mountain State. *State* NE USA
Wetar, Pulau 139 F5 *island* Kepulauan Damar, E Indonesia
Wetzlar 95 B5 Hessen, W Germany
Wevok 36 C2 *var.* Wewuk. Alaska, USA

Wewuk *see* Wevok
Wexford 89 B6 *Ir.* Loch Garman. SE Ireland
Weyburn 37 F5 Saskatchewan, S Canada
Weymouth 89 D7 S England, UK
Wezep 86 D3 Gelderland, E Netherlands
Whakatane 150 E3 Bay of Plenty, North Island, NZ
Whale Cove 37 G3 Nunavut, C Canada
Whangarei 150 D2 Northland, North Island, NZ
Wharton Basin 141 D5 *var.* West Australian Basin. *Undersea feature* E Indian Ocean
Whataroa 151 B6 West Coast, South Island, NZ
Wheatland 44 D3 Wyoming, C USA
Wheeler Peak 48 D1 *mountain* New Mexico, SW USA
Wheeling 40 D4 West Virginia, NE USA
Whitby 89 D5 N England, UK
Whitefish 44 B1 Montana, NW USA
Whitehaven 89 C5 NW England, UK
Whitehorse 36 D4 *territory capital* Yukon Territory, W Canada
White Nile 72 B4 *Ar.* Al Baḥr al Abyaḍ, An Nīl al Abyaḍ, Bahr el Jebel. *River* SE Sudan
White Nile 72 B4 *var.* Bahr el Jebel. *River* S Sudan
White River 44 D3 *river* South Dakota, N USA
White Sea *see* Beloye More
White Volta 75 E4 *var.* Nakambé, *Fr.* Volta Blanche. *River* Burkina faso/Ghana
Whitianga 150 D2 Waikato, North Island, NZ
Whitney, Mount 47 C6 *mountain* California, W USA
Whitsunday Group 148 D3 *island group* Queensland, E Australia
Whyalla 149 B6 South Australia
Wichita 45 F5 Kansas, C USA
Wichita Falls 49 F2 Texas, SW USA
Wichita River 49 F2 *river* Texas, SW USA
Wickenburg 48 B2 Arizona, SW USA
Wicklow 89 B6 *Ir.* Cill Mhantáin. *Cultural region* E Ireland
Wicklow Mountains 89 B6 *Ir.* Sléibhte Chill Mhantáin. *Mountain range* E Ireland
Wieliczka 99 D5 Małopolskie, S Poland
Wieluń 98 C4 Łódzkie, C Poland
Wien 95 E6 *Eng.* Vienna, *Hung.* Bécs, *Slvk.* Videň, *Slvn.* Dunaj; *anc.* Vindobona. *Country capital* (Austria) Wien, NE Austria
Wiener Neustadt 95 E6 Niederösterreich, E Austria
Wierden 86 E3 Overijssel, E Netherlands
Wiesbaden 95 B5 Hessen, W Germany
Wight, Isle of 89 D7 *island* S England, UK
Wijchen 86 D4 Gelderland, SE Netherlands
Wijk bij Duurstede 86 D4 Utrecht, C Netherlands
Wilcannia 149 C6 New South Wales, SE Australia
Wilhelm, Mount 144 B3 *mountain* C PNG
Wilhelm-Pieck-Stadt *see* Guben
Wilhelmshaven 94 B3 Niedersachsen, NW Germany
Wilkes Barre 41 F3 Pennsylvania, NE USA
Wilkes Land 154 C4 *physical region* Antarctica
Willard 48 D2 New Mexico, SW USA

Willcox 48 C3 Arizona, SW USA
Willebroek 87 B5 Antwerpen, C Belgium
Willemstad 55 E5 *dependent territory capital* (Netherlands Antilles) Curaçao, Netherlands Antilles
Williston 44 D1 North Dakota, N USA
Wilmington 41 F4 Delaware, NE USA
Wilmington 43 F2 North Carolina, SE USA
Wilmington 40 C4 Ohio, N USA
Wilrijk 87 C5 Antwerpen, N Belgium
Winchester 89 D7 *hist.* Wintanceaster, *Lat.* Venta Belgarum. S England, UK
Winchester 41 E4 Virginia, NE USA
Windhoek 78 B3 *Ger.* Windhuk. *Country capital* (Namibia) Khomas, C Namibia
Windorah 148 C4 Queensland, C Australia
Windsor 41 G3 Connecticut, NE USA
Windsor 148 D1 New South Wales, SE Australia
Windsor 38 C5 Ontario, S Canada
Windsor 89 D7 S England, UK
Windward Islands 55 H4 *island group* E West Indies
Windward Islands *see* Barlavento, Ilhas de
Windward Passage 54 D3 *Sp.* Paso de los Vientos. *Channel* Cuba/Haiti
Winisk 38 C2 *river* Ontario, S Canada
Winisk 38 C2 Ontario, C Canada
Winnebago, Lake 40 B2 *lake* Wisconsin, N USA
Winnemucca 47 C5 Nevada, W USA
Winnipeg 37 G5 Manitoba, S Canada
Winnipeg, Lake 37 G5 *lake* Manitoba, C Canada
Winnipegosis, Lake 38 A3 *lake* Manitoba, C Canada
Winona 45 G3 Minnesota, N USA
Winschoten 86 E2 Groningen, NE Netherlands
Winsen 94 B3 Niedersachsen, N Germany
Winston Salem 43 E1 North Carolina, SE USA
Winsum 86 D1 Groningen, NE Netherlands
Winterswijk 86 E4 Gelderland, E Netherlands
Winterthur 95 B7 Zürich, NE Switzerland
Winton 148 C4 Queensland, E Australia
Winton 151 A7 Southland, South Island, NZ
Wisconsin 40 A2 *off.* State of Wisconsin; also known as The Badger State. *State* N USA
Wisconsin Rapids 40 B2 Wisconsin, N USA
Wisconsin River 40 B3 *river* Wisconsin, N USA
Wisła 98 C2 *Eng.* Vistula, *Ger.* Weichsel. *River* Śląskie, S Poland
Wismar 94 C2 Mecklenburg-Vorpommern, N Germany
Wittenberge 94 C3 Brandenburg, N Germany
Wittlich 95 A5 Rheinland-Pfalz, SW Germany
Wittstock 94 C3 Brandenburg, NE Germany
W.J. van Blommesteinmeer 59 G3 *reservoir* E Suriname
Władysławowo 98 C2 Pomorskie, N Poland
Włocławek 98 C3 *Ger./Rus.* Vlotslavsk. Kujawsko-pomorskie, C Poland
Włodawa 98 E4 *Rus.* Vlodava. Lubelskie, E Poland

Wlotzkasbaken 78 B3 Erongo, W Namibia
Wodonga 149 C7 Victoria, SE Australia
Wodzisław Śląski 99 C5 Ger. Loslau. Śląskie, S Poland
Wōjjā see Wotje Atoll
Woking 89 D7 SE England, UK
Wolf, Isla 60 A4 var. Wenmen Island. Island W Ecuador
Wolfsberg 95 D7 Kärnten, SE Austria
Wolfsburg 94 C3 Niedersachsen, N Germany
Wolgast 94 D2 Mecklenburg-Vorpommern, NE Germany
Wollaston Lake 37 F4 Saskatchewan, C Canada
Wollongong 149 D6 New South Wales, SE Australia
Wolvega 86 D2 Fris. Wolvegea. Friesland, N Netherlands
Wolverhampton 89 D6 C England, UK
Wŏnsan 129 E3 SE North Korea
Woodburn 46 B3 Oregon, NW USA
Woodland 47 B5 California, W USA
Woodruff 40 B2 Wisconsin, N USA
Woods, Lake of the 38 A3 Fr. Lac des Bois. Lake Canada/USA
Woodville 150 D4 Manawatu-Wanganui, North Island, NZ
Woodward 49 F1 Oklahoma, C USA
Worcester 89 D6 hist. Wigorna Ceaster. W England, UK
Worcester 41 G3 Massachusetts, NE USA
Worcester 78 C5 Western Cape, SW South Africa
Workington 89 C5 NW England, UK
Worland 44 C3 Wyoming, C USA
Worms 95 B5 anc. Augusta Vangionum, Borbetomagus, Wormatia. Rheinland-Pfalz, SW Germany
Worms see Vormsi
Worthington 45 F3 Minnesota, N USA
Wotje Atoll 144 D1 var. Wōjjā. Atoll Ratak Chain, E Marshall Islands
Woudrichem 86 C4 Noord-Brabant, S Netherlands
Wrangel Island see Vrangelya, Ostrov
Wrangel Plain 155 B2 undersea feature Arctic Ocean
Wrocław 98 C4 Eng./Ger. Breslau. Dolnośląskie, SW Poland
Września 98 C3 Wielkopolskie, C Poland
Wuchang see Wuhan
Wuday'ah 121 C6 Najrān, S Saudi Arabia
Wuhai 127 E3 Nei Mongol Zizhiqu, N China
Wuhan 128 C5 var. Han-kou, Han-k'ou, Hanyang, Wuchang, Wu-han; prev. Hankow. Hubei, C China
Wuhsi see Wuxi
Wuhsien see Suzhou
Wuhu 128 D5 var. Wu-na-mu. Anhui, E China
Wujlān see Ujelang Atoll
Wukari 75 G4 Taraba, E Nigeria
Wuliang Shan 128 A6 mountain range SW China
Wu-lu-k'o-mu-shi see Ürümqi
Wu-lu-mu-ch'i see Ürümqi
Wu-na-mu see Wuhu
Wuppertal 94 A4 prev. Barmen-Elberfeld. Nordrhein-Westfalen, W Germany
Würzburg 95 B5 Bayern, SW Germany
Wusih see Wuxi
Wuxi 128 D5 var. Wuhsi, Wu-hsi, Wusih. Jiangsu, E China
Wuyi Shan 125 E3 mountain range SE China

Wye 89 C6 Wel. Gwy. River England/Wales, UK
Wyndham 146 D3 Western Australia
Wyoming 44 B3 off. State of Wyoming; also known as The Equality State. State C USA
Wyoming 40 C3 Michigan, N USA
Wyszków 98 D3 Ger. Probstberg. Mazowieckie, C Poland

X

Xaafuun, Raas 72 E4 var. Ras Hafun. Headland NE Somalia
Xaçmaz 117 H2 Rus. Khachmas. N Azerbaijan
Xaignabouli 136 C4 prev. Muang Xaignabouri, Fr. Sayaboury. Xaignabouli, N Laos
Xai-Xai 79 E4 prev. João Belo, Vila de João Bel. Gaza, S Mozambique
Xalapa 51 F4 var. Jalapa, Jalapa Enriquez. Veracruz-Llave, SE Mexico
Xam Nua 136 D3 var. Sam Neua. Houaphan, N Laos
Xankändi 117 G3 Rus. Khankendi; prev. Stepanakert. SW Azerbaijan
Xánthi 104 C3 Anatolikí Makedonía kai Thráki, NE Greece
Xátiva 93 F3 var. Jativa;anc. Setabis. País Valenciano, E Spain
Xauen see Chefchaouen
Xeres see Jeréz de la Frontera
Xiaguan see Dali
Xiamen 128 D6 var. Hsia-men; prev. Amoy. Fujian, SE China
Xi'an 128 C4 var. Changan, Sian, Signan, Siking, Singan, Xian. Shaanxi, C China
Xian see Xi'an
Xiangkhoang see Pèk
Xiangtan 128 C5 var. Hsiang-t'an, Siangtan. Hunan, S China
Xiao Hinggan Ling 128 D2 Eng. Lesser Khingan Range. Mountain range NE China
Xichang 128 B5 Sichuan, C China
Xieng Khouang see Pèk
Xieng Ngeun see Muong Xiang Ngeun
Xigazê see Xigazê
Xigazê 126 C5 var. Jih-k'a-tse, Shigatse, Xigaze. Xizang Zizhiqu, W China
Xi Jiang 124 D3 var. Hsi Chiang, Eng. West River. River S China
Xilinhot 127 F2 var. Silinhot. Nei Mongol Zizhiqu, N China
Xilokastro see Xylókastro
Xin see Xinjiang Uygur Zizhiqu
Xingkai Hu see Khanka, Lake
Xingu, Rio 63 E2 river C Brazil
Xingxingxia 126 D3 Xinjiang Uygur Zizhiqu, NW China
Xining 127 E4 var. Hsining, Hsi-ning, Sining. Province capital Qinghai, C China
Xinjiang see Xinjiang Uygur Zizhiqu
Xinjiang Uygur Zizhiqu 126 B3 var. Sinkiang, Sinkiang Uighur Autonomous Region, Xin, Xinjiang. Admin. region autonomous region NW China
Xinpu see Lianyungang
Xinxiang 128 C4 Henan, C China
Xinyang 128 C5 var. Hsin-yang, Sinyang. Henan, C China
Xinzo de Limia 92 C2 Galicia, NW Spain
Xiqing Shan 124 D2 mountain range C China
Xixón see Gijón
Xizang see Xizang Zizhiqu
Xizang Gaoyuan see Qingzang Gaoyuan
Xizang Zizhiqu 126 B4 var. Thibet, Tibetan Autonomous Region, Xizang, Eng. Tibet. Admin. region autonomous region W China

Xolotlán see Managua, Lago de
Xuddur 73 D5 var. Hudur, It. Oddur. Bakool, SW Somalia
Xuwen 128 C7 Guangdong, S China
Xuzhou 128 D4 var. Hsu-chou, Suchow, Tongshan; prev. T'ung-shan. Jiangsu, E China
Xylókastro 105 B5 var. Xilokastro. Pelopónnisos, S Greece

Y

Ya'an 128 B5 var. Yaan. Sichuan, C China
Yabēlo 73 C5 C Ethiopia
Yablis 53 E2 Región Autónoma Atlántico Norte, NE Nicaragua
Yablonovyy Khrebet 115 F4 mountain range S Russian Federation
Yabrai Shan 127 E3 mountain range NE China
Yafran 71 F2 NW Libya
Yaghan Basin 67 B7 undersea feature SE Pacific Ocean
Yahotyn 109 E2 Rus. Yagotin. Kyyivs'ka Oblast', N Ukraine
Yahualica 50 D4 Jalisco, SW Mexico
Yakima 46 B2 Washington, NW USA
Yakima River 46 B2 river Washington, NW USA
Yakoruda 104 C3 Blagoevgrad, SW Bulgaria
Yaku-shima 131 B8 island Nansei-shotō, SW Japan
Yakutat 36 D4 Alaska, USA
Yakutsk 115 F3 Respublika Sakha (Yakutiya), NE Russian Federation
Yala 137 C7 Yala, SW Thailand
Yalizava 107 D6 Rus. Yelizovo. Mahilyowskaya Voblasts', E Belarus
Yalong Jiang 128 A5 river C China
Yalova 116 B3 Yalova, NW Turkey
Yalpuh, Ozero 108 D4 Rus. Ozero Yalpug. Lake SW Ukraine
Yalta 109 F5 Respublika Krym, S Ukraine
Yalu 125 E2 Chin. Yalu Jiang, Jap. Oryokko, Kor. Amnok-kang. River China/North Korea
Yamagata 131 B7 var. Yamaguti. Yamagata, Honshū, SW Japan
Yamaguti see Yamaguchi
Yamal, Poluostrov 114 D2 peninsula N Russian Federation
Yambio 73 B5 var. Yambiyo. Western Equatoria, S Sudan
Yambiyo see Yambio
Yambol 104 D2 Turk. Yanboli. Yambol, E Bulgaria
Yamdena, Pulau 139 G5 prev. Jamdena. Island Kepulauan Tanimbar, E Indonesia
Yam HaMelah see Dead Sea
Yam Kinneret see Tiberias, Lake
Yamoussoukro 74 D5 country capital (Côte d'Ivoire) C Côte d'Ivoire
Yamuna 134 D3 prev. Jumna. River N India
Yana 115 F2 river NE Russian Federation
Yanbu 'al Baḥr 121 A5 Al Madīnah, W Saudi Arabia
Yangambi 77 D5 Orientale, N Dem. Rep. Congo
Yangchow see Yangzhou
Yangiyūl 123 E2 Rus. Yangiyul'. Toshkent Wiloyati, E Uzbekistan
Yangon 136 B4 Eng. Rangoon. Country capital (Myanmar) Yangon, S Myanmar
Yangtze see Chang Jiang
Yangtze Kiang see Chang Jiang
Yangzhou 128 D5 var. Yangchow. Jiangsu, E China
Yankton 45 E3 South Dakota, N USA
Yannina see Ioánnina
Yanskiy Zaliv 113 F2 bay N Russian Federation

Yantai 128 D4 var. Yan-t'ai; prev. Chefoo, Chih-fu. Shandong, E China
Yan-t'ai see Yantai
Yaoundé 77 B5 var. Yaunde. Country capital (Cameroon) Centre, S Cameroon
Yap 144 A1 island Caroline Islands, W Micronesia
Yapanskoye More see Japan, Sea of
Yapen, Pulau 139 G4 prev. Japen. Island E Indonesia
Yap Trench 142 B2 var. Yap Trough. Undersea feature SE Philippine Sea
Yap Trough see Yap Trench
Yapurá see Caquetá, Río
Yapurá see Japurá, Rio
Yaqui, Río 50 C2 river NW Mexico
Yaransk 111 C5 Kirovskaya Oblast', NW Russian Federation
Yarega 110 D4 Respublika Komi, NW Russian Federation
Yarkant see Shache
Yarlung Zangbo Jiang see Brahmaputra
Yarmouth see Great Yarmouth
Yarmouth 39 F5 Nova Scotia, SE Canada
Yaroslavl' 110 B4 Yaroslavskaya Oblast', W Russian Federation
Yarumal 58 B2 Antioquia, NW Colombia
Yasyel'da 107 B7 river SW Belarus
Yatsushiro 131 A7 var. Yatusiro. Kumamoto, Kyūshū, SW Japan
Yatusiro see Yatsushiro
Yaunde see Yaoundé
Yavarí see Javari, Rio
Yaviza 53 H5 Darién, SE Panama
Yavoriv 108 B2 Pol. Jaworów, Rus. Yavorov. L'vivs'ka Oblast', NW Ukraine
Yazd 120 D3 var. Yezd. Yazd, C Iran
Yazoo City 42 B2 Mississippi, S USA
Yding Skovhøj 85 A7 hill C Denmark
Ýdra 105 C6 var. Ídhra. Island S Greece
Ye 137 B5 Mon State, S Myanmar
Yecheng 126 A3 var. Kargilik. Xinjiang Uygur Zizhiqu, NW China
Yefremov 111 B5 Tul'skaya Oblast', W Russian Federation
Yekaterinburg 114 C3 prev. Sverdlovsk. Sverdlovskaya Oblast', C Russian Federation
Yelets 111 B5 Lipetskaya Oblast', W Russian Federation
Yell 88 D1 island NE Scotland, UK
Yellowknife 37 E4 territory capital Northwest Territories, W Canada
Yellow River see Huang He
Yellow Sea 128 D4 Chin. Huang Hai, Kor. Hwang-Hae. Sea E Asia
Yellowstone River 44 C2 river Montana/Wyoming, NW USA
Yel'sk 107 C7 Rus. Yel'sk. Homyel'skaya Voblasts', SE Belarus
Yelwa 75 F4 Kebbi, W Nigeria
Yemen 121 C7 Ar. Al Jumhūrīyah al Yamanīyah, Al Yaman. Country SW Asia

Yemen 121

Official name Republic of Yemen
Formation 1990
Capital Sana
Population 19.1 million / 94 people per sq mile (36 people per sq km)
Total area 203,849 sq miles (527,970 sq km)
Languages Arabic
Religions Shi'a Muslim 42%, Sunni Muslim 55%, Christian, Hindu and Jewish 3%
Ethnic mix Arab 95%, Afro-Arab 3%, Indian, Somali and European 2%

12-113

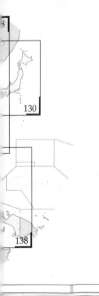

24-125

130

138

Yemen (continued)

Government Multiparty republic
Currency Yemeni Rial
Literacy rate 46.3%
Calorie consumption 2,038
kilocalories

Yemva 110 D4 prev.
Zhelesnodorozhnyy Respublika
Komi, NW Russian Federation
Venakiyeve 109 G3 Rus.
Yenakiyevo; prev. Ordzhonikidze,
Rykovo. Donets'ka Oblast',
E Ukraine
Yenangyaung 136 A3 Magwe,
W Myanmar
Yendi 75 E4 NE Ghana
Yengisar 126 A3 Xinjiang Uygur
Zizhiqu, NW China
Yenierenköy see Agialoúsa
Yenisey 114 D3 river
Mongolia/Russian Federation
Yenping see Nanping
Yeovil 89 D7 SW England, UK
Yeppoon 148 D4 Queensland,
E Australia
Yerevan 117 F3 var. Erevan, Eng.
Erivan. Country capital (Armenia)
C Armenia
Yeriho see Jericho
Yerushalayim see Jerusalem
Yeu, Île d' 90 A4 island NW France
Yevlax 117 G3 Rus. Yevlakh.
C Azerbaijan
Yevpatoriya 109 F5 Respublika
Krym, S Ukraine
Yeya 109 H4 river SW Russian
Federation
Yezd see Yazd
Yezyaryshcha 107 E5 Rus.
Yezerishche. Vitsyebskaya
Voblasts', NE Belarus
Yiannitsá see Giannitsá
Yichang 128 C5 Hubei, C China
Yildizeli 116 D3 Sivas, N Turkey
Yinchuan 128 B4 var. Yinch'uan,
Yin-ch'uan, Yinchwan. Ningxia,
N China
Yinchwan see Yinchuan
Yin-hsien see Ningbo
Yining 126 B3 var. I-ning, Gulja,
Kuldja. Xinjiang Uygur
Zizhiqu, NW China
Yithion see Gytheio
Yogyakarta 138 C5 prev.
Djokjakarta, Jogjakarta,
Jokyakarta. Jawa, C Indonesia
Yokohama 131 D5 Aomori,
Honshū, C Japan
Yokohama 131 A2 Kanagawa,
Honshū, S Japan
Yokote 130 D4 Akita, Honshū,
C Japan
Yola 75 H4 Adamawa, E Nigeria
Yonago 131 B6 Tottori, Honshū,
SW Japan
Yong'an 128 D6 var. Yongan. Fujian,
SE China
Yonkers 41 F3 New York, NE USA
Yonne 90 C4 river C France
Yopal 58 C3 var. El Yopal. Casanare,
C Colombia
York 89 D5 anc. Eboracum,
Eburacum. N England, UK
York 45 F4 Nebraska, C USA
York 41 E4 Pennsylvania, NE USA
York, Cape 148 C1 headland
Queensland, NE Australia
Yorkton 37 F5 Saskatchewan,
S Canada
Yoro 52 C2 Yoro, C Honduras
Yoshkar-Ola 111 C5 Respublika
Mariy El, W Russian Federation
Youngstown 40 D4 Ohio, N USA
Youth, Isle of see Juventud, Isla de
la
Yreka 47 B4 California, W USA
Yssel see IJssel
Ysyk-Köl see Issyk-Kul', Ozero
Yu see Henan
Yuan see Red River
Yuan Jiang see Red River
Yuba City 47 B5 California, W USA

Yucatan Channel 51 H3 Sp. Canal
de Yucatán. Channel Cuba/Mexico
Yucatan Peninsula 35 C7 peninsula
Guatemala/Mexico
Yuci 128 C4 Shanxi, C China
Yue see Guangdong
Yueyang 128 C5 Hunan, S China
Yukhavichy 107 D5 Rus.
Yukhovichi. Vitsyebskaya
Voblasts', N Belarus
Yukon 36 C2 river Canada/USA
Yukon see Yukon Territory
Yukon Territory 36 D3 var. Yukon,
Fr. Territoire du Yukon. Admin.
region territory NW Canada
Yulin 128 C6 Guangxi Zhuangzu
Zizhiqu, S China
Yuma 48 A2 Arizona, SW USA
Yumen 128 A3 var. Laojunmiao,
Yümen. Gansu, N China
Yun see Yunnan
Yungki see Jilin
Yung-ning see Nanning
Yunjinghong see Jinghong
Yunki see Jilin
Yunnan 128 A6 var. Yun, Yunnan
Sheng, Yünnan, Yun-nan. Admin.
region province SW China
Yunnan see Kunming
Yunnan Sheng see Yunnan
Yuruá, Río see Juruá, Rio
Yushu 126 D4 Qinghai, C China
Yuty 64 D3 Caazapá, S Paraguay
Yuzhno-Sakhalinsk 115 H4 Jap.
Toyohara; prev. Vladimirovka.
Ostrov Sakhalin, Sakhalinskaya
Oblast', SE Russian
Federation
Yuzhou see Chongqing
Yylanly see Il'yaly

Z

Zaanstad 86 C3 prev. Zaandam.
Noord-Holland, C Netherlands
Zabaykal'sk 115 F5 Chitinskaya
Oblast', S Russian Federation
Zabern see Saverne
Zabīd 121 B7 W Yemen
Ząbkowice see Ząbkowice Śląskie
Ząbkowice Śląskie 98 B4 var.
Ząbkowice, Ger. Frankenstein,
Frankenstein in Schlesien.
Wałbrzych, SW Poland
Zábřeh 99 C5 Ger. Hohenstadt.
Olomoucký Kraj, E Czech Republic
Zacapa 52 B2 Zacapa, E Guatemala
Zacatecas 50 D3 Zacatecas, C Mexico
Zacatepec 51 E4 Morelos, S Mexico
Zacháro 105 B6 var. Zaharo,
Zakháro. Dytikí Ellás, S Greece
Zadar 100 A3 It. Zara; anc. Iader.
Zadar, SW Croatia
Zadetkyi Kyun 137 B6 var. St.
Matthew's Island. Island Mergui
Archipelago, S Myanmar
Zafra 92 C4 Extremadura, W Spain
Żagań 98 B4 var. Zagań, Żegań; Ger.
Sagan. Lubuskie, W Poland
Zagazig 72 B1 var. Az Zaqāzīq.
N Egypt
Zágráb see Zagreb
Zagreb 100 B2 Ger. Agram, Hung.
Zágráb. Country capital (Croatia)
Zagreb, N Croatia
Zāgros, Kūhhā-ye 120 C3 Eng.
Zagros Mountains. Mountain
range W Iran
Zāgros Mountains see Zāgros,
Kūhhā-ye
Zaharo see Zacháro
Zāhedān 120 E4 var. Zahidan; prev.
Duzdab. Sīstān va Balūchestān,
SE Iran
Zahidan see Zāhedān
Zahlah see Zahlé
Zahlé 118 B4 var. Zahlah. C Lebanon
Záhony 99 E6 Szabolcs-Szatmár-
Bereg, NE Hungary
Zaire see Congo
Zaječar 100 E4 Serbia, E Serbia and
Montenegro (Yugo.)
Zakháro see Zacháro

Zākhō 120 B2 var. Zākhū. N Iraq
Zākhū see Zākhō
Zákinthos see Zákynthos
Zakopane 99 D5 Małopolskie, S
Poland
Zakota Pomorskiea see Danzig,
Gulf of
Zákynthos 105 A6 var. Zákinthos, It.
Zante. Island Iónioi Nísoi, Greece,
C Mediterranean Sea
Zalaegerszeg 99 B7 Zala,
W Hungary
Zalău 108 B3 Ger. Waltenberg,
Hung. Zilah; prev. Ger.
Zillenmarkt. Sălaj, NW Romania
Zalim 121 B5 Makkah, W Saudi
Arabia
Zambesi see Zambezi
Zambeze see Zambezi
Zambezi 78 D2 var. Zambesi, Port.
Zambeze. River S Africa
Zambezi 78 C2 North Western,
W Zambia
Zambia 78 C2 off. Republic of
Zambia; prev. Northern Rhodesia.
Country S Africa

Zambia 78

Official name Republic of Zambia
Formation 1964
Capital Lusaka
Population 10.6 million /
36 people per sq mile (14 people
per sq km)
Total area 290,585 sq miles
(752,612 sq km)
Languages English, Bemba, Nyanja,
Tonga, Kaonde, Lunda, Luvale, Lozi
Religions Christian 63%,
Indigenous beliefs 36%, other 1%
Ethnic mix Bemba 34%, European
1%, other African 65%
Government Presidential
democracy
Currency Zambian kwacha = 100
ngwee
Literacy rate 78.1%
Calorie consumption 1,912
kilocalories

Zamboanga 139 E3 off. Zamboanga
City. Mindanao, S Philippines
Zambrów 98 E3 Podlaskie,
E Poland
Zamora 92 D2 Castilla-León,
NW Spain
Zamora de Hidalgo 50 D4
Michoacán de Ocampo,
SW Mexico
Zamość 98 E4 Rus. Zamoste.
Lubelskie, E Poland
Zancle see Messina
Zanda 126 A4 Xizang Zizhiqu,
W China
Zanesville 40 D4 Ohio, N USA
Zanján 120 C2 var. Zenjan, Zinjan.
Zanján, NW Iran
Zante see Zákynthos
Zanthus 147 C6 Western
Australia
Zanzibar 73 C7 Swa. Unguja. Island
E Tanzania
Zanzibar 73 D7 Zanzibar,
E Tanzania
Zaozhuang 128 D4 Shandong,
E China
Zapadna Morava 100 D4 Ger.
Westliche Morava. River C Serbia
and Montenegro (Yugo.)
Zapadnaya Dvina 110 A4
Tverskaya Oblast', W Russian
Federation
Zapadno-Sibirskaya Ravnina 114
C3 Eng. West Siberian Plain. Plain
C Russian Federation
Zapadnyy Sayan 114 D4 Eng.
Western Sayans. Mountain range
S Russian Federation
Zapala 65 B5 Neuquén,
W Argentina
Zapiola Ridge 67 B6 undersea feature
SW Atlantic Ocean

Zapolyarnyy 110 C2 Murmanskaya
Oblast', NW Russian Federation
Zaporizhzhya 109 F3 Rus.
Zaporozh'ye; prev.
Aleksandrovsk. Zaporiz'ka
Oblast', SE Ukraine
Zapotiltic 50 D4 Jalisco, SW Mexico
Zaqatala 117 G2 Rus. Zakataly.
NW Azerbaijan
Zara 116 D3 Sivas, C Turkey
Zarafshon 122 D2 Rus. Zarafshan.
Nawoiy Wiloyati, N Uzbekistan
Zaragoza 93 F2 Eng. Saragossa; anc.
Caesaraugusta, Salduba. Aragón,
NE Spain
Zarand 120 D3 Kermān, C Iran
Zaranj 122 D5 Nīmrūz,
SW Afghanistan
Zarasai 106 C4 Zarasai,
E Lithuania
Zárate 64 D4 prev. General José
F.Uriburu. Buenos Aires,
E Argentina
Zarautz 93 E1 var. Zarauz. País
Vasco, N Spain
Zarauz see Zarautz
Zaraza 59 E2 Guárico, N Venezuela
Zarghūn Shahr 123 E4 var.
Katawaz. Paktīkā, SE Afghanistan
Zaria 75 G4 Kaduna, C Nigeria
Zarós 105 D8 Kríti, Greece,
E Mediterranean Sea
Zarqa see Az Zarqā'
Żary 98 B4 Ger. Sorau, Sorau in der
Niederlausitz. Lubulskie,
W Poland
Zaunguzskiye Garagumy 122 C2
Turkm. Üngüz Angyrsyndaky
Garagum. Desert N Turkmenistan
Zavet 104 D1 Razgrad, N Bulgaria
Zavidovići 100 C3 Federacija Bosna
I Hercegovina, N Bosnia and
Herzegovina
Zawia see Az Zāwiyah
Zawiercie 98 D4 Rus. Zavertse.
Śląskie, S Poland
Zawīlah 71 F3 var. Zuwaylah, It.
Zueila. C Libya
Zaysan, Ozero 114 D5 Kaz. Zaysan
Köl. Lake E Kazakhstan
Zbarazh 108 C2 Ternopil's'ka
Oblast', W Ukraine
Zduńska Wola 98 C4 Łódzkie,
C Poland
Zeebrugge 87 A5 West-Vlaanderen,
NW Belgium
Zeewolde 86 D3 Flevoland,
C Netherlands
Żegań see Żagań
Zefat 119 B5 var. Safed, Tsefat,
Ar. Safad. Northern, N Israel
Zeist 86 C4 Utrecht, C Netherlands
Zele 87 B5 Oost-Vlaanderen,
NW Belgium
Zelenoborskiy 110 B2
Murmanskaya Oblast',
NW Russian Federation
Zelenograd 111 B5 Moskovskaya
Oblast', W Russian Federation
Zelenogradsk 106 A4 Ger. Cranz,
Kranz. Kaliningradskaya Oblast',
W Russian Federation
Zelle see Celle
Zel'va 107 B6 Pol. Zelwa.
Hrodzyenskaya Voblasts',
W Belarus
Zelzate 87 B5 var. Selzaete. Oost-
Vlaanderen, NW Belgium
Žemaičių Aukštumas 106 B4
physical region W Lithuania
Zemst 87 C5 Vlaams Brabant,
C Belgium
Zemun 100 D3 Serbia, N Serbia and
Montenegro (Yugo.)
Zenica 100 C4 Federacija Bosna I
Herzegovina, C Bosnia and
Herzegovina
Zenjan see Zanján
Zeravshan 123 E3 Taj./Uzb.
Zarafshon. River
Tajikistan/Uzbekistan
Zevenaar 86 D4 Gelderland,
SE Netherlands

Zevenbergen *86 C4* Noord-Brabant, S Netherlands

Zeya *113 E3* river SE Russian Federation

Zgierz *98 C4* Ger. Neuhof, Rus. Zgerzh. Łódź, C Poland

Zgorzelec *98 B4* Ger. Görlitz. Dolnośląskie, SW Poland

Zhabinka *107 A6* Pol. Żabinka, Rus. Zhabinka. Brestskaya Voblasts', SW Belarus

Zhambyl *see* Taraz

Zhanaozen *114 A4* Kaz. Zhangaözen, prev. Novyy Uzen'. Mangistau, W Kazakhstan

Zhangaözen *see* Zhanaozen

Zhangaqazaly *see* Ayteke Bi

Zhang-chia-k'ou *see* Zhangjiakou

Zhangdian *see* Zibo

Zhangjiakou *128 C3* var. Changkiakow, Zhang-chia-k'ou, Eng. Kalgan; prev. Wanchuan. Hebei, E China

Zhangzhou *128 D6* Fujian, SE China

Zhanjiang *128 C7* var. Chanchiang, Chan-chiang, Cant. Tsamkong, Fr. Fort-Bayard. Guangdong, S China

Zhaoqing *128 C6* Guangdong, S China

Zhe *see* Zhejiang

Zhejiang *128 D5* var. Che-chiang, Chekiang, Zhe, Zhejiang Sheng. Admin. region province SE China

Zhejiang Sheng *see* Zhejiang

Zhelezndoroznyy *106 A4* Ger. Gerdauen. Kaliningradskaya Oblast', W Russian Federation

Zheleznogorsk *111 A5* Kurskaya Oblast', W Russian Federation

Zhengzhou *128 C4* var. Ch'eng-chou, Chengchow; prev. Chenghsien. Henan, C China

Zhezkazgan *114 C4* Kaz. Zhezqazghan; prev. Dkaraganda. Karaganda, C Kazakhstan

Zhlobin *107 D7* Homyel'skaya Voblasts', SE Belarus

Zhmerynka *108 D2* Rus. Zhmerinka. Vinnyts'ka Oblast', C Ukraine

Zhodzina *107 D6* Rus. Zhodino. Minskaya Voblasts', C Belarus

Zhovkva *108 B2* Pol. Żółkiew, Rus. Zholkev, Zholkva; prev. Nesterov. L'vivs'ka Oblast', NW Ukraine

Zhovti Vody *109 F3* Rus. Zhëltyye Vody. Dnipropetrovs'ka Oblast', E Ukraine

Zhovtneve *109 E4* Rus. Zhovtnevoye. Mykolayivs'ka Oblast', S Ukraine

Zhydachiv *108 B2* Pol. Żydaczów, Rus. Zhidachov. L'vivs'ka Oblast', NW Ukraine

Zhytkavichy *107 C7* Rus. Zhitkovichi. Homyel'skaya Voblasts', SE Belarus

Zhytomyr *108 D2* Rus. Zhitomir. Zhytomyrs'ka Oblast', NW Ukraine

Zibo *128 D4* var. Zhangdian. Shandong, E China

Zielona Góra *98 B4* Ger. Grünberg, Grünberg in Schlesien, Grüneberg. Lubuskie, W Poland

Zierikzee *86 B4* Zeeland, SW Netherlands

Zigong *128 B5* var. Tzekung. Sichuan, C China

Ziguinchor *74 B3* SW Senegal

Žilina *99 C5* Ger. Sillein, Hung. Zsolna. Žilinský Kraj, N Slovakia

Zimbabwe *78 D3* prev. Rhodesia. Country S Africa

Zimbabwe 78

Official name Republic of Zimbabwe
Formation 1980
Capital Harare

Zimbabwe (continued)

Population 12.9 million / 86 people per sq mile (33 people per sq km)
Total area 150,803 sq miles (390,580 sq km)
Languages English, Shona, Ndebele
Religions Syncretic (Christian and traditional beliefs) 50%, Christian 25%, Traditional beliefs 24%, other 1%
Ethnic mix Shona 71%, Ndebele 16%, other African 11%, Asian 1%, White 1%
Government Presidential regime
Currency Zimbabwe dollar = 100 cents
Literacy rate 88.7%
Calorie consumption 2,117 kilocalories

Zimnicea *108 C5* Teleorman, S Romania

Zimovniki *111 B7* Rostovskaya Oblast', SW Russian Federation

Zinder *75 G3* Zinder, S Niger

Zinjan *see* Zanjān

Zipaquirá *58 B3* Cundinamarca, C Colombia

Zittau *94 D4* Sachsen, E Germany

Zlatni Pyasŭtsi *104 E2* Dobrich, NE Bulgaria

Zlín *99 C5* prev. Gottwaldov. Zlinský Kraj, E Czech Republic

Złotów *98 C3* Wielkopolskie, C Poland

Znam"yanka *109 F3* Rus. Znamenka. Kirovohrads'ka Oblast', C Ukraine

Żnin *98 C3* Kujawski-pomorskie, C Poland

Znojmo *99 B5* Ger. Znaim. Brněnský Kraj, SE Czech Republic

Zoetermeer *86 C4* Zuid-Holland, W Netherlands

Zolochiv *108 C2* Pol. Złoczów, Rus. Zolochev. L'vivs'ka Oblast', W Ukraine

Zolochiv *109 G2* Rus. Zolochev. Kharkivs'ka Oblast', E Ukraine

Zolote *109 H3* Rus. Zolotoye. Luhans'ka Oblast', E Ukraine

Zolotonosha *109 E2* Cherkas'ka Oblast', C Ukraine

Zomba *79 E2* Southern, S Malawi

Zongo *77 C5* Equateur, N Dem. Rep. Congo

Zonguldak *116 C2* Zonguldak, NW Turkey

Zonhoven *87 D6* Limburg, NE Belgium

Żory *99 C5* var. Zory, Ger. Sohrau. Śląskie, S Poland

Zouar *76 C2* Borkou-Ennedi-Tibesti, N Chad

Zouérat *74 C2* var. Zouérate, Zouîrât. Tiris Zemmour, N Mauritania

Zouérate *see* Zouérat

Zouîrât *see* Zouérat

Zrenjanin *100 D3* prev. Petrovgrad, Veliki Bečkerek, Ger. Grossbetschkerek, Hung. Nagybecskerek. Serbia, N Serbia and Montenegro (Yugo.)

Zubov Seamount *67 D5* undersea feature E Atlantic Ocean

Zueila *see* Zawīlah

Zug *95 B7* Fr. Zoug. Zug, C Switzerland

Zugspitze *95 C7* mountain S Germany

Zuid-Beveland *87 B5* var. South Beveland. Island SW Netherlands

Zuidhorn *86 E1* Groningen, NE Netherlands

Zuidlaren *86 E2* Drenthe, NE Netherlands

Zula *72 C4* E Eritrea

Züllichau *see* Sulechów

Zundert *87 C5* Noord-Brabant, S Netherlands

Zunyi *128 B5* Guizhou, S China

Županja *100 C3* Hung. Zsupanya. Vukovar-Srijem, E Croatia

Zürich *95 B7* Eng./Fr. Zurich, It. Zurigo. Zürich, N Switzerland

Zürichsee *95 B7* Eng. Lake Zurich. Lake NE Switzerland

Zutphen *86 D3* Gelderland, E Netherlands

Zuwārah *71 F2* NW Libya

Zuwaylah *see* Zawīlah

Zuyevka *111 D5* Kirovskaya Oblast', NW Russian Federation

Zvenyhorodka *109 E2* Rus. Zvenigorodka. Cherkas'ka Oblast', C Ukraine

Zvishavane *78 D3* prev. Shabani. Matabeleland South, S Zimbabwe

Zvolen *99 C6* Ger. Altsohl, Hung. Zólyom. Banskobystricky Kraj, C Slovakia

Zvornik *100 C4* E Bosnia and Herzegovina

Zwedru *74 D5* var. Tchien. E Liberia

Zwettl *95 E6* Wien, NE Austria

Zwevegem *87 A6* West-Vlaanderen, W Belgium

Zwickau *95 C5* Sachsen, E Germany

Zwolle *86 D3* Overijssel, E Netherlan

Zyōetu *see* Jōetsu

Żyardów *98 D3* Mazowieckie, C Poland

Zyryanovsk *114 D5* Vostochnyy Kazakhstan, E Kazakhstan

KEY TO MAP PAGES

NORTH & WEST ASIA

SOUTH & EAST ASIA

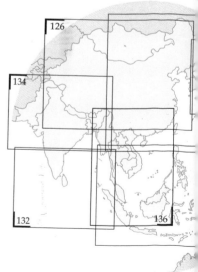

KEY TO MAP PAGES

NORTH & WEST ASIA 112-113

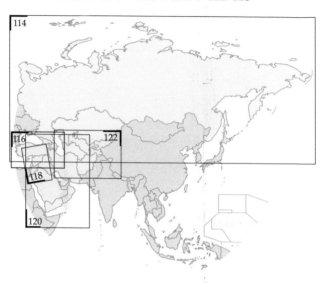

SOUTH & EAST ASIA 124-125

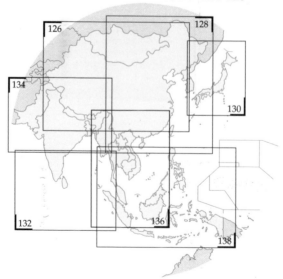